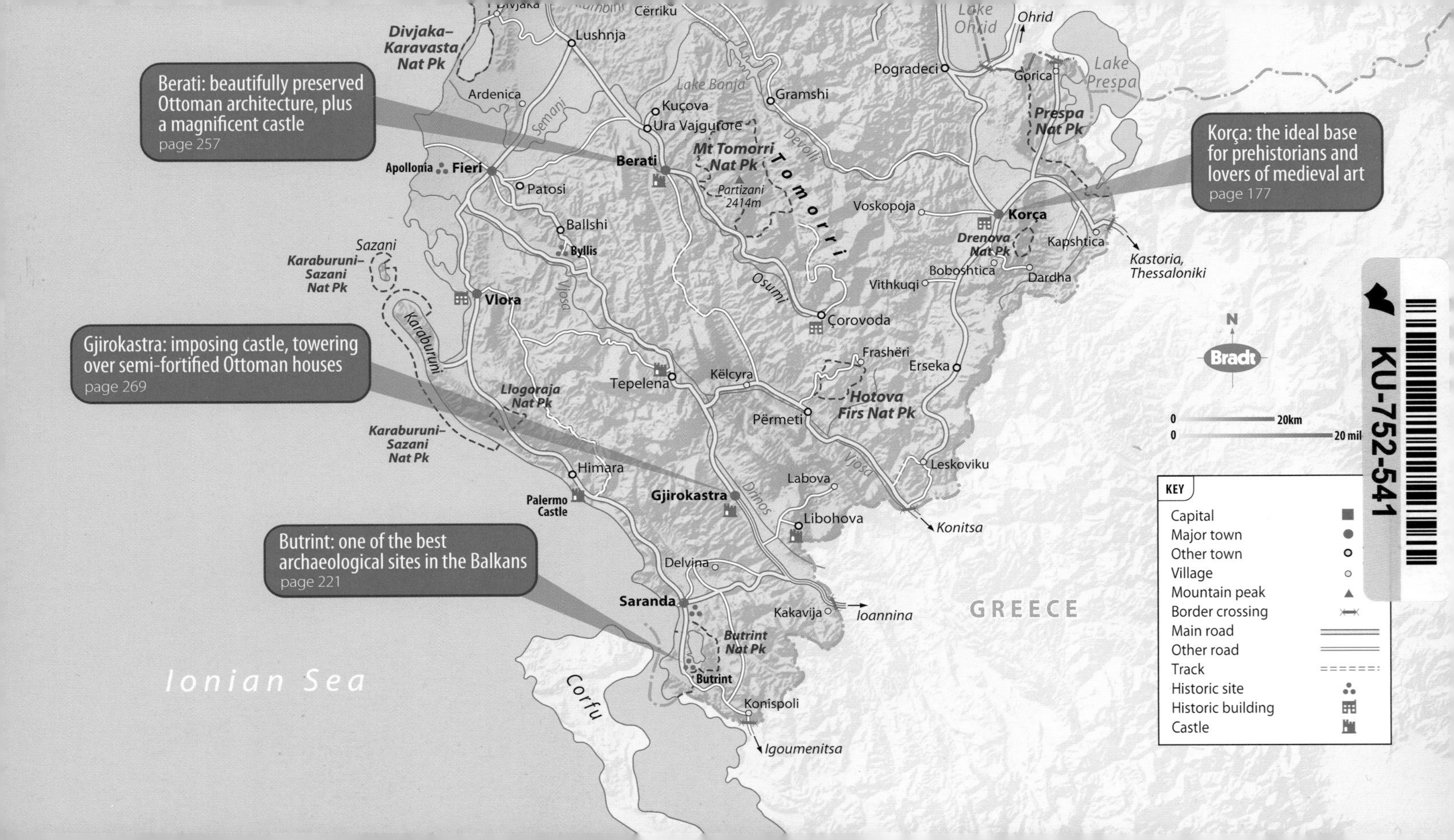
Berati: beautifully preserved Ottoman architecture, plus a magnificent castle
page 257
Korça: the ideal base for prehistorians and lovers of medieval art
page 177
Gjirokastra: imposing castle, towering over semi-fortified Ottoman houses
page 269
Butrint: one of the best archaeological sites in the Balkans
page 221
Divjaka–Karavasta Nat Pk
Lushnja
Cërriku
Ardenica
Semani
Lake Banja
Kuçova
Ura Vajgurore
Gramshi
Devolli
Mt Tomorri Nat Pk
Tomorri
Partizani 2414m
Berati
Apollonia
Fieri
Patosi
Ballshi
Byllis
Sazani
Karaburuni–Sazani Nat Pk
Vlora
Vjosa
Karaburuni
Osumi
Çorovoda
Llogoraja Nat Pk
Tepelena
Këlcyra
Frashëri
Hotova Firs Nat Pk
Përmeti
Himara
Palermo Castle
Gjirokastra
Drinos
Labova
Libohova
Konitsa
Delvina
Saranda
Kakavija
Ioannina
Butrint Nat Pk
Butrint
Konispoli
Igoumenitsa
Corfu
Ionian Sea
Lake Ohrid
Ohrid
Pogradeci
Gorica
Lake Prespa
Prespa Nat Pk
Voskopoja
Korça
Drenova Nat Pk
Kapshtica
Kastoria, Thessaloniki
Boboshtica
Dardha
Vithkuqi
Erseka
Leskoviku
GREECE
N
Bradt
0 20km
0 20 mil
KEY
Capital
Major town
Other town
Village
Mountain peak
Border crossing
Main road
Other road
Track
Historic site
Historic building
Castle

KU-752-541

Albania Don't miss...

Communist heritage
Vlora's Independence Monument is an imposing bronze cast in the Socialist Realist style (o/S) page 244

Gjirokastra
The restored clock tower is an icon of this beautiful Ottoman town (k/S) page 276

Albania

the Bradt Guide

Gillian Gloyer

edition
7

www.bradtguides.com

Bradt Guides Ltd, UK
The Globe Pequot Press Inc, USA

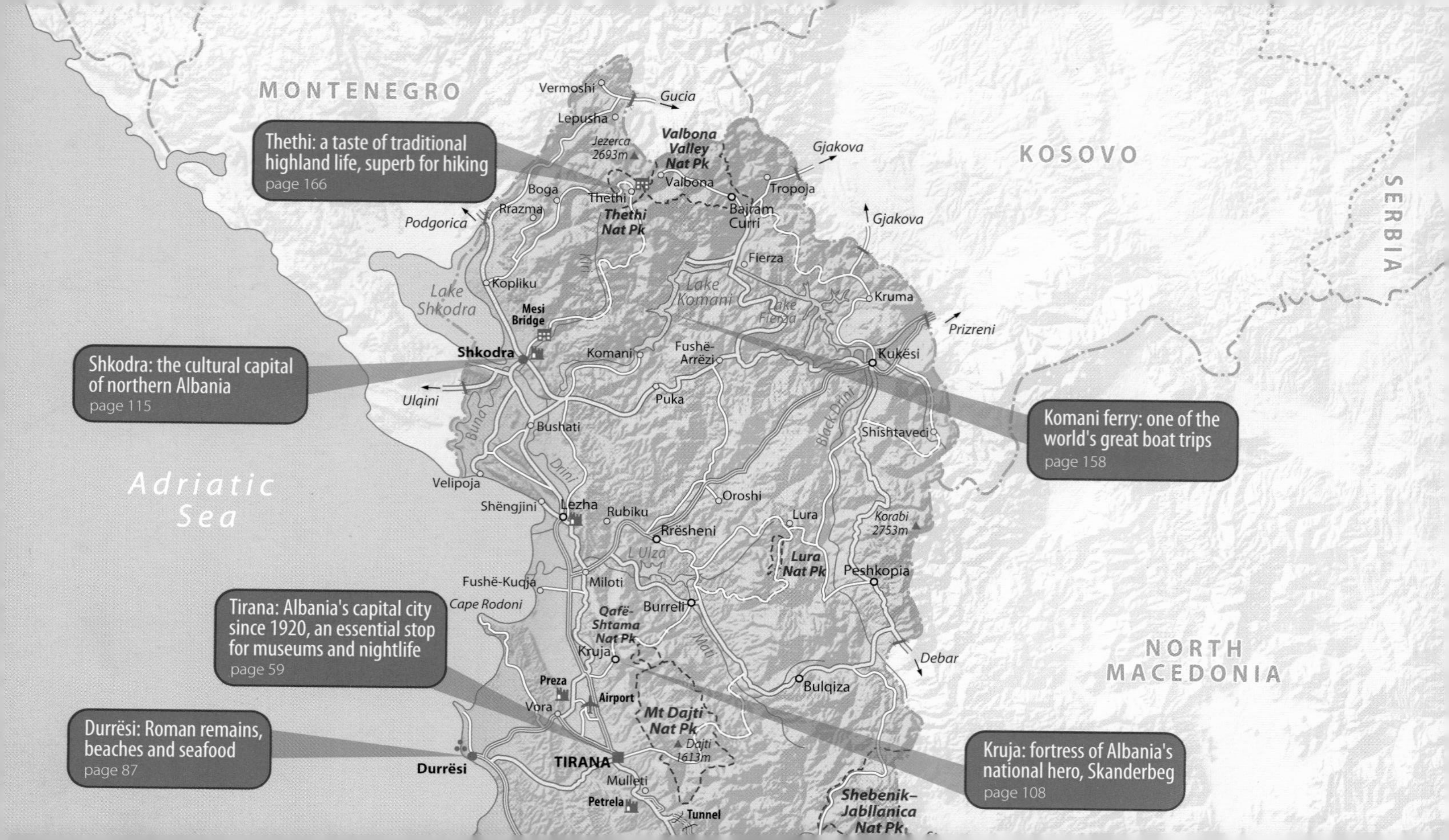

Thethi: a taste of traditional highland life, superb for hiking
page 166
Shkodra: the cultural capital of northern Albania
page 115
Komani ferry: one of the world's great boat trips
page 158
Tirana: Albania's capital city since 1920, an essential stop for museums and nightlife
page 59
Durrësi: Roman remains, beaches and seafood
page 87
Kruja: fortress of Albania's national hero, Skanderbeg
page 108
MONTENEGRO
KOSOVO
SERBIA
NORTH MACEDONIA
Adriatic Sea
Vermoshi
Gucia
Lepusha
Jezerca 2693m
Valbona Valley Nat Pk
Valbona
Gjakova
Tropoja
Boga
Thethi
Bajram Curri
Rrazma
Podgorica
Thethi Nat Pk
Gjakova
Kiri
Fierza
Kopliku
Lake Shkodra
Lake Komani
Lake Fierza
Kruma
Mesi Bridge
Prizreni
Shkodra
Komani
Fushë-Arrëzi
Kukësi
Ulqini
Puka
Buna
Bushati
Black Drini
Shishtaveci
Drini
Velipoja
Oroshi
Shëngjini
Lezha
Rubiku
Lura
Korabi 2753m
Rrësheni
L Ulza
Lura Nat Pk
Peshkopia
Fushë-Kuqja
Miloti
Cape Rodoni
Burreli
Qafë-Shtama Nat Pk
Mati
Kruja
Debar
Bulqiza
Preza
Airport
Vora
Mt Dajti Nat Pk
Dajti 1613m
Durrësi
TIRANA
Mulleti
Petrela
Tunnel
Shebenik-Jabllanica Nat Pk

Thethi
The 'lock-in tower' in Thethi was used during negotiations to resolve blood-feuds (GG)
page 166

Orthodox frescoes
The beautifully restored frescoes in Shelcani were painted in 1554 by the great Albanian icon-painter Onufri (DD)
page 106

Butrint
The theatre at Butrint, still used for drama festivals, was built in the 2nd century BC (V/S) page 221

Albania in colour

above Warriors, intellectuals and workers rally around Mother Albania in the 1981 mosaic above the National Historical Museum (p/S) page 73

left Tirana is full of surprises; this Bektashi shrine, the Tyrbe of Kapllan Pasha, nestles below a modern business hotel (GG) page 78

below The Mosque of Et'hem Bey dates from the 18th century and is one of the best-preserved old buildings in the capital, with frescoes inside and out (f/S) page 73

above left **The Tanners' Bridge is one of the few remnants of Tirana's Ottoman past** (JG/S) page 78

above right **The statue of Mother Albania looks down over Tirana from the Martyrs' Cemetery** (o/S) page 83

below right **Tirana retains a handful of communist sites, such as Bunk'Art 2 – a museum housed in a bomb-proof tunnel** (p/S) page 80

above **Borshi is one of many superb beaches found along Albania's Riviera** (AL) page 229

left **Rafting is popular on the crashing waters of both the Vjosa and Osumi rivers** (VE) pages 203 & 266

below **The boat-trip along Lake Komani is a highlight of any visit to northern Albania** (PW/S) page 158

AUTHOR

Gillian Gloyer studied ancient languages at Wadham College, Oxford. This turned out to be surprisingly useful when she came to learn Albanian. She now speaks the Albanian language well and reads its literature for pleasure.

Gillian lived in Tirana for four years, directing a long-term training programme with political parties. Now based mainly in Edinburgh, she returns to Albania at least once a year. Pre-pandemic, she led tour groups to the country for several UK-based tour operators.

CONTRIBUTORS

M C Barrès-Baker is a military historian. He lives in the UK and has visited Albania several times.

Catherine Bohne is a naturalist. She lives in Tropoja, in the Albanian highlands, where she is active in defending the region's wild spaces from inappropriate development.

Carolyn Perry leads archaeological and cultural tours of Albania and Greece. She lives mainly in Durresi.

AUTHOR'S STORY

I first tried to visit Albania in 1982, when it was one of the world's most closed countries. Needless to say, this early attempt was a resounding failure; it would be another 16 years before Albania and I became acquainted. The four years that I went on to spend there were professionally rewarding and politically exciting, but also gave me the opportunity to travel to more parts of the country than most Albanians ever do. While I was preparing to leave my post in the spring of 2002, a couple of Albanian friends suggested that my knowledge of their country made me the ideal person to write a travel guide to it.

The seed was sown. Back in Scotland, I contacted Bradt Guides, who, fortuitously, were already thinking of commissioning a guide to Albania. Bradt had published earlier guides, in 1989 and 1995, but since then the country had changed beyond recognition and they realised that a completely new book was called for. I knew nothing about writing travel guides, but I thought I knew a lot about Albania. Unfortunately, much of what I knew turned out to be of little practical use to the traveller – the political affiliation of the mayor, for example, or how many members of the local election commission were women – and I swiftly discovered that the project was going to require quite a lot more work than I had anticipated. It was fortunate that Bradt's editorial staff were such skilled hand-holders, coaxing out of me what was needed without plunging me into total despair.

For most visitors, the greatest revelation about Albania is the hospitality and kindness of the Albanian people. They won my heart long ago; having to update this book is an excellent reason for me to go back to the country again and again.

COVID-19

Please note that research for this guide was carried out during the Covid-19 pandemic. Because of the impact of the crisis on tourism, some businesses or services listed in the text may no longer operate. We will post any information we have about these on **w** bradtguides.com/updates. And we'd of course be grateful for any updates you can send us during your own travels, which we will add to that page for the benefit of future travellers.

Seventh edition published June 2022
First published 2004
Bradt Guides Ltd
31a High Street, Chesham, Buckinghamshire, HP5 1BW, England
www.bradtguides.com
Print edition published in the USA by The Globe Pequot Press Inc,
PO Box 480, Guilford, Connecticut 06437-0480

Text copyright © 2022 Gillian Gloyer
Maps copyright © 2022 Bradt Guides Ltd; includes map data © OpenStreetMap contributors
Photographs copyright © 2022 Individual photographers (see below)
Project Manager: Laura Pidgley
Cover research: Ian Spick, Bradt Guides

The author and publisher have made every effort to ensure the accuracy of the information in this book at the time of going to press. However, they cannot accept any responsibility for any loss, injury or inconvenience resulting from the use of information contained in this guide. All rights reserved. No part of this publication may be reproduced, stored in a retrieval system, or transmitted in any form or by any means, electronic, mechanical, photocopying, recording or otherwise without the prior consent of the publisher.

ISBN: 9781784779122

British Library Cataloguing in Publication Data
A catalogue record for this book is available from the British Library

Photographs Albert Kaleci (AK); Derek Drescher (DD); Getty Images: RilindH (R/G); Gillian Gloyer (GG); Alma Lahe (AL); Shutterstock.com: Rimgaudas Budrys (RB/S), Dardan18 (D/S), Dritan Zaimi Albania (DZA/S), fkaymak (f/S), Justinas Galinis (JG/S), Pargovski Jove (PJ/S), kobeza (k/S), milosk50 (m50/S), MehmetO (MO/S), ollirg (o/S), posztos (p/S), Ppictures (Pp/S), Elzbieta Sekowska (ES/S), Shoovar (S/S), taranzhenya (t/S), VVlasovs (V/S), Przemyslaw Wasilewski (PW/S), Tomasz Wozniak (TW/S); SuperStock (SS); Vjosa Explorer (VE)

Front cover Mesi Bridge, near Shkodra (R/G)
Back cover Borshi (AL)
Title page Thethi (D/S); Lake Komani (t/S); Berati (m50/S)

Maps David McCutcheon FBCart.S

Typeset by Ian Spick, Bradt Guides and www.dataworks.co.in
Production managed by Jellyfish Print Solutions; printed in India
Digital conversion by www.dataworks.co.in

Acknowledgements

Many people have helped in the preparation of this book from the earliest days of the project. Alban Zusi, Elvis Mataj and bison-grass vodka are responsible for the original idea, now – alarmingly – two decades ago. Rather than again listing everyone who contributed to previous editions, I thank them all collectively. However, I do want to single out two friends for special thanks: Gjon Pjetri and Alma Lahe, who have been a constant source of advice, information and logistical help from the very beginning.

I am grateful to everyone at Bradt Guides, past and present, who were far-sighted enough to undertake the first edition. Thanks to Laura Pidgley and the rest of the (sadly depleted) Bradt team for shepherding this edition to publication.

Albania is an exceptionally difficult country for which to obtain accurate maps. The Albanian Military Geographical Institute (IGUS) kindly gave permission, many years ago, to use its town plans and maps. Some of these have since been updated using w openstreetmap.org. Mimoza Hysaj, Egda Rapo and Gjorgj Kasarosi drew the maps which served as the basis for the town plans of Durrësi, Himara and Shkodra, respectively. Ylli Asllani, Arben Hoxha, Daniel Lee and Gjergj Mano provided source maps for Gjirokastra, Korça, Përmeti and Saranda, respectively.

The research for this seventh edition has been unusually difficult because of the restrictions in Albania, the UK and throughout Europe as a result of the Covid-19 pandemic. Some of the hotels and restaurants that I have listed may not survive beyond the expected publication date of this guidebook.

I am grateful to Sandi Gale for her advice on ornithology; Carolyn Perry for her advice, hospitality and readiness for adventures; Ilir Hysaj for New Year's Day in Pëllumbasi; Gjergj Mano for introducing me to his home village of Mursi and facilitating my visits to Phoinike and Konispoli; Egda Rapo in Himara; Përparim Laçi in Puka; and Juxhin Shishko in Korça. In and around Përmeti, Giorgio Ponti, Julian Elezi and their colleagues at CESVI and Vjosa Explorer were exceptionally generous with their time, local knowledge and logistical support of all kinds. Thanks to Gjon and Drane Pjetri for their hospitality and logistical help with my visit to the Lura Lakes; and Pavlin Nikolli for his skilful driving. In Shebenik-Jabllanica National Park, Alma Lahe set the trip up and kept me company there. Fatmir Brazhda, Albert Koleci, the Hasa family and Endrit Polaska made sure we saw as much of the national park as possible on a too-short visit. Last but not least, thanks for their help and support to my friends Kristina Fidhi in Gjirokastra, Ardian Dine in Vlora, Catherine Bohne in Tropoja, Roland Bejko, Alban Zusi and Etleva Bisha in Tirana.

I always appreciate input from readers. My thanks to all those who took the trouble to write with updates and corrections to the last edition.

Contents

LIST OF MAPS

HOW TO USE THIS GUIDE

AUTHOR'S FAVOURITES Finding genuinely characterful accommodation or that unmissable off-the-beaten-track café can be difficult, so the author has chosen a few of her favourite places throughout the country to point you in the right direction. These 'author's favourites' are marked with ✷.

PRICE CODES Throughout this guide we have used price codes to indicate the cost of those places to stay and eat listed in the guide. For a key to these price codes, see page 47 for accommodation and page 50 for restaurants.

MAPS

Keys and symbols Maps include alphabetical keys covering the locations of those places to stay, eat or drink that are featured in the book. Note that regional maps may not show all hotels and restaurants in the area: other establishments may be located in towns shown on the map.

Grids and grid references Several maps use gridlines to allow easy location of sites. Map grid references are listed in square brackets after the name of the place or site of interest in the text, with page number followed by grid number, eg: [62 C3].

A NOTE ABOUT PLACE NAMES Albanian has two forms of every place name. The definite form is that used in the text of this book. The indefinite form is used on road signs and maps. The forms are usually similar enough to be easily recognisable; a glossary on page 290 of this book lists the definite and indefinite forms of those towns or districts that are less obvious.

The name 'Kosovo' is used in this book for the state that borders Albania to the northeast. The Albanian form of its name is Kosova (indefinite 'Kosovë'). It declared its independence on 17 February 2008; at the time of going to press, its sovereign status has not been recognised by the United Nations. The country that borders Albania to its east, whose official name is the Republic of North Macedonia, is referred to in this book as 'North Macedonia'.

EXTRACTS The excerpts on pages 82 and 83 are from Bradt's first guide to Albania, Peter and Andrea Dawson's *Albania: A Guide and Illustrated Journal*, which charted their travels in the country towards the end of the communist period. First published by Bradt in 1989, this book is now out of print.

The extracts of Albanian folk tales on pages 124 and 137 are translated (by me) from the versions by Mitrush Kuteli, first published in 1965 as *Tregime të Moçme Shqiptare* and republished in Tirana in 1998 by Shtëpia Botuese Mitrush Kuteli.

Introduction

Albania has been independent only since 1912. It was the last country in Europe, apart from North Macedonia, to gain its independence from the Ottoman Empire and, in its first 30 years as a modern state, it was invaded and occupied, at different times, by all its neighbours. The government that took over in 1944 used a combination of terror, nationalism and isolation to retain power until long after the communist regimes elsewhere in Europe had fallen. Civil unrest bordering on anarchy overwhelmed the country in 1991–92 and 1997.

Given this history, it is not surprising that Albania is so little known. During the communist period, practically the only Westerners who visited the country were in organised groups – ornithologists, art historians or curious adventurers coming in on bus tours from neighbouring Yugoslavia – which were carefully escorted by watchful 'tour guides'. During the turbulent 1990s, most holiday companies were understandably wary of including Albania in their itineraries. It is only in recent decades that travellers in any numbers have started to discover Albania's beauty; its hidden medieval churches and very visible castles; its magnificent archaeological sites, with remains dating back two-and-a-half millennia; and, of course, its delicious fruit, vegetables, lamb and fish. Many visitors are drawn to Albania's spectacular, remote wildernesses and, as in previous editions, I have continued to pay special attention to these and to the outdoor activities which can be enjoyed in them.

Albania is easy to get to, by land, sea or air. There are hotels of at least reasonable standard everywhere. Road infrastructure continues to improve across the whole country. Increasing numbers of visitors are coming to Albania in their own cars or mobile homes, or renting a vehicle to give them more flexibility to explore. However, inter-city buses are a reliable and low-cost option for getting around the country (advice on how to use them can be found on page 43). To make it easier for those who choose to travel by public transport, I have structured the regional sections of this book so that they align with the bus routes from Tirana.

FEEDBACK AND UPDATES REQUEST

At Bradt Guides we're aware that guidebooks start to go out of date on the day they're published – and that you, our readers, are out there in the field doing research of your own. You'll find out before us when a fine new family-run hotel opens or a favourite restaurant changes hands and goes downhill. So why not write and tell us about your experiences? Contact us on 01753 893444 or e info@bradtguides.com, and we will forward your email to the author. Alternatively, you can add a review of the book on Amazon.

Please also share your photos and stories in Albania on Twitter, Instagram and Facebook and we'll share our favourites: f/🐦/📷 BradtGuides.

KEY TO SYMBOLS

- International boundary
- Railway
- Footpath
- Car / passenger ferry
- Steps
- Pedestrian street
- Railway station
- Airport
- Petrol station/garage
- Car park
- Bus station/taxis
- Border post
- One-way street
- Acccommodation
- Tourist information
- Museum/art gallery
- Theatre/cinema
- Important/historic building
- Castle/fortress
- Statue/monument
- Bank/bureau de change
- Post office

- Hospital/clinic
- Pharmacy/dentist
- Restaurant
- Café
- Bar
- Nightclub
- Church/cathedral
- Mosque
- Tomb/mausoleum
- Teqe
- Archaeological/historic site
- Historic gate
- Battle site
- Cave
- Viewpoint
- Fountain
- Bird watching
- Skiing
- Vineyard
- Stadium
- National park
- Urban park
- Market/square

Part One

GENERAL INFORMATION

ALBANIA AT A GLANCE

Location Balkan peninsula
Neighbouring countries Montenegro, Kosovo, North Macedonia, Greece
Area 28,748km^2
Climate Mediterranean
System of government Parliamentary democracy
Head of state President, elected by parliament every five years
Population 2,829,741 (2021 estimate)
Median age 37.6 years (2021)
Life expectancy Males 75.2 years; females 79.6 years (2020)
Population growth rate (annual) -0.6% (2021)
Capital city Tirana (Tiranë)
GDP per capita €4,819 (semi-final 2019 data)
Official language Albanian
Alphabet Roman
Currency Lek
Exchange rate £1 = 145 lek, €1 = 122 lek, US$1 = 111 lek (April 2022)
International telephone code +355
Time zone GMT +1
Electrical voltage 220V
Weights and measures Metric
National anthem *Himni i Flamurit* (*The Flag Hymn*), written in 1880
National flag Black double-headed eagle on red background
National holidays 1 January, 1 May, 28 November (see page 52 for other public holidays)

1

Background Information

GEOGRAPHY AND CLIMATE

Albania is in the southwest of the Balkan peninsula, bordered by Greece, the former Yugoslav republics of North Macedonia and Montenegro, and Kosovo. It is separated from Italy by the Adriatic and Ionian seas, which divide at the Bay of Vlora, about 170km up the Albanian coast; at the narrowest point, the Straits of Otranto, the two countries are only 72km apart.

Albania's surface area of 28,748km^2 (11,100 square miles) makes it slightly smaller than Belgium and slightly larger than the US state of Maryland. About 75% of its territory is mountainous – the average height above sea level is 708m, and its highest peak, Mount Korabi on the North Macedonian border northeast of Peshkopia, is 2,751m high. Most of the population lives in the remaining 25%: the coastal plain, traversed by large rivers which irrigate farmland and create wetlands where they meet the sea.

The climate is Mediterranean, with hot dry summers and mild rainy winters in the lowlands. The higher altitudes further inland make temperatures lower, and winter precipitation there often falls as snow. In the highest mountains, snow lies in the northeastern corries all year round. The lowlands have between 270 and 300 days of sunshine a year, and the sea is warm enough to swim in (comfortably) from May to October. The coldest month is January, when the mean lowland temperature is 5–10°C and inland it can fall to below –10°C. The hottest month, July, can be very hot indeed, sometimes topping 40°C inland. Sea breezes keep the coastal towns cooler.

The southern Balkans are located on the boundary between the Eurasian and African tectonic plates, which makes them susceptible to seismic activity. Albania's most recent major earthquake (6.4 on the Richter scale) was in November 2019. The epicentre was slightly north of Tirana. It caused over 50 deaths and considerable damage to buildings.

Albania's complex geological development means the country has rich mineral resources – its silver mines were probably one of the attractions for the Greek colonists of the 7th century BC. It has fairly large oil reserves, which in recent years have attracted some Western investment. Under communism, Albania was the world's second-biggest producer of chrome, although production is now a fraction of what it was then.

Albania has 362km of sea coast, with the Adriatic running from the Montenegrin border south to the Bay of Vlora, where the Ionian Sea begins. In all but a few stretches the Adriatic coast is low-lying, with large protected bays (such as those of Vlora and Durrësi) that have been used as harbours since ancient times. The Ionian coast is very rugged, with rocky coves along the narrow coastal strip and steep mountains rising almost straight up along much of its length. The highest point is at the Llogoraja Pass, over 1,000m high. Abrasion and karstic activity have created many caves at the base of the cliffs, some of which were inhabited in prehistoric times.

The country is criss-crossed with rivers, which rise in the high mountains and pass through steep gorges, before reaching the plain and making their way to the sea. The main rivers – and, increasingly, many smaller ones – are managed to generate hydro-electricity. The country's largest hydro-electric system is powered by its longest and most constant stream, the River Drini, which is 285km long and drains nearly 6,000km^2 within Albania. The longest rivers in southern Albania are the Semani, formed by the confluence of the Devolli and Osumi, and the Vjosa, which rises as the Aoos in northern Greece and runs northwestwards through the beautiful gorges between Përmeti and Tepelena.

NATURAL HISTORY AND CONSERVATION

Over a third of the territory of Albania – more than a million hectares – is forested, and the country is very rich in flora. More than 3,000 different species of plant grow in Albania and about 5% of those are either endemic or sub-endemic (meaning they also grow in neighbouring countries, but the centre of their distribution is in Albania). The box on page 170 has more information about the flora of northern Albania. Many plants are used for medicinal purposes, in cities as well as villages; more information about these can be found in the box on page 6.

The natural vegetation in the coastal strip is *maquis*, the scrubby bushes found all around the Mediterranean; in the north, where the coastal plain is wider, it is

BATS IN ALBANIA

Albania has no fewer than 32 species of bat, including some which are quite rare elsewhere in Europe. However, if you are not looking for them, you might never know they are there. They fly at night, they live in caves or bunkers, or roost high up in trees. This explains the dearth of data about bats compared with other species such as birds. Many areas of Albania have not been surveyed and about half of the country has no bat data at all.

Specialist researchers use ultrasound equipment to identify the species and number of individual bats and what use they are making of the location, for example whether they are hunting or merely passing through. Radio-tracking can also be used to collect data. Without this specialist equipment, the best way to identify bats is in their homes – caves or bunkers. Gjirokastra Castle (page 274) hosts one of the largest bat colonies in Albania, with seven different species recorded and thousands of specimens.

Perhaps the easiest bats for the amateur to identify are the horseshoe bats (*Rhinolophus*), which typically wrap their wings around their bodies as they hang from roofs or walls. Albania has all five Rhinolophus species: the greater horseshoe bat (*R. ferrumequinum*), the lesser horseshoe (*R. hipposideros*), the Mediterranean horseshoe (*R. euryale*), Blasius's horseshoe (*R. blasii*) and the very rare Mehely's horseshoe (*R. mehelyi*).

Other species of bat prefer forests to caves; in Albania, even less information has been gathered on these bats. They include Natterer's bat (*Myotis nattereri*) and Bechstein's bat (*M. bechsteinii*); the latter has recently been found in caves and in a church, perhaps because the loss of its forest habitat has forced it to adapt to new roosts. The mouse-eared bats (*M. myotis* and *M. blythii*) are found almost entirely under cultivation, while in the south many of the hillsides have been terraced and planted with olive trees. As the land rises, the scrub gives way to deciduous forest of beech and oak, with scattered patches of the rare Macedonian pine (*Pinus peuce*). Birch, fir and pine begin to predominate until the treeline is reached at around 2,000m; thereafter only mountain pastures break the harsh landscape. This subalpine and alpine zone occupies about one-eighth of Albania's territory. The forests are home to a great variety of wild animals, including wolves, bears, wild boar and chamois.

The rivers that flow into the low-lying Adriatic coast have created fertile alluvial plains and, at their mouths, exceptionally rich wetlands, which are home to many waterfowl and migratory birds. The coastal marshes were extensively drained in the 20th century to create agricultural land and eradicate malaria. Albania's flora and fauna have also been affected by pollution, as well as unregulated hunting and fishing. The Albanian government introduced a moratorium on hunting in 2014, which has subsequently been extended. However, illegal hunting continues, especially in the more easily accessible coastal wetlands.

The largest of Albania's freshwater lakes is Lake Shkodra – indeed, at 370km^2 it is the largest lake in the Balkans – which straddles the border between Albania and Montenegro. Thousands of pygmy cormorants (*Microcarbo pygmaeus*) winter on Lake Shkodra. It is relatively shallow (44m at its deepest point) and is rich in underwater flora, with more than 200 types of water plants.

By contrast, the Ohrid and Prespa lakes, in the southeast of the country, are tectonic lakes. Lake Ohrid, which is shared between Albania and North Macedonia,

all over Albania; in spring 2014, nearly 9,000 specimens were recorded during surveys throughout the country, often in mixed roosts with other species. Albania is key for the conservation of the long-fingered bat (*M. capaccinii*), which has been found to use a network of roosts in caves around Prespa Lakes, shared by three countries.

Another very common genus in Albania is the pipistrelle (*Pipistrellus*); four species have been recorded. The common pipistrelle (*P. pipistrellus*) is generally the first species to fly in Albania's main cities, which makes it easy to spot against the early evening sky.

Data collected for Schreiber's bent-winged bat (*Miniopterus schreibersii*) show that Albania hosts extensive hibernating populations. These bats roost in large clusters in caves, mixed together with other species.

The main risk to bats in Albania comes from the destruction of their habitats and roosts. Most use forests to hunt in and, as mentioned above, some also roost there. Illegal logging is an obvious threat, but the lack of data means that even legal loggers are often unaware that bats are present. In Albania, bats often use disused bunkers (see box, page 197), many of which have been destroyed. People visiting the caves where bats roost are also a threat, however good their intentions. You should take care not to pollute their environment, for example by smoking or using candles, and leave the bats in peace as soon as you have enjoyed looking at them. Don't use flash if you want to photograph the bats. Under no circumstances should you ever try to catch a bat.

More information about bats in Albania (some of it in English) can be found at w chiropteralb.wordpress.com or f Lakuriqët e Natës - Bats in Albania.

is exceptionally deep and fed mainly by karstic springs around the edges of the lake and on its bed. Unique species of fish have evolved in Lake Ohrid, among them the delicious *koran* (*Salmo letnica*) and *belushka* (*Salmo ohridanus*). The two Prespa Lakes straddle the borders of Albania, North Macedonia and Greece; in 2000 the governments of the three countries announced the creation of the Transboundary Prespa Park. Prespa is especially important for its large populations of Dalmatian and white pelicans (*Pelecanus crispus* and *Pelecanus onocrotalus*), as well as hundreds of cormorants (*Phalacrocorax carbo*).

There are 801 **protected areas** in Albania, covering about 18% of its territory. Some of them are very small, but there are 14 national parks (IUCN Category II) which cover about 8.6% of the country. The establishment in 2015 of the National Agency for Protected Areas (NAPA; **w** akzm.gov.al) has improved the management

MEDICINAL PLANTS

With thanks to Anika Dede

Albanians use many different plants for medicinal purposes; stalls selling them can be found in every town's market and villagers sometimes also sell them from the roadside. In recent years, producers have started to package the more common varieties of medicinal herb in a more controlled and hygienic environment, for sale in shops and supermarkets in Tirana and other towns.

The most popular herbal tea in Albania is *çaj mali*, a type of ironwort (*Sideritis raeseri*), which translates as **'mountain tea'**. Its medicinal effectiveness is a matter of some dispute, but Albanians of all ages drink *çaj mali* to treat virtually any kind of minor ailment, from the common cold to indigestion.

Some of the most widely used herbal remedies are described below, with their Albanian and Latin names. It should be borne in mind, however, that some of them are toxic in the wrong doses or if the wrong part of the plant is used; this list should not be used for self-medication.

Wild **chamomile** (*lule kamomili, Matricaria chamomilla*) is one of the most widely used medicinal herbs, and is native to southern and southeastern Europe. The flower heads with their stalks are gathered in the summer and dried – bundles of the herb can be bought all over Albania. Chamomile is used for digestive and nervous disorders, and as an anti-inflammatory; it is usually drunk as an infusion, but it can also be added to bathwater to soothe dermatitis.

St John's wort (*lule basani, Hypericum perforatum*), used in northern Europe as an anti-depressant, is very widely used in Albania to treat a variety of other ailments. Bundles of its long stems can often be seen on market and street stalls. It is used to treat diseases of the digestive and respiratory tracts, as well as kidney problems. It improves the circulation of the blood and helps against sleeplessness. St John's wort also has antiseptic properties, and an extract made from its flowers is used externally to prevent infection of wounds or burns.

The **lime** tree (*bliri i bardhë, Tilia*) has about 20 documented species, two of which are used medicinally. The flowers have anti-inflammatory, diuretic and mild anti-spasmodic properties, and also induce perspiration. The infusion made from them is used to treat colds and flu, and diseases of the kidneys and urinary tract. It helps to lower high temperatures and soothes nervous complaints.

The blue flowers of **borage** (*shaja, Borago officinalis*) have diuretic, antiseptic and anti-inflammatory properties, as well as being a culinary herb. Infusions of borage are used to treat urinary infections and problems of the nervous system; borage solution can also be applied externally to skin injuries and inflammations.

of these vulnerable areas. The agency has regional administration offices (RAPA) in each of the country's 12 prefectures, which are responsible for the day-to-day management of the protected areas in their own region. Unfortunately, despite the efforts of the agency's staff, the Albanian government has shown little commitment to safeguarding these protected areas from inappropriate development. Indeed, in order to proceed with plans such as the Vlora airport, the government simply redraws the boundaries of any protected areas that might get in the way.

Albania's internationally important wetlands – its **Ramsar** sites – are Lake Shkodra, Karavasta Lagoon, Prespa Lakes (three separate Ramsar sites, one for each country) and Lake Butrint. Even non-ornithologists will enjoy observing the spectacular birds in these wetlands, including pelicans, cormorants, spoonbills and flamingos (see the box on page 138 for more on waterbirds). The Albanian

Marsh mallow (*mullanjadhja, Althaea officinalis*) has been cultivated in Europe for its medicinal properties since the Middle Ages, when it was grown in monasteries. Albanians use marsh mallow, as an infusion of the roots and leaves, to treat coughs and stomach disorders; the leaves are made into poultices to heal external wounds and soften bruises.

Extracts of **hawthorn** (*murrizi, Crataegus laevigata* and other *Crataegus* species) are used commercially in drops and pills for the treatment of heart and vascular problems. In Albania, the flowers and leaves of hawthorn are made into an infusion that improves heart rhythm and lowers blood pressure.

Fennel (*maraja, Foeniculum vulgare*) is a component of many commercially available herbal tea mixtures. As an infusion, the fruit is used to treat diseases of the digestive system and respiratory tract; a similar infusion can also be used as an eye wash for minor inflammations of the eyelid or conjunctivitis.

White horehound (*kapinoku, Marrubium vulgare*) has anti-inflammatory and antiseptic properties, and its flowering stems are used to treat mild digestive disorders and inflammation of the upper respiratory tract.

Cowslip and **oxlip**, both members of the primrose family (Primulaceae) contain complex organic substances called saponins, which have an expectorant effect. Their roots or flowers are made into decoctions or infusions that are drunk to ease bronchitis and other diseases of the respiratory tract.

Blackthorn, or **sloe** (*kullumbria, Prunus spinosa*), is a spiny shrub whose white flowers have mildly diuretic and laxative properties. In Albania it is administered as an infusion to those suffering from problems of the digestive system, kidneys and urinary tract; it is also good for preventing chills and treating the symptoms of rheumatism.

Lungwort (*pulmonaria, Pulmonaria officinalis*) is one of the oldest medicinal herbs, used since the Middle Ages to treat respiratory problems. In Albania, its flowering stems are administered in the form of an infusion to treat those suffering from bronchitis.

Heartsease (*manushaqja tringjyrëshe, Viola tricolor*) is used internally and externally for its antiseptic and anti-inflammatory properties. The flowering stems are steeped in water and either administered as an infusion, to treat inflammation of the upper respiratory passages and infections of the urinary tract or kidneys; or used to soak gauze pads, which are applied as compresses to treat external wounds and dermatitis.

Ornithological Society has a wealth of information, in English, on its website: **w** aos-alb.org. Ornithologists or others wishing to access the most sensitive areas of the national parks (or the two Category I Strict Nature Reserves) should request permission in the respective RAPA.

HISTORY

PREHISTORY The country now known as Albania has been inhabited for more than ten millennia. The first Palaeolithic settlements to be excavated were in caves at Gajtan, near Shkodra, and Konispoli in the far southwest. More recent work has identified some open-air sites: Shkreli in the northwest and the area around Apollonia in central Albania, for example. The Neolithic period in this region is c6000–c2100BC and the Bronze Age is c2100–c1200BC; southeast Albania is full of sites from these periods, including the tumulus site at Kamenica (page 188). It is in the Iron Age, starting around 1200BC, that it begins to be possible to recognise the culture known as Illyrian. Some archaeologists take the view that, during the Bronze Age, the inhabitants of the Balkan peninsula began to develop tribal differences and that one of the tribes that emerged as a result was the Illyrian people, who are the ancestors of modern Albanians. Others think that the Illyrians came from elsewhere and invaded Albania at some point between the 13th and the 10th centuries BC.

There is also considerable controversy over the question of where the boundary was between Hellenes (Greeks), Epirotes (whom the Hellenes considered to be sort of Greek, in the same way as Macedonians were) and Illyrians (who were definitely barbarians, ie: not Greek). It may be that Illyrian and Epirote settlements were interspersed in what is now southern Albania and northern Greece.

ILLYRIANS What is not in question is that Illyrian culture had many distinctive features and that the ancient Greeks considered the various Illyrian tribes as similar enough to each other to form a distinct group. They built large, well-fortified cities (almost all of which were in stunning locations with magnificent views), they traded with the Greek colonies on the Adriatic coast and beyond, and they minted coins. The silver and copper that they mined was also used for personal adornments: *fibulae* (brooches) in spiralling figure-of-eight shapes; metal coils, which women twisted into their hair; and the unique *byzylyk*, bracelets that were placed on the arms and legs of a dead person as part of the burial process. In one tumulus a skeleton was found with no fewer than six *byzylykë* on each limb.

In the 3rd century BC, a northern Illyrian tribe called the **Ardiaeans** established its capital in Shkodra. The Ardiaeans were seafarers – their coins (and the modern 20-lek coin) show a small, fast galley called a *liburnis*, which was a particular favourite of pirates – and in 229BC their attacks on Italian ships brought them to war with Rome, then emerging as the most powerful state in Italy. Queen Teuta of the Ardiaeans was forced to make terms, and the Romans gained their first foothold on the other side of the Adriatic. Sixty years later, in 168BC, they defeated the Ardiaeans in battle and besieged their king, Genti (known to the Romans as Gentius), in Rozafa Castle until he surrendered. Genti was the last Illyrian king.

ROMANS From the middle of the 2nd century BC, Roman control brought peace and prosperity to Albania. To connect the Adriatic coast with Thessalonica and Byzantium, the Romans built one of their great arterial roads, the Via Egnatia (page 295). The road was named after a Roman proconsul of Macedonia, Gnaeus Egnatius, who laid it and built bridges along it in the 2nd century BC, using an ancient route that linked southern Illyria with Macedonia. The starting points were Dyrrachium (now Durrësi) and Apollonia, and at the place where these two branches joined a town grew up, which later acquired the name of Elbasani. The Romans built other roads too – one down the coast from Shkodra through Durrësi to Butrint and beyond, another from Shkodra east through Prizreni to Niš.

Julius Caesar visited the province of Illyricum in 56BC, while it was under his command, but the first time he is known to have come specifically to what is now Albania was in 48BC, pursuing his opponent in the Civil War, Pompey. Octavian studied in Apollonia before he became the Emperor Augustus, and rewarded the city afterwards with tax-free status. Many Roman citizens bought estates or settled in Albania. Lissus (Lezha) had a community of Roman citizens when Mark Antony landed there with Caesar's reinforcements in 48BC; a friend of Cicero's owned land near Buthrotum (Butrint). Dyrrachium, a free city in the Republic, became a Roman colony under Augustus, who also founded colonies at Byllis and Buthrotum.

On the final division of the Roman Empire in AD395, Albania came under Constantinople's authority, rather than Rome's. This meant that when the Western Empire collapsed in the 5th century, Albania became part of the Byzantine Empire.

BYZANTINES The 4th, 5th and 6th centuries saw destabilising invasions of Albania by Visigoths and then Ostrogoths, who occupied Dyrrachium in AD480 and used it as a base from which to invade Italy and set up a kingdom there. Shkodra was sacked in AD380 and Onchesmus (now Saranda) was completely destroyed in AD551. However, in between invasions, life went on. Bishops were installed and churches were built. The great builder-emperor, Justinian (AD527–65), ordered the fortification or refortification of several cities, including Dyrrachium and Byllis.

In the 10th century, Bulgaria captured large swathes of the Balkans, including all of Albania. The Byzantines were only able to recover this territory after 1018. However, the respite was short. In 1081, a large Norman army, under Robert Guiscard, landed at Avlona (Vlora) and proceeded up the coast to Dyrrachium. The ensuing battle is described in great detail by Anna Comnena, the daughter of the Byzantine emperor Alexius I Comnenus. (Among his allies were a people called the Albanoi.) Despite initial success, the Battle of Dyrrachium was a crushing defeat for Byzantium. Many of the empire's officers were killed; the European troops who had formed the backbone of its army proved to be undisciplined and useless and were replaced with foreign mercenaries. The decisive moment in the battle was a shock charge by the Norman cavalry, holding their lances ahead of them instead of throwing them. This innovation had been tested at the Battle of Hastings, and would be used to even more devastating effect in the First Crusade 15 years later.

After a siege lasting several months, the Normans went on to take Dyrrachium and other coastal towns, as a prelude to an advance to the east two years later; by the middle of the following year, the whole of Illyria was in their hands. Alexius I fought back, however. Allied with the Venetians, who wanted (and got) control of Dyrrachium and Corfu, Byzantium had retaken most of its Balkan territories by the end of 1083.

Constantinople fell to the Fourth Crusade in 1204, and for the rest of that century competing successor states vied for pre-eminence. One of these became known as the **Despotate of Epirus**, whose capital was at Arta (now in northwestern Greece) and whose boundaries extended north to Dyrrachium and, at times, east to Macedonia and Thessalonica. It was founded soon after the fall of Constantinople by Michael I Comnenus Ducas, an illegitimate grandson of Alexius I Comnenus. His own illegitimate son, Michael II Comnenus Ducas, who ruled from about 1237 to 1271, seems to have been the first to use the title of Despot of Epirus. A despot was a kind of imperial regent and provincial administrator, and the title was usually awarded by the emperor.

In 1256, Michael II embarked on a campaign to capture Thessalonica, a city then held by one of the other mini empires, that of Nicaea, and by early summer he was at the city's gates. Early in 1258, however, Durrësi, Vlora and Butrint fell to Prince Manfred of Sicily; Michael II reacted by offering him his daughter in marriage, with the conquered territory as her dowry, and forming an alliance with the kingdoms of Sicily and Achaia against Nicaea. The newly crowned co-Emperor of Nicaea, Michael Palaeologus, dispatched a large army to the Balkans which took the Epirote army by surprise at Kastoria. Michael II Comnenus Ducas regrouped with his allies at Vlora, but they were conclusively defeated at Pelagonia (now Bitola, in North Macedonia) in the summer of 1259. The Nicaeans captured Arta and Michael II took refuge on the island of Cephalonia. He made his way back to Arta the following year, but it was too late for the Despotate of Epirus to reassert itself. On 15 August 1261, Michael VIII Palaeologus entered Constantinople in triumph after the fall of the Latin Empire.

Meanwhile, Albania continued to be tussled over. Manfred Hohenstaufen, by then King of Sicily, died in battle in 1266 against the crusade of Charles of Anjou, the younger brother of King Louis of France. In 1275, the Byzantines retook Butrint and Berati, driving the Angevins back to the Adriatic coast. Five years later, Charles dispatched an army of about 8,000 eastwards across Albania to Berati; the garrison and people in the fortified citadel there held out until a relief army from Constantinople reached them in March 1281 and inflicted a crushing defeat on the Angevin troops. Albania was now back in Byzantine hands.

However, the Byzantine Empire had been fatally weakened during its years of exile from Constantinople and, in the 14th century, it was able to devote less and less energy to its western periphery. The Angevins recaptured Durrësi in 1307; the Serbian king Stefan Dušan invaded Albania in 1343, and got as far south as Vlora and Berati. The Serbs never exercised full control over the country, however. Instead it became a patchwork of semi-independent states run by powerful Albanian families; on Stefan Dušan's untimely death in 1355, they were left as the only functioning authorities. They included the Balshajs in northern Albania, the Muzakajs in and around Berati, and the Topias in central Albania – in the 1380s, Karl Topia rebuilt the church of St Gjon Vladimir near Elbasani (page 106).

THE OTTOMAN CONQUEST The Ottomans had first settled on European soil in 1354, much to the alarm of John VI Cantacuzenus, the Byzantine historian and – at the time – co-emperor. In 1371, Sultan Murad I's troops routed the Serbian army at the river Maritsa; and in June 1389 a coalition of Serbs, Hungarians, Bosnians, Bulgarians and Albanians, under the leadership of the Serbian prince Lazar, met the Ottoman troops on the Field of Blackbirds (Kosovo Polje, in Serbian). The sultan was killed, but the coalition was routed and Prince Lazar executed. The few Serbian nobles who survived were obliged to swear a personal oath of allegiance to the new sultan, Murad's son Bayezid.

Bayezid marched against Constantinople in 1394, and the city remained under siege for eight years, until the Mongol army under **Tamurlane** swept into Asia Minor and defeated the Ottomans in 1402. Bayezid was taken prisoner and died in captivity. His successor as sultan, Mehmed I, returned to Albania; in 1417, Ottoman forces captured Vlora and then Gjirokastra. But their grip on the country was weak and Albania had not yet given up. The early 1430s saw rebellions, put down in 1433. In 1443, the Ottoman army was defeated at the Serbian town of Niš, by a crusade under a multi-national leadership, which included the Hungarian hero János Hunyadi. At this point Skanderbeg, an Albanian nobleman who had been trained as a soldier in the Ottoman army, raised a rebellion from his family seat at Kruja (see box, page 136). Thanks to Skanderbeg's ability to unify the Albanian clans against the enemy, they resisted the occupiers until 1479 – 26 years after the Ottomans had taken the Byzantine capital.

Under Islamic law, non-Muslims living under Muslim sovereignty are treated as 'protected infidels', a status quite different from that of non-Muslims under non-Muslim sovereignty, who can legitimately be killed or enslaved. The Christians in Albania (and elsewhere) were not obliged to convert to Islam, but they did have to pay a capitation tax. It was by virtue of this tax that their lives and property enjoyed legal protection.

Perhaps even more significant for Christian peasants was the **'Collection'**, or *devshirme*, whereby non-Turkish families throughout the empire were required to give up one of their sons to the sultan. Between the 14th and late 16th centuries, the Collection was the main source of recruitment into imperial service, and it must have been a huge sacrifice for peasant families who needed their sons to work their land (although if a family had only one son, he was spared). The best-looking youths in each intake were educated in the Palace Schools and sometimes worked their way up to become governors or other senior officials. Most of the 'collected' boys, though, became Janissaries, members of the sultan's personal infantry corps. Originally, the Janissaries consisted of a few hundred men who served as the sultan's bodyguards. Although their numbers grew over the years, they remained a small, elite corps – during the 16th century, they numbered around 10,000 at any one time. They were fiercely loyal to the Ottoman dynasty, although not necessarily to individual sultans; Janissary rebellions forced at least two sultans to abdicate.

As for those selected for the Palace Schools, after their education was complete they could become pages to the sultan, serve in the military palace guard or join one of the cavalry divisions attached to the palace; if they had a particular interest in Islamic law, they could become *imams*; if their aptitude lay in languages, they might become clerks. It was the sultan's personal pages, however, who stood the best chance of achieving the great offices of the empire – *viziers*, imperial treasurers and chancellors. Many Albanians became Grand Viziers, such as Daud Pasha, who was Grand Vizier from 1485 to 1497, and Koja Sinan Pasha a century later.

INDEPENDENCE In many cases, in fact, it was Ottoman civil servants who provided the intellectual framework and the creative impulse for the **Albanian nationalist movement** that began to emerge in the late 19th century. Abdyl Frashëri (see box, page 206), for example, was Director of Finance for the *vilayet* (province) of Ioannina. He was a senior figure in the Prizren League, whose original goal was merely the unification of the four Albanian-speaking *vilayets*, but which by 1881 was campaigning for autonomy within the Ottoman Empire. The League succeeded in expelling the imperial administrators from Kosovo, but it was crushed shortly afterwards and its leaders were imprisoned.

The nationalist movement now realised that the Albanian language could be a tool with which to build a sense of national unity, and the focus of its campaigning shifted to cultural and linguistic demands. Albanian books and magazines were published and Albanian-medium schools (ie: schools that taught subjects in the Albanian language) were opened (page 184). A generation of great Albanian poets emerged, who embodied the national cultural renaissance (Rilindja Kombëtare) under way.

One obstacle to national unity was the fact that Albanians of different religious faiths wrote their language in different alphabets – Muslims used the Arabic script, Orthodox southerners the Greek alphabet, and northern Catholics the Roman. Agreement on a common alphabet therefore became a pressing aim of the Rilindja movement, and in 1909 a congress in Elbasani formally adopted the Roman alphabet used to this day.

The **First Balkan War** started on 8 October 1912 when Montenegro attacked northern Albania, which was still part of the Ottoman Empire. The other Balkan countries immediately joined in, the Ottoman army crumbled and Albania found itself invaded from all sides. Practically abandoned by their Ottoman rulers, the Albanians realised that if they did not obtain independence their territory would be swallowed up by their Balkan neighbours. Meanwhile, Austria-Hungary had become concerned that Greek, Serb and Italian designs on Albania would reduce its own influence in the Balkans – its southern backyard. Ismail Qemali, who had been one of 26 Albanians elected to the Istanbul parliament after the Young Turk revolution of 1908, travelled to Vienna and Budapest to obtain diplomatic support for Albanian independence.

By the time the war began, much of Albania was already up in arms and Albanian soldiers were deserting the Ottoman army, although others fought bravely with the Ottoman forces against the Montenegrins. Rebels led by the Kosovar Isa Boletini occupied Skopje, took control of Kosovo and captured large tracts of what is now Albanian territory. When Ismail Qemali returned from his diplomatic tour, he learned that Serbian troops were approaching the Adriatic. Northern Albania was being invaded by the Balkan League and the Greek navy was attacking in the south – it was in difficult circumstances indeed that on 28 November 1912, 83 delegates from all parts of Albania gathered in Vlora and proclaimed Albania's independence.

The Great Powers – Austria-Hungary, Britain, France, Germany, Italy and Russia – formally recognised independent Albania in May 1913. In June, after 500 years, the last Ottoman troops left Albanian soil. The Great Powers appointed an International Commission of Control to draft a constitution, and Frontier Commissions to demarcate its borders. They refused to recognise the provisional government set up in Vlora and appointed a German prince as a puppet monarch. Prince Wilhelm of Wied never governed beyond Durrësi and gave up altogether after only six months (for more about this interlude, see box, page 94). Albania sank into anarchy as its leaders fought among themselves for power and, during World War I, it fragmented into a mess of 'autonomous' statelets under the influence of the various countries that had designs on its territory. It would not begin to recover until the 1920s.

KING ZOG One of the leaders who emerged during this chaotic period was Ahmed Zogu, a clan chief from the Mati district in northern central Albania. He participated in the Congress of Lushnja in January 1920, which appointed a senate and a cabinet to restore political order and a High Council of State to oversee them. Zogu was made Interior Minister in the new government. Over the next few years he went on to consolidate his power base, and in December 1924 – after a brief period out of power – he marched on Tirana and overthrew the Democratic Party government of Fan Noli. He quickly abolished the High Council of State, became president, and set about rewriting the constitution and eliminating his opponents.

By the mid 1920s, Italian influence over Albania was increasing. Italian companies were building roads and improving harbours, Italian colonists were settling in parts of the south and, in November 1927, a large Italian military mission was installed in the country, with Italian officers attached to Albanian military units. In 1928, Zogu

SPECIAL OPERATIONS EXECUTIVE (SOE) – THE EARLY YEARS

M C Barrès-Baker

The Special Operations Executive (SOE) was created in July 1940. Placed under the Minister of Economic Warfare and intended 'to co-ordinate… subversion and sabotage, against the enemy overseas', it combined Section D of MI6, the propaganda branch of the Foreign Office and a research branch of the War Office.

In November 1940, the exiled King Zog planned a revolt in northern Albania. SOE feared, possibly wrongly, that Zog was so unpopular that supporting him would actually weaken Albanian resistance. In any case the plan was opposed by the Greeks and just about everybody else; nothing came of it.

In April 1941, SOE sent Lieutenant-Colonel Dayrell Oakley-Hill, who had helped organise Zog's gendarmes before the war, into northern Albania, along with 300 resisters. He was to foment a rebellion but, when Germany invaded Yugoslavia, the operation turned into a diversion to support the Yugoslavs. The tiny invasion received little support and the situation rapidly became hopeless. Oakley-Hill eventually surrendered to the Germans in Belgrade.

In early 1942, SOE headquarters in Cairo began to plan subversion in Albania again. Until 1944, the ethnographer Margaret Hasluck (see box, page 104) ran the SOE Albania desk from Cairo. Since the British didn't recognise an Albanian government-in-exile, they were prepared to work with all Albanian resisters. In April 1943, Major Neil 'Billy' McLean and Captain David Smiley entered from northern Greece and contacted the National Liberation Movement (LNÇ, predominantly partisan) and the anti-communist, anti-Zog Balli Kombëtar. Weapons drops began in June. Initially the aircraft flew from Cyrenaica, moving in December to Italy from where sea sorties were also made. Most supplies went to the partisans, despite McLean and partisan leader Enver Hoxha having developed a growing mutual antipathy. A series of meetings between the LNÇ and Balli Kombëtar, possibly brokered by SOE and the Zogist Abas Kupi, led to the short-lived Mukje Agreements in August.

The Italian surrender exacerbated the divisions between the LNÇ and the nationalists, and civil war threatened. In October 1943, SOE sent in an enlarged mission under Brigadier E F 'Trotsky' Davies, withdrawing McLean. Davies and his men continued to work with the resistance and carry out sabotage, despite growing civil conflict and large-scale German anti-partisan offensives over the winter. He was also charged with uniting the Albanians, or with recommending which group Britain should recognise. 'It sounded so simple,' Davies wrote later. 'In Albania I was to find the whole matter very complex and difficult.' Initially Davies recommended supporting all groups that fought the Germans, but in December he recommended limiting support to the partisans – by far the most active resisters. Davies was captured in January 1944.

SOE, now based in Bari, followed his first recommendation. Norman Wheeler, and later Alan Palmer, took over in the south. In April 1944, McLean and Smiley, along with Julian Amery, returned to northern Albania as part of a mission to Kupi. McLean became very close to Kupi, and hoped he could be built up as an alternative to the partisans. The aims of the two SOE missions rapidly diverged.

crowned himself Zog I, King of the Albanians, and promulgated a new constitution that gave him practically unrestricted powers.

Meanwhile, Italian 'advisers' were installing themselves in the ministries, Italian architects were redesigning Tirana and Italian businessmen were taking over the country's economy. By 1938, Italy accounted for 68.4% of Albania's exports and 36.3% of its imports. Eventually, on 7 April 1939, Mussolini annexed Albania and Italian troops invaded and occupied it. The king sent his wife, Queen Geraldine, and two-day-old son, Leka, to safety across the Greek border, following them himself later in the day. Zog would never return to Albania; he died in Paris in 1961, from where his remains were repatriated in 2012, the centenary of Albanian independence. His widow and son both died in Tirana: Geraldine, who by then styled herself the Queen Mother (Nëna Mbretëresha), in October 2002; Leka, in 2011.

WORLD WAR II Events in Albania during World War II are a matter of extreme controversy and political polarisation. The various liberation groups can be broadly

SPECIAL OPERATIONS EXECUTIVE (SOE) – LIBERATION

M C Barrès-Baker

By April 1944, the partisans were organised like a regular army. They had 13,000 soldiers, formed into 12 brigades. Despite their communist leadership, they were a broad-based popular resistance movement. Abas Kupi had only 5,000 men, and they were far less active than the partisans. Hoxha clearly mistrusted his SOE liaison officers, but his troops killed Germans. 'Billy' McLean's attempt to convince SOE in Bari to consider Kupi as a serious alternative to the partisans was therefore doomed. Although Bari officially supported both groups, the partisans continued to receive the bulk of air-dropped supplies.

Between spring 1943 and late 1944, about 50 British officers were sent to Albania. They were a varied group: Smiley was happiest when 'blowing things up'; Peter Kemp had fought as a nationalist volunteer in the Spanish Civil War; Davies ended the war in Colditz; Reginald Hibbert would become British Ambassador in Paris; and Julian Amery went on to become a Conservative MP. Amery got into trouble for wearing a beard while in uniform at Bari and, while moving in disguise around a Tirana full of occupying German soldiers in light summer uniforms, had a sudden insight into what it must be like to be a colonial subject of the British Empire. A sort of *Boy's Own* adventure atmosphere comes across in some SOE men's memoirs, but this was frustrating, gruelling and dangerous work. Several SOE men (not just officers) have graves in the Tirana Park Memorial Cemetery. The highest-ranking man buried there, Brigadier Arthur Nicholls, developed severe frostbite during the German offensive over the winter of 1943/44. Despite medical assistance from his Albanian colleagues, he died three days after his 33rd birthday. He was awarded a posthumous George Cross.

In July 1944, the partisans launched a major offensive, entering Kupi's heartland. Fearing all-out civil war, SOE stopped supplying them, but further partisan successes against the Germans led to this decision being reversed. Bari now signed military agreements with the LNÇ. Faced with this clear British move towards the partisans, Kupi and the Ballists both engaged the Germans more forcefully, but SOE was not impressed. In September 1944, it gave up on them completely. McLean and Smiley were ordered to return to Bari. Dismayed by the lack of support for Kupi, Smiley and Amery later claimed that SOE was bedazzled categorised as 'nationalist', meaning those who wanted the post-war borders of Albania to include Kosovo and other Albanian-speaking lands, and 'partisan', meaning those who ultimately came out on top and took power after liberation. The former group included supporters of King Zog, such as Abas Kupi, who came to call themselves the Legality (Legaliteti) Movement, and supporters of the Noli government, such as Mit'hat Frashëri, who founded the National Front (Balli Kombëtar) Party in April 1939, immediately after the Italian invasion. The latter group included Enver Hoxha and Mehmet Shehu, and its core was the Albanian Communist Party.

Albania remained part of Italy for more than four years, although the Greek army occupied parts of the south when the Italian invasion of Greece went awry in late 1940. When Italy surrendered in September 1943, the occupying army in Albania disintegrated – some Italian soldiers became servants on Albanian farms in order to get enough food to survive. As in Italy itself, the Wehrmacht stepped into the gap; a Council of Regency was set up, consisting of four Albanian politicians

by the partisans and infiltrated by communist agents. The books in which they made these claims were widely read, unlike Hibbert's memoir of his work with the partisans, and for many years their views became the accepted version.

Fearing a partisan victory, many nationalists were by now fighting alongside the Germans. Kupi refused to do this, disbanding his forces instead. The British authorities in Italy refused to evacuate him, but he still managed to get out of Albania and across the Adriatic.

In October, British commandos helped liberate Saranda, making Hoxha very suspicious. Long Range Desert Group forward observers directed RAF air support during the battle for Tirana and SOE men accompanied the partisan brigades into the city.

The end of the war was not the end of British involvement in Albania. From 1949 to 1953, the American CIA and British military intelligence attempted to overthrow Hoxha by covert means. It has been claimed that Cambridge spy Kim Philby gave Moscow details of the operation, but the plans overestimated the ability of ordinary Albanians to rise up against the regime. Many infiltrators, code-named 'pixies' by their Anglo-American handlers, lost their lives.

After the war, Hoxha denied, or greatly played down, British aid to the partisans. Indeed, he destroyed all trace of the British War Cemetery, moving the bodies to an unmarked collective grave, with the result that, until 1995, men who had died in Albania were commemorated at Phaleron War Cemetery in Greece. Even now, most of the grave markers at Tirana Park Memorial Cemetery do not correspond precisely to where these men lie. On the other hand, some in the West accused the SOE of having enabled the communists to seize power. Most historians now accept that the aid was very useful to the partisans, but that they would have defeated the other groups anyway. Several SOE agents who served in Albania subsequently wrote memoirs. For details of these, see page 293.

Initially, the post-communist government recognised the achievements only of SOE personnel who had worked closely with Kupi, but for the Liberation Day celebrations in November 1994 they invited all the wartime British Liaison Officers they could. Only two managed to attend – Hibbert and Smiley. Both men were awarded the Order of Liberty, First Class.

who were prepared to collaborate with the Germans, and the country was formally independent once more.

Many Albanians, however, refused to accept the German occupation. In the vicious war that followed, Albanians fought both against and alongside the Germans, and against each other. Beyond the intellectual elite of Tirana, Albanian politics is still essentially based on who did what to whom during World War II.

Both nationalists and partisans were assisted by British officers, infiltrated into Albania from 1943 by the Special Operations Executive, or SOE (see boxes on pages 13 and 14). Gradually, however, Britain gave greater support to the partisans, supplying them with weapons, ammunition and clothing. In May 1944, at a congress in the southern town of Përmeti, a provisional government was elected. The Congress of Përmeti consolidated the exclusion that had begun the previous year of the non-communist forces, annulled various decisions and agreements made by the pre-war monarchist government, and specifically banned King Zog from returning to Albania.

In September, partisan brigades began to advance on Tirana. The Battle for the Liberation of Tirana lasted 19 days, from 29 October to 17 November; intense street fighting raged up and down the city, with the partisans receiving some air support from RAF Beaufighters. By the end of November, the Germans had been driven out of Shkodra, their last foothold in Albania, and the communist government controlled the whole country.

COMMUNISM Albania was impoverished and devastated at the end of World War II. An estimated 28,000 people had been killed and thousands more were homeless. The United Nations implemented a relief programme and the new government, under its prime minister, Enver Hoxha, organised brigades of peasants to repair roads and rebuild houses. Meanwhile, industry, banking and transport were nationalised, the property of those who had fled the country for political reasons was confiscated and, in 1945, an agrarian reform law broke up and redistributed privately owned estates. The following year all surplus agricultural land was taken over by state farms or co-operatives.

At this time, the relationship between Albania and Yugoslavia was still good – Belgrade gave generous economic assistance to its neighbour, despite its own need for reconstruction. As far as Britain and the USA were concerned, however, Albania suspected their embassies of encouraging opponents of the regime (probably with some justification) and started to restrict their diplomats' movements. Britain withdrew its diplomatic mission in April 1946, followed later that year by the USA.

Relations between Britain and Albania became even worse after the **Corfu Channel incident** of October 1946, when two British destroyers hit mines in the narrow strait between Ksamili and Corfu, and more than 40 crew members were killed. The mines had been recently laid, rather than forming part of a wartime minefield, and Britain accused Albania of deliberately laying them. The matter was the first-ever case referred to the International Court of Justice, which ruled against Albania and ordered it to pay compensation. Many historians now think that Yugoslav ships were responsible, although Albania's (and Britain's) role in the episode is still far from clear.

When Yugoslavia was expelled from Cominform (the post-war body that replaced Comintern) in 1948, Albania immediately sided with the Soviet Union and annulled all its economic agreements with its neighbour. This was also the year that the Albanian Communist Party changed its name to the Party of Labour (Partia e Punës së Shqipërisë; PPSH).

The 1950s was a decade of **industrialisation**, with hydro-electric plants built to provide power for the new factories and mines. In 1954, the year after Stalin's death, Mehmet Shehu took over the position of prime minister, although Enver Hoxha stayed on as First Secretary of the party and continued to wield considerable power. Shehu had been one of the partisans' most illustrious generals; before the war he had attended Italian military school, been expelled for left-wing activities and fought in the Spanish Civil War. He was interned in France and returned to Albania on his release in 1942.

By the late 1950s, relations between China and the Soviet Union were deteriorating and Albania took China's side. In 1961, this culminated in a complete severance of diplomatic links between Albania and the USSR and, in 1968, Albania withdrew from the Warsaw Pact. In 1967, in the wake of the Chinese Cultural Revolution, Albania banned the practice of religion and declared itself the world's first **atheist state**. Christian and Muslim clerics were shot or imprisoned, and churches and mosques were demolished or converted into warehouses or sports halls. Only a few very old or exceptionally beautiful religious buildings were spared.

After Mao's death in 1976, China lost interest in Albania and in 1978 it ended its aid programmes there. Albania now had no powerful ally to protect and subsidise it, and had little option but to begin to improve relations with its neighbours – first with Yugoslavia and later, after the restoration of democracy there, with Greece. However, most Albanians – those who did not take part in sporting or cultural delegations or get to attend trade fairs – were almost completely cut off from the rest of the world.

Rapprochement with Yugoslavia caused divisions within the party and the government, which Hoxha usually resolved by eliminating those who disagreed with him. Mehmet Shehu fell out of favour and was found dead in December 1981. It was rumoured that Hoxha had shot him, but Shehu's own sons believe their father committed suicide. They and their mother were imprisoned; Shehu's widow died in prison, while his sons were released in 1991. Hoxha himself died in 1985 and was succeeded as First Secretary by Ramiz Alia (1925–2011), one of the few northerners to have gained prominence in the PPSH.

Alia attempted to improve relations with Albania's neighbours, but internally there was little liberalisation of any sort until after the Berlin Wall had fallen. Then a few minor political reforms were announced and religious worship was again tolerated. In 1990, thousands of Albanians climbed over the walls of the Western embassy buildings in Tirana, in an attempt to flee the country. Students began demonstrations and hunger strikes, demanding, first of all, better living conditions in their halls of residence, then the removal of Enver Hoxha's name from that of the national university, and finally 'freedom [and] democracy'. On 11 December 1990, the government at last agreed to allow independent political parties. When the Democratic Party (DP) was formed the following day, it was the first opposition party in Albania for half a century.

THE 1990S In February 1991, a march in support of the striking students turned into a symbolic and historic event, when the demonstrators poured into Skanderbeg Square and pulled down the 10m-high statue of Enver Hoxha which dominated it. A few weeks later tens of thousands of young men climbed aboard ships docked in the ports of Durrësi and Vlora, and forced their crews to take them across the Adriatic to the Italian port of Brindisi. It was in this tense environment that, on 31 March 1991, Albania's first multi-party elections were held. The DP and other newly formed parties contested the elections, but were unable to make much headway against the PPSH electoral machine. Despite the parliamentary arithmetic, however, the PPSH government was brought down only weeks later by a general strike. A cross-party government took over and new elections were held on 22 March 1992, which the DP won by a landslide.

The PPSH subsequently rebranded itself as the Socialist Party and carried out internal reforms, in particular allowing considerable autonomy to its youth wing, whose members were not tainted by association with the party's communist past.

The DP governed until 1997, when it, too, was brought down. This time the cause of the unrest was the failure of pyramid investment schemes, which had sprung up in 1995 and 1996. The 'pyramids' offered a rate of return that people with any experience of Western capitalism would have known was unsustainable. The Albanians, however, isolated as they had been, were easily convinced to deposit their savings there; some sold their houses or farms to raise cash to invest in the pyramids. Even educated people who knew deep down that it was too good to be true allowed themselves to be carried along. Towards the end of 1996, some of the smaller pyramid 'banks' began to fail, as was inevitable, and savers began to panic, which was also inevitable.

Street demonstrations spread and soon became riots. In the generally anti-DP cities of the south, the riots grew from simple protests against the disappearance of people's savings to a full-scale rebellion against the government, which quickly spread to other parts of the country. Police and army officers fled and looters broke into their weapons stores. Anything connected to the state was ransacked and destroyed, from DP offices and police stations to state-owned hotels and children's swing-parks.

The anarchy lasted for weeks and was only brought under any sort of control by the arrival of an international peacekeeping force, the promise of new elections, and the establishment of a caretaker, cross-party government. The elections of June 1997 were conducted in circumstances in which normal campaigning was impossible and voter intimidation was widespread. Nonetheless, the results were accepted by the DP president, who resigned just before the new, socialist-dominated parliament convened.

The incoming government restored its authority gradually over central Albania, but there was still considerable instability in much of the rest of the country. Over half a million weapons had been looted in the spring of 1997, and attempts to persuade people to hand them back were largely unsuccessful. In September 1998, the political situation took a turn for the worse with the assassination of a DP Member of Parliament, Azem Hajdari. For a few days, violence returned to the streets of Tirana, fortunately without spiralling out of control.

Gradually Albania pieced itself back together. Its central and local authorities won widespread praise for their response to the crisis in Kosovo, which brought half a million refugees across its borders. Its Interior Ministry and police chiefs cleared the car-jackers off the highways and locked up the armed gangs who controlled some towns and cities. Ordinary Albanians were horrified by what happened to their country in 1997. This, perhaps more than anything else, has ensured that Albania has subsequently avoided sliding into similar turmoil, even when political tensions have run high.

GOVERNMENT AND POLITICS

Albania is a parliamentary democracy, governed by a constitution passed in 1998. One hundred and forty members, elected through regional party lists, sit in its parliament. Their mandate runs for four years and the last elections were held in April 2021, when the Socialist Party retained its overall majority. The largest opposition parties are the Democratic Party and the Socialist Movement for Integration (LSI). Every five years, the parliament elects the country's president, who is the head of state.

Local government is conducted by 61 municipal councils and their directly elected mayors. In addition, there are 12 prefectures, each headed by an appointee of central government. The prefects co-ordinate the regional departments of the various ministries and have some oversight over the local councils' work. For macro-planning purposes, each local council elects delegates from its number to a regional authority (*qark*) whose boundaries correspond with those of the prefecture.

ECONOMY

The Democratic Party government elected in 1992 inherited an economy in ruins, where GDP had fallen by more than 50% since 1989. It launched an economic reform programme that included price and exchange system liberalisation, fiscal consolidation, monetary restraint and an incomes policy. These were complemented by a comprehensive package of structural reforms, including privatisation, enterprise and financial sector reform, and creation of the legal framework for a market economy and private sector activity.

These reforms were similar to those applied in other newly democratic countries of central and eastern Europe, and were popularly known as 'shock therapy'. The growth and currency stabilisation that they brought were accompanied by unemployment and a sharp reduction in state benefits. In 1995, GDP growth began to stall and inflation to increase – in 1996, it approached 20% and in 1997, the year of the civil uprising, it reached 50%.

Since 1998, however, the economy has stabilised and GDP has steadily increased (although probably not in the 2020–21 financial year), thanks mainly to the expansion of the services sector, which accounts for nearly half of GDP. Agriculture, mostly on small family farms, accounts for about half of employment but about 20% of GDP. The construction industry has fallen back from its peak in 2008 to about 9% of GDP. The economy is further bolstered by remittances from Albanians abroad, mainly in Greece and Italy, which, although they have declined in recent years, still account for 7% of GDP.

The grey economy may be as large as 50% of official GDP. Much of this comes from the cultivation and export of cannabis, which is widely grown throughout the country. Spectacular police raids on cannabis plantations make international headlines from time to time.

ETHNIC GROUPS

Most people who live in Albania are ethnically Albanian. Nine national minorities are officially recognised, but accurate figures for their numbers are not available. The most recent census, conducted in 2011 (the Covid-19 pandemic delayed the next census until 2022), was the first to include a question about ethnic and cultural affiliation, but this was one of several optional questions and nearly 16% of respondents chose not to answer it. The nationwide figures also give a misleading impression because most ethnic minorities are clustered in specific districts, rather than being evenly spread throughout the country.

The largest minority is the Greek-speaking community, which is concentrated in southern Albania. There are state-funded Greek-medium schools in that part of the country, and ethnic Greeks are active in the political and commercial life of Albania. The nationwide figure for the Greek community in the 2011 census is 0.87%, although it is likely that there is some underreporting. The Roma and Vlach (Aromanian) communities make up the second-largest ethnic groups, with 0.3% each at national level. As in most other countries, Roma are almost completely excluded from the political process and many live in extremely precarious conditions of great poverty.

Vlachs were originally transhumant shepherds and they are found all over the Balkans. The main centres of Vlach population in Albania are in villages in the Korça district (Voskopoja is one; Mborja is another) and across the central lowlands in towns such as Lushnja and Berati. Their language is very similar to Romanian and many Albanian Vlachs have emigrated to study or work in Romania. It is not known when the two groups divided, but the languages are close enough that a modern Romanian and an Albanian Vlach can converse with each other.

Egyptians and various Slavic groups are the other main minorities in Albania. The Egyptian, or Jevg, community claims to be descended from Egyptian mercenaries who came to Albania with Alexander the Great's army. This community, too, exists in other Balkan countries; in Albanian-speaking lands their mother tongue is Albanian. Egyptians are often lumped in with Roma, but they look different and are more integrated into Albanian society. The main thing the two communities have in common is the extreme discrimination they face.

There are Slavic-speaking settlements around Lake Prespa, where they are ethnically (North) Macedonian; in the border area between Peshkopia and Kukësi, where they are Gorani, like their cousins (often literally) across the border in Kosovo; and around Lake Shkodra and in Malësia e Madhe, where they are ethnically Montenegrin.

Local government reform in 2014 created three municipalities where national minorities are the majority community locally. Two have ethnically Greek majorities: Finiq and Dropull, in the southwest of the country. The third is Macedonian-speaking Pustec, around Lake Prespa.

LANGUAGE

Albanian is an Indo-European language, in the same large family as Greek, Italian and Serbo-Croat (and English), but in a separate linguistic branch from all of them. It shares certain grammatical features with Romanian, and the point at which the two languages diverged is a matter of great controversy among philologists of both countries.

Albania was part of the Ottoman Empire for more than 400 years (page 10) and many Turkish words, often themselves derived from Arabic, thus became assimilated into the Albanian language, including *reçel* (jam), *koltuk* (armchair), *sahat* (clock), *çantë* (bag) and *para* (money). Greek words have also made their way into Albanian, and are used particularly in the south (eg: 'Are you hungry?', '*A ke oreks?*').

The grammatical structure of Albanian is instantly recognisable to anyone who has studied other Indo-European languages. People who speak French or another Romance language will notice cognates such as *furrë* (*four*, oven), *qen* (*chien*, dog) and the numbers *dy* and *katër* (two and four). That said, however, it must be admitted that Albanian grammar is difficult and much of its vocabulary does not look familiar on first acquaintance.

Albanians themselves are rather pleased that their language is reputed to be so difficult. They will waste no time in telling you with glee that the Albanian alphabet has 36 letters; they will regale you with stories of elderly peasants from opposite ends of the country who are unable to understand each other's dialect. They will be delighted if you learn some of their language, but somewhat taken aback if you speak it well.

THE ALPHABET The 36 letters of the alphabet include two letters with diacritic marks (*ë* and *ç*) and nine digraphs, meaning letters that are written using two consonants but that are considered to be a single letter (*dh*, *gj*, *ll*, *nj*, *rr*, *sh*, *th*, *xh* and *zh*). This makes the printed language look scarier than it really is – most of the 36 letters will cause no difficulty at all. Each of the consonants is always pronounced in the same way, wherever it appears in the word; vowels can be short or long, but the language is fairly phonetic, which makes it very easy to learn phrases. A guide to pronunciation and a list of everyday words and phrases can be found on page 284.

DIALECTS A dialect is a language variant that is sufficiently different from another variant of the same language, and sufficiently consistent within itself, to be more than just an accent. Three dialects of Albanian are normally recognised: Arbëresh is spoken in parts of southern Italy, where Albanians settled after the Ottoman conquest of their country; Gheg is spoken in northern Albania, Kosovo, Montenegro and northwestern North Macedonia; and Tosk is spoken in southern Albania, Skopje and the south of North Macedonia, and in some mountain villages of northern Greece. Some argue that the language used in central Albania (Durrësi and Tirana) also qualifies as a dialect.

Within Albania a standard form of the language is used, known as 'the literary language' (*gjuha letrare*). The literary language was an official attempt to combine elements of Gheg and Tosk, although northern Albanians would contend that Tosk elements preponderate in it. It has been taught in Albanian schools for more than 50 years and is universally understood. People may use their own dialect when talking among themselves, but with anyone who is not local (ie: not only foreigners) they will switch to this standardised Albanian. Of course, it is true that an elderly shepherd is likely to be less fluent in 'literary language' than a 30-year-old bank clerk, but the chances are the shepherd will also make more of an effort to ensure that, as a guest in his or her land, you are happy and understand what is going on.

RELIGION

E mos shikoni kisha e xhamia/feja e shqyptarit asht shqyptaria!
(Pay no attention to churches and mosques/the Albanian's faith is Albanian-ness!)
O Moj Shqypni!, Pashko Vasa (1825–92)

During the five centuries that they formed part of the Ottoman Empire, Albanians converted to Islam in larger numbers than anywhere else in Ottoman Europe. Catholicism survived in the high mountains of the north and in coastal cities such as Shkodra; Orthodox Christians clung to their faith in the south. However, it is fairly clear that many (if not most) of those who converted did so for entirely pragmatic reasons, such as reducing their tax demands, gaining the right to bear arms or keeping their sons from the *devshirme* (page 11). Often the man of the household would convert, while his wife retained her Christian faith. There were also cases of 'crypto-Christianity', where people would adopt Islamic names and attend prayers in the mosque, but in private would follow their old Christian rituals.

Perhaps this attitude helps to explain how it was possible for religion to be completely banned in 1967. In that year, Albania's communist government prohibited religious worship and the country became the world's only officially atheist state. Churches and mosques were demolished or turned into warehouses or sports halls, and the practice of religion remained an offence until 1990. Albania remains an extremely secular society today.

The 2011 census was the first to include a question about the respondent's religious affiliation, but it was one of several optional questions and over 16% of people chose not to answer it. Unreliable though the data may be, they reveal an interesting shift from the traditional breakdown of 70% Muslim, 20% Orthodox and 10% Catholic. The 2011 figures show just under 57% Muslim, with a further 2% answering 'Bektashi', 10% Catholic and only 7% Orthodox. A fraction of 1% identified themselves as belonging to another Christian religion – the evangelical Protestant churches that have become popular in the cities in the past decade or so – and 2.5% continue to describe themselves as atheists.

THE AUTOCEPHALOUS CHURCH The Albanian Orthodox Church is autocephalous, meaning that it ordains its own bishops and is its own authority. Autonomy from the Greek Church was a campaign issue for Orthodox Albanians in the Rilindja years of the early 20th century, particularly in Korça and among diaspora Albanians in the USA (many of whom were originally from Korça). The first liturgy in Albanian was celebrated in Boston in 1908, by a priest who had been ordained two weeks before by the Russian Archbishop of New York. The Albanian priest's name was Fan Noli, and in 1924 he also served for six months as Prime Minister of Albania.

After the end of communism and the restoration of religious freedom, a new archbishop was enthroned in 1992, and the Albanian Church has regained its autocephalous status. The website of the Orthodox Autocephalous Church (w orthodoxalbania.org) has information about the Church's history and activities, although not all of it is translated into English. There is also a breakaway Orthodox Autocephalous Church, based in Elbasani (page 103).

THE CATHOLIC CHURCH Albania's Catholics are mostly concentrated in the northwest of the country: Shkodra, Mirdita and villages hidden in the mountains, too remote for the Ottomans to have bothered trying to convert them to Islam. Their perceived allegiance to Rome brought them under particular suspicion from the communists who came to power in 1944. Priests were arrested and shot; others were imprisoned and died in labour camps. Lay Catholics were arrested too, including a young woman from Mirdita called Marije Tuci, who had been a postulant with the Stigmatine Sisters in Shkodra until the government closed the convent. Imprisoned in 1949, she died the following year, aged only 21. Some of the Catholics who died for their faith under communism are commemorated in Shkodra Cathedral and (in Albanian) on the website of the Catholic church in Shkodra (w kishakatolikeshkoder.com).

Albania's best-known Catholic was Mother Teresa (1910–97), canonised in 2016 as Saint Teresa of Calcutta. She was in fact born in Skopje (now the capital of North Macedonia) but, thanks to her Mirdita ancestry, Albanian Catholics claim her as their own. The date of her beatification, 19 October, is a public holiday in Albania.

JUDAISM The earliest trace of a Jewish community in what is now Albania is in Saranda, where a synagogue was built in the 5th century (page 220). Jews started to arrive in significant numbers after the community's expulsion from Spain in 1492. They were attracted by the Adriatic ports of Vlora and Durrësi, with their trading links with the rest of the Mediterranean. There were smaller communities in Berati (page 264) and Elbasani.

Despite the German occupation of Albania, the country's Jewish community survived World War II; indeed, during the war, Albania provided a haven for Jewish refugees from other countries. Some of the Albanians who sheltered Jews are honoured at the Yad Vashem Holocaust memorial in Jerusalem as 'Righteous among the Nations'. Nor were Jews treated any worse than members of other religions during the atheism campaign. The Jewish community emigrated en masse to Israel as soon as the borders opened, not because they had been badly treated in Albania but simply because, unlike most Albanians, they were lucky enough to have a country that would welcome them. A Holocaust Memorial in Tirana's Lake Park (page 79) was inaugurated in 2020.

BEKTASHISM Albania's 'fourth religion' is Bektashism, a Sufi order of Islam founded in the 13th century. The Ottoman Empire's 'official' Islam was Sunni, and was followed mainly by the intelligentsia, the civil servants and functionaries. Ordinary people in the Balkan provinces were much more attracted by the Sufi sects, whose rituals and rite system were closer to folk beliefs. The followers of Sufism believe that individuals can achieve communion with God through their own personal qualities and experience, with the help of contemplation.

Bektashism came to Albania gradually, brought by clerics known as dervishes or *babas* (fathers) travelling alone or in very small groups. They actively sought to assimilate local traditions into the religious ideas they taught, including relics of paganism such as mountain worship. Their religious centres – places of preaching, study and initiation called *teqe* (spelt '*tekke*' in Turkish, and sometimes in English too) – were often established near the tomb of some righteous person, who with time became venerated in the same way as Christian saints.

Bektashism took hold in Albania and began to expand dramatically in the early 19th century. Alarmed by the sect's popularity, the Ottoman authorities attempted to suppress it; in response, the *babas* moved up into the mountains and built *teqes* in high, remote places such as Mount Tomorri in Skrapari and Melani, above Libohova. Many of these *teqes* are still used today, especially for pilgrimages on holy days.

The Bektashi order was expelled from Turkey in 1925 and its leadership of the time decided to move its world headquarters to Albania. The World Bektashi Centre, in the outskirts of Tirana, welcomes visitors (page 85).

EDUCATION

School education in Albania follows a pattern that is unfamiliar to British visitors. Most children attend the same school for nine years, then go on to either a General High School (Shkolla e Mesme e Përgjithshme) or a Professional High School (Shkolla e Mesme Profesional). The latter trains students for specific professions – for example, economics and accounting, mechanics, construction, hotel management or sports. In very rural areas, the elementary schools tend to take only five classes; after their fifth year, the children have to commute to school in a larger village or town, or even board with relatives or in a school dormitory (*konvikt*).

More than half of those who finish high school go on to higher education. Albania's state university was founded in the 1950s. It has branches in each city, offering a range of faculties such as engineering, medicine, science, law and economics; the Agricultural Institute in Kamza and the Conservatoire (both in Tirana) are also part of the state university system. The first private university in the country opened its doors in 2002 and since then there has been a huge increase in the number of such institutions. They are of varying quality; some are very good and have close academic relations with universities in Italy, France or other western European countries. Many Albanian families continue to make huge sacrifices so that their children can study in universities abroad.

CULTURE

LITERATURE The earliest documents written in Albanian were religious works produced by Catholic priests – a 16th-century missal and some doctrinal poetry survive. However, Albanian literature did not emerge until the 19th century, in a cultural phenomenon known as the National Renaissance (Rilindja Kombëtare), which was closely linked to the rise of Albanian nationalism.

The 19th-century writers included essayists and dramatists, but the predominant literary form was lyric poetry, and its exponents came from all parts of the Albanian-speaking world. Pashko Vasa (1825–92) and Gjergj Fishta (1871–1940) were Shkodran; Çajupi (1866–1930) and Naim Frashëri (1843–1900) came from the south; the birthplace of the essayist Faik Konica (1875–1942), who served as King Zog's ambassador to the US, was Konitsa, now in northern Greece; Jeronim de Rada (1814–1903) was Arbëresh; and Fan Noli (1880–1965), briefly Albania's prime minister, was born in an Albanian settlement near Adrianople, now the Turkish city of Edirne. The poem that later became Albania's national anthem, *The Flag Hymn*, was written in 1880 by Asdreni (1872–1947), from Drenova near Korça.

The lyric tradition continued into the 20th century, represented by the Shkodran poets Migjeni (1911–38) and Martin Çamaj (1925–93), and was complemented with novels, plays and short stories. The extracts from Albanian folk tales throughout this book are translated from the versions by Mitrush Kuteli (the pseudonym of Dhimitër Pasko, 1907–67). Dritëro Agolli (1931–2017) made delightful translations into Albanian of some of Robert Burns's poems. These writers, like others such as the poet and novelist Fatos Arapi (1930–2018) and the novelist and screen-writer Vath Koreshi (1936–2006), are almost unknown in the English-speaking world.

The only novelist of that generation who is at all widely read in English translation is Ismail Kadare, born in Gjirokastra in 1936. Kadare's works, in addition to being fine literature, make very good background reading if you are planning to visit Albania. *Chronicle in Stone*, *Broken April* and *The General of the Dead Army* are perhaps the most accessible. These novels are available in English, but most of the translations available were made from the French versions rather than directly from the Albanian. Those who read French may well prefer those direct translations, which were made by the great Albanian–French translator Jusuf Vrioni (1916–2001) and give a more accurate flavour of the original. Affordable paperback editions are published in Fayard's *Le Livre de Poche* series. See the box on page 276 for further information about Kadare and his work.

Other living Albanian writers include Besnik Mustafaj (b1958), Preç Zogaj (b1957) and Visar Zhiti (b1952), whose first volume of poetry in 1973 was deemed to denigrate socialist reality and brought him a 13-year prison sentence. More recently, women writers have at last started to gain recognition: the poet Irma Kurti (b.1966) and the novelists Lindita Arapi (b.1972) and Majlinda Nana Rama (b.1980), among others.

FILM In the 1960s and 1970s, Albania developed a thriving film industry. A film studio, Kinostudio, was opened in 1952 and *Skanderbeg*, a Soviet–Albanian co-production, was released the following year. Initially, post-production was done in the Soviet Union or Yugoslavia; the first feature film entirely produced in Albania was *Tana*, in 1958. By the 1970s, Kinostudio was making 14 films a year. There were 26 cinemas, in towns all over the country, and portable cinemas took films to the villages.

The Albanian National Film Archive (Arkivi Qendror Shtetëror i Filmit; Rr Aleksandër Moisiu 76/1; w aqshf.gov.al) holds a huge stock of communist-era films, much of it in very precarious condition. Work is under way to conserve, restore and digitise the whole of the archive's collection of 35mm films. Many of these, including *Skanderbeg* and *Tana*, can be viewed online on its website. The small but comfortable cinema at the Film Archive's HQ has regular screenings of historic Albanian films as well as classic world cinema; consult its website for details.

In the late 1990s, Albanian scriptwriters and directors began to produce films again and several have had international success. Directors to look out for include Kujtim Çashku (*Magic Eye*, 2005; *Colonel Bunker*, 1996), Iris Elezi (*Bota*, 2014), the late Gjergj Xhuvani (*Slogans*, 2001; *Dear Enemy*, 2004; *East West East*, 2009) and Fatmir Koçi (*Amsterdam Express*, 2014; *Time of the Comet*, 2008). Art-house cinemas in Britain and other western European countries screen modern Albanian films from time to time, and some can be streamed from the internet.

MUSIC There are three distinct strands to Albanian folk music – the diatonic music of the north, the pentatonic tradition of the south and the chromatic intervals of the traditional music of the country's cities.

The music of northern Albania (and of Albanians in Montenegro and Kosovo) is characterised by solo male singers, accompanied on long-necked stringed instruments called *çiftelia* and *lahuta*. The *lahutë* is a bowed instrument, making it suitable for accompanying diatonic melodies, while the *çifteli* has frets and is used to create a kind of drone effect, which is very atmospheric. A single-drone bagpipe called *gajda* is also played in northern and central Albania.

Albanian polyphonic music, known as iso-polyphony, is a sophisticated form of unaccompanied group singing. The 'iso' in its name is a vocal drone, sung either as a continuous note or rhythmically. Above the drone, other singers carry a melody and a counter-melody. This kind of polyphonic singing is found not only in southern Albania, but also across the modern borders in Greece and North Macedonia, and in the Arbëresh settlements in southern Italy. Albanian iso-polyphony is listed by UNESCO as part of the Intangible Cultural Heritage of Humanity. The most characteristic instrument of the south is the Epirote clarinet, which often accompanies the dancing at weddings and similar social events.

The chromatic intervals of Albanian urban folk music (*ahengu qytetar*) were inherited from Turkish musical traditions during the Ottoman period. This type of music is found mainly in the towns of central Albania, especially Elbasani, and also in Shkodra and Berati. It can be sung with an instrumental accompaniment, or played by a small orchestra. Musical instruments typical of this tradition are the accordion, the mandolin, the tambourine and a fretted instrument called the *sharki*. Urban folk music has heavily influenced the development of 'popular music', *musika popullore*, which is the only type of traditional music that can readily be heard live in Albania.

The folklore festivals at Gjirokastra (every four years, more or less) and Peshkopia (annually, in September) are the best places to hear all the different Albanian musical traditions, including performers from other Albanian-speaking lands. Smaller festivals of traditional music take place from time to time in other parts of the country; the Përmeti Folk Festival, held annually in June, brings together traditional musicians from all over the Balkans, with a special focus on a different country each year.

Windows on
EUROPE
Estonia 8
Neil Taylor
with Juhan-Markus Laats
Bosnia & Herzegovina 6
Tim Clancy
Bulgaria 3
Annie Kay
Montenegro 6
Norm Longley
Annalisa Rellie
North Macedonia 6
Thammy Evans
Serbia 6
Laurence Mitchell
Bradt GUIDES
TRAVEL TAKEN SERIOUSLY
bradtguides.com/shop
BradtGuides
@BradtGuides
@bradtguides

2

Practical Information

WHEN TO VISIT

For most purposes, the best times of year to visit Albania are spring and autumn. In early spring, apple and cherry blossoms form little pastel-toned drifts by the roadside. By May, the snow is melting on the high mountain passes, water starts to flow again in the rivers and roses bloom in the lowlands. The long evenings of early summer are a good time to enjoy the terrace cafés in Tirana and the coastal towns. In June and September, the beaches are at their best, without the crowds of the peak tourist season, and the sea temperature is still comfortably high. By late autumn, the orchards start to blaze with bright orange persimmons and golden pomegranates.

Albania has a Mediterranean climate and in the lowlands it never gets really cold, although most buildings are poorly insulated and it often feels colder indoors than out. In Tirana, it is unusual for temperatures to stay below zero for more than a few days at a time. The southwest coast in particular is very clement, with average winter temperatures of 8–10°C. Most of Albania's annual rainfall occurs between late autumn and early spring. Minor roads are not well drained and can become muddy and slippery during and after rain.

In the highlands, winter is a much more serious proposition. High-level hiking should only be attempted between June and September. Snow on arterial highways is usually cleared quickly, but the high passes on minor roads are normally closed for two or three months – or even longer in a harsh winter. Mountain towns such as Korça and Peshkopia are very cold at this time of year.

July and August are the warmest months and inland towns can become oppressively hot. In Gjirokastra and Berati, for example, summer temperatures are usually in the high 30°Cs and, with climate change, there are increasingly more days when the thermometer tops 40°C. Hotels and restaurants of a reasonable standard have air conditioning, but museums do not. Sightseeing in high summer is an exhausting business. On the coast, sea breezes keep the average temperatures down to a more tolerable 25–30°C. The best place to be at the height of summer is in the high mountains. Hikers and cyclists should be sure to have enough water with them; everyone else will never be far from a café.

HIGHLIGHTS

Albania has something for almost everyone. Lovers of the **outdoors** will be happy just about anywhere in the country. The Albanian Alps in the far north and the mountains between Berati and Përmeti in the south are the best organised in terms of accommodation, guides and so forth. Those who are more interested in watersports will find many exciting opportunities for river rafting and sea kayaking. Birdwatchers will want to head straight for the coastal wetlands at Karavasta, Narta and Shëngjini.

Albania is also full of delights for anyone with a passion for **archaeology and history**. In the southwest of the country, the ancient city of Butrint richly deserves its status as the country's best-known archaeological site, but there are many other interesting prehistoric, Hellenistic and Roman sites throughout the country. Tirana has the cream of the country's archaeological collections, while Berati and Korça have the best museums of medieval icons and other Orthodox Christian art.

No visit to Albania would be complete without at least a couple of **castles**. In the south, the 'museum cities' of Gjirokastra and Berati have ancient fortifications and fascinating Ottoman architecture. In the north, the castles of Shkodra and Kruja give an insight into the many centuries of Albanian history.

Albania has beautiful **beaches**, from Velipoja and Rana e Hedhun in the north to Buneci and Ksamili in the south. However, if your only reason for visiting Albania is to spend your holiday on one or more of these beaches, this is probably not the right guidebook for you.

SUGGESTED ITINERARIES

Where you go in Albania depends not only on what you like doing, but also where you enter the country. The itineraries that follow are based on an arrival into Tirana International Airport and, in the case of the 'long weekend' option, also into Saranda from Corfu. Those who approach Albania from other directions can easily tweak these suggested routes to suit their starting points. All the itineraries that follow can be done by public transport, although the occasional taxi or hire-car will speed things up considerably.

LONG WEEKEND

Coming from Corfu For such a short visit, it is advisable to hire a car in Saranda (page 216).
Friday: Take the morning hydrofoil (you gain an hour coming to Albania from Greece) and head straight for Butrint. Overnight either at the Livia Hotel there or in Saranda.
Saturday: Gjirokastra: visiting the castle and one or two of the traditional houses; staying overnight there or returning to Saranda in the evening.
Sunday: The Riviera: Ali Pasha's fortress at Porto Palermo; Borshi Castle and/or Old Himara; a swim at Borshi or Himara; back to Saranda for the Monday-morning hydrofoil to Corfu.

Flying into Tirana

Friday: Day in Tirana: one or more museums, walk around town.
Saturday: Mount Dajti (cable car and hiking); Pëllumbasi (cave, hiking, lunch); or Durrësi (beach or archaeological sites and museum, depending on weather and preferences). Overnight in either Tirana or Durrësi.
Sunday: Travel to Kruja; visit the castle and museums; overnight either in Kruja or at an airport hotel, depending on flight times.

ONE WEEK

Day 1: Day in Tirana: National Historical Museum; National Gallery of Arts; Bunk'Art2 or House of Leaves or Kadare museum; walk around town.

Day 2: Berati: visit the castle and Ethnographic Museum; walk around town; stay overnight.
Day 3: Gjirokastra: visit the castle and one or two of the traditional houses; stay overnight.
Day 4: Butrint; overnight in Saranda.
Day 5: The Riviera: overnight in Himara, Dhërmiu or Llogoraja, depending on interests (history, beaches, hiking).
Day 6: Continue north to Vlora (for museums) or Divjaka (for beach and/or birdwatching).
Day 7: Kruja.

TWO WEEKS

Day 1: As Day 1 for *One Week*
Day 2: Tirana (perhaps a trip up Mount Dajti or to Pëllumbasi, or more museums).
Day 3: Berati (two nights).
Day 5: Vlora or Divjaka, stopping en route at Ardenica and/or Apollonia.
Day 6: The Riviera: overnight in Himara, Dhërmiu or Llogoraja.
Day 7: Butrint; overnight in Saranda.
Day 8: Gjirokastra (two nights): add Antigonea and/or Libohova.
Day 10: Durrësi (archaeological sites and museum and/or beaches).
Day 11: Lezha and Shkodra (two nights).
Day 13: Kruja.

THREE WEEKS Using the two-week itinerary as a basis, add to it with a focus on either (a) cultural and historical heritage or (b) outdoor activities:

Option (a) From Gjirokastra, travel to Korça through the Gramoz Mountains; three nights in Korça, including a day trip to Voskopoja. Then to Elbasani via Lini and/or the Illyrian tombs at Selca. One night in Elbasani and onwards to Durrësi for one night, as above. After Durrësi, add two nights in Mirdita and/or Mati, then an additional night in Shkodra, to allow more time there or a day trip to Thethi.

Option (b) From Berati, continue to Çorovoda for rafting or hiking, depending on the time of year (one additional night). From Gjirokastra (one night), travel to Përmeti; two nights there, hiking, rafting and/or thermal baths at Bënja. Continue through the Gramoz Mountains to the Prespa Lakes (two nights). From Prespa, travel to Librazhdi and onwards to the Shebenik-Jabllanica National Park (two nights). Then to Shkodra and onwards to Thethi; hike to Valbona; return to Shkodra on Komani ferry (four or five nights in total).

TOUR OPERATORS

Organised tours to Albania from western Europe had been increasing until the shock of the Covid-19 pandemic and the travel restrictions that resulted. At the time of writing, their range and number are understandably more limited. Some of the longest-standing operators are listed here; as international travel returns to pre-pandemic levels, other tour operators will certainly return. Tours range from general introductions, often including one or more of Albania's neighbouring countries, to specialist archaeological or cultural visits. Most international and Albanian operators can also tailor-make individual itineraries.

The Albanian tour operators listed here act as ground agents for incoming tours and are responsive to the requirements of foreign travellers. Businesses that call themselves travel agencies in Albania, even if they have a 'tourist information' sign outside the shop, tend to cater for the outbound market, booking flights and package holidays. Of course, this does not mean they will not do their best to help a foreign client, but their knowledge of their own country can be limited. There are horror stories, for example, of foreign hikers being encouraged by a 'tourist information office' to hike from Thethi to Valbona in March (see page 172 for why this was terrible advice).

UK

Andante Travels 01722 713800; e tours@andantetravels.co.uk; w andantetravels.co.uk. Specialises in tours of Albania's archaeological sites.

Drive Albania 020 3393 9989 (UK); m 069 81 17 716 (Albania); e info@drivealbania.com; w drivealbania.com. Off-road driving, mountain-biking & hiking tours.

Regent Holidays 01174 538 957; e regent@regentholidays.co.uk; w regent-holidays.co.uk; see ad, inside back cover. The doyen of UK-based tours to Albania, leading trips since 1971, now able to offer a far wider range of options than was possible 50 years ago.

Travel Editions 020 7251 0045; e tours@traveleditions.co.uk; w traveleditions.co.uk. Albania tours, some including neighbouring countries, focusing on culture, history & art.

Voyages Jules Verne 020 3811 5939; e sales@vjv.co.uk; w vjv.com. Shorter tours of Albania's cultural & archaeological highlights.

Walks Worldwide 0845 301 4737, 01962 737565; e sales@walksworldwide.com; w walksworldwide.com. Offers several hiking tours in northern & southern Albania & can also arrange tailor-made walking holidays there.

IN ALBANIA

Cultural and historical tours

Albania Holidays Tirana; 04 223 5688, 04 223 5498; e contact@albania-holidays.com; w albania-holidays.com; see ad, 1st colour section

Elite Travel Elbasani; 05 424 4094, 425 9934; e info@elitetravel-albania.com; w elitetravel-albania.com

Gjolek Mera Elbasani; m 069 21 22 555; e gjolekmera@yahoo.com

Past & Present Journeys Tirana; 04 237 3957; e info@pastandpresent.al; w pastandpresent.al; see ad, inside front cover

Tours Albania & Balkans Tirana; m 068 40 29 914; e info@tours-albania.com; w tours-albania.com; see ad, page 58

Outdoors tours

Caravan Travel Gjirokastra; m 069 53 75 743, 069 22 34 137; e travelcaravan@ymail.com; f Caravan Riding Centre Albania. Offers guided horseback tours through the mountains of southwest Albania, eating & sleeping in village homes. Experienced riders only; local horses & kit provided. English spoken.

Cycle Albania Tirana; 04 432 4884; m 069 24 75 728; e info@cyclealbania.com; w cyclealbania.com; see ad, 2nd colour section. Guided or self-guided tours on bicycles or motorcycles; bikes & motorbikes also available to hire.

Outdoor Albania Tirana; 04 222 7121; e info@outdooralbania.com; w outdooralbania.com. Albania's pioneers in specialist outdoors activities. Guided hiking holidays of varying durations, climbing expeditions, rafting, kayaking etc. throughout spring & summer. In winter, guided ski tours & snowshoeing trips, led by an experienced climber & skier. Self-guided tours for individuals or small groups. English & other languages spoken.

Vjosa Explorer Përmeti; m 068 39 30 797; e infovjosaexplorer@gmail.com; w vjosaexplorer.com; f Vjosa Explorer. Offers hiking & cycling tours, at various levels of difficulty, around the villages & mountains of Përmeti & Këlcyra; rafting on the River Vjosa; 4x4 excursions to traditional villages. English & other languages spoken.

Zbulo! (Discover Albania) Tirana; m 069 21 21 612, 069 69 31 932; e welcome@zbulo.org; w zbulo.org; f Zbulo - Discover Albania; see ad, page 56. Offers a range of interesting hiking itineraries beyond the usual routes, including in southern Albania; guided 'Peaks of the Balkans' &

'High Scardus' hikes; in winter, ski tours in various locations. Also offers self-guided hiking tours. Can arrange visas for independent cross-border hikers. English & other languages spoken.

RED TAPE

Citizens of many countries are not required to obtain Albanian visas in advance. Countries to which this visa-free system applies include all those in the European Union (EU) and European Free Trade Association (EFTA), all of Albania's neighbours, the UK, Australia, Canada, Japan, New Zealand and the US.

The Albanian Foreign Ministry's website (w punetejashtme.gov.al) carries information in English about visa requirements; a full list, with contact details, of diplomatic representation in Albania, including for countries that cover Albania from their embassies in other countries; and information on Albanian embassies throughout the world. Albanian embassies do not provide tourist information, beyond visa requirements and similar queries.

WESTERN EMBASSIES IN TIRANA

E **Czech Republic** Rr Skënderbeu 10; 04 223 4004, 223 2117
E **Netherlands** Rr Asim Zeneli 10; 04 224 0828
E **Poland** Rr e Durrësit 123; 04 451 0020
E **UK** Rr Skënderbeu 12; 04 223 4973/4/5
E **USA** Rr Stavro Vinjau 14; 04 224 7285

GETTING THERE AND AWAY

BY AIR

Tirana Airport Albania's main (and, until 2021, only) international airport is officially called Mother Teresa International Airport but more often referred to simply as Tirana Airport, even by the airport authorities themselves. Albanians often refer to it as 'Rinas', from the name of the village that once existed there. The IATA code is TIA.

From the UK, direct flights to Tirana are operated by British Airways (w ba.com), EasyJet (w easyjet.com) and Wizz Air (w wizzair.com). A full list of airlines that operate scheduled flights into Tirana Airport, with their websites and the telephone numbers of their local offices, is available on the airport's website (w tirana-airport.com). This also has real-time listings for arrivals and departures, details about flight schedules and other useful information.

Tirana Airport has a modern passenger terminal with all the usual facilities, including free Wi-Fi. Smoking is prohibited throughout, apart from an airside smoking lounge in departures. ATMs in the baggage reclaim area accept Visa, MasterCard and Maestro cards, and issues Albanian lek. There is also a bureau de change. There are reasonable toilets just beyond passport control, in the baggage reclaim area. The landside section of the terminal has mobile-phone shops, cafés, toilets, another ATM and a bookshop. The car-hire kiosks are just outside the exit from the terminal. There are several hotels in the vicinity of the airport (page 32).

On the way out of Albania, airport check-in and security procedures are usually efficient. Leks can be changed back into euros, US dollars or sterling at the landside bureau de change, but the rates are as poor as one might expect. It is likely to be a better deal to spend any surplus leks in the airside duty-free shops. These sell Albanian souvenirs and foodstuffs such as olive oil and mountain tea (see box, page 6), as well as the usual things one finds in international airports.

Naturally, they accept euros and credit cards as well as leks. Prices in the airside bars are eye-watering.

Transport from Tirana Airport Subject to traffic, it takes about half an hour by car from the airport to Tirana, 17km away. A slip road in the opposite direction leads to the Fushë-Kruja junction of the main north–south highway, 2.8km from the airport; this is the most convenient route from the airport to northern Albania.

Approved airport **taxis** can be booked online in advance (w tiataxi.al) or simply arranged on arrival; the drivers wait at the exit from the terminal and can be identified by their yellow lanyards. You should agree a fare with the driver before accepting his services – the going rate into Tirana or Durrësi is €20. A taxi to Shkodra from the airport should cost no more than €50. Unofficial taxis wait in the car park across the road from the airport perimeter fence and may be susceptible to haggling.

From 07.00 to 23.00, an hourly **bus** service runs from the airport into the centre of Tirana, dropping passengers off at intermediate points (eg Casa Italia for the North/South bus station) on request and terminating at the bus park behind the Palace of Culture. The one-way fare for this journey is 300 lek. There are also less-frequent bus services from the airport to Durrësi (480 lek; 052 225 539), Fieri (1,000 lek; 034 222 408; m 069 67 40 073) and Vlora (1,000 lek; m 067 60 97 542); details can be found on the airport website.

The **railway** line between Durrësi and Tirana is due to be upgraded and a new spur built to the airport; the contract was awarded in February 2021, to an Italian company, and trains may start running within the lifetime of this guidebook.

Where to stay at Tirana Airport *Map, page 58*

Ark Hotel (56 rooms) 450 0515/0616; m 068 80 30 234; e info@arkhotel.al; w arkhotel.al. Part of Best Western's Premier chain, just beyond the airport perimeter fence & 5 mins' walk from the terminal building. The quiet, generously sized rooms have good-size beds, AC, TV, & nicely designed en suites with bath & separate shower. Good English spoken at reception; lifts; restaurant; bar; well-equipped gym, spa & sauna; plus a small outdoor pool (summer only). B/fast served from 03.30 to 10.00, bar & restaurant open until 23.00. **$$$$**

Hotel Airport Tirana (50 rooms) 450 0190; m 068 20 04 243, 068 20 47 964, 068 20 55 133; e info@hotel-airportirana.com; w hotel-airportirana.com. Located just outside airport perimeter fence; hotel shuttle service provides free pick-up & drop-off on request. Restaurant, garden bar, outdoor pool (summer only) with wooden loungers, lift, laundry service, free parking. Nicely furnished, soundproofed rooms all en suite with AC, flatscreen TV, balcony, hairdryer & Wi-Fi; some have minibar, spa shower. **$$$$**

Jürgen (8 rooms) m 069 22 30 663; e hoteljurgen@yahoo.com. Right at entrance to airport perimeter fence; free parking; friendly, efficient reception staff; English spoken. Restaurant with terrace; bar; speedily served b/fast inc. All rooms w. nicely fitted en-suite shower-room, AC, TV & good Wi-Fi. **$$**

Verzaçi (30 rooms) m 068 20 25 542; e verzaci_hotel@yahoo.com. 10 mins' walk from airport; pick-up & drop-off on request. Restaurant, terrace bar; lift; English spoken at reception; free parking; good Wi-Fi. Bedrooms on airport side have great views of parked planes & Kruja; all en suite with excellent shower; flatscreen TV, AC, small balcony. **$$**

Other airports A second international airport at **Kukësi** in northeast Albania became operational in 2021. The IATA code is KFZ. At the time of writing, it has flights from only a few European cities; up-to-date information can be found on the airport's website (w kuiport.al). Cars can be hired at the airport, but there is no public transport; it is a short distance by taxi from the town and onward buses (page 153).

Another new airport is due to be built between Vlora and Fieri (page 211); it is highly controversial because of its environmental impact, but it may open during the lifetime of this guidebook. There is also a proposal to build an airport in Saranda.

It is worth considering the option of a **budget flight** to Podgorica, Prishtina or Thessaloniki and crossing into Albania by land. As the airline industry recovers from Covid restrictions, Ohrid airport may become a feasible option again. See page 34 for more on travel to Albania from its neighbours.

BY SEA For many northern Europeans, the cheapest and most convenient way to get to southern Albania is to take a flight to Corfu and from there the hydrofoil to Saranda. The journey takes about 40 minutes. There is at least one hydrofoil crossing a day, all year round (page 214).

Albania has good sea connections with Italy. The busiest route is Bari–Durrësi (page 87), with several ferry companies operating throughout the year. The crossing takes about 9 hours. There are also ferries to Durrësi from Ancona and Trieste (18 and 24 hours, respectively), and to Vlora from Brindisi (8 hours overnight; page 237). The Italian website w traghetti.it has details of all routes between Italy and Albania. A passenger route has been proposed between Durrësi and the Croatian ports of Rijeka and Zadar, and may start operating in the lifetime of this book.

Those fortunate enough to have the use of a **private yacht** will find their mooring options rather limited in Albania. The country's only marina (at least at the time of writing) is at the southern end of the Bay of Vlora, between Orikumi and Radhima (page 234). It is also possible to anchor or berth in Durrësi, Shëngjin, Vlora and Himara. Official port fees and other information are available from the National Coastal Agency (Agjencia Kombëtare e Bregdetit). Sail Albania, based in Vlora, are port agents for Vlora and the Orikumi marina; they also charter yachts and motorboats. There are other maritime agents in Albania, though most of them focus on commercial shipping.

National Coastal Agency m 067 60 96 010; w bregdeti.gov.al

Orikum Yachting Club (Marina e Orikumit) t 0391 22248; t +39 05 6525 2040 (Italy); m 069 53 50 233; e marinaorikum@hotmail.it; w orikum.it

Sail Albania Rr Murat Terbaçi, Uji i Ftohtë, Vlora; m 069 73 24 138, 069 77 10 739; e sailalbania@gmail.com; w sail-albania-vlore.com

BY LAND Visitors who bring their own **cars** into Albania should ensure that their vehicle insurance is valid there. There is no longer a 'circulation tax'. Petrol and diesel are widely available everywhere except the most remote mountain areas. Liquid Petroleum Gas (LPG) is available in petrol stations on major highways and in cities. For those with an electric vehicle, public chargers are not widespread – there are a few in Tirana, including one on Embassy Row, Rruga Skënderbeu – but availability will probably improve in the near future.

If crossing into Albania from Kosovo, there are practically no formalities beyond showing your passport. Women aged under 18 travelling without either of their parents should carry a notarised authorisation; this is intended to make life difficult for criminals trafficking women, rather than for the legitimate female traveller. In the other direction, because Kosovo is not part of the Green Card system, drivers of foreign-registered vehicles must buy a minimum of 15 days' insurance at the border (€15 for a saloon car, at the time of writing). See page 114 for further information about public transport on this route.

Crossing into Albania by **bus** is usually a straightforward process. There are buses from all neighbouring countries to Tirana and other Albanian cities. Finding out about cross-border buses from Greece, however, can be a challenge. At Greek bus stations and tourist information offices, staff will often deny the existence of any public transport to Albania, even though there are buses every day from practically every city in Greece to practically every city in Albania. If you are unable to find reliable information about through buses, the alternative is to take a Greek KTEL bus to the border at Kakavija or Kapshtica, go through both passport controls on foot, and continue onward in one of the taxis or minibuses that will be waiting on the Albanian side.

There are no international passenger **trains** at the time of writing, although the line from Podgorica to Shkodra is open and used for freight.

HEALTH *With thanks to Dr Felicity Nicholson*

BEFORE YOU GO Albania is no more dangerous from a health point of view than any other country in southeastern Europe. It is a good idea in general to keep up to date with **vaccinations** against tetanus, polio and diphtheria. In the UK these are normally given together and should be boosted every ten years. Other vaccinations that are worth considering, depending on what you plan to do in Albania, are those against hepatitis A and B. There have been no cases of human rabies in Albania since the 1970s. Malaria was eradicated from Albania in the 1930s.

HEALTH CARE IN ALBANIA If you are involved in an accident or a medical emergency, call an ambulance on ☎ 127. Outside the big cities, however, it may be quicker to use a taxi; say to the driver '*tek urgjenca*', meaning 'to accident and emergency'. You will be given the best treatment possible.

In Tirana and other cities, there are now good non-state hospitals, with the latest technological equipment, which offer a full range of medical services up to and including heart bypasses and neurosurgery. The standard of dental practices is very variable – there are some good ones in Tirana – and you should seek local advice, perhaps at your hotel.

✚ **American Hospital** ☎ 04 235 7535/7011; **w** spitaliamerikan.com. 3 hospitals in Tirana (☎ 04 235 7535), medical centre in Durrësi (☎ 05 222 2333) & hospital in Fieri (☎ 034 232 123).

✚ **Hygeia Hospital** ☎ 04 232 3000 (emergency), 04 239 0000 (info); **w** hygeia.al

In small towns and rural areas, health care can be a problem. State hospitals are often short-staffed, with equipment that is old and sometimes does not work at all; many rural clinics have closed altogether. If you intend to travel outside the cities and are reliant on a specific medication, you should ensure you take an adequate supply with you. During the Covid-19 pandemic, summer health centres opened at places popular with tourists, such as beach resorts; it is possible that this innovation may continue in future years.

For minor ailments, remedies such as painkillers or antiseptic ointment can be bought over the counter in pharmacies. Opticians can make repairs to spectacle frames or replace lenses fairly quickly. Disinfecting solution for contact lenses is stocked by a few opticians in Tirana and other big cities. The international-style supermarkets in Tirana and other large cities stock tampons.

COVID-19

This guide was researched and sent to print during the Covid-19 pandemic. By comparison with many better-resourced countries, Albania dealt relatively well with the pandemic. One factor is that frail, elderly people in Albania live with their families, not in care homes. Of course, elderly, frail Albanians have died of Covid-19, but the disease did not have the opportunity to rampage through this vulnerable group as it did in the UK and elsewhere. The government imposed stringent restrictions very early on, closing the country's borders completely, even to Albanian citizens, closing all non-essential businesses and banning movement by private or public transport, apart from a few specific exemptions. At the end of March 2020, a strict stay-at-home order was imposed under which only one member of each household was allowed to leave the house for only one hour each day. These measures meant that, by mid-June, only 34 deaths from Covid-19 had been registered and the state of emergency was lifted.

After so many weeks of such harsh restrictions, people understandably wanted to socialise, spend time at the beach, or attend long-postponed weddings. Unfortunately, just as it did elsewhere, this had the predictable effect of causing a spike of cases in the autumn of 2020. This time the death rate was higher. All hospital treatment was centralised in dedicated Covid hospitals in Tirana, but many people suffered at home, with oxygen or ventilators if they could afford them. Evening and night-time curfews were introduced in an attempt to stop people socialising; in February 2021, all schooling was taken back online.

Vaccination got off to a slow start but, by late April 2021, mass vaccination was under way, starting with those working in the tourism and hospitality sectors. Gradually the restrictions were relaxed and case rates remained relatively low. By 3 March 2022, the total number of deaths attributed to Covid-19, since the start of the pandemic, was 3,476. By the end of 2021, most adult Albanians had received two doses of the vaccine.

At the time of writing, all travellers entering the country, including Albanian citizens, must show proof of vaccination or recovery or a negative test. Up-to-date information on travel restrictions and testing requirements is available on the Albanian Foreign Ministry's website (w punetejashtme.gov.al).

HEALTH RISKS IN ALBANIA

Hepatitis A This viral infection is transmitted by contaminated food or water, or by direct contact with an infectious person. Washing your hands before and after eating, and taking care over what you consume will greatly reduce the risk of contracting hepatitis A. If you plan to camp wild or stay in mountain-village homes, where it may be more difficult to take these precautions, you might consider being vaccinated before you travel.

Hepatitis B Hepatitis B is transmitted by sexual contact with an infected person, or by puncture wounds from contaminated instruments, such as needles. In the UK, the course of vaccinations is usually given only to health workers and other people who are likely to be at high risk. For travellers, the risk of hepatitis B can be avoided by not indulging in risky behaviour such as unprotected sex, body piercing, tattooing or acupuncture. There is also an increased risk when working with small children or playing contact sports. There are two types of vaccination. The shorter course (Engerix) must be started at least 21 days before travel, for those aged 16 or over.

Tick-borne encephalitis This viral infection, like other, rarer diseases, is spread through the bites of infected ticks. You can protect yourself to a large extent by preventing ticks from attaching themselves to you, and removing any that succeed. If you are hiking in the forests, you should cover your arms and legs; wear long trousers tucked into your boots, and a hat. There is some evidence that insect repellents containing DEET or permethrin can discourage ticks. Tick repellent and tick-removal gadgets can be bought before you travel, but they are not available in Albania.

Always check for ticks at the end of your day out. Ticks should be removed as soon as possible; the longer they are on your body, the greater the chance of infection. Grasp the tick as close as you can to your skin, with tweezers or your fingernails, and then pull it steadily and firmly away, at right angles to your skin. The tick will come away complete, as long as you do not jerk or twist. Clean the skin, and your hands, afterwards with soap and water or skin disinfectant, if possible. Don't try to burn the tick off or remove it with Vaseline, alcohol or other irritants, since they can cause the ticks to regurgitate and therefore increase the risk of disease. If you are travelling with a companion, you can check each other for ticks; if you are hiking with small children remember to check their heads, and particularly behind the ears.

Seek medical attention if you feel flu-like symptoms within one to four weeks after being bitten by a tick. In 20–30% of cases, the disease can then progress, with symptoms including a high fever and headache. There is a safe and effective vaccine (TicoVac and TicoVac Junior) that is recommended for people whose activities might put them at increased risk: for example, foresters or farmers.

OTHER PRECAUTIONS Albanian **tap water** is treated and is fine for brushing teeth, but the pipes are old and most urban Albanians prefer mineral water. In the mountains, everybody drinks spring water, often piped from their own spring.

You should try to avoid drinking **unpasteurised milk** while you are in Albania; there is TB and brucellosis in the Albanian dairy herd. Dairy products in supermarkets and restaurants are commercially produced and properly pasteurised. Safe UHT milk is always available, even in small shops which stock homemade butter and cheese. The problem only really arises if you are staying with a family in a rural area, when you will almost certainly be offered fresh milk for breakfast and soft cheese or yoghurt at lunch or dinner. If you are concerned, you might want to think in advance about how to refuse it tactfully; the Albanian for 'I don't eat dairy products' is '*nuk ha bulmet*'.

SAFETY

Albania is a safe country for visitors. Its traditions of hospitality mean foreigners are treated with great respect; almost all Albanians will go out of their way to help you if you are lost or in trouble. In general, violent crime in Albania happens either within the underworld of organised crime or in the context of a blood feud. A foreign visitor is highly unlikely to come into contact with either of these categories.

Nevertheless, there are poor and desperate people in Albania, as there are in any other country, and thefts and muggings do occur. It is foolish to flash expensive watches, phones or cameras around, especially in the peripheral areas of towns where the poorest people tend to live. Some travellers carry a dummy wallet with a small amount of cash in it, so that in the event of a mugging they can hand this over instead of their 'real' wallet full of dollars or euros.

The greatest risk most people in Albania face is on the roads, where traffic accidents are very frequent and the fatality rate is one of the highest in Europe. Until a decade or so ago, Albanian roads were so bad that it was difficult to drive fast enough to kill anyone. Now, though, cars zip along newly upgraded highways which are also used by villagers and their livestock. There is no stigma attached to drink-driving and little attempt is made to check it.

WOMEN TRAVELLERS

Foreign women are treated with respect in Albania, although the same respect is not always shown to Albanian women. Domestic violence, in particular, is very prevalent and almost always unreported. Outside the home, however, women are at less risk of sexual assault or rape than in any northern European country. Of course, these crimes are not completely unknown, but they are rare enough to make headline news when they happen.

BLACK AND MINORITY ETHNIC TRAVELLERS

Black and minority ethnic (BAME) visitors to Albania sometimes find themselves on the receiving end of treatment that, although not racist in its intent, can make the visitor feel uncomfortable – for example, children or even adults stroking or pinching your skin out of curiosity. Occasionally, however, BAME visitors have been verbally and even physically abused by groups of racists. There have also been sporadic reports of racist behaviour by some hotel owners.

LESBIAN AND GAY TRAVELLERS

Homosexuality is legal in Albania. A law passed in 2010 specifically protects its citizens against discrimination on grounds of sexual orientation, while a 2013 amendment to the criminal code added sexual orientation and gender identity to the grounds for charges of hate crimes. However, it is still rather taboo and the LGBTI community generally keeps a low profile. Almost no public figures are openly gay. That said, however, lesbian or gay travellers are unlikely to encounter hostility or discrimination in Albania, assuming they behave with reasonable discretion (as they probably would in an unfamiliar town in their own country). A couple of bars in Tirana advertise 'gay-friendly' evenings.

The lead organisation for LGBTI rights in Albania is the Pink Embassy/LGBT Pro Albania (**w** pinkembassy.al), which has been active since the mid 2000s. Their website has extensive information, in English and Albanian, about their advocacy and advice work.

TRAVELLERS WITH A DISABILITY

In 2013, Albania ratified the UN Convention on the Rights of People with Disabilities, which sets targets for improving legislation, access and employment for people with disabilities. This was a positive step and progress has been made since then. However, Albania is still a challenging destination for people with physical

INFORMATION FOR TRAVELLERS WITH A DISABILITY

The UK government's website (w gov.uk/government/publications/disabled-travellers) provides general advice and practical information for travellers with disabilities preparing for overseas travel. **Accessible Journeys** (w disabilitytravel.com) is a comprehensive US site written by wheelchair users who have been researching wheelchair-accessible travel full-time since 1985. There are many tips and useful contacts (including lists of travel agents on request) for slow walkers, wheelchair travellers and their families, plus informative articles, including pieces on disabled travelling worldwide. The company also organises group tours. The **Society for Accessible Travel and Hospitality** (w sath.org) also provides some general information.

disabilities, particularly users of wheelchairs. Most communist-era museums and other public buildings were built with steep stairs and other obstacles, although more and more now have ramps which provide access at least to the ground floor. Outside the central areas of the larger cities, few pavements in Albania have dropped kerbs and pedestrian crossing lights rarely have acoustic signals. Braille is not widely used. Public buses and most taxis are completely inaccessible for wheelchair users. All that said, however, people with reduced mobility will find Albanians eager (possibly overeager) to assist when necessary.

Some more recent buildings have been designed to take people with disabilities into account. In Tirana, for example, the MAK Albania and Rogner Europapark hotels are accessible and have specifically designed guest rooms. Tirana Airport is accessible throughout, including the toilets, and has dedicated parking spaces at the entrance to the terminal. The modern shopping malls in Tirana and other big cities are generally accessible. See page 55 for contact information for the Albanian Disability Rights Foundation.

TRAVELLING WITH CHILDREN

Older children are likely to have a wonderful time in Albania, as long as they are reasonably flexible when things do not go exactly as planned. Travelling with young children, however, does present some practical problems. Pavements tend to be rather high, which can make pushchairs awkward to manoeuvre. Outside Tirana, health care is not up to Western standards and it may be hard to find exactly the medication you need, should this be required. Entertainment specifically for children is not usually available, apart from the swing-parks that abound in every town. On the outskirts of Tirana, strung out along the Elbasani road, there are several day resorts that have pools and other activities for children. Many beach resorts have play areas and sometimes children's pools.

Two particularly appealing places for children of almost any age are the Llogora Tourist Village, between Vlora and Saranda, and Farma Sotira, in the mountains between Përmeti and Korça. The Llogora resort (page 234) has sports facilities including tennis courts and a large indoor swimming pool. Activities are organised for youngsters and a babysitting service is offered. The whole resort, over 1ha in extent, is designed to blend in harmoniously with the natural beauty of the park. Several roe deer live in a large enclosure at the edge of the forest and are let out during the day to wander freely around the complex. Farma Sotira (page 201) is a working farm, with sheep, cattle, chickens and horses. There is an outdoor pool with a separate shallow section for children. It is surrounded by meadows and forests; more strenuous hikes are also possible.

WHAT TO TAKE

It is not strictly necessary to take anything at all to Albania; imported toiletries, first-aid items, standard chargers for mobile phones and alkaline batteries can all be bought in any reasonable-sized town. Tampons are available in the Western-style supermarkets in Tirana and other cities, and the street markets have the same cheap imported clothes as those sold in Western supermarkets, at similar prices.

The most useful item to bring is undoubtedly a pocket- or head-torch (flashlight). The electricity supply in towns is much more reliable than it used to be, but there are still power cuts from time to time. In rural areas, these are more frequent and the lights can occasionally be out for several hours. Even if you are not planning to venture out of the cities, you may find a torch useful. Museums are sometimes badly lit and a torch can come in very handy for seeing what is in the display cases.

Electrical sockets are usually the European two-pin standard; British travellers should remember to pack an adaptor for their phone, camera or other electronic equipment. An older type of two-pin socket is very occasionally found in hotels, hostels or guesthouses; where it is encountered, the management will almost certainly have an adaptor they can lend to guests. For trips into the mountains of more than a day or two, a portable solar charger is a good way to keep phones and cameras powered up.

Mosquitoes can be a problem in the summer, especially on the coast. Insect repellent can be purchased in Albania, but you may prefer to come prepared with an extra-powerful brand. Plug-in devices which emit repellent are useful at night; if you are likely to be staying anywhere with an uncertain power supply, a mosquito coil is more practical.

In 2020, all of us became accustomed to having antibacterial hand gel with us at all times. Those travelling around Albania by public transport may also want to carry some biodegradable wet-wipes. The toilets of the roadside restaurants where the inter-city buses stop for breaks have running water, but not always soap or anything with which to dry your hands. Grabbing a couple of paper napkins from the restaurant table on your way to the toilet is a useful precaution.

In the cities, especially Tirana, the summer dust can irritate eyes and throats; eye drops and cough sweets help, and some contact lens wearers give up and revert to wearing glasses.

MONEY

CURRENCY The Albanian monetary unit is called the lek, which is also one of the words for 'money'. The currency floats freely but is fairly stable; at the time of going to press, there are 146 lek to the pound sterling, 120 to the euro, and 110 to the US dollar. On the rate boards in banks and bureaux de change, the initials 'ALL' are sometimes used instead of the word 'lek'.

In the 1970s, the lek was revalued and a zero was dropped. Albanians of all ages still insist on using the old number of zeros, although people who have regular dealings with foreigners sometimes try to remember not to. The systems are differentiated by the adjectives 'old' (*të vjetra*) and 'new' (*të reja*). In modern supermarkets the prices are displayed in 'new' lek; in markets and small shops, particularly outside the cities, if prices are displayed at all they might be in either system. While it is fairly easy to guess that the price of a bottle of mineral water is about 30p rather than £3.00 (50 'new' lek rather than 500), it can in some cases be quite unclear which is meant. Fortunately, most Albanians are very honest about this and will put you right if you try to give them ten times more money than they expect.

Matters are made even more confusing by a tendency to quote large numbers without mentioning the word 'thousand' – so a hotel receptionist might well quote a room rate simply as 'fifty'. The only way to find out if this means 50 euros or 5,000 (new) lek is by asking.

CHANGING MONEY All towns have ATMs (known in Albanian as *bankomat*). A few ATMs can issue euro notes as well as Albanian lek; for example, the ProCredit bank on Rruga Ded Gjo Luli in Tirana.

Credit cards can be used to withdraw cash from ATMs and, increasingly, to pay for goods or services in city shops, hotels and the more upmarket restaurants. Some hotels have card readers that accept payment only in lek, even if the room rate is quoted in euros; the conversion rate is usually worse than the bank rate. The receptionist really ought to ask first that you are happy with this, but you may wish to double-check before authorising the payment, especially if you are using a Eurozone card.

Outside the cities, you should not rely on being able to use your credit card at all. Card readers are not always able to connect with the card issuer to authorise the payment and sometimes they are simply out of order. In the Albanian mountains, you will need sufficient cash to pay for all your accommodation and, if you are driving, fuel. The Albanian Riviera also has long cash-only stretches. Locations of ATMs in the Albanian Alps and Riviera are given in the relevant sections of this guidebook.

Foreign currency can be changed in banks, at bureaux de change, and on the street; the euro is by far the most widely accepted. The more upmarket hotels offer currency-exchange services, although often only for euros and usually at a less favourable rate than on the street. Banks and bureaux de change will have rates for major currencies other than the US dollar and the euro. Bureaux de change provide a speedier, less bureaucratic procedure than banks, and offer practically the same rate for the amounts most visitors will be changing. Where a bureau de change exists, the money changers on the street do not offer a significantly better rate. In Tirana and other big cities a minority of unscrupulous on-street changers circulate counterfeit notes.

You will almost certainly be able to pay for your hotel room in euros even if you have been quoted a price in lek, although the hotel will use a rule-of-thumb exchange rate which may not be in your favour. Restaurants also sometimes accept euros, especially in the far north where they are used to visitors from Montenegro and Kosovo, where the euro is the official currency.

Travellers' cheques are not accepted as payment and cannot be cashed anywhere in Albania (younger readers may wonder what on earth a 'travellers' cheque' is!).

BUDGETING

How much you spend in Albania depends on what you want to do and where you want to sleep. If you base yourself in Tirana, stay in one of the top-of-the-range hotels, hire a car with a driver to move around in, and eat in the best fish restaurants, you could just about get through €400 a day (hotel: €150–200; car: €100 a day, if long tours are involved; meals with wine in top-of-the-range restaurants: €40–50 per head). If, at the other budgetary extreme, you stay in backpackers' hostels (€12–15 per person), travel everywhere by bus (you can get a very long way for 1000 lek, less than €10; for example Tirana to Bajram Curri or Gjirokastra), buy lunch from the market (bread, cheese, tomatoes and fruit for under €5), and dine on pasta or pizza (€10 maximum), you could equally easily keep within a budget of a tenth of that amount.

Most people will probably fall somewhere between these two extremes. A 1.5-litre bottle of local mineral water in a shop (as opposed to a café) costs between 50 and 70 lek; a half-litre bottle of Albanian beer in a bar usually ranges from 150 to 200 lek; a small loaf of bread from a bakery is 50 lek; small, triangular *byrek* (page 49) cost between 30 and 50 lek; and a medium-sized Mars bar, or similar imported chocolate, costs 60 lek in a supermarket, a bit more in a kiosk. Bars and cafés on the coast tend to charge more, especially in summer, than their inland equivalents.

Most museums, castles and archaeological sites have a small admission charge, usually 200–300 lek. A few of the most recently remodelled museums charge 500 or even 700 lek per visitor. Some sites are still unstaffed and do not have any explanatory information for visitors; when access is possible, it is free. Increasingly, mosques and churches charge a fixed admission fee; where they do not, a contribution of 100 or 200 lek per person is expected.

GETTING AROUND

MAPS It seems to be impossible for map publishers to produce reliable road maps of Albania. The speed of Albania's road improvement programme is admittedly hard to keep up with (this warning even applies to the maps in this guide), but there is no obvious explanation for the wild variations from one map to another in distances and spot heights. Some published maps even fail to show long-established border crossings. Google Maps is not updated for Albania regularly enough to be reliable beyond the centres of the large cities. For example, it took over a year for it to show the Fieri bypass, which opened in June 2019. Other map apps and satnavs are equally unreliable. For self-drivers, the best strategy is to consult various sources, check them against the information in this book and, whenever possible, ask locally.

The only commercially available **hiking and cycling maps** are published by the German company Huber Kartographie (w cartography-huber.com). There are 1:50,000 maps of Tropoja, Thethi and Kelmendi, Puka and several parts of southern Albania, and a 1:60,000 map of the cross-border Peaks of the Balkans trail (page 45). The maps have contours at 50m intervals and include descriptions, in English and Albanian, of selected hiking trails and cycling routes. Better still, they show, in grey dotted lines, the routes of old paths; these were the best routes 40 years ago and many of them are still used by local people.

Excellent hiking maps of the Albanian Alps, at 1:30,000, have been developed by Journey to Valbona, a multi-faceted organisation based in Bajram Curri. The only reliably marked trails in Valbona are maintained by a group of local volunteers, and these maps are produced in tandem with that work. They differentiate between marked trails, unmarked but clear trails, and invisible but plausible routes for confident navigators. Contours are shown at 10m intervals, 4x4 tracks are also indicated and there are extensive trail notes. The maps are printed to a high quality on waterproof paper. They can be bought online (w journeytovalbona.com) or in Journey to Valbona's shop in Bajram Curri (page 159). Part of the purchase price goes to finance the work of maintaining and expanding the trail system.

Downloads of the Soviet military maps of Albania, at 1:50,000, can be purchased at w mapstor.com. Although based on very old data, these maps are still useful for planning hikes or cycling tours in many areas of Albania. They should be used with caution, however, because in some parts of the country the topography has changed quite substantially since they were produced – for example, the old village of Kukësi is now under Lake Fierza – and elsewhere, new roads and dams have been built and old tracks have become blocked by landslides or washed away by floods. The names on the maps are in the Cyrillic alphabet. It should also be noted that the projection used is one from which amateur GPS equipment is unlikely to be able to set co-ordinates.

Commercially available maps

Freytag & Berndt *Albania*, 1:400,000, single-sided, index on reverse, some topographical detail, also covers all of Montenegro & Kosovo, most of North Macedonia & part of northern Greece.
Freytag & Berndt *Albania*, 1:200,000, double-sided, index booklet, some topographical detail, shows administrative boundaries.
Huber Kartographie GmBH *Peaks of the Balkans*, 1:60,000, contoured, GPS-compatible, relief shading, shows national park boundaries & recommended overnight stops. Detailed route description on reverse, with GPS waypoints.
Huber Kartographie GmBH 1:50,000, contoured at 50m intervals, spot heights, GPS-compatible, extensive topographic information. Recommended hiking & cycling routes are prominently marked & cross-referenced to descriptions on the reverse of each map. The old, traditional paths are also shown.
ITMB *Albania*, 1:210,000, double-sided, indexed, some topographical details, street plans of 7 cities & towns. Not a hiking map, but shows many of the old, traditional paths. Inexplicably, some well-established roads are missing altogether, including at least 2 border crossings.
Reise Know-How *Albanien*, 1:220,000, double-sided, indexed, waterproof, tear-resistant, good topographical detail with contour colouring & spot heights. Awkward to use on the road.

CAR HIRE Self-drive cars can be hired at Tirana and Kukësi airports, outside the ferry terminal in Saranda, and in other cities and larger towns. A few companies offer the option of dropping the vehicle off in a different town from where it was picked up. For some of the routes described in this book, a small saloon will not be adequate. Many car-hire agencies have 4x4 vehicles available, although of course these are more expensive.

At least some of the car-hire kiosks at Tirana Airport stay open until the last flight of the day has arrived. However, if you want to be sure of being able to rent the model you want as soon as you arrive, you should book it in advance. Several small, local companies also offer car hire from offices located just beyond the airport perimeter fence, across the road.

Another option, reasonably affordable in Albania, is to hire a taxi with its driver, which can be arranged for a specific trip or for several days. Taxis can be hired either through a local tour operator (page 30) or your hotel, or independently (if you can establish a common language with a driver) at the main taxi rank in each town.

Avis 04 223 5011; w avis.com
Europcar 04 222 7888; w europcar.com
Hertz 04 226 2511; w hertz.com
Sixt Tirana Airport & Durrësi; m 068 20 68 500; w sixt.com
Tirana Car Rentals Tirana & Durrësi; 04 630 1255; m 068 40 30 505; w tirana-car-rentals.com

CYCLING *Thanks to Bruce Logan, Jaap de Boer and others for their contributions*
Adventurous cyclists will be spoilt for choice with all the ancient tracks across Albania's mountain passes and along remote valleys. Some ideas for routes are suggested in the relevant chapters. For short excursions on reasonably surfaced roads, bikes can be hired in several cities.

Road surfaces are very variable and, for longer tours, 'touring' or off-road tyres are essential. Gradients are often much steeper than cyclists used to the Alps, for example, might expect. The unreliability of maps of Albania (page 41) can make these gradients even more of a surprise (or shock). The cobbled surfaces of some of the pre-WWII Italian-built roads become very slippery with rain and may not be rideable in wet conditions.

Albanian drivers are now more used to sharing their roads with foreign cyclists and, in the main, they are reasonably courteous to them. However, it is safer as well as more enjoyable to travel as much as possible during the day and on roads with light traffic. On busy highways, extreme caution and defensiveness are advisable. On some of the new highways, there are signs indicating that cyclists are not allowed. If there is an alternative route, it will probably make for more enjoyable riding; if there is not, the prohibition is not always enforced, at least not on foreign cyclists.

As for security, if you are camping you should remove all loose items and lock the bike as securely as you possibly can, perhaps by chaining it to a tree. Hotel owners will be happy to find a space for your bike in the courtyard or somewhere else secure, although you should nonetheless lock it and keep loose items with you.

PUBLIC TRANSPORT Public transport in Albania falls broadly into one of three categories, which for convenience in this guidebook are referred to as 'inter-city buses', 'rural buses' and 'city buses'. They all operate daily, except in some remote areas where there is no Sunday service. The rail network is restricted to a couple of trains a day between Durrësi and Elbasani and Shkodra. The fares are cheap, but the trains are so slow and infrequent that they are not a realistic option for most travellers. There are no internal civilian flights at the time of writing.

Inter-city buses Inter-city buses vary in size, from full-size coaches to minibuses with as few as half a dozen seats. Their common denominator is that they run to timetables. On busy routes to or from Tirana, this can be as often as once or twice an hour; on less heavily travelled routes, there may be only one bus a day in each direction. The schedules change from time to time and those that are specified later in this book are for guidance only. The best way to confirm bus times is to go to the terminus for where you want to go – some cities have proper bus stations, elsewhere you have to ask locally. Whether it is a formal bus station or a street corner, the Albanian name for it is '*agjencia*'. Bus stations often seem rather chaotic but, implausible though it may seem to the foreign observer, there is always someone whose job it is to co-ordinate passengers with the correct bus. Either tell the co-ordinator which city you want to go to, and they will advise you (possibly even in English), or look around the terminus for yourself. Inter-city buses have signs in their dashboards showing their destination.

Bus schedules often start very early in the morning, at 06.00 or even earlier. Apart from routes to and from Tirana, you are unlikely to find any inter-urban buses much after midday. The earlier you present yourself at the bus terminus, the more choice you will have. The departure time of the last bus depends to some extent on how far away the destination is – Tirana–Shkodra, for example, is only a couple of hours, and there are buses until 17.00. The latest departures from provincial towns tend to be earlier than those from Tirana; for example, the last bus from Shkodra to Tirana leaves at 16.00. Albanians confirm bus times and reserve seats by phoning the driver's mobile, but it is difficult for foreign travellers to ascertain this number without physically locating the bus; some drivers helpfully post their mobile number on their dashboard sign.

On heavily travelled inter-city routes, especially for shorter distances, buses are supplemented with **shared vehicles** – minibuses or cars. They leave only when there are enough passengers to make it worth the driver's while or, if he is not in his home-city, when he needs to get home. These shared vehicles have fixed fares. Again, the earlier you can set off, the better; later in the day, you will probably have to hang around for quite a while, waiting for the optimum number of passengers to materialise.

Rural buses The rule about transport being infrequent after midday is turned on its head when it comes to rural buses. This is because Albanian villagers travel to towns only when they have administrative tasks to carry out or special shopping to do, or if they are connecting on to an inter-city bus. In all these cases, they want to arrive in the town early, so that they can accomplish everything they need to do. Their rural bus is driven by one of their neighbours and it leaves at whatever time will get the villagers to town when the government institutions open. As for its return trip to the village, in some cases there is a scheduled departure time, while in others, the bus will leave when everyone the driver is expecting has returned to it with their shopping (the villagers will all have the driver's phone number saved in their mobiles and will let him know if their plans have changed). If you want to get a rural bus to a village, perhaps to visit one of the many remote archaeological sites described in this book, or to do some hiking, or for whatever other reason, you will probably spend quite a lot of time hanging around. If you can establish a common language with the driver, you can exchange mobile numbers so that at least you can go off and have some lunch; or you can sit in the nearest café until the driver shows up (he may turn out to have been in the same café all along). With few exceptions (some are covered in the relevant sections of this guidebook), you are unlikely to be able to find any transport (including hitchhiking) back to the town from the village until early the following morning.

On school days, rural buses also provide transport for the village kids to and from their elementary school. The drivers are contracted to provide this service and, in the most remote places, it is probably what keeps the rural bus operating at all. The consequence is that, on school days, there is sometimes an extra bus service, from the town back to the village, at about 13.00. Space on the school bus can almost always be found, if required, for one or two foreign travellers and their luggage. In very remote areas, it is sometimes possible to hitch a lift on the school buses that ferry the teachers, first thing in the morning, from the district capital to the elementary schools in the villages.

City buses In most Albanian towns and cities, the urban bus system is – frankly – opaque. It is designed for people who live in that town and who know that Ilir's boy drives the bus that goes up past the tractor factory. Visitors who do not know Ilir, or what his son looks like, or that those ruined buildings on the hill used to be the tractor factory, until it was burned down in 1991, have little chance of identifying the bus which will take them where they want to go. In Tirana things are somewhat easier – at least there the buses display their routes – but the buses get so crowded at peak times of day that using them then is not a comfortable option. The appropriate sections in this guidebook include guidance on city bus routes that the author has found most useful.

Street names are rarely used in Albania and, even when they are, matters are complicated by the fact that everybody still uses the old, communist-era names instead of the new ones that are on street maps. Albanians navigate by landmarks rather than addresses so that, if you ask for directions to, say, the Vila Bekteshi restaurant in Shkodra, you will not be told it is on Rruga Hazan Riza Pasha, but that it is behind the mosque, near the Orthodox cathedral.

Taxis There are plenty of taxis in every town of any size. They usually have a meter or a flat fare for short journeys within the town centre; for longer journeys you should agree a fare before getting into the car. Taxis can be hired for half a day, or a day, or even longer – the Albanian expression for this is '*në dispozicion*' – and again the rate should be negotiated in advance. If meal breaks are involved you will be expected to pay for the driver's food.

Taxi licences are issued by the relevant local council. Licensed taxis have yellow registration plates and a shield-shaped sticker on the door with the licence number on it. In Tirana and some other cities, the cars themselves are often yellow too. In very small towns the cars might have only the council's stickers, not the yellow number plates. Unlicensed 'pirate' taxis operate in some places and undercut the licensed taxis. Licences are quite expensive and the legitimate taxi drivers are understandably resentful of the 'pirates'.

HIKING AND SKIING Albania offers magnificent opportunities to explore wild, remote places, on foot, on skis or with snowshoes. However, only a few of the national parks have any kind of infrastructure in place to support outdoor activities; accommodation, where it exists at all, is usually in family homes with conditions that are sometimes rather basic. Indeed, just reaching many of Albania's national parks and nature reserves involves a difficult journey by 4x4 or several hours' walk from the nearest village served by public transport.

The mountain areas of Albania are now very sparsely populated, because many villagers have given up subsistence farming in exchange for a slightly less tough life in a town or city. If you sprain your ankle or run into other problems, the nearest help could well be several hours' walk away. Remote mountain areas do not usually have mobile-phone coverage. You should never set off on a hike alone. Great caution is also needed when approaching sheepdogs in the mountains; they are trained to attack anything which they think might be a threat to the livestock they are protecting. If you are confronted by a sheepdog, stop; if you have the presence of mind, back slowly away from it. Do not go any further into the dog's territory until the shepherd, who will be somewhere around, makes his or her way to you and calls the dog off.

Long-distance hiking The long-distance, cross-border hiking trail called Peaks of the Balkans (w peaksofthebalkans.com) is now well-established and justifiably popular. A new cross-border trail is in development (at the time of writing): the High Scardus Trail, linking North Macedonia and Kosovo via Shebenik-Jabllanica National Park (page 193) in Albania (w highscardustrail.com), and designed to link into the Via Dinarica (w viadinarica.com). The main problem with these initiatives is that it is practically impossible for an independent hiker to obtain permission to cross the borders between Montenegro, Kosovo and Albania. In theory, all three countries have systems in place to enable this; the snag is that you need to be physically present in the relevant border town in order either to pay the permit fee (Montenegro) or to process the paperwork (Albania and Kosovo). Zbulo! (page 30) can submit your paperwork, chase up your applications and inform you when your permit is approved, for a small fee. If you are travelling as part of an organised hiking tour, the agency you have booked with will deal with permits for the whole group.

Hikers are unlikely to be robbed, but it is not completely unheard of; if you are attacked, your assailant is almost certain to be armed with a gun.

An increasing number of guesthouses in the Albanian mountains provide space and facilities for **campers**. Often these will be shared with people travelling in campervans or mobile homes. The two groups tend to have different views of what time days should start and finish, which can sometimes lead to friction. There are also campsites on the Riviera beaches, most of them open only in summer.

Wild camping is tolerated, but you should follow the usual codes of conduct (the Mountaineering Council of Scotland's website – **w** mcofs.org.uk/assets/pdfs/wildcamping.pdf – has useful guidelines, although obviously its legal advice does not apply in Albania). In particular, it is not always easy to tell if you are pitching your tent on private property. If there is an inhabited house within sight, you should make yourself known to the inhabitants. Apart from anything else, if they discover in the middle of the night that there are strangers roaming around their property, they are almost certain to reach for their guns before leaving the house to find out who is there. Albanian highlanders have ancient traditions of hospitality and may well invite you to sleep in their house. If you prefer to be in your tent, a polite compromise might be for you to camp in their garden. If the head of the family refuses payment, it is a nice gesture to press a few hundred lek, 'for the children' ('*për femijët*'), into the hand of the oldest child.

Sleeping rough in the Albanian mountains might also bring you into closer proximity with the carnivorous fauna of the country than you would like. Wolves do not eat people, although hearing them howl around your tent is probably quite disconcerting; bears, on the other hand, have been known to attack humans and they don't howl first. Albania also has some venomous snakes, among them the dangerous nose-horned viper (*Vipera ammodytes*).

Skiing In the communist era, skiing was quite a popular pastime and several small resorts were developed. They do not have Western-style infrastructure, but for adventurous skiers they can be interesting to visit. The first snow usually falls in November and lasts until March or April, with average snowfall of 40–60cm and low maximum temperatures. At the time of writing, the best place to ski in Albania is **Puka**, in the north of the country. The Marenglen Laçi outdoor sports resort, just out of town, has a simple ski-lift, good accommodation, and skis (and ice skates) available to hire (page 133). For those who are able to bring their own skis, other resorts are:

Dardha 20km south of Korça; page 182. A traditional village, 1,344m above sea level; a tourist attraction in the summer, too. Hotel & guesthouse accommodation is available.

Shishtaveci 31km from Kukësi; page 155. The plateau is over 2,000m above sea level. There are several guesthouses & a small hotel in the village.

Voskopoja 26km west of Korça; page 187. The Akademia Hotel, 2,286m above sea level, was used in the communist period to accommodate groups of students on skiing trips. Alternative accommodation is available with local families in Voskopoja.

ACCOMMODATION

HOTELS Communist-era hotels in Albania were built to provide accommodation either for individuals travelling on official business or for families on holiday at the beach or in the mountains. Very few foreign tourists visited Albania and so – unlike other communist countries in central and eastern Europe – there were no hotels specifically built for them.

ACCOMMODATION PRICE CODES

Prices are based on the cost of a double room per night or, in the case of backpacker hostels, two beds in a dorm.

$$$$$	Luxury	€100+
$$$$	Upmarket	€70–100
$$$	Mid-range	€45–70
$$	Thrifty	€30–45
$	Budget	under €30

Every provincial capital had a centrally located hotel, with its own bar and restaurant, and usually with a large number of rooms. This was invariably referred to as 'Turizmi' ('The Tourism'), and it was where foreign tour groups stayed as well as Albanian sports teams or cultural ensembles. In coastal and mountain resorts, there were similar hotels to accommodate student groups and holidaying families. Because these hotels had been state-owned, they were often targeted by rioters during the civil uprising of spring 1997 and several were completely destroyed. Of those that survived, all have now been privatised. Most of these hotels now meet reasonable international standards, with en-suite bathrooms, constant hot water, air conditioning, TV and Wi-Fi as a minimum. In some towns, the former 'Turizmi' is of a very high standard indeed.

Hotels and guesthouses built since the end of communism – often referred to as 'private hotels' – are more variable in quality. The minimum standard that can be expected of a mid-range hotel is an en-suite bathroom with shower, air conditioning, TV and Wi-Fi. In Tirana, such hotels typically charge €60–70 a night; in the rest of the country it is usually €10–20 less. Rooms in more upmarket hotels may have balconies, bathtubs and/or minibars. At the beach resorts in July and August, hotels charge whatever they think they can get away with; demand exceeds supply at the height of the Albanian holiday season and so haggling is unlikely to be successful at that time of year. When the quoted price is for the room, not per person, single travellers can often negotiate a discount.

In mountain villages, accommodation is usually in family homes. The welcome is always hospitable, but conditions range from quite comfortable to rather basic. Typically, each room will have three or four beds and the bathroom will be shared, sometimes also with the family. It is very unusual for there to be no Wi-Fi, but TV and air conditioning are not standard. Breakfast is always included and usually lavish; other meals or packed lunches can be provided on request.

Room rates are usually given in euros, except at the budget end of the market where they tend to be quoted in lek. It is always possible to pay in either currency, although you may be given your change in lek. Breakfast is sometimes included, sometimes not; it will almost always be available, even if you have to pay extra for it. Albanian hotel breakfasts usually consist of toast or bread with a hard-boiled or fried egg, cheese, jam, honey and/or ham. Milk or tea is traditionally served with breakfast; coffee is not always included but can be paid for as an extra.

Some hotels in Albania have their own websites through which rooms can be booked. Otherwise, hotel accommodation throughout the country can be reserved through the Tirana-based agency **Albania Holidays** (☎ 04 223 5688, 04 223 5498; w albania-hotel.com) and through international websites such as w hostelworld.com and w booking.com.

CAMPING AND CARAVANNING Sites for mobile homes started to appear in Albania only about a decade ago, and the standards are variable. Most open only in the tourist season, roughly June to September. Details of some recommended sites can be found in the relevant chapters. The advice of the late Charlie Nuytens was invaluable in keeping this information up to date in this and previous editions.

In summer, many of the beaches on the Riviera have tented sites, of varying degrees of comfort, where travellers can either rent a tent or pitch their own. Information about these seasonal campsites is available on the usual travellers' websites. Some mobile-home sites also provide spaces where tents can be pitched. Advice on wild camping is given on page 46.

EATING AND DRINKING

FOOD Albanian cuisine is rich in Mediterranean ingredients such as olive oil, tomatoes and pimentos. Lamb, as you would expect in a mountainous country, is excellent, as is fish from Albania's rivers, seas and lakes. Those who like offal will welcome the chance to try dishes that changing consumer tastes have all but eliminated from northern European menus.

Fruit and vegetables Fruit and vegetables in Albania are delicious. The tomatoes taste of tomato, the watermelons remind you of something other than water, and the citrus fruit is tangy and refreshing. Aubergines, courgettes, green beans and okra figure prominently in summer, with cabbages, carrots and potatoes taking over in winter. It is a frequent boast in restaurants that all the food is organic (*bio*), but there is no system in Albania yet for certifying organic produce.

Meat The classic way to eat lamb is spit-roasted (*mish në hell*), and the classic place to eat it is in a village restaurant; see pages 86, 233 and 236 for a couple of suggestions. At weekends and on public holidays these places are filled with extended families at huge tables, tucking into lamb, salad, chips and carafes of wine. Traditional food in Albania is still seasonal, which means that spit-roasted lamb is not available until early summer; kid is a little earlier. An all-year-round variant is *paidhaqe*, lamb or veal ribs grilled over charcoal. Veal calves are not kept in crates and are slaughtered older than the milk-fed veal calves which used to be eaten in Britain; *biftek* is a cross-cut steak from the shoulder or loin, which can be fried or braised; and *rosto* is boned shoulder, oven-roasted and served with gravy.

Sheep's heart, liver, kidneys, brains and other organs are very popular. In the big cities, it is not always easy to find restaurants that serve these things, but they always exist and can be tracked down by asking. Albanian specialities include *paçë koke*, a thick soup made with sheep's head that is a traditional breakfast dish, and *kukurec*, chopped innards in a gut casing.

Fish and seafood The lake fish *koran* (a species of trout unique to Lake Ohrid) and carp are usually available only near the lakes where they are fished, although you can sometimes find them in Tirana, at a price. River trout, too, seldom travel far. Fresh sea fish is readily available all along the coast and in the inland cities. The varieties that appear most frequently on menus are *levrek* (sea bass) and *kocë* (sea bream), both usually farmed, *barbun* (red mullet) and *merluc* (hake). Eels (*ngjalë*) are caught in the lakes and coastal lagoons and are much sought after there; they rarely make it to the cities. Prawns (*karkalec*) are landed by Albanian fishermen, and on the coast they are likely to be fresh; elsewhere you may wish to ask if they are frozen (ie: imported).

Fresh lobster is sometimes available, although it is not cheap. Mussels (*midhje*) are farmed in Butrint Lagoon. Clams seem to be served only with pasta dishes in Italian restaurants. Finally, although it is not a fish, the edible variety of frog (*bretkosë*) is bred and its legs eaten – usually grilled – in central and southern Albania.

Traditional meals Traditional Albanian home cooking uses vegetables, yoghurt and cheese to make meat go further. Potatoes, aubergines, courgettes, peppers and cabbage are all stuffed with minced meat. Pieces of veal are simmered with aubergine, spinach or green beans, or braised in a terracotta pot with pickling onions (*mish çomlek*). For *turli*, different vegetables – carrots, aubergines, potatoes, okra or anything else the cook has to hand – are layered with slices of tomato around a veal joint and simmered. *Fergesë* is made with green peppers and onions, fried together and then mixed with egg and *gjizë*, a dry curd cheese, before being baked. Pieces of meat or liver are sometimes added to *fergesë*. In *tavë Elbasani*, or *tavë kosi*, yoghurt and eggs are beaten together and poured over pieces of lamb or mutton, before the whole thing is baked in the oven.

Shish qebap is cubes of meat – lamb, pork or beef – marinated and then grilled on skewers, alternated with onion slices; *qebap në letër* is the same ingredients plus chunks of feta cheese, wrapped in tinfoil and baked in the oven. *Qofta* are rissoles of minced lamb bound with egg: sometimes they are round and flat, like hamburgers, and sometimes they are cylindrical; sometimes they are served grilled with salad and chips, and sometimes with a tomato-based sauce, when they are usually called *qoftë Korçe*.

Albanian housewives preserve vegetables in vinegar for the winter, when salads consist mainly of different sorts of pickle – not only the familiar gherkin, but also preserved peppers, aubergines and other treats.

Albanian fast food *Qofta* also appear as fast food, sold at street kiosks straight from the grill. Doner kebab, called *sufllaqë* in central Albania and *pita* in the south, is served either in a circular piece of unleavened bread or in a hot-dog roll, topped with salad, chips and tomato ketchup or mustard. The other big player in the Albanian fast-food world is the *byrek*, which comes in many guises but is essentially filo pastry with something inside. The classic *byrek* is round and flat, and alternates layers of pastry with *gjizë*, or minced meat fried with chopped onions, or leeks. As a starter for the family lunch, it can be bought whole at the *byrektore* or made at home; as fast food, it is cut into quarters and eaten on the street. Another variant is the small triangular *byrek*, which can contain meat, or *gjizë*, or spinach, or tomato and onion, and is crispier and lighter than its circular relative. Finally there is the *pita*, for which the filo pastry is rolled up around the filling to make a long sausage shape, then coiled around itself and baked. All of these are tasty options when a full meal is not required.

Desserts Desserts are not usually eaten after meals in Albanian homes. On special occasions *xupa* might be served, a kind of blancmange sprinkled with walnuts. Sweetmeats are more often eaten with coffee during the *xhiro*, the early evening promenade. *Kadaif* and *halva* will be familiar to anyone who has visited Turkey or Greece, or indeed ever been in a Turkish café. *Tullumba* are cylinders of dough, deep-fried and tossed in syrup. *Sheqerpare* is made from little balls of sweet dough, baked in butter. *Shëndetlli* is a kind of fruit cake, steeped in honey; *kaçavure* is a light sponge cake infused with oranges and syrup. *Hashuref* is made with cornstarch, sugar and butter, brought to the boil and then baked (nicer than this makes it sound).

RESTAURANT PRICE CODES

Prices are based on the average cost of a main course.

$$$$$	Expensive	1,500 lek+
$$$$	Above average	1,000–1,500 lek
$$$	Reasonable	500–1,000 lek
$$	Good deal	under 500 lek
$	Cheap	snacks, less than 200 lek per item

Vegetarians and vegans Except in upmarket, Westernised establishments, there is almost never a specifically vegetarian option among the meals on offer in restaurants. In restaurants that are used to foreigners, vegetarians will always be offered something they can eat; elsewhere, it will generally be possible to persuade the kitchen to rustle up an omelette or a simple tomato sauce for pasta. Fish-eaters will be fine in the cities and on the coast. The Albanian highlands are resolutely carnivorous; non-meat-eaters will struggle to convince their puzzled hosts that all they want is cheese or eggs. Delicious though the cucumbers and tomatoes are, vegans are likely to have become quite tired of them after a couple of weeks in Albania.

Vegetarians in search of a tranquil countryside retreat will want to know about Ferma Grand Albanik, in the mountains above Këlcyra (page 204), which offers fully vegetarian menus (and meat for guests who want it). The owners themselves are vegetarian and can also cater for vegans.

DRINK The draught **wine** in provincial restaurants is normally rather young, but can be very drinkable. Albanian wine in bottles is often excellent. The main wine-producing areas are around Korça and Berati and between Lezha and Shkodra. The Bardha vineyard near Tirana produces outstanding wine in small quantities, difficult to track down but on the wine lists of a few Tirana restaurants. Most Albanian vineyards use well-known grapes such as Sauvignon and Cabernet, which are easy for them to sell in quantity. A few, however, are now moving towards a more high-end product using indigenous grapes such as Shesh (red and white), Pulës or Dëbinë (white) and Kallmet (red). Some of these vineyards, listed below, can arrange tours of their production facilities and offer tastings of their own wines. For those who are unable to visit the vineyards, these wines are usually on sale in the duty-free shops at Tirana Airport.

Alpeta Roshniku, near Berati; m 069 748 4361; e alpetawinery@gmail.com; f Kantina e Veres Alpeta

Arbëri Rrësheni; 0216 22486; e info@kantina-arberi.com; w kantina-arberi.com

Çobo Ura Vajgurore, near Berati; 0361 22088; e info@cobowineryonline.com; w cobowineryonline.com

Nurellari Fushë-Peshtani, near Berati; 032 238 551; e fatosnurellari@yahoo.com; w nurellariwinery.com

Beer is brewed commercially in several towns and cities. Korça is home to the oldest brewery in Albania (page 186); others that are widely available outside their home region include Tirana, Kaon and Puka beers. The Tirana and Korça breweries produce dark beer as well as the more widely available lager; Puka offers an unfiltered version and Kaon a Weissbier.

Of the other Albanian alcoholic drinks, **raki** is the most widely consumed. Despite its Turkish name, Albanian raki is not flavoured with aniseed as it is in Turkey. It is a clear spirit, usually distilled from grape juice, and drunk as a morning pick-me-up, an aperitif, a digestif, or at any other time of day. Albanians also make raki from mulberries (*mani*), brambles (*manaferre*) and practically any other soft fruit they can lay their hands on. In Slav-speaking villages raki is distilled from plums, as it is across the border in former Yugoslavia. The Berati-based vineyard Çobo makes excellent walnut raki. Another unusual raki is that made from the fruit of the strawberry tree (*Arbutus unedo*) called *mare* in Albanian. The best raki is homemade; commercially bottled products are widely available in shops.

Albanian brandy (*konjak*) can be quite good, or it can be appalling; the commercially available Skënderbeu brand is in the former category. *Fernet*, a drink made from herbs that tastes nothing like the Italian Fernet-Branca, is a popular aperitif, though something of an acquired taste.

Coffee is an even more integral part of Albanian life than raki. Over coffee, deals are done, jobs are offered and marriages arranged. Having a coffee with an Albanian takes an absolute minimum of half an hour. Traditionally it was made in the usual Balkan way, with very finely ground coffee, water and sugar all boiled together in an individual pot – in Albanian it is called *kafe turke*. This is usually what you will be offered in Albanians' houses. In cafés and restaurants in towns and cities, Italian espresso machines are the norm, when there is electricity to operate them. During power cuts, *kafe turke* comes back into its own. You will be asked how you take it, meaning how much sugar you want. Four possible answers are: '*e ëmbël*' (sweet); '*e mesme*' (standard, which is quite sweet); '*me pak sheqer*' (with a little sugar); and '*sade*' (unsweetened). In recent years, self-service coffee shops have become popular in cities; two national chains are Mulliri and Mon Chéri.

Herbal **teas** are also popular in Albania (see box, page 6). Some widely available brands are BioTea, Bumi and Kraco. In winter, a warming alternative to coffee is **salep**, of Ottoman origin. Traditionally it is made from the tubers of orchids, ground into powder and mixed with warm milk. Nowadays it is much more likely to come out of a packet.

PRACTICAL INFORMATION Most restaurants in Albania do not have fixed opening hours. They are family-run and open when the owners think people might want to start eating – in the countryside this will be around 09.00 or 10.00, when Albanian farmers have breakfast (*paçë koke*, for example), while in towns it is usually a bit later. They close when there are no more customers – in the countryside this tends to be quite early in the evening, in small towns it will be around 21.00 and in cities an hour or so later. Some restaurants, particularly those that serve very traditional food, are open only in the mornings and at lunchtime; the listings in each section of the guide specify where this is the case.

It is rarely necessary to book a table in advance; indeed, most restaurants do not even have telephone numbers, other than the mobile phone of the owner. Where reservations are advisable, numbers are given in the listings in each section.

Restaurant bills are always in lek, although euros are usually accepted if necessary; however, the exchange rate is unlikely to be in the customer's favour. In restaurants, tips are expected though not obligatory – rounding up to about 10% of the total bill is fine. Tipping practice in cafés is to leave a couple of coins on your table after you have paid your bill.

PUBLIC HOLIDAYS

Albania shuts down pretty much completely on 1 and 2 January (New Year) and 28 November (Independence Day). Particularly on 1 January, only a handful of cafés and restaurants open and all shops are closed.

On other public holidays, banks, museums and government offices are closed, while shops, restaurants, bureaux de change and other private businesses generally stay open. The major feast days of each of Albania's religions or, if they fall on a Sunday, the Monday following them, are public holidays. The two which have fixed dates are the Bektashi festival of Nevruz, on 22 March, and 25 December, when both the Catholic and Albanian Orthodox churches celebrate Christmas. Moveable religious holidays are Catholic and Orthodox Easters (usually on different Sundays), Eid al-Fitr (*Bajram i Vogël*, the end of Ramadan) and Eid ul-Adha (*Bajram i Madh*). Other holidays include Summer Day (14 March), International Workers' Day (1 May), Mother Teresa Day (19 October) and Liberation Day (29 November). The last commemorates liberation from the Germans at the end of WWII which, since it was immediately followed by 45 years of communist rule, not everybody in Albania agrees is a reason for celebration.

'National' museums close on Mondays; others are more likely to be closed on Saturdays and Sundays. The difference is not always obvious.

SHOPPING

The best places in Albania to shop for souvenirs are Kruja (page 112) and Gjirokastra (page 273), where all the shops are close together in the bazaar. In Kruja, there are traditional felt-makers, who produce slippers and the felt caps called *qeleshe*; shops selling hand-woven *qilime* (this is the same word as the Turkish *kilim*, a woven rug); and antique dealers. Many of the Kruja shops sell small souvenirs such as Albanian flags, copper plates and ashtrays in the shape of bunkers. Gjirokastra's bazaar has a stonemason, a woodworker, lacemakers and shops selling woven textiles and *qilime*, as well as other souvenirs.

Elsewhere it can be quite difficult to find traditional crafts for sale. Please refer to the relevant chapters of this guide for further information. If all else fails, small souvenirs and bottles of wine, raki and cognac can be purchased at the airport.

ARTS AND ENTERTAINMENT

Albania, like many formerly communist countries, has a strong tradition of classical music. The country's main venue for this is the National Theatre of Opera and Ballet on Tirana's Skanderbeg Square; forthcoming concerts, operas and ballet performances are usually advertised outside the theatre. Classical recitals also take place in the Academy of Arts in Tirana and, occasionally, in other venues around the country (eg: the theatre at Butrint). Plays and similar performances are staged, generally in Albanian, in the main theatres in Tirana, Shkodra, Durrësi and Korça. It is far from easy to find out about these events; asking at the nearest tourist information office might yield results. Public institutions, such as theatres and museums, cannot normally deal with telephone enquiries from members of the public. The cinemas in several towns and cities usually screen Hollywood films, in the original version with Albanian subtitles. Screenings of Albanian films are much rarer.

It is almost as difficult to find performances of traditional Albanian music or dance. The best way to stumble across them is to be staying in a hotel where a wedding is being celebrated; Albanian weddings last three days, with the final big celebration always on a Sunday night. There are folk festivals at Gjirokastra (every four years, roughly), Peshkopia (annually, in September) and Përmeti (annually, in June). Please refer to the relevant chapters of this guide for further information.

PHOTOGRAPHY

Albanians are usually delighted to have their photographs taken but, like people in any other country, they prefer to be asked first. Once permission has been requested, you may well end up having to take photos of the entire family.

Again like everywhere else, the security and armed forces tend not to be very happy about people taking photos of military or government buildings. Bunkers are fine, as long as they are not surrounding a military base.

MEDIA AND COMMUNICATIONS

MEDIA Albania's state-owned public broadcaster, RTSH, is partly funded through a levy charged through residents' electricity bills. In addition, several privately owned stations are licensed to broadcast nationwide, with locally licensed channels in many cities. Albania converted all its terrestrial TV channels to digital in 2017. Almost all private media are owned by a few media groups, each of which operates TV channels, radio stations and newspapers. The individual businesspeople who head each media group are often well-known, and usually have other business interests as well as media, but there is no real transparency of ownership.

Practically all hotels have a TV in every guest room. The 24-hour news channels have rolling headlines in English and occasional English-language news summaries. One or other of BBC World, Euronews or CNN are often available. Channels in other languages vary, depending on the digital subscription service used by the hotel. There are usually several Italian channels and a few in German, plus sometimes France24.

Radio plays a less significant role in Albania than in some other countries. The public broadcaster has three radio stations (Radio Tirana); two privately owned radio stations have national licences. The BBC World Service can be picked up on medium wave in Tirana and online elsewhere. To the great dismay of many Albanians, the World Service ended its Albanian service in 2011. The Voice of America broadcasts to Albania on medium and short wave; its website (w *voa.gov*) has details of frequencies.

Newspapers are rather a niche product these days, apart from the sports papers. Most Albanian newspapers also publish their content online. There are several English-language news websites; those interested in reading up on Albanian current affairs before visiting the country will probably find the best coverage in the *Tirana Times*, which is linked to the Albanian Institute for International Studies (w aiis-albania.org).

PEOPLE Communicating with Albanians is much easier than might be expected. They are among the most polyglot people in Europe, perhaps because the country was isolated for so long and so few foreigners speak their language. It is not at all unusual for a young Albanian to have a good command of three or four languages. Most older people do not know English, but they may well speak good French, Greek or Italian.

Italian is widely spoken in coastal towns, such as Shkodra, Durrësi and Vlora, thanks to their historical links with, and geographical proximity to, Italy. Even during the later years of the communist regime, Albanians on the coast and in Tirana could watch Italian television, and so people now in their 30s and 40s more or less grew up with the language and often speak it extremely well. Younger people, however, are more likely to have English as their first foreign language.

Enver Hoxha (see box, page 84) studied in France, at the University of Montpellier, and during communism the French *lycées* in Korça and Gjirokastra continued to operate. Particularly in these towns, therefore, but also elsewhere, a sizeable number of Albanians speak French. In the south of the country, Greek is very widely spoken, including by people who are ethnically Albanian rather than Greek.

Those who were at school or university in the 1950s and 1960s learned Russian, although many of them have not used the language for 40 or more years and have forgotten most of it. In areas that border the former Yugoslavia, there are Slavic-speaking ethnic minorities (page 20). Some people who are now in their 60s learned Chinese, usually because they studied in China; some academic exchanges have resumed since the advent of democracy in Albania, and one occasionally comes across younger people, too, who have studied in China and learned the language.

POST AND TELEPHONES The fixed network in Albania is run by a privatised monopoly, called Albtelecom but known locally as 'Telekomi'. Numbers in Tirana have seven digits; numbers elsewhere in the country have five or six. However, most people prefer to use their mobile phones.

There are several **mobile phone** companies in Albania. Between them, they have agreements with most other European companies, so if you have roaming enabled on your phone you should be able to use it in Albania. Alternatively, if your phone is network-unlocked, an Albanian prepay SIM card will cost a few hundred lek, most of it as call time. Tariffs have come down in recent years and coverage is as good as it is ever likely to get in a mountainous country like Albania.

To make a phone call in Albania, other than from a mobile phone, the cheapest option is Albtelecom, where you can book your call, have it transferred to a booth in the phone centre and pay for it after you have made it. In cities, the other option is to use a public phone in the street. These take cards, not coins; you can buy a card at Albtelecom agencies. Luxury and many upmarket hotels offer guests the facility to make calls, directly or through their switchboard, but – like hotels everywhere – they add a hefty charge for this facility.

The Albanian **postal service** (Albapost) is reasonably reliable. Western Union, DHL and FedEx all have offices in Tirana and other cities.

ALBANIAN TIME AND BUSINESS

Albania is 1 hour ahead of GMT from October to March, and 2 hours ahead in summer; this is the same time as Italy and most of mainland Europe, but 1 hour behind Greece.

The traditional Albanian working day begins at 08.00, or in rural areas even earlier, and ends at 15.00, when everybody goes home for lunch, the main meal of the day. Many people then take a siesta, particularly in summer when the tarmac on the streets is melting, and re-emerge in the early evening for the *xhiro*. This is when families go out together and walk up and down the town's boulevard or – if it has a waterfront – its promenade. The *xhiro* may include an ice cream or a coffee, or a chat with casually met friends, but it does not have to involve anything other than walking.

In cities, especially in national and local government offices, working hours have increasingly moved closer to a northern European norm of 08.30 or 09.00 to 16.30 or 17.00. However, if you have government business to do in Albania, it is best accomplished early in the day. If you wish to meet the owner or manager of a privately owned business, it is almost always possible to do this over a coffee at any reasonable hour.

Doing business or buying property in Albania is fraught with difficulty owing to the prevalence of corruption, the presence of organised crime, and the weakness of the judicial system. Anyone considering investing in the country should seek the advice of the commercial attaché at their embassy in Tirana.

CULTURAL ETIQUETTE

Albanians traditionally shake hands not only on being introduced to somebody but also on greeting or leaving people they already know. This etiquette has begun to break down a little, however, due to the influence of the Covid-19 pandemic. With friends, a kiss on both cheeks is exchanged by men as well as women. This is often combined with a hand on the other person's shoulder. After a long separation, or with really close friends, the number of kisses increases.

The usual way to indicate 'yes' is by moving the head horizontally from side to side. During a conversation, this movement is also used to indicate general agreement with what the other person is saying, or simply to show that you are listening. The usual sign for 'no' is a slight raising of the eyebrows, sometimes accompanied by a gentle click of the tongue. Raising the whole chin is a very emphatic 'no'. Unfortunately, exposure to foreign visitors has confused this simple state of affairs and people (especially in Tirana) sometimes try to be helpful by using non-Albanian head signals. The result is that it can be hard to tell whether the person shaking his or her head at you is saying 'yes' in Albanian, or 'no' in your language. Sometimes you just have to ask.

Albanians usually remove their shoes inside their homes or other people's houses. If you are visiting an Albanian home, you will be offered a pair of slippers or plastic sandals to wear while you are indoors.

Smoking is widespread. A ban on smoking in enclosed public places was introduced in 2007, but it is not always fully enforced in restaurants and bars. People almost always respect the smoking ban on public transport. On long journeys, the bus will stop for a couple of cigarette breaks.

As might be expected in a country that for 50 years was starved of contact with foreigners, Albanians are always very keen to engage visitors in conversation, for example, on bus journeys. Their questions often become very personal very quickly, although usually they do not mean to be intrusive.

TRAVELLING POSITIVELY

The charitable sector in Albania is very weak compared with northern Europe or (especially) North America. Most Tirana-based not-for-profit organisations conduct research or lobbying rather than hands-on humanitarian assistance. The main organisations that actually help people on the ground are the churches and mosques.

Albanian Disability Rights Foundation (ADRF) Rr Mujo Ulqinaku 26, Tirana; 04 226 6892, 04 226 9426; e adrf@albmail.com; f Fshdpak Adrf. Set up by Oxfam GB in 1994,

ADRF (its Albanian acronym is FSHDPAK) promotes the rights of people with disabilities, mostly through lobbying & training.

Albanian Red Cross 04 225 7532/3; e kksh@albaniaonline.com; w kksh.org.al. The oldest humanitarian organisation in Albania, founded in 1921. It has been a member of the Federation of the International Red Cross & Red Crescent since 1923.

THE ENVIRONMENT AND SUSTAINABLE TOURISM One area where there are some organisations actively trying to make a difference is that of the environment and sustainable tourism; they tend to call themselves 'Associations' (*Shoqata*) to differentiate them from the lobbying and research NGOs.

Organisation to Conserve the Albanian Alps (TOKA) m 067 30 14 638; e contact@toka-albania.org; w toka-albania.org. Grown from the campaigning efforts of a group of activists in the Valbona Valley National Park for several years, TOKA (meaning 'earth') focuses on protecting & managing the natural resources of the Albanian Alps; ensuring respect for & implementation of Albania's environmental laws; creating & promoting sustainable growth; & representing local stakeholders.

Protection and Preservation of Natural Environment in Albania (PPNEA) 04 562 8954; e contact@ppnea.org; w ppnea.org. Focusing on research & policy advocacy, PPNEA is an active partner in the Balkan Lynx Recovery Programme (page 171) & Save the Blue Heart of Europe, a campaign to protect the wild rivers of the Balkans from unbridled hydro-electric developments. PPNEA also has a number of smaller-scale but no less important projects, including monitoring monk seals & campaigning against the keeping of bears in captivity. Donations can be made through its website.

Hiking
Trekking
MTB
Albania, Kosovo, Montenegro, Macedonia
ZBULO
ALBANIA & BEYOND
Tour leaders
Local guides
Self-guided
Private groups
Group tours
Tailor-made
Zbulo! Albania & Beyond
Human-powered adventures in the Balkans handcrafted by local travel specialists.
www.zbulo.org / welcome@zbulo.org / +355 69 2121 612

Part Two

THE GUIDE

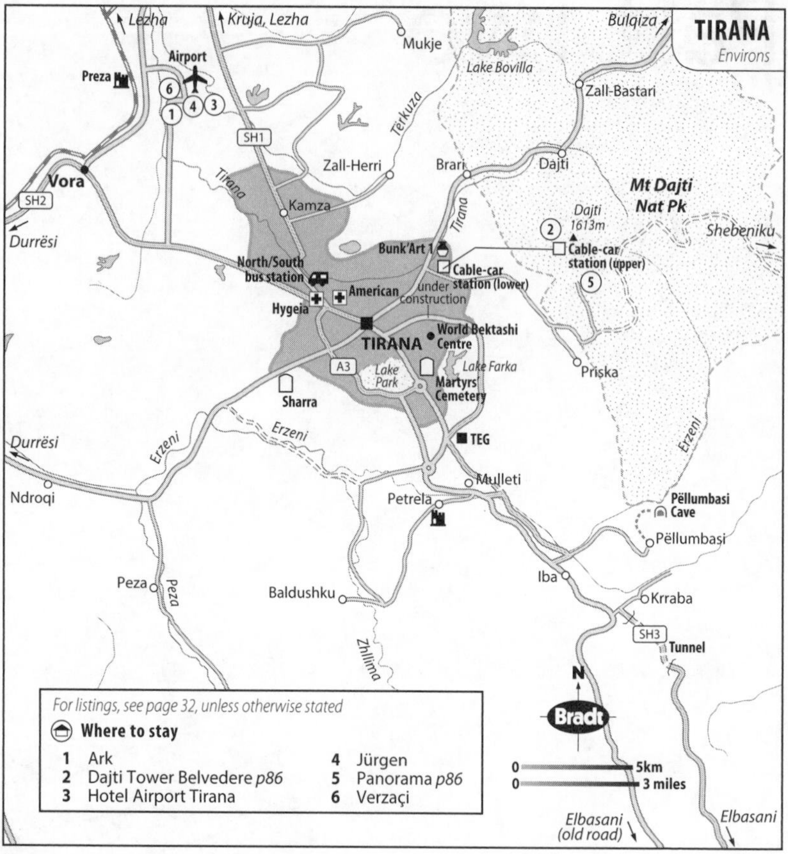

TOURS ALBANIA & BALKANS
Tour Operator & DMC

Tours Albania

Holiday packages & tours to Albania & the Balkans

www.tours-albania.com
info@tours-albania.com
Str, Luigj Gurakuqi 47/8, Tirana, Albania 1017

3

Tirana

Telephone code: 04

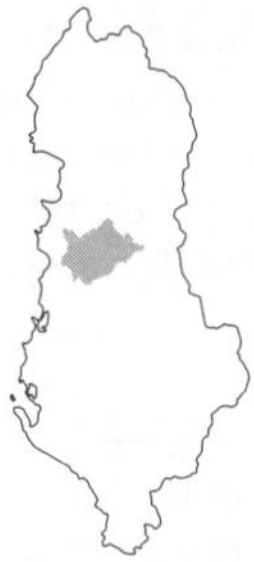

Tirana was founded in the early 17th century by Sulejman Pasha Mulleti, who built a settlement in the area around the modern intersection of Rruga e Barrikadave and Rruga Luigj Gurakuqi. His statue stands today in the little square near that crossroads. Until it was designated as Albania's capital in 1920, Tirana was a small, unimportant town. Its main virtue for the country's political leaders was its geographical position more or less in the centre of the recently independent country, on the fault line dividing the northern Ghegs from the southern Tosks. The new capital remained a bit of a sideshow for several years afterwards, as Albania struggled to stabilise itself in the face of internal lawlessness and invasions by its hostile neighbours.

It was not until Italian influence became pervasive in the late 1920s that the centre of Tirana took on the appearance of a capital city. Italian planners created the huge new square – given the name of the national hero Skanderbeg – and the wide, typically Fascist Boulevard leading off it; Italian architects designed the ministry buildings, the National Bank and the City Hall around the square, as well as the Dajti Hotel, the royal palace on Rruga e Elbasanit, and some of the embassies. During the communist era, the few pre-Italian buildings still standing on Skanderbeg Square were demolished and the opera house, the National Historical Museum and the Hotel Tirana (now the Tirana International Hotel) were added, as were the public buildings further down the Boulevard. All these 20th-century accretions, plus the destruction caused by various earthquakes and by the Battle for the Liberation of Tirana in 1944, means that not much is left of Ottoman Tirana. A good deal of what survived into the 1990s has subsequently disappeared under glittering high-rise office blocks and shopping centres.

Tirana has become well known for its brightly painted apartment buildings. This initiative began in the wake of the 2000 local elections, which saw an artist and former Minister of Culture becoming Mayor of Tirana. The new mayor, Edi Rama (at the time of writing, he is the country's prime minister), began by restoring to the ministries on and around Skanderbeg Square the ochre colour that they had when they were first built in the 1930s; he went on to give a lick of paint to the tatty apartment blocks in the streets nearby, choosing bold colours which – although they did not convince everybody – at least had the merit of brightening up the city. The colours and patterns became livelier and livelier, until even the more progressive of Tirana's citizens began to complain that their city was starting to look like a circus. Happily for them, the fierce summer sun bleaches out the most migraine-inducing colours after a year or two.

As well as its intriguing mix of architectural styles, Tirana has several very good museums and a range of cultural activities. It has hundreds of cafés; dozens of modern bars; numerous clubs, some with live music, particularly at the weekends; and an array of restaurants, many of them excellent. New bars and restaurants open all the time, and a complete list would certainly become out of date in the lifetime of a guide such as this. The more ephemeral *Tirana in Your Pocket* (w inyourpocket.com/albania) is a good resource of restaurants, nightlife and events.

Tirana also has some infuriating aspects, mainly the appalling traffic congestion and noise. In general, however, the city centre is an attractive place to stay, and its excellent public transport links make it the best base for exploring the rest of Albania.

GETTING THERE AND AWAY

BY AIR Tirana is Albania's main international airport. Its website (w tirana-airport.com) has real-time arrival and departure data, as well as flight schedules and other useful information. The airport is 17km from the city centre, but the journey time is entirely dependent on traffic congestion in Tirana; anything between 20 minutes and an hour. Approved airport taxis can be booked online (w tiataxi.al) or hired on arrival. The vehicles wait just outside the exit from the terminal. You should agree a fare with the driver before accepting their services – the going rate into Tirana is €20. Car-hire kiosks are located immediately outside the terminal building.

The airport bus station is just beyond the car-hire kiosks. The one-way fare to Tirana is 300 lek. The timetable changes every so often but, at the time of writing, the service operates hourly from 08.00 to 24.00. The bus can drop off passengers at the Casa Italia shopping mall, for the North/South bus station (see below). It terminates at the bus park behind the Palace of Culture [69 E2]. To return to the airport, the bus leaves from the same stop between the hours of 07.00 and 23.00. A rail link from the airport to Tirana and Durrësi may become operational within the lifetime of this guidebook.

There are several hotels located near the airport, useful for early-morning departures or late-night arrivals (page 32).

BY BUS Buses and/or minibuses run to Tirana from all other parts of Albania. In Tirana, they depart from one of two inter-city bus stations according to destination. For Elbasani, Korça and other destinations in the southeast, the **Southeast (Juglindor) bus station** [63 H6] is behind the university's Faculty of Economics (Fakulteti i Ekonomisë) on Rruga e Elbasanit. Buses to northern and southwestern Albania, including Durrësi and Berati, leave from the **North/South (Veri/Jug) Terminal**, at the junction known as Kthesa e Kamzës ('the Kamza Turning'). It is a long way from the city centre and there is nothing there apart from the buses and a poorly stocked kiosk. A better kiosk– unlike the other, it stocks items such as bottles of mineral water and packets of tissues – is across the pedestrian crossing just outside the bus terminal. The nearest food, coffee and (barely acceptable) public toilets are on the other side of the roundabout, in the Casa Italia shopping mall. Unlicensed minibuses to the larger cities operate from locations closer to the city centre; hotel reception staff may be able to obtain details.

The **international bus station** [62 B3] is behind the Asllan Rusi Sports Centre (Pallati i Sportit) on Rruga e Durrësit. International buses run to and from the main cities in all the neighbouring countries (Greece, North Macedonia, Kosovo and Montenegro), and further afield. The Ring shopping mall at Zogu i Zi is a good place to kill time while waiting for international bus departures, with excellent, clean, free public toilets, air conditioning and a reasonably priced café, as well as, obviously, lots of shops.

City buses for Kamza pass the North/South Terminal. The Tirana e Re service also calls at this terminal; it is a good option for destinations to the southwest of the city, not so good for the centre. Whichever bus you take, the traffic in Tirana is so congested that you should allow an hour from the city centre to the bus station.

Several city buses, such as the Qendër–Sauk line, stop at the Faculty of Economics on Rruga e Elbasanit, a few minutes' walk from the Southeast bus station. All city buses that go along Rruga e Durrësit will drop off or pick up passengers near the international bus station.

BY RAIL Tirana's railway station, at the northern end of Boulevard Zogu I, was demolished in 2013 and the railway lines were asphalted over to build what will eventually become the new Tirana ring road (Unaza e Re). The section already built at the time of writing has been planted with trees and shrubs, separating the cycleway and footpaths from the highway; while of course these are nice for the environment, a functioning rail network would have been even better.

GETTING AROUND

City **buses** are run by private companies and licensed by the Municipality of Tirana. They have a flat fare of 40 lek, which is collected by a conductor on the bus; they get very crowded at peak times. There are bus stops around the edges of the pedestrianised Skanderbeg Square: behind the National Museum, for buses to Kamza and the many other services that ply along Rruga e Durrësit; opposite the National Bank for buses up Rruga e Elbasanit and the Southeast bus station; and behind the Palace of Culture for, among others, the airport bus and buses to the lower station of the Dajti cable car.

Licensed Tirana **taxis** are metered, although it is worth checking that the driver has turned the meter on when you set off. A short journey in the city centre should cost between 400 and 500 lek. For longer journeys, you should agree a fare before setting off. There are taxi ranks at several places in the city centre: along the sides of 'The Block'; behind the National Historical Museum on Bulevardi Zogu I, convenient for getting to the airport and the bus stations on that side of the city; and beside the Academy of Arts on Mother Teresa Square. Taxis can also be hailed on the street. Green Taxi has an all-electric fleet (☎ 0800 2000; w green.al) and another reliable firm is City Taxi (☎ 0800 0000; m 069 99 99 111; w citytaxi.al).

Car-rental agencies are mostly based at the airport; some of the larger international agencies also have pick-up points in the city centre. Bicycles and e-scooters can be hired at various points around the centre; the backpacker hostels also have bikes available to rent. There are some segregated cycleways in the city centre but, as a rule, cycling, or indeed driving, in the centre of Tirana is not for the faint-hearted.

TOURIST INFORMATION

Tirana's tourist information office [68 D2] (Rruga Ded Gjo Luli, behind the National Historical Museum; ⏲ 08.00–16.00 Mon–Fri) stocks a range of free leaflets and brochures about Tirana and other towns in Albania. English is spoken.

Tirana in Your Pocket (w inyourpocket.com/tirana) is updated (a bit) about twice a year and is a good source of information about new restaurants, bars and clubs. The PDF version can be downloaded from its website.

The local travel agencies listed on page 30 can arrange one-day (or longer) tours of Tirana on request. The city's backpacker hostels organise one-day hikes and cycling tours in the countryside around Tirana. Favourite destinations are Mount Dajti and Pëllumbasi Cave. These day trips are an excellent option for outdoors enthusiasts with too little time in Albania to embark on a more ambitious trek. Walking tours of Tirana can also be arranged.

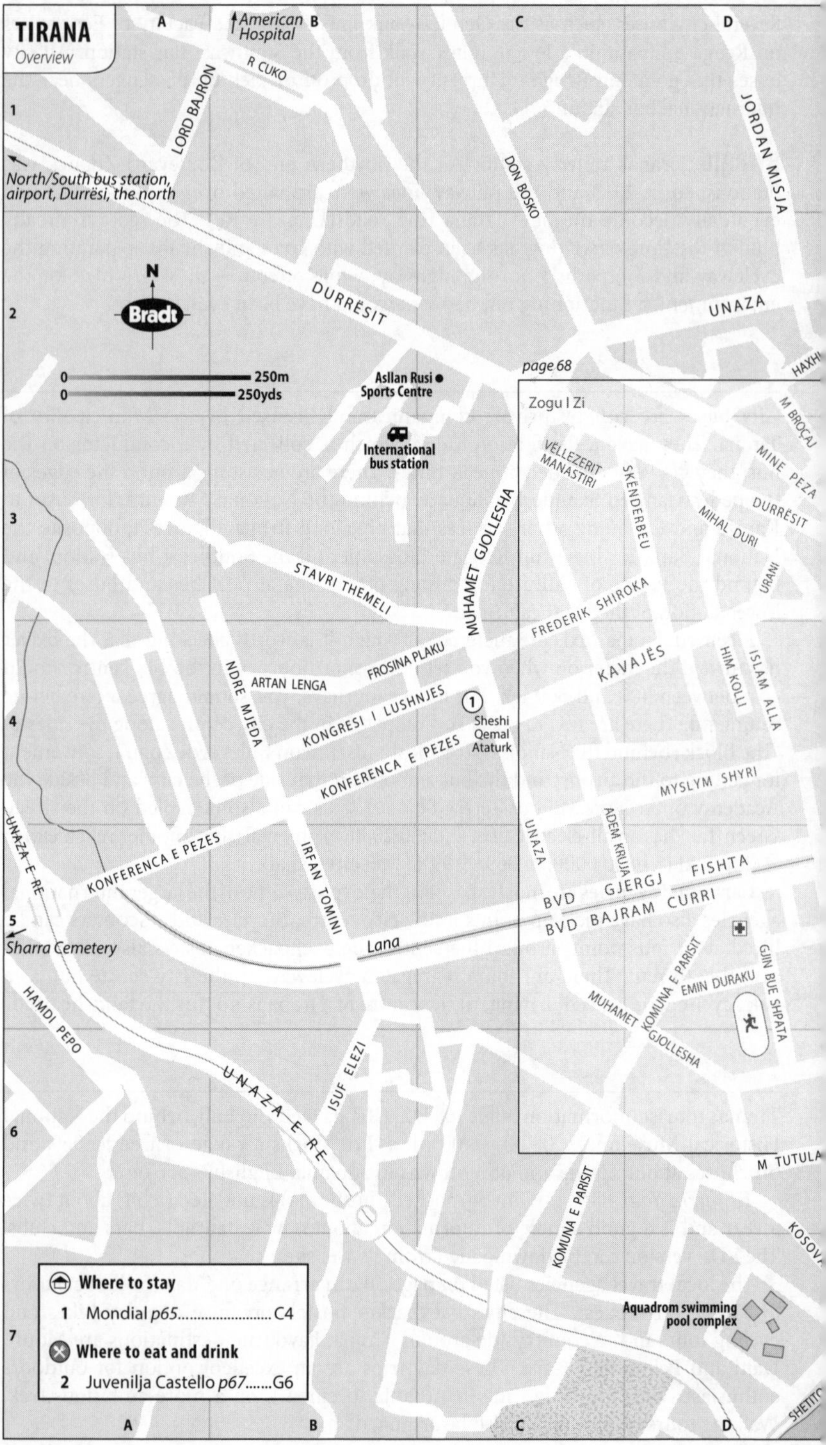
TIRANA
Overview
American Hospital
North/South bus station, airport, Durrësi, the north
Sharra Cemetery
Bradt
N
0 250m
0 250yds
Asllan Rusi Sports Centre
International bus station
page 68
Zogu I Zi
Sheshi Qemal Ataturk
Aquadrom swimming pool complex
LORD BAJRON
R CUKO
DON BOSKO
JORDAN MISJA
DURRËSIT
UNAZA
M BROÇAJ
MINE PEZA
VELLEZERIT MANASTIRI
SKENDERBEU
MIHAL DURI
URANI
MUHAMET GJOLLESHA
STAVRI THEMELI
FREDERIK SHIROKA
KAVAJËS
HIM KOLLI
ISLAM ALLA
NDRE MJEDA
ARTAN LENGA
FROSINA PLAKU
KONGRESI I LUSHNJES
KONFERENCA E PEZES
MYSLYM SHYRI
ADEM KRUJA
BVD GJERGJ FISHTA
BVD BAJRAM CURRI
IRFAN TOMINI
Lana
KOMUNA E PARISIT
EMIN DURAKU
GJIN BUE SHPATA
UNAZA E RE
HAMDI PEPO
ISUF ELEZI
M TUTULA
Where to stay
1 Mondial p65........................C4
Where to eat and drink
2 Juvenilja Castello p67.......G6

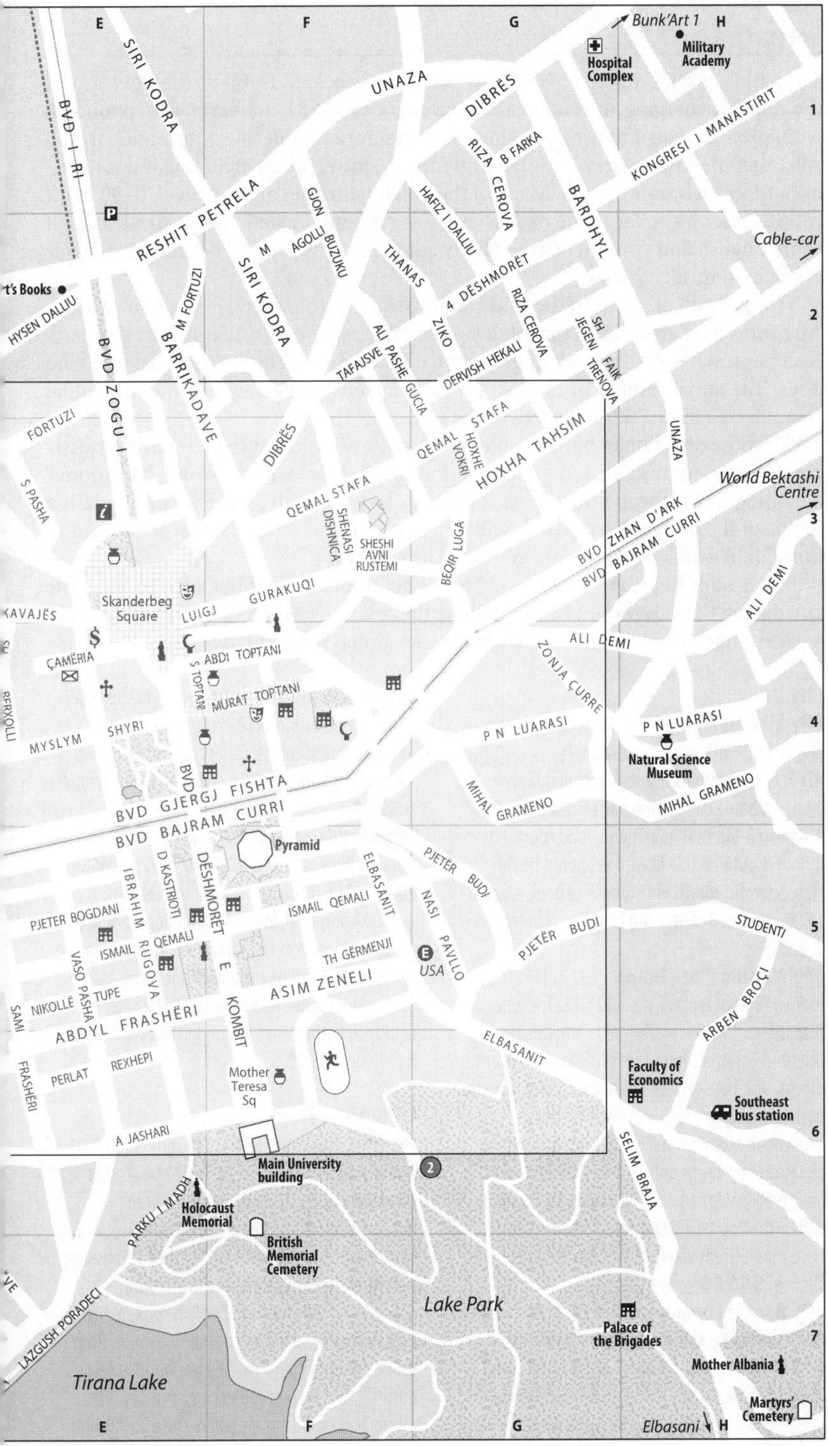

E
F
G
H
1
2
3
4
5
6
7
Bunk'Art 1
Military Academy
Hospital Complex
UNAZA
DIBRËS
SIRI KODRA
BVD I RI
KONGRESI I MANASTIRIT
RIZA
B FARKA
CEROVA
HAFIZ I DALLIU
BARDHYL
GJON BUZUKU
M AGOLLI
RESHIT PETRELA
P
Cable-car
THANAS ZIKO
4 DËSHMORËT
RIZA CEROVA
SH JEGENI
FAIK TRENOVA
'rt's Books
HYSEN DALLIU
M FORTUZI
BVD ZOGU I
BARRIKADAVE
ALI PASHE GUCIA
TAFAJSVE
DERVISH HEKALI
FORTUZI
DIBRËS
QEMAL STAFA
HOXHE VOKRI
HOXHA TAHSIM
UNAZA
World Bektashi Centre
S PASHA
i
SHENASI DISHNICA
SHESHI AVNI RUSTEMI
BEQIR LUGA
BVD ZHAN D'ARK
BVD BAJRAM CURRI
ALI DEMI
KAVAJËS
Skanderbeg Square
LUIGJ GURAKUQI
ÇAMËRIA
S TOPTANI
ABDI TOPTANI
ALI DEMI
ZONJA ÇURRE
MURAT TOPTANI
P N LUARASI
P N LUARASI
Natural Science Museum
MYSLYM SHYRI
BVD GJERGJ FISHTA
MIHAL GRAMENO
MIHAL GRAMENO
BVD BAJRAM CURRI
Pyramid
IBRAHIM RUGOVA
D KASTRIOTI
DËSHMORËT E KOMBIT
ELBASANIT
PJETËR BUDI
PJETER BOGDANI
ISMAIL QEMALI
ISMAIL QEMALI
NASI PAVLLO
PJETËR BUDI
STUDENTI
VASO PASHA
TH GËRMENJI
E USA
SAMI NIKOLLË TUPE
ASIM ZENELI
ABDYL FRASHËRI
ARBEN BROÇI
ELBASANIT
FRASHËRI
PERLAT REXHEPI
Mother Teresa Sq
Faculty of Economics
Southeast bus station
A JASHARI
SELIM BRAJA
Main University building
2
PARKU I MADH
Holocaust Memorial
British Memorial Cemetery
Lake Park
LAZGUSH PORADECI
Palace of the Brigades
Tirana Lake
Mother Albania
Martyrs' Cemetery
Elbasani

WHERE TO STAY

Tirana has a wide range of hotels to suit every pocket. Those at the very top of the market, charging in excess of €100 a night (**$$$$$**), are very well appointed, with professional, English-speaking staff, restaurants offering international and Albanian menus, business facilities and fitness centres, often including indoor and/or outdoor swimming pools. Many of the hotels with rates around the €70–90 mark (**$$$$**) offer a similar range of services. Their reception staff always speak at least some English and you can be reasonably confident that you will be able to use your credit card in such hotels.

Tirana is full of hotels in the mid-range category, around €60 for a double (**$$$**). All rooms have air conditioning and a reasonable range of TV channels as standard. Reception staff usually speak English and, if not, there will be someone around who does. The small sample in the listings here includes hotels with some individual character, each in a different area of the city.

For those on a tighter budget, hotels in the €40–50 price range (**$$**) have perfectly comfortable rooms, if sometimes on the small side, with en-suite bathrooms. Anything much cheaper in Tirana is likely to be a bit seedy; dorm accommodation in one of the backpackers' hostels will be a better option. Practically every hotel and hostel in Albania provides free Wi-Fi for its guests.

If you want to escape Tirana's noise and pollution at night but need to be in the city during the day, Mount Dajti might be the solution (page 85). There are hotels in a wide range of categories near Tirana International Airport (page 32).

LUXURY

MAK Albania [69 F7] (151 rooms) Sheshi Italia, off Mother Teresa Sq; 227 4707; e reservations.tirana@makalbania.com; w makalbania.com. Piano bar, restaurants with Albanian & international menu, food court, lifts. Indoor & outdoor (May–Sep) pools, health club. Spacious rooms with king-size beds, satellite TV, AC, safe, coffee-making facilities, minibar. **$$$$$**

Maritim Plaza Tirana [69 E3] (190 rooms) Rr Abdi Toptani 18; 221 1221; e info@plazatirana.com; w plazatirana.com. Business-oriented hotel; conference facilities with 8 event rooms; also has serviced apartments; underground parking, lift, gym, spa, same-day laundry service. All-day informal restaurant, fine-dining restaurant evenings only, lounge bar. All rooms have well-equipped en suite, smart TV, minibar, coffee-making facilities & safe. Deluxe rooms have magnificent views of Mt Dajti. Good English spoken. **$$$$$**

Rogner Europapark [69 E6] (178 rooms) Bd Dëshmorët e Kombit; 223 5035; e info.tirana@rogner.com; w hotel-europapark.com. Good restaurant with Albanian & international cuisine; bar popular with politicians & expats; lift, newsagents, business centre, spa, gym. Open-air pool (heated in winter) & terrace bar in lovely gardens, tennis courts, fitness centre. All rooms have AC, TV, safe, minibar, coffee-making facilities. **$$$$$**

Xheko Imperial [69 E7] (71 rooms) Rr Ibrahim Rugova 56; 225 9574/5/6/7; m 068 20 29 777; e contact@xheko-imperial.com; w xheko-imperial.com. Lift to all floors; wine bar; restaurant; rooftop restaurant & bar with great views of city; parking; spa with pool & massage; conference rooms. Rooms have AC, TV, safe; well-equipped bathrooms with underfloor heating & hairdryers. **$$$$$**

UPMARKET

* **Colosseo** [68 A1] (43 rooms) Sh Adem Jashari, Rr e Durrësit; 222 0010, 223 0004; m 069 20 32 666; e reservations@hotelcolosseotirana.com; w hotelcolosseotirana.com. Very convenient for UK & other embassies; sister to hotel of same name in Shkodra (page 117). Helpful staff, English spoken, lift. Restaurant, terrace bar, conference room. Room service, laundry service, free parking. Generous buffet b/fast inc, served in conservatory. All rooms have well-equipped en-suite bathroom;

TV, AC, safe, minibar, coffee/tea-making facilities. **$$$$**

Grand Spa [68 D6] (31 rooms, 3 suites) Rr Ismail Qemali 11; 225 3219/20; e info@grandhoteltirana.com; w grandhoteltirana.com. Great location in the Block. Lobby bar, good Italian-inspired restaurant; spa & gym with indoor pool & Turkish bath. All rooms have AC, minibar, safe & balcony. **$$$$**

Iliria [69 G7] (20 rooms) Rr e Elbasanit 1; 237 1700; m 068 40 27 112; e info@iliriahoteltirana.com; w iliriahoteltirana.com. Handy for US embassy & buses to southeast. Restaurant & terrace bar, secure parking, lift; conference rooms; laundry service. Good-sized rooms, with well-appointed en suite, CH, AC, TV, minibar, safe; some have balcony overlooking Lake Park. **$$$$**

Mondial [62 C4] (36 rooms) Rr Muhamet Gjollesha 90; 223 2372; m 068 20 04 642; e info@hotelmondial.al; w hotelmondial.al. Away from the busy centre, convenient for the airport & highways to the west & north. Helpful reception staff; lift. Good restaurant, rooftop & indoor bars, rooftop pool (in summer), sauna, laundry service. All rooms have TV, AC, safe, minibar; suites have balcony. **$$$$**

Tirana International [69 E2] (158 rooms, 12 suites) Skanderbeg Sq; 223 4185; m 068 22 34 185; e reservation@hoteltirana.com; w tiranainternational.com. Ground-floor bar; restaurant with Albanian & international menu & terrace with view over the square; secure parking; lift. Spa centre with hydromassage pool, gym, sauna; extensive conference room capacity; business centre. All rooms have AC, HD TV, minibar, safe; many rooms have unbeatable views over Skanderbeg Square. 35-storey extension expected to open in 2025. **$$$$**

MID-RANGE

Arbër [69 E2] (24 rooms, 1 suite) Rr Bardhok Biba 59; 227 3811; e reservation@hotelarber.com; w hotelarber.com. Very close to Skanderbeg Sq. Lift, laundry service, parking; terrace bar, restaurant with Albanian & Italian menu. Good-sized rooms with en suite, CH, AC, TV, minibar; 1 suite has 1 dbl bedroom, 2 bathrooms & a sitting room. **$$$**

Brilant Antik [69 F3] (10 rooms) Jeronim de Rada 79; 251 166; m 067 31 98 888; e reservation@hotelbrilant.com; w hotelbrilant.com. In a side street off Rr Xhorxh W Bush, central but surprisingly quiet. A modern building decorated & furnished in traditional style. Restaurant, bar, homemade b/fast & secure parking inc. All rooms with spacious en-suite bathroom, AC, TV, safe, minibar. **$$$**

Gloria [69 F2] (5 rooms, 1 suite) Rr Qemal Stafa; 222 0036; m 069 52 40 707; e brpgloria@hotmail.com, info@hotelboutiquegloria.al; w hotelboutiquegloria.al. Near central market. Helpful, English-speaking reception staff; secure parking; laundry service; room service. Good, long-established restaurant/pizzeria on top floor (separate entrance, also direct access from hotel). All rooms have AC, flatscreen TV, safe, minibar with free water, well-equipped bathroom with luxurious shower; 4 rooms have balcony. **$$$**

Green House [69 F5] (6 rooms) Rr Jul Variboba 6; 222 2632, 225 1015; e info@greenhouse.al; w greenhouse.al. In quiet street, handy for US & Italian embassies & Albanian governmental buildings. Secure parking. Good restaurant with tables in courtyard, sometimes has game dishes such as hare ($$$$). All rooms en suite, dbl, with AC, TV; some have bathtub, some have balcony. **$$$**

Theranda [68 C5] (14 rooms) Rr Andon Z Çajupi 6&7; 227 3766; m 069 20 72 900; e therandahotel@outlook.com; f HotelTheranda. On the edge of the Block; slightly tricky to find, signposted off Rr Çajupi. 2 quiet villas linked by an attractive courtyard garden; bar, secure parking, conference room. All rooms with alarmed door locks, good-sized en-suite bathroom, minibar, AC, TV. **$$$**

* **Villa Tafaj** [68 C2] (25 rooms) Rr Mine Peza 86; 222 7581 (reception), 223 4287 (restaurant); m 068 20 21 013, 068 20 78 055; e reservations@villatafaj.com; w villatafaj.com. Once the home of one of Tirana's oldest families, built in the 1920s, & still run by the Tafaj family. Professional, English-speaking reception staff, very helpful; café-bar; restaurant, with tables outside in shaded courtyard; parking; laundry service inc. The historic building's many stairs would be a challenge for those with reduced mobility; some rooms easier to access than others. Wi-Fi generally fast & reliable, but patchy in some rooms. All rooms en suite (some with bathtub), AC, fridge, flatscreen TV; some have balcony. **$$$**

THRIFTY

✱ **Freddy's** [68 D1] (18 rooms) Rr Bardhok Biba 75; 226 6077; m 068 20 35 261, 068 20 26 205; e hotelfreddys@gmail.com; freddyshotel. Centrally located, very good value; good English spoken at reception; friendly, helpful staff & management. Fast reliable Wi-Fi throughout; laundry service; generous buffet b/fast inc. Airport transfers can be booked through website, excursions can be arranged; small library with guidebooks (including this one) & Albanian literature in translation. Sgl, twin, dbl, trpl & 4-bed rooms, all en suite with good shower-screen & toiletries, TV, fridge; most have AC; ample electrical sockets; bedside light. **$$**

Millennium [69 E3] (7 rooms) Rr Murat Toptani 5; 225 1935; m 069 95 97 629; e tiranahotelmillennium@gmail.com. Good location on pedestrian street, opposite Millennium cinema. English spoken at reception; generous b/fast inc. All rooms have AC, TV, nice en-suite bathroom; 2 have balcony. **$$**

Primavera [68 B7] (14 rooms) Rr Grigor Heba; 268 098; m 068 46 99 781. 5-min walk from the Block without Block prices; also close to Lake Park. Friendly English-speaking reception staff; secure parking; quiet; Wi-Fi throughout. Café-bars nearby for b/fast. 10 dbl/twin & 4 trpl rooms, all en suite with AC, TV. **$$**

BUDGET

✱ **Backpacker Hostel** [68 B2] (48 beds) Rr e Bogdanëve 3; m 068 46 82 353, 068 31 33 451; e tiranabackpacker@hotmail.com; w tiranahostel.com. Albania's pioneer backpackers' hostel, in an Italian pre-war villa; large garden with bar, hammocks, relaxing area; camping possible. Well-equipped kitchen & dining area; water from the house's own well; laundry at small extra charge; sheets & towels provided; b/fast inc; vegetarian dinners by arrangement. Mountain bikes available to hire; car hire can be arranged; day trips organised. 6 dorms (1 with AC, 1 with wood-burning stove) with lockers; 1 dbl (**$$**); all sharing 3 toilets & 3 showers on each floor. **$**

Hostel Albania [68 A3] (24 beds) Rr e Kavajës 80/7; m 069 67 48 778; e hostelalbania@gmail.com; w hostelalbania-homestel.com. Slightly tricky to find, but directions & downloadable map on website. Kitchen, laundry at small extra charge; sheets & towels provided; b/fast inc. Rooftop terrace with hammocks, BBQ, bar, camping in summer. Free city tours & day trips organised; vegetarian dinner nights. 1 dbl en suite; 3 dorms with lockers & AC; 1 en suite, 2 share toilets & 3 showers. **$**

Milingona City Center [69 G2] (44 beds) Rr Vehbi Agolli; m 069 20 49 836, 069 40 96 304, 069 20 70 076; e milingonahostel@gmail.com; w milingonahostel.com. Off Rr Hoxha Tahsim, map & directions on website, look out for the yellow & green gate. Kitchen, washing machine; large garden with fruit trees, 1st-floor terrace, bar, piano; parking; sheets & towels provided; lockers; b/fast inc. Day trips & airport transfers organised. Camping possible in garden. 6 dorms of varying sizes, each named after an Albanian town, plus 1 dbl (**$$**). **$**

WHERE TO EAT

Tirana has many excellent restaurants. In all but the most expensive establishments listed here, a main course with a salad or soup and a beer or a glass of wine should come in at under €15. Fish and seafood are always more expensive than meat. Clusters of good restaurants are located in the Central Bazaar (Pazari i Ri), which is particularly recommended for fish or seafood, and in Kalaja e Tiranës (w kalajaetiranes.com), which has a range of upmarket restaurants offering traditional Albanian dishes, sushi, Italian cuisine and even truffles (the fungi, not the chocolates).

Tirana may be the only capital city in Europe that does not have a McDonald's. The Albanian fast-food option is a 'grill' – cafés serving grilled *qofta* (meatballs) or *sufllaqë* (doner kebab, the Greek *souvlaki*), traditionally washed down with beer. There are many such grill restaurants; a couple of the best in Tirana are listed here. Nationally, the Zgara Korça chain is reliable. For those who cannot survive without burgers, Kolonat has branches across the country. Vegetarians will have to make do with *byrek*.

At weekends, Tirana families head out to one of the restaurants on Mount Dajti (page 86) or Pëllumbasi (page 107) for spit-roasted lamb accompanied by huge salads, chips and red wine.

EXPENSIVE

Amor [68 B6] Rr Muhamet Gjollesha; 224 1573; m 069 26 84 952, 068 40 10 403; Restoranti Amor; Mon–Sat. Haute cuisine in a weirdly out-of-the-way corner of Tirana. No printed menu; the waiter tells you what the chef proposes, based on what they liked the look of in the market that morning. Difficult to find, in an alleyway among residential buildings behind the Dinamo Stadium. $$$$$

Otium [68 C5] Rr Brigada VIII; 222 3570; m 069 20 50 778; Tue–Sun. Small, intimate restaurant; excellent service; unusual but effective menu blending high-quality Albanian ingredients with Western culinary inventiveness. $$$$$

Panevino [69 E3] Rr Abdi Toptani. Part of Maritim Plaza hotel (page 64). High-quality Italian-inspired menu, good wine list with some Albanian wines, very professional service, not overly formal. $$$$$

Piazza [68 D2] Rr Ded Gjo Luli, in the corner behind the fountain; 223 0706. Possibly the best fish restaurant in Tirana; extensive menu also includes meat & vegetable dishes; outstanding wine list with the best Albanian wines; highly professional service; formal atmosphere. $$$$$

ABOVE AVERAGE

Juvenilja Castello [63 G6] Rr Gjeneral Niko Pushkini; 226 660; w juvenilja.com. Lovely setting, in a curious castle-style building just on the edge of the Lake Park. The usual range of salads & Italian dishes, with an unusually interesting selection of Albanian-style antipasti. Tables in garden right next to the park are for drinks only; the restaurant has a roofed gallery overlooking the garden & the park. $$$$

Oda [69 F2] Rr Luigj Gurakuqi; 224 9541; m 069 20 94 911. The best selection of traditional Albanian food in Tirana, with specialities from southern & central Albania, inc various offal dishes. In an old house near the central market; 2 small dining rooms, 1 with *sofra* (traditional low tables), the other with Western tables & chairs; English spoken. Excellent selection of raki, inc *mani* & *mare*. $$$$

* **Vila Era** [69 F6] Rr Papa Gjon Pali II; m 068 90 24 561; w era.al. Light, modern interior; tables in courtyards to front & rear, large 1st-floor terrace. Traditional Albanian specialities, plus a range of Italian & other international dishes; good wine list with several Albanian vineyards represented; professional service. $$$$

REASONABLE

Era [68 C6] Rr Ismail Qemali 13/2; w era.al. At the western edge of the Block; one of Tirana's longest-standing restaurants. Has a good selection of traditional Albanian food, plus salads, pizzas & pasta. Also home delivery, English menu on website. $$$

Juvenilija [68 C5] Rr Sami Frashëri; w juvenilja.com. Another long-standing Tirana restaurant on edge of Block. Offers vast range of pizzas; escalopes, steaks & fish; traditional Albanian dishes; pasta, risotto, salads. $$$

King's House [69 E7] Rr Ibrahim Rugova 12; KingHouseRestorant. Fairly formal restaurant with a good range of traditional Albanian dishes, salads, pasta, seafood, meat, etc. Extensive wine list, including Kallmet. $$$

London [68 D1] Bd Zogu I, on the left of the first block coming from Skanderbeg Sq. Short but interesting menu, in English & Albanian; some English spoken. Wooden-beamed ceiling, wood-burner, British-themed photographs on the walls; smoking ban enforced in restaurant; separate, ventilated area for smokers. The bar stocks a particularly good range of raki. $$$

Lulishte 1 Maji [69 F4] Bd Xhorxh W Bush; lulishte1maji.tirane. Huge garden-terrace with play area for children; live music on summer evenings. Menu (in English on FB page) inc some traditional Albanian dishes, fish, meat, pizza, pasta. $$$

Odisseas Greek Taverna [69 E3] Rr Murat Toptani. Family-run, real Greek food as well as international dishes, friendly service. On a pedestrian street, good value for such a central location. $$$

* **Paidhaqe Dajkua** [69 E2] Signposted from corner of Rr Uran Pano, in an alleyway behind

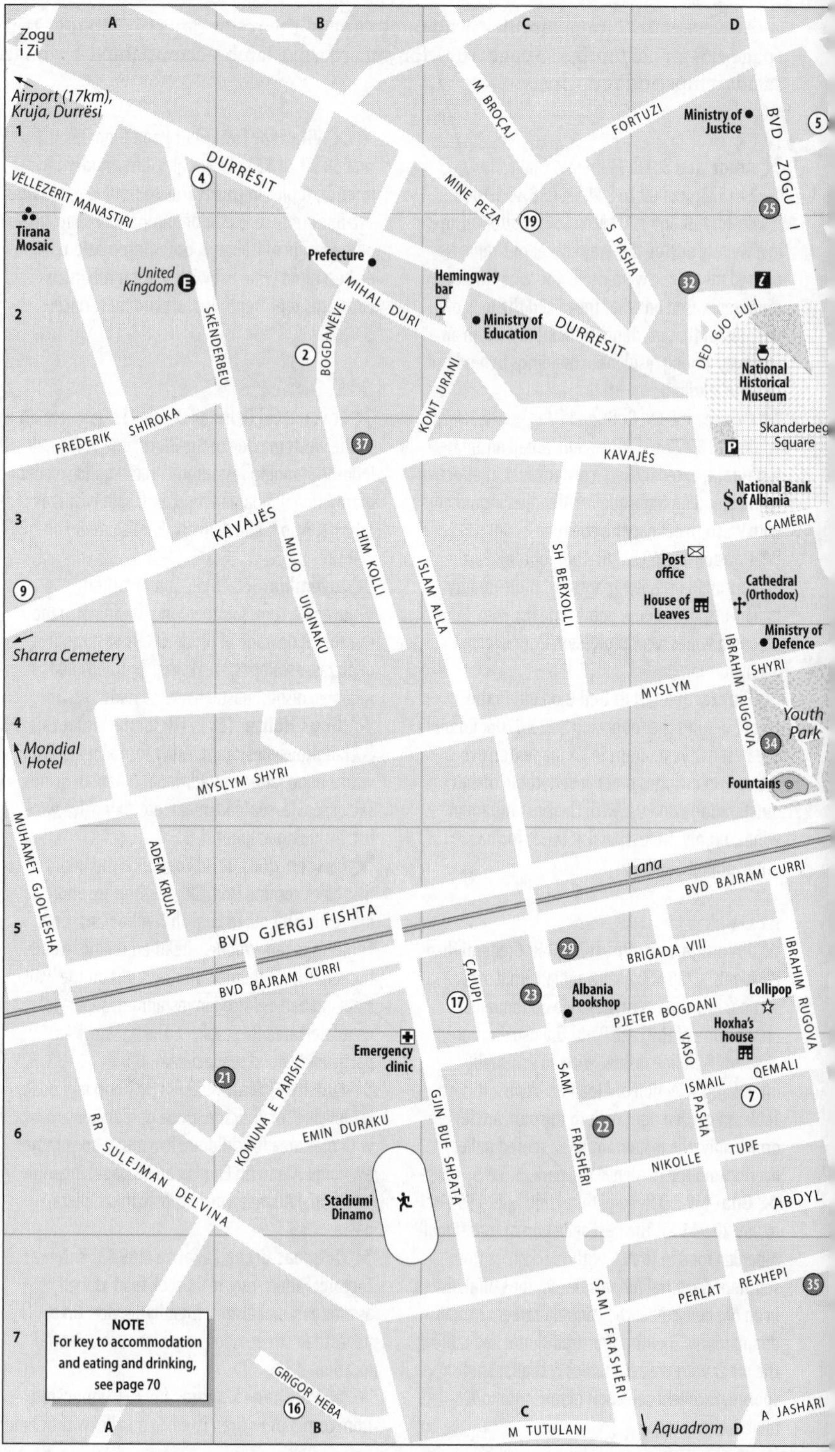
A
B
C
D
1
2
3
4
5
6
7
Zogu i Zi
Airport (17km), Kruja, Durrësi
Sharra Cemetery
Mondial Hotel
Aquadrom
DURRËSIT
VËLLEZERIT MANASTIRI
Tirana Mosaic
United Kingdom
SKËNDERBEU
Prefecture
MIHAL DURI
BOGDANËVE
Hemingway bar
Ministry of Education
M BROÇAJ
MINE PEZA
FORTUZI
S PASHA
Ministry of Justice
BVD ZOGU I
DED GJO LULI
National Historical Museum
Skanderbeg Square
KONT URANI
FREDERIK SHIROKA
KAVAJËS
National Bank of Albania
ÇAMËRIA
MUJO UIQINAKU
HIM KOLLI
ISLAM ALLA
SH BERXOLLI
Post office
Cathedral (Orthodox)
House of Leaves
Ministry of Defence
IBRAHIM RUGOVA
MYSLYM SHYRI
Youth Park
Fountains
MUHAMET GJOLLESHA
ADEM KRUJA
Lana
BVD GJERGJ FISHTA
BVD BAJRAM CURRI
BRIGADA VIII
ÇAJUPI
Albania bookshop
PJETER BOGDANI
Lollipop
Hoxha's house
VASO PASHA
ISMAIL QEMALI
Emergency clinic
KOMUNA E PARISIT
EMIN DURAKU
GJIN BUE SHPATA
SAMI FRASHËRI
NIKOLLE TUPE
ABDYL
Stadiumi Dinamo
RR SULEJMAN DELVINA
PERLAT REXHEPI
GRIGOR HEBA
M TUTULANI
A JASHARI
NOTE
For key to accommodation and eating and drinking, see page 70

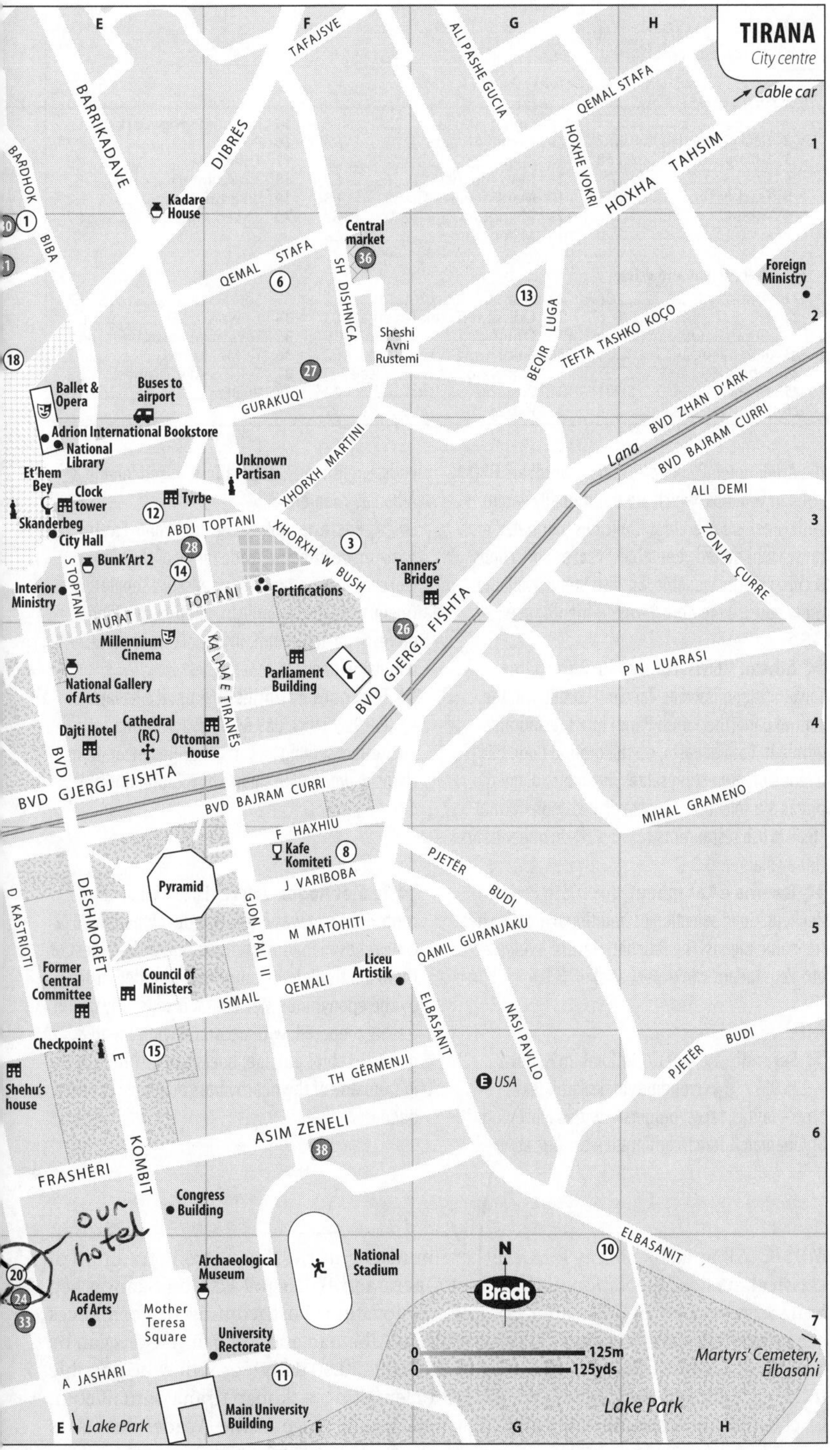
TIRANA
City centre
Cable car
E
F
G
H
1
2
3
4
5
6
7
TAFAJSVE
ALI PASHE GUCIA
QEMAL STAFA
HOXHE VOKRI
HOXHA TAHSIM
BARRIKADAVE
DIBRËS
BARDHOK
BIBA
Kadare House
Central market
QEMAL STAFA
SH DISHNICA
Foreign Ministry
Sheshi Avni Rustemi
BEQIR LUGA
TEFTA TASHKO KOÇO
GURAKUQI
Ballet & Opera
Buses to airport
Adrion International Bookstore
National Library
XHORXH MARTINI
Unknown Partisan
Lana
BVD ZHAN D'ARK
BVD BAJRAM CURRI
ALI DEMI
Et'hem Bey
Clock tower
Tyrbe
Skanderbeg
ABDI TOPTANI
XHORXH W BUSH
ZONJA ÇURRE
City Hall
Bunk'Art 2
S TOPTANI
Interior Ministry
Fortifications
TOPTANI
Tanners' Bridge
MURAT
BVD GJERGJ FISHTA
Millennium Cinema
KA LAJA E TIRANËS
Parliament Building
National Gallery of Arts
P N LUARASI
Dajti Hotel
Cathedral (RC)
Ottoman house
BVD
BVD GJERGJ FISHTA
BVD BAJRAM CURRI
MIHAL GRAMENO
F HAXHIU
Kafe Komiteti
PJETËR BUDI
Pyramid
J VARIBOBA
D KASTRIOTI
DËSHMORËT
GJON PALI II
M MATOHITI
QAMIL GURANJAKU
Former Central Committee
Council of Ministers
Liceu Artistik
ISMAIL QEMALI
ELBASANIT
NASI PAVLLO
Checkpoint
E
PJETËR BUDI
Shehu's house
TH GËRMENJI
USA
ASIM ZENELI
FRASHËRI
KOMBIT
Congress Building
our hotel
ELBASANIT
Archaeological Museum
National Stadium
N
Bradt
Academy of Arts
Mother Teresa Square
University Rectorate
0 125m
0 125yds
Martyrs' Cemetery, Elbasani
A JASHARI
Main University Building
Lake Park
Lake Park
1
6
13
18
27
36
12
28
14
3
26
8
15
38
10
20
24
33
11

TIRANA *City centre*

For listings, see from page 64

Where to stay

1 Arbër.....E2
2 Backpacker Hostel.....B2
3 Brilant Antik.....F3
4 Colosseo.....A1
5 Freddy's.....D1
6 Gloria.....F2
7 Grand Spa.....D6
8 Green House.....F5
9 Hostel Albania.....A3
10 Iliria.....G7
11 MAK Albania.....F7
12 Maritim Plaza Tirana.....E3
13 Milingona City Center.....G2
14 Millennium.....E3
15 Rogner Europapark.....E6
16 Primavera.....B7
17 Theranda.....C5
18 Tirana International.....E2
19 Villa Tafaj.....C2
20 Xheko Imperial.....E7

Where to eat and drink

21 Amor.....B6
22 Era.....C6
Green House.....(see 8)
23 Juvenilija.....C5
24 King's House.....E7
25 London.....D1
26 Lulishte 1 Maji.....F4
27 Oda.....F2
28 Odisseas Greek Taverna.....E3
29 Otium.....C5
30 Paidhaqe Dajkua.....E2
Panevino.....(see 12)
31 Pastaría.....E2
32 Piazza.....D2
33 Serendipity.....E7
34 Taiwan.....D4
35 Taverna e Kasapbeut.....D7
36 Te Met Kodra.....F2
37 Tek Zgara e Tironës.....B3
38 Vila Era.....F6

the Arbër hotel. *Paidhaqe* (a Greek word) are BBQ lamb or veal ribs, which are traditionally eaten with Greek salad & chips. Delicious marinated or (in season) grilled vegetables; veal or pork chops & chicken also available; English menu available. Good house wine from Përmeti; friendly service. $$$

Taiwan [68 D4] Rr Ibrahim Rugova. The Taiwan (Albanicised as 'Tajvani') complex in the central park (the 'Youth Park') has 3 restaurants within it. Casa di Pasta, on the ground floor, has a range of interesting salads, fresh bread, good pizzas & a selection of pasta dishes. More formal steak & fish restaurants ($$$$$) on upper floors (lift available). $$$

Taverna e Kasapbeut [68 D7] Rr Perlat Rexhepi. Good selection of traditional meat dishes (its name means 'The Butcher's Tavern'), *fergesë*, etc. Vegetarians can expect a salad. $$$

GOOD DEAL

Serendipity [69 E7] Rr Ibrahim Rugova; 225 9377; serendipitymeksikani. Tex-Mex – fajitas, tacos, burgers – with a leavening of Albanian & Italian options. Live music at w/ends. English-speaking waiters, mixed foreign & Albanian clientele. $$

✷ **Pastaría** [69 E2] Rr Uran Pano. Fresh pasta made in-house, wide range of sauces; you choose your pasta shape & sauce separately (menu available in English). English-speaking, professional table staff; informal atmosphere; popular with expat Italians. $$

Tek Zgara e Tironës [68 B3] R e Kavajës; m 069 94 75 953, 069 94 84 792. A Tirana institution, serving all sorts of grilled meat, from chops to *qofta*, with salad, chips & draught beer. $$

BUDGET

Te Met Kodra [69 F2] Pazari i Ri. The central market was entirely redeveloped in 2017 & now has many smart restaurants. The oldest of them all, though, has survived: founded in 1957 by the eponymous Met Kodra, it sells only *qofta*, freshly prepared, with accompanying bread & garnish. Tables outside; beers can be brought in from any of the nearby bars or shops. Expect queues. $

ENTERTAINMENT AND NIGHTLIFE

MUSIC Albania, like many formerly communist countries, has a strong tradition of **classical music**. The National Theatre of Opera and Ballet [69 E2], on Skanderbeg Square, reopened in 2021 after complete renovation. Forthcoming performances are promoted on its website (w tkob.gov.al), in Albanian and English. Tickets can be bought at the box office (⌚ 10.00–14.00 & 16.00–20.00 daily), or it may be possible to reserve by phoning m 067 63 27 313 or emailing e tkobap.tirana@gmail.com. Orchestral and chamber concerts occasionally take place in the Academy of Arts (the national Conservatoire) [69 E7] and in the music high school (Liceu Artistik) [69 F5], on the corner of Rr Ismail Qemali and the Elbasani road.

It is hard to find live **folk music** in Tirana. The National Ensemble of Folk Song and Dance (Ansambli Kombëtar i Këngëve e Valleve Popullore) performs at the Theatre of Opera and Ballet. It also tours around the country and performs at the regular folk festivals held around Albania; w tkob.gov.al may have details. The Hemingway bar [69 C2] (m 069 20 22 303; @hemingwaytirana), on the corner of the little square at the junction of Rruga Mihal Duri and Rruga Kont Urani, sometimes has live **jazz**.

THEATRE Theatre performances in languages other than Albanian are rare and it is quite difficult to even find out about plays in Albanian. The National Theatre, built in 1938 by an Italian architect, was demolished in 2020, after a lengthy and impassioned campaign to save it. It was probably not a coincidence that the demolition took place at the height of the Covid-19 lockdown, when potential protesters were not allowed to leave their homes. From time to time, the various western European cultural institutes hold festivals of their own countries' films, theatre or music. These festivals tend not to be well publicised; the best way to find out about them is through the websites of the respective embassies.

NIGHTLIFE Before the Covid-19 pandemic, which closed the doors of all nightclubs in Albania, Tirana was becoming a thriving nightlife destination. Word of mouth is likely to be the best source of information about the constantly changing trends in the club scene. The longest-standing dance club in the city centre is **Lollipop** [68 D5], on Rr Pjetër Bogdani.

SPORTS The most popular sport in Albania is unquestionably **football**. In 2016, the national team qualified for the UEFA European Championship for the first time ever, generating huge excitement throughout the country. Albanian matches are interesting cultural experiences, even for people who are not big football fans. The home of the national side is the 22,500-seater Air Albania Stadium [69 F7], which opened in 2019 and is still referred to almost universally by its old name, 'Qemal Stafa'. The new building is a vast complex that includes a high-rise hotel and a shopping mall. A more traditional alternative is the small stadium on the other side of town [68 B6], whose official name is 'Selman Stërmasi' but which is always called by its communist-era name of Stadiumi Dinamo.

The **Aquadrom swimming pool complex** [62 D7] (04 246 5521; w aquadrom.al; May–Oct) has several separate pools, including Albania's only Olympic-standard pool and a 'family' pool with a flume. Within the complex are an Irish pub, a beer garden and fast-food restaurants.

SHOPPING

The centre of Tirana is full of shops, and the outskirts full of shopping malls, selling imported goods at higher prices than in the UK. For souvenirs, the best options are the central market, the souvenir shops on nearby Rruga Luigj Gurakuqi, and Kalaja e Tiranës.

Formerly a charming but slightly chaotic warren of stalls, the **central market** [69 F2] (Pazari i Ri), between Sheshi Avni Rustemi and Rruga Qemal Stafa, is now as much of an eating and drinking destination as a market, with several good restaurants and bars surrounding the stalls in the central area. As well as fruit and vegetables, there are stalls and shops selling different sorts of olives and nuts, honey, olive oil and raki, and a few traders who sell communist-era badges and other memorabilia. Meat, fish and dairy products are displayed in the indoor section. Small neighbourhood fruit and vegetable markets can still be found elsewhere in the city; there is one along Rruga Mihal Grameno, for example, and another on Rruga Fortuzi.

The shops in **Kalaja e Tiranës** [69 E/F4] stock high-quality products including traditional folk costumes, hand-carved wooden utensils and Albanian edibles such as honey and mountain tea. The Çobo vineyard (page 266) has a wine bar near the entrance, serving its range of wine by the glass or bottle, along with food to soak it up. There are also several upmarket restaurants.

The Albania bookshop [68 C5] (Rr Sami Frashëri), Adrion International Bookstore [69 E3] (Skanderbeg Sq) and Art's Books [63 E2] on Boulevard Zogu I, stock **books** in English about Albania and the Balkans, and translations of Albanian literature.

OTHER PRACTICALITIES

OBTAINING CASH There are ATMs (cashpoints, known in Albanian as *bankomat*) all over the city. Cash euros, sterling, Swiss francs and dollars of the Australian, Canadian and US varieties can all be changed in Tirana. There are many bureaux de change throughout the city, with clusters on Bulevardi Zogu I and around the junction of Rruga Myslym Shyri and Rruga Ibrahim Rugova. In general, they stay open until at least 17.00; some close earlier on Saturdays and almost all are shut on Sundays. Foreign currency can also be changed in any of the numerous banks in the city, although the process is swifter in the bureaux de change. Euros are widely accepted in hotels and larger restaurants, usually at a slightly rounded rule-of-thumb rate.

POST OFFICE The central post office [68 D3] is on Rruga Çamëria, behind the National Bank of Albania. It is open from 07.30 to 20.00 Monday to Saturday, and from 07.30 to 14.00 on Sundays.

MEDICAL The city's **accident and emergency clinic** (*Urgjenca* in Albanian) is on Rruga Gjin Bue Shpata [68 B6], near the Dinamo Stadium. Tirana has good private **hospitals**; see page 34 for details.

Tirana is a safe city, and the biggest danger is being struck by a bike or motorcycle jumping a red light, or whizzing the wrong way up a one-way street. Outside the city centre, pavements are often rather uneven and, although young Albanian women seem to negotiate them flawlessly in precipitous heels, the less gazelle-like will find it easier to get around in flatter shoes. Along the main shopping streets in the city centre, an unexpected risk is that of falling down the (often) unfenced steps of one of the many basement shops.

WHAT TO SEE AND DO

SKANDERBEG SQUARE [68 D3] Skanderbeg Square was once the hub of Tirana's commercial and social life. Before World War II, the main market was here; the 18th-century mosque was where men met to chat, as well as to worship; and around the edges of the square were small shops and cafés. In the 1920s and 30s, the square became the city's administrative centre, with imposing new buildings designed by

Italian architects. Tirana's citizens still refer to it as 'the centre'. Now it has been completely closed to traffic and an underground car park has been built beneath its paved expanse.

On Skanderbeg Square's northern side are the National Historical Museum and the Tirana International Hotel; to the west are the National Bank and the arterial roads called Rruga e Kavajës and Rruga e Durrësit; and the eastern side is entirely taken up with what was once known as the Palace of Culture, which still houses the opera house and the National Library. On the southeastern corner of the square, the 18th-century **Mosque of Et'hem Bey** [69 E3] is one of the few really old buildings left in Tirana, and is perhaps also the most beautiful. Its minaret was shattered in the Battle for the Liberation of Tirana (page 16), but it was subsequently repaired, and the mosque's status as a Cultural Monument kept it from being damaged or destroyed during the atheism campaigns of the late 1960s. There are frescoes on its exterior walls and more wall paintings inside the mosque, all painstakingly restored in 2019–20. Visitors are admitted except during prayers; shoes must be removed at the entrance, before stepping on the carpet, and women must cover their hair.

Next to the mosque is Tirana's **City Hall** (*bashkia*) [69 E3], one of the institutional buildings around the southern edge of the square and its surrounding streets that were designed by Italian architects in the 1920s and '30s. An equestrian statue of **Skanderbeg** [69 E3] (see box, page 136) stands at the southern end of his eponymous square. The sculptor was Odhisë Paskali (1903–85), who created many of the imposing statues and monuments in towns and cities throughout Albania. To Skanderbeg's south, the wide **Boulevard**, designed by Italian urban planners in the 1930s and perfect for Fascist parades, begins its route through the city centre to Mother Teresa Square.

Excellent views of the square and the Boulevard can be enjoyed from the top of the 35m-high **clock tower** [69 E3] (🕘 09.00–18.00 Mon–Fri, 09.00–14.00 Sat), just behind the Mosque of Et'hem Bey. The tower was built in the 1820s; its collection of scale models of clock towers in Albania is not on display at the time of writing, but has been promised a purpose-built museum once construction work has finished on the skyscraper that now dwarfs clock tower, mosque and City Hall.

MUSEUMS AND GALLERIES

National Historical Museum

[68 D2] (Muzeu Historik Kombëtar; **w** mhk.gov.al; 🕘10.00–17.00 Tue–Sat, 09.00–14.00 Sun, last admission 30mins before closing; 200 lek) Dominating Skanderbeg Square is the National Historical Museum, with its huge mosaic mural above the entrance. The museum was opened in 1981 and the mural is an excellent example of the nationalist narrative fostered during the communist period. It depicts the sweep of that version of Albanian history: Illyrian warriors, smiling peasants, the fighters and intellectuals who won independence from the Ottoman Empire, and brave male and female partisans, all being led into the glorious future by a Mother Albania figure.

You should allow an absolute minimum of 2 hours to look round the whole museum. There are many interesting things on display, with helpful maps and information on multilingual panels. Each display case usually has a summary in English and French. On the ground floor – the prehistory, antiquity and late antiquity sections – some of the individual exhibits are labelled in English and French as well as Albanian. The exhibition is arranged in rough chronological order, and starts with prehistoric finds from the Stone, Copper, Bronze and Iron ages. There are maps of Illyrian tribes and city-states at different points in time, and examples of Illyrian jewellery, coins and votive objects in terracotta and bronze from the 3rd to the 1st centuries BC. Two outstanding works of art date from the 4th century BC: a head of Apollo, discovered in the *orchestra* of the theatre at Butrint and known as 'The Goddess of Butrint'; and the first mosaic ever discovered in Albania, which portrays a woman's head and is called 'The Belle of Durrësi'. There is pottery from the Greek colonies in what is now Albania, 3rd-century armour and reconstructions of 2,000-year-old agricultural implements. Maps on the walls show the sites of uprisings and invasions during the turmoil of the 11th and 12th centuries.

The first floor covers the rise of the feudal states in the medieval period, the Ottoman conquest and Albania under Ottoman rule. The highlight of the medieval section is the 'Epitaph' of Gllavenica, a beautiful embroidered altar-cloth from 1373. The complete doorway of the church of St Gjon Vladimir, near Elbasani, has been re-erected and a relic of the saint is in a display case nearby. There are also interesting exhibits from other medieval churches, including a fragment of fresco from the 13th-century church at Vau i Dejës, near Shkodra, which was demolished (by art students!) during the atheism campaign of 1967. A whole room is devoted to the role of Skanderbeg as leader of the Albanian resistance to the Ottomans. The section covering the 16th to 18th centuries gives a good overview of Ottoman administration and the development of Albania's cities.

The second floor of the museum covers the National Renaissance (Rilindja Kombëtare), the cultural and political movement of the late 19th and early 20th centuries, which culminated in Albania's declaration of independence on 28 November 1912. The explanatory panels are in English and French, although some prior knowledge of the Rilindja movement would be an advantage in understanding the exhibition. There are attractive displays of 19th-century textiles, weapons and ethnographic items. The icon gallery on this floor is home to the magnificent iconostasis from the church of St Gjon Vladimir, by the 17th-century artist Kostandin Ieromonaku. There is a good selection of icons, including works by Onufri; however, the cream of Albania's Byzantine art is in Korça, home of the National Museum of Medieval Art (page 182), and in the Onufri Museum in Berati Castle (page 262).

Although the World War II exhibition still predominantly consists of displays about the communist-led liberation movement and the activities of the partisans, the curators have made an effort to include other sides of the story. There are panels explaining the parts played by Balli Kombëtar and the Legalitet movement, for example, and a display of photographs of the Councils of Regency that governed Albania in the period between Italy's capitulation and liberation. The role of SOE (see boxes, page 13 and 14) and the contribution made during the war by the USA are also presented. The World War II section is quite extensive and it could easily take over an hour to study it all in detail. It is possible to access it by the back stairs, without passing through the whole of the rest of the museum, and those with a particular interest in this period might want to consider visiting it separately.

The final hall of the museum is devoted to a fascinating exhibition about Albania during the communist period. Unfortunately, the information panels in the display cases are not translated, which makes it difficult for non-Albanian visitors to follow the historical development of the exhibition. A life-size mock-up of a solitary confinement cell brings home the terrible conditions in which so many Albanians were imprisoned. A rolling video, with some English subtitles, includes film of the student protests in 1991 that ultimately brought about the end of communist rule in Albania.

The museum shop stocks postcards, souvenirs and books. There are reasonable toilets on the ground floor.

THE MYSTERY OF THE MARTINI RIFLES

With thanks to M C Barrès-Baker

Fans of the 1964 film *Zulu* may wonder why the .45" Martini-Henry rifle, the weapon used to defend Rorke's Drift, appears in so many Albanian paintings and museum display cases. The answer is that they are not Martini-Henrys at all.

The British adopted the Martini-Henry in 1871, naming it after Friedrich von Martini, who designed its breech mechanism, and Scotsman Alexander Henry, who designed the barrel. In 1872, Khedive Ismail of Egypt gave the Ottoman sultan 50,000 Martini-Henrys. The sultan was so impressed that he ordered 600,000 copies from the Providence Tool Company of Rhode Island, USA. These were called Peabody-Martinis, after Henry O Peabody, an American who had patented the earliest version of the Martini breech.

Peabody-Martini rifles played a significant role during the 1877 siege of Plevna, inflicting heavy casualties on the attacking Russian and Romanian troops. Turkish payments for the rifles were constantly in arrears, however, and in 1885 this drove Providence Tool bankrupt. Its president was reduced to burning Peabody-Martini rifle butts to keep warm.

A few years later the Turkish army went over to using Mauser magazine rifles; Edith Durham, however, travelling in the early years of the 20th century, describes Albanian gendarmes 'armed with Peabody-Martini rifles of American pattern, which they call "Martinas" and cherish dearly'. By then the rifle had also become the weapon of choice among the Albanian civilian population, both because the cartridge cases were easy to refill and because it was a better man-stopper than more expensive bolt-action rifles.

Martinis could be used as part-payment in a *besa* (see box, page 128) or to buy a wife; but keeping one's Martini in powder and lead could be nearly as expensive as keeping a wife. Men often decorated their Martinis with silver filigree or with silver coins, one for each life taken. In *High Albania*, Durham describes a man singing a song to his Martini, 'in which he addressed it as his wife and his child, for he wanted no other.'

Archaeological Museum [69 E7] (Muzeu Arkeologjik; ⌚ 10.00–16.00 Tue–Sun; 300 lek) Although the National Historical Museum holds the best-known objects from Albania's archaeological heritage, the collection in the Archaeological Museum, located within the Centre for Albanology Studies in Mother Teresa Square, is much more extensive. Few of the artefacts are labelled in English, but in most cases the labels merely indicate provenance, so geographical rather than linguistic knowledge is what is required. Some of the curators speak good English and, their time permitting, they are usually pleased to explain the collection to visitors.

The first two rooms are devoted to the Stone, Bronze and Iron ages, with some particularly nice spear- and axe-heads, and a fine iron helmet. Then the artefacts from Illyrian cities begin, which will be of greater interest to visitors who are not prehistory specialists. Lovely little figurines in bronze and terracotta, including a delightful little bronze dog from Antigonea (page 280), are perhaps the most attractive items in these cases, but there is also jewellery and pottery to admire, and a well-preserved helmet complete with nose and cheek guards. The Roman period is represented with statuary, some fine glassware, inscribed tombstones (some with identifiably Illyrian names), and inscriptions from Victorinus's Wall, built around the ancient city of Byllis.

On the walls there are enlarged photographs of archaeological sites and of some of the mosaics that have been discovered there. The museum has a selection of publications for sale, some of them in English translation, about Albanian archaeology and archaeological sites.

National Gallery of Arts [69 E4] (Galeria Kombëtare e Arteve; Bd Dëshmorët e Kombit; w galeriakombetare.gov.al; see website for opening hours; 200 lek) The National Gallery of Arts has a fascinating collection of Albanian art, which puts into context the Socialist Realist work that can be seen in so many public spaces around the country. The building was completely reconstructed in 2021–22 and, once it reopens, the exhibition may no longer follow the chronological order described here.

Modern Albanian art begins in the late 19th century, with the portraits and depictions of idealised rural life of Albania's first non-religious painters, which give an insight into the cultural atmosphere in Albania at that time. Albania's first art school was founded in 1931 and the paintings from the pre-war period show greater realism; for example, the Korçan painter Vangjush Mio (1891–1957, page 185). The next rooms move Albanian art into the communist period, with the historical tableaux of artists such as Fatmir Haxhiu (1927–2001) and the Socialist Realist portrayals of idealised workers, including some splendid sculptures.

At the beginning of the 1970s, Albanian artists began to experiment with Formalism and produced some outstanding work in this genre. Their experimentation was not without risk: several of their number were arrested for creating works opposed to the principles of Socialist Realism and being influenced by decadent Western art. One of these was the painter and architect Maks Velo (1935–2020), arrested in 1978 and condemned to the prison camp at Spaçi (page 147). The court ordered 246 of his paintings to be burned. The permanent exhibition ends with a display of post-1990 Albanian painting and sculpture, with work by artists including Edi Rama (b1964), who at the time of writing is the Prime Minister of Albania.

Hidden behind the building is a collection of discarded communist-era statues: Lenin, Stalin, Hoxha, a couple of idealised workers and Shote Galica, a heroine of the struggle for Albanian independence. It is not always possible to gain access to this part of the gallery's grounds; it seems to depend on the mood of the security guard on duty at the time.

The gallery's website was not functioning at the time of writing, while the reconstruction work is under way, but in the past has provided an excellent introduction not only to the collection, but also to the history of Albanian art. The gallery also houses a reference-only art library, with over 4,200 titles in various languages, which is open to the public free of charge.

Kadare House Studio [69 E1] (Rr e Dibrës 85; e shtepiakadare@tirana.al; ⌚ May–Oct 09.00–19.00 Tue–Sat, Sun 10.00–17.00 Sun, Oct–Apr 10.00–17.00 Tue–Sat, 10.00–15.00 Sun; 500 lek) This is the apartment where Albania's best-known novelist, Ismail Kadare, and his wife Elena lived and worked from 1974 to 1990. The apartment block was designed in the Bauhaus style by the architect and artist Maks Velo (1935–2020); the Kadares were allocated a double apartment on the second floor. As such, it had two entrance doors; they used one as their official address, while the other was known only to their friends. The Kadares asked Velo to make some alterations to their apartment, including installing glass folding doors and a fireplace in Ismail's study, both of which are still in situ.

These alterations were among the charges laid a few years later against the architect; see opposite for his punishment.

The original plans of the building and apartment are on display in the apartment, along with a collection of the author's books and periodicals, and photographs of the Kadare family and of Tirana at that time. Some of the rooms have their original furniture. A film showing daily life in communist-era Tirana plays in a screening room where books of stills from Ismail's and Elena's films can also be studied. Knowledgeable curators can provide a tour of all the rooms, in English and other languages, included in the admission charge. A new lift has been installed, connecting the ground floor with the landing a few stairs below the entrance to the museum.

The Tirana Mosaic [68 A2] (🕘 08.00–17.00 daily; free admission) Tirana's only visible Roman remains, the Tirana Mosaic, was discovered during construction work in 1972. The original Roman building seems to have been the villa of a 1st-century AD winemaker. Two of his (or her?) amphorae are on display at the site, along with other items excavated there. The mosaic floor was laid in the 4th or 5th century AD, when the villa was converted into a basilica. It has been conserved and stabilised to make it one of the few mosaics in Albania that can be viewed in situ by the general public (others are in Saranda, page 220, and Lini, page 191).

The mosaic site is slightly to the south of Rruga e Durrësit, just inside the ring road (Unaza). It is hidden among residential buildings and is a little tricky to find, although it is signposted from the ring road. It should take about 15 minutes to walk there from Skanderbeg Square, or you could board any of the buses that go from the centre to the Zogu i Zi roundabout.

Natural Science Museum [63 H4] (Muzeu i Shkencave të Natyrës; Rr Petro Nini Luarasi; m 068 69 46 691; 🕘 08.00–16.30 Mon–Fri; 200 lek) Now housed in a modern building, the Natural Science Museum has a collection of over 5,000 items from Albania and around the world. The display is organised in seven galleries over two floors, to illustrate the process of evolution: corals; insects; fish (including the skeleton of a Mediterranean whale, captured by the communist-era border guards who mistook it for an enemy submarine) and reptiles; over 200 species of birds, including a stuffed Dalmatian pelican; and various stuffed mammals, including a brown bear. Those with a particular interest in a specific aspect of life science would be well advised to arrange their visit in advance, by calling (or having an Albanian-speaker call on your behalf) the telephone number above, to ensure that someone with whom you have a common language will be available to receive you.

WALKS AROUND TIRANA

History and architecture A 45-minute walk around some of Tirana's architectural highlights starts at the clock tower [69 E3] just off Skanderbeg Square. Following the alleyway between the clock tower and the rear entrance to the Italian-designed City Hall will bring you out on to Rruga Abdi Toptani. The Toptanis were one of the Albanian families that rose to power in the 18th and 19th centuries, during the Ottoman period. These feudal lords were known as *pashas;* there is more information about this phenomenon in the box on page 218. The Toptani family's original power base was Kruja and one of their houses can be visited there (page 111). Directly across Rruga Abdi Toptani from the City Hall is a replica bunker that forms the entrance to Bunk'Art 2. This and its sister-installation, Bunk'Art 1, are dedicated to the interpretation of aspects of the communist period (see page 80 for details of the two Bunk'Art sites).

If (for now) you continue past the replica bunker, you will reach Rruga Murat Toptani, a pedestrianised street (in Albanian it is known universally as Pedonalja, from the Italian for 'pedestrianised street'). One of the entrances to the grounds of the National Gallery of Arts is across the street and the Boulevard is visible on your right. To continue this walking tour, though, turn left on to Rruga Murat Toptani, lined with restaurants and bars and, in summer, lively with stalls and street performers. On the right, just beyond the Millennium Cinema, is the only remaining stretch of Tirana's Ottoman-era city wall. A stone archway and information panels mark the entrance to the upmarket leisure complex called Kalaja e Tiranës ('Tirana Castle'), developed in the space between the city wall and the Toptani family's ancestral home. A paved path leads through shops, restaurants and wine bars to the beautiful house at the end of the pedestrian area. A helpful map at the entrance shows the location of each of the businesses. There are even public toilets.

Beyond the Toptani house, through the car park, you reach the Lana, the little river that bisects the city centre. Turning right here would let you combine this walk with the 'Tirana's parks' walk described below, joining it at the Youth Park. To continue with this shorter walk, however, turn left along Boulevard Gjergj Fishta, past the huge new mosque, cross Rruga Xhorxh (the Albanicised spelling of 'George') W Bush and continue until you get to the cute little 19th-century **Tanners' Bridge** (Ura e Tabakëve) [69 G3]. Turn left up this street, past the Lulishte 1 Maji restaurant. On the corner is an attractive Italian-period villa, now the headquarters of the Association of Politically Persecuted People; across Rruga Xhorxh W Bush is the **Albanian Parliament** [69 F4], built in 1924 to an Italian design and set in attractive gardens. The city's main mosque stood in these gardens until it was destroyed in 1944, during the Battle for the Liberation of Tirana; the large new mosque that has replaced it is not on exactly the same site.

Back on Rruga Murat Toptani, information panels at the northern entrance to the Parliament gardens show the location of the various buildings within them. The fortifications excavated and preserved here date from the struggle for control of Tirana in the 18th century between the Toptanis and another feudal family. From here, turn right alongside the modern shopping mall, to emerge on to Rruga Abdi Toptani at the side of the Maritim Plaza Hotel. Preserved under a curving roof of the hotel is a circular construction called the **Tyrbe of Kapllan Pasha** [69 E3]. A *tyrbe* is a Bektashi shrine commemorating the burial place of a holy person. Kapllan Pasha was the son of Ismail Toptani, who built the beautiful house in Kruja that is now the Ethnographic Museum there. Kruja was the northernmost stronghold of Bektashism and Kapllan Pasha was the first Toptani to settle in what is now Tirana. It is thanks to the tyrbe's designation as a Cultural Monument that it survived the frenzy of building that overwhelmed Tirana in the first 15 years of this millennium. It now nestles incongruously in the shadow of the modern architecture that has been built above and around it. A little further along Rruga Abdi Toptani, another Ottoman house can be seen through the fence that surrounds its tree-shaded courtyard. It was built in the early 19th century and, in the 1920s, it housed the legation of the United States. From here it is a few minutes' walk back to the City Hall and the clock tower where the walk began.

Tirana's parks The relentless pace of construction over the last decade or so has meant the loss of many of Tirana's green spaces, but two of the city's best-loved parks have survived: they were known in the communist era as the Youth Park

(Parku i Rinisë) and the Big Park (Parku i Madh).The walk described here includes both of these parks.

From Skanderbeg Square, walk down the wide Boulevard Dëshmorët e Kombit (Boulevard of the Martyrs of the Nation). On the left of the Boulevard, just beyond the ministries that line the south of the square, is the National Gallery of Arts (page 76); across the road is the central park, which older Tirana residents still refer to as the **Youth Park** [68 D4].

In fine weather, the park fills with people of all ages, relaxing with their friends or family. A massive monument to Albania's centenary of independence, set in a pool whose water then flows through the upper section of the park, stands at the corner where the Boulevard meets Rruga Myslym Shyri. The large building on the opposite side of the park – facing on to Rruga Ibrahim Rugova – is a recreation complex known as 'Taiwan' (albanicised as 'Tajvani'), in honour of the country that donated the splendid fountains beside it. The park was re-landscaped in 2019–20; an information panel indicates the intended purpose of each of its new sections.

Once you have looked around the Youth Park, continue beyond the Pyramid and the governmental buildings, the Rogner Europapark hotel and the Congress Building. The square where the Boulevard ends is **Mother Teresa Square** [69 E7]; the building that occupies most of the southern end is the rectorate of the **University of Tirana**. In 1990, it was students from this university, then called Enver Hoxha University, who lit the spark that eventually ended single-party rule in Albania (page 17). If you now cross the square and turn right at the university, then slightly uphill to your left, you will find one of the entrances to the **Lake Park** [69 G/H7], once known simply as the Big Park. Albania's Holocaust Memorial, inaugurated in 2020, stands at this entrance to the park. Now there are two main options: keep going uphill or bear right.

If you keep going uphill (bearing left), you will get to an attractively painted wooden sign indicating the start of the 'Memorials'. The first memorial you come to is the graveyard of German soldiers who died in Albania during World War II; a little further on are the graves and busts of four highly influential figures in the Albanian cultural renaissance (Rilindja Kombëtare) of the late 19th and early 20th centuries – the three Frashëri brothers, Abdyl, Naim and Sami (see box, page 206); and, a little apart from them, Faik Konica (page 24).

A little beyond the Frashëris, the **British Memorial Cemetery** [63 F6] commemorates 47 British and Commonwealth soldiers and airmen who died in Albania during World War II. Most are not buried here, however; their remains were painstakingly collected and reburied by the British Army's Graves Registration Unit in 1946, but were later dug up and moved. Nobody knows where those bodies now lie. The exception is the grave of Sgt Peter Twiddy, who was one of nine servicemen to die in 1943, when their plane crashed on its way to drop supplies and SOE agents into southern Albania. The crash site was located in 2021; Sgt Twiddy's remains were identified using relatives' DNA, and he was reburied with full military honours in the Memorial Cemetery, on what would have been his 100th birthday. The British Embassy organises a memorial service here on Remembrance Sunday (around 11 November) every year, which anyone can attend. See the box on page 13 for further information about the work of the brave men remembered here.

If you bear right instead of left at the park entrance, you will come to **Tirana Lake** [63 E7], the reservoir around which the park was created, and the promenade along the top of its dam. It is possible to walk around the lake, although this southwestern corner is an unpromising start, with a huge (and very controversial) apartment complex right next to the dam, followed by a stretch of Tirana's outer ring road before the lakeside path veers back into the park.

Of course, you might choose simply to stroll around the park and see what you come across; it might be a fine Socialist Realist statue, the small Catholic church, a restaurant or a chess match. Wandering from west to east, you will emerge on Rruga e Elbasanit, from where you can catch a bus or walk back into the centre.

COMMUNIST HERITAGE For the first 25 years of Albania's post-communist history, the last thing people wanted to be reminded of was the political repression and economic hardship they had so recently succeeded in getting rid of. Recently, however, national and local authorities have begun to invest in conserving some of the more notable communist sites and curating them so that Albanians and visitors can learn about this difficult and controversial period. There are three such sites in Tirana, each described here.

Bunk'Art 1 [map, page 58] (Rr Fadil Deliu; m 068 48 34 444; w bunkart.al; ⌚ 09.00–16.00 Wed–Mon; 500 lek) A fascinating exhibition about how the repressive and isolationist regime developed has been installed within a bunker complex in the northwestern outskirts of Tirana. Built in the 1970s but never used, this vast network of underground tunnels was intended to shelter the entire government apparatus in the event of invasion or nuclear attack (as with similar bunkers built in the UK and elsewhere, one can only wonder whom they expected to be governing after a nuclear attack). There were offices and dormitories for government officials, apartments for the party leaders, communications rooms, an assembly hall and a canteen: 106 rooms in total. A state-of-the-art air purification system was installed and a telephone network linked the party leaders with their officials. You can explore the apartment set aside for Enver Hoxha (see box, page 84): an office, with an anteroom for his secretary (and a wonderful communist-era map of Albania), a sparsely furnished bedroom and an equally sparse en-suite bathroom. The only touch of luxury was the carpeting throughout and the lino cladding over the reinforced concrete walls. The whole complex was top-secret at the time; even the commanders of the military base above ground, which is still operational, did not have access to it.

As you go through the tunnels, each room has a display of photographs and other archive material, illustrating the phases of World War II and the subsequent chilling of relations with one set of former allies after another. Some rooms are used for modern art installations inspired by this aspect of Albania's history. You can download an app at the site to access additional information about the exhibits as you go round; free Wi-Fi is provided.

Bunk'Art 1 is in the northwestern outskirts of Tirana. From the city centre, the 'Linzë' buses leave from behind the Palace of Culture and stop near the entrance to a tunnel, with spooky piped sound effects, which leads to the ticket kiosk. Those arriving by private transport or taxi miss out on the tunnel; cars can be parked at the ticket kiosk. A fair bit of walking is involved, including several flights of steps. A minimum of 2 hours is recommended; it would take the best part of a day to look attentively at the whole exhibition.

Bunk'Art 2 [69 E3] (Rr Abdi Toptani; m 067 20 72 905; w bunkart.al; ⌚ 09.00–16.00 Wed–Mon; 500 lek) In the 1980s, the communist authorities constructed a bomb-proof tunnel under the Ministry of the Interior, home to the police force in its various incarnations throughout Albania's 100-year history. In the museum created in this space, archive photographs and film illustrate the development of policing in the country, from the Dutch-trained gendarmerie (see box, page 94) of the first years after independence, through the Italian occupation (the ministry itself was built by Italian architects in the 1930s), to the terrifying period from 1944 to 1991. Between 1949 and 1990, nearly a thousand Albanian citizens were killed by the Border Forces; the so-called State Security (Sigurimi i Shtetit) spied on, tortured and imprisoned Albanians on the flimsiest of pretexts.

You can visit the interrogation rooms and the holding cells in the tunnel, as well as the decontamination room that would have been used in the event of a nuclear or chemical attack. There are 24 rooms, including a far-from-luxurious apartment for the Minister of the Interior and a telecommunications centre. The exhibition of photographs and artefacts is very extensive and it would take over 2 hours to absorb all the information presented. As in Bunk'Art 1, there are also contemporary art installations. Additional information can be accessed in each room by means of Bunk'Art's free phone app, downloadable at the site.

As you leave the tunnel, there is a chance to see the original structure that would have protected it from attack: nearly 2.5m of reinforced concrete. The current exit and entrance were installed when the exhibition site centre was opened. The decision to erect a replica bunker in the centre of Tirana, when the country was not exactly short of the real thing, generated considerable controversy at the time.

The House of Leaves [68 D3] (Shtëpia e Gjethëve; Rr Ibrahim Rugova; ☎ 222 2612, 225 0055; 🕘 09.00–19.30 daily; 700 lek) The House of Leaves is the former surveillance centre of the Sigurimi, Albania's secret police. It was built in 1931 as a maternity clinic, founded by Zog I's personal physician, and taken over secretly by the Sigurimi, for use mainly by the technicians who tapped people's telephones and installed bugs in their apartments. Also based there was the department responsible for spying on foreign visitors and residents, intercepting communications in hotels and embassies in Tirana and maintaining detailed notes about every foreigner in the country.

The museum displays original items used by the Sigurimi to spy on 'the enemy within' (ie: virtually everyone in Albania) and 'the external enemy' (everybody else). The collection includes original recording devices, photographic equipment and bugs, along with illustrations of how the bugs were concealed. Archive film screened in various rooms document statements given by individuals under interrogation, show trainers explaining how to use the equipment and give a voice to some of the survivors. In a video room, you can watch and listen through headphones to a huge number of further films, documentaries, feature films and interviews. Photographs, reproduced documents, plans and diagrams complement the films and artefacts. A replica living room with made-in-Albania household items from the communist period provides a moment of light relief.

Like the Bunk'Art exhibitions, the House of Leaves presents a vast amount of information, and at least 2 hours should be allowed to look around it.

Historic buildings In Skanderbeg Square, the Tirana International Hotel and the Palace of Culture, the huge building that occupies the whole of the eastern side of the square, were both designed by Soviet architects in the 1960s. Only the exterior of these buildings reminds one of those times. The hotel has been completely overhauled and a towering new extension is under construction behind it (expected to open around 2025). The opera house was renovated more recently, reopening in 2021, and although it is now more comfortable than before, it has lost its faded communist grandeur in the process.

Back on the Boulevard, the **Dajti Hotel** [69 E4] played a pivotal role in its first half-century. Designed by Italian architects in the 1930s, it was the only hotel in Tirana until what is now the Tirana International Hotel opened in the 1960s. In the communist period, almost all foreign visitors were accommodated in the Dajti. Ordinary Albanians were not allowed through the doors until the advent of democracy. Countless treaties were negotiated and plots hatched in the Dajti Hotel. Peter and Andrea Dawson described the Dajti in Bradt's first guide to Albania, in 1989; 10 years later, it was little changed, although obviously the statues of Lenin and Stalin had gone by then.

> We decide that the other large hotel in Tiranë, the Dajti, is worth investigation. We walk down the Avenue of the Martyrs of the Nation, past the bronze Lenin statue and the National Art Gallery, and, behind the trees opposite the statue of Stalin, are the party cars: Mercedes and black Volvos. The red 'Dajti' lettering fronts a heavy stone and glass canopy, shielding the steps to the entrance.
>
> Inside, a vast reception area and hall contains a bookshop, a souvenir shop and, in a lounge, a television is showing Albanian programmes, watched by some of the foreign businessmen, who, along with trade and political delegations, form the bulk of the Dajti's clientele.
>
> A corridor to the right leads to the bar, and we have cappuccinos and bottled Albanian beer, sitting in comfortable armchairs at a low walnut table.
>
> Peter and Andrea Dawson, *Albania: A Guide and Illustrated Journal*

The doors of this historic hotel closed in December 2005 and the building was left to fall into disrepair. In 2021, work began at last to redevelop the building as offices for the National Bank of Albania. The original tiles from the floors and walls were painstakingly removed and numbered and will be replaced; some of the original furniture and doors will be conserved and re-used. Members of the public will have access to the main reception area, mentioned in the extract above, and to the Bank's library on the ground floor.

The **Pyramid** [69 E5], just across the little River Lana from the Dajti, was a remarkable piece of architecture, with sloping walls at the front leading round to vertical faces at the back, all clad in white marble. It was commissioned as a memorial museum to Enver Hoxha (see box, page 84) and was designed by Hoxha's daughter, Pranvera, and her husband; they were also the architects of the **Congress Building** (Pallati i Kongresëve) [69 E6], further down the Boulevard, and of the Skanderbeg Museum in Kruja (page 110). After the end of one-party rule and until the end of the first decade of the 21st century, the Pyramid was used for conferences and trade fairs, with a nightclub in the basement and offices at the rear let to various companies, including a privately owned national TV station. There were threats that the Pyramid would be completely demolished, the tenants of the offices gradually moved out, and the building became increasingly derelict. In 2021, it was stripped out and its transformation began into a shopping and recreation centre.

The large bell hanging above the walkway outside the Pyramid is the Bell of Peace, an initiative of schoolchildren from northern Albania who collected spent bullet casings from the 1997 uprising (page 18), and used them to cast this testimonial to the country's near-collapse.

Just across the street that runs behind the Pyramid, Rruga Gjon Pali II ('John Paul II') is a communist-nostalgia bar called **Kafe Komiteti** [69 F5] (Rr Fatmir Haxhiu), furnished and decorated with original items from Albanian households of the 1970s and 80s. It offers an excellent selection of different kinds of raki.

On the Boulevard next to the Pyramid is the government building known as the **Council of Ministers** [69 E5] – a Socialist Realist bas-relief has been preserved on the wall facing the Boulevard. The building directly opposite is where the Albanian Party of Labour's Central Committee used to meet and where its senior members, including Hoxha, had their offices; it now houses various state institutions, such as the Parliament and the Constitutional Court. The **Checkpoint** memorial [69 E6], an installation commemorating Albania's isolation under communism, includes a segment of the Berlin Wall, one of the pillbox bunkers that once lined many of Albania's roads and covered much of its countryside, and – most chilling of all – part of the concrete mineshaft supports from the prison camp at Spaçi (page 147). The memorial has been installed in a little garden on the corner of the Boulevard with Rruga Ismail Qemali: one of the entrances to the area known as **the Block** (Blloku). The Block covered almost a square mile and was reserved for the families of the Party elite. Ordinary Albanians gained access to it for the first time after the fall of the communist regime. The bunker in the Checkpoint memorial came from one of the entrances to the Block.

It is said that there is a tunnel from the Central Committee building to **Enver Hoxha's house** [68 D6], in the next block along Rruga Ismail Qemali. Part of the house has now been taken over by an English-language school, while another is occupied by one of the Block's trendy bars, both of which must have the xenophobic Hoxha turning in his grave (read on to find where that is). Mehmet Shehu's house (page 17) is on the left between the Checkpoint and Rruga Ibrahim Rugova.

Statues and cemeteries Tirana has several good examples of Socialist Realist statues, apart from those in and behind the National Gallery of Arts (page 76). The monument to the **Unknown Partisan** [69 F3] stands in a little square beside the junction of Xhorxh W Bush and Luigj Gurakuqi. The partisan rises above the people and the traffic, waving his comrades on into battle with one hand and gripping his rifle in the other. In the Lake Park, there is a charming statue of a partisan girl offering water to a soldier. Most imposing of all is **Mother Albania**, who overlooks the city at the **Martyrs' Cemetery** [63 H7] (Varreza e Dëshmorëve; ⌚ Mon–Fri). A flight of steps on the left of the path leads up to the *parvis* where Mother Albania stands, clutching a laurel wreath with a star and looking out over Tirana spread below her.

> In April 1985 Enver Hoxha, former teacher of French, tobacconist and partisan leader, secretary of the Party of Labour, was buried here, and his polished red granite tombstone is on the stepped platform next to Mother Albania. A small red and black double-eagle flag flies at the head of the tombstone, and it is guarded by two soldiers at attention, with high black polished boots and automatic rifles: the smartest soldiers in Albania, according to Andrea.
>
> Nearby are the graves of the party officials, and down the gentle slopes are the graves, many with star and laurel denoting a People's Hero, of 900 men and women killed during the War of National Liberation.
>
> From here you can look down on Tiranë, with the minaret, clock-tower and Hotel Tirana clearly visible. On the left, almost hidden by poplars, is the former palace of King Zog, which was an important seizure for the partisan brigades liberating the capital.
>
> Peter and Andrea Dawson, *Albania: A Guide and Illustrated Journal*

The inscription below Mother Albania reads 'Eternal Glory to the Martyrs of the Fatherland', a reminder that this cemetery is much more than a relic of communism – it commemorates many of those who died in World War II, struggling against Fascist Italy and then Nazi Germany. Resistance fighters who were opposed to the

ENVER HOXHA

Enver Hoxha was born in Gjirokastra in 1908; his reconstructed family home is now that city's Ethnographic Museum. Hoxha studied in Gjirokastra and Korça and was then given an Albanian state scholarship to attend the University of Montpellier. During his time in France, he met Ali Kelmendi, the most senior of the small number of Albanian communists at the time. When Hoxha returned to Albania in 1936, he got a job teaching at his old school, the French *lycée* in Korça, and became involved in the fledgling Communist Party there.

The party remained very small and fragmented until, in 1941, the Yugoslav communists sent two delegates to help reorganise it and recruit new members. The Albanian Communist Party was officially founded in November 1941, and the following year Enver Hoxha was appointed party secretary. He became Prime Minister of the Provisional Government of Albania in October 1944, and went on to consolidate his power within the party over the next few years. He continued as prime minister until 1954, when he handed over the position to his wartime comrade Mehmet Shehu (page 17); but Hoxha continued to exercise considerable authority over the government, the party and the country until his death in April 1985.

nascent Communist Party were not buried here (see page 15 for more information). The rows of graves run down the hillside beyond the statue, beginning with the best-known partisan fighters, including women such as Margarita Tutulani, who was shot by the Italians in 1943 aged only 19. Hundreds of others follow in alphabetical order of their first names, as is standard practice in Albania. Beside Mother Albania is the tomb of the young partisan Qemal Stafa, a founding member of the Albanian Communist Youth; next to that is a rectangular patch where Enver Hoxha's body lay until April 1992, when it was exhumed and reburied in the public cemetery (Sharra Cemetery), on the other side of the city.

The 'former palace of King Zog', referred to in the extract above, can be glimpsed through its gates on the opposite side of the Elbasani road, just before the gate into the Martyrs' Cemetery. As the authors say, its capture was a key point in the Battle for the Liberation of Tirana in 1944; after liberation, it was renamed the **Palace of the Brigades** [63 H7] and was used for government receptions. It is now the official residence of the President of Albania.

The Martyrs' Cemetery is a long and, until you get to the Palace of the Brigades, not particularly interesting walk from the city centre. Any bus that shows 'TEG' as its destination will let passengers off and pick them up at the nearest stop to the gates (TEG is Tirana East Gate, the huge shopping mall at the junction of the Elbasani road and the new Tirana bypass). A taxi from the city centre would take between 15 and 45 minutes, depending on how bad the traffic congestion is.

Sharra Cemetery (Varreza e Sharrës) is just off Rruga Konferenca e Pezës, in the southwestern outskirts of Tirana. The turn-off uphill to the cemetery can easily be identified by the flower stalls just before it. The graves are grouped chronologically, but you need to bear in mind that Hoxha's coffin was exhumed and reburied in 1992, and so that is his chronological position, rather than the date of his death, 1985. Once you are in roughly the right section, the large brown marble headstone is easy to spot; there may be fresh flowers on the grave. Mehmet Shehu, Albania's prime minister until his fall from grace in 1981, has also been reinterred in the main cemetery. The whereabouts of his remains were unknown until 2001, when one of his sons tracked down his unmarked grave in a village near Tirana. To get to Sharra by public transport from the city centre, the best option is to take a bus for Kombinat, from where it is about a 10-minute walk from the cemetery.

WORLD BEKTASHI CENTRE (Kryegjyshata; Rr Dhimitër Kamarda; ☎ 235 5090; ⏱ 10.00–13.00 daily; free admission) The Sufi order known as Bektashism has had its world headquarters in Albania since 1929, when King Zog gave it land for a *teqe* and associated buildings. When Albania was declared an atheist state in 1967, these buildings were confiscated and converted into an old people's home. In 1991, most of the property was returned to the Bektashis, the elderly residents were relocated to another care home, and the *teqe* was reopened in the presence of Mother Teresa.

In 2015, the crowning glory of the World Bektashi Centre was inaugurated: a great prayer-hall known as the Odeon. Around the entrance stand 16 black pillars, representing the 16 children killed at the Battle of Karbala, a central event in Shi'a tradition. Visitors may enter the Odeon and admire the exquisite architecture and decoration – the columns of Indian marble (one for each of the 12 martyrs of Islam), the magnificent wall paintings and, an architectural curiosity, pillars on either side of the *qibla* that spin on their axis. This has nothing to do with Bektashi beliefs but is an ingenious seismic warning system; in the event of an earthquake, the pillars will freeze in place, thus alerting the building's caretakers that there is a problem with the building.

In the basement of the Odeon is an interesting museum with artefacts and panels (in Albanian) illustrating the history of Bektashism. The order's website (w kryegjyshataboterorebektashiane.org) has some information in English about the exhibition; click on the 'Museum' button.

The World Bektashi Centre is in the eastern suburbs of Tirana, south of Rruga Ali Demi. It is not at all easy to find and the quickest way to get there is by taxi.

MOUNT DAJTI At 1,613m, Mount Dajti is not very high by Albanian standards, although it is 269m higher than Britain's highest mountain, Ben Nevis. It is only 25km from the centre of Tirana and makes a great day out, especially for those who would like to do some hiking but are short of time to explore Albania's higher but less accessible mountains. There is forest – mostly beech – almost all the way to the summit, which makes for very pleasant, shady walking, especially in the heat of summer. A map of the path network is posted at the exit from the upper cable-car station. You should wear sensible footwear and have sufficient water with you.

The cable-car company operates an adventure park (⏱ 09.30–17.30 daily), a short walk from the upper cable-car station, with zip-lines, bungee jumps and other activities (€12/8 adult/child). It also has an 18-hole mini-golf course.

Getting there and away By far the best way to get up to Mount Dajti, unless you are very uncomfortable with heights, is on the cable car (w dajtiekspres.com; ⏱ summer 09.00–21.00 Wed–Mon, winter 09.00–19.00 Wed–Mon, weather permitting; 500/800 lek sgl/return; bicycle transport €7). The upper station is at just over 1,000m above sea level; the lower station is in the eastern suburbs of Tirana. It takes about 15 minutes to travel between the two cable-car stations. The website has helpful 'Getting Here' information, in English, including guidance on public transport. Tickets can be bought only at the lower station.

The lower station is tricky to find if you are driving or cycling on your own. The website has good directions. The free car park at the lower station fills up quite early on fine days, especially at weekends or when there is snow. By public transport, the 'Qendër–Porcelan' buses leave from the clock tower in the city centre and terminate at the *Teleferiku* stop, a few minutes' walk from the lower cable-car station.

It is also possible to drive up Mount Dajti. It takes about an hour from the western side of the city, through urban sprawl and then into forests with occasional views out over Tirana. There is a car park at the upper cable-car station.

Where to stay *Map, page 58*

Dajti Tower Belvedere (24 rooms); m 067 40 11 035; e marketing@dajtiekspres.com; w dajtiekspres.com. Right next to upper cable-car station & under same management; magnificent views over Tirana on one side, forested mountainside on the other. English spoken. Panoramic restaurant, revolving bar on top floor, free transport on cable car for hotel guests. All rooms en suite with AC, satellite TV, free Wi-Fi, minibar **$$$**

Panorama (5 rooms, 4 chalets); 236 3124; m 069 20 23 936, 068 20 23 936; e panorama@albaniaonline.net. Friendly staff, some English spoken; shuttle bus runs between hotel & upper cable-car station. Dbl rooms below the restaurant, chalets to the side, all at ground level. All have beautiful views (when clear, to the Adriatic), en-suite bathroom, TV. **$$**

Where to eat

Ballkoni i Dajtit Part of the complex around the upper cable-car station. Standard Albanian restaurant fare – pasta, salads, pizza, grilled meat. Outdoor terrace with viewing platform, amazing views over Tirana &, on clear days, to Adriatic. **$$$**

Gurra e Përrisë m 068 20 60 720. Trout farm; fish raised in pools in the restaurant's grounds. In season, spit-roasted lamb also offered. In summer, tables outside around the trout pools; in winter, traditional-style dining room with log fire. Lovely views of the forested hillsides. **$$$**

Panorama Restaurant of the hotel of the same name. The house speciality is spit-roasted lamb, served with chips, salad & red wine; also well known for its game dishes, such as hare & pheasant. Spectacular views of Tirana from dining room & terrace. **$$$**

4

Central Albania

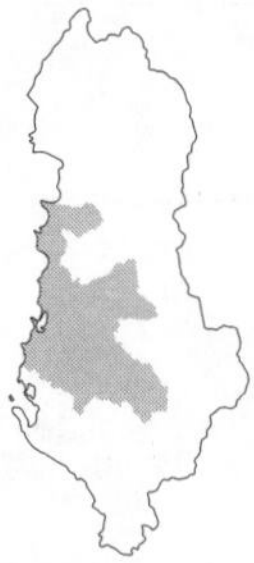

Central Albania epitomises the country's image of itself. The largest city in the region, Durrësi, was the independent Albania's first capital and is still its largest port; its second city, Elbasani, was the venue for a famous congress of Albanian intellectuals, where it was decided that the Roman alphabet would be used thenceforth to write the Albanian language; and the castle at Kruja was the seat of Albania's national hero, Skanderbeg. All of these places are close enough to Tirana to be feasible as day trips, even by public transport, but they also have enough attractions of their own to merit a longer stay.

GETTING THERE AND AWAY

BY AIR Durrësi and Kruja are each less than an hour's drive from Mother Teresa Airport. Durrësi has an airport bus service; see page 32 for details. At the time of writing, there is no public transport between the airport and other towns in this chapter.

BY SEA Durrësi is served by three different ports in Italy. The most frequent – and cheapest – crossing is the 9-hour journey from Bari. Several operators run ferries on this route; up-to-date schedules can be found on the Italian ferry website w traghetti.it. In addition to the crossings from Bari, car ferries operate to Durrësi from the Italian ports of Ancona (16 hours) and Trieste (26 hours). These routes are operated by **Adria Ferries** (+39 (0)71 5021 1621; w adriaferries.com). The ferries run all year round, with more frequent departures in summer. A new ferry service to Durrësi from the Croatian ports of Rijeka and Zadar may commence during the lifetime of this guidebook.

DURRËSI *Telephone code: 052*

The headland at the north of Durrësi Bay forms a natural harbour in which ships have anchored since the 7th century BC. In antiquity it was known as Epidamnos, and the city that was built around it was called Dyrrhachion. In the 5th century BC, a popular uprising in Dyrrhachion helped to start the Peloponnesian War, which engulfed the whole of Greece from 431BC to 404BC.

Under Roman rule, Dyrrachium (as it was by then known) became a vital staging post, one of the two starting points of the Egnatian Way (Via Egnatia), the great road that linked the Adriatic coast with Byzantium. The city thrived during the Roman and Byzantine periods, and the amphitheatre that the Romans built there was the largest in the Balkan peninsula. In the Middle Ages Dyrrachium was coveted by Normans, Angevins and Venetians, and for a few years after independence Durrësi was the capital of Albania. This rich past is reflected in the town's Archaeological Museum, with its collection of Illyrian, Greek and Roman artefacts.

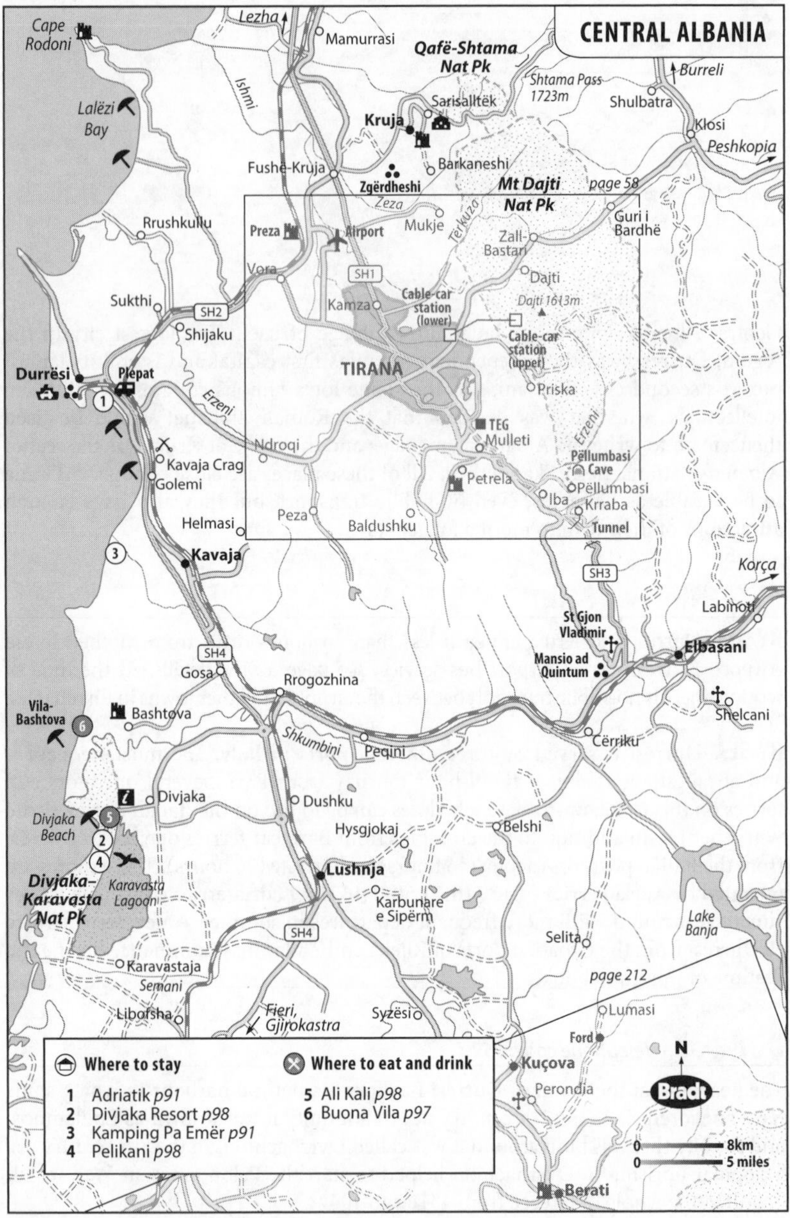

Most Albanians visit Durrësi not for its history but for its beaches, with their golden sand and safe swimming. In the summer, these beaches become very crowded; out of season, in late spring and early autumn, the sea is still warm enough to swim in and the evenings are pleasantly cool. The beaches to the north of the city, known as Currilat, are quieter.

HISTORY Durrësi has probably been inhabited for about 3,000 years, but it enters history in 627BC, when it was colonised by settlers from the Greek island of Corfu

(Corcyra), who may have been attracted by the silver mines further inland in Illyria. The new colony prospered for many years, until internal political unrest led to a war between Corcyra and Corinth. The Athenian historian Thucydides describes the aftermath of this war as one of the causes of the great war fought, between 431BC and 404BC, between Athens and its allies on the one hand, and the Peloponnesians, including Sparta, on the other.

Dyrrhachion flourished during the 4th–2nd centuries BC. The city continued to benefit from Greek cultural influence, and temples were built to Greek deities such as Aphrodite and Artemis. The late 4th-century mosaic known as the 'Belle of Durrësi' is the best example of the Hellenistic art of this period. Politically and economically, too, Dyrrhachion was thriving. The Illyrian kings Glaukias (late 4th century BC) and Monun (around 280–270BC) ruled over a city whose population was growing and which had minted its own coins since the middle of the 4th century BC – some of these can be seen in Durrësi's Archaeological Museum.

After the Roman conquest of 229BC (page 8) the city, its name by now Latinised to Dyrrachium and with a population of around 40,000, became a major transit point between Italy and points further east. The Via Egnatia was built by Roman engineers along the route of an already ancient road that had been used by Illyrian and other traders for centuries; its two starting points were Dyrrachium and Apollonia (page 250), and it carried goods and people all the way to Byzantium, later called Constantinople. Excavations in 2016 revealed stonework which is thought may be the starting point of the Via Egnatia. The Roman poet Catullus (84–54BC), mentions the city in one of his poems (C36.15), calling it – as one might expect of a port – 'the road house of the Adriatic'.

In the second phase of the Roman Civil War, between Julius Caesar and Pompey, Dyrrachium was the Pompeian forces' main arsenal and therefore a key target for Caesar after he landed in Albania in 48BC. Caesar managed to cut Pompey off from his arsenal, but in response Pompey entrenched his army in what must have seemed an impregnable position – the crag to the south of the city which is now called Shkëmbi i Kavajës and which the Romans called Petra. With typical audacity, Caesar decided to blockade Petra and, although his forces were much smaller than Pompey's, not to mention less well fed, he almost succeeded in starving the Pompeian troops into surrender. Pompey then broke through Caesar's lines and, in the ensuing battle, inflicted heavy losses on the opposing side. Caesar managed to free his army and retreated east, where the third and final phase of the civil war would unfold in Thessaly.

GETTING THERE AND AWAY

By land Buses to Durrësi leave Tirana from the North/South bus station and terminate at the bus park outside the railway station. There are frequent departures throughout the day until 18.00; the fare is 150 lek and the journey takes about half an hour.

There are buses to Durrësi from all other cities in Albania. From the south, any bus going to Tirana will drop passengers off at Plepat bus station, where the city bypass leaves the coast road (SH4) a few kilometres south of Durrësi. A shuttle bus runs between Plepat and the city centre, or there are always taxis waiting.

Throughout the communist period, Durrësi was the country's main rail terminus. Since then, the railway network has gradually shrunk and, at the time of writing, there are only a couple of trains a day, to Elbasani and Shkodra. Departure times are shown on the timetable outside the station. These trains are agonisingly slow – it takes nearly 3 hours from Durrësi to Elbasani and nearly 4 hours to Shkodra.

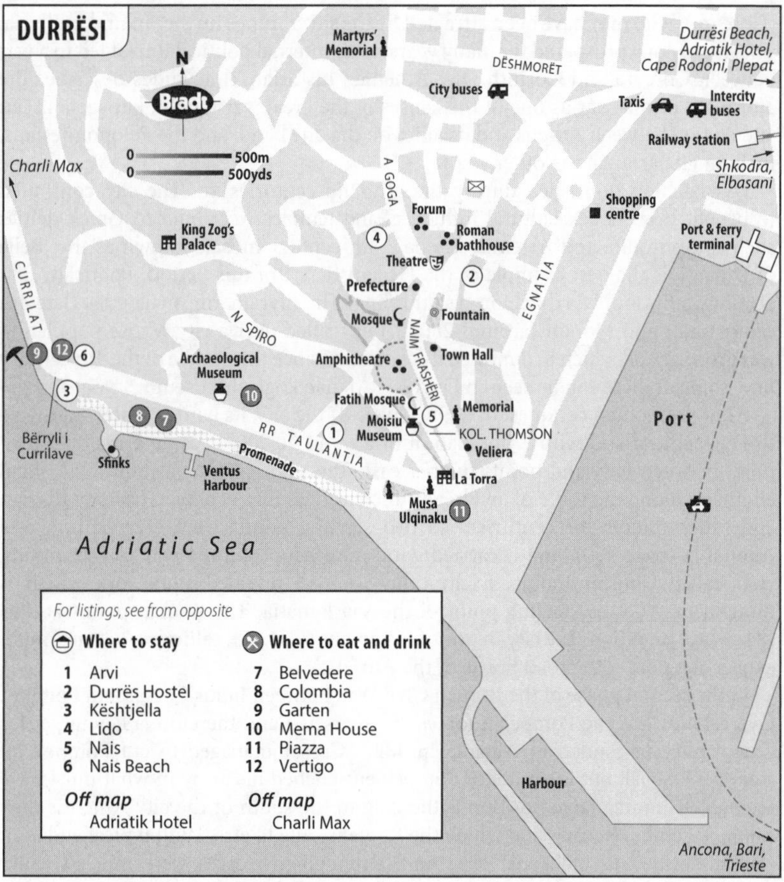

Devotees of rail travel might like to try a shorter run, such as Durrësi to the Vora junction. The railway between Durrësi and Tirana is due to be upgraded and a new spur built to Mother Teresa Airport; the contract was awarded in February 2021 and trains may start running within the lifetime of this guidebook. Durrësi station has a certain scruffy charm and the trains themselves are worth a look, even when they are stationary.

By air Durrësi is less than an hour's drive from Mother Teresa Airport, and a bus connects the two; the schedule is on the airport website (w tirana-airport.com) and can be checked by calling the bus company on 052 225 539. The one-way fare is 480 lek.

By sea Durrësi is Albania's largest port and is served by ferries from three different ports in Italy. See page 87 for details.

GETTING AROUND The main sights in the city are all fairly central and walking between them is not at all arduous, except in very hot or very wet weather. There is a **taxi rank** at the bus station in Durrësi, where a driver can be hired for a single journey or for a day's or a half-day's sightseeing.

Most city buses stop near the inter-city bus station in the centre, then terminate on the little square on Rruga Dëshmorët. The flat fare is 40 lek. A useful route passes the Archaeological Museum (page 93) and continues, beyond the restaurants and hotels at the end of Rruga Taulantia, to the Currilat beaches.

WHERE TO STAY *Map, opposite, unless otherwise stated*

There is no shortage of hotels in Durrësi, ranging from the expensive and luxurious to the cheap and cheerful. The coast to the south of the town has become heavily built up as far as Kavaja, with dozens of hotels lining the beaches and climbing inexorably higher up the hillside on the other side of the road. In high summer (July and August), these southern beaches are crowded and dirty, and there are often problems with the water supply in cheaper hotels during this time. The hotels to the west of the city centre, on Rruga Taulantia, are a better option for those looking for quieter sea views.

Adriatik [map, page 88] (63 rooms, 6 suites) Rr Pavarësia, Plazh; 260 850; m 069 20 21 778; e info@adriatikhotel.com; w adriatikhotel.com. 2 restaurants, bars, large swimming pool in palm-fringed garden, reserved section of sandy beach with sun-loungers & parasols, casino, tennis court, spa, gym, children's pool & playgrounds. Wi-Fi throughout; free parking, business facilities, souvenir shop. Airport pick-ups & tours can be arranged for guests. All rooms have en-suite bathroom with tub or jacuzzi; AC, satellite TV, minibar, safe; 'standard' rooms have view of gardens, others have sea view, 'executive' rooms have balcony. **$$$$$–$$$$**

Arvi (35 rooms, 7 suites) Rr Taulantia; 230 403; m 068 60 47 177; e info@hotelarvi.com; w hotelarvi.com. Modern & well appointed, excellent location on the seafront but close to city centre; English spoken. Restaurant, bars, secure parking. Twin & dbl rooms all en suite, AC, satellite TV, Wi-Fi, direct-dial phone & minibar, some with sea view, some also with balcony. **$$$$**

Kështjella (13 rooms) Rr Taulantia, Bërryli i Currilave; 221 817; m 067 52 03 681; e keshtjella01@hotmail.com; f Hotel Keshtjella. Large beachside restaurant, terrace bar, friendly service. Room rate inc secure parking & use of sun-loungers & parasols on the hotel's section of the beach. Pedalos & boats for hire. All rooms have 1 dbl & 2 sgl beds, en suite, Wi-Fi, TV, AC, phone, hairdryer, balcony with sea view. **$$$**

Lido (13 rooms, 1 suite) Rr A Goga; 227 941; m 068 20 43 719. Opposite Byzantine forum, set back from main road. Friendly, helpful staff; English spoken; bar & restaurant. Spacious rooms, twin & dbl, all en suite with Wi-Fi, AC, TV & fridge. **$$$**

Nais (16 rooms) Rr Naim Frashëri 46; 230 375, 224 940; e hotelnais@hotmail.com; f NaisHotel. Lift; friendly, helpful staff, English spoken; bar & conference room. All rooms en suite with Wi-Fi, flatscreen TV, fridge, phone, AC, some have balconies. **$$$**

Nais Beach (24 rooms) Rr Taulantia, Bërryli i Currilave; 223 130; e info@hotelnais.al; w hotel-nais-beach.durres.hotels-al.com. Lift; free parking; English spoken; b/fast room; arrangement with Vertigo restaurant (page 92). All rooms en suite with Wi-Fi, flatscreen TV, fridge, AC, radio, balcony; upper floors have sea view. **$$$**

Durrës Hostel (2 en-suite dbls, 6 dorms) Sheshi Liria; m 069 46 36 852; e hosteldurresgmail.com; f hosteldurres. Superb location, just off Durrësi's main square, but quiet, in a modernised old villa with beautiful tree-shaded gardens. Bar open to public; garden areas reserved for hostel guests; balconies at front & rear of building; roof terrace; fully equipped kitchen; indoor sitting area; laundry; lockers. English spoken; Wi-Fi throughout; bikes available to hire; day trips organised. All rooms high-ceilinged & airy; ample shower & toilet facilities. **$$** *dbls*, **$** *dorms*

Kamping Pa Emër [map, page 88] Synej-Karpen, near Kavaja; m 066 41 51 502, 066 41 52 854; e reservation@kampingpaemer.com; w kampingpaemer.com; year-round. About 10km from the highway, set in lovely grounds 30m from the beach. Bar & restaurant overlooking the sea; boats for hire. Chalets (**$$$$**) & rooms (**$$$**) also available. Beachside pitches **$**

WHERE TO EAT *Map, page 90*

Durrësi's promenade, which runs between the roundabout at La Torra and the junction known as Bërryli i Currilave ('the Currilat elbow'), is lined with restaurants, most of them offering standard Italian dishes such as pasta, risotto and pizza, all of which Albanian chefs often do very well, plus fish, which is usually fresh and good. All the promenade restaurants have outside tables during the summer months.

Piazza Rr Taulantia; 2 37 601. At the eastern end of the promenade, opposite the Musa Ulqinaku statue. Italian menu, good-quality seafood & fish; professional service. $$$$$

Vertigo Rr Taulantia, Bërryli i Currilave; m 069 60 15 580. On the top floor of the Nais Beach Hotel (under different management); spectacular sea views, Italian-inspired menu, good service, live music at w/ends. $$$$

Belvedere On the promenade; m 069 20 96 123. Reasonably priced fish, meat, pizza & pasta; efficient service; outside tables overlook sea. $$$

Charli Max Beyond Currilat; m 067 20 80 021. Great location overlooking a little harbour, with views towards Durrësi from the terrace. Sea-themed décor; friendly service. Excellent fresh fish & seafood, grilled, in salads or pasta. $$$

Colombia On the promenade; m 068 65 15 999 Excellent fresh fish, farmed & wild, plus seafood pasta, pizza & salads; friendly, English-speaking staff. $$$

Garten Rr Taulantia, Bërryli i Currilave; 500 018. Great location right on Currilat beach. AC indoors, shady terrace with plants & water feature outdoors, both with sea view. Friendly, English-speaking staff. Fish, seafood, pasta etc. $$$

Mema House Rr Taulantia; 228 4408; m 069 75 41 068; f memahouse.al. Traditional Albanian meat dishes; a good choice for those tired of eating fish (although they also serve it). Friendly, professional service. $$$

WHAT TO SEE AND DO

The amphitheatre

The amphitheatre (09.00–19.00 daily; 200 lek; English-speaking guides sometimes available) The huge Roman amphitheatre, which is one of Durrësi's main attractions, was built in the early 2nd century AD. The largest in the Balkans, it is elliptical in shape, about 130m at its longest point, with the arena itself measuring about 60m by 40m across. On the terraced seats there would have been room for about 15,000 spectators, about a third of the capacity of the Colosseum in Rome.

You can go down into the vaults below the rows of seats – the original steps, supplemented with less slippery modern ones, are just after the ticket booth – and see how the amphitheatre was constructed. The Romans alternated rows of brick with *opus incertum*, a mixture of stones and mortar, a technique designed to resist earthquakes. You can see this *opus incertum* in several places around the amphitheatre, including three full rows, well over 2m high, in one of the galleries. The technique was evidently quite successful, since most of the amphitheatre is still standing, despite Durrësi being hit by several strong earthquakes over the centuries. Behind the gallery, you can see the pens where the wild animals were kept; leading out from it is the tunnel through which the gladiators entered the arena. When the site was first excavated, 40 skeletons were discovered with their necks broken – could they have been unsuccessful gladiators?

When gladiatorial combat was banned in the 5th century, the amphitheatre took on a new life as a Christian funerary space. The arena became a cemetery and small chapels were created in the galleries. One of these has 10th- or 11th-century mosaics of saints and archangels on the walls. They are the only wall mosaics ever found in Albania, and those on the back wall are rather badly damaged. The mosaic on the side wall is thought to depict the sponsor of the whole chapel, a man identified only as Alexandros, and his wife. There is a baptismal well at the entrance.

Back out in the arena, the entrance halfway round the terracing is where Dyrrachium's aristocracy arrived in their carriages. The horses were led off to the left while their owners took their seats above the entranceway. The tunnel through which they rode is said to extend right to where the town centre is now, nearly half a kilometre away. Further round to the left, through the beautifully built tunnel where the horses were led, is another chapel, with faint traces of badly damaged fresco still just about visible.

The amphitheatre was discovered only in 1966 and has not been fully excavated, because people still live in the houses which were unwittingly built on top of it. The Albanian Institute of Archaeology and various Italian universities continue to research the site. Excavations between 2004 and 2007 revealed the southern exit from the amphitheatre, which was destroyed by an earthquake in the 13th century. Several important medieval structures have also been discovered in this area, including shops that were still in use within living memory.

Archaeological Museum (Rr Taulantia; 🕘 winter 09.00–16.00 Tue–Sat, summer 09.00–14.00 & 16.00–19.00 Tue–Sat, 09.00–14.00 Sun; 300 lek) Durrësi's Archaeological Museum covers the prehistoric, Hellenistic and Roman periods; the museum's Byzantine collection will eventually be displayed on the upper floor. There are helpful information panels in English and Albanian.

The fact that the city has been more or less continuously inhabited throughout its history means that most of it has never been systematically excavated. Many of the items in the museum were discovered by chance, as local people ploughed their land or as foundations were dug for the new high-rise apartment blocks.

The port that is now Durrësi was colonised by Greek settlers in the 8th century BC. These colonists and the local people interacted and intermarried; evidence of this can be seen in the display of cylindrical grave markers. Their inscriptions, in Greek, have names that mingle Greek and Illyrian. One is to a certain Quintus Dyrracinus Phileros, the middle name showing that people were beginning to identify themselves as being from this city.

Around the middle of the 4th century BC, Dyrrhachion began to mint and circulate its own coins. The silver *stater* bore the old Corcyran emblem of a cow suckling a calf, with the Greek initials DYRR. Lower-denomination bronze coins were also minted. Dyrrhachion's currency has been found as far away as the Danube territories of Dacia (modern Romania) and Thrace.

A highlight of the museum is a whole case of terracotta faces and other body parts. These were votive offerings and were excavated in the 1970s at a sanctuary site northwest of the city. An incredible 1,800kg of fragments were recovered, of which those on display are obviously a selection. Many of the figurines represent Aphrodite, the Greek goddess of love; Catullus indicates, in the same poem referred to on page 89, that Dyrrachium was a centre of worship of Venus (the Roman name for Aphrodite). Other female deities are represented too, including Artemis, the goddess of the hearth. Some scholars believe that the sanctuary was dedicated to her rather than to Aphrodite.

The development of the Via Egnatia, one of whose branches began in Dyrrachium, consolidated the city's position as a major trading centre. A fascinating map shows the extent of this trade route and how it connected with other Roman roads. A collection of amphorae (two-handled urns), some of them encrusted with shells from centuries of immersion in the sea, illustrates the city's importance as a maritime trading centre – their lids are marked with the initials of the exporter. Milestones from the Via Egnatia are displayed nearby.

MAJOR LODEWIJK THOMSON AND THE DUTCH PEACEKEEPERS

With thanks to the late Charlie Nuytens

Albania declared its independence on 28 November 1912, shortly after the outbreak of the First Balkan War (page 12). However, the armed forces of the Balkan League continued to invade and attack their newly independent neighbour. In December, a Conference of Ambassadors was hastily convened in London; its remit was to consider the organisation of the new Albanian state and its international status. It was May 1913 before the London Conference concluded its deliberations and formally recognised Albania. It decided that Albania would be ruled not by the government established in November 1912 under Ismail Qemali, but by a foreign prince chosen by the Great Powers, and that its internal order would be maintained by a gendarmerie under Dutch officers.

The Dutch mission arrived in Albania in October 1913, commanded by Major Lodewijk Thomson, whose military career had included postings in Aceh, South Africa and Greece. (Tintin fans will be happy to learn that Edith Durham, who met him in June 1914, spells his surname 'Thompson'.) The Dutch officers' task was far from easy. Not only did they have to try to create a disciplined Albanian force, changing ingrained habits such as looting after a victory; they were also supposed to oversee the handing in of the weapons that practically every Albanian man held. The only real incentive at their disposal was that anyone who volunteered as a gendarme could keep his weapons.

Prince Wilhelm of Wied, Albania's appointed ruler, landed at Durrësi on 7 March 1914, and made the mistake of appointing Essad Pasha as his Minister of National

Other interesting exhibits are a large kiln for firing pottery, found intact in Currilat, a limestone door frame with elegantly carved dolphins, and a case of locally produced glassware, mostly the long-necked jars in which, it was popularly supposed, the tears of a deceased's loved ones were collected so that they could be interred with the body (in unromantic fact, they probably just contained ointments and perfumes). Fragments of fresco came from the rescue excavation of a domestic bathhouse, discovered while the foundations were being dug for one of the new high-rise apartment blocks.

At the ticket desk, there are attractive replicas for sale of some of the artefacts on display, as well as books in Albanian and English about the history of Durrësi and other archaeological sites. The museum building was damaged in the earthquake of November 2019, but fortunately the damage was not structural and the only exhibit to suffer was one of the glass jars.

The city walls Durrësi was first fortified in the Hellenistic period and then refortified shortly after the Roman conquest, in the 1st century BC. However, the oldest surviving walls are Byzantine, built during the reign of the Emperor Anastasios (AD491–518) to replace earlier fortifications that a catastrophic earthquake in AD348 had destroyed. These walls protected the city for several centuries, until the Byzantine Empire began to collapse and Dyrrachium and its valuable port fell prey to one invader after another. The medieval city within the walls covered an area of around 120ha.

Dyrrachium – or Durazzo, as it was by then known – was part of the Venetian Republic for the whole of the 15th century. One of the towers that the Venetians built, at the southern corner of their walls, is known as **La Torra,** now dwarfed by the high-rise Veliera development. Finally, in 1502, the Ottomans rebuilt the old

Defence. Essad had previously been the military commander of Shkodra who surrendered the city to Montenegro in 1912; since then Essad had done his best to undermine the Qemali government, with encouragement – and probably also financial support – from Serbia. Almost as soon as Wied arrived in Albania, fighting broke out between supporters of Qemali (who was by now in exile in Italy) and Essad.

By early June, the political and military situation was deteriorating. Insurgents were advancing on Durrësi; the Dutch-trained gendarmerie tried to contain them by firing on the crowd, killing several people. In the early hours of 15 June, Edith Durham awoke to the sound of rifle fire and rushed to find out what was happening. She soon learned that Thomson had been fatally wounded in the first hours of the battle; he died in a roadside guardhouse, in the arms of *The Times's* correspondent, Arthur Moore.

Thomson's remains were taken back to the Netherlands, where he was buried in the city of Groningen. A few weeks later World War I broke out and the Dutch mission was ordered back home. Prince Wilhelm of Wied left Albania on 3 September, never to return. Thomson, however, is still remembered in the country of his death as well as that of his birth. On Rruga Naim Frashëri, a group of columns forms a memorial to Thomson and to the others who died that day; a plaque affixed to one of the columns dates the inauguration of this memorial to Independence Day 1927. The parallel street, where Alexander Moisiu's house stands, is called Rruga Koloneli Thomson.

fortifications and garrisoned their troops within them. An information panel at the city gate, which leads to the amphitheatre, shows an outline map of the fortifications as they changed over the centuries.

The forum and baths Cutting behind Veliera from La Torra and up Rruga Naim Frashëri will bring you to Durrësi's main square, with the town hall and the theatre facing each other across it and the city's main mosque to your left. Behind the theatre is the circular forum, thought to date from the end of the 5th century AD. This may have been a *macellum*, or food market, rather than a traditional multi-purpose forum. A paved area, 40m in diameter, was surrounded by 40 marble Corinthian columns. In its centre was a stepped podium, which may have marked the start of the Via Egnatia. Shops were built around the perimeter of the colonnade; this area was excavated as recently as 2019. The whole complex had fallen out of use by the 7th century.

While the modern theatre on the main square was being built in 1957, a Roman bathhouse was discovered. It was excavated and preserved below the new building, which forms a protective canopy over it. A helpful illustrated panel at the entrance shows the layout of the *caldarium* and *tepidarium*, with a cheerful-looking slave stoking the fire. The first section of the baths is the *caldarium*, the hot room, with its black-and-white tiled floor. Further in are the remains of the hypocaust, the warm transitional area called the *tepidarium*, the black-and-white tiles of other sections of the baths, a drainage channel and part of the Roman street. In the Byzantine period, a complex drainage system was added and part of the bathhouse was used as a burial site. Recent excavation has revealed part of the Hellenistic floor. Access to the bathhouse is by a gate which is generally kept locked; the café next door should be able to locate the key-holder.

Ottoman buildings Durrësi was occupied by the Ottomans in August 1501, and a period of economic and cultural decline began. The harbour that had been such an important link across the Adriatic was of little interest to an empire centred far to the east. For the next 200 years, Durrësi became an insignificant little town of no more than 120 houses.

Almost immediately after the occupation, the Ottomans built a mosque on the site of a 10th- or 11th-century basilica, which they called the **Fatih Mosque**; Sultan Mehmed II, who was called the Conqueror (Fatih) after he took Constantinople in 1453, was dead by then, but his memory was not. The mosque is on a corner of a side street off Rruga Naim Frashëri, a restrained, whitewashed building with intricate wrought-iron windows. The minaret is a recent addition.

Just before the corner on which the mosque stands, a left turn will bring you to one of Durrësi's few remaining Ottoman houses, a delightful building with a traditional *çardak* or enclosed balcony. This was the home of Alexander Moisiu, an Albanian actor who was renowned across Europe in the early part of the 20th century. Moisiu was born in 1879, to an Italian mother and Albanian father in Trieste. He applied for Albanian citizenship five years after the country became independent, but was awarded it only in 1934. He died in Switzerland the following year, aged 55. Alexander Moisiu's house is now a **museum** (◷ 08.00–13.00, 17.00–19.00 Tue–Sun; 100 lek), which contains an exhibition of photographs and documents relating to the actor's family and professional career, and (perhaps of greater interest to most non-Albanian visitors) a display of folk costumes and other ethnographic material.

Those with a particular interest in Alexander Moisiu might like to visit his father's family home in nearby Kavaja, which has also been preserved as a museum.

King Zog's Palace It was not until the Balkan Wars and Albania's independence that the city re-emerged from obscurity; it was the new nation's capital in 1914, under Prince Wilhelm of Wied (see box, page 94), and then again from 1918 until the final decision to site the capital in Tirana. King Zog I had a palace built here in 1927, a cream-and-pink villa up on the hill with marvellous views over the city and the bay. The building has now been returned to Zog's descendants and is not open to the public.

Monuments On 7 April 1939, Italian troops disembarked in Durrësi as part of their mission to occupy Albania. British-trained gendarmes, under the command of Abas Kupi (page 15), resisted the invasion but were outnumbered and eventually defeated. Across from La Torra (page 94) stands a Socialist Realist monument to this attempt which the anti-communist Kupi would probably have hated. Perhaps it is just as well, therefore, that it is not a statue of Kupi, but of one of his fellow resisters, **Musa Ulqinaku**. Nearby, a fierce **partisan** brandishes his rifle at the enemy across the sea.

The coast A walk along Durrësi's **promenade** takes about half an hour end to end, although most people will want to stop for an ice cream or a drink in one of the many bars and restaurants that line it. Two structures have been built out into the sea. The **Ventus Harbor** complex has trendy bars in the section nearest the beach and a hotel with a fish restaurant ($$$$$) at the end of the pier. Further west, the so-called **Sfinks** (ie: 'sphynx') is a public space, where locals come to sit and chat, fish from the steps or skateboard. In summer there are often live concerts there.

The beaches to the **south** of Durrësi have become very built up. Particularly in the peak tourist season (July and August), huge numbers of Albanians from landlocked Kosovo and North Macedonia fill the hotels and holiday apartments with which the coast is lined. At this time of year you should expect to find crowded beaches covered in litter, with the sea full of empty plastic bottles and crisp packets. On the positive side, this stretch of the coast has lively nightlife during the tourist season. If you are staying in the town centre and want a quick dip, the best option is one of the small beaches along **Rruga Currilat**, at the northern end of the city, beyond the Archaeological Museum. The hotels and restaurants along this stretch have reserved sections of sandy beach, with sun-loungers and parasols for which there is a small charge.

Further north still is the upmarket resort on Lalëzi Bay (Gjiri i Lalëzit). The northern end of Lalëzi Bay is bounded by a peninsula called **Cape Rodoni** (Kepi i Rodonit). The road to the cape is asphalted as far as the luxury beach resort on the northern coast of the peninsula. It is possible to kayak to remoter beaches and to Rodoni Castle, the medieval sea fortress said to have been built, in 1465, by Skanderbeg (see box, page 136). There is no public transport to Lalëzi Bay or Cape Rodoni.

BASHTOVA CASTLE

The imposing remains of Bashtova Castle tower over the flat fields that surround it. The castle is thought to have been built between 1467 and 1478, but an earlier phase of building is obvious in the walls that stand today. Roman materials – columns and tiles – are clearly visible and may have been re-used from a fortification on exactly the same site. It is certainly a very good choice of site, commanding not only the land around but also the River Shkumbini, which coils around three sides of it. It meets the sea only 3km to the west.

On three sides, the walls have survived to nearly their original 9m height, with two well-preserved wall-towers at the northern and eastern corners. There are stone steps up to the battlements on the northern and southern side. You can climb up and walk around the top of the walls for good views of the surrounding area; note that there are no handrails or any other kind of protection. It is also possible to walk all around the outside of the castle. The southern wall, although it is more damaged than the others, has beautifully worked arrow-slits.

There is an information panel, in Albanian and English, at the entrance. The castle is unattended and free to enter. To reach it, leave the SH4 at the turn-off for Gosa (the signpost shows the indefinite form, Gosë). At the time of writing, the first section of the road is very rough; 4x4 is advisable although, in dry weather, not essential. It takes about half an hour to reach the castle from the highway junction, through the village of Vila; accommodation, if required, can be found at the Panorama Hotel there.

Half an hour's drive beyond Bashtova Castle, the beach of **Vila-Bashtova** is sandy and relatively quiet, even in high summer, thanks to the poor state of the road. The **Buona Vila** restaurant (map, page 88; $$$) at the beach serves generous portions of fresh grilled fish and seafood, including mussels, seafood pasta and excellent salads. It has sea-themed décor indoors; outdoors, on a wooden terrace, tables have a view of the beach and sea. The staff are friendly and efficient, and English is spoken.

DIVJAKA-KARAVASTA NATIONAL PARK

The national park centred on the Karavasta Lagoon is an internationally recognised wetland area – a Ramsar Site, the first in Albania, designated in 1995 – sandwiched between the Semani and Shkumbini rivers. Home to around 250 bird species, 18 of which are globally threatened, it is the most westerly breeding ground of the Dalmatian pelican (*Pelecanus crispus*). Pelicans like building their nests away from the shore, to protect their eggs and chicks from predators such as rats, and the Karavasta Lagoon is full of small, low islands, ideal for the pelicans' purposes. In the 2020 breeding season, 85 nesting pairs of pelicans were recorded here.

The inner lagoon is quite well protected, as a Category II National Park. A proposal to build a huge development at the heart of the park, with thousands of holiday apartments, several hotels and a golf course, was defeated in 2019, thanks to a vigorous campaign by the Albanian Ornithological Society and other non-governmental organisations (see page 7 for more on the Albanian government's policies on wildlife and national parks).

The lagoon is separated from the sea by a forested sandbar on which there are fish restaurants and hotels. Divjaka-Karavasta's biggest drawback, reasonably enough given it is in the middle of the largest wetland in Albania, is that it is infested with huge, thirsty mosquitoes from late spring to early autumn. If you visit at these times of year, you should take strong insect repellent.

GETTING THERE AND AWAY Divjaka-Karavasta National Park is pretty much due east of the town of Lushnja. Coming from the north on the SH4 highway, the turn-off for Divjaka is signposted at the first roundabout after the roundabout where the SH7 (for Elbasani) and SH3 diverge (this is the Rrogozhina roundabout). From the south, the turn-off for Divjaka is the second small roundabout after the Lushnja turn-off. The village of Divjaka is about 15 minutes' drive down this minor road; to get to the entrance to the national park, 3–4km further on, follow the signs for '*Plazh*' ('beach'). The road leads through the pinewoods and ends at the beach resort.

To get to Divjaka by public transport, you can take any inter-city bus whose route passes that roundabout and ask the driver to let you off there. Local taxis wait near the junction until at least midday (probably later in the summer). The usual fare is 1,500 lek. You should specify at the outset that you are going to Divjaka Beach (Plazhi i Divjakës), to avoid arguments about the fare when you get to the village.

WHERE TO STAY AND EAT *Map, page 68*

Divjaka Resort (68 rooms) m 067 60 00 505, 067 60 00 004; e info@divjaka-resort.com; f divjakaresort1. Fully renovated, set in extensive landscaped grounds, direct access to beach; children's play area; tennis court; large outdoor pool. Helpful, English-speaking reception staff. Restaurant & bar on 1st-floor terrace with sea view; poolside bar; conference room; free secure parking; Wi-Fi throughout; laundry service. All rooms are nicely furnished with fridge, balcony with forest or sea views & well-fitted-out en-suite shower room. **$$$**

Pelikani (10 rooms) m 068 85 56 310; f Bar Restorant hotel Pelikani. In centre of resort; English spoken; friendly, helpful staff; room service available. All rooms have good en-suite shower room, TV, fridge & small balcony. Good restaurant ($$$) with tables on terrace & in garden. **$$**

Ali Kali ('Ali the Horse') m 068 83 71 111; f Restorant-Ali Kali. This memorable dining experience lies in the forest between the visitor centre & the main resort area. A statue of a rearing horse marks the start of the track through the trees. There is no menu; Ali rides up to your table on a white horse (hence the name) with your food & serves it to you from horseback. Then he brings you more, & more, until you can convince him to stop. Fresh fish, meat & bread, all grilled, feature prominently, perhaps thanks to their aerodynamic qualities. Good toilets, with running water & hand wash. *Full meal, with wine* $$$

WHAT TO SEE AND DO The best place to start a visit to Divjaka-Karavasta National Park is the **visitor centre** (free), on the right as you enter the park. It has an excellent exhibition about the national park, with extensive information in English and Albanian.

There are maps showing the places of interest around the park and displays about its flora and the birds and animals in it – pelicans, of course, but also flamingos (in winter) and otters in the River Shkumbini. Interactive exhibits, such as a panel where touching the image of each bird generates a recording of its call, are designed for schoolchildren but are fun for adults too. Bicycles can be hired at the centre and there are public toilets. A tame pelican called Johnny roams the grounds and poses for photos.

An **observation tower** has been erected beside the visitor centre (100 lek) and is well worth the climb for the 360° views of the park from the top. There are viewing platforms on the way to the top.

The shoreline at the Divjaka resort has changed substantially over the last 20 years. The sea is now further away from the resort and a new island, **Turtle Island** (Ishulli i Breshkave), has emerged. A walkway leads to it from the Divjaka Resort Hotel, over a bridge, from where the huge nets the villagers use as fish traps can be seen. There are sun-loungers and a beach bar on the island, and the sand slopes very gently into the sea.

Entrance to the inner lagoon, where the pelicans nest, is strictly controlled, but there are no restrictions on walking along the beach or through the forests outside the protected area, where wooden walkways have been constructed among the pinewoods. There is an access point to the edge of the protected area: follow the track out of the resort, beyond the hotels and shops.

THE BIRDS OF KARAVASTA

The 2019 International Waterbird Census recorded 250 individual Dalmatian pelicans at Karavasta, while in the 2020 breeding season no fewer than 85 pairs were observed, with about 65 fledglings – the highest number of breeding pairs for 40 years. The Dalmatian pelican's numbers are on the increase throughout Europe, not only at Karavasta, and the species is no longer classified as 'vulnerable'.

Karavasta also has Albania's largest heronry, in a tamarisk forest to the north of the national park. When it was discovered in 2015, there were 400–600 nests, including pygmy cormorants (*Microcarbo pygmaeus*), black-crowned night herons (*Nycticorax nycticorax*), squacco herons (*Ardeola ralloides*) and little egrets (*Egretta garzetta*).

The park is very important for wintering waterbirds – the 2019 Waterbird Census recorded over 35,000 individual birds, with 47 distinct species. Unfortunately, this continues the downward trend seen since waterbirds were first systematically monitored at Karavasta; 45,000 individual birds were recorded in 1996 and 68,171 in 1997. The most common species are coots (*Fulica atra*), gulls (Laridae) and at least a dozen species of duck (Anatidae). There are also thousands of flamingos (*Phoenicopterus roseus*), cormorants (*Phalacrocorax carbo*) and pygmy cormorants. The spotted eagle (*Clanga clanga*), classed as 'Endangered' within Europe, regularly winters here. Other interesting birds to look out for include great crested grebes (*Podiceps cristatus*), spoonbills (*Platalea leucorodia*) and curlews (*Numenius arquata*).

Life scientists who would like access to the more protected areas of the national park should request authorisation at the park administration office (m 069 89 00 540; f Administrata-e-Zonave-te-Mbrojtura-Qarku-Fier). Further information can be obtained at the visitor centre in the park.

ELBASANI *Telephone code: 054*

Elbasani's origins lie in the 2nd century BC, when a trading post called Scampa grew up at the junction of the branches of the Via Egnatia, the great Roman road running between the Albanian coast and Byzantium, whose starting points were Dyrrachium and Apollonia. By the 2nd century AD, this had developed into a sizeable way-station called Mansio ad Quintum. During the upheavals and invasions of the 4th century AD, the Romans fortified the settlement and stationed a legion there to protect the Via Egnatia. The castle that they built is right in the centre of the modern town of Elbasani and covers almost $1km^2$.

The castle walls were rebuilt by the Ottomans in 1466, during Mehmed II's expedition against Skanderbeg (see box, page 136). Their plan was to use the fortress as a base for extending their conquest and they gave it the name 'Elbasan', which in Turkish means 'the place for raiding other people's territory'. The town flourished under the Ottomans, and by the 17th century it had become an important commercial centre, exporting its leather, fabrics and silverwork throughout the Ottoman Empire.

In the early 20th century, the town hosted a meeting of intellectuals – the Congress of Elbasani – who agreed to adopt the Roman alphabet as the script for the Albanian language and selected Elbasani as the site of Albania's first teacher-training college. Later, it became the home for many years of Margaret Hasluck, a British archaeologist and ethnographer who went on to direct wartime Special Operations in Albania (see box, page 13). The metallurgical complex called 'The Steel of the Party' was built in 1974, with technical and financial support from China, and it employed over 8,000 people in its heyday. Now, most of the plant lies idle; a Turkish company has taken over part of it, but it is a shadow of its former glory.

GETTING THERE AND AWAY The SH3 highway, with tunnels blasted through the mountains, has cut the journey time between Tirana and Elbasani to under an hour. **Buses** leave Tirana from the Southeast bus station, behind the Faculty of Economics; the fare is 150 lek. There are buses to Elbasani from every other major town in central and southern Albania.

The main **bus station** in Elbasani is rather far from the town centre, on the other side of the railway line. It is not particularly easy to find and it looks quite chaotic once you arrive – but, fortunately, it is better organised than first impressions indicate. Confusingly, Tirana buses terminate in and leave Elbasani not from the bus station, but from the square in front of the sports centre. From the bus station, there are services to every other major town in the country, including to Llixhat (page 107) and to the surrounding villages, such as Shelcani (page 106).

For those with their **own transport**, the old Tirana–Elbasani road is slow and precipitous, but has spectacular views over the Martanesh Mountains. The highest point of the road is almost 931m above sea level; it then hairpins back downhill, passing a series of large Socialist Realist murals on the hillside wall, until the vast steel plant comes into view, spreading for miles at the foot of the mountain.

WHERE TO STAY *Map, opposite*

Guri (12 rooms) Bd Aqif Pasha, Rr Isuf Ibershimi; 257 608; m 069 20 83 089, 069 66 22 626; e hotelguri01@gmail.com; Hotel Guri. Traditional house within the castle walls, nicely renovated, with a small art gallery & museum within one of the towers of the wall. Courtyard

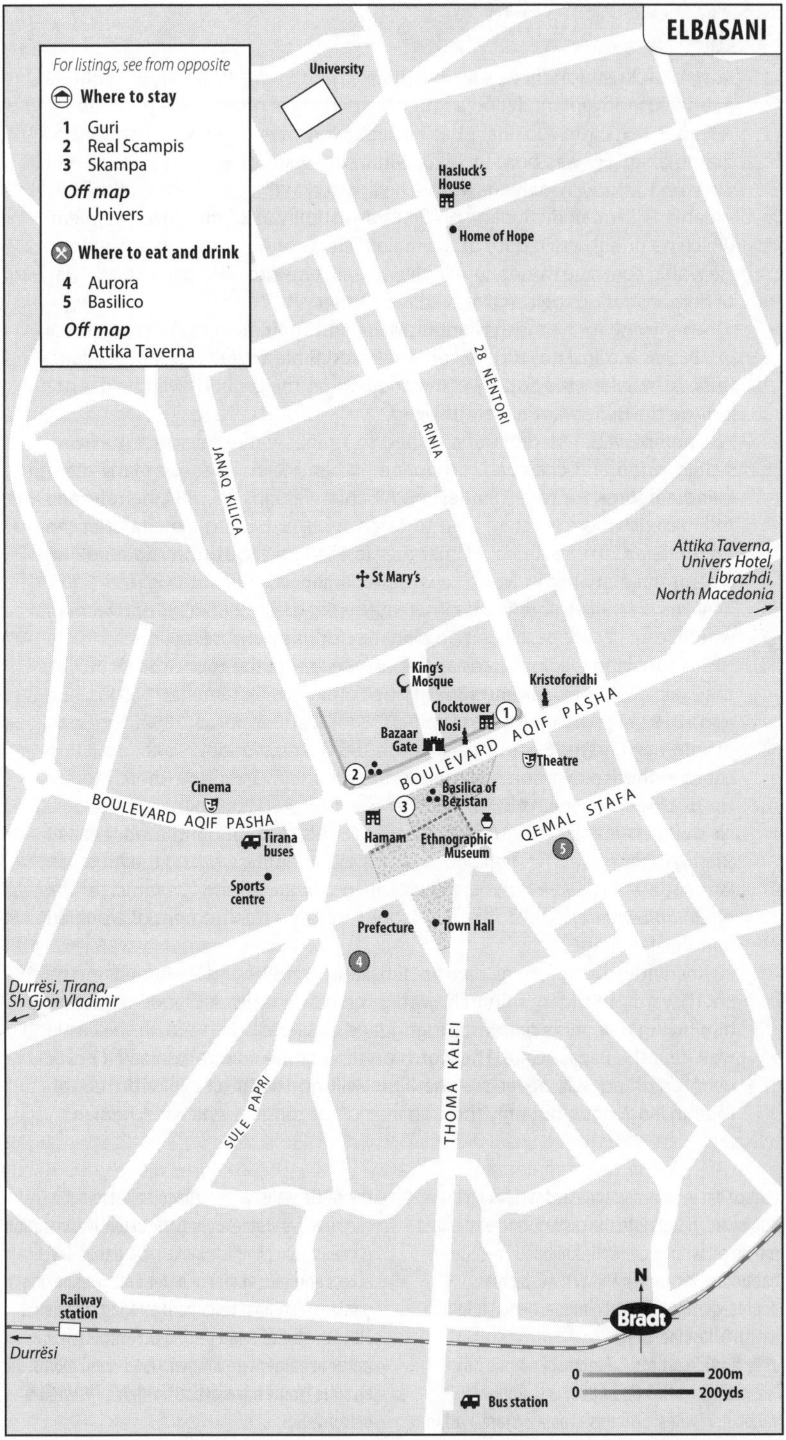
ELBASANI
For listings, see from opposite
Where to stay
1 Guri
2 Real Scampis
3 Skampa
Off map
Univers
Where to eat and drink
4 Aurora
5 Basilico
Off map
Attika Taverna
University
Hasluck's House
Home of Hope
28 NËNTORI
RINIA
JANAQ KILICA
St Mary's
Attika Taverna, Univers Hotel, Librazhdi, North Macedonia
King's Mosque
Kristoforidhi
Clocktower
Nosi
Bazaar Gate
BOULEVARD AQIF PASHA
Theatre
Cinema
Basilica of Bezistan
BOULEVARD AQIF PASHA
Hamam
Ethnographic Museum
QEMAL STAFA
Tirana buses
Sports centre
Prefecture
Town Hall
Durrësi, Tirana, Sh Gjon Vladimir
SULE PAPRI
THOMA KALFI
Railway station
Durrësi
N
Bradt
0 200m
0 200yds
Bus station

KOSTANDIN KRISTOFORIDHI

Kostandin Kristoforidhi was an illustrious figure in the 19th-century cultural nationalist movement, Rilindja Kombëtare. He was prolific as a translator of religious texts into Albanian, but his life's work was as a lexicographer and grammarian. He was born in 1826, within the walls of Elbasani's castle, and went on to study in Ioannina, where he assisted in the preparation of the first Albanian–German dictionary. His first translation was of the New Testament, which he published in both of the main dialects of Albanian, Gheg and Tosk. He would continue throughout his life to translate into both dialects, as a way of demonstrating their similarity to each other.

After living for a time in Istanbul, Malta and Tunis, he returned to Istanbul in 1865 as a translator for the London-based Bible Society. He worked for it until 1874, when the Society dismissed him on the grounds that he did not believe the Bible was divinely inspired.

Unemployed, Kristoforidhi returned to Tirana, where he scraped a living selling wood and charcoal, and opened a bar. Meanwhile, like many other Rilindja figures, he gave clandestine Albanian lessons. In 1884, he returned to Elbasani, where he continued to teach secretly. He was a member of the Commission on the Alphabet that met in the late 1860s to try to agree on a common alphabet in which to write Albanian; it would not be until 1909, 14 years after Kristoforidhi's death, that the congress held in his native town would formally adopt the Roman alphabet for this purpose.

His surviving religious translations are versions of the Four Gospels (1866), the Psalms (1868 in Tosk and 1869 in Gheg), the New Testament (1869 in Gheg and 1879 in Tosk), Genesis and Exodus (1880), Deuteronomy (1882), the Song of Solomon and the Book of Isaiah (both 1884). Kristoforidhi's Tosk translation is the authorised version still used in the Albanian Orthodox Church today. He published a Gheg ABC in 1867, and a Tosk ABC the following year. He also wrote Albanian-language textbooks for his students, and a story called *Gjahu i malësorëve* (*The Highlanders' Hunt*). His scientific work on the Albanian language – his *Dictionary of the Albanian Language* and *Grammar of the Albanian Language* – laid the foundations for the establishment of a unified national language.

Kostandin Kristoforidhi died in Elbasani in 1895 and is buried in the churchyard of St Mary's Church, within the castle walls. A plaque depicting him giving one of his clandestine language classes can be seen on the castle wall near the Bazaar Gate. The words on the plaque read: 'Albania will never learn anything, will never see the light, will not be at all civilised through foreign languages, but only through its mother tongue, which is Albanian.'

terrace bar in summer; some rooms look on to Boulevard, others into the castle. Generously sized rooms, all with large, well-equipped en-suite bathrooms inc superb shower; AC, biomass CH, double-glazing; TV, Wi-Fi, fridge, period furniture. Lavish b/fast inc. **$$$**

Real Scampis (7 rooms) Rr Janaq Kilica; 255 575; m 069 82 22 880; e scampisreal@yahoo.it; f Real Scampis - Faqja Zyrtare. Within the castle walls, with archaeological remains conserved & visible around the extensive, beautiful gardens. Good English spoken; car park & level-access entrance at rear of hotel. Café overlooking gardens; excellent restaurant offering traditional Elbasani dishes & interesting chef's specials; live music in gardens in summer. Good-sized rooms, all en suite (some have jacuzzi) with AC, TV, Wi-Fi & balcony. **$$**

Skampa (7 rooms) Bd Aqif Pasha; 512 661. Part of the former 'Turizmi', renovated in 2012. Wi-Fi throughout, strongest in rooms closest to router; fantastic views of castle or mountains. Bar, restaurant; some English spoken at reception. All rooms en suite with AC, TV. **$$**

Univers (14 rooms) Lagja Emin Matraxhiu, Ura e Bakallit; 256 193; m 069 40 71 278, 069 40 71 277; e univers.hotel@yahoo.com, univershoteli@gmail.com; w univershotel.eu. On the eastern outskirts of town, ideal for those with their own transport. Quiet, modern & comfortable; good restaurant, bar; free secure parking; Wi-Fi throughout; conference room; outdoor swimming pool (in summer); peaceful gardens. English spoken; 24-hour reception. All rooms en suite with AC, TV, fridge; most have balcony or terrace. **$$**

WHERE TO EAT *Map, page 101*

Attika Taverna Rr Kozma Naska (near Ura e Bakallit); 243 583; m 068 20 71 290. A range of unusual & delicious dishes, neither traditionally Albanian nor, despite the restaurant's name, noticeably Greek. Carnivores will enjoy Sofra e Pashait ('the Pasha's Table'); lots of cheese treats for vegetarians. $$$

Aurora Central location, behind Prefecture & Town Hall; 1st-floor terrace with view of city & mountains. $$$

Basilico Rr Rinia; m 068 85 40 000. The best pizzas in town, plus other Italian-inspired dishes. $$$

WHAT TO SEE AND DO

The old town The surviving castle walls run along one side of Rruga Aqif Pasha and down the streets perpendicular to it. Within them lie Roman remains, including traces of the Via Egnatia, one of the oldest mosques in Albania, and a fine Orthodox church. The 60m-high clock tower, set into one of the bastions of the wall, was built in 1899. The castle had four entrances through the walls, one of them now the pedestrian entrance to the Real Scampis hotel.

To find the **King's Mosque** (Xhamia e Mbretit), enter the old town through the **Bazaar Gate** – the archway with lion fountains on either side. The street forks just inside the entrance; the left-hand fork will bring you straight to the King's Mosque – one of the oldest in Albania. Construction began in 1492, the year Columbus discovered the New World. The building was neglected under communism, though not deliberately damaged, and the interior has been substantially, though faithfully, renovated.

From the mosque, **St Mary's Church** (Kisha e Shënmërisë) is a couple of hundred metres deeper into the old town, bearing in the same direction. A church was first built on this site in 1486, with renovations and additions made over the centuries. In the garden, as you enter the churchyard, is the tomb of the 19th-century lexicographer and grammarian Kostandin Kristoforidhi (see box, opposite). The church was used by the army for storage after the atheism campaign of 1967, but the fabric of the building was saved from wanton destruction by the cobbled streets of Elbasani's old town, which are too narrow for bulldozers. The interior walls of the church were covered in frescoes until they were whitewashed during the atheism campaign; the only ones that survive are the Pantocrator in the dome and the early 20th-century fresco on the south wall. The iconostasis, however, is the original, intricately carved in boxwood in 1870 by craftsmen from the district of Dibra, famous at the time for the skill of its woodworkers. The icons of St Michael and St Gabriel were painted in 1659 by the great Albanian artist Onufri (page 262).

The Basilica of Bezistan Across the street from the Bazaar Gate, next to the Skampa hotel, stands a plane tree (*rrapi*) known locally as Rrapi i Bezistanit. 'Bezistan' is a word from Ottoman times, meaning 'a covered marketplace'.

Elbasani's covered market is long gone, but the plane tree remains and has traditionally served as a meeting place for locals. Now it has given its name to the archaeological remains that lie below it: a 5th-century basilica, discovered and excavated as recently as 2007.

The church was of the usual paleochristian layout, with a central nave, subsidiary naves on either side and a narthex, or entrance porch. Beautiful mosaics paved the floors of the narthex and nave; photos of some of them can be seen on the information panel at the entrance to the site, which is fortunate since – as is almost always the case in Albania – they are covered to protect them and cannot be viewed. The site, however, is open for anyone to look around; it is unattended and there is no admission charge.

In the late 17th century, the Ottomans built a **bathhouse** (*hamam*) opposite the castle. It is so close to the Bezistan plane – although now it is separated from it by the modern hotel building – that it must have been linked to the market. The surviving structure mostly dates from the 19th century. Unfortunately, it is not open to the public at the time of writing and it is difficult to get close enough for a good view of the attractive tiled domes on its roof.

MARGARET HASLUCK

The combination of archaeology, ethnography and wartime special operations is not a classic career path, yet Margaret Hasluck achieved success in all three fields. She spent 16 years in Albania, researching and publishing on topics as diverse as Roma customs, Albanian grammar and blood feud. In 1935, she settled in Elbasani, where she is remembered to this day as *anglezka*, 'the little Englishwoman'.

The 'Englishwoman' was born in northeast Scotland in 1885, the daughter of a farmer, John Hardie. Despite her humble origins, she went on to study classics at Aberdeen, one of Scotland's four ancient universities, which had opened its faculties to women in 1892. She graduated from Aberdeen in 1907 and continued her studies at Cambridge University, where (it should be recalled) women were not awarded degree titles until 1921.

This remarkable young woman then turned her attention to archaeology. She studied at the prestigious British School in Athens (the BSA) and took part in excavations in Turkey. In 1912, she married Frederick Hasluck, whom she had met at the BSA.

Their married life would be short, however; Frederick Hasluck died of tuberculosis in 1920. He had published research on the followers of Bektashism (page 23), and his widow used a travel grant from Aberdeen University to return to Albania and conduct her own ethnographic fieldwork there. She became an expert on the customs and traditions of the northern clans, including blood feud – her comprehensive study, *The Unwritten Law in Albania*, was published posthumously; she learned the language well enough to publish *Këndime anglisht-shqip*, a collection of stories which illustrate points of Albanian grammar and vocabulary; and she conducted extensive field research in the mountain villages of Shpati, near Elbasani (page 106). There, she became friendly with Lefter (Lef) Nosi, an intellectual and politician who was a signatory of Albania's Declaration of Independence and had served in the country's first government. Over the years, they worked together investigating Albanian folklore and ethnography. In 1936, Nosi sold her a plot of land in Elbasani on which she had a house built.

Ethnographic Museum (⌚ 08.30–15.30 Mon–Fri, 09.15–13.45 Sat–Sun; 100 lek) At the edge of the town's central park, a characteristic Ottoman house with a covered balcony (*çardak*), built in the 18th century, sits in an attractive garden. In 1908, it became Elbasani's first Albanian-medium school and, in 1986, it was converted into the Ethnographic Museum you see today. There are explanatory panels throughout the museum, in Albanian and English.

Traditionally, the ground floor of an Albanian house was used for workshops, storage and – in rural areas – the stabling of livestock. The museum has used this space to present the early history and archaeological record of the region. The first mention of the town – as Scampis – is on the *stela* (tombstone) of a Roman legionary, Marcus Sabidus, which is on display here.

In the 17th century, Elbasani was an important commercial centre, exporting its leather, fabrics and silverwork throughout the Ottoman Empire. Its craftsmen were organised in no fewer than 45 guilds; the Tanners' Guild had a written statute as early as 1658. These guilds, and the work in which each of them specialised, are presented in two side rooms on the ground floor. One room is devoted to wool-working, including the making of felt. The different types of *qeleshë*, or fez, are displayed and explained.

In April 1939, just before Italy invaded and annexed Albania, Margaret Hasluck was expelled from the country. She ended up in Cairo where, in early 1942, SOE (see boxes, pages 13 and 14) recruited her to explore possible ways to encourage resistance in occupied Albania. By 1943, she was the head of SOE's Albanian section. She briefed SOE operatives before they were parachuted into Albania, taught them the rudiments of the language, and provided and collated intelligence.

As SOE came to concentrate on supporting the partisans, at the expense of the non-communist resistance, Margaret Hasluck became increasingly disillusioned. She resigned from SOE in 1944, around the same time as she was diagnosed with leukaemia and told she had only a short time left to live. She was awarded the MBE for her services in 1944.

Meanwhile, Lef Nosi had agreed to participate in the Council of Regency, the Albanian quisling government set up by the Germans after Italy's capitulation. After Albania's liberation, not surprisingly, he was tried and shot. Margaret Hasluck wrote a personal letter to Enver Hoxha, pleading for clemency for her friend. Not only was her appeal unsuccessful, but the communist government put it about that she and Nosi had been lovers, in an attempt to destroy both of their reputations.

Margaret Hasluck died of her leukaemia in October 1948, and is buried with her parents, brothers and sisters in the churchyard of the Scottish village of Dallas. Her house in Elbasani, built on the land she bought from Lef Nosi, is now a state kindergarten. Across the street, also on her land, is a children's home, where there is a plaque on the wall outside, unveiled by her nephew in 2010 in commemoration of the 125th anniversary of her birth. A statue of her friend Lef Nosi now stands on Rruga Aqif Pasha, in front of the castle walls.

She sent many ethnographic artefacts back to her *alma mater*, Aberdeen University, including unusual items such as medicinal minerals and herbs, amulets and children's toys; over 100 of these items can be viewed in the university's image database (w digitool.abdn.ac.uk). Some of the folk tales that she and Nosi collected and translated together have been published; see page 294 for details of this and *The Unwritten Law in Albania*.

The other is 'the room of metal and wood', including tobacco production, which started locally in the early 18th century. An intriguing bladed device is a tobacco-cutter, of a design still used in the Albanian countryside today – the whole leaves are bundled into the hopper and pushed through with one hand while the other hand works the chopper. Elbasani was famous for the skill of its gunsmiths, whose guild was already established by the second half of the 16th century, and there are several examples of locally made rifles. Another interesting exhibit is a set of bells, in different sizes for different animals, including an extraordinarily heavy cow bell.

Upstairs, the covered balcony has photographs, displays and costumes illustrating Elbasani traditions and culture. The rooms leading off this central space each had their own function. The 'bride's room' has a 250-year-old mirror and dowry chests from the 1930s, while the 'men's room' has a fine plaster fireplace (*oxhak*), an ornately carved wooden ceiling and storage cupboards with carved doors. Finally, the 'girls' workroom' has information about the making of lace and silk, with a silk-weaving loom and examples of the beautiful finished products.

EXCURSIONS FROM ELBASANI Top of the excursions list, for anyone with even the slightest interest in religious art, is the Church of St Nicholas at **Shelcani**. This 14th-century church somehow escaped the whitewashers of the atheism campaign. Its interior walls are completely covered with magnificent frescoes painted, in 1554, by the great Albanian artist Onufri. Better still, the frescoes have been cleaned by specialists from the Albanian Institute of Monuments. Images of saints and scenes from the New Testament, such as Lazarus rising from the grave and Christ entering Jerusalem on Palm Sunday, glow in radiant colours. Shelcani is in the Shpati Mountains to the southeast of Elbasani, where Margaret Hasluck conducted much of her ethnographic research (see box, page 104). The road is asphalted most of the way, apart from the last 100m or so up to the church, and it takes about 45 minutes to get there from Elbasani. At the start of the track up to the church, there is a small signpost ('Kisha Shën Kollit') and space to park.

The National Historical Museum in Tirana (page 74) has the original doorway and several icons from the church of **St Gjon Vladimir**, part of a medieval monastery about 5km from Elbasani on the old road to Tirana. According to the inscriptions on the lintel, the church was built by Karl Topia, 'lord of Arbër', in 1382, after an earthquake had destroyed the church that previously stood on the site. Karl Topia was one of the powerful feudal princes who, between them, ruled Albania from the middle of the 14th century until the Ottoman conquest. The church itself is set in a peaceful garden, with the monastic buildings to the side. They are attractive buildings, but the church has been completely restored internally, apart from a large fresco which survives in poor condition behind the altar. It is known locally (for example, by taxi drivers) as Kisha e Shijonit, the Church of Shijoni.

The best-preserved piece of Elbasani's Roman heritage is **Mansio ad Quintum**, a few minutes' drive southwest out of town. The original trading post that grew up at the junction of the Apollonia and Dyrrachium branches of the Via Egnatia developed over the years into something much more substantial – an official roadhouse, or *mansio*. Every major Roman road had these; they were intended to provide accommodation and entertainment for government officials and others travelling on important business. Mansio ad Quintum had a bathhouse (how could it not?) and shops as well as accommodation; the baths' hypocausts are particularly impressive. The site is up a track just off the main road towards Durrësi, near the village of Bradasheshi. It is unattended and can be accessed at any time.

Llixhat, the Albanian word for 'spa', is an area of thermal springs about 12km from Elbasani. The water here was first analysed scientifically in 1924, at the behest of Lef Nosi's brother, Grigor. In 1932, he built the very first spa hotel in Albania, to an Austrian design. The surrounding grounds – over 50,000m^2 – are partly wooded and partly laid out as gardens. This lovely historic building is still standing at the time of writing, but it has been on the market for some time and requires major investment to bring the accommodation up to international standards. Llixhat is about 30 minutes' drive from Elbasani, following the road towards Gramshi. 'LLixha' buses operate from the bus station in Elbasani.

Two nice places for **day hikes** around Elbasani are Lake Banja, an artificial lake created in the 1980s for hydro-electric power generation, although it was never operational; and the gently rolling hills around the (natural) lakes of Belshi, both about an hour's drive away. For those who would prefer to spend longer in these attractive spots, there are hotels in Belshi and in Gramshi, at the southern end of Lake Banja. Buses to both towns leave several times a day from the bus station in Elbasani. If you have your own transport (with two or four wheels), you could continue from Gramshi to Korça (page 190), along the River Devolli, or from Belshi to Kuçova, in the Berati region. The road between Gramshi and Maliqi is rather rough and a 4x4 would probably be needed, particularly in wet weather.

PËLLUMBASI

The small village of Pëllumbasi sits at the southernmost tip of the Dajti massif, which runs southeast–northwest to Kruja (page 108). It can easily be visited in a day trip from Tirana or on a detour en route to or from Elbasani, but it would also make a good base for a few days' hiking or relaxing in the mountain air.

Pëllumbasi has several restaurants and guesthouses, which have developed quite recently in response to increasing numbers of visitors to its eponymous cave, also known as the **Black Cave** (Shpella e Zezë). The cave is 360m long and has a series of chambers filled with wonderful stalagmites and stalactites. Archaeological research has shown that it was inhabited by humans at various points between the Stone Age and the early Middle Ages, and by cave bears (*Ursus spelaeus*) a long time before that. (Cave bears became extinct about 27,500 years ago.) There are also, as one would expect, many bats (see box, page 4). Unfortunately, there are many fewer now than there were before the cave started to attract visitors –in the 1990s, a colony of 5,000 specimens was reported in the cave, whereas more recent monitoring has found as few as 100. The use of candles within the cave is particularly dangerous for the bats, as is lighting fires at the entrance.

The 'Black Cave' Info-Point in the village has a map of the cave on display and English-speaking staff who can explain its history. Torches can be rented here. It takes about an hour to walk up to the cave entrance from the village; the path climbs steeply through the villagers' fields, emerging into the beautiful Skorana Gorge, with the River Erzeni flowing far below you. There are wooden signs, steps at the steepest parts and handrails at the most slippery parts.

Returning to the village afterwards, you can walk down to the river for a swim (there is a path to the river from the cave, but it is very steep), or enjoy a meal of traditional central Albanian specialities, perhaps at the restaurant run by the managers of the Info-Point (vegetarian meals available). A short leaflet about the various things to do in the area can be downloaded from w pellumbascave.weebly.com.

GETTING THERE AND AWAY To get to Pëllumbasi from Tirana, take the highway towards Elbasani and turn off at the village of Iba; from there it is a couple of kilometres up an asphalted road to Pëllumbasi. There are three buses a day to Pëllumbasi from Tirana; they leave the Southeast bus station at 07.00, noon and 17.00. The last bus out of Pëllumbasi leaves around 18.00 and goes only as far as Iba; buses for Tirana or Elbasani can be flagged down on the main road.

WHERE TO STAY

The House in the Village (2 rooms) m 069 32 19 555; w thehouseinthevillage.org. A superb base for a short (or longer) stay in Pëllumbasi. A simple guesthouse operated by the people behind the Tirana Backpacker hostel, set in extensive grounds with fruit trees & olives. 2 small dorms on 1st floor; 1 has traditional open fireplace (*oxhak*); 2 shared showers & toilets downstairs; landscaped campsite (**$**) above orchard. Kitchen, laundry facilities, communal rest area, firepit, interactive 'museum' with traditional artefacts & activities; water from well; bicycles available; large balcony with wonderful views. **$$**

PETRELA CASTLE Petrela is a small but historically interesting castle. It was a strategic link in Skanderbeg's system of communication (page 112) and is said to have been where his sister Mamica lived. The earliest phase of the castle is the Roman watchtower. The fortifications were expanded in the late Roman period and it became an important fortress in the 12th century.

To reach the castle from Elbasani, the best option is to leave the SH3 highway at Iba and take the old road north to the Petrela turn-off, just before the bridge over the River Erzeni. From Tirana, take the SH3 highway towards Elbasani and leave it at Mulleti. Cross the Erzeni and take the first right for Petrela. The castle is clearly visible from the highway, perched high up on a crag on the other side of the river. Cars can be parked in the village square, from where it is a 5-minute walk up to the castle.

KRUJA *Telephone code: 0511*

Kruja has been fortified since ancient times – ceramics and coins from the 3rd century BC have been excavated there. The name comes from the Albanian word for the spring (*krua*), within the castle, which provided its inhabitants with water. The castle of Kruja was the centre of Albanian resistance to the Ottoman invasion in the 15th century, which was led by the great national hero Gjergj Kastrioti, also known as Skanderbeg (see box, page 136). The buildings and museums within the castle walls, combined with the attractively restored bazaar area just outside them, provide an excellent introduction to Albanian history and traditions. Kruja is the only town in Albania, apart from Saranda in the far south, which is really geared towards tourists; it is one of the best places in the country to shop for souvenirs.

Kruja was the northernmost stronghold of Bektashism (page 23) – it was the Kruja *baba* (father) who is said to have converted Ali Pasha Tepelena (see box, page 218). Apart from the lovely *teqe* within the castle, Kruja is linked with the 13th-century Sufi saint Sari Salltëk: a *teqe* above the town is dedicated to him and, just off the road that leads up to the town, is a rock where his foot is supposed to have left its print in the stone as he strode up from the plain. There is an asphalted road to the *teqe* and also a steep footpath; it takes about an hour to get there on foot.

GETTING THERE AND AWAY Kruja is about an hour's drive from both Tirana and Durrësi. The town at the junction with the SH1 highway is called Fushë-Kruja

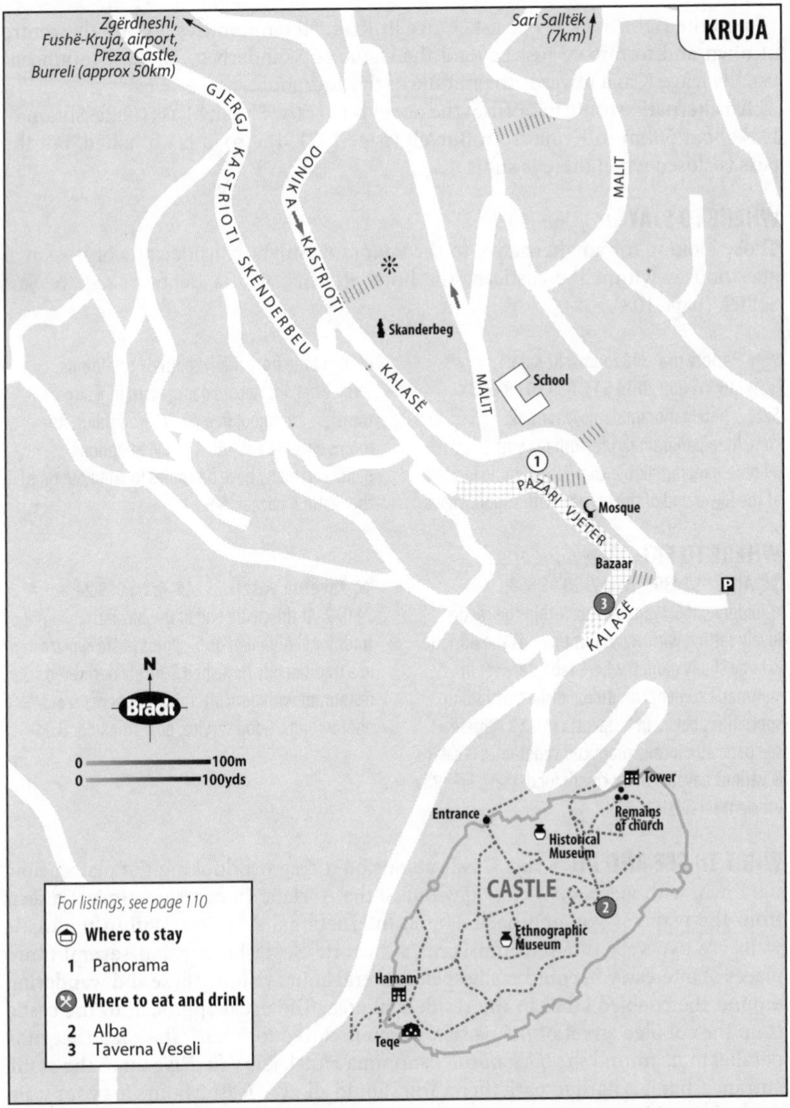

('Kruja on the Plain'); if you are driving yourself, it is worth pausing briefly in Fushë-Kruja to take a look at the statue of US President George W Bush, who visited the town in 2007 (and allegedly had his watch stolen during his visit).

Kruja is less than an hour's drive from Tirana International Airport. This makes it an attractive option to spend your last night, or your last morning, in Kruja and go from there directly to the airport. A taxi from Kruja to the airport should cost €15–20.

Minibuses leave Tirana from the North/South bus station (page 60), with departures from early morning to late afternoon; the fare is 200 lek. You should take care to board a vehicle that is going all the way up the hill to Kruja; there are more frequent minibuses that go only as far as Fushë-Kruja. The drivers will keep you on the right track if you ask. Once in Kruja, the minibuses go into the centre of town and terminate just beyond the statue of Skanderbeg. The last minibuses usually leave Kruja towards the middle of the afternoon.

An alternative route to or from the north is over the Shtama Pass (Qafë-Shtama). It is about 50km to Kruja from Burreli (page 142). The road is asphalted, but the pass is closed when there is snow.

WHERE TO STAY *Map, page 109*

Those looking for an alternative to the Panorama might consider one of the small guesthouses within the castle or the hotel attached to the Bektashi *teqe* of Sari Salltëk (page 108).

Panorama (18 rooms) Rr Kala; 24336; m 069 20 34 533, 069 20 98 528; e hotelpanoramakruje@hotmail.com, hotelpanoramakruje@gmail.com; w hotelpanoramakruje.com. Unbeatable location at the lower end of the bazaar, with superb views of the castle from many rooms. Restaurants, terrace bar, lift, secure garage parking, airport transfers arranged, free Wi-Fi throughout. All rooms en suite with AC, LCD TV, telephone, hairdryer; many have balconies looking out on to the castle & bazaar. **$$**

WHERE TO EAT *Map, page 109*

Alba 24390; m 069 20 95 858; e lulderveni66@yahoo.com. Within the castle; lovely setting with views out towards the Adriatic & large shady garden where tables are set in summer. Excellent traditional dishes, including specialities baked in terracotta (*tavë* & *fergesë* – see page 49), locally produced vegetables & salads & various flavours of ice cream for dessert. Friendly, efficient service. **$$$**

Taverna Veseli 24416; m 069 24 24 079. At the castle end of the bazaar. Traditional Albanian dishes, plus pasta & pizza, in a traditionally furnished & nicely decorated restaurant with agricultural implements & old photographs. Good service; non-smoking. **$$$**

WHAT TO SEE AND DO Kruja Castle stands on a crag overlooking the plain below the town, with views on a clear day out to the Adriatic (it can sometimes be seen from the plane as you approach Tirana International Airport). Within the castle walls are two very different museums, a historic Bektashi *teqe* and several other places of interest; you could easily spend several hours visiting these and wandering around the cobbled lanes in the residential area. The usual approach to the castle is up the cobbled street of the bazaar, which is closed to traffic. The road that runs parallel to it, around the back of the Panorama Hotel, lets you drive up to the castle entrance, but it is hard to park there. You should allow at least 2 hours for your visit, more if possible.

Historical Museum (09.00–14.00 & 16.00–19.00 Tue–Sat, 09.00–19.00 Sun; 200 lek) On your left as you emerge from the vaulted entranceway is the Historical Museum, designed in 1982 in a sort of castle-ish style by the architects Pranvera Hoxha – daughter of the communist leader Enver – and her husband. The displays on the ground floor cover the Illyrian city-states, the Roman and Byzantine periods and the development of Albania's medieval principalities. Then comes the story of Albania's struggle against the Ottomans, told through maps, murals, books and replicas. On the upper floors, there are scale models of Kruja and other castles, in a room with an etched-glass window showing the second siege of Kruja, and an exhibition focusing on Skanderbeg's diplomatic efforts to rally support from other

European countries for the resistance. In clear weather, there are good views from the upper terrace over the Kruja Plain towards the sea.

The Historical Museum is sometimes criticised for its idolatry of Skanderbeg and the implied parallel with the personality cult around Enver Hoxha, and it is true that the relentless 'Skanderfest' can become a little wearing. In fairness, however, he was probably the most significant single individual in the entire history of Albania and the museum is a well-presented introduction to this period of Albanian history. Almost none of the information is translated; non-Albanian visitors are expected to use the services (free of charge) of one of the museum's guides, who are knowledgeable and multilingual. The ticket desk stocks publications in a range of languages about Skanderbeg and the items in the museum.

Ethnographic Museum (🕘 09.00–13.00 & 16.00–19.00 Tue–Sun; 300 lek) One of the most interesting ethnographic museums in the country lies opposite the entrance to Kruja Castle (from where the sign is clearly visible). Its interest is partly due to the house in which it is located, designed for the prosperous and influential Toptani family (page 77) and built in 1764. Laminated information sheets, in English and Albanian, explain the items on display.

The ground floor of the house is where the livestock were kept, the produce from the family's lands was processed and the tools were made or repaired. There is a raki still (page 51), an olive press and equipment for making felt, one of Kruja's traditional industries. The herdsman slept in the stable, with the sheep and/or goats, while the family lived upstairs, in rooms accessed from the covered balcony that was used as the living space in summer. The doorways off the balcony have a stepped threshold, to keep out draughts once the door was closed, and an arch so that those entering had to lower their heads, thus showing respect to those within. Some of the rooms have been maintained with their original 18th-century furniture, frescoes and carved wooden panelling. The reception room, where (male) visitors would be welcomed and entertained by the men of the house, has a beautifully painted ceiling and an enclosed gallery, with a couple of small windows, where the women could sit without being seen by their male relatives' visitors. The room in which the family ate and slept also has a gallery, although it is not walled; this was where the children slept and played, out from under their parents' feet. The large fireplace heated not only the room, but also the water for the house's own steam bath, or *hamam*. The museum also has a rich collection of traditional costumes and jewellery.

A walk around the citadel Ordinary families still live within Kruja Castle, although in less luxurious houses than the Toptani house. A network of cobbled alleyways spreads downhill from the open area where the museums are. Down one of these is the castle's beautiful little Bektashi ***teqe*** (100 lek). Bektashism is a Sufi order, founded in Persia in the 13th century; it was introduced to Albania in the wake of the Ottoman conquest and became widespread there in the early 19th century. The Kruja *teqe* was built in 1770 (1191 in the Islamic *hijri* calendar) and is one of the oldest in the country. The olive tree in its garden is said to have been planted by Skanderbeg himself, as part of his campaign to encourage the other landowners of Kruja to plant olives.

A *teqe* is not a mosque, but it is a holy place; visitors must remove their shoes before entering. The Kruja *teqe* was used for storage after religion was banned in 1967; it was restored by local Bektashis after freedom of worship was regained in 1990. It is a small, simple building, housing the tombs of past *babas* and is decorated inside with rugs, embroideries and pictures given to the *teqe* by Bektashis around the world.

To find the *teqe* from the open area between the museums, look for its dome and head down the winding paths aiming for it. It is reached up a flight of steps through a stone arch. Across from the foot of the steps is a **bathhouse** (*hamam*), five centuries old; the earthenware pipes which can be seen were installed, it is said, by Skanderbeg as a technological innovation that he had learned during his years at court in Constantinople.

At the other end of the citadel, up at the top beyond the museums, the **tower** was originally a lookout and signalling post. Skanderbeg used this castle as part of a chain of communication running the length of Albania. In a mountainous country like this, beacons had to be strategically located so that each could be seen, along valleys or passes, from two others in the chain. From Kruja, the beacon could be seen by troops in the fortresses at Preza and Rodoni (opposite and page 97, respectively). Beside the tower, on the other side of a retaining wall, are the **remains of a medieval church**, with a couple of surviving fragments of fresco. The lack of maintenance of this church is disgraceful and the frescoes are unlikely to survive much longer.

The bazaar The bazaar was restored in the mid 1960s, but the wood-built shops and cobbled streets have a very authentically Ottoman feel. The extra-long eaves and the gutter in the middle of the road mean that rain, or wet snow, falls off the roofs and drains downhill straight away – an unusual but effective architectural device. Many of the shops sell small souvenirs such as Albanian flags, copper plates and ashtrays in the shape of bunkers. There are also traditional felt-makers, who produce slippers and the felt caps called *qeleshe*; carpet shops, in some of which you can watch the local women weaving the next batch of *qilime* (woven rugs; this is the same word as the Turkish *kilim*) with their ancient patterns; and antique dealers, where wooden butter paddles, cradles and intricately carved dowry chests pause in their journeys from highland villages to modern cities. Kruja's bazaar is a laid-back place and nobody will mind if all you want to do is window-shop.

AROUND KRUJA

Zgërdheshi Archaeologists think that the Illyrian ruins at Zgërdheshi may have been the city of Albanopolis, mentioned by Ptolemy (in the 2nd century AD) as the capital of Arbanon, the name from which Albania has taken its modern name. Built, like all Illyrian cities, on a hilltop, Zgërdheshi was fortified in two stages – first the acropolis, in the early Iron Age (c1000BC), and then a larger area, with the construction of defensive walls, in the 4th or 3rd century BC. A third phase, in the 2nd century BC, saw the city expand beyond the western fortifications. The first section you come to is the Illyrian circuit wall, built with the huge stone blocks characteristic of Illyrian fortification, and the remains of watchtowers that were positioned along this wall. The main fortified area covers 10ha and the buildings within it were constructed on terraces. Traces of the terrace walls are still visible, as are postholes and drainage channels in the bedrock. The acropolis is difficult to interpret without a specialist guide, but it is worth the climb for the views westwards to the Adriatic. Wild flowers and herbs grow all around. (I am grateful to Oliver Gilkes for the information on Zgërdheshi in his *Archaeological Guide*; see page 295 for bibliographical details.)

The turn-off for Zgërdheshi is about 5km out of Fushë-Kruja on the road towards Kruja itself. It is signposted at the junction, but not thereafter. You can drive as far as the circuit wall and towers, although the road is unpaved most of the way.

Any Kruja minibus will let you off at the junction; it takes 15–20 minutes to walk up to the circuit wall.

Preza Castle Preza was one of the strategic links in the communications system mentioned opposite. It occupies a splendid position, with sightlines to Kruja to its northeast and, beyond Tirana, Petrela Castle (page 108). Preza Castle was first fortified in the 14th century by Karl Topia (page 106), ready for Skanderbeg to use in the following century. It is rectangular in form, with a watchtower at each corner. The western wall, which was most vulnerable to attack, also had a square tower; the ruins of this and of two of the round towers can still be clearly seen. The only gate was in the southern wall; after the Ottoman conquest, a mosque was built at this spot.

On the site of the northeastern watchtower, a café has been built, with a viewing platform above it. This offers magnificent views all around, including of the planes on the airport runway; binoculars are provided. The café toilets are clean and have running water. There are steps up to the castle and the café from the car park; there is also a restaurant, entered from the car park. Even for those who are not particularly interested in castles, Preza is so close to the airport and has such good views that it makes a nice farewell stop before checking in.

5

The North

The unspoilt wildernesses of northern Albania are a magnet for hikers and other lovers of the outdoors. It is rich in wildlife, with waterbirds in its coastal wetlands, wildcats and lynx in its mountains. Yet the north also has cultural riches: the traditional stone houses and watermills in its villages; its Illyrian castles and Ottoman bridges; the 19th-century artists and architects of its Italian-influenced cities. The north is the heartland of the Catholic faith in Albania. Great poets have written in Albanian's northern dialect, Gheg. All this and more is to be found in this chapter.

GETTING THERE AND AWAY

BY AIR Northern Albania is very accessible from Tirana Airport. A right turn at the exit from the airport will lead you to the SH1, the main north–south highway. From there it is about 20km to the Miloti interchange, where you turn right for Mati, Mirdita and Tropoja, or continue straight on for Shkodra, Lake Komani and Puka. At the time of writing, there are no buses from the airport to northern Albania. The junction with the main highway is 2.8km from the airport – a short taxi ride, or even walkable – from where inter-city northbound buses can be flagged down.

A new airport opened in 2021 at Kukësi (page 152); up-to-date information about flights there can be found on its website: w kuiport.al.

BY LAND From **Tirana**, buses to all the towns in this chapter leave from the North/South bus station. The junction of the coastal highway (SH1) and the highway to Kosovo (A1) is known as Miloti. Any bus will drop off or pick up passengers at Miloti; it is often quicker to change there than to wait for a through bus to or from some of the more remote towns. For **Peshkopia**, the quickest route from Tirana is the new road called Rruga e Arbërit, provisionally inaugurated at the end of 2021.

There are many bus services between all the main cities of **Kosovo** and Tirana. They use the A1 highway and can drop passengers off at Kukësi as well as Miloti. Those with their own transport have the alternative of the old road from Kukësi, via the beautiful district of Puka. This road is in poor repair, but has almost no traffic; it is justifiably popular with foreign motorcyclists.

From **Montenegro**, the main border crossing is at Hani i Hotit; on the Montenegrin side the crossing is called Božaj. The Montenegrin company Old Town Travel (☎ +382 32 520 495; e info@kotortotirana.com; w kotortotirana.com) operates a daily bus service between Kotor and Tirana, with stops in Budva, Podgorica and Shkodra. The whole trip takes about 6 hours; between Shkodra and Podgorica, about 2 hours, depending on how long it takes to get across the border. The departure time from both Shkodra and Podgorica is 10.00 (Tirana and Kotor 2 hours earlier). The bus leaves from outside the Rozafa Hotel in Shkodra and from the main bus terminal in Podgorica. The one-way fare is €10 between

Shkodra and Podgorica; €25 between Tirana and Kotor. Tickets can be bought online (w busticket4.me), at Osumi travel agencies or from the bus driver. A taxi from Shkodra to Podgorica airport costs around €35.

Other vehicular routes into northern Albania from Montenegro are from Ulqini, via the border post at Muriqani (see below), and from Plava via Kelmendi (page 164). On **foot** only, the border can also be crossed between Vuthaj (Vusanje) and Thethi or Valbona; see pages 171 and 157 for details of these hiking routes and page 45 for the difficulties of arranging border-crossing permits. There are no passenger trains across any of Albania's borders, although the Albanian government has announced an ambition to reinstate the service between Shkodra and Podgorica some day.

BY SEA Information about entering Albania by private yacht can be found on page 33. For lesser mortals, there are two ways to get to northern Albania by sea from Italy: one is to take a ferry from Ancona or Bari to Bar (called Tivari in Albanian) in Montenegro, then continue to Shkodra via Ulqini, 26km away. The other is to take a ferry to Durrësi and drive or take a bus from there to any of the destinations in this chapter.

SHKODRA *Telephone code: 02*

Shkodra has been a highly significant city during most of its long history. It was the capital of the Illyrian state of the Ardiaeans from the 3rd century BC until the Roman conquest in 168BC. The city was part of the Venetian Republic from 1396 until it was surrendered to the Ottomans, after a long siege, in 1479. During the Ottoman occupation, Shkodra was the seat of a semi-autonomous *pashalik* under the Bushati family, which at one point stretched east into what is now Kosovo, and south as far as Berati (there is more about the Bushati pashas in the box on page 126). Shkodrans were prominent in the Albanian cultural and political renaissance (Rilindja Kombëtare) which led ultimately to independence from the Ottomans.

In terms of visitor attractions, Shkodra has one of Albania's best castles (which is saying a lot), attractive domestic architecture and several excellent museums: the archaeological display in the Historical Museum, the huge collection of 19th- and 20th-century photographs in the National Museum of Photography, the Cathedral's Diocesan Museum and the chilling Site of Witness and Memory.

The city is a good starting point for excursions into the wild and beautiful Albanian Alps. On the coast, there are important wetland habitats at Velipoja and Kune-Vaini, where many rare and attractive waterfowl and other birds can be observed. See page 140 for further information about birdwatching in these reserves.

GETTING THERE AND AWAY

To/from Tirana There are frequent buses from Tirana to Shkodra, running at least once an hour from 07.00 to 17.00. The journey takes about 2 hours and the one-way fare is 300 lek. In Shkodra, buses to Tirana depart from Sheshi Demokracia. They can be boarded or alighted from at almost any point along their route: for example, at the bridge leading from the highway to Lezha, the junction at Miloti or the slip-road for the airport.

To/from Montenegro Buses run between Ulqini (called Ulcinj in Serbo-Croat) and Shkodra all year round, at least three times a day. It takes 1½ hours; the one-way fare is €6.50 (w busticket4.me or from the driver). Helpfully, the Montenegrin and Albanian authorities operate a joint border post at Muriqani, 14km from Shkodra. In Shkodra,

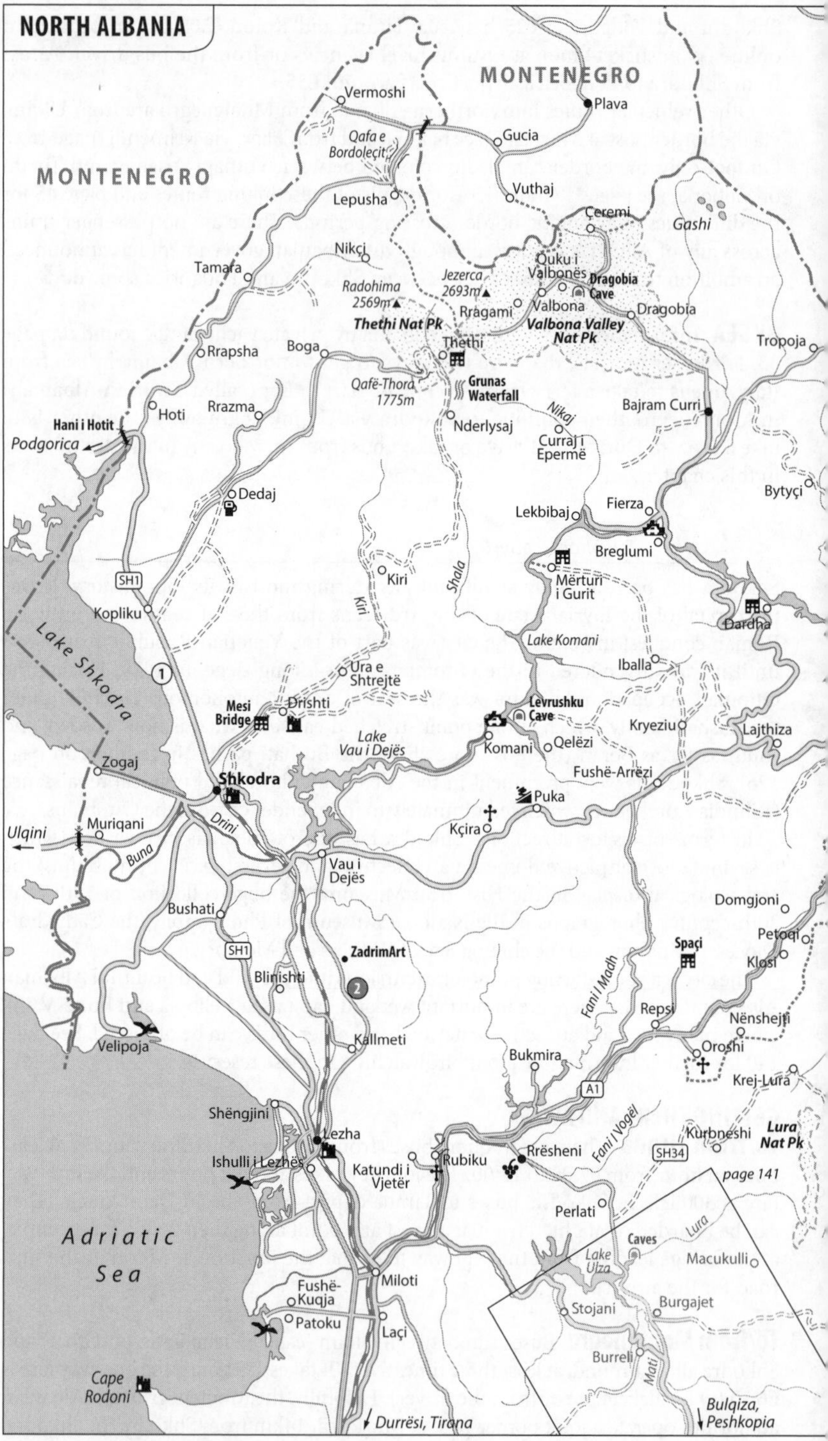
NORTH ALBANIA
MONTENEGRO
MONTENEGRO
Vermoshi
Plava
Qafa e Bordoleçit
Gucia
Lepusha
Vuthaj
Çeremi
Gashi
Nikçi
Tamara
Quku i Valbonës
Jezerca 2693m
Dragobia Cave
Radohima 2569m
Rragami
Valbona
Dragobia
Thethi Nat Pk
Valbona Valley Nat Pk
Tropoja
Rrapsha
Boga
Thethi
Qafë-Thora 1775m
Grunas Waterfall
Hoti
Razma
Nderlysaj
Nikaj
Bajram Curri
Hani i Hotit
Podgorica
Curraj i Epermë
Dedaj
Bytyçi
Lekbibaj
Fierza
Breglumi
Kiri
Mërturi i Gurit
SH1
Kopliku
Shala
Kiri
Lake Shkodra
Dardha
Lake Komani
1
Ura e Shtrejtë
Iballa
Mesi Bridge
Drishti
Levrushku Cave
Kryeziu
Lajthiza
Lake Vau i Dejës
Komani
Qelëzi
Zogaj
Shkodra
Fushë-Arrëzi
Puka
Muriqani
Drini
Kçira
Ulqini
Buna
Vau i Dejës
Domgjoni
Bushati
Petoqi
SH1
ZadrimArt
Spaçi
Klosi
Blinishti
2
Fani i Madh
Repsi
Nënshejti
Velipoja
Kallmeti
Oroshi
Bukmira
Krej-Lura
A1
Shëngjini
Lezha
Kurbneshi
Lura Nat Pk
Ishulli i Lezhës
Katundi i Vjetër
Rubiku
Rrësheni
Fani i Vogël
SH34
page 141
Perlati
Adriatic Sea
Caves
Lura
Lake Ulza
Macukulli
Miloti
Fushë-Kuqja
Patoku
Stojani
Burgajet
Laçi
Burreli
Mati
Cape Rodoni
Durrësi, Tirana
Bulqiza, Peshkopia

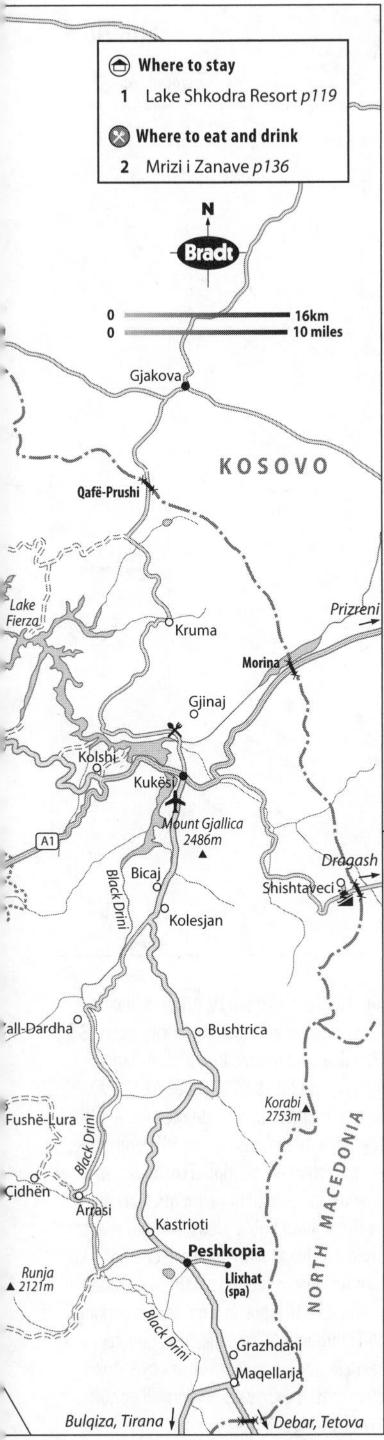

the buses leave from outside the Rozafa Hotel; in Ulqini, from the bus station. Taxis also do this run; they charge €8 per person, or €25 for the whole car. In Shkodra, the drivers tout for passengers outside the Rozafa Hotel. The taxi fare from Shkodra to Podgorica airport is around €35.

See page 114 for details of the bus service to/from Kotor via Shkodra and Podgorica, and page 164 for information about Kelmendi, with its border crossing into the southern Montenegrin district of Plav.

GETTING AROUND As elsewhere in Albania, Shkodrans are more likely to give directions with reference to neighbourhoods and landmarks. Most people, if they use any street names at all, still use the old, communist-era names. The municipal police are friendly and helpful to lost tourists.

Many agencies now organise hiking in the Albanian Alps; see page 30 for information about specialist hiking companies. Buses from Shkodra to Vermoshi, Kopliku and other destinations to the north, including Thethi, leave from Rus Maxhar, in the city's northern suburbs.

WHERE TO STAY *Map, page 120, unless otherwise stated*

Colosseo (41 rooms) Rr Kolë Idromeno; 224 7513/4; m 068 20 07 751; e info@colosseohotel.com; w colosseohotel.com. Centrally located on a pedestrian street, opposite a mosque (light sleepers beware the combination of late-night music & early-morning call to prayer). English spoken; lift; free parking; indoor pool, gym, sauna (extra charge). Good, long-established restaurant offering Albanian & Italian dishes, separate entrance; bar on top floor with great city views. Good Wi-Fi throughout; business facilities available. Large well-fitted rooms, all with stylish en-suite bathroom; AC, bedside light, safe, minibar, hairdryer, flatscreen TV, desk, phone, good mirrors, thick curtains; some have balcony. **$$$$**

Grand Hotel Europa (50 rooms) Sh 2 Prilli; 224 1211, 224 6381; m 069 20 68 492; e info@

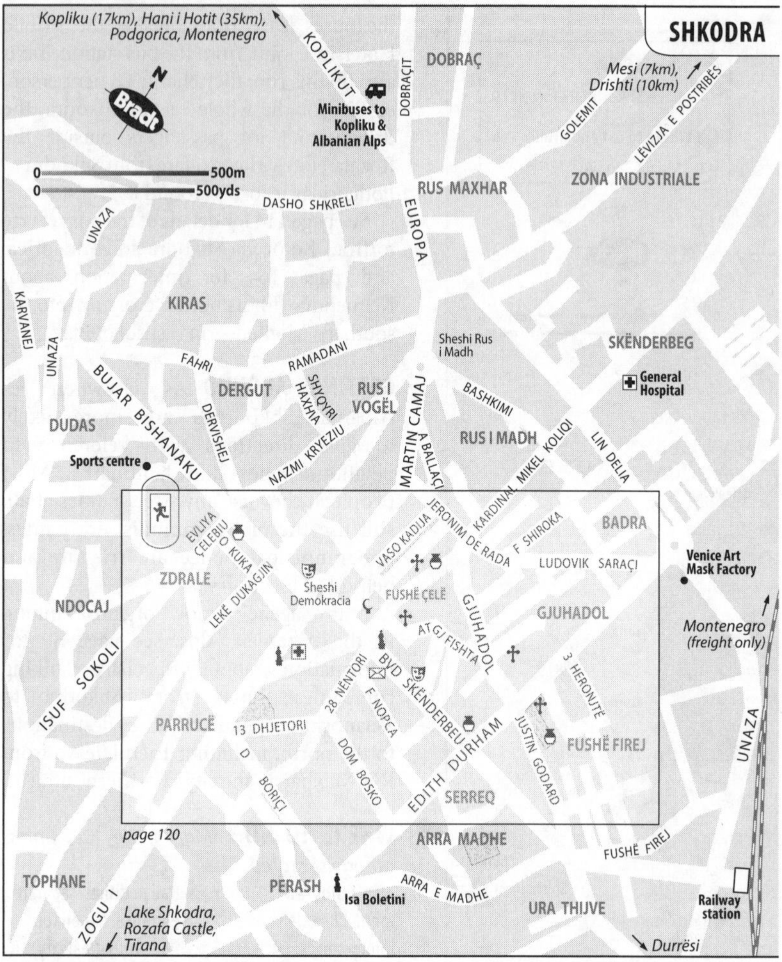

europagrandhotel.com; **w** europagrandhotel.com. Restaurant with international & Albanian cuisine; lobby bar & cocktail bar. Lift, free parking, laundry service; outdoor pool, garden; gym, sauna, Turkish bath, spa (extra charge); casino; in-house travel agency, business centre, ATM, free Wi-Fi throughout. English spoken. Suites, dbl & twin, all en suite with hairdryer, direct-dial phone, flatscreen TV, AC, safe. **$$$$**

Rozafa (77 rooms) Rr Teuta; 224 2767; **m** 067 40 29 369; **e** info@hotelrozafa.al; **w** hotelrozafa.al. Built in 1971 as Shkodra's 'Turizmi' hotel, it was completely renovated in 2020. Central location; English spoken at reception; lifts, free parking; restaurant, bar, Wi-Fi. All rooms en suite, some with bathtub as well as shower; good double-glazing; minibar, flatscreen TV, AC, desk, hairdryer; some have balcony with panoramic city views. **$$$**

Tradita (12 rooms) Rr Edith Durham 4; 224 0537; **m** 068 20 86 056, 068 62 63 770; **e** info@traditagt.com; **w** traditagt.com. A 17th-century, stone-built house in the Shkodran style; owner's collection of traditional costumes, musical instruments, household implements & art on display throughout public areas; cultural events organised. Lively bar with good selection of raki; excellent restaurant serving northern Albanian specialities. English spoken. Free secure parking, free Wi-Fi throughout, free bike use; laundry service. Bedrooms in modern annex overlooking attractive central courtyard garden, all en suite with Wi-Fi & fridge. **$$$**

Kaduku (15 rooms) Rr Studenti 84/1, Sh Demokracia; 242 216; m 069 25 51 230; e info@hotel-kaduku.com; w hotel-kaduku.com. Good location, just off the central square, but quiet because set back from the street (signposted). Friendly, very helpful staff; English spoken; luggage storage possible. Free parking; free bike use; restaurant with some traditional dishes. Range of room sizes, all en suite with hairdryer, AC, CH, flatscreen TV, Wi-Fi. Substantial b/fast inc. **$$**

Red Bricks (14 rooms) Rr Studenti, Sh Demokracia; 290 0888, 157 0035; m 067 52 42 200, 069 89 43 200; e info@theredbricks-al.com; w theredbricks-al.com. Centrally located; all rooms have en-suite bathroom with scales, hairdryer, shower with screen & alarm; plus AC, big flatscreen TV, safe, daybed, iron, minibar, mineral water inc, tea- & coffee-making facilities. English spoken; lift; business facilities; parking. Indoor & outdoor bars; free Wi-Fi. B/fast inc. **$$**

Lake Shkodra Resort [map, page 116] Vraka; n 42° 08′30.2″N 19° 27′93.8″E; m 069 27 50 337, 067 41 17 947; e faye@lakeshkodraresort.com; w lakeshkodraresort.com. Campsite on the lakeside, about halfway between Kopliku & Shkodra, signposted from highway. Bike & kayak hire, fishing, sandy beach. Free Wi-Fi; laundry service; ample showers & toilets; lakeside restaurant & bar. Glamping tents available (**$$**); also 2-bedroom chalet (**$$$$**). **$**

Mi Casa Es Tu Casa (30 beds) Bd Skënderbeu; m 069 38 12 054; e hostelshkoder@gmail.com; w micasaestucasa.it. Old Shkodran house (photographed by Marubi in 1912), with a lovely garden with fruit trees, tortoises & comfortable veranda. Beware of the dog! English spoken; bike hire; kitchen; big sitting room; bar; washing machine; free Wi-Fi; sheets & towels provided. Bike & horseriding tours arranged. Camping possible in garden; separate shower & toilet for campers. *Studio apt with en-suite bathroom & kitchen* **$$**, *dbl room* **$$**, *dorms share toilets & showers* **$**

WHERE TO EAT *Map, page 120*

The local speciality is carp (*krap*) from Lake Shkodra, although it is not always available. It is easier to find in the restaurants on the lakeshore, on the other side of the River Buna; the closest are just before the old bridge (eg: the Beer Garden), or there is public transport to the lakeside villages of Shiroka and Zogaj (bus stop opposite the Rozafa Hotel).

Piazza Park Sh Nënë Tereza. Upmarket pizza, pasta, salads, etc. Tables outside on large terrace in summer. $$$

Rozafa Rr Marin Beçikemi; m 068 60 15 026. Across from cathedral; tables outside in summer; friendly service. Seafood, excellent pasta, risotto, pizza. $$$

San Francisco Rr Kolë Idromeno. English spoken & English menu; big terrace on 1st floor, overlooking pedestrian street. Meat, seafood, carp, pasta, good pizza. $$$

Tradita Rr Edith Durham 4; 240 537; m 068 20 86 056. It is well worth eating here even if you are not staying at the hotel. Restaurant in 17th-century stone-built house, open hearth where meat is grilled, excellent menu with local specialities inc game, wild fungi & forest fruits in season. Some English spoken; service can be rather slow. Interesting exhibition of traditional costumes & other items. $$$

Vila Bekteshi Rr Hasan Riza Pasha; 240 799; m 069 28 67 445, 066 66 63 558. Near the Orthodox church; also known as 'Çoçja'. Tables outside in internal courtyard & upstairs in formal dining room. Good service, some English spoken. Italian-inspired menu, excellent meat dishes, pizzas good even by high Albanian standards. Locally brewed beer on draught; good house wine. $$$–$$

ArtiZanave Rr Berdicej, Gjuhadol. Social enterprise, community-run restaurant; part of Slow Food movement. Simple, tasty salads & grilled meat. $$

WHAT TO SEE AND DO

Rozafa Castle

(09.00–14.00 Tue–Sun; 200 lek) Shkodra's castle stands above the confluence of its three rivers, the Drini, the Kiri and the Buna, and thus controls all but the northern approach to the city. It is an excellent place for a castle and has been fortified since Illyrian times, when the Ardiaean queen Teuta launched her

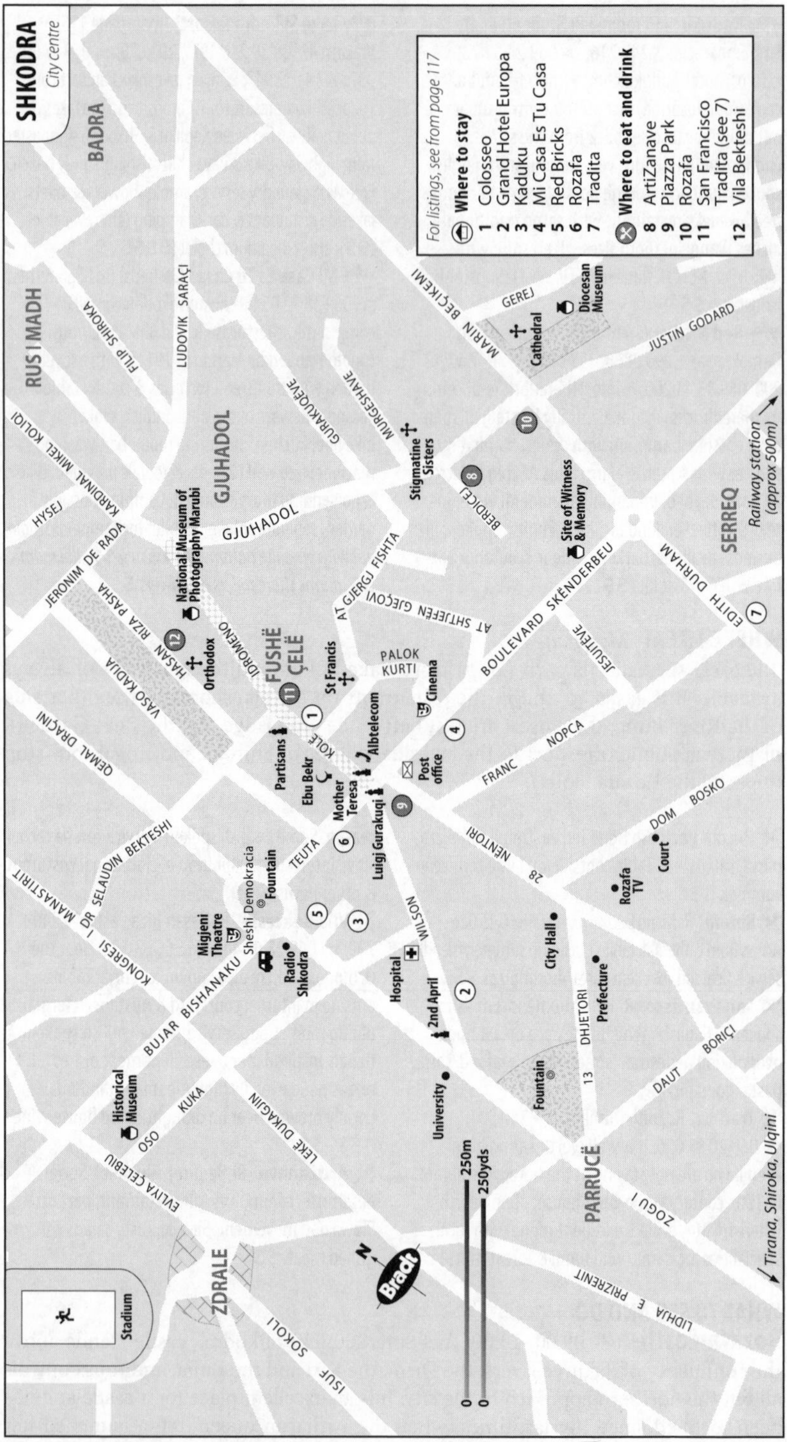
SHKODRA
City centre
For listings, see from page 117
Where to stay
1 Colosseo
2 Grand Hotel Europa
3 Kaduku
4 Mi Casa Es Tu Casa
5 Red Bricks
6 Rozafa
7 Tradita
Where to eat and drink
8 ArtiZanave
9 Piazza Park
10 Rozafa
11 San Francisco
Tradita (see 7)
12 Vila Bekteshi
BADRA
RUS I MADH
GJUHADOL
FUSHË ÇELË
SERREQ
PARRUCË
ZDRALE
LUDOVIK SARAÇI
FILIP SHIROKA
KARDINAL MIKEL KOLIQI
HYSEJ
JERONIM DE RADA
HASAN RIZA PASHA
VASO KADIJA
QEMAL DRAÇINI
DR SELAUDIN BEKTESHI
KONGRESI I MANASTIRIT
BUJAR BISHANAKU
OSO KUKA
EVLIYA ÇELEBIU
LEKË DUKAGJINI
ISUF SOKOLI
GJUHADOL
GURAKUQËVE
MURGESHAVE
MARIN BEÇIKEMI
GEREJ
JUSTIN GODARD
BERDICEJ
AT GJERGJ FISHTA
AT SHTJEFEN GJEÇOVI
PALOK KURTI
IDROMENO
KOLE
TEUTA
WILSON
BOULEVARD SKËNDERBEU
FRANC NOPCA
NËNTORI 28
DOM BOSKO
JESUITËVE
EDITH DURHAM
DHJETORI 13
DAUT BORIÇI
ZOGU I
LIDHJA E PRIZRENIT
National Museum of Photography Marubi
Orthodox
St Francis
Stigmatine Sisters
Cathedral
Diocesan Museum
Site of Witness & Memory
Partisans
Ebu Bekr
Mother Teresa
Albtelecom
Post office
Cinema
Luigj Gurakuqi
Fountain
Sheshi Demokracia
Migjeni Theatre
Radio Shkodra
Hospital
2nd April
City Hall
Rozafa TV
Court
Prefecture
Fountain
University
Historical Museum
Stadium
Railway station (approx 500m)
Tirana, Shiroka, Ulqini
250m
250yds
0
0
N
Bradt

attacks on the Romans from it (page 8). Traces of the Illyrian walls, constructed of large stones with no mortar, can still be seen at the entrance to the castle.

Most of what remains is Venetian and Ottoman. The outer walls follow the line of the hill; within, successive lines of fortification create three distinct areas, of which the most secure and easily defensible is the section at the narrowest part. The views from the citadel are wonderful, across Lake Shkodra to Montenegro, out to the Adriatic, and down towards Lezha.

Rozafa Castle was twice besieged by Ottoman armies. When it finally surrendered in January 1479, it was only after a lengthy blockade, supervised for a time by Sultan Mehmed II in person, had brought Venice to the realisation that it had no choice but to make peace. Rozafa was the last fortress in Albania to fall to the Ottomans. Two-and-a-half thousand Shkodrans chose to leave under the terms of the surrender and were granted pensions by Venice. The new rulers continued to use the castle as a military and administrative centre; it was the vizier's residence and, from 1840, was the capital of the whole northern Albanian province (*vilayet*). It was last used for military purposes in 1913, when it operated as the Ottoman command centre during yet another siege, this time by Montenegrins.

You enter through the vaulted barbican gate to the first courtyard. A trickle of lime down the wall of this courtyard marks where people believe the eponymous Rozafa was walled up alive to guarantee the strength of the walls (see box, page 124). Local women still gather here to acknowledge Rozafa's sacrifice and to pray for their own fertility. The second enclosure was the main living area, with the barracks, stores and prison; the latter was in use until the early 20th century. The **ruined church** on your right was once Shkodra's cathedral, a 13th-century building that remained in use even after the Ottoman occupation, until it was converted into a mosque in 1869. The circular, chimney-like structures here and there are the access points for water cisterns, constructed in the 15th century and fed by pipes running into them from all over the castle.

The third section was the real fortress, with underground stairways and tunnels connecting to different parts of the citadel. Some of the entrances to these secret passageways can still be seen, although the tunnels themselves are not open. The wellhead is original; it was stolen in the civil unrest of 1997 and reappeared mysteriously ten years later. The three-storey Venetian building at the end of the third courtyard was the garrison commander's residence in the 14th and 15th centuries and now houses the **museum** (150 lek). This covers not only the history of the castle but also of the surrounding area. It is perhaps the only museum in Albania that is designed to be accessible to blind visitors, with information in Braille (in Albanian and English) and tactile displays. The exhibition includes a 3rd- or 4th-century mosaic, discovered at the foot of the castle hill; this is the only mosaic ever found in northern Albania. There is stonework from this castle – including a Venetian lion that may once have been over the entrance gate – and from the nearby castle of Drishti (page 130); coins from various periods, including some minted in Shkodra by the Nemanjić dynasty of medieval Montenegro, and others with the symbol of the Balsha family, the feudal power in northern Albania in the 13th to 15th centuries; and copies of documents including a map from 1600, the Statute of the city of Shkodra, written – in Latin and Dalmatian – in 1346 and discovered in Venice only in 2002, and interesting political cartoons from the early 20th century. Next to the museum is an atmospheric **restaurant**, which has excellent views from the balcony to its rear.

From the castle walls, you can see the **Leaden Mosque** on the floodplain below, an 18th-century building in classical Ottoman style. It was the first mosque to reopen after freedom of religion was restored in 1990. However, problems with flooding

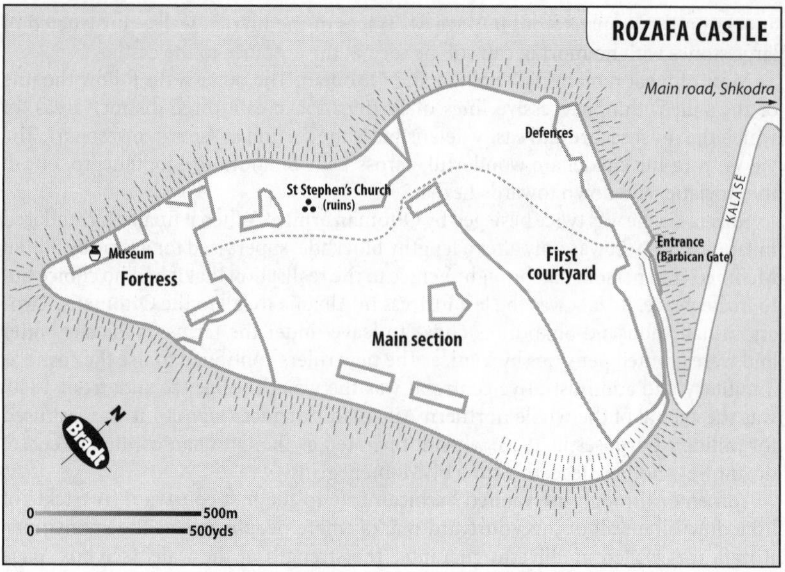

then forced it to close for many years. It reopened in 2016 and the imam, who lives nearby, is happy to show visitors around his beautiful mosque (he does not, however, speak English).

It is a long way to the castle from the centre of town, and a stiff climb up from the main road; if you do not have your own transport, you could take a taxi up and walk back down to catch a bus back into town.

Historical Museum (Rr Oso Kuka 12; 243 213; 09.00–15.00 Mon–Fri, groups at other times by arrangement 1 day ahead; 150 lek) The house of Oso Kuka, who died defending Shkodra against Montenegrin attackers in 1861, is now home to the town's Historical Museum, and provides an opportunity to see traditional domestic architecture. From the street, a Shkodran house is just a windowless wall with a thick wooden door; once through this door, you find yourself either in a narrow entrance hall or, as in the case of Oso Kuka's house, in a courtyard, with the house in the centre, far away from the surrounding walls. The courtyard always had a well and this one has two: the original, from when the house was built in 1840, and a Venetian wellhead from the 15th century. Various large items recovered from the castle or found elsewhere in the area are displayed in the courtyard and in the garden behind the house. One of the most interesting is an Ottoman coat of arms, intricately carved in stone, which dates from the late 19th century and was found in the castle.

The archaeological collection is exhibited on the ground floor of the house, which – like traditional houses all over Albania – was originally used for storage or workshops. The prehistory section includes finds from the Mesolithic site at the Gajtan Cave; Bronze Age goods from Mycenae and the Celtic world, which demonstrate the extent to which Shkodra was then trading with other civilisations; and a cute 'family' of terracotta figurines, discovered in a burial mound. The museum has a good collection of coins and medals, including a rare *denarius* bearing the head of Brutus, Julius Caesar's rival, and coins struck in Shkodra in the 2nd century BC, during the reign of the last Illyrian king, Genti; these bear on their reverse a *liburnis* – a small, fast ship – like that on the modern 20-lek coin.

In the days when this house was lived in, the living quarters were on the first floor, reached by a flight of wooden stairs up to a large wooden landing, with doors leading off it to the rooms within. One of these rooms, the *oda e miqve* or guest room, now houses the museum's ethnography collection. Beautifully carved wood decorates the walls, and the room is overlooked by a gallery, where the women of the house could sit while their menfolk were entertaining guests. The hosts and their guests sat on either side of the huge stucco chimney, made in a style unique to Shkodra. Traditional costumes are displayed in glass cases in this room: those worn by Muslim and Catholic men and women in the city, alongside the outfits characteristic of Shkodra's mountainous hinterland.

National Museum of Photography Marubi (Muzeu Kombëtar i Fotografisë Marubi; Rr Kol Idromeno; ☎ 240 0500; e info@marubi.gov.al; ⏲ 09.00–14.00 & 15.00–18.00 Tue–Sun; 700 lek) The Marubi photographic archive (Fototeka) is a marvellous record of historical events and ordinary people in northern Albania. It is housed in a specially renovated museum on Shkodra's main pedestrian street, where high-quality prints, glass negatives and photographic equipment are now displayed in airy, light exhibition rooms.

The earliest of the photographs in the collection were taken by Pietro Marubbi (1834–1903), an Italian Garibaldist who came to Shkodra as a political refugee and albanicised his name to become Pjetër Marubi. One of the oldest is a self-portrait of Marubi himself, in wet collodion, which was discovered during an inventory of the archive in 2013. Kol Idromeno (1860–1939), who went on to become one of Albania's most eminent painters, took his first art lessons in Marubi's studio. Idromeno was also responsible for screening the first film ever shown in Albania, in 1912.

Pjetër Marubi had no children of his own, so he adopted his gardener's sons and trained them in photography. The elder boy died tragically young, of TB; the younger, Kel (1860–1940), followed in his adoptive father's footsteps and, by the end of the 1920s, had been appointed as King Zog's official photographer.

Kel's son Gegë (1907–84) also trained as a photographer. During the communist period, the Marubi studio was incorporated into the Kooperativa e Artizanatit Shtetëror, the 'State Cooperative of Creative Artists'. The studio filmed and photographed staged 'prisoner escapes' and 'weapon caches' for Albania's secret police, the Sigurimi, which helped to justify executions and imprisonment of the regime's political opponents. In 1970, Gegë Marubi donated his family's archive to the state, which remains responsible for its conservation. The collection also includes work by other Albanian photographers.

The exhibition displays fascinating images of people and places in the northern highlands, views of the cities of Durrësi and Shkodra in Ottoman times, interwar portraits of ordinary Shkodrans and of prominent men and women, including Edith Durham (see box, page 148), and the photographic record of many historic events, from as far back as 1878. There are examples of early photographic equipment and a mock-up of Pjetër Marubi's studio, where the great and the good of Shkodra vied to have their portraits taken.

The permanent exhibition is on the first floor of the museum, while the ground floor hosts temporary exhibitions. All the labelling is in English and Albanian. At least an hour should be allowed to look around the whole museum. There is also a short video, with soundtrack in English or Albanian, which explains more about the context in which some of the early photographs were taken, and a small library of books about photography.

ROZAFA CASTLE *From Mitrush Kuteli's* Old Albanian Tales

On top of Valdanuz Hill, three brothers were working. They were building a castle. The wall that they made by day, at night was destroyed, and so they could not raise it at all.

One day a good old man came by. 'Work well, you three brothers!' he said.

'You too, you good old man, go well! But what do you see that's good with us? By day we work, by night it falls down. Can you give us any advice? What can we do to keep the walls standing?'

'I know,' said the old man, 'but it would be a sin for me to tell you.'

'Let the sin be on our heads,' they replied, 'because we want this castle to stay up.'

The old man reflected and asked them: 'Are you married, brave lads? Do the three of you have your brides?'

'We are married,' they said. 'The three of us have our brides. Tell us, then, what to do to keep this castle standing.'

'If you want it to stand firm, promise each other this in a solemn oath: don't tell your brides, don't discuss at home what I am going to tell you. Whichever of the three sisters-in-law brings you your lunch tomorrow, take her and wall her up alive in the wall of the castle. Then you will see that the wall will endure and will remain for ever and a day.'

So said the old man, and he left: one moment they saw him, the next they didn't.

Alas! The oldest brother broke his oath. He discussed it at home, he told his own bride just as it had happened, he told her not to go there the following day. The middle brother also broke his oath: he told his bride everything. Only the youngest kept his promise: he did not discuss it at home, he did not tell his own bride.

In the morning, the three of them rose early and went to work. The hammers struck, the stones were crushed, their hearts pounded, the walls grew high.

At home, the boys' mother knew nothing. She said to the oldest: 'Oldest daughter, the masons want bread and water; they want a gourd of wine.'

The oldest wife replied: 'Upon my word, mother, I cannot go today, for I am ill.'

She turned and said to the middle one: 'Middle daughter, the masons want bread and water; they want a gourd of wine.'

The Marubi archive holds nearly half a million glass-plate negatives and films. About 100,000 of the photographs have been digitalised in high resolution. Some of them can be seen in the Marubi Virtual Museum (w marubi.gov.al).

Site of Witness and Memory (Vendi i Dëshmisë dhe Kujtesës; Bd Skënderbeu; (⌚09.00–14.30 Mon–Fri, 09.30–12.30 Sat–Sun; 150 lek) From 1946 to 1991, a rather unassuming 19th-century house on Shkodra's main boulevard became the regional headquarters of the Ministry of Internal Affairs. This innocuous name belies the political persecution and terror that emanated from this building for 45 years. The storerooms of the former Franciscan seminary were transformed into detention cells and interrogation rooms for the Sigurimi, communist Albania's secret police. Thousands of people passed through these cells before they were sentenced; they were then either executed or sent on to other prisons or prison camps such as Spaçi (page 147).

Now the building has been transformed again, this time into a museum that commemorates those who suffered there. Panels in English and Albanian explain

The middle wife replied: 'Upon my word, mother, I cannot go today, for I am spending the night with my parents.'

The boys' mother turned to the youngest wife: 'Youngest daughter. . . '

The youngest daughter leapt to her feet: 'Tell me, honoured mother!'

'The masons want bread and water; they want a gourd of wine.'

'Upon my word, mother, as for me, I have my baby boy. I am afraid he will want my breast and he will cry.'

'Out you go, on you go, for we will take care of your son, we won't let him cry,' said her sisters-in-law.

The youngest stood up, the good girl, she took the bread and water, she took the gourd of wine, she kissed her son on both cheeks and she went out. She climbed up Valdanuz Hill, she drew close to the spot where the three were working – her two brothers-in-law and her husband.

'Work well, masons!' she said.

But what was this? The hammers stopped striking, but their hearts beat ever more strongly. Their faces grew pale. When the youngest saw his wife, he threw the hammer from his hand, he cursed the stone and the wall. His wife said to him: 'What is the matter, sir? Why do you curse the stone and the wall?'

Her oldest brother-in-law cut in: 'Black was the day when you were born, sister. We have sworn to wall you up alive in the wall of the castle.'

'Here's to you, my brothers-in-law!' she said. 'But I have one request for you: when you wall me up, leave my right eye out, leave my right hand out, leave my right foot out, leave my right breast out. For I have my baby son. When he starts to cry, with one eye I will see him, with one hand I will caress him, with one foot I will rock his cradle, and with one breast I will give him milk. May my breast turn to stone, may the castle endure, may my son be brave, may he become king and rule!'

They took the youngest bride and walled her up in the foundations of the castle. And the walls were raised, they grew high, they did not fall down as before. Yet at their foot, even today the stones are wet and mossy, because the mother's tears still fall for her son.

various aspects of Albanian communism, including the destruction of religious buildings, the anti-communist uprisings in northern Albania, and the public trials that took place in buildings around Shkodra. The events are brought to life through photos, documents, press cuttings and personal items belonging to prisoners. Finally, a walk of 50m leads to the corridor of prison cells, 29 of them plus a reconstructed interrogation room (a euphemism for 'torture chamber').

The purpose behind the Site of Witness and Memory is to provide an opportunity for Albanians to understand and learn from their past. It is a welcome by-product that it also helps non-Albanians to learn about this terrifying period of the country's history. It takes at least an hour to give the exhibition the attention it deserves. The admission charge includes an information booklet in Albanian and English.

Diocesan Museum (Muzeu Dioqezan; Sh Gjon Pali II; **m** 067 55 52 076; **e** muzeudioqesansp@gmail.com; **w** kishakatolikeshkoder.com; ⌚ 09.00–13.00 Mon–Sat, summer also 15.00–17.00 Mon–Fri; free admission) Shkodra is the centre of Albanian Catholicism, the seat of the archdiocese of Shkodra and Pulti.

THE BUSHATI DYNASTY

By the 17th century, the gradual weakening of Ottoman authority over the empire's peripheral areas led, in Albania, to the rise of feudal lords known as *beys* or *pashas*, all anxious to control as much territory (and therefore revenues) as possible – the territory controlled by each pasha was called a *pashalik*. The rivalry between the pashas gave rise to wars and, ultimately, to a period of anarchy. This was brought to an end, in the middle of the 18th century, by the emergence of two powerful pashas, one in northern Albania and one in the south, who managed to gain control of almost all the small pashaliks and merge them into two huge ones. The southern pashalik was ruled by Ali Pasha Tepelena, about whom there is more information in the box on page 218.

The northern pashalik was created in 1757 by Mehmet Bey Bushati (the surname is alternatively spelt 'Bushatlli'). It was Mehmet Bushati who, in 1773, built the Leaden Mosque, below Rozafa Castle (page 121). His ambitious son, Kara Mahmoud Bushati, extended the territory of the pashalik of Shkodra east to what is now Kosovo and south as far as Berati, the border with Ali Pasha Tepelena's territory. In 1785, Kara Mahmoud invaded Montenegro and captured the pirate stronghold of Ulqini. The Ottoman authorities besieged his troops in Rozafa Castle for three months in 1787, but Kara Mahmoud managed to secure an imperial pardon by threatening to switch his allegiance to Austria-Hungary. Like his southern counterpart Ali Pasha, however, he ended up overstretching Ottoman tolerance. When he launched a second attack on Montenegro in 1796, he was defeated and – again, like Ali Pasha – beheaded. The Ottoman authorities appointed his brother Ibrahim Pasha as the governor of Shkodra, which, thanks to Kara Mahmoud's policies, had become an important trading centre.

The pashalik remained under the control of the Bushati family, effectively autonomous until 1830, when Sultan Mahmoud II determined to break the independence of the Albanians. Another siege of Rozafa ended in the surrender of the Bushatis and the end of the pashalik of Shkodra. This did not mean the end of the family's influence, though, and nor did it do much to improve the Porte's control of its restless Albanian subjects.

The current archbishop, Angelo Massafra, is from the Albanian-speaking Arbëresh community of southern Italy.

St Stephen's Cathedral was built in 1858, to replace the cathedral in Rozafa Castle which had been closed by the Ottoman authorities and converted into a mosque. The Russian tsar helped to fund its construction and Shkodra's leading artists of the time designed and decorated it.

Slightly hidden behind the cathedral, in its former sacristy, the Diocesan Museum provides fascinating insights into the history of Catholicism in northern Albania, from its earliest traces in the 12th century. The exhibition is organised thematically, starting with archaeological finds from medieval monasteries and religious medallions. Documents, maps and photographs help to put the items on display into their proper context.

In 1946, the country's new communist government closed all Catholic schools and confiscated the buildings. In 1967, matters became even worse for Albania's Catholics (and those of other religions) when the government declared the world's first atheist state. Churches and mosques were demolished or used for secular purposes;

St Stephen's Cathedral was converted into a sports hall and used for basketball and volleyball matches. Priests and imams were imprisoned or executed. The Diocesan Museum displays astonishing items such as a secret, handwritten baptismal certificate, hand-carved rosaries and a miniature 'Mass kit'. The latter has everything needed to celebrate a clandestine Mass, including a model of a bishop, all kept hidden in a little wooden chest under the floorboards of the home of its owners. A beautiful wooden statue of the Franciscan saint Rocco, dated to the 16th or 17th century, was hidden within the wall of another family's home to protect it from the atheism campaigners.

Shkodra was chosen as the location for the national Atheism Museum, which began as a temporary exhibition in 1967 and displayed relics and artefacts looted from closed or demolished religious buildings. Some of the church bells on display in the Diocesan Museum – at the foot of the bell tower, in fact – were recovered from the Atheism Museum after it closed in 1982.

Venice Art Mask Factory (Rr Lin Delia; m 068 20 47 291; e edmondangoni@gmail.com; f Venice Art; ⌚ Mon–Sat by arrangement) In an intriguing twist on the historic links between the two cities (Shkodra was part of the Venetian Republic for almost a century), many of the masks worn by revellers at the Venice Carnival are produced in a factory on the outskirts of Shkodra. They are handmade with papier-mâché (*cartapesta* in Italian): sheets of paper are soaked in glue and layered over a mould to make the basis of the mask. Once it is dry, it is then painted, decorated with sequins, gold leaf, lace and feathers, and finally varnished to give it an antique look – the whole process has 15 stages. Visitors can watch the masks being made and admire – or buy – the finished products in the factory showroom.

A walk around town Although Shkodra is a large and rather straggly town, the historic centre is quite compact and easy to walk around. The circuit described here should not take much more than an hour, excluding time to look around. Alternatively, do as the Shkodrans do, and cycle. Several hotels and hostels provide bikes for their guests.

The main **mosque** is as good a place to start as any, since it occupies practically a whole block of the town centre and is impossible to miss. The original mosque on this site had been destroyed in an earthquake in 1905 and was rebuilt by the Ottoman authorities in 1910; it was then known as the Ebu Bekr Mosque. Its beautifully engraved minarets and copper roofs were not enough to save it from the atheism campaigners, however: the mosque was razed to the ground in the late 1960s, the graves in its gardens were levelled and olive trees were planted over them. It was rebuilt in 1995, with funding from the Saudi El-Zamil family.

Behind the mosque, in the large garden that surrounds it, is a rather weather-beaten and neglected partisan monument.

Leaving the mosque grounds, turn left out of the gate and then left again towards the road junction called Mother Teresa Square, with a recent statue of the nun herself, outside the Albtelecom building. Albania claims **Mother Teresa** (1910–97) as its own – although she was born in what is now North Macedonia – thanks to her father's Mirdita origin. Shkodra, with its large Catholic community, is especially proud of her; on Mother Teresa Day in October, the people decorate the statue with flowers. Across the junction, with his hands in his pockets, is **Luigj Gurakuqi** (1879–1925), one of Shkodra's most illustrious sons, who served Albania in various capacities including as Minister of Education in the independent country's first government.

The statue of Gurakuqi stands on the spot that was graced by a bust of Stalin until January 1990. Following the street to Gurakuqi's left will lead you to the **2nd of April**

BLOOD FEUD

Blood feud is an ancient mechanism for resolving serious conflicts between clans or other social groupings. It has been (and still is) used in many cultures, but rarely has it achieved the degree of formal codification as it did in Albania. The codes that govern blood feud and other matters of clan administration were transmitted orally until recent times, and are known by the Turkish (from Arabic) word for 'law', Kanun. There were several versions of these codes in different parts of highland Albania; the best known are those of Lekë Dukagjin and of Skanderbeg. The latter, of course, is Albania's national hero, the chieftain who united all the northern clans against the Ottoman invaders in the 15th century (see box, page 136, for more about Skanderbeg). The Dukagjins were another of the powerful clans of medieval Albania, and the Lekë concerned is thought to have been the clan chief in the 15th century, although many of the laws in his Kanun must date from earlier times.

The Kanun regulated all aspects of life in the northern clans, including marriage, property and taxes. It also attempted to regulate the practice of revenge killing, or *gjakmarrja* ('blood-taking'), by setting out ways in which feuds between clans could be reconciled. In a society governed by revenge, if a member of your clan is killed by a member of a rival clan, you are duty bound to avenge that killing. The family of the man you kill (in such societies, women and children do not count) is then obliged to kill either you or – if that proves impossible – one of your close male relatives. It is perfectly obvious that if no mechanism is found for stopping this cycle, your clan and that of your enemy will both die out.

The Kanun way to end a blood feud was *besa*, an Albanian word that means many things ranging from 'word of honour' (its usual modern meaning), through 'sacred oath', to its Kanun meaning of a truce between clans. Besa could be cemented with a marriage between the two families concerned, or by the payment of a tribute, or not at all, since the word itself was enough – but it was not necessarily permanent and, if the feud revived, the male members of the families involved would begin the cycle again. The lock-in tower in Thethi (page 166) is a reminder of the devastating effect that blood feud had on northern Albanian families.

The communist government managed to suppress blood feud fairly thoroughly, presumably through the same mechanisms of fear and suspicion

Monument. This commemorates the date in 1991 when Shkodran students and others demonstrated in protest against the result of the elections two days earlier, which had been won by the (communist) Albanian Party of Labour. Security forces opened fire on the demonstrators and four students were killed.

From the 2nd of April Monument, a short cut across the grounds of the Grand Hotel Europa will bring you to some attractive 19th-century governmental buildings: the **Prefecture**, pretty much straight ahead of you, and the **City Hall** round to the left. Following this street beyond the City Hall will bring you back to Mother Teresa Square.

Now cross the main road to the pedestrian street named after Shkodran painter Kol Idromeno. It is full of cafés, restaurants and souvenir shops, many of them in restored 19th-century houses. Towards the end of the pedestrianised area, a street down to the right, Rruga Gjuhadol, will bring you out at Sheshi Gjon Pali II ('John Paul II Square') and the **Catholic Cathedral**. Kol Idromeno (1860–1939) designed the ceiling and Pjetër Marubi (1834–1903) made the wall paintings: see page 123 for more about them and page 126 for more about the history of the building.

which it used to suppress activities such as listening to the BBC World Service. In the 1990s, however, blood feud re-emerged and has once more become a serious problem, although foreigners are extremely unlikely to be even tangentially affected. Feuds have been revived from several generations back, and because there is now freedom of movement, the young men who are at risk have left their mountain villages for Albanian cities, for Italy or Greece, or for further-flung destinations. Unfortunately, freedom of movement also means that the feud can follow them, thus spreading the problem from the highlands into the poor suburbs of the big cities.

Shkodra has been particularly badly affected by blood feud, with certain streets in the city functioning effectively as a 'lock-in neighbourhood', populated by people who have fled their villages and who allow no stranger to enter, lest he bring death to one of the families there. Having an enclave like this means that the men need not be confined to their houses, but can at least walk up and down the street and drink coffee with their neighbours. The women, of course, fulfil the same role as they would in the village, except they can buy food in the market instead of ploughing the fields on their own. There is even a 'lock-in apartment building' in the centre of Tirana.

The traditional codes exclude women and children from revenge killing. However, because they were maintained orally, by the elders of each clan or village, there was nobody left to interpret them according to the ancient custom when they were revived after 50 years of suppression. Since the resurgence of blood feud in the 1990s, therefore, it has taken on quite anarchic aspects. Young boys are prevented from attending school because they might be the target of a blood feud, and the old besa systems of feud reconciliation have almost completely broken down. The botched land privatisation of the early 1990s has not helped; the majority of revenge killing cycles nowadays are started over disputes about property or water rights.

One group that offers advice to families involved in blood feud and helps with reconciliation, when this is possible, is the Diocesan Commission in Albania of the Catholic organisation Justice & Peace (Sh Papa Gjon Pali II; 022 248 795; e p&dshkod@albnet.net; w kishakatolikeshkoder.com).

The cathedral was reconsecrated in 1991 at a mass attended by, among many others, Mother Teresa. To the left of the altar is a display of photographs commemorating the dozens of Albanian Catholics – priests and lay people – who were executed during the communist regime. The bell tower, designed by Kol Idromeno and his father Arsen, was demolished in 1968 and rebuilt in 1999.

Returning to the centre by a slightly different route, turning off Rruga Gjuhadol on to Rruga At Gjergj Fishta, will take you past the **Franciscan convent and church**, with its lovely vaulted ceiling, and back to the start of the pedestrian street.

Drishti and the Mesi Bridge About 7km upstream from Shkodra, on the River Kiri which rises far up in the mountains that surround Thethi, is a spectacular Ottoman bridge called Ura e Mesit, or the **Mesi Bridge**. There are lots of old bridges in Albania called Ura e Mesit, which just means 'the Bridge in the Middle' – that is, the place that joined people from communities on opposite sides of the river. This particular bridge was built in 1868 by Mehmet Pasha Bushati, a member of the family which administered northwestern Albania on behalf of the Ottoman authorities. At 108m long, it is the longest Ottoman bridge in Albania, with 13 arches, and it is the only one with a curve. It was built for the transport of timber down from the mountains to the River Buna and on to Ulqini, which at the time was Shkodra's main port. Until 1965, when the modern bridge next to it was built, it was the only substantial bridge across the Kiri upriver of Shkodra itself. But Mehmet Pasha built his bridge at a crossing that had been used for many centuries before him, a link in a much older route connecting Shkodra with Drishti.

Drishti – or, as it was known at the height of its power, Drivasto – had an importance in the past which is hard to imagine nowadays. A fortress was built there in late antiquity; it was the seat of a bishopric until the end of the 9th century, and the citadel whose ruins can still be seen dates from the 14th century. Rozafa Castle outside Shkodra is clearly visible from the citadel; Drishti and Rozafa were both important links in the chain of communication by beacon, used by Skanderbeg and, no doubt, by earlier lords. In 1396, Drivasto was acquired by the Venetian Republic; the wellhead that can still be seen, surrounded by a ramshackle wall, is thought to be Venetian, from the mid 15th century. By then, around 100 families lived in the town. But in 1478, during the final siege of Shkodra, the houses within the castle walls and the fields below it were destroyed by Ottoman troops, as part of their strategy of starving out the city's defenders. Edith Durham visited Drishti in 1908 and was entertained in the imposing house of the head of the village, the one with the covered balcony (*çardak*), on your right as you come through the castle walls from the main road. The house had two entrances, each with its own flight of stone stairs, one for men and the other for women; the front steps are ruined now, but the back flight is still visible.

The road is in reasonable condition as far as the castle entrance, although a 4x4 would probably be needed in wet weather. Minibuses ply several times a day between Shkodra and Mesi, where the bridge is. From Mesi, a minibus runs early every school-day morning and then again at lunchtime to the school in the modern village of Drishti, below the castle; it takes the school teachers to work and brings them back again, but they will probably be prepared to squeeze up and make room for one or two foreign tourists, if necessary. It is quite a long way from the village up to the castle, but if you are on foot you can use the cobbled path that leads up to the main gate – the entrance on the other side of the castle from the gate where the asphalt road passes.

PUKA *Telephone code (Puka town): 0212*

The district of Puka nestles in the corner formed by the spectacular lakes created by the hydro-electric damming of the River Drini. The old road from Shkodra to Kukësi, which more or less bisects Puka, follows much of the line of an ancient trade route along which the Romans built one of their great arterial roads, the Via Publica. This connected the Adriatic ports of Dyrrachium (now Durrësi) and Apollonia with Prizreni, Niš and, eventually, Odessa on the Black Sea. Traces of the Roman road can still be seen in the district. In the Ottoman period, the route became even more important: there was a customs post at Vau i Spasit, the ford by which travellers crossed the Drini from Puka to Hasi (page 156). Fortifications were built to protect the road at Qafa e Malit and at Vau i Spasit.

These hundreds of years of Puka's history are reflected in the variety of its textiles as well as its castles, bridges and fortified houses. Ringed by mountains and fjord-like lakes, Puka also has magnificent scenery and, thanks to its good infrastructure, this can be enjoyed in winter as well as summer. The town of Puka, 838m above sea level, has long been the best place to ski in Albania.

GETTING THERE AND AWAY The main road that cuts across the district of Puka makes much of its territory surprisingly accessible and, happily for cyclists, the heavy traffic that used to congest it has now transferred on to the A1 highway to the south. Beyond the turn-off for Komani (page 159), the road climbs higher and higher, in tight hairpin bends; the scenery is wild and desolate, with spectacular views of the River Drini below.

From Tirana, **buses** to the towns of Puka and Fushë-Arrëzi leave from the North/South bus terminal at roughly hourly intervals from early morning until mid afternoon; the last bus of the day leaves Tirana at 16.00. Buses going to Fushë-Arrëzi can drop off passengers in Puka. The journey to Puka takes about 3½ hours and the fare is 500 lek. There are also buses in the mornings between Puka and Shkodra, a journey time of 1½–2 hours. In Puka, the bus station is on the northern edge of the town, a short walk from the pedestrianised main square, Sheshi Tërbuni.

With **bikes** or **4x4** vehicles, an alternative route into Puka is by the old road up from Mirdita (page 145), following the River Fani i Madh. The road is almost deserted, now that all the traffic uses the highway, and the surface is reasonable; it is a beautiful run of about 60km from Rrësheni in Mirdita to Fushë-Arrëzi in Puka.

WHERE TO STAY AND EAT

Puka town

Hani i Përparim Laçit (25 rooms) Rr. Ismet Uke Laçi, Puka; m 069 22 19 985; e haniperparimlacit@gmail.com; f HaniPerparimLacitPuke. Hotel & ski complex in a countryside setting, a short walk or longer drive from the town centre. 2 stone-built hotels & wooden chalets, all set in extensive grounds; excellent restaurant with traditional menu & huge open fireplace, very popular locally; bar service; conference/private dining room. Family-run, very welcoming & friendly; some English spoken; good Wi-Fi throughout. Access to ski-run & climbing wall (page 133) from grounds; skis & skates for hire; hiking, climbing & jeep excursions around Puka district can be arranged. Camping also possible. All rooms en suite with CH, TV. FB available. **$$**

Hotel Turizëm Puka (HTP) (32 rooms) Puka Qendër; 22822; m 067 20 70 306; e info@hotel-puka.com. Central location overlooking lake. Lift; ample parking; Wi-Fi. Restaurant; popular bar serving Puka beer, brewed next door. Conference room with traditional fireplace; excursions with guide can be arranged. All rooms en suite with hairdryer, TV, CH; some have balcony. **$$**

Dardha

Alpin (6 rooms) On main road above Dardha village; m 068 20 60 361; e hoteldardha@gmail.com; f Hotel Alpin Dardha. Sympathetically designed modern chalet-style building; beautiful setting on the edge of the forest with views of Lake Fierza; landscaped gardens with trout pond & water features; restaurant offering local specialities. Motorboat available for lake excursions. All rooms en suite; 1 has balcony. **$$**

Kunora (4 rooms) On main road above Dardha village; m 068 23 13 943; e Albano-Uka@hotmail.com; f Hotel Bar Kunora. Beautiful location overlooking Lake Fierza, with views on clear days to Bajram Curri & Kukësi. Renowned restaurant with traditional specialities, menus available in English & Italian; popular bar with selection of local drinks, inc cornelian cherry raki; private dining room with *sofra* (low, circular table), fireplace & balcony. Boats available for lake excursions & fishing trips. Simple twin rooms, shared toilet & basic shower. Camping possible. **$**

WHAT TO SEE AND DO In the last few years, Puka town centre has been spruced up and partly pedestrianised. Information boards at various locations introduce some of the notable people from the town and suggest places to visit in the area. A good place to start is the town's **museum** (free admission), housed within the Cultural Centre in the main square, with its excellent exhibition of traditional costumes and other local textiles, richly embroidered with ancient designs. There is a small display of locally made musical instruments, *lahuta* and *sharki*, while the historical section gives an overview of the archaeology of the area, from prehistory through the Roman and Byzantine periods to the Middle Ages.

A short walk from the square, past the Hotel Turizëm Puka, leads to the **lake**. Walkways and wooden bridges have transformed this into a very pleasant place for a stroll, even on a grey winter's day. In summer, rowing boats can be hired. Benches at various points around the lake provide spots to rest and enjoy the views of the town and the mountains. Wooden steps at the northwestern edge of the lake join a footpath, which leads up to the main road and is a short cut to the Hani i Përparim Laçit complex.

Most of Puka's historic churches were demolished in the late 1960s (see page 21 for more about the atheism campaign of those years). Some have been rebuilt since the restoration of freedom of worship; one of these is at **Kçira**, where the foundations of the destroyed church have been lovingly walled around and planted with herbs and flowers. The Catholic community of Kçira runs an interesting agricultural improvement programme, with experimental plantations of cereals, fruit and herbs. They are testing different kinds of crops, to see which do best in the local soil, and they dry herbs for use as medicinal infusions. They also keep pigs, which end up being turned into sausages, prosciutto and salami in the project's kitchens, and breed sheepdogs. Kçira is on the main road, 15 minutes' drive from Puka town; coming from there, the church is visible down a track to the right just after Kçira, indicated with a large cross at the junction.

Puka is famous for the quality and quantity of its ceps (called in Albanian by their Italian name, *porçini*) and other fungi. Most of these are exported fresh to Italy; **Agropuka**, a farmers' association based in Puka, is spearheading an attempt to add value locally to these and other sought-after products. In modern dryers, they prepare ceps, fruit such as apple and persimmon, and herbal teas, which are then packaged in-house and sold locally and in Tirana, including in the airport duty-free shops. The factory outlet in the outskirts of Puka town is an excellent place to stock up on these treats, whose great advantage for the traveller is that they are very light and unbreakable. Agropuka also sells fruit conserves and local honey. Finally, no visit to the town would be complete without sampling a beer from **Birra Puka**. The brewery is just behind the Hotel Turizëm Puka; ask at reception if a tour can be arranged.

Once you have bought all these goodies, a nice spot for a picnic is **Mrizi i Memajve**, signposted up a reasonable track off the main road about halfway between Puka and Fushë-Arrëzi. A *mriz* is a shady grove where livestock can shelter from the heat of the afternoon; Mrizi i Memajve is now used by the people of Puka for barbecues in summer. There are beautiful views of the surrounding mountains. It is also possible to camp here.

Puka district has many surviving fortified houses, or *kulla* (see box, page 143). Some fine examples can be seen on the way to one of Puka's most exciting attractions: the **Levrushku Cave** (Shpella e Levrushkut), above Lake Komani. This cave was used as a hermitage and it has a tiny chapel at the entrance, built into the rock; for this reason, it is also known as 'the Christian's Cave' (Shpella e Kaurrit). The exciting thing about it is that it can only be accessed from the lake; you clamber up the rock face from a small boat, as the hermits would have done, a 5–10m climb depending on the water level in the lake. At the entrance to the cave, in front of the rock chapel, the hermits built a wall with an embrasure, just like a fortified house. The interior of the main cave – 20m long – is divided into two levels, each with a balcony from which the inhabitants could keep an eye out for intruders. The Christian's Cave can be reached by boat from the dam at Komani, but a more interesting option is to hike (with a guide) from Qelëzi, an hour or so's drive up rough roads from Puka town. From Qelëzi, a path leads down to and then along the river which you will follow almost to the point where it joins Lake Komani. The path rises high above the river and provides lovely views of the mountains and of *kulla*, in clusters or standing alone. Two abandoned *kulla* can be explored just beyond the village of Levrushku, on either side of a smaller river (which you have to ford). Finally, you reach the place where the boatman will meet you and take you across the river and around into the lake, where the entrance to the Christian's Cave is marked by a high, tumbling waterfall. A whole day should be set aside for this excursion; it is one for which a guide is advisable, even for travellers who like to be very independent, because co-ordination with the boatman is essential and the path is not always clear.

Right on the other side of the district, on Lake Fierza, is **Dardha**. With two hotels above the village (page 131), this is an ideal base for a couple of days' hiking or boat trips on the lake. It is about 55km from Puka town, on the road to Fierza from where one can continue up to Tropoja or take the ferry down Lake Komani (page 158) and back to the coast. The descent from here down to Fierza is very steep, with many hairpin bends; cycling in the opposite direction would be very hard work, possibly more than 2,000m ascent in total. There are old fortified houses in Dardha, one said to be 300 years old, right down on the lakeside. Near the top of the hill that leads down to the lake from the main road is a three-storey *kullë* whose owners can show you around. From the outside you can see the niche built into the wall of the guests' room; coffee and the implements to make it were kept here, so the head of the household could reach them easily from where he sat, to prepare and serve coffee for his guests. Below it is a *frëngji*, the embrasure from which unwanted visitors could be shot; the owners of the house have bricked it up to keep out draughts, but its shape is still clear. The owners do their best to maintain this fascinating old house, but the upkeep costs are very high and they would appreciate a small donation towards this.

In the dry weather of a normal summer, it would also be possible to get to Mërturi i Gurit, which has more than a dozen fortified houses, although only two of them are inhabited. A good base for hiking and exploring in summer, including to Mërturi, is **Iballa**, tucked into the centre of a ring of high mountains. Huber Kartographie's series of hiking **maps** (page 42) includes a useful map of the district of Puka.

WINTER SPORTS Puka has long been the best place to ski in Albania. It has good accommodation and, in most years, there is snow from October to March, with over 1m in the winter months. Përparim Laçi (**m** 068 20 56 472; **e** haniperparimlacit@gmail.com), who is a registered ski instructor with the Albanian Ski Federation, runs a ski resort a short drive from the town centre. A 600m piste has been cut through the forest; there is a simple ski-lift and a snow-making machine. Skis can be hired and training can be provided for children aged five or over and adults. Ice skates can be hired too, for use when the nearby lake is frozen over. For summer visits, there is a climbing wall. Clay-pigeon shooting is also offered.

In his younger days, Përparim climbed in the Himalayas. He can offer advice and guiding to climbers who wish to explore some of the peaks in Puka district or beyond.

LEZHA *Telephone code: 0215*

Albanians are always very keen for foreigners to visit Lezha, because it is where their national hero Skanderbeg, or Gjergj Kastrioti, brought the Albanian clan chieftains together to swallow their differences and unite against the Ottoman threat.

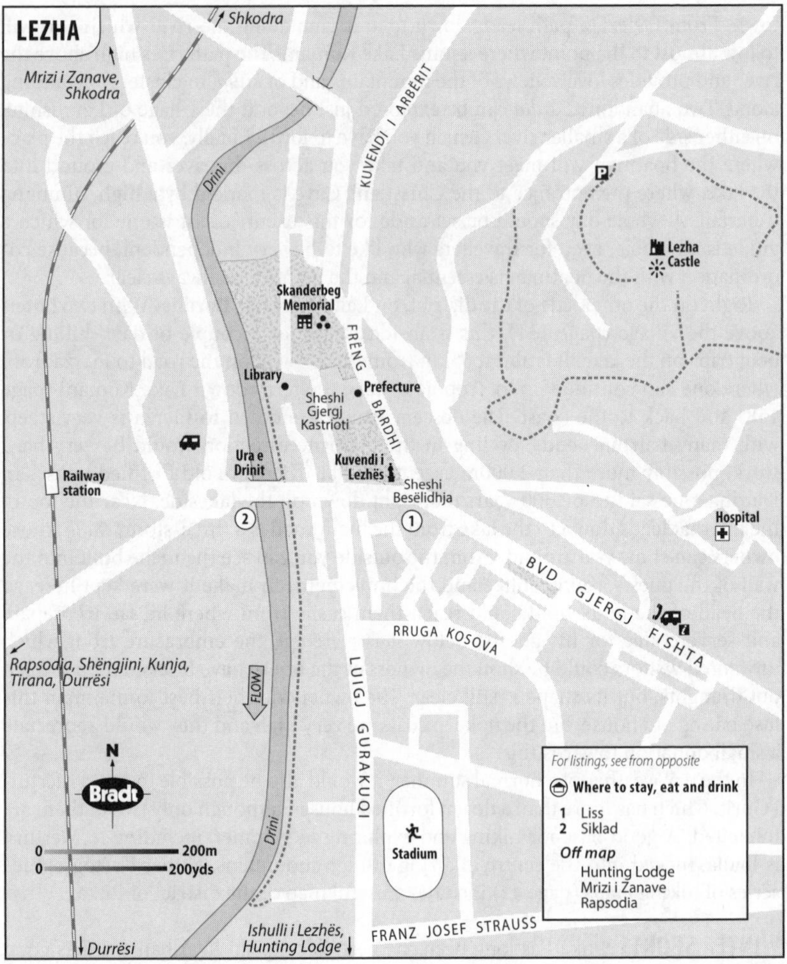

When Skanderbeg died in 1468, after 24 years successfully resisting the Ottomans, he was buried in Lezha's cathedral.

Lezha has Illyrian fortifications, including the citadel above the town, which can be visited. During the Roman period, it was called Lissus and was an important river port. In 48BC, Mark Antony landed at what is now Shëngjini (then called Nymphaeum) on his way to link up with Julius Caesar in their campaign against Pompey. Lezha was part of the Venetian Republic for most of the 15th century, and in this period the town – by then called Alessio – and its port thrived. In the Ottoman period Lezha, like Durrësi and other Adriatic-facing Albanian towns, fell into decline, and it did not really begin to recover until Italy's economic and political influence began to grow in the 1930s.

Shëngjini, known in Italian as San Giovanni di Medua, is the second-largest port in Albania, after Durrësi. To the south of the port, a beautiful sandy beach stretches for several miles to the Merxhani Lagoon, part of the wetlands that make up the Kune-Vaini Nature Reserve. In the summer months, this resort is a very popular destination for Albanian-speaking tourists, and it can become rather busy.

The Kune-Vaini reserve straddles both sides of the River Drini, and offers magnificent birdwatching opportunities (page 140). It is within easy reach of both Shëngjini and Lezha, either of which would make an ideal base for day trips into the reserve.

GETTING THERE AND AWAY Lezha is just off the SH1 coastal highway, about halfway between Shkodra and Tirana. It is a little less than an hour from Shkodra and about the same, depending on traffic, from Tirana.

Buses ply the route constantly until at least 17.00. They leave Tirana from the North/South bus terminal and Shkodra from Sheshi Demokracia. If there is no transport specifically for Lezha at the time you want to travel, you can catch any bus up or down the coastal highway and get off at the Lezha junction; from there, it is a 5-minute walk across the bridge into the centre of Lezha. In Lezha, the bus station is on Bulevardi Gjergj Fishta.

In summer, there are frequent buses to Shëngjini from Lezha and also from Shkodra, leaving in the morning and returning in the afternoon. There is no public transport to the Vaini area of the nature reserve, but a 4x4 is not required and any Lezha taxi driver could take you.

WHERE TO STAY *Map, opposite*

Liss (21 rooms, 2 suites) Sheshi Besëlidhja; 24700; m 067 20 09 841, 069 66 90 799; e hotel-liss@uldedajgroup.al; w hotelliss.al. Right in the centre of town, the former 'Turizmi', completely renovated, is comfortable, well run & with some English spoken. Good restaurant, popular bar, terrace; free parking, free Wi-Fi; laundry service. All rooms en suite with hairdryer, TV, AC, phone, minibar. **$$$**

Siklad (14 rooms) Pranë urës së Drinit; 22333; m 068 20 33 445, 069 25 91 848. At the bridge from the highway into town; restaurant on ground floor; friendly management; free parking, free Wi-Fi throughout. B/fast inc. All rooms en suite with good shower, hairdryer, flatscreen TV, AC. **$$**

WHERE TO EAT *Map, opposite, unless otherwise stated*

The restaurant at the Liss Hotel is open to non-residents and offers an Italian-inspired menu of pasta, pizza, escalopes and grilled meat ($$$–$$). Weather permitting, the sunken garden outside the restaurant is a very pleasant place to eat or drink, with the tables arranged around a fountain. In Shëngjini, there are good fish restaurants ($$$) near the entrance to the port.

The wider Lezha area has several excellent restaurants and is becoming a culinary destination in its own right. Visitors who are interested in gastronomy should try to sample at least one of the restaurants listed here.

Rapsodia On the Shëngjini road, about 4km out of Lezha; m 068 29 47 771; e info@hotelrapsodia.com; w hotelrapsodia.com. A fairly formal restaurant with excellent antipasti & fish, as well as Italian-influenced meat dishes. Has 9 en-suite guest rooms (**$$**). Once a month, the chef prepares a special gastronomic menu, sometimes cooking with flowers, sometimes reversing the order of courses; phone for details. $$$$$

Hunting Lodge (Hoteli i Gjuetisë) Ishulli i Lezhës; m 068 90 66 660; e info@hoteligjuetise.al; w hoteligjuetise.al. Built in the 1930s by Mussolini's son-in-law, Count Galeazzo Ciano, who also served as Fascist Italy's foreign minister, it was used by party functionaries during the communist period & ransacked by rioters in 1997. Now fully renovated, also has 4 en-suite guest rooms. Specialising in traditional Albanian cuisine, inc excellent fresh fish, the restaurant a good choice for a leisurely lunch after a long morning's birdwatching in the Vaini marshlands. $$$

Mrizi i Zanave [map, page 116] Fishta, Blinishti; **m** 069 21 08 032; **e** info@mrizizanave.com; **w** mrizizanave.com. Beautiful setting in the countryside northeast of Lezha, in the birthplace of the priest & Gheg poet Gjergj Fishta (the restaurant takes its name from the title of his masterpiece). Part of the Slow Food movement, it uses local ingredients, many from its own farm or foraged, to prepare perfectly grilled meat, exquisite salads, unusual side dishes & desserts. The good house wine is also locally produced. In summer, there are tables outside on shady terraces. English spoken; also has 9 guest rooms (**$$**). The owners' environmental commitment extends to having installed a solar-powered flour mill. Blinishti is signposted off the main Lezha–Shkodra highway; homemade signs direct you to Mrizi i Zanave; phone the restaurant if lost. **$$$**

WHAT TO SEE AND DO

Skanderbeg Memorial (⌚ 09.00–13.00 & 15.00–18.00 Tue–Sun; 100 lek) Lezha's main claim to fame is as the place where Albania's national hero, Skanderbeg united

SKANDERBEG

Albania's national hero was born Gjergj (George) Kastrioti, the son of a powerful Albanian chieftain who controlled a large swathe of what is now northern Albania from his citadel at Kruja. When the Ottomans advanced towards Kruja in 1433, Gjergj's father struck a deal with them to be allowed to continue ruling his lands as a vassal – this was not untypical of the decentralised way in which the Ottoman Empire administered Albania in later years too. As part of the deal, Gjergj was sent to be brought up in the sultan's court, where he was trained as a soldier and given the name Skënder (Alexander), with the honorific ending 'beg' (or 'bey').

In 1443, the Ottomans suffered a serious defeat at Niš, in Serbia. Skanderbeg seized the moment and raised his family's standard – the double-headed eagle on a red background which is the national flag of modern Albania – from the castle at Kruja. The exact circumstances in which he did so are unclear, but the traditional version is that he and his men deserted the Ottoman army at Niš and rode from there to Kruja, where Skanderbeg tricked the Ottoman guards into letting him into the citadel.

He then achieved the feat that has given him his place in history. The Albanian clans, like their Scottish counterparts of the same period, spent most of their time fighting each other, which made them easy prey for better-organised invaders. Skanderbeg managed to gather all the clan chiefs together, in Lezha, on 2 March 1444, and made them undertake to put their differences aside. A solemn undertaking of this sort is known in Albanian as *besa*, an expression that is still widely used in modern times to mean something like 'word of honour'. The agreement of the besa at Lezha is called *besëlidhja* in Albanian, and has given its name to the town's main square.

The Lezha besa allowed the clans to concentrate on fighting the invaders, and they held them at bay for an astonishing 34 years. Kruja came under siege in 1449–50, and many died before the Ottoman forces withdrew. The sultan, Murad II, died soon after the retreat from Kruja. His successor Mehmed II turned his attention to Constantinople, and it was not until he had conquered that city that he returned to Albania. Meanwhile, Skanderbeg tried to rally support for his beleaguered country from other European nations, but his diplomatic initiatives brought little success. In 1466, the Ottoman army returned to Kruja; Skanderbeg sought military assistance from Naples, which enabled him to break the siege the following year.

Skanderbeg died of malaria in Lezha in 1468, leaving only a son who was too young to take over his father's command; yet the besa held and the clans stayed united against the Ottomans. Kruja finally fell in 1478. The last citadel to be lost the country's feuding clan chiefs against Ottoman attack, and where he was buried after 24 years of resistance. There is a monument to the gathering of the clan chiefs – known in Albanian as Kuvendi i Lezhës, the Assembly of Lezha – at the corner of Sheshi Besëlidhja ('Pledge-bond' Square), as you enter Lezha over the bridge from the highway.

When Skanderbeg died, in January 1468, he was buried in St Nicholas's Cathedral in Lezha. His death marked the beginning of the end for the Albanian resistance, and when the Ottomans occupied Lezha, they ransacked Skanderbeg's tomb and converted the cathedral into a mosque. Between 1880 and 1905, the site was used by the local Bektashi community (page 23) as a *tyrbe*, or shrine; Bektashis believe that the young Gjergj Kastrioti converted to Bektashism while he was in Constantinople. For the quincentenary of Skanderbeg's death, shortly after Albania had been declared the world's first atheist state, the mosque was

was Rozafa Castle in Shkodra (page 119), the following year. Folk legend has it that Skanderbeg's son led a group of Albanians across the Adriatic to settle in southern Italy. To this day there are villages there in which an archaic form of Albanian is spoken; the dialect, and the people who speak it, are called Arbëresh.

The year after the Ottomans had taken Shkodra, they crossed the Adriatic and captured the castle of Otranto. They were unable to hold it for more than a few months, thanks in part to a revolt in Albania that occupied their troops there, and under the next sultan, Bayezid II, they gave up on their plans to expand their conquests westwards beyond the Balkans. It is often said that had it not been for János Hunyadi, the Turks would have taken Vienna and the political fault-lines of Europe would have been hundreds of miles further north than they are. Less attention has been given to the possibility that without Skanderbeg and the Albanian resistance, much of what is now Italy would have fallen, and the fault-lines would have been several hundred miles further west.

THE DEATH OF SKANDERBEG

They brought [Skanderbeg] his son – small and tender, with long golden hair. Skanderbeg took him in his arms and said: 'Oh, my little flower, who has bloomed amid the surge of battle; oh, flower of my broken heart! When I die, my comrades will continue the war. And if it turns out that you are not big enough to hold and wield a sword, take care that the Turks do not imprison you alive and lock the door. I know the Turks well. They try to distort a man's spirit, to turn him against himself and his clan, to make him an oppressor of his own land. And then honour is blanketed in disgrace.

'And so, if you see that you are in trouble, take your mother and three ships, the best we have, and set off across the sea. Then, when you grow up, come back to your land and carry on my struggle. I say this to you not to save you from death, but to save the clan from defilement; because defilement is worse than death.'

'When you reach that pebbly beach over there, you will see a shady, mournful cypress. There, to the trunk of that cypress, tie my horse; and above the horse, raise my flag so that it ripples; and under the flag, tie my sword. When the sea breeze blows, my horse will whinny, the flag will flutter and my sword will resound under the shady cypress. The Turks will hear it. They will be afraid of the death which my sword brings, and they will not dare to throw themselves into battle.'

From Mitrush Kuteli's Old Albanian Tales

requisitioned, its minaret was removed and Lezha's former cathedral became a shrine to Skanderbeg.

The Skanderbeg Memorial is protected by a modern pillared structure that surrounds and roofs the ruined cathedral. As you pass through the carved wooden doors into the cathedral, there is a bronze bust of the hero directly ahead of you. Behind it, on a red mosaic background, is the double-headed eagle which was Skanderbeg's flag and is now the national flag of Albania. Below the bust are replicas of his sword and his helmet topped with a roebuck's head; the 15th-century originals are in the New Imperial Palace (Neue Burg) in Vienna, part of the Kunsthistorisches Museum's Arms and Armour Collection. On each of the side walls hang shields,

BIRD SPECIES IN THE WETLANDS

By far the most common birds in the wetlands of Albania are coots (*Fulica atra*), and there are also many species of duck (Anatidae), but the following is a selection of the more spectacular birds that can be observed in Albania's coastal wetlands. Serious birdwatchers may like to contact the Albanian Ornithological Society (**e** aos@aos-alb.org; **w** aos-alb.org).

GREAT CORMORANT (*Phalacrocorax carbo*) This black, long-bodied, long-necked waterbird swims and dives for fish, and may perch on rocks and in dead trees. It characteristically stands with its wings outstretched, to dry them. In spring it has white feathers on its head and neck, and bold white patches on its flanks.

PYGMY CORMORANT (*Microcarbo pygmaeus*) About half the size of *P. carbo*, the pygmy cormorant otherwise looks similar. It nests in trees, preferably willow (*Salix*), and feeds in reed beds and in the transition zones between reed beds and open waters. Pygmy cormorants occasionally forage together in flocks. It is thought that they may drive shoals of fish towards the edge of reed beds, in order to catch them more easily.

SQUACCO HERON (*Ardeola ralloides*) This beautiful small heron is rather shy and often solitary, feeding either by 'standing and waiting' or walking slowly along. The breeding plumage is mainly golden, with long brown streaked nape plumes and a greenish-blue bill, but in flight it is surprisingly white.

LITTLE EGRET (*Egretta garzetta*) These white, medium-sized herons have black legs and bright yellow feet, and in the breeding season have long white nape plumes. They are sociable, often boisterous, birds and nest with other herons in trees. They feed mostly on fish and small shore-dwelling animals.

BLACK-CROWNED NIGHT HERON (*Nycticorax nycticorax*) The size of the little egret, but stockier, adults are a soft grey colour, with a black back and crown, and white head plumes in spring. Young birds are brown-buff and spotted. The legs are raspberry-pink at the start of the breeding period and yellowish the rest of the year. It rests by day in clumps of trees or bushes and is easiest to see at dusk, when it flies around and feeds.

SPOONBILL (*Platalea leucorodia*) The long, broad, spatulate bills that give spoonbills their English name make them unmistakable. They are white, but much larger than little egrets. They feed with a graceful side-to-side sweeping action, catching each representing one of the battles he waged against the invaders. On the back wall of the cathedral, a fragment of fresco has survived from the 15th century.

Recent excavations have revealed a 12th-century baptistery just next to the memorial, which shows that there was a church on this site long before the cathedral was built. In the surrounding park, remains of Illyrian and Roman fortifications can be seen, which once extended all the way up the hill to the citadel.

Lezha Castle (🕘 09.00–noon & 15.00–20.00 daily; 100 lek) Lezha was one of the links in the chain of castles used by Skanderbeg to communicate information up and down the country; a beacon lit here can be seen from Rozafa Castle, 45km to

small aquatic animals. In the breeding season, adults have a yellow patch round their necks and a bushy crest at the back of the neck.

GREATER FLAMINGO (*Phoenicopterus roseus*) These large, distinctive birds are a fairly recent arrival in Albania but can now be seen in large numbers in the three main wetland sites, especially Narta. Saline lagoons are their typical habitat, although they bathe and drink in freshwater inlets. Flamingos nest in large, dense colonies, on mudflats or small islands. They fly with their long necks and legs extended, revealing the striking pink-and-black pattern under their wings.

GLOSSY IBIS (*Plegadis falcinellus*) The size of a little egret, the glossy ibis is very dark, with a long, down-curved bill. The rich chestnut plumage has beautiful green and purple highlights. Glossy ibis eat small water-dwelling animals and, like spoonbills, they fly with their necks stretched out, often in single file. In Albania, they breed at the heronry in the Divjaka-Karavasta National Park.

EURASIAN CURLEW (*Numenius arquata*) Europe's largest wading bird, the curlew is easily identifiable by its long, down-curved bill. In the breeding season, the males can often be heard before they are seen, with the evocative 'bubbling' call they use to attract mates and defend their territories. The curlew population is in global decline, because of habitat loss and egg predation, and it is classified as 'near threatened'. The slender-billed curlew (*Numenius tenuirostris*), which has previously been recorded in Albania, is now thought to be possibly extinct in Europe.

GREATER SPOTTED EAGLE (*Clanga clanga*) The spotted eagle is a medium-sized eagle (wingspan 1.53–1.77m), with dark brown plumage and slightly paler flight feathers. Juveniles have rows of white spots along the upper wing. It occurs in lowland forests near wetlands, where it nests in tall trees, and hunts – sometimes soaring to 100m high – for small mammals, waterbirds, frogs and snakes. In Europe, its population is declining rapidly, as a result of extensive habitat loss, poaching and electrocution, and it is classified as 'critically endangered'.

WHITE-TAILED EAGLE (*Haliaeetus albicilla*) White-tailed sea-eagles are huge birds (wingspan 1.90–2.40m). The adults are easily identified from their white tails and large yellow bills. However, it takes about five years for adult plumage to be acquired and immature birds can be confused with other eagles. They require large expanses of lake, coast or river valley and are usually seen on their own.

the north, and at Kruja, 54km south. In dry weather it is possible to drive up to the castle in any reasonably robust car; when the track is wet, a 4x4 will be needed. It is a pleasant, though steepish, walk of 30–45 minutes, with good views of the Drini Delta on the way and, of course, from the castle itself, at the top. There is another well-preserved section of the ancient wall about halfway up.

The interior of the citadel is very interesting, especially if you have previously visited Rozafa. Like its bigger and better-preserved neighbour, Lezha Castle has a church that was converted into a mosque, a cistern for storing rainwater, and a dungeon, complete with air hole so that the unfortunate prisoners could breathe. The citadel was first fortified in the 4th century BC; the surviving buildings and the watchtowers are medieval, built between the 15th and 17th centuries. A helpful information panel has been installed near the entrance to the castle, with a timeline and information about the main buildings within.

ZadrimArt (m 068 28 28 582; f ZadrimArt-Krajen Lezh) The ZadrimArt workshop creates and sells beautiful ceramics. It was set up by the priest of this Catholic district, Zadrima, to generate employment for the villagers so that they would not have to leave the area in search of work in Tirana or Italy. They will show you the whole process, from treating the clay, forming the items on the potter's wheel, painting them with traditional or modern designs and, finally, firing them. Then you can browse in the sale-room for bowls, jugs, plates and smaller souvenirs. Examples of the workshop's products are shown on its Facebook page. The staff will wrap your purchases carefully, so that you have a chance of getting them home in one piece. ZadrimArt is a 10-minute drive from Mrizi i Zanave (page 136); ask at the restaurant for directions.

BIRDWATCHING IN THE NORTHERN ALBANIAN WETLANDS The wetlands surrounding the mouths of the Buna and Mati rivers are important sites for wintering and migratory waterbirds. Some 700ha around Velipoja and 2,300ha in Kune-Vaini, south of Shëngjini, have been designated as Protected Landscapes (IUCN Category V). The 2019 International Waterbird Census in these two protected areas recorded many cormorants, herons and flamingos. There are also many species of duck, including the common pochard (*Aythya ferina*) which, despite its English name, is not very common in Europe.

Both Velipoja and Shëngjini are easy to get to and have good accommodation nearby. Room rates in these beach resorts increase substantially in July and August, when all the hotels there are likely to be fully booked several weeks in advance.

The habitats The river called the Buna in Albanian forms the border between Albania and Montenegro, where it is known as the Bojana. Where it meets the sea, it divides into two branches between which is the little (Montenegrin) island of Ada Bojana. Both sides of the river are under pressure from tourism. On the Albanian side, a large expanse of inland marshes and reed beds make up the Dumi Marsh (Këneta e Dumit), which gives way to a sandy beach and the resort of Velipoja. At the eastern end of the beach is the Viluni Lagoon (Laguna e Vilunit), a large, shallow coastal lagoon of about 300ha. The beach then continues along the coast of the Drini Bay to the port of Shëngjini.

The southern end of the Drini Bay marks the beginning of a complex of coastal lagoons, sandbars and marshes that extend south to the mouth of the River Mati and the Patoku Lagoon, a good place to observe curlews (*Numenius arquata*). Draining of these marshes began in the 1930s, in King Zog's efforts to eradicate malaria. After World War II, the area was cultivated and networked with an extensive irrigation system, although since the fall of communism this has not been well maintained and, in some places, the marshes are beginning to reclaim the land. An even greater threat to the wetlands now comes from the development of beach tourism. At Shëngjini, there are restaurants and hotels even within the protected area.

MATI *Telephone code (Burreli): 0217*

Mati was the home district of Ahmed Zogu, the clan chieftain who became King Zog (page 12), and it is full of history, fortified houses and caves. The district capital, Burreli, is only 36km from the main Tirana–Shkodra highway. There are several interesting places to visit in Mati and it is well worth a short detour.

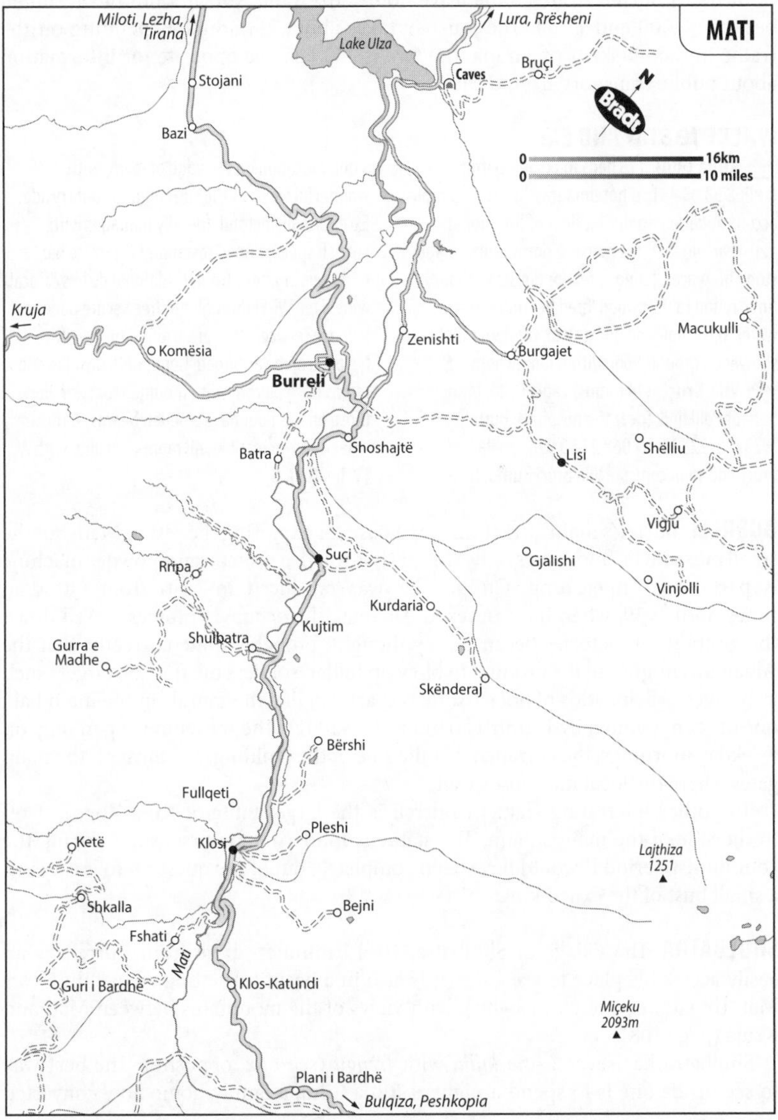

GETTING THERE AND AWAY The turn-off for Burreli is signposted off the A1 highway that links the Albanian coast with Kosovo, the Rruga e Kombit or the 'Road of the Nation'. From the junction with the SH1, the coastal highway, the drive to Burreli takes about an hour through spectacular scenery. For those with their own transport, an alternative route is the narrow, mountainous road from Kruja (page 110) over the Shtama Pass (Qafë-Shtama), about 50km. There is no public transport and the pass is closed when there is snow.

The new highway connecting Tirana and Dibra, **Rruga e Arbërit,** was provisionally inaugurated in late 2021. Once it is completed, the new highway will cut the journey time between Tirana and Peshkopia to less than an hour, but it will leave Mati in a kind of cul-de-sac.

Buses to Burreli from Tirana leave hourly from the North/South bus terminal between 07.00 and 17.00. The journey takes about 2½ hours, depending on the traffic in the outskirts of Tirana; the fare is 400 lek. See opposite for information about public transport around Mati.

WHERE TO STAY AND EAT

Kulla Gjini (16 beds max) Shulbatra; m 068 53 03 481; e hotelmagra@live.com. Simple accommodation on the 1st floor of traditional 120-year-old fortified house. 2 dorms with carved stone fireplaces, lounge area for guests with *sofra* (low, round table); wood-fired heating & hot water; basic toilet on guest floor, modern toilet & shower on ground floor within family home. **$**

Vila Bruçi (14 rooms) Lagja Drita, pranë Spitalit Poliklinik (near the hospital), Burreli; t 23266, 22387; m 068 21 59 926; e vila-bruci@hotmail.com; f Vila Bruci Burrel. In a quiet location on the edge of town, with wonderful views of the surrounding countryside. Exceptionally helpful, friendly management; English spoken. Good restaurant & terrace bar (**$$**) serving fresh trout, traditional dishes & local wine. Free Wi-Fi throughout; free secure parking; laundry service. Tours of surrounding area & beyond can be arranged. Generous b/fast inc. Most rooms have balcony with mountain or river views; those on top floor have wooden beams; some are wheelchair-accessible. All rooms en suite, with AC, TV, heating. **$**

BURRELI Burreli's main attraction is as a base for exploring the rest of Mati, but the small **museum** (⌚ mornings only Mon–Fri) is worth a visit; the gunpowder machine is particularly interesting. Gunpowder was produced in Mati from Ottoman times until 1939, when Italy annexed Albania. The occupying forces closed down the gunpowder factories because they thought, probably quite correctly, that the Albanians might use the product to blow up Italian soldiers or strategic targets such as bridges. Aficionados of Socialist Realist art will like the murals in the main hall, one of them painted by Fatmir Haxhiu (1927–2001). The museum is open only on weekday mornings; the entrance is at the side of the building, not through the main gates where the local minibuses wait.

The other interesting sight in Burreli is the large **statue** of King Zog, just off to the side of the main square. The statue is modern, of course, since during the communist period it would have been completely out of the question to erect even a small bust of the exiled king.

SHULBATRA The village of Shulbatra, 10–15 minutes' drive from Burreli, is an easily accessible place to see *kulla*. It is also in a beautiful setting, above the River Mati (in summer, one can swim), with views of the mountains between Mati and Kruja (page 108).

Shulbatra has several fine *kulla* with *frëngji* (see box, opposite). The best way to see inside one is to spend a night at **Kulla Gjini**, a family home now converted

KULLA

The traditional family houses of northern Albania were highly defensible stone buildings, usually two or three storeys high, called *kulla*, whose literal meaning is 'tower'. The word is often translated into English as 'tower house', which is confusing because these houses are not towers at all. *Kulla* are big enough for a traditional extended family to live in; the living quarters are usually on the first floor, accessed with an external staircase; where there is a third storey, this will have been used for bedrooms. The windows are small – hard to fire into and easy to shoot out of – and are often protected with stone embrasures, called *frëngji*, instead of wooden shutters.

Mati has several well-preserved *kulla*, some built as recently as the 1930s – these later buildings have windows of a more normal size, because by then security was better.

The imposing cluster of *kulla* where the Zogu family lived, in Burgajet just across the river from Burreli, was razed to the ground after World War II. The site can be seen from the terrace of the Vila Bruçi (see below). An easily accessible place to see *kulla* is the village of Shulbatra which has several fine *kulla* with *frëngji*, one of which, Kulla Gjini, has been converted into a guesthouse.

Other villages in Mati with *kulla* are Guri i Bardhë and Macukulli. However, the roads up to them are very rough and a 4x4 vehicle is needed. A rural bus leaves Macukulli early in the morning for Burreli and returns to the village around lunchtime. It would probably be possible to find accommodation in one of the village homes, or of course one could camp (see page 46 for advice on wild camping).

into a simple guesthouse. In the older part of this house, built 120 years ago, there is an inscription, carved into the stonework, in Ottoman Turkish (the family does not know what it means). The owner's grandfather built an extension in 1934 and carved his name, with the date, into the wall, as well as making sure to add built-in rifle holes. There are also stone fireplaces carved with stylised eagles.

To get there by public transport, you can take any minibus for Klosi, from the main bus terminus outside the museum in Burreli, and ask the driver to let you off at Ura e Shulbatrës ('the Shulbatra Bridge'). The turn-off can be identified from the large sign for 'Kulla Gjini'. From the main road, cross the bridge over the green River Mati and follow the asphalted road to the centre of the village. The asphalt ends here, although the road up to the guesthouse is just about drivable. It is better to park and explore the village on foot.

CAVES Another fascinating excursion in Mati is to a cluster of three caves in the north of the district, on the border with Mirdita. Recent archaeological research has found evidence that one of these, the Neziri Cave, was inhabited in the Neolithic period.

The first of the caves, **Shpella e Blasit**, is 240m deep, through a short but very confined opening. Once you have wriggled through this rather scary tunnel, you emerge into a long, high cave, full of beautiful stalactites. The second, **Shpella e Keputës**, is also long, with thousands of sleeping bats; the end of this cave is blocked with earth, not bedrock as in Shpella e Blasit, and it is thought that it might ultimately link up with Shpella e Valit, across the district border in Mirdita. Finally, **Shpella e Nezirit** was home to those Stone Age people, who cooked and ate at the entrance to the cave. Nails in the floor of the cave show where the archaeologists measured out their trenches. Lake Ulza and the mountains of Kruja can be seen from the entrance to the cave, a good choice by the Neolithic inhabitants.

The hike up to the caves starts in the village of Bruçi, about half an hour's drive from Burreli, off the road to Rrësheni. The turn-off for Bruçi is at the petrol station in Uraka, 20km or so from Rrësheni and about 15km from Burreli. This main road is fully asphalted; after the turn-off, the asphalt continues for a while after Uraka and then peters out.

The hike takes about 2 hours, plus however long you spend in the caves, and requires reasonable fitness and sensible shoes. A good torch is essential; a local guide is highly recommended. The owner of the hotel in Burreli (page 142) is originally from Bruçi and can either organise a tour to the caves for you or contact one of his relatives in the village in advance, to meet you there. Alternatively, you can ask the staff in the café in Bruçi to contact a guide for you.

MIRDITA *Telephone code (Rrësheni): 0216*

The district of Mirdita is an enchanting blend of wild mountain scenery and centuries of unique religious and cultural history. The first of these unique features is the institution called the Captaincy, or Kapedania, a hereditary position that combined the roles of judiciary and head of state. The chiefs of all of Mirdita's clans accepted the authority of the Captain, not as first among equals, like the *bajraktarë* of the rest of highland Albania, but as their judicial authority and their head of state. Edith Durham (see box, page 148) attended a council of the Mirdita clans in 1908 and took a famous photograph of the highlanders gathered, all armed to the teeth, on the lawns of St Paul's Church. The Captain resolved legal disputes according to the traditional Code, or Kanun – the version used in Mirdita was the Code of Skanderbeg – and represented the region to the Ottoman authorities and, eventually, those of independent Albania. The Captaincy's palaces were in Mirdita's ancient capital, Oroshi.

Also in Oroshi was the seat of the Abbacy of Mirdita, with special Nullius status (the only one in Albania) that made it directly dependent on the Vatican, not on any of the archbishoprics covering the rest of Albania. Mirdita has always been fiercely independent and managed to keep the Ottomans from establishing their authority over it, dealing with it instead as practically an autonomous state. Because of this resistance, almost the entire population of Mirdita is still Catholic. Most of its churches, including the Abbey at Oroshi, were burned to the ground during the atheism campaign of 1967 and have been rebuilt since freedom of worship was restored in 1990.

There was some industrialisation during the communist period, most of it linked to the copper mines in the area. At its peak, the copper industry employed 5,000 people in Mirdita alone; there were small copper-processing plants all over the district, feeding into the main plant at Rubiku. From there, the copper was sent on to Shkodra to be further processed into wire and other industrial materials. The mines closed in the 1990s and the plants that processed the minerals now generally lie idle. Mirdita experienced very high emigration as a consequence of the lack of local employment but, thanks in part to the job opportunities created by tourism and other small-scale businesses, this trend is now beginning to reverse.

Until 2010, most of the district was difficult to get to; but the construction of the A1 highway, which cuts straight through Mirdita, and improvements to minor roads have made formerly wild and remote places much more accessible. Hotel accommodation is limited, but it would be perfectly feasible for hikers or cyclists to base themselves in Rubiku or Rrësheni and explore the district from there. Those with tents could base themselves in whichever remote corner took their fancy; see page 46 for advice on wild camping in Albania.

GETTING THERE AND AWAY The A1 highway connecting Kukësi (and Kosovo) with the Adriatic port of Durrësi begins at the Miloti interchange on the coastal highway (SH1), about halfway between Tirana and Shkodra, and cuts pretty much due northeast, straight through Mirdita, with state-of-the-art tunnels blasted through inconveniently located mountains. Cyclists can avoid almost all of the highway as far as Repsi by crossing the River Fani i Madh just after Miloti, on a bridge built during King Zog's reign, and then using the old road that runs more or less parallel to the highway.

There is good **public transport** to the district capital, Rrësheni, from Tirana and Lezha. In Tirana, buses leave from the North/South bus station from early morning until mid afternoon, usually on the hour; the journey takes about 1½ hours. From Kukësi (130km), any bus heading for Tirana could drop passengers at the turn-off for Rrësheni or Rubiku. Those with their own transport could also enter Mirdita from the district of Mati, on the recently asphalted road from Burreli around the western tip of Lake Ulza.

With **bikes** or a **4x4** vehicle, an alternative route is the old road north to the district of Puka, following the River Fani i Madh. Before the new highway this was the shortest, although not the quickest, way from Rrësheni to Kukësi; now all the traffic whizzes up and down the highway and this old road, although now asphalted, is almost deserted. It is a beautiful run of about 60km between Repsi, in Mirdita, and Fushë-Arrëzi, in Puka. This would make a very attractive little circuit around a fascinating part of highland Albania for those who do not have the time or inclination to venture further north.

TOURIST INFORMATION On the SH1 highway, just beyond Rubiku on the right coming from the coast, the Infokulla, or 'Information Tower' (m 069 56 02 970; e info@hikingmirdita.com; w hikingmirdita.com; ⏲ 09.00–17.00 daily) stocks a range of publications, including hiking maps of various parts of Mirdita. The helpful, English-speaking staff can provide information about accommodation, places to see and events throughout the district. Hiking tours of varying lengths can be arranged. There is also a small museum (admission €2) with an interesting exhibition about Mirdita's history, culture, flora and fauna. There is ample parking.

WHERE TO STAY

Bujtina Dini (6 rooms) Katundi i Vjetër, Rubiku; m 068 46 52 952; f Bujtina Dini. Restaurant & bar with terrace on the ground floor & rooms above. All rooms en suite with nice wooden furniture, TV, fan & CH. **$$**

* **Marub** (19 rooms) Katundi i Vjetër, Rubiku; t 028 450 013; m 068 20 77 424, 068 24 64 009; e info@hotelmarub.com, hotelmarub@yahoo.com; w hotelmarub.com. 2km from Rubiku, set in forested hills on the (asphalted) road towards the village of Katundi i Vjetër. Modern alpine-style building, designed as a pilot project for sustainable tourism & to meet exacting environmental standards; beautiful views, ample car parking; biomass CH. Excellent restaurant using locally produced ingredients; bar; Wi-Fi. Guides & horses can be arranged for excursions in the area. Nicely furnished rooms, all en suite with water-saving shower, AC, satellite TV, fridge, ample power points, bedside lights, balcony with mountain view. **$$**

Arbëri (7 rooms) Rrësheni; t 23376; m 069 21 83 887. Opposite the cathedral, convenient for buses. Friendly management; good restaurant; bar with terrace above street. En-suite rooms. **$**

Bujtina Jaku (2 rooms) Katundi i Vjetër, Rubiku; m 068 64 39 608. Basic accommodation in village home in mountains above Rubiku, surrounded by forest. Veranda bar, simple restaurant. **$**

Kamping Lakosa Rruga Rrëshen-Perlat; m 068 68 37 504; f Kamping Lakosa. About

1km outside Rrësheni on the riverside; lovely landscaped grounds with secluded spots for mobile homes & tents. It has an excellent restaurant specialising in local traditional dishes, with service at wooden tables in garden. $

WHERE TO EAT

Eksklusiv Rrësheni; 23375. Just off main, pedestrianised square. Standard menu of *qofta* or steak with chips & salad; if given prior notice, they can also prepare locally caught trout. Excellent local wine, made from the indigenous Kallmet grape. $$

Europa Rubiku. On the main street, on the right if coming from Tirana. Exceptionally good food inc, astonishingly, vegetarian dishes other than salad. Carnivores should (also) try the grilled pork. Excellent, locally produced, Arbëri Kallmet wine. $$

Sofra e Kthellës Perlati; m 068 47 71 640. About halfway between Rrësheni & Burreli. Superb traditional dishes: chargrilled meat & vegetables, homemade sausages, grilled vegetables. $$

WHAT TO SEE AND DO

Rubiku Rubiku is a pleasant little town, with well-maintained public spaces and a commendable absence of litter. Above it, prominent on a white crag, stands a beautiful old church.

Rubiku was one of four Benedictine foundations in Mirdita – the others were Ndërfani, Shalla and Oroshi (see opposite). The church at Rubiku, St Saviour's (Kisha e Shelbuemit), was founded in 1166 and later transferred to the Franciscan order whose property it still is. There have of course been extensions and alterations made to the building over the centuries. In the 15th century, the oldest part of the church, above and behind the altar, was decorated with frescoes that, although damaged, still have the power to inspire those who worship here. The best way to be sure of being able to see inside the church is to go there on a Sunday or a major feast day. There are good views from the terrace behind the church. Both the church and the monastic buildings beside it were damaged during World War II, then allowed to fall into disrepair during the years of official atheism (page 21). The monastery is still in ruins; the church was reroofed and repaired in the 1990s and, later, the Stations of the Cross were installed along the road leading up to it.

Rrësheni The district capital, about 20 minutes' drive beyond Rubiku, is the only other town of any size in Mirdita. Rrësheni has a technical college, a Western Union office and the last ATMs before the Lura Lakes. It is the main hub for public transport out to the rest of the district and for inter-city buses to and from Lezha, Tirana and Shkodra. Buses leave from and terminate on the street outside the cathedral.

Places of interest in Rrësheni include a small historical museum, a fascinating ethnographic collection and one of Albania's finest wine producers. It is also worth visiting the cathedral. For hundreds of years, until the abolition of religion under communism, Mirdita's cathedral was the Abbey at Oroshi. It was only in December 1996 that Rrësheni was made the seat of the diocese. Construction of the new cathedral began almost immediately and continued in defiance of the destructive civil unrest that overwhelmed Albania at the beginning of 1997. It was finally completed and consecrated in 2001.

The ethnographic exhibition is in the **Cultural Centre**, just off the main pedestrianised square. The traditional costumes of Mirdita are instantly recognisable from the preponderance of red, rather than the range of colours used elsewhere in highland Albania. The Cultural Centre has a display of more than 20 different types of costume, as well as a good collection of traditional musical instruments. It is also the home of the Mirdita Ensemble, nationally and internationally renowned performers of folk music and dance. The **historical museum** is at the other end of town, beside the Europa café. The displays illustrate the themes of Mirdita's development as a state, the importance of Catholicism and the region's ethnological heritage.

Kantina Arbëri (Zona Industriale Mirditë, in the outskirts of Rrësheni; ☎ 22486; m 069 20 57 553; e info@kantina-arberi.com; w kantina-arberi.com) produces the Kallmet wine served in many restaurants in northern Albania and Tirana. Kallmet is an indigenous red-wine grape and Arbëri's are grown in Bukmira, in the hills to the north of Rrësheni. They also use Kallmet for high-quality, cask-matured raki. From the indigenous Shesh i Bardhë grape, Arbëri produces white wine and sparkling wine made using *méthode champenoise*. The house offers wine-tasting tours (from 1,000 lek per person); these should be booked three days ahead.

Oroshi The traditional capital of Mirdita, Oroshi was the seat of both its ecclesiastical and temporal powers: the Abbacy (Abacia), first mentioned in Vatican documents of 1703; and the Captaincy (Kapedania), Mirdita's unique system of government. The Captain was recognised by all other clan chiefs as the leader who could negotiate on Mirdita's behalf with foreign powers, such as the Ottoman authorities, and who was the last court of appeal in legal disputes, which were resolved according to the traditional Code (see box, page 128). The Captaincy was a hereditary position, although it did not automatically pass to the eldest son (of course it was always a man; Mirdita was not *that* different from the rest of Albania!). The Captain and his household had two palaces at Oroshi, one of them right next to the Abbey.

The importance of Oroshi as a symbol of Mirdita's unity and resistance meant that aspiring oppressors have completely destroyed it no fewer than three times. The first was during a sustained assault by the Ottomans in the 1870s, described by Edith Durham (page 148) in *High Albania*. The church was then rebuilt by the energetic abbot Prend Doçi, who also successfully negotiated with the Vatican to be brought under the direct jurisdiction of the pope (as a 'territorial prelate' or 'prelate *nullius*'). This meant that, from that point on, the abbots of Oroshi would report directly to the Vatican, rather than via an archbishop – Oroshi was the only diocese in Albania that had this special Nullius status. The church and palace were burned down again during the Second Balkan War, then demolished by the Albanian government in 1967. The church that now stands on its historic site in Oroshi was built in 1994–95, using old photographs to create an exact replica of the building destroyed by the atheism campaigners. The individuals who represented Mirdita's traditional institutions were also eliminated by the communist government: Gjon Markgjonaj, the last Captain of Mirdita, led an insurrection against it and was killed in 1946; the Abbot of Oroshi, Monsignor Frano Gjini, was shot in 1948, one of dozens of Catholics executed in northern Albania who are commemorated in Shkodra Cathedral (page 129).

The village of Oroshi, scattered across the hillside across from the church and the ruins of the palace, is now home to 20 families. It is served by two buses a day from **Repsi**, 7–8km away. Further up in the mountains is **Nënshejti**, a beautiful village with a 500-year-old church, set in magnificent scenery. It is 23km from Repsi, but the road is so bad that it takes at least 2 hours to get there. There is no public transport and a 4x4 vehicle is essential. There is no accommodation in Nënshejti at the time of writing, but it would be a wonderful place to camp.

Spaçi In 1968, the Albanian government decided to use the copper mine at Spaçi as a forced-labour camp for political prisoners. Over the next 24 years, thousands of men were imprisoned at Spaçi, behind three rings of barbed-wire fence that enclosed the whole 12ha of the mine. An unknown number died, sometimes of exhaustion and malnutrition, sometimes shot. Not all the bodies were returned to their families

– the guards would take corpses across the river and bury them in unmarked graves on the hillside opposite. The author Fatos Lubonja, who spent 11 years in Spaçi, survived (just) and has written about his experience in a book translated into English as *Second Sentence* (I B Tauris, 2009). Spaçi was not the only forced-labour camp in Albania, but it was the only one that used exclusively political prisoners. There were also a few non-prisoners employed at Spaçi. Their job was to handle the explosives, which for obvious reasons were not made available to the prisoners.

At any one time there was an average of 800 prisoners in the camp; when it closed, in 1991, 830 men were freed. They were kept, 50 to a room, in cells measuring 5m by 6m. The slightest breach of discipline could mean a stay in the isolation cell, where prisoners were left for days with no food or blankets, even in the sub-zero

EDITH DURHAM

Edith Durham, like many other travellers to the Balkans, came to the region almost by accident. She was born in London in 1863, into a comfortably off professional family. Her father was a distinguished surgeon, and her seven brothers and sisters later became eminent in their various professions. She herself studied fine art and exhibited twice at the Royal Academy. However, when her mother became ill in the 1890s, it fell to Edith, as the eldest daughter in the family, to abandon her artistic career and devote herself to her mother's care.

Understandably enough, she became depressed and ill herself – 'The future stretched before me in endless years of grey monotony, and escape seemed hopeless,' she wrote – and, in 1900, she was advised by her doctor to take two months' holiday every year, as a complete break from her duties as a carer. She decided to take a cruise, with a friend, down the Dalmatian coast from Trieste to Kotor, in Montenegro. From there, she followed Baedeker's advice to drive up to Cetinje, then the Montenegrin capital, in order to 'be able to say ever afterwards, "I have travelled in Montenegro"'. Durham was struck both by the picturesqueness of this tiny, mountainous princedom and by what she described as its 'impossibly feudal views'.

That first short trip to Cetinje and Podgorica, where she saw Albanians for the first time, had sown the seeds of a lifelong engagement with the Balkans. When she returned to London, she learned the Serbian language and studied Balkan history. In subsequent years, her travels grew increasingly adventurous; she visited Montenegro four times, travelled extensively in Serbia, and ventured into the Ottoman province of Kosovo. In 1904, she published an account of these journeys, *Through the Lands of the Serb*. She hoped that her ethnographic studies of the region might help to solve the vexed question of Balkan borders, which continued to give rise to so much diplomatic intrigue and military skirmishes.

In 1903, she visited Albania, the least known of all the Balkan provinces and the only one without a sponsor in one of the Great Powers. She discovered a growing feeling of national unity among Albanians that belied their religious and cultural differences, and realised that Albanian national aspirations would need to be taken into account if the problems caused by the decline of the Ottoman Empire were to be adequately addressed. She returned to Albania in 1908 and embarked on a remarkable journey through the northern highlands. Very few foreign men had ever travelled in this remote and mountainous region; for a foreign woman to undertake such a journey was completely unprecedented. Durham recorded it in her book *High Albania*, a combination of travelogue, ethnographical observations and political reporting of the historical events that affected Albania during her stay.

temperatures of winter. The sulphur used in copper mining increased the heat in the mineshafts to over 30°C, while outside in winter the temperature can fall to -15°C.

This eerie place, in its bleak setting amid bare, harsh mountains, is a depressing but fascinating place to visit. Information panels in English have been installed around the site and work has begun to stabilise the buildings so that the the prison camp can be transformed into a museum, along the lines of Robben Island in South Africa. A Turkish mining company has built new installations, on the hillside directly opposite the historic site, and is using the same mineshafts that were once worked by the political prisoners. The mining company has also upgraded the road up to Spaçi from the highway. The 17km from Repsi are on an unasphalted but well-maintained road, signposted at every junction. There is no public transport beyond Repsi.

In 1911, the Catholic clans of northern Albania, encouraged and armed by Montenegro, rebelled against Ottoman rule. The uprising did not last long – the clans were obliged to make terms with the Ottomans when Montenegro withdrew its support – but during and after it Edith Durham organised the provision of humanitarian aid from her base in Scutari (the Italian name for Shkodra). She distributed flour, roofing materials and money, and gave medical treatment to sick highlanders who would often travel for days to find her. She remained in Montenegro and Shkodra during the two Balkan Wars of 1912 and 1913, and described the events of the wars and her own experiences in *The Struggle for Scutari*.

Edith Durham was in Vlora when Greek troops occupied southern Albania in October 1914, and in Korça when it was taken the following year. She and a friend tried to save Korça by pleading on its behalf with the Council of Ambassadors in London; this involved their walking for three days across the mountains to Berati, the nearest place from where a telegram could be sent. After the war, she became the Secretary of the Anglo-Albanian Association, a pressure group promoting Albanian interests. Her final visit to the country, in 1921, was cut short by illness, but during her stay she was greeted by cheering crowds and fêted by Albanian politicians. In Shkodra, delegations of clansmen came down from the mountains to welcome her.

Although she did not return to Albania after her 1921 trip, she continued to write about the Balkans. She was a council member of the Royal Anthropological Institute and wrote an ethnological study entitled *Some Tribal Origins, Laws & Customs of the Balkans* (published in 1928), as well as political-historical accounts of her travels such as *Twenty Years of Balkan Tangle* (1920). King Zog awarded her the Order of Skanderbeg and offered her a home in Albania. However, she remained in London, where she died in 1944.

Edith Durham is still revered in Albania, where she is sometimes referred to as 'The Highlanders' Queen' (Krajlica e Malësorëve; *krajlica* is an archaic word used in folk epics, and so the Albanian expression has a kind of fairy-tale sound to it). Streets still bear her name – sometimes they are the only streets that have signs – as do schools.

It is now very much easier to obtain copies of Edith Durham's books than it was before the advent of print-on-demand OCR reproductions (page 292). Images of some of the items she collected on her travels can be viewed on the British Museum's website (w britishmuseum.org).

Caves and *kulla* The easiest of Mirdita's **caves** to visit is the Vali's Cave (Shpella e Valit), near the district boundary with Mati. (A *vali* was a provincial governor in the Ottoman administration.) The cave is 3–4km from the road and has stalagmites and stalactites. To its south, in Mati, is a cluster of three further caves. One of the longest of these is blocked with earth and it is thought that it may be connected with the Vali's Cave. The Marub Hotel near Rubiku (page 145) and Vila Bruçi in Burreli (page 142) can organise excursions to these caves.

There are also caves in the commune of Fani, in the far northeast of Mirdita. Fani is the most traditional part of Mirdita, due to being completely surrounded by high mountains (nearly 2,000m above sea level). Until a few years ago, it was almost impossible to get to. Now, though, the main village, **Klosi** is right next to the new highway and slip roads have been built along it to provide access for the villagers. These include exits on either side at the entrance to the Kalimashi Tunnel, which is 5.6km long and cuts through the mountains to Kukësi district. Fani has 17 villages, many in spectacular settings, with traditional fortified houses (*kulla*) still occupied. One that can be reached in an ordinary car is **Petoqi**, 800m above sea level. The village of **Domgjoni** is less accessible, but has a 4th-century aqueduct system, a very unusual structure that provided water to the ancient settlement of Sukbukëra.

THE LURA LAKES

The Lura National Park covers 1,280ha of mountainous terrain around the Crown of Lura (*Kunora e Lurës*) massif, which rises at its peak to 2,121m. The area was designated as a national park because of the beautiful lakes that lie within it, 1,600–1,720m above sea level, with the mountains rising high above them. Each of the seven main lakes has a subtly different atmosphere. Several of them are covered in white and yellow water lilies, and huge dragonflies dart around them. Others have no flowers in them; the stillness of their water is dappled with the reflection of the surrounding trees.

The Lura Lakes were a popular destination for Albanian holidaymakers during the communist period. Then, for 25 years, illegal logging within the park (and throughout Albania) reached calamitous levels, destroying large swathes of forest and causing serious erosion by clear-felling on the hillsides. The Albanian government introduced a ten-year ban on logging in January 2016 and some reforestation was attempted in Lura, although many of the trees do not seem to have thrived. Before they were chopped down, the trees were mainly beech, up to about 1,700m above sea level, and above them pines (*P. heldreichi, nigra* and *silvestris*).

Despite the logging companies' efforts, the lakes are lovely, tranquil places. Three are close enough to the largest settlement within the park, Fushë-Lura, to be reasonably easy to reach on foot. The road up to the lakes is completely impassable to any vehicle less robust than a Land Rover.

The first of the seven lakes is Slate Lake (Liqeni i Rrasave), 7.7km from the end of the asphalt, so named because of the flat stones in and around it. The next lake you come to is Great Lake (Liqeni i Madh), large and dark, where local children swim. Less hardy adults might find the water a bit too cold.

The third of the closest lakes is Little Lake (Liqeni i Vogël, also called Liqeni i Bruçit), perhaps the prettiest of the three, filled with water lilies and reeds and ringed with beech trees. At certain times of year, huge, electric-blue dragonflies live around the water. It is an ideal spot for a picnic. Just beyond it, Great Lake comes back into view.

From Little Lake, it is 8.4km back to the asphalt road and almost 5km to the next lake in the chain. For those on foot, it is probably not worth the hike to the remaining four lakes until the trees have had a chance to regenerate. The bare hillsides give way to clear-felled lakesides, a shocking legacy of mismanagement and corruption. However, those with suitable transport – only the most rugged 4x4 or motorbikes – may like to carry on and see more of the park.

The next two lakes along the road are Hoti Lake (Liqeni i Hotit) and, a couple of kilometres further on, Black Lake (Liqeni i Zi), so-called because it is very deep and steep. Finally, 16.5km from the asphalt, the small Kallaba Lake (Liqeni i Kallabës) and, just beyond it, Flower Lake (Liqeni i Lulëve), carpeted with yellow and white water lilies, were once a breathtaking climax to the Lura Lakes. Nowadays, unfortunately, one's breath is likely to be taken away by the appalling sight of the denuded shores.

Golden eagles (*Aquila chrysaetos*) and hoopoes (*Upopa epops*) can be spotted, the latter quite low down towards the village. Capercaillie (*Tetrao urogallus*) and rock partridge (*Alectoris graeca*) were formerly reported as breeding in the park, although no recent data are available. There are roe deer, red squirrels, hares, foxes and polecats; wolves, wildcats and bears may have returned now that the neighbourhood is quieter, with fewer chainsaws.

GETTING THERE AND AWAY Access to the Lura National Park is from the neighbouring districts of Mirdita or Mati, using the asphalted SH34 that links Rrësheni and Burreli. The turn-off for Lura is signposted, at the village of Perlati, for Kurbneshi; it is a distance of about 40km from the junction to the village of Fushë-Lura. At the time of writing, the road is bad and a 4x4 is highly advisable; upgrading of the road between Perlati and Fushë-Lura has been tendered and may happen within the lifetime of this guidebook. Until it does, the journey from Rrësheni takes about 2½ hours. About 40 minutes after Kurbneshi, the road passes through Krej-Lura, a Catholic village that used to be administratively part of Mirdita district, and, 15 minutes or so later, you reach Fushë-Lura.

One **bus** a day connects Lura with Tirana. It leaves the North/South bus terminal in Tirana at 07.00 and, if there is space, it can pick up passengers in Rrësheni; the fare is 1,000 lek regardless. This is the only way to reach the Lura Lakes by public transport.

Lura belongs administratively to the district of Dibra (page 174) and some maps show a road connecting Lura with Peshkopia (38km). This should not be attempted in anything other than the most rugged of 4x4 vehicles or motorbikes.

GETTING AROUND THE PARK The road that runs roughly south from Fushë-Lura along the eastern edge of the Lura National Park is exceptionally bad – parts of it are more like a dry riverbed, with large stones and deeply rutted sections. One of the worst stretches is right at the start, just beyond the former communist-era hotel. A resilient and high-axled 4x4 vehicle is essential, or rugged, powerful motorbikes. A Land Rover with driver can be hired in Rrësheni (the author recommends Pavlin Nikolli, on m 068 26 02 058, also with WhatsApp), but not in Lura itself. The road is not passable at all in winter or after heavy rain. An information panel, with distances, stands at the start of the track up to the lakes.

If you are walking, there are short cuts up through the trees, although it is easy to lose the path and end up battling through the forest. You might consider hiring a local guide in the village – ask the hotel staff or the family you are staying with to find someone to show you the quickest way to the lakes.

The start of the route, however, is straightforward. From the former hotel, head roughly southwest straight uphill. The walking is considerably more pleasant than along the stones and boulders of the road, over rough grass and past thickets of wild fruit – raspberries, blackberries, strawberries and blaeberries. The track rejoins the road at a flat, open area which would be a good place to camp overnight. It takes 30–40 minutes to reach this point from the former hotel. It is best to follow the road for the next stretch, until you come to a waterfall that runs under the road. A few metres after the waterfall, a clear path leaves the road to the right, and then rejoins it near Slate Lake. There are also large pipes carrying water downhill, and where these meet the road, their line can be followed as short cuts.

WHERE TO STAY AND EAT The hotels listed here are in the village of Fushë-Lura. They are open all year round, although in winter the access road from Perlati is sometimes blocked with snow for several days at a time. Breakfast is included and other meals can be provided on request. There is no Wi-Fi in Fushë-Lura at the time of writing.

There are several places in the park where a tent could be pitched, in clearings in the steep, forested terrain; one is suggested above. Other possible sites are around the main section of Great Lake and around the area of Kallaba and Flower lakes. Please see page 46 for advice on wild camping in Albania. If you plan to camp, you should bring adequate supplies of food and water with you. It should be possible to buy basic foodstuffs such as bread and cheese from local families in Fushë-Lura.

Lura (18 rooms) m 068 21 87 497. Restaurant/bar; large terrace overlooking village with views of mountains; English spoken in summer; guides can be arranged & transport to/from Rrësheni. Various sizes of room, all en suite with TV & CH (solar). Wraparound shared balcony for rooms on village side of hotel. Campsite below terrace; power & water points for mobile homes; space for tents (**$**). **$$**

Oxhaku i Doçit (11 rooms) m 068 45 40 342. Restaurant with fresh trout; home-produced honey with b/fast; bar service. The owner is a guide to historic & archaeological sites in area. Bedrooms are spread across three buildings: 2 above restaurant, 1 on ground floor, shared bathroom; 5 dbl/twin en suite in neighbouring building; 3 rooms in historic kulla with *frëngji*, 1 with balcony, shared bathroom & kitchen with washing machine. **$**

KUKËSI *Telephone code: 024*

Kukësi's principal attraction is its dramatic setting, surrounded by mountains and overlooking vast Lake Fierza. At 72km long, this is the largest in a chain of three interconnecting lakes that generate most of Albania's electricity. The damming of Lake Fierza in 1978 created the Light of the Party hydro-electric plant but inundated several settlements, including the old town of Kukësi. The existing town was built to rehouse the people whose homes are now underwater and so it is entirely modern. In dry years, when the water level in the lake is unusually low, the roofs of the old town appear above the surface and the old people go down to the lakeside to sit and look at their former homes.

While Kukësi is not a top tourist destination in itself, it is a convenient base from which to explore further afield: north to Tropoja, south to Peshkopia, west to Puka or Mirdita, or east to Prizreni and the rest of Kosovo.

GETTING THERE AND AWAY

By air Kukësi Airport opened in 2021. At the time of writing, it has flights from only a few European cities; up-to-date information can be found on the airport's website: w kuiport.al.

albania holidays DMC

...loving the Balkans

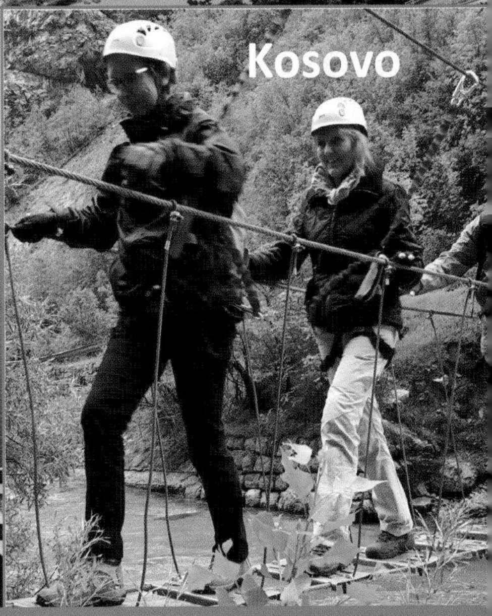

www.albania-holidays.com

www.macedonia-holidays.com

www.kosovo-holidays.com

left Southern Albania is studded with beautiful, neglected churches like this one at Kosina, near Përmeti (DD) page 208

below left The Unknown Partisan advances on the enemy, above a plaque commemorating the Battle for the Liberation of Tirana (TW/S) page 83

below right Kruja's attractively restored bazaar and buildings make the city an excellent place to get a feel for Albanian history and traditions (Pp/S) page 108

above Atmospheric Rozafa Castle has three layers of fortification, with the most secure section here, at its narrowest part (PJ/S) page 119

right The galleries around Durrësi's Roman amphitheatre contain a Byzantine chapel with wall mosaics, the only examples of their kind ever to be found in Albania (SS) page 92

below Shkodra's Catholic Cathedral was designed and decorated by the city's foremost 19th-century artists (ES/S) page 128

above left A weaver at work in her house in Jagodini, near Elbasani (AL)

above right Traditional *qilime* – woven rugs – on sale at the bazaar in Kruja (RB/S) page 112

below Iso-polyphony, a southern Albanian musical genre, is listed by UNESCO as part of Humanity's Intangible Cultural Heritage (SS) page 25

above Driving in rural Albania means sharing the road with livestock; this is on the way to Thethi (MO/S) page 166

right The artisans' cooperative in Gjirokastra includes a stonemason's workshop (AL) page 273

below Relaxing in the thermal waters at Bënja, near Përmeti (DZA/S) page 208

above **The little town of Peshkopia is surrounded by spectacular mountains** (GG) page 174

below **Hiking on Mount Kallkan, in Shebenik-Jabllanica National Park** (AK) page 193

bottom left **The 18th-century Gorica Bridge links two of Berati's UNESCO-listed museum zones** (m50/S) page 265

bottom right **The ancient city of Apollonia was a major port for many centuries, until the course of the Vjosa River shifted** (S/S) page 250

Cycle Albania

Rr. Bardhok Biba , Pall Trema A Tirana, Albania
Telephone : +355 67 30 8000/+355 69 24 75728
Website : www.cyclealbania.com
E-mail : info@cyclealbania.com

FARMA SOTIRA

Stay at our working animal farm, with sheep, cattle, pigs, horses, chickens and ducks, located 70km from Korça and 15km from Leskoviku in the tourist area of Germenj-Shelegur

- Self-catering bungalows or camping facilities, organic breakfast included
- Bar and restaurant serving home-cooked organic traditional dishes
- Cookery classes, apitherapy and fishing
- Guided hiking and horse-riding excursions to the thermal waters of Leskoviku
- Open-air swimming pool and playground
- English spoken and Wi-Fi included

Web: farmasotira.com Email: info@farmasotira.com Tel: +355 (0) 69 23 42 529

JOIN
THE TRAVEL CLUB
THE MEMBERSHIP CLUB FOR SERIOUS TRAVELLERS
FROM BRADT GUIDES
Be inspired
Free books and our monthly e-zine, packed with travel tips and inspiration
Save money
Exclusive offers and special discounts from our favourite travel brands
Plan the trip of a lifetime
Access our exclusive concierge service and have a bespoke itinerary created for you by a Bradt author
Join here:
bradtguides.com/travelclub
Membership levels to suit all budgets
Bradt GUIDES
TRAVEL TAKEN SERIOUSLY

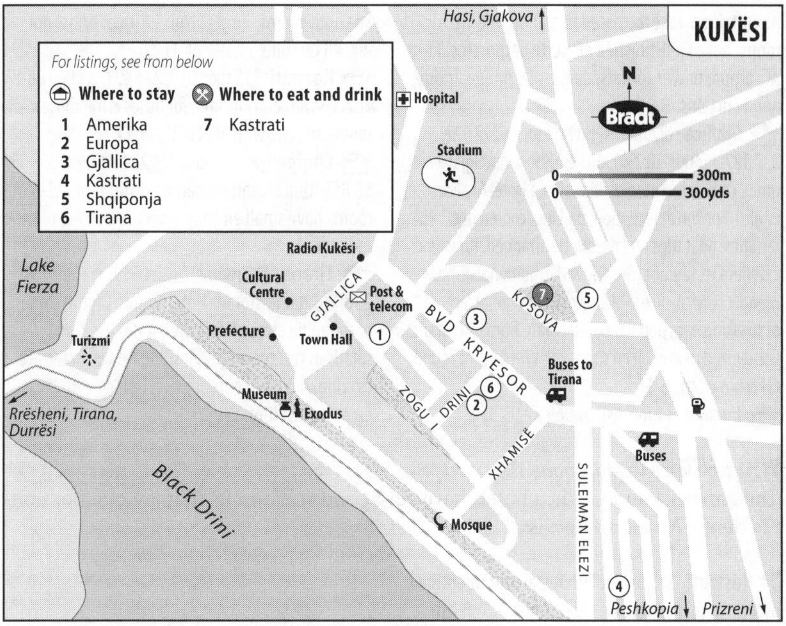

By land

From Kosovo Kukësi is only 42km from Prizreni, in southwestern Kosovo. Border formalities are minimal; see page 33 for further information.

An alternative route, for those with their own transport, is from Gjakova (Đakovica, in Serbian) through the border crossing at Qafë-Prushi and via the district of Hasi (page 156).

From elsewhere in Albania Kukësi is less than 3 hours' drive from Tirana on the A1 highway. In Tirana, **buses** leave from the North/South bus terminal station more or less every 2 hours from early morning to late afternoon. The fare is 400 lek. Buses between Tirana and **Bajram Curri** go via Prizreni and Kukësi and can drop off passengers on the highway below Kukësi. Slightly rickety metal stairs lead up from the highway to the town (negotiating these stairs with a large rucksack in heavy rain is an interesting experience).

There is one bus a day between **Peshkopia** and Kukësi (800 lek); it leaves Peshkopia at 07.30 and returns from Kukësi at noon.

The main bus terminus in Kukësi is along the street that runs from the eastern junction of the main boulevard down towards the lake (Rruga Suleiman Elezi). The best chance of obtaining information of any reliability about bus departure times is to ask in the cafés here. The buses to Tirana wait on the boulevard itself, 100m or so around the corner from the main terminus, opposite the junction with the street down to the mosque (Rruga e Xhamisë).

WHERE TO STAY *Map, above*

✷ **Amerika** (42 rooms) Lagjia 5; ☎ 223 278; m 068 20 37 874; e office@baramerika.com; w baramerika.com. Boutique hotel; professional, friendly service; English spoken; secure key-card lift to all floors. Generous cooked b/fast inc. Excellent restaurant ($$$) menu inc game & other specialities & bar on ground floor; cocktail bar on top floor, with beautiful 360° views of mountains & lake, accessed by panoramic lift. All rooms have well-finished en-suite bathrooms, TV, AC, ample power sockets, direct-dial phone, fridge, good curtains. $$$

Gjallica (22 rooms) Bd Kryesor; 222 527, 222 327; m 068 20 23 096/098/099; e hotelgjallica@gmail.com, info@hotelgjallica.al; Hotel Gjallica. English spoken at reception; parking; conference facilities; boat trips on lake can be arranged. B/fast inc. Excellent restaurant ($$$), with traditional dishes, friendly service, nice table decoration & enforcement of smoking ban; popular bar, separate from restaurant. Good-sized rooms, all en suite with Wi-Fi, TV, AC, good CH & hot water. $$

Europa (4 rooms) m 069 22 93 391. Spacious rooms: 1 sgl, 2 trpl, 1 4-bed; b/fast not inc. All en suite, TV, AC, Wi-Fi. $

Kastrati (15 rooms) 224 403; m 069 68 17 762. Conveniently located for buses & minibuses. All rooms en suite with AC, CH, Wi-Fi, TV. $

Shqiponja (5 rooms) 224 343; m 068 55 58 855. Quiet location; bar; no restaurant; Wi-Fi. All rooms have small en suite with shower; AC, electric radiator. $

Tirana (10 rooms) 224 819; m 069 20 44 280; Bar Restorant Hotel Tirana. On the corner of the main street. Wi-Fi; b/fast not inc. Good salads in restaurant ($$), some tables on terrace overlooking city-centre bustle. Rooms with basic en-suite facilities. $

WHERE TO EAT *Map, page 153*

The Amerika and Gjallica hotels have very good restaurants that are open to non-residents. An alternative is:

Kastrati Rr Kosova. Fish restaurant (identified by 'Fish' sign on street outside); superb fresh fish from river & lake, generous portions; professional service; good house wine, range of specialist raki. $$$

WHAT TO SEE AND DO The area around modern Kukësi has been settled since Neolithic times. The first people in the region for whom there is archaeological evidence lived at Kolshi (excavated in the 1970s) and were part of the Starçevo cultural community, the earliest settled farming society in the western Balkans (6000BC). Later, as in southeastern Albania, the people began to bury their dead in tumuli (barrows), such as those found at Çinamaku. No fewer than 80 tumuli were identified there, ranging in date from the 12th to the 7th centuries, then used again between the 4th and 2nd centuries BC, with the latest burials of all dating from the 1st century AD and even the early medieval period. Excavations at Çinamaku also uncovered Attic white-figure pottery (6th century BC) and coins minted by the Ardiaean king Genti (168–147BC).

The Romans built one of their great arterial roads through this region, to link the Roman port of Lissus (now Lezha, page 134) with the cities that are now called Prishtina and Niš. Romans settled in the Kukësi region too, but it was only in the 9th century that the town began to develop. Its location on the River Drini and on the Roman road made it an important link in the trading network between the Adriatic and the Danube.

The town **museum** (free admission) presents all this history through maps and artefacts, with most of the information translated into English. There is a section about the history of the town in the 20th century, including fascinating photos of Old Kukësi, now under the waters of Lake Fierza, and information about the flora and fauna of the district. Upstairs is a small ethnographic exhibition.

Exploring the town A walk around Kukësi takes an hour at most. The information panel in the piazza outside the museum is as good a place to begin as any. It has a map of the town and another of the surrounding region, with information about the main places of interest. The administrative buildings for the town and region are in the main square beyond.

The imposing **tower** beside the museum, overlooking the lake, is a monument to the exodus from Kosovo during the 1998–99 war. Most of the 500,000 refugees who fled Kosovo entered Albania at Kukësi, which – despite its own poverty and lack of infrastructure – somehow managed to cope not only with its Kosovar cousins but also with the hordes of foreign aid workers and journalists who descended on the town. The monument was erected by a group of grateful Kosovars in 2009, the tenth anniversary of the refugees' return to their homes (also via Kukësi) after NATO had driven out Slobodan Milošević's forces.

The town's **lakeside promenade** is a pleasant walk on a fine evening, when it fills with strolling families and couples. To the right are fine views of the lake; to the left is a park, with swings and other amusements for children. The A1 highway runs below the promenade, along the lakeside. Towering above the town, lake and highway, Mount Gjallica rises to the southeast, 2,486m high.

Towards the end of the promenade, at the mosque, turn left to reach the main street, Bulevardi Kryesor or (its new name, which nobody will know) Rruga Dituria. The buses for Tirana wait for passengers near this junction. Turning left on to Boulevard Kryesor, you will pass the Gjallica Hotel and come to the Radio Kukësi building, with a wonderful Socialist Realist bas-relief above its door. Turning left down Rruga Gjallica here brings you back to the main square, with the Cultural Centre, town hall and regional government building, or Prefecture.

The minor road up to the north, beside the Cultural Centre, leads through trees and above fields to the ruined shell of the former 'Turizmi' hotel, used as offices by international organisations during the war in Kosovo and, since then, left to decay and crumble. From the other side of the ruins, there are marvellous views of Lake Fierza, the Black Drini coming into it from the south and the confluence of the White Drini just visible to the north. The White Drini rises near the Kosovo–Montenegro border and flows down to Albania through Kosovo; the Black Drini begins its overland life at the northern end of Lake Ohrid and flows through North Macedonia before entering Albania to the south of Peshkopia. From here there is also a good view of the bridge over the Black Drini and the highway that continues to Rrësheni, Durrësi and Tirana.

The Black Drini (Drini i Zi) The Black Drini runs through spectacular gorges, wild rocky mountains and pretty hillside villages, making for a magnificent drive or bike run. A new road, further to the east, is now the main route between Kukësi and Peshkopia and there is no longer any public transport on the Black Drini road. The old road is not maintained and a 4x4 vehicle is likely to be required.

From Kukësi, the road runs first through pretty woodland, with good views behind of the town and the lake, and past the airport (page 32). The old and new roads separate at the village of Kolesjan, about 10km south of Kukësi. On the old road, the scenery now starts to become quite dramatic, with breathtaking views of the river far below and tributaries tumbling down towards it through willows and alders. There are clusters of houses fortified in the traditional style, using the slope of the hill to protect the back of the building, with small windows on the upper floors and none at all at ground level. Along the way, birds of prey hang on the thermals and spectacular white cliffs tower on the other side of the river.

Shishtaveci Shishtaveci is the largest of a group of eight villages on the Shishtaveci Plateau, 31km southeast of Kukësi right on the border with Kosovo. The plateau is over

2,000m above sea level at its highest point and, in the communist period, Shishtaveci, with its natural ski-slope, was one of the country's ski resorts. In the summer, the countryside is beautiful. The road from Kukësi is asphalted all the way to the border crossing to Dragash (in Kosovo). A minibus leaves the village for Kukësi first thing in the morning and returns to Shishtaveci in the early afternoon. There are several guesthouses and a small hotel in the village.

Hikers should exercise caution in this part of Albania and avoid straying off beaten tracks. This is because there may still be some unexploded ordnance remaining from the 1999 war in Kosovo. The mines were laid by Kosovar fighters to stop the Serbs following them into Albanian territory; it is thought that all of them have now been cleared, but it is impossible to be certain that none has been missed. The northeastern border is the only part of Albania where landmines present even the most remote risk.

Hasi The district of Hasi is wild, desolate country, dotted with traditional *kulla*. The lack of employment opportunities has led to very high emigration since the 1990s; there are many Hasians among the Albanian community in the UK. The district capital, officially called **Kruma** but usually also referred to as Hasi, is connected to Kukësi and to the border crossing at Qafë-Prushi by a good, asphalted road. Elsewhere in the district, including towards Tropoja, the roads are rough (although some may be upgraded within the lifetime of this guidebook) and most require 4x4.

The route between Kukësi and Kruma offers wonderful scenery and beautiful views over Lake Fierza. Just off the main road at the junction for the village of Gjinaj, a simple wooden **restaurant** serves fresh *zander* (pike-perch) and grilled meat dishes (**$$$**). There is a good view from here of the confluence of the two Drini rivers. In Kruma, the **Jupa Hotel** offers simple accommodation (**$**) – three rooms, sharing a toilet and shower – and serves good fish and traditional Albanian food. There are several **buses** a day between Kruma and Kukësi; it takes less than an hour and the fare is 150 lek.

TROPOJA

The mountain range that forms the border between Albania and Montenegro is known variously as the Albanian Alps, the Dinaric Alps, the Accursed Mountains or, more usually in everyday Albanian parlance, just 'the Highlands' (Malësia). The western part of the range, Malësia e Madhe or 'the Big Highlands', is covered from page 163. This section covers the eastern part of the highlands.

The district of Tropoja nestles in the top right-hand corner of Albania, cut off physically from the rest of the country by huge lakes and towering mountains. These geographical features, inconvenient though they are for the local people, offer the visitor the chance to see spectacular scenery in unspoilt surroundings rare in Europe. The highlights of any visit to Tropoja are the approach by boat up Lake Komani and excursions in the valley of the River Valbona. There are many mountain tracks for hillwalkers to enjoy, although you should exercise the same caution as you would in any other remote high mountain area – don't go alone, leave your planned route with someone you trust, don't assume your mobile phone will work, and so on.

Tropoja district takes its name from a village in its northeastern corner, which gives some indication of the disastrous effect on it of the Great Powers' decision (page 12) to deprive the newly independent Albania of what is now western Kosovo. The district seems very far from Tirana, but it is very close and accessible to the Kosovar towns of Gjakova, Peja and Prizreni. There can scarcely be a single family in Tropoja that does not have relatives on the other side of the border: in Kosovo, in Montenegro or in both. Yet during the communist period it was completely cut off from these trading centres, while for most of the first decade of democracy, sanctions against Yugoslavia closed the border once again. At the same time, the district was sidelined and starved of resources by successive governments, even when the president of Albania was Sali Berisha, a native of Tropoja village.

In these circumstances, smuggling and criminality flourished during the 1990s, and Tropoja gained a reputation for being violent and unsafe. In a kind of vicious circle, this meant it got even less money from central government and none at all from foreign donors, who were afraid to go there. A clampdown by central government during 2001–02 saw the security situation improve dramatically and, like elsewhere in Albania, Tropoja has also benefited from investment in roads and other infrastructure. Valbona in particular has become a thriving destination for Kosovar and international visitors.

GETTING THERE AND AWAY By far the best way to approach Tropoja from the south is on the **ferry** up Lake Komani, a world-class journey through outstanding fjord-like scenery. Details of this route can be found on page 159. The only other feasible option entirely within Albania is the old road through Puka and across the bridge at Fierza (page 133).

There are no roads into Tropoja from the west or the north. To reach the district by **road** from elsewhere in Albania normally requires crossing into and back out of neighbouring Kosovo. The roads have all been upgraded and are in good condition. Border formalities are minimal for holders of most passports (indeed, practically non-existent for Albanian adults). Those driving foreign-registered cars into Kosovo are obliged to buy a minimum of 15 days' vehicle insurance. This can be purchased at the border and, at the time of writing, costs €15.

There are two options by road via Kosovo. The principal route is via Kukësi, Prizreni and Gjakova. All buses use this route. An alternative, for those with their own transport, is the slightly shorter route (also fully asphalted) via Kruma and the border crossing at Qafë-Prushi.

By bus, the fare for the whole journey is 1,000 lek; it takes about 6 hours, or longer if there are delays at the borders. Buses leave Tirana's North/South bus terminal every 2 hours from 06.00 to 14.00. In the other direction, the first minibus leaves Bajram Curri for Tirana at 08.00 and departures continue until 14.00. Passengers can alight at any reasonable spot along the route; from Bajram Curri, it takes about 2½ hours to Kukësi and the fare is 500 lek. Minibuses from Gjakova to Bajram Curri leave frequently during the day and the journey takes about 1 hour. The one-way fare is 300 lek; if the driver is Kosovar, he will probably insist on being paid in euros. For transport between Bajram Curri and Valbona, see page 161.

Properly equipped and prepared **hikers** have other options for getting to Tropoja. From Thethi, the popular hike over the Valbona Pass (1,817m) is covered on page 172 and the more challenging alternatives, through the Nikaj Valley, on page 163. There are no official border crossing points between Vermoshi and the main road from Gjakova, but there are footpaths. One of these comes into Tropoja from the Montenegrin but Albanian-speaking district of Plava and links into the path down from the village of Çeremi to Valbona. The locals apparently do the journey between Çeremi and Vuthaj ('Vuthanje' in Montenegrin) in an hour, but it should be borne in mind that Albanian villagers are very fast walkers. Hikers wishing to cross any of the international borders between Albania, Kosovo and Montenegro should obtain permits in advance, to avoid problems at the exit border. See page 45 for details of how to obtain these permits.

WHERE TO STAY AND EAT The district capital, Bajram Curri, has a range of hotels and a few restaurants (page 160). Most visitors head quickly for Valbona (page 161), where there is a wide choice of accommodation, from boutique hotels to the family homes known as *hans*.

LAKE KOMANI The journey along Lake Komani deserves to be one of the world's classic boat trips, up there with the Hurtigrut along the Norwegian coast or the ferry from Puerto Montt to Puerto Natales in Chile. Lake Komani is narrow and twisting, with sheer cliffs right down to the water in some stretches, complete with breathtakingly high waterfalls. It is part of a huge hydro-electric system constructed in the 1970s and 1980s but, unlike Lake Fierza further upstream, its topography was not much altered by flooding. In some places, the slopes are gentler and small clusters of houses can be seen. Here the people have terraced what little land is available, to pasture their livestock and grow maize and other crops. It must be a desperately harsh existence in these lakeside villages, where the only form of transport is a boat and where in bad weather you can be cut off completely from any shops, schools or medical care. Incredibly, some people apparently choose to live in even more remote spots, in the houses that can be spotted from time to time high up above the lake. Some of these houses are now abandoned, but others are still occupied, at least in the summertime, by hardy souls who work their land and build their haystacks as their ancestors did before them.

Thoughts of the hardship of these people's lives need not deter you from marvelling at the magnificent scenery. Because the lake follows the twisting line of the river on which it is based, the boat at times appears to be heading for an unbroken cliff face. At the last moment, as it begins to turn, the break in the rock appears and the continuation of the lake can be seen through the gorge ahead. In these narrow stretches, the steep rocks on either side of you seem even higher than they really are. The water is a deep jade colour, and the cliffs and trees climbing up above it are reflected in its intensity. In the less steep stretches, you can see the far-off summits of the Dinaric Alps, more than 2,500m high. Herons (*Ardea cinerea*) and pygmy cormorants (*Phalacrocorax pygmeus*) live around the lake, and golden eagles (*Aquila chrysaetos*) and chamois (*Rupicapra rupicapra*) can sometimes be seen up in the surrounding peaks.

Ferries and boats Car ferries and passenger boats operate between Komani and Fierza between April and October or early November. The journey takes about 2 hours. At Komani, car parking is available before the tunnel that leads to the harbour.

The largest car ferry, the **Alpin**, leaves Fierza at 08.00 and returns from Komani at 11.00, but it operates only when it has sufficient reservations. At weekends in the peak summer months, it is fairly safe to assume that it will run; at other times, you should check before travelling to the lake (contact details below). Rates vary according to vehicle size (motorbikes and saloon cars 3,000 lek, 4x4 vehicles 3,500 lek). A further 1,000 lek is payable per passenger. The ferry has a canopied upper deck from which to enjoy the spectacular views, a bar on the lower deck with a rather restricted range of drinks and snacks, indoor lounges (by reservation only) and adequate toilets.

The **Berisha** ferry, with space for ten cars, runs between April and October leaving Komani at 09.00 and returning there from Fierza at 13.00. Rates vary according to vehicle size; foot passengers pay 800lek. Pedestrians and cyclists have the additional option of the **Dragobia**, which leaves Fierza at 06.00 and Komani at 09.00 (800 lek per person one way) all year round, subject of course to weather. Tickets for the Berisha and Dragobia can be bought online (contact details below) in advance, which is slightly cheaper. Other companies do the Komani–Fierza–Komani run in summer, but the departure times tend to be similar.

Several companies offer **lake excursions** in summer, including Komani Lake Ferry and Mario Molla (Komani Lake). Typically they include a stop-off for swimming, at the River Shala or an island in the lake, and lunch in a village restaurant. Kayaking can also be arranged. Prices range from €25 to €29 per person. At additional cost, groups can be picked up in and returned to Shkodra or even Tirana.

The passenger boats leave Fierza not from the old ferry terminal, 3km beyond the town, but from a jetty on the other side of the bridge, called Breglumi ('The Riverbank').

Alpin m 068 80 12 731; e info@alpin.al; w alpin.al; f Trageti-Alpin

Dragobia & Berisha m 068 52 70 934, 069 68 00 748; e kontakt@komanilakeferry.com; w komanilakeferry.com, komanilake-explore.com

Mario Molla 026 373 003; m 068 20 22 686, (WhatsApp) 068 52 63 884, 068 63 74 712; e mariomolla@outlook.com; w komanilake.org; f KomaniLake

Getting there and away To get to Komani, the main road as far as Vau i Dejës is good; after the Komani turn-off, it is rather slow going for 22 mountainous kilometres. At least 2 hours should be allowed by car from Shkodra. **Cyclists** should note that the tunnel leading to and from the jetty at Komani is badly lit and badly surfaced. Cars can be parked for the day or overnight in the car park before the tunnel to the jetty at Komani. There is a small, basic hotel at the Komani jetty (Natyra; **$**) and a campsite before the tunnel (**$**).

Komani Lake Ferry, which operates the Berisha car ferry, offers a **minibus** service from Tirana and Shkodra, to connect with the ferry departure from Komani. They can also take passengers onwards to the hotels in Valbona and pick up from there for the 13.00 ferry from Fierza.

Public **buses** run between Bajram Curri and Fierza in the mornings; the journey takes about half an hour. The going rate for a taxi from Valbona to Fierza is €30.

BAJRAM CURRI *Telephone code: 0213*

The administrative centre of Tropoja district, Bajram Curri was purpose-built during the communist period and named after one of the key figures in the liberation of Albania from Ottoman rule. Bajram Curri was in fact Kosovar, which brought him into conflict with Ahmed Zogu (later King Zog), for whom reunification with Kosovo was not a priority. After two decades in and out of the leadership of Albania, he died in a cave near Dragobia in 1925, probably assassinated on Zog's orders. A large Socialist Realist statue of him looks down over the main square of the town named after him. The museum behind the statue was looted in 1997 and has been closed ever since.

Tourist information In 2021, **Journey to Valbona** (w journeytovalbona.com; Jun–Oct 11.00–22.00 daily; Nov–May check times on website) opened a shop, information and cultural centre in Bajram Curri. It sells its acclaimed hiking maps

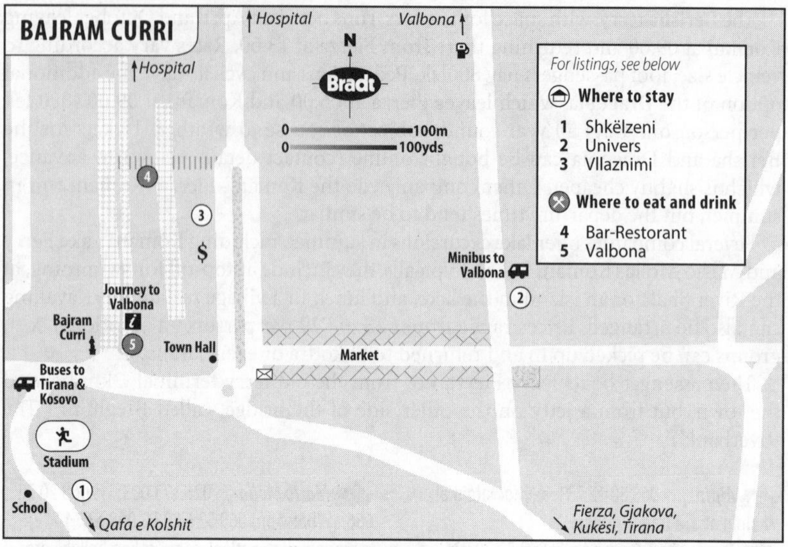

(page 41), postcards and hiking supplies; it is a fair-trade outlet for local artisans and farmers, selling everything from knitted socks to honey and raki; and, in celebration of local culture, it is furnished with traditional antiques, mostly donated by local families. The staff are happy to answer visitors' questions and discuss options for making the most of Valbona and other parts of Tropoja. The environmental NGO TOKA (page 56) has its office upstairs.

Where to stay *Map, above*

Shkëlzeni (36 rooms) Bajram Curri; **m** 068 35 97 178, 067 50 00 093; **e** hotel.shkelzeni@gmail.com; **w** hotelshkelzeni.com. The former 'Turizmi' hotel, completely renovated in 2017, is now of a high standard & wheelchair-accessible throughout. Good restaurant ($$$), indoor & terrace bars; lift; Wi-Fi throughout; free parking; laundry service. All rooms are spacious & nicely furnished; good-sized en-suite bathrooms with rainshower (some have tub), well-lit mirror, toiletries, hairdryer; flatscreen TV, AC, phone, minibar, some have balcony. **$$$–$$**

Aste (4 rooms) Tropoja e Vjetër; **m** 068 58 27 445; **e** hello@asteguesthouse.com; **w** asteguesthouse.com. Beautifully furnished *han* in Old Tropoja, good option for hikers. Living room with balcony; further balcony with views across River Tropoja; double-glazed & heated with wood stove. Bedrooms have different configurations, all en suite with new fittings & good shower. **$$**

Vllaznimi (19 rooms) Bajram Curri; **m** 068 20 79 060, 068 36 19 177. English spoken by some staff. Restaurant ($$) & lively, though very smoky, bar. All rooms en suite with TV, AC; 5 'superior' rooms have small balcony; nice, good-sized bathroom with shower; good-sized dbl bed or twins. **$$**

Univers (5 rooms) Bajram Curri; **m** 067 25 96 335, 067 25 96 366, 068 56 88 189. Above restaurant, Wi-Fi in public area. Twin rooms, all with basic en-suite bathroom, AC, TV. **$**

Where to eat *Map, above*

Bar-Restorant (So-called on sign above door) Behind the Vllaznimi Hotel. Serves good home-cooked Albanian dishes. $$

Valbona Range of grilled & roast meat dishes at lunchtimes, salads & light meals at other times. $$

Other practicalities The town has the usual things you find in Albanian towns, such as grocery stores, ATMs, mobile phone shops, a post office, a hospital and a couple of large mosques. Travellers heading onward to Valbona should note that there are no cash machines, Accident and Emergency facilities, or petrol stations beyond Bajram Curri. Nor are there any shops in the Valbona Valley; there is no shortage of food or drink, but hikers should stock up here on snacks, fruit, cigarettes, batteries, plasters and anything else that might be required. There is a small hardware store near where the minibus for Valbona waits.

There are no fixed-line telephones in the Valbona Valley. Some remote parts of the valley do not even have mobile-phone coverage.

VALBONA The River Valbona is justly famous for its dramatic gorges and plunging waterfalls, as well as for the clarity and the beautiful, light-blue colour of its water. It rises on the slopes of Mount Jezerca (2,694m), which is the highest mountain wholly in Albania (Mount Korabi, near Peshkopia, is partly in North Macedonia, although the summit is on the Albanian side of the border), and flows into the huge northern hydro-electric system at Fierza. The road runs alongside or above it for about 30km, up to Rragami, near its source, a few kilometres beyond the main village of Valbona (Valbona Qendër).

The river comes into view just before the road crosses it a couple of kilometres beyond Bajram Curri; if you are using your own transport it is worth stopping somewhere near the bridge, so that you can enjoy the view up and down the gorge. Dragobia is about halfway between Bajram Curri and the main village of Valbona; by this point, despite the magnificent scenery, cyclists may well be glad of a rest from the relentless uphill paths.

The path up to **Dragobia Cave** (Shpella e Dragobisë), where Bajram Curri was killed in 1925, starts on the other side of the river, a little further on towards Valbona. It is waymarked from the Rilindja guesthouse (page 162); 1:30,000 hiking maps are available from Journey to Valbona's shop in Bajram Curri (page 159).

As you approach the village of Valbona, the valley flattens out, and the river runs between meadows right through the village. Valbona was a thriving little resort until 1997, when it suffered in the civil unrest that engulfed Albania. In recent years, though, tourism has begun to flourish again and the village is quite lively in summer, with lots of visitors who come from Kosovo for the day or the weekend, as well as a smaller number of foreign hikers.

Getting there and away A rural **bus** operates from Valbona down to Bajram Curri in the mornings and back again in the afternoons; the one-way fare is 300 lek. It leaves Valbona punctually at 07.00, from the western end of the village, just down the hill from the Lamthi and Çardaku guesthouses; barring delays, it connects with the Tirana bus that leaves Bajram Curri at 08.00. The Valbona minibus leaves Bajram Curri again at 14.00; it picks up passengers outside a little shop just before the last petrol stations on the road out towards Valbona. The road has been surfaced and widened as far as the main village of Valbona, although it tends to disintegrate in the winter. Beyond the main village, a drivable road goes as far as Rragami, bridging the river just beyond Fusha e Gjesë.

Where to stay and eat

Hotels

Fusha e Gjesë (50 rooms) **m** 067 20 18 005; **w** hotelfushaegjes.com. At the end of the asphalted road from Valbona, lovely setting, can be noisy at w/ends. Large restaurant with traditional dishes, bar, Wi-Fi, parking. Chalets with 1 dbl

& 1 sgl bed, veranda, en-suite toilet & shower, wardrobe, heater. Sgl, dbl & trpl rooms, all en suite with AC, TV & balcony. **$$$**

Jezerca (8 rooms) Valbona Qendër; m 067 30 93 406. Stone-built traditional house with restaurant & Wi-Fi. Dorms & dbl rooms, sharing 4 modern bathrooms. Camping also possible (**$**). **$$**

Margjeka (9 rooms) Ziçi; m 067 33 82 162; e info@hotelmargjeka.al; w hotelmargjeka.al. More or less directly above Fusha e Gjesë, 500m uphill from the main road to Rragami. Restaurant with large terrace, beautiful views over the valley; open fire & TV in lobby; laundry service; German spoken; Wi-Fi in public areas & most rooms. All rooms en suite with CH; 2 family rooms (**$$$**). **$$**

Rezidenca (11 rooms) Quku i Valbonës (also known locally as Quku i Dunishës); m 067 30 14 637; w journeytovalbona.com. Just off the main road from Bajram Curri, 3km before the main village of Valbona. Comfortable rooms in a traditional highland house; English spoken. Sitting room with sofas & open fire, Wi-Fi, laundry service. Dbl & twin rooms, nicely furnished, all en suite with good shower, CH, private balcony with table & chairs. **$$**

Rilindja (5 rooms) Quku i Valbonës (also known locally as Quku i Dunishës); m 067 30 14 637; w journeytovalbona.com. Signposted off the main road up to Valbona; same ownership as the Rezidenca; English spoken; restaurant & bar. Campsite (**$**) with dedicated showers & toilets for campers. 2 twin rooms & 2 family rooms share large bathroom, 1 dbl en suite. **$**

Tradita (5 chalets, 6 rooms) Valbona Qendër; m 067 33 80 014, 067 30 14 567; f Hotel.Tradita.Valbone. Restaurant. Chalets, each with 1 dbl & 1 sgl (**$$**); AC; nice en-suite bathroom with shower. Rooms in stone-built farmhouse share 2 modern bathrooms; 2 dbl, 4 twin. **$**

Guesthouses (han)

All prices are per person with b/fast (**$**); FB & HB options are also available.

Ilirjan Lamthi (12 beds) Rragami; m 069 25 22 486. 1 dorm, shared bathroom; home-cooked food, inc honey from Ilirjan's own bees.

Kol Gjoni (30 beds) Valbona, just beyond the main village; m 069 26 40 836; f GuestHouseKoleGjoni. Some English spoken; a member of the family is the English teacher at the village school. Bar, restaurant with home-cooked food. Dbl, trpl & dorm rooms.

Lazër Çardaku (8 beds) Rragami; m 067 28 86 309, 069 23 11 499. Some English spoken; Lazër is a teacher at the village school. 2 rooms sharing modern bathroom; traditional, home-cooked food & homemade raki & wine; picnic lunches can be provided.

Mark Lamthi (16 beds) Rragami; m 069 25 03 941, 067 30 14 524. 1 twin room with beautiful carved wooden ceiling, 3 dorms, 2 shared bathrooms; camping also possible; home-cooked food.

What to see and do There are plenty of short **hikes** in the Valbona area, to lovely alpine meadows, mountain lakes and spectacular waterfalls. The Journey to Valbona shop and information centre in Bajram Curri (page 159) has good hiking maps for sale, including *Central Valbona* which covers most of the routes suggested here, and can give advice or arrange guides for hikes. Some accommodation providers in Valbona also stock these maps. The management of any of the hotels and the families in any of the guesthouses will also be able to recommend a knowledgeable guide. For a day's guiding, the going rate is €50 a day; for an hour or so, around 1,000 lek. Horses can also be arranged.

Several hiking routes have been waymarked: an easy option is the short stroll to **Liqeni i Xhemës**, a beautiful little lake hidden away among beech trees only a couple of hundred metres from the main road, between the Rilindja and Rezidenca hotels.

A longer waymarked hike – 2.4km from the main road – goes through the forests to **Çeremi**, a tiny traditional village right up on the border with Montenegro. There is also an asphalted road up to the village. For those who have hiked across the border into Albania (page 157), Çeremi is a good place to stop for lunch or for the night. **Berti's** (4 beds; m 067 22 74 913 – use SMS, no mobile signal in village; **$**) offers a single dorm room with four single mattresses on the floor. Solar panels provide electricity and hot water, and there is a toilet and shower in separate cubicles. Camping is possible in a field behind the family house. Berti's mum prepares huge traditional lunches of home-produced ingredients. Some English is spoken.

Beyond the main village, a track across the (usually) dry bed of the River Valbona leads to the village-cluster of **Rragami**. There are several guesthouses here (see opposite). From here, you can continue on foot along the riverbed or return to the asphalted road and continue by car, over the new bridge, to the Fusha e Gjesë Hotel, where the asphalt ends. To drive any further requires a 4x4 vehicle (or two wheels). Users of less rugged cars can park at the hotel and walk the rest of the way to the hamlet of Gjelaj i Rragamit, where the drivable track ends. It is 9km from here to the Rilindja Hotel.

Gjelaj is a beautiful place, nestled right in the angle where the mountains meet, but it is a harsh environment to live in, with 2m of snow every winter and no school or other community facilities. Many families moved away and return only in the summer. There are no shops or bars, but bread, cheese and raki can be bought from the villagers. Some of the local families provide simple accommodation (**$**), which can be booked online at w journeytovalbona.com. A scramble up through the woods above Gjelaj leads to a spectacular waterfall; as usual, Journey to Valbona has a hiking map and guide to this hamlet.

From Gjelaj, an ancient path leads over the Valbona Pass to **Thethi**. See page 172 for details of this hike, which has been waymarked and can easily be done without a guide.

For those who find the Valbona Pass a little too well trodden, an alternative route between Valbona and Thethi goes through the beautiful, wild country of the Nikaj Valley. Cut off from the rest of Tropoja by walls of mountains, the remote village of **Curraj i Epermë** is now uninhabited apart from three or four families who return in summer. From Valbona, the easiest pass into the valley is Qafa e Kolshit, which can be reached by road from Bajram Curri; then you walk down to Bëtosha and up the river to Curraj i Epermë. From there, a stiff hike over a gigantically high pass takes you to Nderlysaj and a comparatively gentle stroll up the River Shala to Thethi. There are also routes into Nikaj over the passes from Dragobia and Rragami, but they are higher and more difficult. If you are coming to Tropoja along Lake Komani (page 158), you can ask to be set down at Lekbibaj. From there, it is a short walk to Peraj i Nikajt and a good, clear path over Qafa e Mrrethit (about 2 hours) and down to Curraj i Epermë. There is no accommodation in Nikaj, although the families in Curraj i Epermë will look after you *in extremis*; wild camping is possible everywhere. Take enough food with you; there is plenty of wonderful spring water.

THE BIG HIGHLANDS

The mountain range that forms the border between Albania and Montenegro is known variously as the Albanian Alps, the Dinaric Alps, the Accursed Mountains or, more usually in everyday Albanian parlance, just 'the Highlands' (Malësia). This section covers the western part of the range, Malësia e Madhe or 'the Big Highlands', and Thethi. The eastern part of the highlands, the district of Tropoja, is covered from page 156.

The best general hiking maps of this area are produced by Huber Kartographie (page 42). For some specific routes, including the popular hike between Thethi and Valbona (page 172), the guide-maps developed by Journey to Valbona cannot be bettered. They can be bought online at w journeytovalbona.com or in the organisation's shop in Bajram Curri (page 159).

Unless otherwise specified, everywhere covered in this section can be reached by **public transport**. With the exception of Thethi, these are 'rural buses' (page 44) and the usual rules apply: the driver leaves the village early in the morning and then returns to the village around lunchtime. Buses and minibuses to the western highland villages leave Shkodra from the northern suburb of Rus Maxhar. It is always worth checking in the morning whether the bus you want has in fact come to Shkodra that day. The bus and its driver are sometimes hired by a group of villagers, for example to go to Tirana or the airport, which means the bus might not be back in Shkodra until the following day.

Kopliku, a small town 17km north of Shkodra, has the last ATMs that you will see before your return from the highlands. It is essential to carry sufficient cash for your trip; credit cards are sometimes accepted, but cannot be relied upon anywhere in the Albanian Alps. Nor are there any landline telephones beyond Kopliku. There are frequent buses from Shkodra to Kopliku, also from Rus Maxhar. The shopkeepers around the street in Kopliku where the minibuses wait are very helpful and will try to find out for you what time the bus you want is likely to depart.

KELMENDI The district of Kelmendi is Albania's northernmost extreme, a finger of territory poking up into Montenegro. The main villages are Tamara (the administrative centre), Lepusha and Vermoshi – each of them a scattering of stone-built houses surrounded by magnificent mountains. Some of these houses have been kitted out as guesthouses, from where day hikes and longer expeditions can be undertaken. The local produce is delicious – fish from the rivers, lamb and pork from the families' own livestock, the special Kelmendi cheese called *mishavinë*, fruit conserves and syrups, and plum raki.

Tamara has shops, a post office and cafés; the Prodhimë të Kelmendit shop stocks a range of local foodstuffs, including honey, raki, different kinds of jam and fruit syrup and mountain tea (*çaj mali*). The tourist information office also sells local produce. In Vermoshi, there is a café and a little shop that sells household goods, fruit and groceries, beer and cigarettes. The Albanian mobile-phone networks are rather intermittent beyond Tamara; a Montenegrin signal can be picked up in some spots. Lepusha and Vermoshi both have internet connections.

Getting there and away The sole road linking Kelmendi with the rest of Albania runs up the spectacular, rugged valley of the River Cemi; it is now asphalted all the way to Vermoshi, which has cut the journey time to less than 2 hours from Shkodra.

A minibus runs from Shkodra up the valley to Vermoshi every day except Sundays. It leaves from behind the Malësia e Madhe restaurant at Rus Maxhar at about 13.30; however, you should check in the morning whether or not the driver has definitely come down that day. The fare to Vermoshi is 700 lek. For Lepusha, you should ask to be dropped off at the Bordoleçi Pass (Qafa e Bordoleçit), on the main road just above the village. Another minibus serves the route between Shkodra and Tamara. It also leaves Shkodra around 13.30; the fare to Tamara is 400 lek.

From Montenegro, a road leads up to the border crossing from the village of Gucia (called Gusinje in Serbo-Croat), in the district of Plava. There is no public transport on the Albanian side; it is about 3km from the border to the main road. The border crossing is open all year round and, in winter, snow is usually cleared fairly quickly from the main road.

In summer, it is possible to hike to Lepusha from Thethi, a two-day trip; there are guesthouses in Nikçi (eg: Prekë Isufi; m 069 52 85 003) where the journey can be broken. Huber Kartographie's *Vermoshi: Tamarë, Razma, Thethi* map gives details of this route, and other suggested hikes in the area. The passes are usually blocked with snow until at least May.

Tourist information The Italian-funded tourist information office in Tamara (m 069 47 24 658; f Kelmend-Shkrel; ⌚ 09.00–18.00) stocks a range of useful leaflets and maps (including the hiking map mentioned above), and sells guidebooks and local foodstuffs. The helpful, enthusiastic staff can advise on accommodation throughout Kelmendi and assist with making reservations. Malësia e Madhe municipality's website (w bashkiamalesiemadhe.gov.al) includes 'The Guide of Kelmend', with extensive information in English about the district, including some accommodation options and contact details for local guides.

Where to stay and eat There are family-run guesthouses throughout Kelmendi, providing simple accommodation with shared toilet and shower facilities. The daily rate for full board is around €25 per person (**$**); some guesthouses also offer half-board or bed and breakfast.

Some of the houses in Vermoshi are across the river from the main road; when the river is low you can ford it in a car, but otherwise there is only a footbridge. The family you are staying with will help you with your luggage if required.

Gjergj Frani (20 beds) Vermoshi; m 066 66 69 022, +382 69 53 06 03 (Montenegro). Up a track off the main road just before Vermoshi; 10 rooms of varying sizes; kitchen; dining room; washing machine; large covered terrace; garden with gazebos. Hiking guides with English & other languages can be arranged.

Kafe Natyra (30 beds) Vermoshi; m +382 69 52 61 18 (Montenegro). Just off the main road; 5 rooms in family house, large dorm & 1 twin in new wood-panelled building. Restaurant in a tree house in a huge cherry tree; all food home produced; outdoor pool with shallow section for children; orchard. Wi-Fi. Camping also possible (**$**).

Leonard Lumaj (7 beds) Vermoshi; m 069 30 30 733. Guesthouse separate from family home, across the river from the road. Modern bathroom, fully equipped kitchen, large sitting room. Wi-Fi in family home. Mr Lumaj operates the minibus to Shkodra, making this a convenient option if that is how you are getting to Vermoshi. Ground-floor dorm with 4 beds. 1 dbl, & 1 dbl & sgl upstairs.

Lepusha (8 beds) Lepusha; m 069 99 35 806, +382 69 27 79 72 (Montenegro); e zef.nilaj@gmail.com; f Bujtina Lepushe Page. Signposted from the main road, asphalted to gate & beyond; landscaped garden; campsite on raised terrace among fruit trees; Wi-Fi. 3 rooms (1 wood-panelled dorm, 1 sgl, 1 twin) sharing large modern bathroom.

Maja e Trojanit (9 beds) Budaçi; m 069 45 19 116. About halfway between border turn-off & Qafa e Bordoleçit. 3 rooms (2 dorms, 1 dbl) sharing 1 shower & toilet; kitchen.

Prelë & Mariana Vuktilaj (28 beds) Vermoshi; m +382 69 55 24 35 (Montenegro); e antonjo_vuktilaj@hotmail.com. Across the river from the road. 7 rooms, 3 dorms & 4 dbls, sharing 5 modern bathrooms; dining room with TV; balcony running the length of the house; small museum of traditional implements & costumes; courtyard with seating & views out across valley. Horseriding can be arranged; Mr Vuktilaj can lead hiking & climbing trips.

RRAZMA Like Thethi, Rrazma became a tourist destination in the 1930s. It never took off in quite the same way, however, and has only recently begun to redevelop its tourism potential. It would be a good base for hiking, especially for those who do not have the time or the inclination to venture further into the mountains to Thethi or Kelmendi. Rrazma is much closer to Shkodra and the road is good all the way. There is a range of accommodation and a good choice of places to eat, although the village does close down to some extent outside the peak summer months. In the winter, cross-country skiing is possible, although there is no piste.

Where to stay

Natyral Rrazma Resort (27 rooms)
m 068 60 45 455/7; e info@natyralrazmaresort.com; w natyralrazmaresort.com. Modern building in traditional style; English spoken at reception; free Wi-Fi throughout; restaurant (**$$$$**); bar. 25m indoor, heated swimming pool (open year round), sauna, cinema; skis available. All rooms non-smoking, nicely decorated, with flatscreen TV, minibar, AC, CH; en-suite bathroom, some with tub. 3 rooms have balcony, 1 suite has large terrace, all with mountain views. Cash only. **$$$$**

Where to eat There are several restaurants around Rrazma, serving everything from traditional northern Albanian dishes to pizza. They are a better (and less expensive) option than the restaurant in the Natyral Rrazma Resort, which – although beautifully designed, with traditional open fireplace and attractive art on the walls – offers very average Italian cuisine, imported wine only and slow, erratic service.

THETHI About 50km northeast of Kopliku, at the head of the River Shala, lies the national park named after its largest settlement, the village of Thethi. The area was a tourist resort during (and, indeed, before) the communist period and its attractive, traditional features were accordingly maintained, while in other parts of highland Albania they were destroyed either deliberately or through neglect. Edith Durham (see box, page 148) visited Thethi in 1908, and described her stay there in her book *High Albania*. 'Life at Thethi was of absorbing interest,' she wrote. 'I forgot all about the rest of the world, and… there seemed no reason why I should ever return.' The modern visitor's reaction is likely to be similar.

There are 200 houses scattered across the valley, although only a handful of families live there all year round. Most people spend the winter in either Shkodra or Kopliku, and return to Thethi in April or May, for the start of the tourist season; they leave again in September or October, before the harsh winter weather sets in. The traditional houses are built of stone, and roofed with shingles (wooden tiles). They were designed to be easily defensible – these mountains were once the heart of blood-feud territory (see box, page 128) and every family needed to be able to defend its menfolk against revenge. A traditional house of this kind is now the village museum. Of especial interest is the 'lock-in tower' (*kulla e ngujimit*), the only one remaining of its kind that is easily accessible to visitors. The beautiful little church dates from 1892. See below for details of these buildings; they are all in the main settlement and can easily be visited during a day trip. A longer stay in Thethi will allow you to explore further afield and see some of the beautiful natural phenomena in the park. There are also many longer treks for the fit and well equipped, including the popular hike across the Valbona Pass to Tropoja.

Getting there and away The main road to Thethi is clearly signposted from the highway north from Kopliku to the border with Montenegro. Just over an hour from Shkodra is the village of Boga, which was photographed by Marubi in the late 19th century (page 123). Boga has guesthouses and a campsite; given the relentless climb that lies ahead, these may be especially appealing to those intending to cycle to Thethi. A series of increasingly steep and alarming hairpin bends leads up to the pass, Qafë-Thora, 1,775m above sea level. The road is asphalted as far as the summit, but not (at the time of writing) much beyond it. The views on the way are outstanding on a clear day, with towering mountain peaks on either side. There is a viewpoint at the pass and a café nearby.

The 15km from the pass to the main settlement of Thethi (known as Qendër, 'Centre') are equally steep and switchbacked, and the road is rough, despite constant governmental promises of asphalt. A 4x4 vehicle is preferable, although in dry weather it is possible to make the trip, with caution, in a reasonably robust car. About 20 minutes' drive beyond the pass, a dignified stone memorial to Edith Durham looks down over the village she found so fascinating. It takes about 3 hours to drive from Shkodra to the main settlement of Thethi.

If you do not have your own transport, the most convenient option is one of the many **jeeps** that take passengers to and from Thethi in the summer. Your hotel or hostel in Shkodra (or Thethi) should be able to find a driver for you. Typically, they take three or four passengers and charge €10 a head each way; the driver will usually collect you from your accommodation in the morning. A **bus** runs up to Thethi and back to Shkodra every day in summer. It leaves at around 07.00 from Rus Maxhar, in the northern outskirts of Shkodra, and returns from Thethi between noon and 14.00; the fare is also €10 each way. It is best to reserve a seat in advance; your hotel or guesthouse can help you with this.

Outside July and August, getting to or from Thethi without your own transport will be more difficult. It may be possible to hitchhike; expect to pay something towards the driver's fuel. There are daily rural buses to Boga from Kopliku or Shkodra. To walk between Boga and Thethi, the footpath called the Sheep Track (page 172) is a much shorter route than the road; it takes the locals 6 hours. There are half a dozen places to stay overnight in Boga (eg: Boga Alpine Resort; m 067 37 06 462; w bogaalpine.com; **$$–$**).

All but the hardiest cyclists will find the 25km from Boga to Thethi quite challenging, with gradients averaging about 10%. In particular the unasphalted stretch between Qafë-Thora and Thethi would be very rough going on a bike.

Snow and ice close Qafë-Thora for between four and six months every year. The only way out of Thethi then is south, along the Shala and Kiri rivers, to approach Shkodra from Drishti and Mesi. This road is unasphalted and the local people rarely use it except in emergencies. Those who spend the winter in Thethi stock up on essentials before winter sets in. However, if you are travelling in your own 4x4 vehicle or by bike, you could return from Thethi by this route, by way of variety. It is about 130km back to Shkodra.

For information about walking into or out of Thethi, see pages 163 and 172.

Where to stay, and other practicalities There is plenty of accommodation all over Thethi. Long acquainted with the requirements of western European tourists, the guesthouses have modern bathroom facilities, now often en suite, and warm, comfortable beds. Many are registered with w booking.com or other international websites. There is always constant running water, often from the house's own spring, but the electricity supply is sometimes interrupted. Some guesthouses have photovoltaic solar panels.

Bed and breakfast, full- and half-board options are usually offered. Meals consist of traditional northern Albanian dishes, with vegetarian options available. Packed lunches can easily be arranged if you want to spend the day hiking. Campers can order meals at the guesthouse adjoining their campsite, or eat in one of the restaurants in the village (eg: Shpella or Zorgji). Food to cook yourself cannot be bought in Thethi.

The health centre, next to the school, is not staffed full-time; you should bring any essential medicines with you. There is good mobile-phone coverage in the main settlement, but not everywhere in the national park.

🏠 **Harusha** (13 rooms) Qendër; m 069 27 70 294, 068 58 33 476; e nikoharusha@hotmail.com; f Bujtina Harusha. Just across the bridge at the entrance to the main settlement; convenient for hiking to Valbona. Open year round (the family winters in Thethi). Some English spoken; free Wi-Fi. Campsite & parking for campervans with 4 dedicated showers & toilets; can be noisy. Various sizes of rooms; 8 dbls & some others en suite. **$$$**

🏠 **Çarku** (19 beds) Gjeçaj; m 069 31 64 211, 068 36 44 788. On the right-hand side of the road as you come down into Thethi from Qafë-Thora, high above the main settlement. Some English spoken. Meals can be taken on terrace; beautiful views across Shala Valley to mountains towards Valbona. 1 dbl en suite, other rooms share 2 bathrooms. **$$**

🏠 **Shpella** (12 rooms) Qendër; m 069 37 74 851; e shpella.family@googlemail.com; f Thethi Shpella Guesthouse. Centrally located below 'lock-in tower'; English spoken. Qualified hiking guide in family; 4x4 available for excursions; airport pick-up possible from Tirana or Podgorica; all-in packages available with sister-hotel in Shkodra. Restaurant (open to non-residents) with tables in garden; free Wi-Fi. Campsite with dedicated shower & toilet indoors. Rooms of various sizes; 10 en suite, 2 share bathroom. **$$**

🏠 **Zorgji** (7 rooms) Qendër; m 068 23 19 610; e pellumbkola@gmail.com. Split location: 2 en-suite trpls above restaurant, centrally located next door to school; 5 en-suite rooms of varying sizes in traditional stone-built house on hillside above (vehicle & foot access; camping possible. Some English spoken. Restaurant & bar (open to public) with tables in large garden; free Wi-Fi. **$$**

🏠 **Dedë Nika** (20 beds) Nderlysaj; m 069 33 46 423. Conveniently located if approaching Thethi from the south or from Curraj i Epermë (page 163). **$**

🏠 **Rupa** (7 rooms) Qendër; ☎ (in Shkodra) 022 244 077; m 068 20 03 393; e rorupaog@yahoo.com. Centrally located between school & church; some English spoken; free Wi-Fi. Camping possible. Various sizes of rooms; 3 en suite, 4 sharing 2 bathrooms. **$**

What to see and do The road into Thethi from Qafë-Thora winds down through beech forest, passing meadows, farmhouses and the lovely **Gjeçaj Waterfall**, which tumbles from its cliff only metres from the road. The main sights in the village (Qendër) are down to the right across the bridge; an information panel with a map of the national park has been installed at the junction here. Wooden signs direct visitors to the places of interest.

The first of the village's public buildings you come to is the **school**, with a memorial stone outside to John Holmes of the Balkans Peace Park Project (see box, page 173), which did so much over the years to support sustainable tourism in Thethi. Adjoining the school is the health centre, the building where Albania's mountaineering community held its first-ever event, in 1956.

Thethi is a Catholic village; the Ottomans left these remote mountain settlements largely to their own devices and the people had no reason to convert to Islam (see page 21 for the reasons why some did elsewhere). The village **church**, built in 1892, was restored and reroofed in 2005–06 thanks to donations from 'the children of Thethi' in the United States. Edith Durham was welcomed to Thethi in 1908 by the Franciscan priest of this church: 'a solid, shingle-roofed building, with a bell-tower.' A footpath leads from the church, across fields and up a stony track, to the stone-built house that is now Thethi's **museum** (200 lek). Like all traditional houses in Albania, the ground floor was used for livestock, workshops and storage; the living quarters were on the first floor. This being the warlike highlands, the rooms on this floor were carefully designed to be defended against attackers, with rifle loop-holes on all sides and, at the corners, the elaborate *frëngji,* embrasures with rests for the gunmen's elbows, and an outer grille of stone. The chute built into another wall was used for slops etc, while the men were 'in blood' – that is, when they were involved in a vendetta – and unable to leave the house. There are a few household items on display, but the main interest here is the building itself.

Perhaps the most interesting building in the village is the **lock-in tower** (*kulla e ngujimit;* 150 lek), which is said to be 400 years old. This highly defensible building was used, until as recently as the 1920s, whenever a Thethi man had committed murder and was therefore subject to blood feud. The killer was allowed a fortnight's grace, incarcerated in the tower, while the village elders negotiated with the wronged family to try to reconcile the feud. Apart from the heavy door, which opens straight on to the bedrock on which the tower was built, there are no openings at all on the ground floor. As long as negotiations were under way, the murderer was protected from reprisals by gunmen on the upper floor, where *frëngji* can still be seen on each wall. If the feud conciliators (*pajtimtarë*) were successful, the man was set free to fulfil his side of the bargain, often by marrying a daughter of his victim. If not, he was released from the tower to seek his own solution, either fleeing the district or being killed in turn by his victim's family.

In the past, every village in northern Albania had a lock-in tower like this. King Zog had many of them destroyed as part of his campaign to modernise the country (and, conveniently, to punish the Catholic clans that opposed him). In the communist period, those that remained were either used for storage, until they collapsed through lack of maintenance, or were deliberately dismantled and the stone re-used for other buildings. Only a few now remain, in very remote parts of the high mountains. They are all designated as Cultural Monuments now, but the preservation and restoration of this tower is thanks to Thethi's history as a magnet for visitors since the days of Edith Durham. The roof was repaired and the building conserved in 2007, with Dutch funding. Photographs of famous *pajtimtarë* decorate the walls on the first floor; they include Sokol Koçeku, grandfather of the current owner. Mr Mark Koçeku also runs a guesthouse next door (**w** thethiguesthouse.com; **$$**).

From the tower, it is a short drive or an easy walk to the Grunas Canyon, a spectacular gorge 2km long and 60m deep, crossed high above by the Gërla Bridge. Anyone who likes waterfalls and can manage a little scrambling should visit the **Grunas Waterfall**. It plunges 25m into a deep pool of ice-cold water. Smaller waterfalls and rapids rush the stream down from this pool to meet the River Shala. You can walk up to the waterfall from the canyon or from the lock-in tower, following a footpath until you see the waterfall up on the left. In 2007, archaeologists discovered a large Bronze Age site near the Grunas Canyon.

Some 3 or 4km further along the road, at the settlement of **Nderlysaj**, the force of the river has carved spectacular formations out of the rocks. A wooden bridge enables visitors to get a good look at these falls. There are natural pools that are good for swimming, although the water is very cold even in summer.

Hiking in the national park Journey to Valbona's *Qafa e Valbonës* map (page 41) indicates hikes around Thethi as well as the route between Thethi and Valbona, with hiking notes, and includes a useful map of the village itself. The most popular hiking routes around Thethi are waymarked. However, it is essential to bear in mind that, away from the scattering of settlements which make up the village, the area is very sparsely populated and there are no friendly mountain rescue helicopters. Minor accidents such as sprained ankles acquire much greater significance when the nearest help is 4 hours' limp away and, although there is mobile-phone coverage in the main settlement (Qendër), it cannot be relied upon elsewhere in the national park. For anything beyond a short stroll around the centre or along the road, suitable footwear and a good map are essential. Less experienced hikers may prefer to hire a guide; the family running your guesthouse will be able to find one for you. For a full day's guiding, you should expect to pay around €50.

In the mountains, **ornithologists** should look out for the beautiful and graceful bee-eater (*Merops apiaster*), the green and great-spotted woodpeckers (*Picus viridis* and *Dendrocopus major*), the rock partridge (*Alectoris graeca*), the hoopoe (*Upupa epops*), with its exotic-looking crest, the capercaillie (*Tetrao urogallus*), and the *balkanica* race of the shore lark (*Eremophila alpestris*), which has a warm pink nape and pale yellow facial markings, as well as its characteristic black horns.

Little herpetological mapping has been done in Albania, but **snakes** that definitely reside in Thethi are the venomous nose-horned viper (*Vipera ammodytes*) and the harmless smooth snake (*Coronella austriaca*). There are fire salamanders (*Salamandra salamandra*) and alpine salamanders (*Salamandra atra*), which like to come out when it rains; the nose-horned vipers like eating them, so they come out in the rain too. There are yellow-bellied toads (*Bombina variegata*), tree frogs (*Hyla arborea*) and agile frogs (*Rana dalmatina*). Hermann's tortoise (*Testudo hermanii*) is also present in the area. (Thanks to Joost Smets for this information.)

FLORA AND FAUNA IN THE ALBANIAN ALPS

Catherine Bohne

The Malësia is a naturalist's dream. The convergence of the central European alpine climate with the Mediterranean produces the richest flora in Europe, with an estimated minimum of 3,200 naturally occurring species of higher plants (compare this with the 1,500 native species of the British Isles). With 14 species of wild thyme, six different mints, lavender and rosemary and 16 different members of the Sage genus, a walk in the highlands simply *smells* good.

Begin with staring at what's under your feet: the limestone rock from which the mountains are formed. Some 50–100 million years old, the mountains were forced upwards when Africa hit Europe (in summary) and so everything around you is formed of sedimentary limestone, which was originally coral on the bottom of a large, shallow inland sea. This same limestone and its tendency to dissolve in strange patterns both above and below ground gives rise to the karst geology, characterised by underground rivers, excellent drainage (not so exciting to you perhaps, but thrilling to the plants) and many, many caves. There should also, of course, be many fossils.

As you stand and stare across a valley, the further peaks and rocky outcrops may appear barren, but closer inspection reveals them to be a riot of tiny gem-like plants, such as alpine succulents, Saxifrage, Sempervivums, Silenes and Sedums (to mention only things beginning with 's'). Moving down from the peaks, you find the grassy meadows of the Bjeshkët ('alps'), an absolutely dizzy fit of flowers from May to July. Here you will find the endemic Albanian lily (*Lilium albanicum*), as well as fritillaries, several species of orchids, and some of the 32 species of *Campanula* (bellflowers) on record. *Dianthus* (22 species of pinks), flowering peas and *Lathyrus* (up to 26 species), *Geranium* (also a possible 26) and let's not forget up to 60 species of clover. And these are just a handful of the things it's *easy* to see.

If you can tear your eyes away from all this, you might look up to spot a golden eagle (*Aquila chrysaetos*) soaring majestically (or dropping a baby goat from a great height to stun it for lunch). Luckily for the eagles, the heights are also hopping with a large population of chamois (*Rupicapra rupicapra*); watching one casually run straight down a seemingly vertical cliff is a heart-stopping thrill not to be missed.

Descending further, these frequently vertical meadows and rock faces will intersect with marginally more gentle slopes formed by millennia of piled rock debris, now blanketed most often with beech forest (*Fagus sylvatica*). Besides being straight out of Grimms' Fairy Tales, these forests also shelter what may well

The River Shala rises high up above Thethi, in the karst of Mount Arapi (2,217m), the cliff that towers over the Thethi Valley from the north, and it flows pretty much north to south until it meets Lake Komani. It emerges above ground just before the settlement of **Okoli**, in a number of little springs surrounded by beech trees, and there are several nice picnic spots in the vicinity. To get to Okoli from the main village of Thethi, turn left instead of right after you have crossed the bridge near the school, and keep going along the road. If you are staying up above the village, on the way down from Qafë-Thora, you can cut across the hillside, through woods and meadows, and come down to Okoli from the west. As you approach the village from this direction, you pass some World War II bunkers, of quite different design from the communist-era pillboxes.

Climbing up the eastern flank of Mount Arapi, the path continues up to **Qafa e Pejës** (the Peja Pass), 1,700m high, which used to link Thethi with the Montenegrin towns of Gusinje (Gucia, in Albanian) and Plava. To cross

be the largest population of *Ursus arctos* – brown bear – left in Europe. Although they will avoid you assiduously, sightings are still frequent and signs of their passing – footprints, scratched trees and droppings – are easy to spot. Other large animals you might see signs of include wild boar (*Sus scrofa*) and, of course, no fairy-tale woods would be complete without… wolves (*Canis lupus*). There are an estimated 400 wolves in these mountains, making this the largest population in Europe. While hard to spot in the summer, when they move up to the meadows to follow the flocks of sheep and goats, in winter they are extremely prevalent, their tracks are easy to follow (particularly as they circle the houses at night) and an enthusiastic observer can begin to recognise the tracks of individual wolves. Things you are almost guaranteed not to see a sign of, but might like to know are around, include the wild cat (*Felis sylvestris*) and the very rare Balkan lynx (*Lynx lynx*). The Balkan Lynx Recovery Programme, which involves Albanian and international biologists, has been using camera traps since 2008, in an effort to monitor the movements of lynx and other wildlife in the Albanian highlands.

Also lurking in the forest are another plethora of rare (elsewhere) and beautiful plants of which the most notable is the *Ramonda serbica*, a sort of Balkan version of an African violet. Badgers (*Meles meles*) make a racket snuffling through the undergrowth, and a rainy day will bring out hordes of fire salamanders (*Salamandra salamandra*). Once down by the riverbanks, strolling through stands of silvery willows, you can look for the round webbed tracks of the common otter (*Lutra lutra*) and peer into eddy pools for the highly prized local trout. Smaller animals you might encounter without ever straying from your hotel or guesthouse include such pleasures as red foxes (*Vulpes vulpes*), the incredibly cute fat dormouse (*Glis glis*) and the noble eastern hedgehog (*Erinaceus concolor*).

All of this of course only touches on a fraction of what's actually here to be seen. Not mentioned yet are such joys as beetles, butterflies, the oddly friendly grasshoppers (pink ones as well as green!), snakes, vipers, cuckoos, woodpeckers – the list goes on and on.

Finally, a word of encouragement. One of the main reasons for this richness is the historical isolation and economic neglect of the area. As this changes, these precious populations will come under threat. The interest and enthusiasm of visitors will be invaluable to the future survival of this last remaining corner of wild Europe.

the international border on foot between Albania, Kosovo and Montenegro, advance permits are needed; see page 45 for advice on obtaining these. There are interesting caves on Mount Arapi, pretty much due north from Okoli, and others above the alpine meadows called Fusha e Dënellit, on the other side of Thethi. The paths are not always easy to identify and the use of a guide is highly recommended.

Further up the main road out of Thethi, a footpath called Shtegu i Dhenve ('the Sheep Track') leads up to a pass at 1,830m and onward to Boga (at least 6 hours' walk). On a clear day there are excellent views from here over the Boga Valley as well as back down across the Shala Valley. Before the road over Qafë-Thora was built in the 1930s, this was the only way for the people of Thethi to get to Boga; instead, their natural links were with Shkodra, using the route along the Shala and Kiri rivers, and with the village of Rragami in the neighbouring district of Tropoja.

Hiking from Thethi to Valbona An ancient track runs between Thethi and Rragami across the Valbona Pass, over 1,800m above sea level; most winters, the pass is snowbound until May or even early June. The track has been waymarked and, in summer, it is quite straightforward to find the route. However, the hike requires a reasonable level of fitness and should not be attempted without adequate footwear and clothing. Horses can be hired in Thethi or Valbona to carry rucksacks; enquire at your guesthouse. The going rate for a horse, with a human to manage it, is €50; each horse can take up to 60 kilos of luggage. Depending on how fit you are and how much kit you are carrying, it takes 4–5 hours to reach the Valbona Pass, and then another 3 hours down to Rragami. Obviously this hike can also be done in the opposite direction, from Rragami to Thethi; it simply comes down to how you choose to organise the rest of your trip.

The path out of Thethi leads fairly gently uphill from the River Shala to meet the very rough vehicle track (difficult even with 4x4) to the settlement of **Gjelaj.** The first of three cafés on the route, just above Gjelaj, is a good opportunity for a breather before a very steep section through beech forest; it is possible to camp at this café.

About an hour beyond Gjelaj, a spring just before the end of the forest is the next place where water bottles can be replenished. Then you emerge on to a beautiful alpine meadow, carpeted with lavender, clover of different colours and little orchids. All these flowers, of course, mean lots of butterflies: blues, arguses and tortoiseshells, among others. Several very rare butterflies can be found in the Albanian highlands, including the apollo (*Parnassius apollo*), large blue and Alcon large blue (*Phengaris arion* and *P. alcon*).

The meadows give way to more beech forest, with patches of tiny, tart wild strawberries. A second café stands in a clearing; camping is also possible here (**m** 068 52 35 920). Members of the family who live here (except in winter) sell cold drinks and slices of the northern Albanian dish called *fli*, layers of filo pastry and butter which might have been invented as a hiking snack. The toilets are impeccable, with running water, soap, clean towel and mirror. This is the last chance to fill water bottles until far down on the other side of the pass.

It takes about an hour from the café to the Valbona Pass. At the top, there are magnificent views across the valley to Qafë-Thora and Qafa e Pejës, and down into Thethi and towards the source of the Shala. However, it is a bleak spot and often very windy. The path down on the other side is steep and feels as if it is going in the wrong direction (it isn't). It will be with relief that you find yourself at the third and

THE BALKANS PEACE PARK PROJECT

With thanks to Antonia Young

Since 1999, a group of international and local organisations and individuals have been working within the Balkans Peace Park Project (B3P) to establish a cross-border park that would straddle the highlands of northern Albania, southern Montenegro and western Kosovo.

There are more than 600 environmentally protected areas in the world that straddle international boundaries; one of them can be found at the other end of Albania, encompassing the two Prespa Lakes shared by Albania, Greece and North Macedonia. About 25 of these cross-border parks are specifically dedicated as 'Peace Parks', symbols of peace and co-operation between countries where sometimes there has been serious conflict. One of the first was the Morokulien Peace Park between Norway and Sweden, set up in 1914. B3P is one of about 400 cross-border projects in the European Green Belt, an initiative of the International Union for Conservation of Nature (IUCN), which runs the length of the old 'Iron Curtain', from Finland to the southeastern Balkans.

The mountains and valleys in the area proposed for the Balkans Peace Park are home to people who have retained their traditional lifestyles to an extent that is unusual in Europe, and are a habitat for exceptional flora and fauna. But the lack of economic opportunity has led to environmental threats, such as illegal logging, and the cultural threat of depopulation as people move to the cities for work. B3P's vision is of a Peace Park where communities from all three countries working together to protect their environment, stimulate local employment and promote sustainable tourism in the region. In Albania, the Peace Park boundaries would cover Kelmendi, the Valbona Valley and Shala, the area that includes Thethi. Its partner organisation, B3P-Albania, is registered as a non-profit organisation in Shkodra.

B3P's earliest initiatives were to support walking, bike and horse treks, researching old and new routes in the proposed Peace Park area and working to help open up cross-border tracks. It has sponsored and organised international conferences, facilitated several significant academic studies in the region, and established regular exchange visits between the communities in the area and the Yorkshire Dales National Park in England. From 2008 to 2015, it ran an annual summer programme in the former village school in Thethi, bringing together Albanian teachers and foreign volunteers. The summer programmes later expanded across northern Albania and into Kosovo and Montenegro. Adults as well as schoolchildren had the opportunity to learn skills that help their community to survive: English, so that they can communicate with foreign tourists; marketable arts and crafts; and agricultural techniques such as permaculture.

More information about B3P's activities can be found on its website (**w** balkanspeaceparkdotorg.wordpress.com).

last of the trail-side cafés, Kafe Simoni, at the source of the River Valbona. Another steep slog downhill brings you to Gjelaj i Rragamit, the twin settlement of Gjelaj i Thethit where the hike began. As on the other side, there is a rough track to this settlement, useable by 4x4 vehicles. It is 3km from here to the asphalted road and the restaurant at Fusha e Gjesë. See page 163 for information about Rragami and page 161 for onward travel to Valbona and Bajram Curri.

PESHKOPIA *Telephone code: 0218*

Peshkopia is set amid spectacular mountains that have made it rather isolated from the rest of Albania. Like Tropoja, it was cut off from its natural hinterland by the border drawn in 1913 and, like Tropoja, it suffered further from many years of neglect by the Albanian government. In recent years though, the town has developed into a thriving and pleasant place. The district of which it is the administrative centre is called Dibër (or Dibra), and the town itself is also sometimes referred to by that name. This can lead to confusion, since the nearest town on the other side of the border is also called Dibër (or, in Macedonian, Debar). The key is to remember that only 100 years ago, before the drawing of the lines that have caused so much turmoil in the Balkans, it was all the same district. Many travellers use Peshkopia as a base from which to visit the Mavrovo National Park, only 26km away, but on the other side of that 1913 border, in North Macedonia.

GETTING THERE AND AWAY

By car The new highway connecting Tirana and Dibra, **Rruga e Arbërit** or the 'Arbëri Road' ('Arbëri' was a medieval name for part of what is now Albania), was provisionally inaugurated in late 2021, after about a decade of construction in fits and starts. The new highway is 70km long and cuts through the mountains, in tunnels and over bridges, between Klosi and Tirana (see the colour map at the beginning of this guidebook). It is scheduled to be completed by May 2022 and will cut the journey time between Tirana and Peshkopia to less than an hour.

The old road to Peshkopia, from the SH1 coastal highway, runs through spectacular scenery, above a precipitous river gorge, past Lake Ulza and through wild, rather bleak terrain dotted with fortified houses. After Burreli, it continues to follow the lovely green River Mati upstream, before climbing over the watershed through forests of beech and conifers, with glimpses through them of the mountain peaks on either side. It is 140km from the junction with the SH1 (the Miloti junction).

Another new road, replacing the old road along the River Black Drini, links Peshkopia with Kukësi, via Kastrioti and Bushtrica. It is asphalted but mountainous – it apparently has no fewer than 760 bends – and the journey takes about 2 hours.

Finally, the Albanian government has promised the asphalting of the road between Dibra and Librazhdi, through the Shebenik-Jabllanica National Park; this may happen within the lifetime of this guidebook.

By public transport From Tirana, buses for Peshkopia leave from the North/South bus terminal from early morning until mid afternoon. Note that buses displaying signs for 'Dibër' will take you to Peshkopia, not North Macedonia! In Peshkopia, they terminate in and leave from the main square. The one-way fare is 600 lek.

From neighbouring North Macedonia, minibuses operate between Peshkopia and Dibra e Madhe (Debar) via Maqellarja, a bustling little transport hub about 13km from Peshkopia. If there is no direct bus at the time you want to travel, there are very frequent minibuses from Maqellarja to Peshkopia, taking about 30 minutes.

A daily bus service operates between Peshkopia and Kukësi; it takes just over 2 hours and the one-way fare is 800 lek. In Peshkopia, the bus departs from the bus park next to the Brazil Hotel. It leaves there between 07.00 and 07.30 and returns from the main bus terminus in Kukësi at noon.

By bike The new road between Kukësi and Peshkopia is very hard going on a bicycle. It has a good surface all the way, but the gradients are very tough – 15–20%

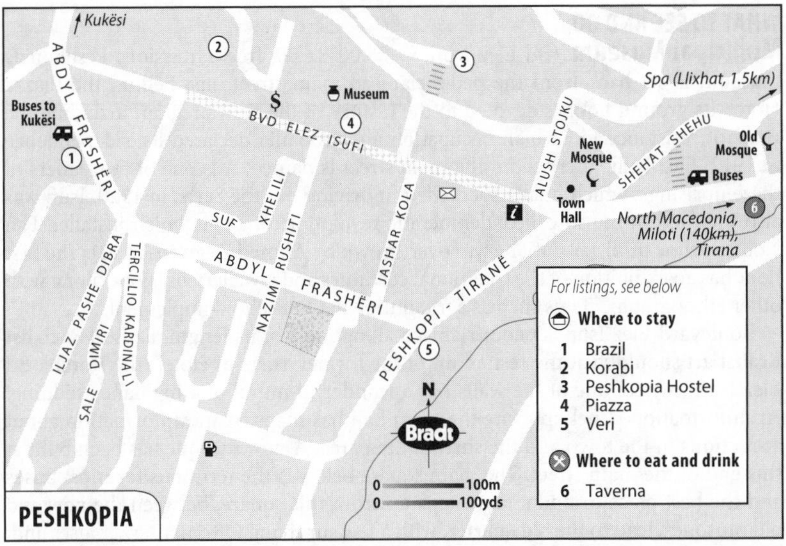

in places. You should allow up to 8 hours on this route. A slightly easier alternative is the old road, which runs above the River Black Drini, another spectacularly beautiful route. For details of the route through the Shebenik-Jabllanica National Park, to Librazhdi, see page 195.

WHERE TO STAY *Map, above*

Veri (48 rooms, 2 suites) 25090; m 069 20 98 186; e verihotel@gmail.com; f HotelVeri. New building with lift, good restaurant ($$$), bar Wi-Fi. B/fast inc. Generously proportioned rooms, all with large, well-equipped en-suite bathroom, king-size bed, desk, bedside lights, flatscreen TV, AC. **$$$**

Piazza (20 rooms) Bd Elez Isufi; 24616; m 069 67 41 378; e info@hotelpiazza.al; w hotelpiazza.al. New building, great location on pedestrianised main street; free underground car park; free Wi-Fi throughout. Excellent restaurant ($$$), all organic, good wine list; terrace bar. B/fast inc. Generously sized rooms, all with large en-suite bathroom, AC, flatscreen TV, desk, balcony. **$$**

Brazil (9 rooms) 23934; m 068 20 90 648. Next to the court (*pranë Gjykatës*), very handy for buses to Kukësi. Bar & restaurant; rooms of varying capacity, basic but clean. All rooms en suite with heater & TV. **$**

Korabi (70 rooms) Bd Elez Isufi; m 069 20 70 107, 068 20 70 107. Refurbished communist-era hotel, central location. Good restaurant ($$$) with separate entrance; in summer, tables outside on lovely raised terrace. Free parking; conference room; laundry service; Wi-Fi; b/fast inc. All rooms en suite with AC, TV, balcony. **$**

Peshkopia Hostel (3 dorms, 2 private rooms) m 068 27 76 848, 068 31 33 451. Renovated villa once used as accommodation for visiting communist leaders. Great location overlooking the town; huge garden with trees & hammocks; ample parking; Wi-Fi. 2 common rooms, 1 with fireplace; fully equipped kitchen; 2 bathrooms on each floor; towels & bed linen provided; b/fast inc. Camping possible. Tours organised, including to Lura & Mt Korabi. **$**

WHERE TO EAT *Map, above*

The restaurants in the Piazza and Veri hotels are open to non-residents. The **Taverna** café ($$), at the western end of the main square (closed in the evenings), offers traditional Albanian dishes, including the local speciality, *jufka*, a kind of fine pasta.

WHAT TO SEE AND DO

Municipal Museum (Bd Elez Isufi; ⌚ 08.00–16.00; free admission) Peshkopia's museum is set back from the pedestrianised main street, just behind the Piazza Hotel. Its ground floor is devoted to the history of the Dibra region, including the years of resistance to Serbian occupation after Albania declared its independence in 1912. Elez Isufi, after whom the main street is named, was one of the leaders of these uprisings, which finally succeeded in driving out the Serbs in 1920. Isufi was also involved in the so-called 'democratic revolution' of 1924, which installed Fan Noli as prime minister until he was overthrown by Ahmed Zogu (page 12). The first floor has an exhibition of the traditional costumes and jewellery of Dibra, along with other ethnographic items such as agricultural and household implements.

Boulevard Elez Isufi is pedestrianised along most of its length. Fans of **Socialist Realist art** should visit the restaurant of the former Turizmi Hotel (the Korabi, Bd Elez Isufi), where one of the walls has a wonderful mural of a highland wedding. An information panel opposite the town hall has maps of and information about attractions in the town and the surrounding area. A new mosque has been built at this end of the main street. The main square below is the terminus for most buses and the best place to find a taxi. Steps up from this square, between the new and old mosques, lead to the **old quarter**, with a few surviving Ottoman-era houses and, from the top, marvellous views over the town and of the mountains to the east.

Towards the end of October each year, Peshkopia hosts an important **festival of traditional music** (Oda Dibrane) from all over the Albanian-speaking world. It is difficult, although not impossible, to get tickets for Oda Dibrane, and it is essential to book accommodation in advance while it is on.

Llixhat e Peshkopisë Just outside Peshkopia is a well-known **spa complex**, 750m above sea level, known by the generic Albanian word for thermal springs: Llixhat. The three sulphurous springs that feed the Peshkopia spa have been exploited since the early 20th century, when two communal baths were built. The current building, opened in 1989, has 44 individual cubicles, a pool and rooms for mud treatment. The ground temperature of the water is 38–40°C.

Full courses of treatment are offered from April to October; the best time is September–October, when up to 3,000 people a day use the facilities. The spa stays open all year round; however, drop-in customers (⌚10.00–16.00; 100 lek) can soak for 10–15 minutes in a bathtub in one of the cubicles (bring your own towel). There are many hotels at the spa, open only in season, eg: Hotel Alpin (45 rooms; **m** 068 23 22 446; all rooms en suite with TV, FB; **$**). Llixhat is 1.5km from Peshkopia – a pleasant walk or a short taxi ride (200–300 lek) from the main square.

6

The Southeast

Southeastern Albania is a fascinating and little-explored corner of the country, with dozens of medieval churches, a wealth of prehistoric sites, the wild Gramoz mountain range and the beautiful Ohrid and Prespa lakes. Korça, the regional capital, is a cultured and attractive city, and its many good hotels make it an ideal base from which to explore the rest of the region. Its altitude (850m above sea level) and inland position make it very cold in winter and spring, and delightfully cool in summer.

GETTING THERE AND AWAY

BY AIR The closest airport to southeastern Albania is **Ohrid**, on the North Macedonian side of Lake Ohrid but, as a consequence of the Covid pandemic, it has few flights at the time of writing.

BY LAND The main border crossing from North Macedonia into Albania is Qafa e Thanë, a few kilometres from Struga on the northern shore of Lake Ohrid. From Greece, the principal border crossing for Korça is at Kapshtica. Those with their own transport might also consider using one of the smaller border crossings to get to Përmeti, Prespa or Pogradeci; for these, please refer to the relevant section in this chapter.

From **Tirana**, the traditional route to Pogradeci, Korça and Kapshtica is via Elbasani and Librazhdi, over the mountains via Prrënjasi and a series of hairpin bends, then down the western shore of Lake Ohrid. By the summer of 2022, upgrading work is expected to have been completed on the road connecting Qukësi, west of Prrënjasi, and Qafë-Plloça, a few kilometres south of Pogradeci. This road will avoid the most difficult section of the traditional route and will be the fastest way between Tirana and Korça.

Buses from Tirana leave from the Southeast bus station, behind the Faculty of Economics (the exception is Përmeti, page 201). There are daily services from Athens and other Greek cities to every city and many of the towns covered in this chapter.

KORÇA *Telephone code: 082*

The people of Korça are justifiably proud of their city's cultured and intellectual traditions. The city is home to the magnificent National Museum of Medieval Art and other interesting museums. Korça was one of the main centres of the Albanian cultural renaissance (Rilindja Kombëtare), which created the sense of national identity that ultimately led to the country's independence from the Ottoman Empire (page 11). The first Albanian-medium school was opened here in 1887, with the first girls' school following four years later, and the town was one of the focal points of the movement to standardise the Albanian alphabet.

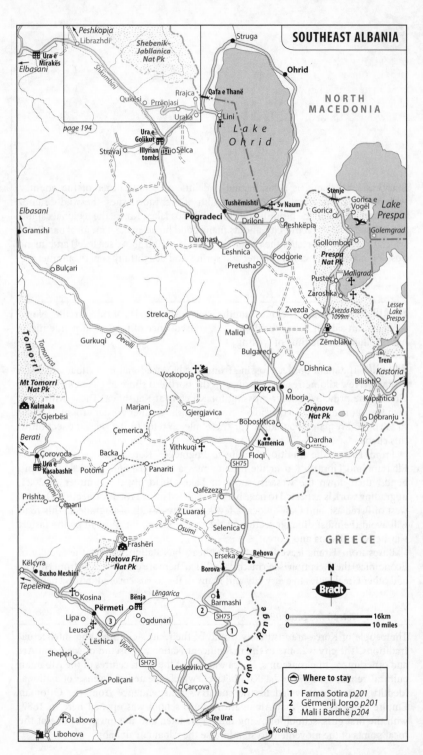

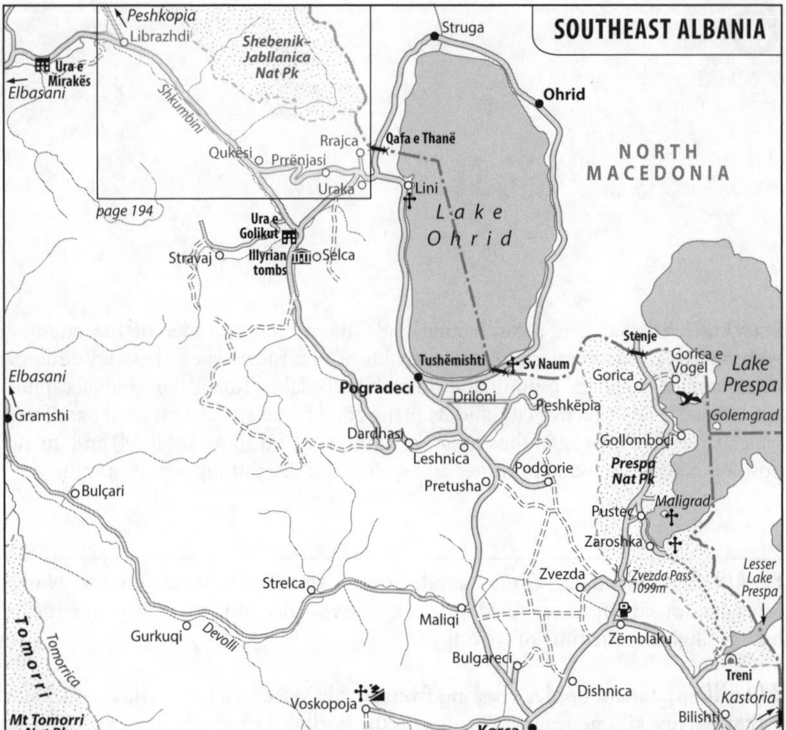
SOUTHEAST ALBANIA
NORTH MACEDONIA
GREECE
Peshkopia
Librazhdi
Shebenik-Jabllanica Nat Pk
Ura e Mirakës
Elbasani
Shkumbini
Qukësi
Prrënjasi
Rrajca
Uraka
page 194
Qafa e Thanë
Struga
Ohrid
Lini
Lake Ohrid
Ura e Golikut
Stravaj
Illyrian tombs
Selca
Tushëmishti
Sv Naum
Pogradeci
Driloni
Peshkëpia
Stenje
Gorica e Vogël
Gorica
Lake Prespa
Golemgrad
Gollomboçi
Prespa Nat Pk
Maligrad
Pusteç
Zaroshka
Elbasani
Gramshi
Dardhasi
Leshnica
Podgorie
Pretusha
Bulçari
Zvezda
Zvezda Pass 1099m
Lesser Lake Prespa
Strelca
Maliqi
Zëmblaku
Gurkuqi
Devolli
Tomorri
Tomorrica
Bulgareci
Treni
Dishnica
Kastoria
Voskopoja
Korça
Bilishti
Mt Tomorri Nat Pk
Mborja
Kapshtica
Kulmaka
Marjani
Gjergjavica
Drenova Nat Pk
Gjerbësi
Dobranju
Boboshtica
Çemerica
Berati
Kamenica
Vithkuqi
Dardha
Çorovoda
Backa
Floqi
Ura e Kasabashit
Potomi
Panariti
SH75
Osumi
Qafëzeza
Prishta
Çepani
Luarasi
Osumi
Selenica
Frashëri
Rehova
Erseka
Këlcyra
Baxho Meshini
Hotova Firs Nat Pk
Borova
Tepelena
Kosina
Bënja
Lëngarica
Barmashi
Përmeti
2
Lipa
3
Ogdunari
SH75
Leusa
1
Lëshica
Vjosa
Gramoz Range
Sheperi
SH75
Leskoviku
Poliçani
Çarçova
Labova
Tre Urat
Libohova
Konitsa
N
Bradt
0 16km
0 10 miles
Where to stay
1 Farma Sotira p201
2 Gërmenji Jorgo p201
3 Mali i Bardhë p204

Korça's history became rather chequered in the early 20th century. The Epirote Insurrection of 1913 saw much of southern Albania raided and terrorised by Greek irredentists who sought its incorporation into Greece. Korça was occupied and its Albanian-medium schools closed, until the Greek government ordered its troops home in June 1914. This respite was short-lived, however. A year later a Greek army returned to occupy Korça and Berati, laying waste to Muslim villages and farmlands and driving streams of refugees across the country to Vlora. In November 1916, the French occupied Korça and set up the so-called Autonomous Albanian Republic of Korça. As leader, they appointed the Rilindja activist Themistokli Gërmenji, who made French and Albanian the official languages of the autonomous republic and set up Albanian schools. The following year, however, he was accused (probably falsely) of collaborating with the Axis Powers, sentenced to death by a French military court and executed in November 1917. Not surprisingly, this turbulent period saw a great deal of emigration, mainly to the USA, where Korçans still make up a large proportion of the Albanian-American community.

GETTING THERE AND AWAY From northern **Greece**, several bus companies run up to Korça from Kastoria (called Kosturi in Albanian), 70km away. There are also buses from Thessaloniki (Selaniku) and Athens.

From **North Macedonia**, the border crossing at Tushëmishti, at the southern end of Lake Ohrid, is a better choice for those with their own transport than the busy crossing further north at Qafa e Thanë. There is also a small crossing on the eastern shore of Lake Prespa, at Gorica.

Within Albania, there are frequent buses to Korça from **Tirana**, running from early morning until early afternoon. They leave from the Southeast bus station, behind the Faculty of Economics. The journey takes about 3 hours (it will be somewhat less once the new road is open); the fare is 500 lek. Buses also serve Korça from other cities, including Durrësi, Vlora and Berati. Korça's bus station is on the main road out of town, at the junction of Boulevard Fan Noli and Rruga Midhi Kostani.

See page 199 for the long but scenic route through the Gramoz Mountains and along the beautiful River Vjosa. Buses serving this route leave Gjirokastra at 07.00 every day except Sundays, and Përmeti at 07.00 every day. In the other direction, they leave Korça every day at 06.00 (for Gjirokastra) and 13.00 (for Përmeti).

For suggested routes on foot or by bike into the Korça area, see pages 190 and 268.

TOURIST INFORMATION The **tourist information office** (🕘 summer 09.00–21.00, winter 09.00–19.00) is in the stone building on the corner of Theatre Square (the pedestrianised main square). The friendly, English-speaking staff can advise on where to stay and what to do, not only in the town but also in the rest of the Prefecture, which includes Pogradeci, Voskopoja, the Prespa Lakes and the Gramoz Mountains. The office stocks maps, brochures and souvenirs; cycling itineraries of various length and difficulty are also available, with a route map which can be downloaded free on to your smartphone. Guided city tours and excursions can be arranged. A good, detailed town plan is posted outside.

Another source of information about the city and its attractions is **Korça Explorer** (m 069 78 32 673; f Korca Explorer), who offer information about accommodation, focusing particularly on the budget end of the market; tours of the city, including a walking tour, and the surrounding area; and bike and car hire. Sister company Discover Prespa Lake provides similar services for the Prespa area.

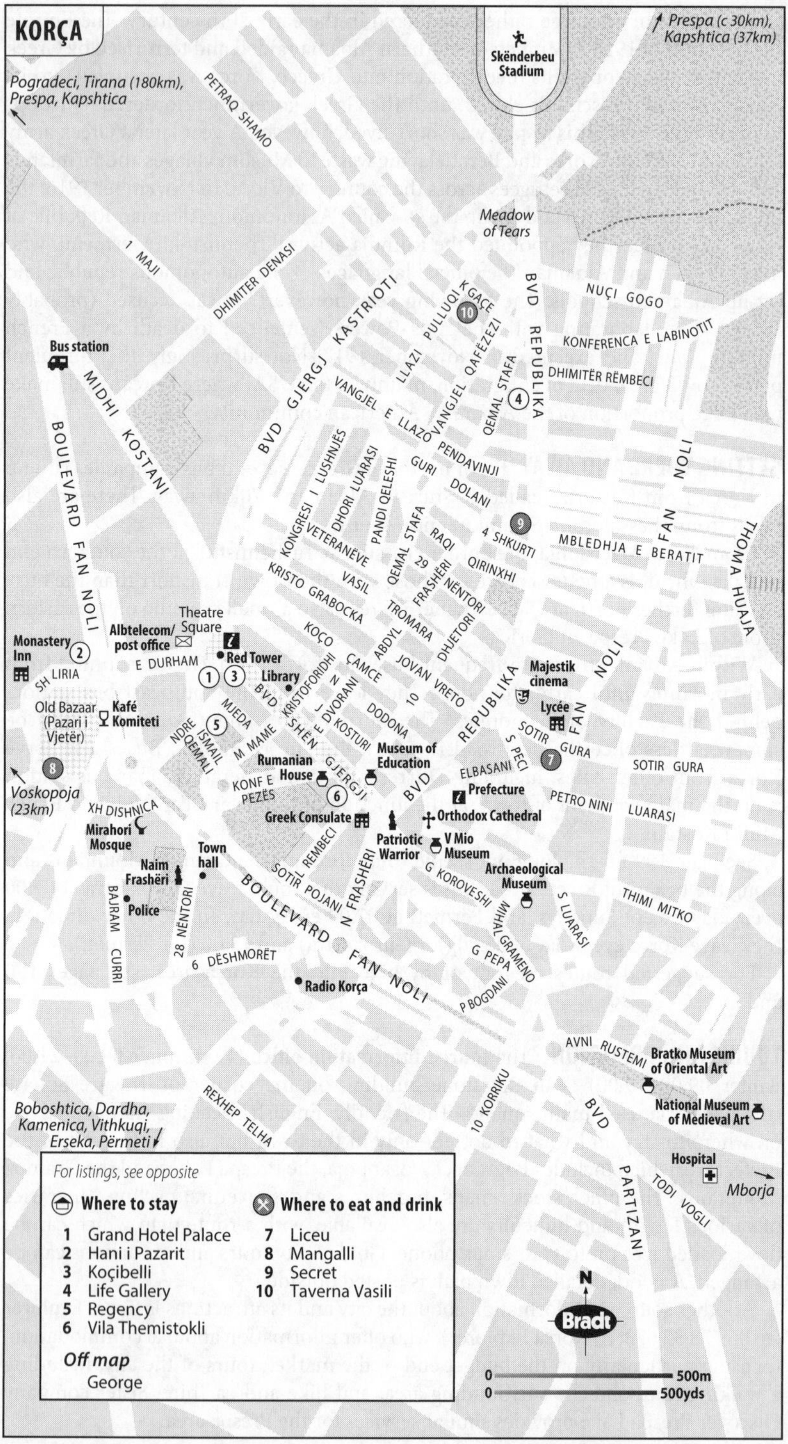
KORÇA
Pogradeci, Tirana (180km), Prespa, Kapshtica
Prespa (c 30km), Kapshtica (37km)
Skënderbeu Stadium
Meadow of Tears
Bus station
Monastery Inn
Albtelecom/post office
Theatre Square
Red Tower
Library
Old Bazaar (Pazari i Vjetër)
Kafé Komiteti
Voskopoja (23km)
Mirahori Mosque
Naim Frashëri
Town hall
Police
Rumanian House
Museum of Education
Greek Consulate
Patriotic Warrior
V Mio Museum
Prefecture
Orthodox Cathedral
Archaeological Museum
Majestik cinema
Lycée
Radio Korça
Bratko Museum of Oriental Art
National Museum of Medieval Art
Hospital
Mborja
Boboshtica, Dardha, Kamenica, Vithkuqi, Erseka, Përmeti
PETRAQ SHAMO
1 MAJI
DHIMITER DENASI
BVD GJERGJ KASTRIOTI
MIDHI KOSTANI
BOULEVARD FAN NOLI
K GAÇE
LLAZI PULLUOJ
VANGJEL QAFËZEZI
QEMAL STAFA
BVD REPUBLIKA
NUÇI GOGO
KONFERENCA E LABINOTIT
DHIMITËR RËMBECI
VANGJEL E LLAZO
PENDAVINJI
GURI
DOLANI
4 SHKURTI
MBLEDHJA E BERATIT
FAN NOLI
THOMA HUAJA
KONGRESI I LUSHNJËS
DHORI LUARASI
PANDI QELESHI
VETERANËVE
VASIL
KRISTO GRABOCKA
RAQI
29 NËNTORI
FRASHËRI
QIRINXHI
TROMARA
DHJETORI
ABDYL
KOÇO
ÇAMCE
JOVAN VRETO
10
E DURHAM
SH LIRIA
BVD SHËN GJERGJI
KRISTOFORIDHI
N DVORANI
J KOSTURI
DODONA
MJEDA
M MAME
NDRE ISMAIL QEMALI
KONF E PEZËS
SOTIR GURA
S PECI
ELBASANI
PETRO NINI
LUARASI
XH DISHNICA
REMBECI
N FRASHËRI
SOTIR POJANI
G KOROVESHI
MIHAL GRAMENO
S LUARASI
THIMI MITKO
G PEPA
P BOGDANI
BAJRAM CURRI
28 NËNTORI
6 DËSHMORËT
AVNI RUSTEMI
10 KORRIKU
REXHEP TELHA
BVD PARTIZANI
TODI VOGLI
For listings, see opposite
Where to stay
1 Grand Hotel Palace
2 Hani i Pazarit
3 Koçibelli
4 Life Gallery
5 Regency
6 Vila Themistokli
Off map
George
Where to eat and drink
7 Liceu
8 Mangalli
9 Secret
10 Taverna Vasili
N
Bradt
0 500m
0 500yds

In the piazza in front of the cathedral is an information board with maps of the town and the surrounding region. Information plaques around the city explain the main places of interest.

WHERE TO STAY *Map, opposite*

Korça has become a popular city-break destination for the well-heeled of Tirana. If visiting over a local holiday weekend, at New Year or in July or August, it is advisable to book accommodation in advance.

Hani i Pazarit (23 rooms) Pazari i Vjetër; 502 222; m 069 70 100 55; e info@hanipazarit.com; w hanipazarit.com. This historic Ottoman *han* in the restored & pedestrianised bazaar, once known as the Hani i Elbasanit, has been beautifully renovated & modernised. Advance booking essential. English spoken; Wi-Fi throughout; fine-dining restaurant (Serenata); café-bar. All rooms very well-appointed, with en-suite wet room &minibar. Deluxe rooms are in what were once the han's stone vaults, while standard rooms line the wooden gallery that surrounds the central courtyard & its well. **$$$$–$$$**

Koçibelli (52 rooms) Bd Sh Gjergji; 243 532, 230 925; m 069 98 17 654; e hotel.kocibelli@gmail.com; f Hotel Kocibelli POOL & SPA. Central location; parking for guests; English spoken at reception. Lifts; restaurant; bars; Wi-Fi; good-sized swimming pool; sauna; conference facilities. All rooms en suite, with AC, CH, minibar, TV. **$$$**

Life Gallery (15 rooms, 4 suites) Bd Republika 55; 246 800, 243 388; m 066 70 90 222; e info@lifegallery.al; f Life Gallery Hotel. Sophisticated contemporary-styled rooms in a traditional 1924 building. English spoken; professional service; lift. Restaurant, bars, courtyard with water feature, conference facilities. All rooms have large, well-equipped bathrooms with superb shower, fluffy dressing-gown & slippers, good toiletries & mirror; excellent lighting, thick curtains, AC, LCD TV, Wi-Fi, well-stocked minibar, phone, desk. **$$$**

Regency (16 rooms, 2 suites) Rr Ismail Qemali 7; 243 868/9, +1 516 520 5227 (US); m 068 20 30 070; e info@hotelregencyalbania.com; w hotelregencyalbania.com. English spoken; professional service. Restaurant, bar, lift, Wi-Fi; conference facilities. All rooms en suite with AC, CH, TV, phone. **$$$**

George (37 rooms) Rr e Mborjës; 243 794; m 069 20 83 112; e hotel.george@hotmail.com; f Hotel George. 1.2km from town centre, quiet & set in attractive grounds; free parking; terrace bar, restaurant; Wi-Fi. All rooms en suite with CH, TV & bedside lights; some have balcony with mountain views. **$$**

Grand Hotel Palace (84 rooms) Bd Ismail Qemali; 243 168, 244 339; e info@grandhotelpalacekorca.com; w grandhotelpalacekorca.com. Great location overlooking the main square. English spoken at reception; lift; good restaurant; good Wi-Fi throughout; free parking for clients; conference facilities. All rooms en suite (some with bathtub), with AC, TV, bedside light. **$$**

Vila Themistokli (2 rooms) Bd Sh Gjergji 7; m 069 94 45 029; e vilathemistokli@gmail.com. Restaurant-with-rooms in former home of Themistokli Gërmenji (page 179).English spoken; good restaurant with fireplace. Excellent cooked b/fast inc freshly squeezed orange juice. Rooms have period furniture, art on walls, thick curtains, CH, flatscreen TV, bedside light, ample electrical sockets, & modern, well-lit bathroom with good shower. **$$**

WHERE TO EAT *Map, opposite*

Korça specialities include *kërnaca*, small cylindrical meatballs, and *lakror*, a large, round *byrek* (filo pastry pie). There are several restaurants in the city that serve these traditional dishes; two of the best are listed here. Korça families, though, are more likely to go out of town for their family lunches at weekends. One popular destination is the village of **Boboshtica**, a few kilometres south of Korça – it is signposted at the turn-off from the main road to Erseka; one option there is **Taverna Antoneta** (m 068 22 64 963; $$$). Boboshtica is also well known for another local speciality: raki distilled from mulberries (*mani*). Another popular destination for family lunches is **Dardha**, in a lovely alpine setting (1,344m above sea level) and with a good hotel (Hotel Dardha; m 068 20 60 362; **$$$**).

Liceu Rr Sotir Gura; 211 208; m 069 23 98 529; 069 36 62 303. Opposite the former Lycée Française, in a traditional Korça house; open fire in winter, tables in garden in summer. Grilled meat, *kërnaca*, *lakror* & other specialities; friendly, informal atmosphere. $$$

✷ **Mangalli** Pazari i Vjetër. Delicious oven-baked specialities, pizza, homemade bread; friendly, efficient service, English spoken; 5 tables above kitchen (warm in winter!); cosy atmosphere. $$$

Secret Bd Republika 31. Grilled meat & fish, pizza, pasta, etc. English menu, English spoken. $$$

Taverna Vasili Rr Kostandina Gaçe 11; 246 610; m 069 21 48 583. Formal dining; interesting photographs of the town displayed in restaurant. Excellent local specialities, good service. $$$

WHAT TO SEE AND DO

National Museum of Medieval Art (Muzeu Kombëtar i Artit Mesjetar; Bd Fan Noli; m 067 51 38 333; 09.00–14.00 & 17.00–19.00 Tue–Sun; 700 lek) Located in a purpose-built gallery, the National Museum of Medieval Art has the largest collection of icons in Albania, with 7,500 objects spanning seven centuries. It also has a fine collection of other liturgical art, such as hammered silver Bible covers and gold-plated crucifixes. Around 400 works are on permanent display, and the new museum provides space for conservation and restoration laboratories. The exhibition is spread over two floors and there is a lift.

The ground floor displays some of the most famous works by Albania's best-known icon-painters: the 16th-century Berati artist Onufri (page 262), the 18th-century David Selenicasi and the 19th-century Katro (Çetiri) and Zografi families. But there was a long tradition of icon-painting before artists began to sign their work – Byzantine painters believed their work was to glorify God, not themselves – and the earliest works in the museum were painted by these anonymous artists. They include a 13th-century icon of St Nicholas, in lovely warm colours, from one of the churches in Vithkuqi, and 14th-century icons from St Mary's Church in Mborja (page 186): another St Nicholas, this one almost monochromatic, and the stunning Archangel Michael in his armour. Dozens of icons fill the full height of the wall of the gallery, with a viewing platform from which to study them.

In the 16th century, a school of artists began to emerge in Berati, a powerful diocese and an economic centre. The best known of the icon-painters there was called Onufri; almost a whole room on the first floor is devoted to his work. They include a set of Royal Doors (the central double doors in the iconostasis, through which only the priest may pass), with six scenes painted on carved, gilded wood. There are several dramatic, complex icons which tell stories such as the Nativity (with a very Albanian-looking shepherd playing a flute), the Raising of Lazarus, the Transfiguration and the Descent into Hell. Many other works by Onufri and other painters of the Berati School are displayed in the Onufri Museum in Berati Castle (page 262).

The Berati School influenced all other Albanian artists right into the 18th century, but new influences were beginning to creep in too. Kostandin Jeromonaku's *Christ Pantocrator*, dated to 1694, portrays Christ seated on a throne decorated with motifs from Islamic art. Contact with western European artistic schools, inspired by the Enlightenment, brought new developments in the 18th century. An early example of this is the complex and detailed *Akathistos Hymn* by the 18th-century artist Kostandin Shpataraku, with its portrayal of the Western image of the Coronation of St Mary.

Two icon-painting families dominated the later 18th and 19th centuries: the Zografi brothers and their sons, and the Katro family. Kostandin and Athanas Zografi worked all over the Balkans and many of their frescoes have survived in the churches of Voskopoja (page 187). Their work shows clear Venetian influence, with careful brushwork and a more realistic portrayal of the human figure than had been seen before. A particularly interesting painting here is Athanas Zografi's depiction of the Council of Nicaea (*The First Ecumenical Council*), dated to 1765. The Zografis' sons worked with the family of Joan Katro (also known as Johannes Çetiri), whose icons of John the Baptist and St George, surrounded by scenes from his life, are displayed in the room at the end of the first floor. Dominating this room is an entire iconostasis, with most of its original icons, salvaged from the Church of St Nicholas in Rehova (page 200) when the churches were closed during the atheism campaign.

The early 19th century marked the end of the old style of Albanian icon-painting. Early 20th-century work, such as the icons on display from Dardha, saw a complete break with the post-Byzantine tradition.

Back on the ground floor, there are civilised toilets and a museum shop, which stocks high-quality publications for sale about Albanian religious art, reproductions of some of the icons in the collection, and smaller souvenirs such as mugs. At least 2 hours should be allowed for this fascinating and beautifully laid-out museum.

Archaeological Museum (Rr Mihal Grameno; ⏱ 09.00–14.00 & 17.00–19.00 Tue–Fri, 09.00–noon & 17.00–19.00 Sat–Sun; 200 lek) The items displayed in Korça's Archaeological Museum come from sites all over the southeast region, including the neighbouring districts of Devolli, Kolonja and Pogradeci. The whole region is a prehistorian's paradise, with many very large tumuli (raised barrows) excavated – one of these, Kamenica, is open to the public and has an excellent site museum (page 188). There is a model of a tumulus in the Korça museum, showing how the graves were arranged concentrically.

The exhibition begins with a display of examples of the different types of tools used by Neolithic people (made of bone and horn as well as stone), their ceramics and their cult figurines. From very early on, they built lake-dwellings, using water to protect themselves from wild animals or human enemies. The site at Maliqi, excavated in the 1960s, was the largest in the Balkans (15ha) and was inhabited continuously from the Chalcolithic (3000–2200BC) to the Archaic period (8th–7th century BC). A scale model of the Maliqi settlement illustrates how these wooden houses were constructed on stilts.

Ceramics from the Bronze and Iron ages (from about 2100BC) show the developing influence of Greek city-states such as Corinth, which began to colonise the coast of what is now Albania in the 7th century BC. Other interesting items on display include bronze and silver bracelets and brooches, grave markers (*stelae*) and one of only three Archaic helmets ever found in Albania. In the courtyard the mosaic floor of a Roman bathhouse has been relaid. Here there are also Ottoman-period gravestones, one with a Star of David, and a sarcophagus from the 1st century AD.

The house in which the museum is located dates from the early 19th century, and is in two separate parts. The main building, where the museum's offices and workshops are, was the family residence, with the traditional covered balcony (*çardak*) on the first floor. The archaeological exhibition is in the *han i mysafirëve*, the guest quarters, where visitors to the family were received and accommodated. The Neolithic section is in what used to be a kind of drawing room, where weddings and other parties were held – the band used to play on the little stage behind the stairwell.

Museum of Education (Bd Shën Gjergji; m 069 28 34 720; ⌚ 09.00–14.00 & 17.00–20.00 daily; 200 lek) The very first school anywhere in which subjects were taught in the Albanian language opened in Korça on 7 March 1887. This was a triumph for the Rilindja campaigners who had focused on the language as the key to building an Albanian national consciousness. The Rilindja's polemicist, Sami Frashëri, wrote:

> The sign of nationhood is language; every nation supports itself on its language. Those who forget their language, and leave it behind, and speak another tongue, in time become people of that other nation whose language they speak, and they abandon their own nationality.

The Korça school went through ups and downs over the years, getting closed down intermittently whenever the country's Ottoman rulers noticed its existence, but the movement it began proved unstoppable. A girls' school was opened in Korça in 1891 – the first girls' school in Albania of any kind, never mind the first to teach in Albanian – and teachers travelled around the country giving lessons in impromptu classrooms or even the open air. The first Albanian-medium teacher-training college (Shkolla Normale) opened in Elbasani in December 1909.

The Korça school is now a Museum of Education, with photographs of the first pupils and teachers of both 'first schools' and an interesting collection of early textbooks. It is easily identifiable from the 'ABC' sculpture in its garden. The museum was renovated in 2019–20 and may now be open to the public rather more reliably than it has sometimes been in the past.

Bratko Museum of Oriental Art (Muzeu i Artit Oriental Bratko; Bd Fan Noli; ☎243056; m 069 21 56 561; f Bratko Museum of Oriental Art; ⌚ 08.00–13.00 Tue, Wed, Sun, 08.00–13.00 Thu, Fri, Sat & 17.00–19.00 daily; small charge) The most unexpected museum in Korça – perhaps in all of Albania – is the private collection of Oriental art donated to his home town by Dhimitër Boria, nicknamed Bratko, who made his fortune in the USA from film and photograph laboratories. The collection is housed in a purpose-built museum, an attractive modern building on Fan Noli Boulevard, just beyond the court buildings. It includes one whole room of lovely Oriental carpets and another of objects from the Far East, India and Africa, all collected by Mr Boria or given to him during his travels around the world. Chinese and Japanese prints and paintings hang on the walls. A third room contains a display of signed photographs of famous Americans and other memorabilia.

The Bratko museum is very much a collector's museum; those who find modern museums too thematic and interactive will love it. Many of the items on display are quite beautiful; the museum's Facebook page has photos of some of them. It takes about an hour to look carefully at everything.

Rumanian House (Bd Shën Gjergji; ⌚ 09.00–14.00 & 17.00–19.00 Tue–Sun; free) This beautiful building now houses a museum devoted to the life and work of the photographer Gjon Mili (1904–14), well worth a visit for anyone with an interest in photography. Mili was born in Korça, but his family emigrated to Romania when he was four years old. From Bucharest, aged only 19, he emigrated again, this time to the United States, where he had a long and successful career with *Life* magazine. His early training as an electrical engineer helped him to develop innovations in stroboscopic and stop-action images. Many of his photographs used these revolutionary techniques and these are displayed in the museum, along with items of his photographic equipment. The exhibition is labelled in English and Albanian, and a 50-minute film about Mili's work and life runs on a loop.

A walk around the town centre The best place to begin exploring Korça is the city's main square, where the tourist information office is (page 179). Dwarfing everything else in the square is the modern **Red Tower** (so-called, although it is not red). A lift (50 lek) takes you to a viewing platform from which there are good views of the city and the mountains that surround it.

From the square, the pedestrianised Boulevard Shën Gjergji leads first to the site of Korça's original **cathedral**, which was built in 1905 and demolished in 1971 to make way for a new city library. The library is still there; however, when the boulevard was being pedestrianised and landscaped in 2014, the outline of the façade of the destroyed cathedral was set into the pavement outside the library. This is an admirable way of commemorating one part of the city's history without destroying another.

Continuing up the boulevard, buildings of note include the house of Themistokli Gërmenji (page 179) now a restaurant-with-rooms, the Museum of Education (page 184), and two beautiful examples of Korça architecture, the Rumanian House (see opposite) and the former **Greek Consulate**, now restored after many years of neglect. Facing down the boulevard, above a water feature, is the statue of the kilted **Patriotic Warrior** (cast by Odhisë Paskali, the sculptor of imposing statues in several other Albanian towns and cities).

The road running across the end of Boulevard Shën Gjergji is Boulevard Republika, which bisects the historic centre of Korça. Directly behind the Patriotic Warrior is the **Orthodox Cathedral**, built in the 1990s to replace the destroyed original. An information panel on the cathedral piazza has maps of the city and the region. Behind it lies a warren of streets of 19th-century houses, built of local stone, slaked with lime and roofed with small, curved tiles. The Archaeological Museum (page 183) is a beautiful example of a traditional house of this period. Another that can be opened to the public (☎ 244 332 for access) is the former house and studio of the Albanian Impressionist painter, **Vangjush Mio** (1891–1957). Many of his paintings are exhibited here; others hang in the National Gallery of Arts in Tirana. Some of the other traditional houses in this neighbourhood have now been restored as hotels.

Along Boulevard Republika, and in the cobbled side streets on either side of it, the buildings are a little later and, with their columns and wrought-iron gates, have a more European feel than the fortress-like houses of Gjirokastra or Berati – a sign of the French influence on Korça in the early 20th century. The **Majestik cinema**, on the right a few minutes' walk down the boulevard, was built in 1926 and restored in the early 2000s. It screens subtitled Hollywood movies and, from time to time, Albanian-language films. Down the side street just before the cinema is the French **Lycée** (Liceu Francez), where Enver Hoxha went to school and was later a teacher.

At the end of Boulevard Republika is the **Meadow of Tears** (Lëndina e Lotëve), a small park that marks the spot where, in the 19th and early 20th centuries, families would gather to wave goodbye to their emigrant men or to wait for them to return – at the time, it was where the town ended and the open road began. At the little shrine here, people still light candles for their faraway loved ones. There are good views of the town and the surrounding countryside from the **Martyrs' Cemetery** (Varreza e Dëshmorëve; access by steps is signposted from Boulevard Republika).

Return to the main square along Boulevard Gjergj Kastrioti, or meander back through the side streets to see more traditional architecture. To the west of the square, across Boulevard Fan Noli, is the **Old Bazaar** (Pazari i Vjetër). Korça's geographical location made it a centre for Ottoman trade with Italy and (after independence) Greece. By the late 19th century, the bazaar had more than a thousand shops. Inns – known by the Turkish word *han* – provided accommodation for different groups of traders: the buildings of the Elbasan Inn (for Muslim traders) and the Monastir Inn (for Christians) have survived. The former has now reopened as a boutique hotel, Hani i Pazarit (page 181).

The Old Bazaar was restored in 2015 in a multi-million-euro project. The square that forms its heart is full of cafés, restaurants and souvenir shops. Kafe Komiteti, like its sister-bar in Tirana, is furnished and decorated entirely with original household items from communist days. It stocks a huge range of artisan raki and liqueurs – 140 different types! – and has three discrete areas, each with a different theme. The ground-floor bar has Illyria radio sets, wooden stools and marquetry on the walls. A second bar is laid out like a country house, with cushions and small tables. Upstairs has old suitcases serving as tables, a rare collection of crockery plates on the walls and, in a quirky touch, a toilet designed to look like a raki still. Events take place in the square throughout the year, including the Spring Fair, beginning in the evening of 28 February and Korça's Carnival, in early June.

A few minutes' walk south from the Old Bazaar is the **Mirahori Mosque**, built in 1484 and thus one of the oldest mosques in Albania, although it was rebuilt in the late 18th century. Crossing the little park behind it will lead you out on to Boulevard Fan Noli, an attractive tree-lined boulevard that runs along the southern edge of the old quarter. If you have any energy left, turn right on to this boulevard and head uphill, past the National Museum of Medieval Art, to the **Birra Korça brewery**, founded in 1928. Guided tours of the brewery can be arranged when staff time permits; ask the security officers at the gatehouse.

St Mary's Church, Mborja The village of Mborja, up beyond the brewery in the southern outskirts of Korça, was once the market town for the whole area, including Voskopoja and Vithkuqi – its name comes from the Greek *emporion*, meaning 'market'. Its little 14th-century church, known locally as Kisha e Ristozit ('Church of the Resurrection'), is a dignified and attractive building of local stone roofed with slates, like so many historic Orthodox churches in southern Albania. Unlike most of them, however, its marvellous frescoes have survived the ravages of time and of the atheism campaign.

The outer section of the church, the narthex, has a particularly enchanting series of frescoes, which begins with a disembodied hand holding a balance in which people are being weighed and found wanting. The unhappy-looking sinners are then whooshed down a chute into the jaws of a dragon, raped by devils, or attacked by serpents. The inner part of the church (the naos) is tiny, with a beautiful dome; this is the original, cross-in-square church. It can be rather dark and a torch will be useful. The frescoes on the walls here show the Resurrection and assorted saints, but they have survived less well and the colours are not as vivid. The original icons, such as the breathtakingly beautiful St Michael, are in the National Museum of Medieval Art.

To reach the church, bear left from the George Hotel, following the small sign for 'Ristozi 200m', and continue up the hill through the village until you see the church on the left. The villagers are used to foreign tourists and will help you to locate the key-holder. It takes about 40 minutes to walk from the town centre. Urban buses run up Boulevard Fan Noli as far as the George Hotel.

VOSKOPOJA

In the early 18th century, when the Industrial Revolution was just getting under way in Britain, Voskopoja was the largest city in the Balkans, bigger even than Athens or Sofia, with a population of about 35,000. It had the first printing press in the region, and an academy where artists were trained to create frescoes and icons for the churches in Voskopoja and elsewhere. Voskopoja itself had no fewer than 24 churches, two in each neighbourhood of the town, plus a basilica in each quarter. This past glory is remarkable. Towards the end of the 18th century, the city was plundered and burned several times, and it was completely supplanted in importance by the rapidly growing Korça. Today Voskopoja is a remote village, with a population of just a few hundred peasant farmers, mostly Vlach (page 20). Only seven churches have survived and some of these are in such disrepair that they are not open to the public.

One of the four basilicas was the Church of St Nicholas, or Shënkoll, which was built in 1726 at the height of Voskopoja's wealth and power. To find it, follow the sign up to the left as you enter the village from Korça, past the local council office. The church is usually kept locked, but the neighbours are used to foreigners trying to visit it and will go and look for the priest if you ask them. While you are waiting for him, you can admire the patterned brickwork of the exonarthex (portico) and the frescoes within it. These were painted by the brothers Kostandin and Athanas Zografi (page 182), whose work was in great demand throughout the Balkans. The bell tower was added later – originally there was another church, to the left as you look from the fence by the bell tower, which joined St Nicholas's to form a U-shape.

The interior frescoes, painted by David Selenicasi (from Vithkuqi), are in better repair than those outside, with beautiful rich colours. The iconostasis is original – the fire damage that can be seen on part of it was caused during World War II – but the icons that were once set in it are now in the National Museum of Medieval Art in Korça. The ornately carved throne was given to the faithful of Voskopoja from the episcopate of Durrësi in 1758, as can be seen from the inscription.

The basilica of St Thanas (Shën Athanas), built in 1724, is down the hill on the other side of the village; you will see its pale stone bell tower before you see the shingled roof of the church, tucked into the lee of a hillock. This technique of 'hiding' the church was more common in the 17th century, when it was a condition imposed by the Ottomans (this is also why the bell tower is often of more recent date than the body of the church). St Thanas's has a beautiful arcaded exonarthex with frescoes depicting scenes from the Apocalypse, painted by the Zografi brothers. Within, extending right around the walls of the naos, is an extended cycle of the martyrdoms of the saints, with lots of grisly detail.

St Mary of the Dormition (Shën Maria e Fjetjes) is one of the largest basilicas in Albania, holding up to a thousand worshippers; its size demonstrates how wealthy and powerful Voskopoja was at the time it was built (1699). The astonishing frescoes around its three-naved naos include a beautiful Pantocrator surrounded by saints, with the four evangelists at the four corners of the dome. There are more frescoes behind the iconostasis. There is a charge of 200 lek per person to visit these two churches.

High up in the forests above the village is the Monastery of St Prodhromi, the oldest building in Voskopoja. The church was built in 1632, with various wings of the monastery added later and now mostly ruined apart from a 20th-century section where the caretaker lives. The church is small, with a beautiful iconostasis; the entrance hall, or narthex, is reminiscent of a Bektashi *teqe* in its layout and furnishings. The monastery is signposted from the centre as 'St John the Forerunner'. The road up to it is in reasonable condition as far as the Akademia Hotel; unless you are in a 4x4 vehicle you should park there and walk the remaining few hundred metres.

Those with a particular interest in art and architecture will also want to visit the eight surviving churches in **Vithkuqi**, which once rivalled Voskopoja in the level of its development. Like Voskopoja, it was destroyed several times before it was finally supplanted by Korça.

GETTING THERE AND AWAY Both Voskopoja and Vithkuqi are about 25km from Korça; the drive takes about an hour each way. There are three or four buses a day between Korça and Voskopoja, so a day trip is unusually straightforward. The buses leave from the bus station in Korça. Vithkuqi, however, is still served by a rural bus, with an early morning departure from the village and a return journey at lunchtime. If you do not want to stay overnight in Vithkuqi, you could agree a fare with a taxi driver to take you up there, wait, and bring you back to Korça. For long-distance hiking routes from Vithkuqi and Voskopoja, see page 268.

WHERE TO STAY In addition to the Akademia, there are several small guesthouses in both villages – the tourist office in Korça will be able to advise on these (page 179). The Akademia is very popular in the summer and advance booking is advisable.

Akademia (29 rooms, 11 chalets) Voskopoja; **m** 069 20 23 047; **e** info@hotelakademia.al; **w** hotelakademia.al. The former 'Pioneers' Camp' above the village of Voskopoja, 2,286m above sea level, has been fully modernised & is set in lovely gardens. English spoken. Good restaurant with traditional dishes; free Wi-Fi; bar, recreation centre, conference room, laundry service; hiking guides, horseriding & skiing can be arranged. Choice of chalets & rooms, all en suite with CH & TV. **$$**

PREHISTORIC SITES

The **Tumulus of Kamenica** (**m** 069 29 08 193, 069 26 87 009; (09.00–14.00 & 17.00–20.00 daily; 200 lek) is one of the most significant prehistoric burial sites in the western Balkans. Three groups of graves have been excavated to date, with the remains of 420 humans in total. The earliest group dates from the late Bronze Age, the 12th or 11th century BC. The bodies were arranged within a circle 13m in diameter and covered by a tumulus (or barrow). During the Iron Age, the tumulus grew as more generations were buried in it. By the 7th century BC, the burial mound was 3m high. The people of Kamenica then began to bury their dead in new sites around the edges of the tumulus, sometimes surrounding the body with stones or even simple walls. These graves seem to have been family burials; DNA analysis of the skeletons in this group has shown that they were related to each other, whereas in the earlier tumulus there is no genetic connection. One of those buried was a woman who was at the start of the ninth month of her pregnancy – the skeleton of the foetus was still in her womb, meaning that she did not die in childbirth but of some illness. This is the only example of such a case found anywhere in Europe.

Unlike most prehistoric sites in Albania, Kamenica is very accessible to non-specialist visitors. The three excavated grave-groups can be viewed and part of the tumulus has been built back up, with earth, to its original height. The site museum has an excellent exhibition, in English and Albanian, which explains the history of the tumulus and the archaeological research that has been done there. A scale model of the site shows its various components. Replicas of some of the human remains and items found during excavation are also displayed. The site is easy to get to – it is only 8km from Korça, just off the main Korça–Erseka road. The turn-off is signposted for 'Tuma e Kamenicës', just before the village of Kamenica, and the minor road (less than 1km) is asphalted all the way to the site entrance. To get there by public transport, you can use any bus for Erseka, or beyond, and ask the driver to let you off in Kamenica.

The tumulus at **Rehova** (page 200) is the largest ever discovered in Albania, with nearly 300 graves. As well as the human remains, 700 pottery objects were excavated, including elegant double-handled jugs and rare double-cupped vessels. The findings have been published, in Albanian with English translation and full illustrations (*Tuma e Rehovës*, Skënder Aliu, Korça, 2012). The small museum in Rehova has an exhibition about this important site.

Another significant prehistoric site is the **Treni Cave** at the western tip of Lesser Lake Prespa (page 198). Excavations within the cave in the 1960s revealed that it was inhabited from the Neolithic period throughout the Bronze Age. On the cliff face opposite the cave, overhanging the lake, there is prehistoric rock art, a wonderful scene of hunters on horseback pursuing a deer. The entrance to the cave is secured by a gate; anyone who is keen to see inside should ask the staff of the Archaeological Museum in Korça if access can be arranged. There is no public transport to this site and some rough walking is involved. A reproduction of the rock art is displayed at the National Historical Museum in Tirana.

POGRADECI *Telephone code: 083*

Pogradeci lies on the southwestern shore of Lake Ohrid (called Ohër or Ohri in Albanian), a large (358km^2) deep lake bisected by the international border between Albania and North Macedonia. Ohrid is a tectonic lake, formed by movements in the earth's crust 2 million years ago, and it has unique species of fish. It is fed by underground streams from Lake Prespa, about 10km away. These streams bubble up in places to form attractive pools and backwaters – one of these is at Driloni, near the border with North Macedonia, and another can be visited at Sveti Naum, just across the border (indeed, Sveti Naum was part of Albania until King Zog gave it to Yugoslavia in 1925). Lake Ohrid's only outlet is the River Black Drini, which leaves it at Struga, on its northern tip, and flows through a corner of North Macedonia before re-entering Albania.

The deepest parts of Lake Ohrid are nearly 300m, and below about 100m its temperature is a constant 6°C. Closer to the shore, however, the water warms up in summer to a pleasant 20°C or so. There are beaches on both sides of the lake and in July and August Pogradeci becomes quite lively. There is a lakeside promenade and sandy beach on the eastern side of town. Further on, towards the border, is Driloni, where the underground streams from Lake Prespa bubble to the surface. There are several restaurants around the pools formed by these springs, where you can sit with your drink and watch the swans go by under the weeping willows.

Pogradeci is a perfect place to relax – strolling around in the sunshine, swimming in the lake and eating fish. The town centre has an attractive lakeside park, with a viewpoint projecting out into the lake. A fountain in the form of a book commemorates two of Pogradeci's literary sons: the poet Lasgush Poradeci and the author Mitrush Kuteli. Each 'page' of the open book has gilded lines from each of these writers. By a rose-garden in the park is an elegant bench with a quotation from Kuteli's *Ancient Albanian Tales*, extracts from which are scattered throughout this guidebook. Both Lasgush and Kuteli are also commemorated with statues in the town.

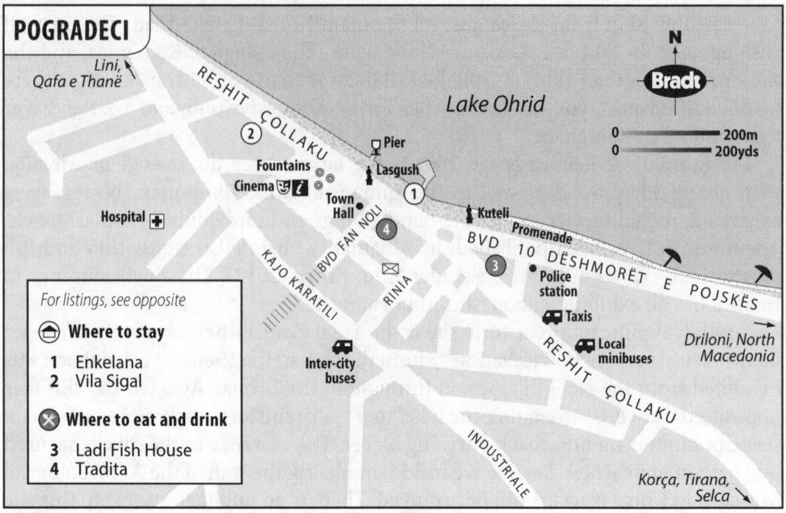

Lake Ohrid is an important site for wintering waterfowl, with over 12,000 coots (*Fulica atra*) recorded in the 2019 International Waterbird Census. Ducks (Anatidae), grebes (*Podiceps cristatus* and *P. nigricollis*), and cormorants (*Phalacrocorax carbo* and *Microcarbo pygmaeus*) are also well represented.

GETTING THERE AND AWAY Pogradeci is only 4km from the Tushëmishti border crossing at the southern end of Lake Ohrid; it is about an hour's drive from Qafa e Thanë, southwest of Struga at the northern end of the lake. The Tushëmishti crossing can be reached on foot from the resort and hotel at Sveti Naum on the North Macedonian side, by means of a path along the lakeshore. If you plan to stay overnight in Pogradeci, you could telephone your hotel in advance and ask the management to send a taxi to come and meet you at the border. There are hotels and guesthouses very close to the border on the Albanian side, in Tushëmishti and Driloni.

To or from **Tirana**, see page 177 for details of the alternative to the traditional route up the western shore of Lake Ohrid. Frequent **buses** run between Tirana and Pogradeci, from early morning until early afternoon (later in the summer). They leave from the Southeast bus station and take about 2 hours; the fare is 450 lek. From Korça, the journey takes about 45 minutes and the fare is 150 lek.

Pogradeci is well situated for several interesting cycle (or motorbike or 4x4) routes. From Maliqi, between Pogradeci and Korça, a minor road goes off to the west and follows the River Devolli until it flows into Lake Banja, just northwest of the small town of Gramshi (about 95km). From Gramshi, you could either continue north to Elbasani, or double back southwards, this time along the River Tomorrica. See page 268 for details of this ancient track around the base of the Tomorri massif to Çorovoda. Another interesting route, starting from either Pogradeci or Elbasani, is the road that links Librazhdi and Peshkopia (about 100km), which runs through the Shebenik-Jabllanica National Park (page 193).

TOURIST INFORMATION The tourist information office (🕘 09.00–17.00 Wed–Mon) is in the piazza with the fountains, where the town hall is. It stocks a range of information leaflets and sells books, postcards and souvenirs. A useful street plan is posted outside the town hall.

WHERE TO STAY *Map, opposite*

Enkelana (100 rooms) Rr Rreshit Çollaku; 222010; m 069 20 94 646, 069 40 52 956; e info@enkelanahotel.com; w enkelanahotel.com. On the lakeside, with direct access to the beach; pedalos for hire; outdoor pool (Jun–Sep) with separate section for children. 2 lifts; restaurant, pizzeria, pier-bar with live music in summer; Wi-Fi throughout; souvenir shop; conference room. All rooms en suite with AC, TV, fridge & balcony, some with stunning views over the lake. **$$**

Vila Sigal (7 rooms) Rr Rreshit Çollaku; 223462; m 069 60 30 415, 069 20 93 815. Attractive pre-war building, bar/restaurant on ground floor; Wi-Fi throughout. Traditionally furnished rooms above, all with good-sized en-suite bathroom, CH, TV, AC, fridge with mineral water, safe. Good cooked b/fast inc. **$$**

WHERE TO EAT *Map, opposite*

Lakes caused by plate tectonics are often home to species that do not occur elsewhere (Loch Ness is a tectonic lake, for example) and Lake Ohrid is no exception. Notably, it has two unique species of trout, both delicious. *Salmo letnica*, called *koran* in Albanian, has a delicate taste similar to that of sea trout; *Salmo ohridanus* (*belushkë*) is smaller and tastes more like its cousin the rainbow trout.

Ladi Fish House Rr Dëshmorët e Pojskës; Fish tavern Ladi. Fish, inc *koran*, *belushkë* & eel; grilled meat of various kinds; some traditional dishes; menu in English & Albanian. Terrace with view of lake. **$$$$**

Tradita Just off Bd Fan Noli. A good place to try traditional offal dishes; also local specialities inc *koran* & *belushkë*; good salads; good local house wine. Menu in English & Albanian; friendly staff. **$$$** (fish **$$$$**)

AROUND POGRADECI

Lini About 15 minutes' drive north of Pogradeci, just before the road starts to climb towards the border crossing at Qafa e Thanë, is the village of Lini, on a promontory that forms a sheltered cove in Lake Ohrid. Above the village, on a bluff with lovely views of the lake and the North Macedonian mountains, are the ruins of a 6th-century church. The walls have been partially restored so that the outline of the building can be seen – a single nave with an apse and two conches on either side, giving it a kind of five-leafed clover shape. Other buildings surround the church, including a deep cistern, brick-built and sealed with cement. The church and some other buildings are paved with fine mosaics. As usual in Albania, some are covered to protect them from the elements; at Lini, however, some are left uncovered. One shows two peacocks (or rather peahens) eating grapes that spring from a *kantharos*, a wine jug: wine is the symbol of the blood of Christ, while peacocks symbolise Paradise and everlasting life.

Getting there and away To get to the church from the village, you can either climb the steps that begin opposite the mosque, or you can drive or cycle up the rough track that begins near the (modern) church. Follow the signs for 'Basilika', if you can. It takes about 20 minutes to walk; a 4x4 would be needed for the last 50–100m.

Where to stay

Rosa B&B (4 rooms) m 069 45 04 577. Near the church; nicely furnished en-suite rooms, all slightly different; shared terrace overlooking lake; garden; Wi-Fi; b/fast incl. Boat trips can be arranged. **$$**

Illyrian royal tombs The magnificent rock-hewn tombs at Selca, in the mountains to the west of Lake Ohrid, offer a rare insight into the funeral rites of Illyrian kings.

Selca was first settled in the Bronze Age and became a royal residence in the 4th century BC. This was the territory of the Dassaretes, whose capital was the modern town of Ohrid, on the other side of the lake. They cut three tombs into the rock face for their kings, the earliest in the second half of the 4th century. It measures 6.5m by 4m, with an antechamber leading into the burial chamber, where a stone bed held the body of the deceased king. The other tombs are from the 3rd century. It is thought that one of these, a two-level tomb with Ionian 'columns' carved above the actual grave, may have held the remains of King Monun (page 89). This is because the bas-relief of a helmet that decorates the entrance is just like a real helmet, discovered in the Ohrid area during World War I and now in Berlin, which is inscribed with Monun's name. A little theatre beside the tombs, also carved out of the rock, may have been used during the funeral rites. The third rock-tomb, which also has carved 'columns' at its entrance, is set a little apart; there are steps up to it and it is linked to the other two by a path. A fourth tomb, below the others, was built with stone blocks, some of them with chiselled decoration. The royal palace must have been on the summit of the hill above the tombs; excavation in this area continues. It is worth climbing at least part of the way up for the views. The Dassaretes chose a beautiful spot to lay their kings to rest.

There is a lovely Ottoman bridge (Ura e Golikut) on the way from Uraka to Selca, one of many built on the sites of much older bridges that formed part of the trade route which, in the 2nd century BC, became the Romans' Via Egnatia (page 8).

Getting there and away By the summer of 2022, upgrading work is expected to have been completed on the road connecting Qukësi with Leshnica, a few kilometres south of Pogradeci. This will make it eminently feasible to include a visit to Selca on the way between Elbasani and Pogradeci or Korça. From the main road, a minor road leads to the village of Selca; the last few kilometres beyond the village, up to the entrance to the site, are paved and can be tackled in any reasonably sturdy car. A path leads across a field and up to the tombs; it can be slippery in wet weather. An alternative road leads from the Uraka junction to the Goliku bridge and on to Selca.

A rural bus connects Selca e Poshtme with Pogradeci, a journey of just over an hour. It leaves Pogradeci around lunchtime and does not return until the following morning. It would be a good option for those who would like to hike along one of the few surviving sections of the (pre)Roman Via Egnatia (for details of the Via Egnatia hiking guide, see page 295), or simply to walk the 15km or so down from Selca to the highway.

LIBRAZHDI

Librazhdi sits on the banks of the River Shkumbin, the traditional dividing line between central and southern Albania. Flanked by mountains on either side of the river, it is an attractive little town and a good base for several very interesting excursions, including to Shebenik-Jabllanica National Park.

Just over halfway between Elbasani and Librazhdi, within walking distance of the Hotel Ballkan, the **Miraka Bridge** (Ura e Mirakës) crosses the river. The structure is Ottoman, but there has been a bridge here since at least Roman times – this is the route of the Via Egnatia, which connected the Adriatic coast with Constantinople.

GETTING THERE AND AWAY Librazhdi is on the SH3 highway between Elbasani and Pogradeci; it is slightly over 30 minutes' drive to Elbasani and about an hour to Pogradeci. It would be a convenient stopping-off point for those travelling with their own transport between Tirana and the Qafa e Thanë border crossing with

North Macedonia. For the old road between Librazhdi and Peshkopia, see page 195; it is suitable only for rugged 4x4 vehicles.

Buses from Tirana, Korça or anywhere else can drop passengers on the highway at either end of Librazhdi. The quickest way into the town centre is from the junction at the eastern end of town, up the partly pedestrianised main street. The bus station in Librazhdi is at the western end of the town, behind a petrol station just to the left as you enter the town from the highway.

WHERE TO STAY

Hotel Ballkan (18 rooms) Miraka (on SH3); m 069 44 39 601; e info@resortballkan.com. Country setting in the hills between Labinoti & Librazhdi, a modern building set in lovely gardens on the River Shkumbini; English spoken at reception. Large outdoor swimming pool, restaurant, terrace bar, contemporary cocktail bar; Wi-Fi throughout. All rooms en suite with AC, TV, minibar, kettle; some have balcony. **$$**

Hotel (so-called on roadside sign) (6 rooms) Librazhdi; m 067 54 77 225. Across the highway from bus station, above the Mobileri Italiane furniture shop. Slightly unpromising exterior belies excellent conditions within; all rooms triple-glazed, with nicely fitted-out en-suite bathroom, AC, TV, minibar, furnished balcony, wardrobe with good hangers, ample power sockets. Wi-Fi throughout; solar-heated water; friendly management; b/fast available in nearby cafés. **$**

WHERE TO EAT

Rahman Biçaku Between the highway & the river. Probably the longest-established restaurant in Librazhdi. Fresh river fish, traditional Albanian dishes; terrace overlooking the river; a pleasant spot to stop just for a drink or coffee. **$$**

Te Fati On a terrace above the pedestrianised street in town centre, opposite Cultural Centre. A good spot for people-watching. Grilled meat, chicken, *qofta* etc; draught beer; friendly staff. **$**

SHEBENIK-JABLLANICA NATIONAL PARK

Albania's most recent UNESCO designation is in the national park known as Shebenik-Jabllanica. In 2017, UNESCO added part of the park to its transnational listing of Ancient and Primeval Beech Forests, a listing which began in the Carpathians and now includes 20 countries in Europe. The beech forests in Shebenik-Jabllanica are the southernmost limit of the UNESCO listing. Some of the beeches are over 40m high and 300 years old.

The park's double-barrelled name combines the protected areas on both sides of the border, Shebeniku in Albania and Jabllanica in North Macedonia. It is not, however, a cross-border park, although negotiations are under way at the time of writing. Its highest point is Mount Shebenik, over 2,200m above sea level. It is one of the largest national parks in Albania. There is magnificent scenery at every turn, fascinating caves and meltwater lakes to visit and, at night, dark skies filled with stars. There are bears, wolves, wildcats, chamois and the very rare Balkan lynx. Over 1,500 species of flora have been identified within the park, including an endemic species of *Lilium albanicum* (information about these and other flora and fauna is on page 170).

In the communist period, Shebeniku was a closed military area because of its proximity to the border with Yugoslavia. Apart from the villagers, who needed special permits, almost nobody was allowed to travel in or out of the area. Nowadays, of course, visitors are free to explore most of the national park, including many of its impressive and beautiful beechwoods. However, the UNESCO-designated beech forest, in the eastern part of the park closest to the border, is highly restricted.

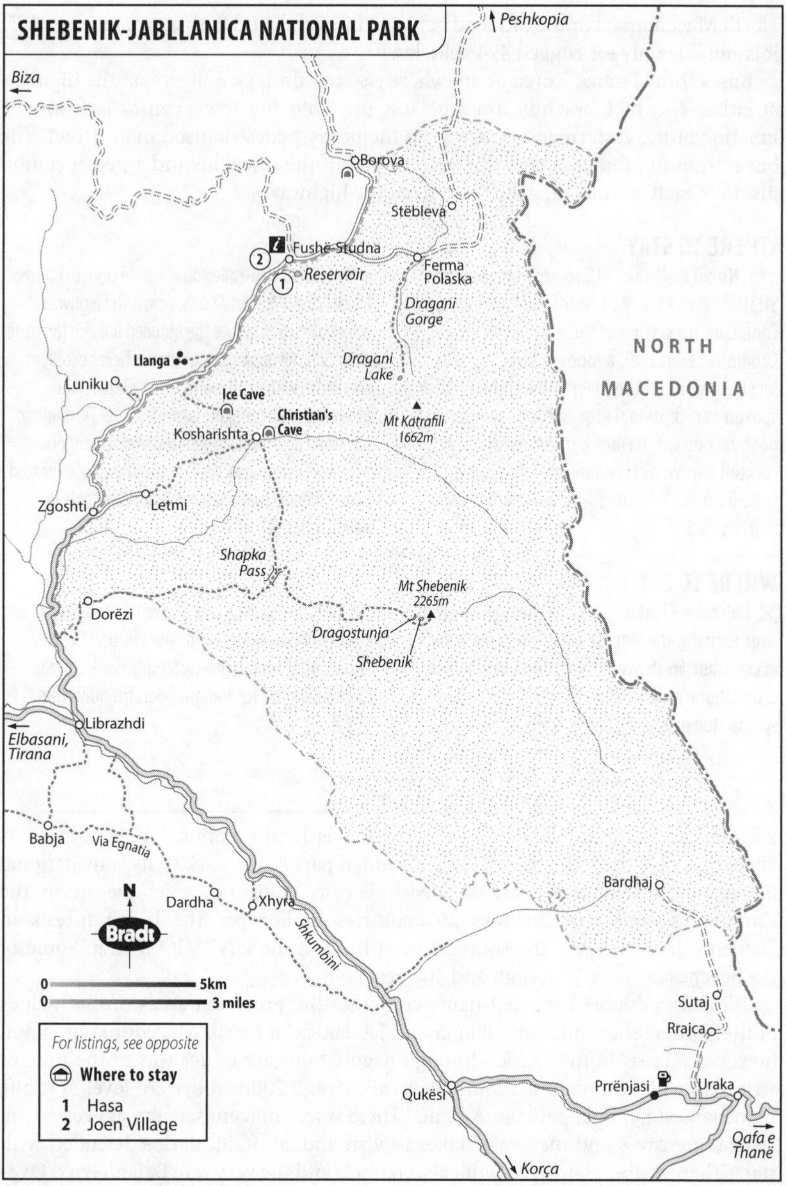

GETTING THERE AND AWAY Shebeniku is culturally and geographically part of northern Albania; it was administratively part of the Dibra region until local government reorganisation in the 1990s. It is covered in this chapter of the guidebook because the feasible routes into the park both start in the southeast. From Prrënjasi, a transitable road (poorly signposted for Rrajca, just east of Prrënjasi) climbs north through the villages of Rrajca and Sutaj to Bardhaj. Various hikes start from here, including a path to the meltwater Rrajca Lakes and onward to the summit of Mount Shebenik (page 193).

The usual access point, however, is from Librazhdi. This road was built by Italians during the reign of King Zog, to connect Librazhdi with Dibra. It runs along the western edge of the national park; at the time of writing, it is asphalted only as far as Zgoshti, but it can be tackled in any reasonably robust car as far as the park's administrative centre, Fushë-Studna, and beyond to Borova. It is 24km from Librazhdi to Fushë-Studna. The most challenging section, known as 'Luniku's Ladder' after the name of the nearest hamlet, comes soon after the end of the asphalt; very twisty with blind bends and, at some points, so narrow that only one vehicle can pass at a time. A rural bus connects Fushë-Studna with Librazhdi.

After Borova, this road should not be attempted at the time of writing in anything other than the most rugged of 4x4s. The Albanian government has promised that the whole road will be asphalted as far as Dibra; this may happen within the lifetime of this guidebook. Adventurous explorers in a rugged 4x4 might also consider the *very* rough road from Fushë-Studna across the Martanesh Mountains to Mount Dajti and on to Tirana. This 'road' passes through Biza, one of the remote areas where SOE agents were parachuted into Albania during World War II (more about them on page 13).

TOURIST INFORMATION The visitor centre, in the centre of Fushë-Studna, has an excellent exhibition about the flora, fauna, geology and culture of Shebenik-Jabllanica. All the information panels are in English as well as Albanian. Good-quality mountain bikes can be hired here (200 lek/hr) and the staff can also arrange local guides. The centre is also an educational resource for schools. The apartment above the exhibition space is used by student groups but can also be rented by casual visitors.

The main paths around the national park have been mapped with GPS; digital hiking maps of seven routes have been uploaded to the Wikiloc platform and can be accessed via w linktr.ee/explorelibrazhd. There are information panels at the start of each of these hikes, each with a QR code that opens the relevant map. Small signposts in English and Albanian indicate the start of each trail and there are more detailed information signs at some of the attractions.

WHERE TO STAY AND EAT Many families in the villages within the national park are set up to provide accommodation and meals to paying guests; the visitor centre in Fushë-Studna can provide contact details. As for food, Shebeniku is renowned in Albania for the excellence of its potatoes and beans (*fasule*).

Joen Village [map, opposite] (3 villas, 12 rooms) Fushë-Studna; m 067 68 80 561; e joenvillage@gmail.com; f JOEN Village; joenvillage. Each villa can be let as a whole; Villas 2 & 3 can also be taken as individual rooms. All bedrooms are en suite & have TV, CH, AC; b/fast inc. Restaurant with traditional menu & open wood-fire, bar, landscaped garden with children's play area; Wi-Fi throughout. Quad bikes & bicycles available for hire; astronomy evenings with professional-standard telescopes can be arranged. **$$$–$$$$**

Hasa Hotel [map, opposite] (9 rooms) Fushë-Studna; m 067 67 58 249; e altinhasa2@gmail.com; Restaurant_Hotel_Hasa. All bedrooms are en suite & have CH; some have covered balcony; 2 have their own fireplace (oxhak); Wi-Fi throughout. Large restaurant with open wood-fire; excellent traditional cuisine, home-grown vegetables, homemade bread; meals can be served on request on traditional circular table (sofër) in garden. Superb b/fast inc. **$**

Visitor Centre apartment (2 rooms) Fushë-Studna; m 069 62 23 130; e fatbrazhda@yahoo.com or enquire at the centre. Each room has 4 bunk beds; shared bathroom with washing machine; shared kitchen with large fridge, wood-burning stove, 2 bed-settees. Conference room; free Wi-Fi. **$**

Trofta e Borovës Borova. Trout straight from the river to your plate, served with local potatoes & salad. You can look round the trout farm while your meal is being prepared. $$$

WHAT TO SEE AND DO The main village in the park, and its administrative centre, is **Fushë-Studna** (some maps refer to it as Fushë-Studa, while others omit it altogether). It is a convenient base from which to explore the rest of the park. The exhibition in the visitor centre is an excellent place to start. As well as the hotels, the village also has a health centre and a couple of small bars: one next to the visitor centre and the other opposite the mosque.

For a first taste of the beech trees for which Shebeniku is famous, a 10-minute walk from the village brings you to its **reservoir**. There are information panels and picnic benches near the lake, and paths through the woods that surround it. A Park Festival is held in the third weekend of May every year, with exhibition stalls, canoeing on the lake and many other activities.

The most accessible of Shebeniku's many caves is the **Ice Cave** (Shpella e Akullit). It is signposted from the main road and there is space to park. It is a 4km hike to the cave, through cool woods and across beech-fringed meadows. Water bottles can be refilled at a spring shortly before the entrance to the cave. The Ice Cave is very deep – speleologists have explored it to a depth of 80m – and nobody knows how far into the karst it extends. A wide tunnel leads from the entrance to a viewing point, from where many stalactites can be seen; a torch will be useful.

Also easy to visit, apart from a challenging rock face climb up to the entrance, is a cave discovered only in 2019, during the construction of the hydro-electric power station at **Borova**. This cave is well worth the climb for its spectacular curtains of stalactites and multi-coloured columns of stalagmites. The road to Borova from Fushë-Studna does not require a 4x4; if you time your visit right, you could enjoy a lunch of fresh fish from the trout farm there (see above).

Finally, the Christian's Cave at **Kosharishta** is so-called because it was a hermit's cave. High on a cliff beyond the village, it is rather small as hermit's caves go, but two circular paintings have survived on its ceiling. The smaller of the two portrays the Virgin Mary, with what are thought to be disciples in the larger one. Naturally there are also wonderful views from the cave. A good 4x4 vehicle, or a mountain bike, is needed to get to the village – take the Letmi (Letëm) turn-off at Zgoshti – where you can park and continue on foot on the newly improved path. On foot, it is a 10km hike from the same starting point as for the Ice Cave.

This footpath is part of the old road that connected Kosharishta and **Llanga**, the oldest villages in the national park area. There are stone houses (*kulla*) in both villages, although very few people live permanently in them nowadays. The stone buildings of Llanga can be seen from the main road, or you can walk from there to explore the village. Some of its *kulla* are said to be 300 years old. However, they were badly damaged in a major earthquake in 1967; only two are still in good condition. In happier times, Llanga had its own mosque – the building with the tiled roof-tower which can be seen from the road – and its own school. Just at the turn-off for the village from the main road, two springs of delicious mountain water have been piped into a stone surround: Çezmet e Llangës.

The **hiking** opportunities in the national park are almost endless. Apart from the beech forests, there are alpine meadows, jagged limestone crags, meltwater lakes (14 of them above 2,000m) and mountains towering above the treeline. From Kosharishta, a waymarked path continues over the Shapka Pass to two of these meltwater lakes: **Lake Dragostunja** and, as if hanging above it, **Lake Shebenik**. A third lake lies a little beyond. The path continues to the peak of Mount Shebenik;

BUNKER STRATEGY

One of the few things people think they know about Albania is that it is covered in bunkers. As so often in this fast-changing country, what everyone knows is no longer the case.

In 1971, the Central Committee of the Albanian Party of Labour (as the ruling Communist Party was called) resolved to create a network of bunkers across the country. The building programme lasted from 1975 to 1983 and saw thousands of small single-person pillboxes sunk into the fields and hillsides, especially in strategic border areas. The exact number is not known; a figure that is often quoted is 173,000.

It is commonplace to sneer at the bunkers, but the military strategy which inspired them is solid. During World War II, the Albanian resistance fighters were generally best at mountain-based guerrilla warfare. They spent most of their time in the hills and came down to the plain only to carry out attacks. This modus operandi proved highly successful and it therefore made considerable sense to try to adapt it to the post-war situation in which Albania found itself.

The idea behind the bunkers was that they enabled this kind of mountain warfare to be conducted down on the plain. The small bunkers were laid out in lines radiating down from a large command bunker and had a line of sight to it. The large bunkers were permanently manned; the small ones were not. In the event of an invasion, every able-bodied male was expected to collect a gun and take up position in his assigned pillbox until ordered to leave it.

The commanders in the large bunkers had radio contact with their superiors, and from their positions high up on the hill they could control the road or valley along which the invaders would be coming. The men further down the hill could receive visual orders by looking through the slit on one side of their pillbox, and shoot the invaders through the other.

Those who consider it paranoid to think that your country is about to be invaded should remember that between 1947 and 1953 Britain and the USA did in fact attempt to infiltrate anti-communist agents into Albania. These attempts failed dismally; all the agents were captured almost as soon as they landed, and were either killed on the spot or executed after being tried as spies.

Until little more than a decade ago, arrays of these small pillboxes, with their command bunkers above them, were very visible all over Albania. They were set 1–1.5m into the ground, a thick concrete casing over a steel framework, and were difficult for individual farmers to remove; they sometimes used them as outhouses or to store animal feed. Then, however, enterprising Albanians realised that the high-quality steel within them can be sold very profitably as scrap metal; explosives are used to break the concrete casing so that the metal can be extracted. There are now very few of the communist-era pillboxes left, although some of the larger ones are being preserved as tourist attractions. The Checkpoint installation in central Tirana (page 83) includes a cross-sectioned pillbox that shows how they were constructed.

At the time of writing, it is still possible to see arrays of bunkers, showing the strategy that lay behind their positioning, on the hillside at the Bay of Palermo, on the Riviera, and around the junction for the border crossing at Qafa e Thanë, at the northern end of Lake Ohrid, among other places. Earlier bunkers can also be spotted, for example the long World War II bunkers at the turn-off to Apollonia (page 249).

it takes about 5 hours from the pass to the summit (thanks to Alma Lahe for her description of this route). Another option starts from part-way along the road that connects Fushë-Studna with the village of Stëbleva. The path climbs through the Dragani Gorge to a limestone outcrop called Dragani Crag and, below it, the lake of the same name, covered in water lilies. A little further on is a grassy plateau from where there are superb views of the mountains rolling upwards to the border.

Between May and October, **Dragani** fills with sheep and activity. Each village has its own alpine pasture (called *stan* in Albanian) and summer dairy. The shepherds/dairymen are often happy to welcome visitors and show them how the various kinds of cheese are produced, as well as offering a taste of them. Ferma Polaska, accessible in a normal car and close to the start of the Dragani path, is a modern dairy producing high-quality cheese from sheep and goat milk.

Finally, Shebeniku's dark skies are perfect for **stargazing** and, probably uniquely in Albania, Fushë-Studna also has its own astrophysicist, with professional-standard telescopes. The visitor centre and the hotels in Fushë-Studna can arrange astronomy evenings.

THE PRESPA LAKES

The water that bubbles up so prettily at Driloni and Sveti Naum has travelled through about 10km of subterranean channels from another tectonic lake. Greater Lake Prespa is separated from Lake Ohrid by Mali i Thatë, which means 'the dry mountain', so-called because the limestone that forms it sucks Lake Prespa's water underground, leaving no visible rivers (this geological formation is called karst). The larger of the two Prespa Lakes, usually called simply Lake Prespa, has a surface area of 273km^2 and straddles the borders between Albania, Greece and North Macedonia. The smaller of the two, Lesser Lake Prespa, is only 45km^2, all but 6km^2 of which are in Greece. The two lakes were once connected, but now the smaller lake is 3m higher; it freezes over in winter.

In 2000, the whole Prespa basin was designated as a Transboundary Park, the first cross-border protected area in the Balkans. The lakes are rich in wildlife and in particular are home to large colonies of Dalmatian pelicans (*Pelecanus crispus*) and white pelicans (*P. onocrotalus*). There are also many cormorants (*Phalacrocorax carbo* and *Microcarbo pygmaeus*), six species of duck, including common pochard (*Aythya farina*), tufted duck (*A. fuligula*) and Eurasian teal (*Anas crecca*), black-necked grebes (*Podiceps nigricollis*) and thousands of coots (*Fulica atra*).

Although it is quite close to Korça, the Albanian part of Greater Lake Prespa used to be rather remote and difficult to reach, which means that the economy of the villages around the lakeshore was based almost entirely on small-scale farming and fishing. Since the road over the mountains was upgraded, however, the improved access has brought the villagers some welcome income from tourism. Prespa is an ideal base for a few days of gentle hiking, birdwatching or just relaxing in the peaceful atmosphere; it is less than an hour's drive from Korça and so a day trip is perfectly feasible for those with their own transport although not, at the time of writing, by public transport.

The main attraction for non-ornithologists is the island of **Maligrad** (meaning 'little town' in Macedonian, the native language of the villagers of the Prespa area). This small, uninhabited island rises steeply from the turquoise water of the lake. In the 14th century, people built a church here within a natural rock shelter, and beautified it with frescoes outside and in. The church was too remote to attract the attention of the atheism campaigners and so both it and its frescoes have survived, although the latter have been badly damaged by modern graffiti. As well as visiting the church, it is fairly straightforward to climb up to the summit of the island, a tranquil spot covered with wild flowers and the remains of another, ruined, church. From the summit, there are good views of the snowy mountains on the western shore and of Lake Prespa's second island, **Golemgrad** ('big town'), which lies in North Macedonian waters. A low spit of land at Maligrad's northwest has tiny beaches where you can swim when the weather is warm enough: Lake Prespa is 850m above sea level and the water is noticeably colder than Lake Ohrid, 150m lower. The boat trip out to the island is a good opportunity to see pelicans and pygmy cormorants up close. Boats can be hired in Pustec or, if you are staying in Zaroshka, your hotel will be able to arrange a boat for you; the price depends on the number of people on the trip and its duration.

The point at which Lake Prespa drains into the karst is up at the northernmost corner of Albania's part of the lake, near the village of Gorica. The cliffs around it are riddled with caves and sinkholes; broken reeds and other lake debris cluster around the outflow, providing sustenance to fish of all sizes. On the other side of the lake, the road ends just beyond Zaroshka, but there is a footpath beyond the (modern) church along the lakeshore and past a tiny chapel built into the rock face. Another, larger, cave church lies just across the border in Greece.

GETTING THERE AND AWAY The hotels and restaurants are all in the village of Zaroshka (Zrnovsko, in Macedonian), about 45 minutes' drive from Korça; the road is asphalted all the way. The Prespa villages are served by a daily **bus** to and from Korça; it leaves Pustec (formerly known as Liqenas) at 07.00 and returns from Korça at midday, continuing to the border village of Gorica. Otherwise, any bus from Korça to Bilishti will drop you at the petrol station (*karburant*) just before the village of Zëmblaku. Informal **taxis** wait at the petrol station for passengers to Pustec, Zaroshka or any of the other villages around the lake; the going rate is 1,000 lek. It is a very steep 17km from the petrol station to Pustec.

Zaroshka is about 30 minutes' drive from the North Macedonian border near Gorica; the border crossing closes at night. Pustec has a health centre but there are no ATMs; bring sufficient cash from Korça or Bilishti.

TOURIST INFORMATION There is a tourist information kiosk in Gorica. The tourist information office in Korça can advise on visits to the Prespa area. Discover Prespa Lake offers information about accommodation and tours of the area (m 069 78 32 673; f Discover Prespa Lake).

WHERE TO STAY AND EAT

Aleksander (10 rooms) Zaroshka; m 068 25 49 759; e hotel-restorant_aleksander@hotmail.com; f Hotel Restorant "Aleksander". On left just before the entrance to the village, in a stunning location overlooking the lake. The owners are exceptionally kind & helpful; boat trips & other excursions can be arranged. Excellent restaurant ($$$) offering fresh fish, grilled meat, salads & North Macedonian wine; tables outside in the garden, shaded under gazebos, with views of the lake & Maligrad Island. All rooms en suite with lake-view balcony. $

THE GRAMOZ MOUNTAINS

The Gramoz range rises like a wall between Albania and Greece, with some of its summits over 2,500m high. These are serious mountains, with harsh weather conditions and a tough life for the people who live among them. Luckily for the visitor, a road runs along the Albanian side of the range, well surfaced for most of the way, which allows the spectacular scenery to be enjoyed in relative comfort. It is a good route for cyclists, although the narrow road means that you have to keep your wits about you. The gradients are much easier southbound, from Korça to Përmeti. It is about 140km. There is public transport along the whole route: a bus leaves Korça for Gjirokastra at 06.00 (not Sundays) and for Përmeti at 13.00 (daily).

About 40km south of Korça is **Erseka**. At 900m above sea level, this is the highest town in Albania and the mountains that surround it give it a very alpine feel. It has a small Ethnographic Museum in the main square. Fans of Socialist Realist art will like the monument outside the museum, with its kilted warriors and the communist star still intact on the Albanian flag. The Inxhujo Hotel (✆ 081 222 474; **$**), in the square where the buses stop, has rooms, a restaurant and reasonable public toilets for customers. Buses leave for Erseka from the bus station in Korça until around midday. You could also take one of the buses that continue through the Gramoz Mountains and tell the driver you want to get off in Erseka. The journey takes about an hour and the fare is 200 lek.

In the mountains just above Erseka, the village of **Rehova** has a small museum, with information about the highly significant Rehova tumulus (page 189), and the church from which the iconostasis and several of the icons in the National Museum of Medieval Art were taken. Rehova is an attractive village in beautiful surroundings, but it is not an easy place to find one's way around. Anyone planning a special visit to see the museum should ask the staff at the Archaeological Museum in Korça (page 183) to phone ahead and arrange for their Rehova colleague to meet you at the entrance to the village (the author wishes she had followed this advice). There are several guesthouses in Rehova – the tourist information office in Korça (page 179) can help with reservations, or there is an information panel at the entrance to the village – and it would make a good base for a few days' hiking. From Erseka, it takes about 20 minutes to reach Rehova on foot, a very pleasant walk through lovely countryside. There are usually taxis waiting where the buses stop in Erseka.

Beyond Erseka the road begins to climb, up startling hairpin bends, and the scenery becomes more and more dramatic. A statue by the roadside, of a partisan with a child, commemorates the **Massacre of Borova**: German reprisals for a partisan attack in 1943, after which the Wehrmacht returned to Borova and slaughtered over a hundred of the villagers, many of them burned alive inside the church. A second partisan statue surveys the valley, just beyond the village of Barmashi. The road rises again, through dense conifer and beech forests, which open out from time to time to reveal the towering mountains on either side. After another descent through more open country, another climb takes the road back over 1,000m, About 45km from Erseka, a turn-off leads to the little town of Leskoviku.

The next stretch of the main road is narrow and in poor condition. It is very slow going and, although the distance is further, it may take less time to drive down from Leskoviku to the border crossing into Greece (signposted for Tre Urat) and then back up to Çarçova. This detour should take no more than 45 minutes; the second section in particular is very pretty, following the River Vjosa as it enters Albania from its source in northern Greece. The Vjosa, known in Greek as the Aoos, is one of the loveliest rivers in Albania, with crystalline, greenish-blue waters. Hill farmers lead their laden donkeys home across precarious wooden bridges and large birds of prey can be seen quite close at hand.

The border crossing closes overnight, at 19.00 Albanian time (20.00 Greek time). If you get to Leskoviku too late to cross the border, simple accommodation (**$**) is available above the two restaurants ($$) on the street that becomes the road to the border: Jorgo (m 068 37 91 134) and Leskoviku (m 069 27 30 716). There is a shop and restaurant at the Çarçova junction. A bus to Athens, via Tre Urat, passes Çarçova around 07.00 on Mondays and Fridays (it leaves Përmeti at 06.30; m 069 81 87 559, 068 23 86 048).

WHERE TO STAY AND EAT *Map, page 178*

Farma Sotira (5 chalets, 5 cabins) m 069 23 42 529; e info@farmasotira.com; w farmasotira.com; see ad, 2nd colour section. 27km from Erseka, 15km (30mins' drive) from Leskoviku, set in meadows fringed with fir & hazel woods; 1,100m above sea level. A working farm, with sheep, cattle, chickens & horses; also trout nursery; water from the farm's own spring. Guided hiking & riding excursions can be arranged; outdoor pool with separate shallow section for children; laundry facilities; English spoken; fast Wi-Fi throughout site. Excellent restaurant with open fireplace: home-reared lamb cooked in *saç* (Dutch oven), trout, *lakror* & other traditional dishes, all genuinely organic. B/fast inc with home-baked bread, honey & eggs from the farm. Campsite (**$**) with 3 charging points for mobile homes, space for tents, 5 wooden sgl-room cabins, with beds but no en-suite facilities (**$**); all sharing good, modern toilets & showers. Each chalet sleeps up to 4 people in 2 rooms with nice en-suite bathrooms; heating & power points. **$$**

Gërmenji Jorgo (6 rooms) m 069 25 49 488; f Vila "Germenji Jorgo". On the main road, 21km from Erseka, just beyond signposted turn-off for village of Gërmenji. Surrounded by glorious scenery; large terrace bar in garden; restaurant with traditional dishes; open fires in winter; Wi-Fi; laundry service. Camping possible; horseriding excursions can be arranged. All rooms have simple en-suite bathroom & balcony. **$**

PËRMETI *Telephone code: 0813*

Përmeti's setting is spectacular. Behind the town rises the Dhëmbel mountain range, 2,050m high at its peak, and all around are other imposing mountains. The road access to the town is over the River Vjosa, which rushes through the city in a dramatic gorge. The journey to it from either direction runs along the valley of this beautiful river.

Përmeti was settled in prehistoric times, but the earliest traces of habitation are the remains of a medieval castle on the City Rock, which overlooks the gorge through which the Vjosa flows out of the town. In the course of World War II, Përmeti was burned down no fewer than four times, by Italians and Germans; the 6th Partisan Brigade, led by Enver Hoxha and Mehmet Shehu (see box, page 14), was mustered here in 1943, and a large **memorial** to its fallen stands at the entrance to the town.

In 1944, the Congress of Përmeti elected the provisional government that took power following liberation later that year. It consolidated the exclusion of the non-communist forces from the country's future, annulled various decisions and agreements made by the pre-war monarchist government, and specifically banned King Zog from returning to Albania. The congress is commemorated with a fine Socialist Realist statue of a partisan, cast by the Përmeti sculptor Odhisë Paskali, which stands at the side of the main square. Përmeti is famous for its roses, which can be admired from late spring throughout the summer, and for its raki, which can be sampled at any time of year.

GETTING THERE AND AWAY Përmeti is about an hour's drive from Gjirokastra (55km). The route leaves the SH4 at the confluence of the River Drinos with the Vjosa and then enters the first of two imposing gorges (Mezhgorani and Këlcyra, known to the Romans as Fauces Antigonenses, the Jaws of Antigonea; see page 280).

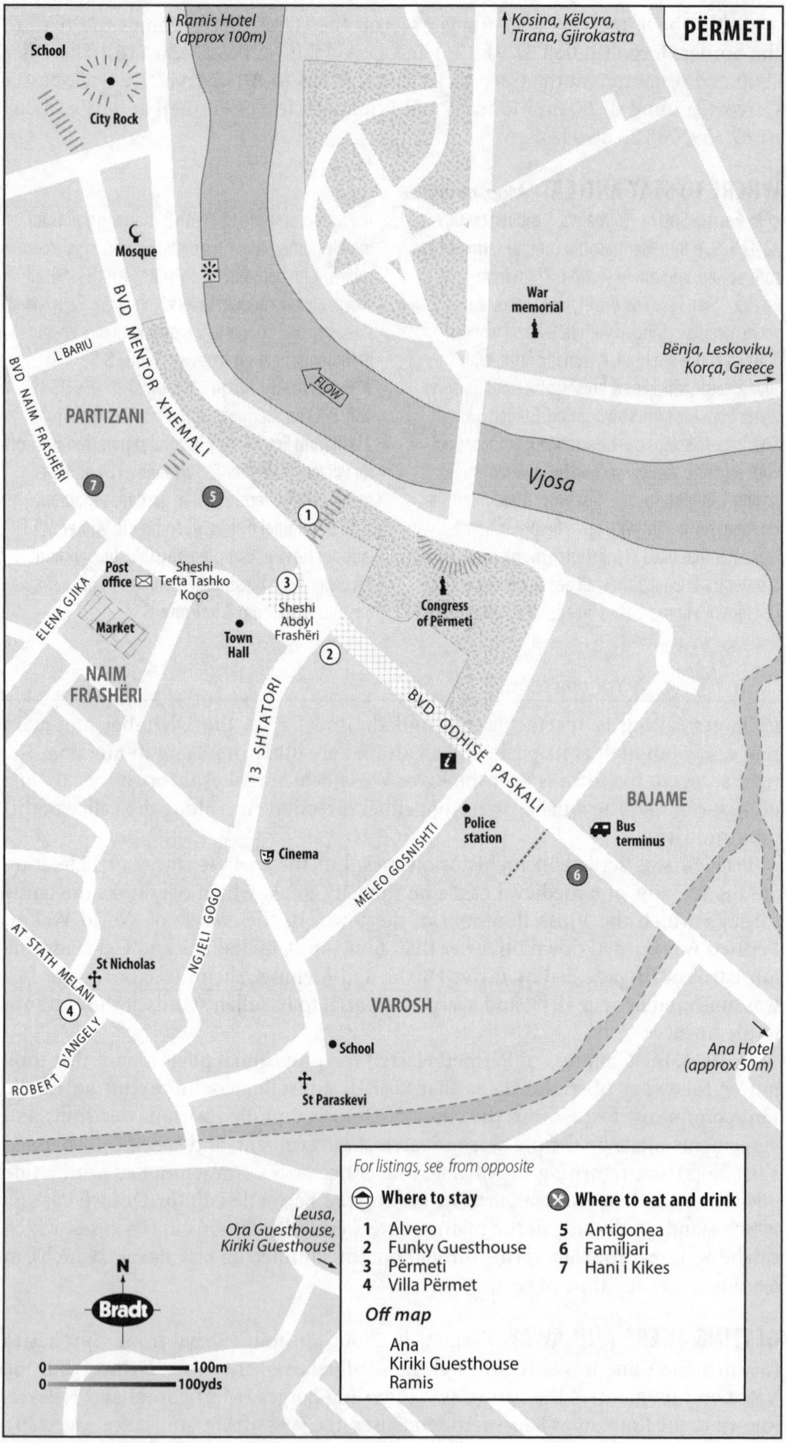

PËRMETI
Ramis Hotel (approx 100m)
Kosina, Këlcyra, Tirana, Gjirokastra
School
City Rock
Mosque
War memorial
Bënja, Leskoviku, Korça, Greece
BVD MENTOR XHEMALI
L BARIU
BVD NAIM FRASHËRI
PARTIZANI
FLOW
Vjosa
Post office
Sheshi Tefta Tashko Koço
Sheshi Abdyl Frashëri
Congress of Përmeti
ELENA GJIKA
Market
Town Hall
NAIM FRASHËRI
13 SHTATORI
BVD ODHISË PASKALI
BAJAME
Police station
Bus terminus
MELEO GOSNISHTI
Cinema
NGJELI GOGO
AT STATH MELANI
St Nicholas
VAROSH
ROBERT D'ANGELY
School
St Paraskevi
Ana Hotel (approx 50m)
Leusa, Ora Guesthouse, Kiriki Guesthouse
For listings, see from opposite
Where to stay
1 Alvero
2 Funky Guesthouse
3 Përmeti
4 Villa Përmet
Off map
Ana
Kiriki Guesthouse
Ramis
Where to eat and drink
5 Antigonea
6 Familjari
7 Hani i Kikes
N
Bradt
0 100m
0 100yds

The SH75 continues along the Vjosa, with mountains on either side of the river, before the signposted turning into Përmeti.

The journey to Korça from Përmeti takes between 4 and 5 hours. It is a spectacular trip, starting with the gorges and rapids of the Vjosa, then climbing on a rough road through forests to Leskoviku, before returning to asphalt for the run through the imposing Gramoz Mountains.

There is a daily **bus** service between Përmeti and Korça; it leaves Përmeti at 07.00 and returns from Korça at 13.00. The Gjirokastra–Korça service (daily except Sundays) passes the Përmeti junction between 08.00 and 08.30. The junction is a short walk to the west of the bridge over the Vjosa. Additionally, a bus for Leskoviku leaves Përmeti daily at 12.30.

The border crossing at Tre Urat – called Mertzani by the Greeks – is about 2 hours' drive from Përmeti (page 200). The route between Këlcyra and Berati, over the Gllava Pass, is unsuitable for any vehicle other than a rugged 4x4 or motorbike.

Unlike the other towns in this chapter, the **buses** from Tirana leave in the mornings from the North/South terminus. If you are travelling from elsewhere to the north or south of Përmeti, the best plan is to ask the bus driver to let you off at Lekli (the indefinite form is Lekël), where the road to Përmeti branches off the highway. The people in the café at Lekli will know if a bus for Përmeti is due. If there isn't going to be another bus that day, you could try hitchhiking; somebody will probably pick you up, although you will usually be expected to pay for the lift.

TOURIST INFORMATION The **tourist information office** (☎ 20015) is on Boulevard Odhisë Paskali, opposite the police station. Friendly, English-speaking staff can advise on where to stay and what to do. The office stocks free maps of the town and brochures; a small exhibition highlights some of the traditions of the area. Hiking maps may also be available. The staff can arrange guided city tours that include the City Rock, the historic churches and other attractions covered here. Visits to *gliko* producers and to vineyards can also be arranged (page 205).

Vjosa Explorer (m 068 39 30 797; e infovjosaexplorer@gmail.com; w vjosaexplorer.com), a Përmeti-based tour operator, offers a plethora of outdoor activities at various levels of difficulty. They have qualified guides who speak English and several other languages. Guided walks range from a short city tour or a half-day hike to a waterfall, through longer hikes to mountain passes or traditional villages and churches, to long-distance treks or overnight camps in shepherds' summer pastures. A similar range of cycling tours is offered, as is rafting on the Vjosa, from half a day to two days. There are also 4x4 excursions to the Hotova Firs National Park, traditional villages and the Vjosa valley.

WHERE TO STAY *Map, opposite, unless otherwise stated*

Villa Përmet (12 rooms, 2 family suites) Rr At Stath Melani; m 069 21 66 646; e info@villapermet.com; w villapermet.com. This historical house opposite St Nicholas' Church has been externally restored & sympathetically renovated internally. Heat-pump, good insulation, winter heating from wood-burner. Restaurant; large terrace with views of the city & beyond; bar service; lounge with wood-burning stove. All rooms en suite with handmade wooden furniture & traditional tiling, TV, CH, AC & fast fibre-optic Wi-Fi with separate router in every guest room; minibar & wood-burner will be added in every room. **$$$**

Alvero (16 rooms) Sh Abdyl Frashëri; ☎ 23514; m 068 23 39 508, 068 20 81 334; e vnikolla@yahoo.fr; w hotelalvero.com. Modern & comfortable; English & French spoken; very helpful owner; tours, fishing trips & drop-off/pick-up transport for hikers can all be arranged. Panoramic lift; large terrace bar overlooking river; conference room. All rooms have good, well-equipped en-suite bathroom, AC, TV, Wi-Fi, fridge; some have balcony. **$$**

Ana (10 rooms, 2 suites) m 069 28 94 536, 069 33 93 391; e hotelana@hotmail.com. Entrance behind grocery shop on main street. Bar/b/fast room with French windows opening on to balcony; Wi-Fi throughout. All rooms en suite with AC, TV, fridge; most have balcony. **$$**

Ferma Grand Albanik [map, page 213] (3 rooms) Ballabani; m 069 36 52 422; e ferma.grand.albanik@gmail.com; w ferma-albanik.com. A tranquil spot in extensive grounds, high in the mountains above Këlcyra; beyond Ballabani, not accessible in normal saloon car, but horses can be sent to meet guests & transport luggage. Hiking, swimming or fishing in nearby lakes, yoga; dark skies for stargazing; hiking guides can be arranged. Communal relaxation areas indoors & out. B/fast inc, other meals on request; almost all ingredients sourced locally; vegetarian menus available; permaculture garden. Rooms have 4,5 or 6 beds; 2 dbl rooms planned; all en suite. Camping area (**$**) with separate terraces for campervans, motorists with tents & backpackers. **$$**

Mali i Bardhë [map, page 178] (9 rooms) 1km from main road on way to Bënja; m 069 95 55 011; e taseapostol@yahoo.com. Good restaurant with traditional menu; tables on terrace, fringed with 400-year-old plane trees; open fire indoors. Hiking & climbing tours can be arranged. All rooms en suite with CH, TV, balcony with view of either mountains or forest & stream; HB possible. **$$**

Përmeti (30 rooms) On the main square; 22611; m 069 78 34 572. The former 'Turizmi'; fully renovated & upgraded. Lift; parking; terrace bar on main square, good for people-watching; Wi-Fi; some English spoken. All rooms en suite with AC, TV, good-sized dbl or twin beds, views of either City Rock or main square. **$$**

Funky Guesthouse (6 rooms, 1 family suite) Sh Abdyl Frashëri; m 067 46 67 795; e avenird@yahoo.co.uk; f funky-guest-house-adventures. Above a bar on the main square. Buffet b/fast included, served indoors or on terrace overlooking square (reserved for hotel guests until 10.00); separate Wi-Fi routers for hotel & bar; good English spoken. Horse treks can be organised by the owner (page 206). All rooms triple-glazed against noise, with nice en-suite shower room, AC, TV; family suite (**$$**) has 2 bedrooms & kitchenette. **$**

Kiriki Guesthouse (7 rooms) Leusa; m 069 21 66 079. This traditional village house has been sympathetically restored in stone & wood with new insulation & heating system; large living room with terrace & fireplace; kitchen for guests' use; meals can be ordered in from local families. Landscaped garden with camping area. All rooms en suite, good-sized, can be dbl or twin, CH. **$**

Ora! Guesthouse (5 rooms) Leusa; run by Vjosa Explorer; m 068 39 30 797; e infovjosaexplorer@gmail.com. Renovated stone house; garden with lovely views over Leusa; kitchen for guests' use; meals can be ordered in from local families. All rooms en suite, each with 2 bunk beds. **$**

Ramis (18 rooms) Lagja Mejden; 23858; m 069 77 88 682; e hotelramizi@yahoo.com; w hotelramis.business.site. Just beyond the City Rock, a few minutes' walk from centre. Restaurant, bar; free parking; wine & raki made on-site; rafting trips, other outdoor activities & visits to *gliko* producers can be arranged. Free Wi-Fi throughout; conference room. All rooms en suite with AC, TV, fridge, balcony, shutters; 4 on top floor are wood-panelled alpine-style rooms. **$**

WHERE TO EAT *Map, page 202*

Antigonea 22566; m 068 23 12 957, 068 40 51 373. Excellent menu; fresh fish from the river, game dishes such as rabbit & partridge, baked veal with mushrooms. Good, professional service, menu in English & Albanian; some English spoken. **$$$**

Familjari Bd Odhisë Paskali; 22537; m 069 52 06 292. Baked veal, grilled meat, pasta & risotto; excellent local wine. Menu in English & Albanian; friendly, efficient service. Attractively decorated interior with wooden ceilings & murals of traditional scenes; very handy for inter-city buses. **$$$**

Hani i Kikes Rr Naim Frashëri; 22163; m 069 23 61 570. Friendly, welcoming atmosphere; good range of traditional southern Albanian meals; menu in English & Albanian; draught beer in summer. **$$**

✕ **Sarajet** Këlcyra; m 069 41 08 086, 069 21 88 008, 069 73 74 441; restaurantsarajet. Attractive wood-panelled interior, heated in winter with modern wood-burner. Grilled meat, salads, local specialities; menu on blackboards in English & Albanian. $$

WHAT TO SEE AND DO A good way to begin a visit to Përmeti is with a stroll along the left bank of the River Vjosa as it flows through the town. In summer, local children swim and sunbathe on the shingle riverbanks. A huge boulder – the **City Rock** – sits by the gorge and can be climbed to enjoy the view of the river from the top; a metal staircase leads up the western face of the rock. A viewpoint, just before the City Rock, has an information panel about the river's biodiversity.

The town has two attractive 18th-century churches. **St Paraskevi** is a Greek saint who was martyred by decapitation; she is often shown in icons with one head on her shoulders and another in a bowl. Her name is the Greek word for Friday; in Albania, she and her churches are usually referred to as Shënepremtë, 'St Friday'. This St Friday's Church was built in 1776, a long, low building with an attractive whitewashed exonarthex (a colonnaded porch). The roof is unusual: normally the roof of the narthex is lower than that over the nave, but here it is on a single level. Another interesting architectural feature is a channel, under the paved floor, which took water from the font out into the rainwater drain outside. The frescoes were painted in 1808, by Tërpo Zografi; they are lovely, but in sore need of conservation. Flooding in 1963 damaged the women's gallery so badly that, ever since, women have worshipped in the nave, although they sit separately from the men. The entrance door is modern, carved by a local craftsman to replace the original door that was destroyed during the atheism campaign.

St Nicholas (Shënkoll) is slightly older, built in 1757, and set in a peaceful garden, surrounded by cypresses and flowers. It is usually possible to get into the courtyard and see the bell tower and exonarthex; the interior was whitewashed in 1967.

Every June, Përmeti hosts a **folk festival**, 'Multicultural Përmeti', in which traditional musicians come together from all over the Balkans. The Summer Day (Dita e Verës) festival, on 14 March, is a celebration of Përmeti's gastronomic and agricultural traditions.

The region is well-known within Albania for the quality of its food products. It is especially famous for its ***gliko***, a syrup preserve of fruit, walnuts or even certain vegetables, which is also made in Greece and elsewhere. The communist-era gliko factory has been converted into a centre for small gliko businesses, mostly run by women. Visits to these businesses and demonstrations of gliko-making can be arranged. It is also possible to visit the wine producers in the area, including Bualioti in the town itself. To arrange these visits, contact the tourist information centre or Vjosa Explorer (page 203).

The Përmeti area also produces excellent cheese and other dairy products. **Baxho Meshini** (m 068 23 25 618, 069 72 44 512; e baxho.meshini@gmail.com; f Punishte Meshini) offers tastings of different kinds of cheese, all made with sheep or goat milk, from a converted World War II bunker and on a shady terrace outside. In the cheese-making months between February and August, visitors can also observe the production process. The owner is active in the local business association, ProPërmet, and the shop in the bunker sells gliko, wine and other local products, as well as the dairy's own cheese, yoghurt, etc. The Meshini dairy is just off the main road between Përmeti and Këlcyra, near the village of Kuqari. It has toilets for visitors' use. Groups of more than four people should book at least one day ahead. In addition to cheese tasting, full lunches can be arranged.

OUTDOOR ACTIVITIES The wider Përmeti area is one of the best in Albania for hiking and other outdoor activities. About 200km of hiking routes, of varying levels of difficulty, have been mapped and waymarked. Some of the easier highlights include the Sopoti waterfall, above the village of Strëmbeci, and a circular hike through the villages of Lipa, Leusa and Lëshica. More ambitious walkers might like to tackle the path to or from Leusa to Sheperi, 11.6km away on the other side of the Dhëmbel and Nemerçka mountain ranges, or from Piskova to Çorovoda (page 268). There are interesting options for cyclists too, such as the route from the thermal baths to the village of Bënja, or around Hotova Firs National Park, where there are several guesthouses. Vjosa Explorer (page 203) can provide advice on these and many other routes and can arrange qualified, multilingual guides. They plan to have mountain bikes available for hire. A good hiking map has been published and should be available from Vjosa Explorer.

Guided horse treks, for beginners as well as experienced riders, start in the village of Ogdunari, near Bënja, organised by the owner of the Funky Guesthouse

THE FRASHËRI BROTHERS

Abdyl, the oldest of the three famous Frashëri brothers, was born in 1839 and became a fairly senior civil servant in the Ottoman administration. In 1877, he was elected to represent Ioannina in the Ottoman parliament. By this time, he was already actively involved in the movement for Albanian autonomy. He set up a secret Albanian Committee, which submitted a memorandum to the Ottoman government in the spring of 1877; it called for the unification of the four Ottoman provinces (*vilayets*) into which the Albanian-speaking lands were divided, and for the establishment of Albanian schools. The memorandum met with no response.

Abdyl Frashëri gave the opening address at a meeting of Albanian nationalist leaders held in Prizreni in June 1878, which soon became known as the Prizren League. Most of the delegates at Prizreni were from Kosovo or the Albanian highlands; Frashëri was one of only two from southern Albania. The meeting was timed to coincide with the Congress of Berlin, which had been convened by the European Powers – Britain, France, Austria-Hungary, Russia, Germany and Italy – to try to find a solution to the imminent disintegration of the Ottoman Empire and Russia's eagerness to fill the void left by it.

The 'solution', in the end, was the Treaty of Berlin, which returned Macedonia to Ottoman control, kept Serbia out of Kosovo, handed Bosnia-Herzegovina over to Austrian administration, and gave part of Kosovo to Montenegro. This last concession caused great resentment in Kosovo, and radicalised the Prizren League. Abdyl Frashëri, who was Bektashi (page 23), used the network of the Bektashi order to rally support for Albanian autonomy among the Muslims of southern Albania, who were not affected by the Treaty of Berlin. As the Albanians' demands developed and became more radical, Abdyl Frashëri travelled around the capitals of Europe, lobbying on their behalf.

In early 1881, the Prizren League began to organise real resistance to Ottoman authority, capturing Prishtina and expelling the Ottoman administrators from the whole of Kosovo. The empire belatedly realised the danger the League posed, and moved swiftly to suppress it. Abdyl Frashëri was captured and imprisoned, but the national awareness that the League had awakened could not be crushed so easily. He was released in 1886 on condition that he lived in Istanbul and took no part in political activity. His health was broken by his imprisonment and he died in 1892.

in Përmeti (page 204), who is originally from Ogdunari. They offer 4x4 transfers in the morning from Përmeti up to the stables and back again in the afternoon. There are eight different routes to suit differing riding abilities; lunch is provided by families in the villages the treks pass through. Longer treks of three to four days can also be organised, sleeping in village homes or camping.

Several companies offer **rafting** excursions on the River Vjosa, including Vjosa Explorer (page 203) and the Ramis Hotel (page 204), in Përmeti, and Outdoor Albania (page 30) in Tirana.

HISTORIC CHURCHES The churches at Leusa and Kosina have lovely architecture and frescoes. **Leusa** is only 1½km from the centre of Përmeti, a stiff walk uphill and about 45 minutes down. The road is in very poor condition and only passable in four-wheel drive. Leusa's church, 23m long, was built at the end of the 18th century, but it stands on the site of a much earlier church. During restoration work in 2000, traces of that church were discovered, a cross-in-square church

The youngest of the three brothers, Sami Frashëri (1850–1904), edited an influential daily newspaper in Istanbul, which in 1878 published an article by Abdyl Frashëri outlining the demands of the Prizren League – a single *vilayet*, Albanian-speaking officials, elected local authorities and Albanian-language schools. Sami led the Albanian Committee of Istanbul, and went on to become the nationalist movement's chief propagandist. His essay entitled *What Albania has been, what it is, and what it will become* was effectively its manifesto. On the Albanian language, he wrote:

> How can it be that Albanians do not have the right to write and read their language, when every nation has this right and nobody forbids it? Why are Albanians deprived of a right which every nation on earth has? Not to be able to write and learn their language, but to have foreign nations coming and opening schools in their languages?

After the crushing of the Prizren League, the emphasis of the nationalist movement shifted to cultural and linguistic demands. Cultural societies in Istanbul and Bucharest printed and distributed books in Albanian and raised funds for Albanian-medium schools (page 184). Naim Frashëri (1843–1900) was active in the Albanian Committee of Istanbul, but more importantly became one of the Albanian language's greatest poets. He wrote allegorical nationalistic works, such as *The Candle's Words* (*Fjalët e Qiririt*), and a paean of homesickness, *Livestock & Agriculture* (*Bagëti e Bujqësi*):

> O Albania, my mother, while I am in exile
> my heart has never forgotten your love.
> When the lamb, wandering from the flock, hears its mother's soft voice,
> it bleats two or three times and rushes off;
> even if twenty or thirty people block its way
> and frighten it, the lamb does not turn back, but goes through them like an arrow.
> In the same way, my heart too leaves me here, where I am,
> and hurries with longing to your lands.

from the 5th or 6th century. Some of its columns can be seen below the floor of the existing church; trapdoors have been installed which visitors can lift to trigger lighting and see the columns.

The paintings on the wall of the exonarthex have been damaged with graffiti, but there are some charming compositions among them, including a cute pelican. Inside, the frescoes on the narthex walls include gruesome scenes of sinners being tortured in various ways. A wooden staircase leads up to a screened gallery with more frescoes. From here there is a good view of the ceiling of the body of the church (the naos). Ask the tourist information centre or Vjosa Explorer (page 203) to arrange for the key-holder to let you into the church.

Kosina church is just off, and visible from, the main road towards Këlcyra, about halfway between the two towns. This beautiful little cross-in-square building, with its patterned brickwork, is typical of churches of the 12th and 13th centuries. The fresco in the dome, of Christ Pantocrator surrounded by his saints, has survived reasonably well, but the whole church urgently needs conservation work. You can park in the village, from where it is 45m or so up to the church; ask locally for the key-holder.

Frashëri The village of Frashëri, where the illustrious brothers Abdyl, Naim and Sami Frashëri came from, is about 40km from Përmeti, high in the mountains beyond Hotova Firs National Park. It is a lovely drive (or cycle, for those with good leg muscles) through forests of fir and spruce that open up from time to time to reveal towering mountains on all sides. The road is not asphalted, but it is in reasonable condition and a 4x4 is not required. There is no public transport; the turning off the main Përmeti–Këlcyra road, between Kosina and Piskova, is signposted for 'Bredhi i Hotovës' and the Bektashi *teqe* of Alipostivan. Note that some commercial maps of Albania show a completely fictitious route. The tourist information office in Përmeti can supply hiking maps of the trails around Hotova Firs.

In the 19th century, Frashëri was a sizeable place, with 22 distinct neighbourhoods. The village's most famous sons were the three brothers who contributed in different ways to Albania's Rilindja Kombëtare, the cultural movement that led ultimately to the country's independence (see box, page 206). Their family home is now a museum, with interesting photographs and maps of the village and surrounding district as it was in the past. There are displays about the family and each of the three brothers, and paintings representing various events in which they played a part. Ask locally for admission.

Frashëri is a largely Bektashi village – indeed, the three famous brothers were Bektashi. The local *teqe*, built in 1781, was used as a school in the communist period. It is a single-storey, whitewashed building, with a *tyrbe* on the hillside above. It is indicative of the religious harmony that generally prevails in Albania that the caretaker of the *teqe* is a Christian.

There is no hotel in Frashëri; accommodation could probably be arranged with a local family, or you could ask to pitch your tent on their land. The road onward to Erseka is not suitable for cars, but it can be cycled. It takes the villagers 8–10 hours to walk. Hikers might alternatively head northwest to Çepani, in the district of Skrapari, and on to Çorovoda and Berati.

Bënja The thermal baths at Bënja are a popular day trip for the people of Përmeti. Below an elegant Ottoman bridge over the River Lengarica, the water from several thermal springs collects in a large pool, wide and deep enough to swim in. The water

THERMAL BATHS

Albania's thermal baths have been enjoyed since Roman times. In the 20th century, some of them were developed into spas – they are known generically by the Albanian word Llixhat (the indefinite form is Llixhe).

The first to have its waters scientifically tested in 1924 was in Llixhat e Elbasanit (page 107). A spa was built there in 1932 by a businessman from Elbasani, Grigor Nosi (brother of the politician Lef Nosi; page 104). Detailed research into the chemical components of the water was conducted by a Czech scientist between 1932 and 1936; the main elements are sodium, magnesium, calcium and potassium. The spa treats a range of ailments, including rheumatism, circulatory problems and skin complaints such as eczema. The water is also said to aid fertility. The springs rise from 13,000m below the surface and emerge at 56°C. Nowadays, many spa hotels have been built at Llixhat e Elbasanit, although some of them pump their water from underground, rather than allowing it to emerge naturally, as is supposed to be better for the conservation of its medicinal properties.

Another spa resort, built during the communist period, is near Peshkopia (page 176). The water here emerges, from three springs, at just above blood temperature (39–40°C); it comes from the same source, far underground, as Llixhat e Elbasanit and a similar (but much more expensive) spa across the North Macedonian border in Kosovrasti. It is so full of sulphur that clients are not allowed to wear jewellery while bathing, because everything except gold will dissolve in it. The original spa here was built in 1964; the current building, with 50 individual bathing cubicles, was one of the last hurrahs of the communist period, inaugurated in 1990. The peak season is September and October, when 3,000 people come through the doors every day. Most people come for a course of treatment of five to seven days, increasing the length of time they soak in the water each day. Hot mud therapy is also available, said to be helpful in the treatment of gynaecological problems and scoliosis. The baths are kept open all year round, for drop-ins by local people or anyone who happens to be visiting Peshkopia. Full courses of treatment are offered from April to October.

The prices at these spas are astonishingly low by northern European standards. A 15-minute soak in a private cubicle at Llixhat e Peshkopisë costs less than €1. Medically trained staff, often with decades of experience, supervise the spa facilities at all times.

There are free thermal baths, open to the elements, in various places around the Albanian mountains. One of these is at Bënja, near Përmeti, a large open-air pool in a beautiful setting, fed by several thermal springs. (See page 210 for details of how to get there.) Finally, there are numerous drinking-water springs, which are also said to have beneficial medical effects; these are often known as Uji i Ftohtë, the Albanian for 'cold water'. If you are making long-distance bus journeys in Albania, you will find that buses often stop at these famous spots so that passengers can fill their plastic bottles with this health-giving spring water.

temperature of the springs is 23–32°C. At the time of writing, there is no charge to use the Bënja pools, although that may change within the lifetime of this guidebook.

There is a café just before the bridge, where coffee, water and other drinks can be bought and which has a toilet for customers' use. At the time of writing, there are plans to open a campsite at Bënja, to address the problem of the minority of thoughtless campervan users who park up free and leave their rubbish (or worse) behind for someone else to deal with. A minibus between Përmeti and Bënja operates in the summer, starting when enough local people want to go there (usually in June) and continuing until summer turns to autumn. Vjosa Explorer (page 203) offers hiking, cycling and jeep excursions to the pools and to the village of Bënja, higher up in the hills and with a lovely old church.

Wanderlust®
Taking The Road Less Travelled Since 1993

Exclusive Bradt Offer!

One Year of Print, Digital & Club Benefits
Only £35 (free UK P&P)
Including a £50 Travel Voucher & Free Gift

SAVE £10 with code **'BRADT35'**
Visit **shop.wanderlust.co.uk** or call us on **01371 853641**

7

The Southwest

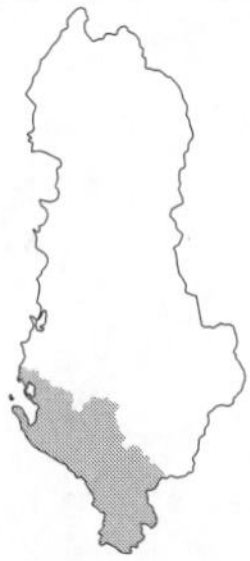

Southwestern Albania has destinations that are on the itinerary of almost every guided tour of the country. The magnificent complex at Butrint is far and away the most-visited archaeological site in Albania, the Ottoman cities of Berati and Gjirokastra are also UNESCO World Heritage sites and the beautiful Ionian coastline draws gasps from every visitor who drives along it.

GETTING THERE AND AWAY

BY AIR For many northern Europeans, the cheapest and most convenient way to get to southern Albania is to take a flight to Corfu and then take the hydrofoil to Saranda, a short hop of around 40 minutes. See page 214 for details.

Construction has begun on a new airport near Vlora at the time of writing. The site is in a formerly protected area just to the north of the Narta Lagoon (page 246), a hugely significant habitat for waterbirds including pelicans and flamingos, and the plans were bitterly opposed by Albanian and international conservation organisations. The Albanian government also intends to build an airport at Saranda.

BY LAND From Greece, the principal border crossing into southwestern Albania is at Kakavija, 60km from Ioannina. There are daily bus services from Athens and other Greek cities to every city and many of the towns covered in this chapter. Alternatively, Greek KTEL buses run several times a day up to the border at Kakavija; there are always taxis and minibuses on the Albanian side of the border.

The Fieri bypass has cut the journey time between Tirana and the southwest by at least half an hour. The Vlora bypass, once it is fully operational (expected in time for the summer of 2022), will reduce travel time by at least as much for those travelling between Tirana and Llogoraja or the Riviera. Buses from Tirana to the southwest leave from the North/South Terminal in Tirana's western suburbs.

BY SEA As well as the hydrofoils and ferries between Corfu and Saranda, there are also daily ferries to Vlora from the southern Italian port of Brindisi (see w traghetti.it for details).

SARANDA *Telephone code: 0852*

Southwestern Albania has many unmissable attractions: the wonderful archaeological site and national park at Butrint; the imposing Ottoman city of Gjirokastra; the beautiful beaches and crystalline waters of the Riviera. Sadly, though, Saranda – the point of entry to Albania for many foreign visitors – is no longer the attractive little port it once was. Before the Covid-19 pandemic,

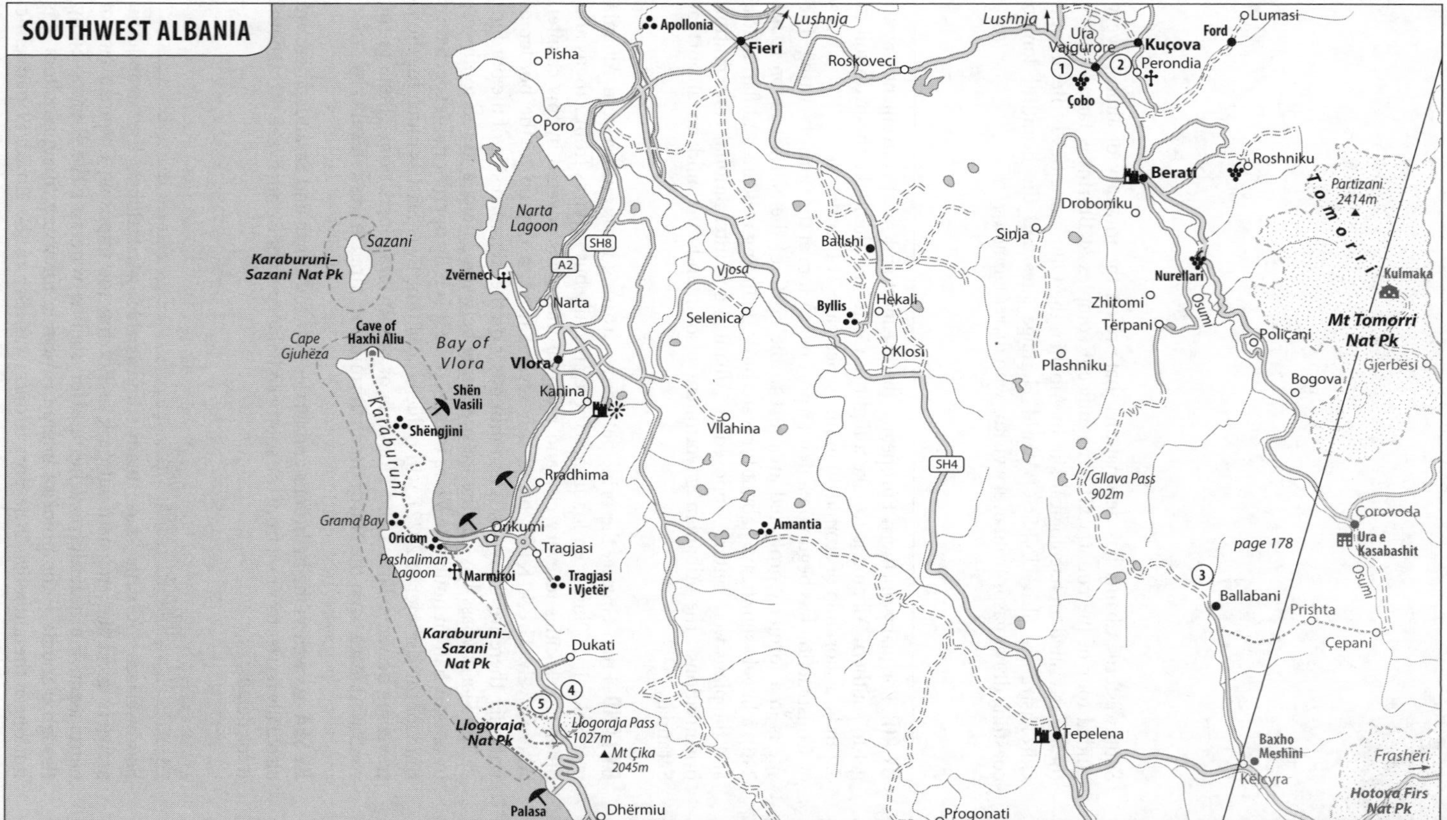

SOUTHWEST ALBANIA
Apollonia
Lushnja
Fieri
Lushnja
Ura Vajgurore
Kuçova
Ford
Lumasi
Pisha
Roskoveci
1
2
Perondia
Çobo
Poro
Roshniku
Berati
Tomorri
Partizani 2414m
Narta Lagoon
Droboniku
Sazani
SH8
Sinja
Ballshi
Karaburuni–Sazani Nat Pk
A2
Vjosa
Nurellari
Kulmaka
Zvërneci
Narta
Hekali
Zhitomi
Byllis
Selenica
Tërpani
Osumi
Mt Tomorri Nat Pk
Cape Gjuhëza
Cave of Haxhi Aliu
Bay of Vlora
Vlora
Klosi
Poliçani
Plashniku
Gjerbësi
Bogova
Shën Vasili
Kanina
Karaburuni
Shëngjini
Vllahina
SH4
Rradhima
Gllava Pass 902m
Çorovoda
Grama Bay
Orikumi
Amantia
Oricum
Tragjasi
page 178
Ura e Kasabashit
Pashaliman Lagoon
Marmiroi
Tragjasi i Vjetër
3
Osumi
Ballabani
Prishta
Karaburuni–Sazani Nat Pk
Çepani
Dukati
4
5
Llogoraja Pass 1027m
Llogoraja Nat Pk
Tepelena
Baxho Meshini
Mt Çika 2045m
Frashëri
Këlcyra
Hotova Firs Nat Pk
Palasa
Dhërmiu
Progonati

Ionian Sea
Gjipe
Jala
Himara
Bay of Palermo
Palermo Castle
Qeparoi
Borshi
Lukova
Shën Vasili
Nivica
Bay of Kakomeja
Cape Qefali
Othoni
Ereikoussa
Mathraki
Saranda
Bay of Saranda
Çuka
Metoqi
Kassiopi
Ksamili
Butrint Nat Pk
Butrint
Corfu
Vrina
Xarra
Mursi
Shkalla
Cape Stillo
Corfu
Qafebota
Konispoli
Igoumenitsa
Janjari
Kardhiqi
Mashkullora
Kardhiq Strict Nature Reserve
Dhoksati
Gjirokastra
Lazarati
Derviciani
Vërgoi
Delvina
Phoinike
Finiqi
Mesopotami
Blue Eye
SH99
Muzina
Rahulla
Dhrovjani
Dhivra
Jergucati
Sofratika
Terihat
Hadrianopolis
Libohova
Melani
Nepravishta
Glina
Peshkëpia
Kakavija
Sotira
Ioannina
GREECE
Antigonea
Asim Zeneli
Labova
Poliçani
Sheperi
Leusa
Përmeti
Korça
Kosina
N
Bradt
0 16km
0 10 miles
Where to stay
1 Berat Caravan Camping p261
2 Familja p261
3 Ferma Grand Albanik p204
4 Hotel Alpin p234
5 Llogora Tourist Village p234

thousands of people made the trip across the Corfu Channel every summer, most of them taking advantage of the day trips to Butrint organised by tour operators and the ferry companies on Corfu. It is a pity that their first encounter with Albania is the unappealing concrete jungle that Saranda has become. Nonetheless, it is still the most practicable base from which to visit the beautiful and interesting places in its vicinity.

Saranda has an excellent climate, averaging around 290 sunny days a year, with pleasantly warm temperatures rarely exceeding 30°C. Some of the hotels have outdoor pools, generally open only in the peak summer months, while some are linked to one or other of the beach resorts along the coast towards Butrint. The beach in the town is a pleasant enough place to catch a few rays in between sightseeing. If a day at the beach is what you are after, though, it is better to head south to Ksamili (page 226) or north to the Albanian Riviera (page 228).

The Greek name for the town – Ayia Saranda, 'forty saints', from which the Albanian name comes – springs from a legend of 40 Christian legionaries who were put to death here (and in other places in the Balkans and Asia Minor) in the 4th century. A pilgrimage church dedicated to the 40 saints was built on a hill behind modern Saranda in the 5th century, rebuilt in the early 9th century and, unfortunately, used as a base by German troops during the Battle for the Liberation of Saranda in 1944 – unfortunate, because it led to the church's destruction by British bombers. The neighbouring hill of Lëkurësi is the site of an early 19th-century castle, which has been converted into a popular restaurant and bar. From the terraces of the restaurant there are magnificent views over the Ksamili Peninsula to the Butrint Lagoon and across to Corfu.

GETTING THERE AND AWAY

By sea Daily hydrofoils connect the towns of Saranda and Corfu all year round. See page 216 for contact details for the operators. In peak season (July–mid-September), there are at least six crossings a day in each direction. The journey by hydrofoil takes about 40 minutes. The one-way fare is €18–19 off-season, €20–23.80 in July and August. There are also car ferries; see operators' websites for details.

The hydrofoils and ferries to Albania leave from the far end of the main port in Corfu town, where the cruise ships berth. Tickets must be purchased before boarding, from one of the ticket agencies near the entrance to the port. Economical hotels (**$$$**) for an overnight stay in Corfu include Atlantis (☎ +30 266 103 5560; w atlantis-hotel-corfu.com), convenient for the seaport, and Bretagne (☎ +30 266 103 0724; w hotelbretagne.gr), within walking distance of the airport. Corfu city buses operate hourly between the airport and the seaport (w corfucitybus.com).

Passport control in Saranda is usually swift and efficient. The centre of Saranda is 10 minutes' walk from the passenger terminal and the bus terminus is about 15 minutes away. Yellow, licensed taxis wait just beyond the barrier at the entrance to the port. Various agencies offer car hire, all clustered around the exit from the port on Rruga Mit'hat Hoxha. Saloons and 4x4 vehicles are available as well as smaller options.

Several companies operate one-day tours to Albania from Corfu. These typically comprise a visit to Butrint, a restaurant lunch and some free time in Saranda. Pre-pandemic, Finikas operated a summer-only hydrofoil service between Corfu and Himara (page 230), excursions by boat from Saranda, and bus tours to Butrint, Gjirokastra and Parga.

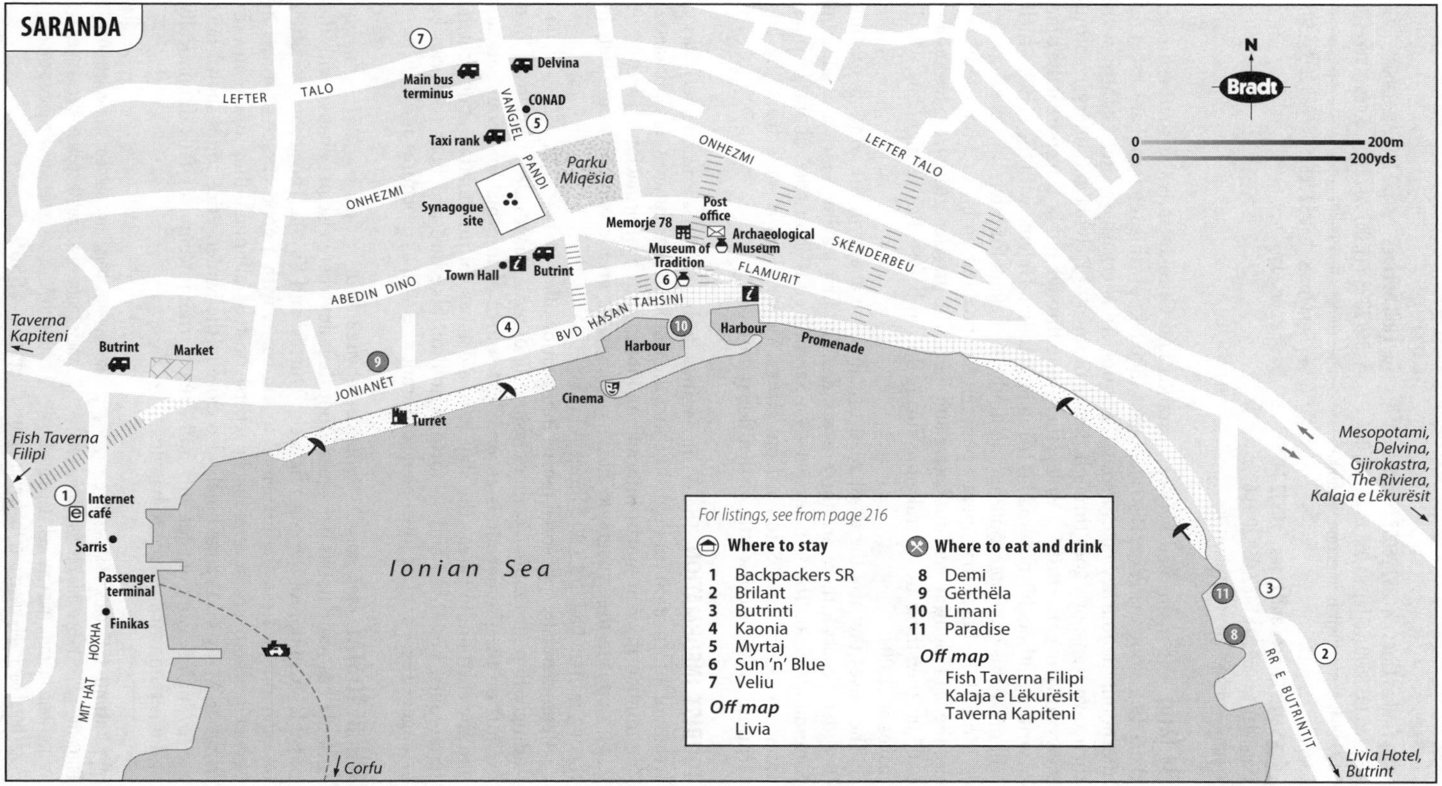
SARANDA
Bradt
N
0 200m
0 200yds
LEFTER TALO
ONHEZMI
ABEDIN DINO
JONIANËT
BVD HASAN TAHSINI
VANGJEL PANDI
SKËNDERBEU
FLAMURIT
MIT'HAT HOXHA
RR E BUTRINTIT
Main bus terminus
Delvina
CONAD
Taxi rank
Parku Miqësia
Synagogue site
Memorje 78
Post office
Archaeological Museum
Museum of Tradition
Town Hall
Butrint
Harbour
Harbour
Promenade
Cinema
Turret
Market
Internet café
Sarris
Passenger terminal
Finikas
Ionian Sea
Corfu
Taverna Kapiteni
Fish Taverna Filipi
Mesopotami, Delvina, Gjirokastra, The Riviera, Kalaja e Lëkurësit
Livia Hotel, Butrint
For listings, see from page 216
Where to stay
1 Backpackers SR
2 Brilant
3 Butrinti
4 Kaonia
5 Myrtaj
6 Sun 'n' Blue
7 Veliu
Off map
Livia
Where to eat and drink
8 Demi
9 Gërthëla
10 Limani
11 Paradise
Off map
Fish Taverna Filipi
Kalaja e Lëkurësit
Taverna Kapiteni

Ferries

Finikas Lines 0852 26057 (Saranda), +30 266 103 8690 (Corfu); m 069 20 73 711, 067 20 22 004; e info@finikas-lines.com; w finikas-lines.com

Sarris Cruises and Lines 0852 24751 (Saranda); m 069 20 81 182, 069 20 91 699; e info@sarrislines.gr; w sarrislines.gr

Car hire

Finikas Lines 0852 26057 (Saranda), m 069 20 73 711, 067 20 22 004; e info@finikas-lines.com; w finikas-lines.com

Sipa Tours 0852 26675; m 068 20 35 250; w sipatours.com

By land The main road between Saranda and Gjirokastra is the southern one, the SH99, along the River Bistrica. Buses (300 lek) ply this road until at least early afternoon; the journey takes about 1¼ hours. An alternative route, for those with their own transport, goes through the small town of Delvina and offers beautiful views down over the Bistrica Valley; there is no through public transport at the time of writing, although a new road is being built to link Delvina with the SH99, which will make this the faster route and no doubt the default for inter-city buses.

Most of the buses that operate between Saranda and Tirana (a 5-hour journey) use the SH4 highway via Gjirokastra and Fieri. The first departure from Saranda is at 05.00, then there are several more during the day before the overnight bus, which leaves at 22.00.

The buses that use the coast road usually have a sign in the window reading 'Bregdet' ('coast'); there are three every day, the first leaving Vlora at 06.45 and Saranda at 06.00. The journey between Saranda and Vlora takes about 4 hours. Inter-city buses leave Saranda from Rruga Vangjel Pandi; some from the bus terminus, others from a little further down the street.

TOURIST INFORMATION The **Visit Saranda** website (w visitsaranda.net) has a wealth of information (in English) about the whole area, as far away as Gjirokastra. The municipally run **tourist information kiosk** (Zyra e Informacionit Turistik, or ZIT), opposite the synagogue site, has somewhat erratic opening hours but, in theory, is open 08.00–15.00 Monday–Friday.

A commercially sponsored **tourist information office** (m 069 27 91 052; 08.00–midnight in high summer, earlier closing out of peak season, Dec–Feb closed Wed & Thu) on the promenade is an excellent source of information about Saranda and the surrounding area. The staff have a database of information about hotels, restaurants, bus times and so forth. Car hire, bike hire and boat trips can be arranged. There are free town plans of Saranda, as well as brochures and leaflets.

WHERE TO STAY *Map, page 215, unless otherwise stated*

Saranda has more hotels per square foot than anywhere else in Albania, with the possible exception of the coast between Durrësi and Kavaja. The accommodation on offer ranges from the luxurious to the basic, with a good choice of hotels in between. There are several backpackers' hostels, although they open only in summer. Many mid-range hotels also close in the winter. Price codes shown here are for high season; outside July and August, room occupancy falls dramatically and it is then worth trying to haggle.

Butrinti (54 rooms, 33 suites) Rr e Butrintit; 25593–6; e info@hotelbutrinti.com; w hotelbutrinti.com. This very well-appointed 5-star hotel has lovely views over the bay to Corfu. Restaurants, bars, large outdoor swimming pool, fitness centre, spa. English spoken. All rooms en suite with AC, suites come with Nespresso coffee machine. **$$$$$**

Brilant (18 rooms, 2 suites) Rr Bilal Golemi; 26262; m 069 20 53 533, 069 20 57 354; e info@brilanthotel.com; w brilanthotel.com. Just beyond the promenade; with magnificent views from upper floors. Lift, lounge on ground floor, free Wi-Fi throughout, b/fast bar on 5th floor with great sea views; English spoken. Most rooms have balcony; all are en suite with TV, AC, minibar, full or partial sea view **$$$**

Kaonia (24 rooms) Rr Jonianët; 22600; m 067 20 54 944; e kaoniahotel@yahoo.com, dgjoni@bkt.com.al; Hotel Kaonia; summer only. On the promenade a few mins' walk from the town centre. Bar with terrace, lift, free parking. All rooms en suite with AC, flatscreen TV & balcony; some have sea view. **$$$**

Livia [map, page 222] (11 rooms) Butrint; 0891 22040; m 067 34 77 077; e info@hotel-livia.com; w hotel-livia.com. 90m from entrance to Butrint site, overlooking Vivari Channel. Good restaurant serving fresh fish & mussels (**$$$$**), tables in peaceful garden. Free parking, free Wi-Fi throughout. All rooms en suite with AC, flatscreen TV, hairdryer, iron, mosquito net, fridge, balcony. **$$$**

Sun 'n' Blue (7 rooms) Rr e Flamurit; m 069 24 15 460; e sunnbluehotel@gmail.com. Centrally located, overlooking the little harbour. Panoramic lift with city views; good English spoken at reception; friendly, helpful staff. All rooms have sea view; nicely furnished, en suite, good-sized balcony, AC, fridge, TV, balcony. **$$$**

Myrtaj (14 rooms) Rr Onhezmi; 24411; m 069 93 26 555; Hotel V.Myrtaj. On the corner opposite the central park; can be rather noisy with traffic early in the morning. Bar; free parking; Wi-Fi. All rooms en suite with AC & TV; some have balcony with sea view. **$$**

Backpackers SR (14 beds) Rr Mit'hat Hoxha 10; m 069 43 45 426; w backpackerssr.hostel.com. Good location near port terminal. Kitchen with fridge & cooker; washing machine; luggage storage; lockers; lift. Free Wi-Fi & bed linen; 3 dorms, all with balcony with sea view. B/fast inc. **$**

Veliu Rr Lefter Talo; m 069 32 67 026. Convenient for inter-city buses. English spoken at reception, helpful staff; lift; generous b/fast inc. Good value. All rooms with small en-suite bathroom, AC, TV, fridge, small balcony (some with view of Corfu). **$**

WHERE TO EAT *Map, page 215*

Mussels, the local speciality, have been farmed in the Butrint Lagoon since the 1960s. They are usually available all year round. Sea bream and sea bass will be farmed unless the menu specifies otherwise. The seafront promenade restaurants are, as one would expect, more expensive than those in the town centre. Out of season, many restaurants tend to close quite early in the evening (or altogether). To be sure of a table in high season (July and August), booking is essential.

Gërthëla Rr Jonianët; m 069 28 54 281. An exclusively fish & seafood menu, inc a wide selection of wild fish. Nice sea-themed décor; professional service; pleasant atmosphere. **$$$$$**

Paradise Rr e Butrintit; m 069 63 93 446. At the eastern end of the promenade, suspended over the water on stilts. A bit pricier than elsewhere, but lots of people think the view is worth it. Good range of fish & seafood, professional service. **$$$$$**

Demi Rr e Butrintit; m 069 20 84 900, 069 20 60 700; w demi.al. Large, covered terrace built out over the sea, at the eastern end of the promenade. Fresh fish, various mussel dishes, seafood risotto & pasta. Also a hotel (**$$$$$**). **$$$$**

Kalaja e Lëkurësit m 069 53 72 300. Behind the town, just off the main road (signposted). Built on the ruins of an Ottoman castle; fabulous views right down the Butrint Lagoon & up the coast to the north of Saranda. Traditional southern Albanian dishes. Large terrace bar; open-air concerts in summer. **$$$$**

Limani Bd Hasan Tahsini; 25858; m 069 40 77 471; Bar-Restaurant-Limani. A lovely setting on the town harbour, in among the little boats & looking out across the bay. Fish, seafood pizza, risotto & pasta, some wild fish. **$$$$**

Taverna Kapiteni Rr Idriz Alidhima; Taverna Kapiteni - Sarandë. More or less across road from football stadium. Fresh fish, some wild; English menu; can get busy. **$$$$**

Fish Taverna Filipi Rr Ismail Qemali; m 069 56 11 071; f TavernaFishFilipi. Neighbourhood restaurant attached to fishmonger's shop; on foot, easiest way to get there is up the steps from the port. Superb fresh fish & seafood, interestingly prepared; excellent grilled vegetables & salads; generous portions. $$$

OTHER PRACTICALITIES The tourist information office on the promenade (page 216) doubles as a **bookshop**, with a wide selection of publications in Albanian, English and other languages – including (usually) this guidebook. It also stocks children's books and games, postcards and stamps. Credit cards are accepted.

The **post office** (08.00–20.00 daily) is up the steps from the little harbour.

ALI PASHA TEPELENA

By the middle of the 17th century, the old system of provincial government in the Ottoman Empire had broken down. No longer did the governors of *vilayets* and *sanjaks* (provinces) work their way up through the ranks of the imperial administration. Instead, increasingly, they were appointed directly by the palace or by other great households; by 1630, only about a quarter of *sanjak* governors and governors-general had previous experience of provincial government. Rapid turnover in the administration also became common, with more than half of the governors-general in 1630 staying in their posts for less than a year.

In Albania, one outcome of these changes was the emergence of near-autonomous local rulers who were known as *pashas*. It was in the *pasha's* interest to expand the territory he controlled – his *pashalik* – whether by war or payment, because the larger it was, the greater his income and power. Towards the end of the 18th century, practically all of these small *pashaliks* had come under the control of two powerful *pashas*, one in southern Albania and the other in the north. See page 126 for information about the northern *pashalik*, whose capital was Shkodra.

The southern *pashalik* was centred on the city of Ioannina, which is now in northern Greece but at the time was in the same administrative region as much of southern Albania. In 1788, the sultan appointed as Governor of Ioannina a man from Tepelena called Ali. He had started his career as a brigand, and used his knowledge of other robber bands to curry favour with the sultan (ie: he shopped his friends), who rewarded him first with a small *pashalik* and then with Ioannina.

From there, Ali Pasha Tepelena used a combination of skilful diplomacy and ruthless violence to extend his authority throughout southern Albania and a large part of the Greek mainland. This was the period of Napoleon's expansions into Italy and Dalmatia, and Ali Pasha played the French and the British off against each other, consolidating his own power as he did so. In 1809, he captured Berati, and then Vlora and Gjirokastra. In that same year, Lord Byron visited Ali Pasha's court at Tepelena and described him in a letter to his mother:

> His highness is 60 years old, very fat, and not tall, but with a fine face, light blue eyes, and a white beard; his manner is very kind, and at the same time he possesses that dignity which I find universal amongst the Turks. He has the appearance of anything but his real character, for he is a remorseless tyrant, guilty of the most horrible cruelties, very brave, and so good a general that they call him the Mahometan Buonaparte.

WHAT TO SEE AND DO Saranda is an ancient town, first settled in the 4th century BC by the Chaonians, who called it Onchesmus. Cicero mentions it as a convenient harbour with a favourable prevailing wind. It was never a Roman colony, but it must have been reasonably prosperous in the 2nd and 3rd centuries AD, since mosaics from that period have been found at various sites in the town.

In the 4th century AD, Onchesmus was fortified with a roughly semicircular wall, about 850m long and 6m high. These fortifications were further strengthened with turrets and, in one of these, coins were found that date the tower's useful life to the period from AD334 to AD578. The remains of one of the **turrets** can be seen on the town beach. The waterfront itself was not fortified, presumably because it could be defended from the sea, so this tower marks where the wall ended. The British artist

Throughout the territory that Ali Pasha controlled, he built castles, aqueducts, bridges and mosques, many of which can still be seen. He was interested in learning about new construction techniques, and hired European architects and builders to work for him. He converted to Bektashism (page 23) in about 1810, around the time when it was taking hold in Albania. His conversion allowed the Bektashi *babas* to preach more freely and to establish *teqes* throughout the territory under his rule.

By 1820, the huge area that he controlled was beginning to alarm the imperial authorities. He was dismissed as governor and ordered to hand his *pashaliks* back to the sultan's authorities. In a last audacious move, Ali Pasha then threw in his lot with a Greek revolutionary organisation. This was the last straw for the Ottomans. They besieged his castle at Ioannina and, after 17 months, in January 1822, he was killed and beheaded. His head was sent to Istanbul and his body was buried in Ioannina, next to that of his wife Emine.

AN ALI PASHA TOUR It would be relatively easy to self-assemble a short Ali Pasha tour, starting from either Ioannina or Corfu. Ioannina Castle houses Ali Pasha and Emine's tomb, next to the Fatih Mosque that he rebuilt in 1795. You can also look at the double-walled fortifications that his European engineers built. From Ioannina it is a short bus journey across the border to Gjirokastra, where Ali Pasha extended the fortifications and built a 10km-long aqueduct (demolished in 1932, sadly, although some traces are still visible).

Two impressive castles built for Ali Pasha, at his home town of Tepelena and at Libohova, are within easy reach of Gjirokastra and could be visited from there on day trips. See page 281 for information about these towns and their castles.

At Butrint, on an island at the mouth of the Vivari Channel, which connects the Butrint Lagoon with the Corfu Channel, is a small fortress that Ali Pasha is said to have built in 1814, in response to Britain's capture of Corfu and the other Ionian islands. This castle can be visited by boat from Butrint; while you are there anyway, it would be perverse not to visit the main Butrint site, which is packed with wonderful things (page 225). Another Ali Pasha fortress stands at Porto Palermo, less than 2 hours north of Saranda up the beautiful coast road (page 230).

Fairly frequent buses link Ioannina with Igoumenitsa, just across the strait from Corfu. Ferries and hydrofoils run every day from Corfu to Saranda (page 214). There are direct buses from Ioannina to Gjirokastra (page 271). If you have your own transport, you could return to Ioannina directly from Tepelena, via Përmeti and the Tre Urat border crossing (page 200).

and poet Edward Lear sketched the city walls in 1859, when they were practically intact. Even into the 1990s, it was still possible to see stretches of the fortifications. The relentless pace of new building in Saranda since then has destroyed almost all of them and only a couple of small sections remain.

The **Museum of Tradition** (Muzeu i Traditës; ⌚ summer 09.00–14.00 & 19.00–22.00 Mon–Fri, 19.00–22.00 Sat–Sun, winter 09.00–14.00; 100 lek, also giving admission to Archaeological Museum), on the promenade, is an excellent place to learn about Saranda's history. The exhibition begins with a reproduction of Lear's sketch and a 1930 photograph from roughly the same vantage point, by which time only eight of the 20 original watchtowers survived. More photographs from the 1930s show the Forty Saints Church before its destruction in World War II. Nothing of the original church remains above ground, although it is possible to visit the crypt (enquire at the tourist information office or in the Archaeological Museum), which has some surviving frescoes.

The exhibition continues with very interesting photographs of Saranda between the wars. The town was built on a grid system in the 1930s; the buildings were deliberately kept low-rise so that the whole town could be seen from the sea, rising uphill like the seats of a theatre. A collection of ethnographic objects illustrates everyday life during this period. Upstairs, textiles and musical instruments are displayed alongside photographs of people producing and playing them. The final room of the exhibition gives a fascinating glimpse into life in the 1960s and 1970s, in the town and the surrounding area, through more photographs and household utensils.

A whole corner opposite the main square has been excavated to reveal the remains of a 5th- or 6th-century **synagogue complex**, with a mosaic floor depicting Jewish symbols such as a menorah (candelabrum) and a ram's horn (page 22). Earlier mosaics on the same site appear to have formed the floor of a Roman villa. Towards the end of its life in the last quarter of the 6th century, part of the synagogue was converted into a Christian church and a third layer of mosaics was laid. The panel at the entrance to the site is very informative, with a helpful map; photographs are displayed of the menorah mosaic, which is usually kept covered to protect it from the elements.

Another of Saranda's mosaics can be seen in the **Archaeological Museum** (Rr e Flamurit; ⌚ summer 09.00–14.00 & 16.00–21.00 daily; 100 lek, also giving admission to Museum of Tradition). This mosaic was discovered in the 1960s, during building work at the neighbouring post office, and the museum was built specifically to protect it. It has been dated to the 6th century AD and is thought to have been the floor of a basilica. The museum also has a small display of photographs and information about the archaeological and historical sites in the Saranda area, including Butrint, of course, but also Phoinike and the Islamic buildings around Delvina (pages 226 and 228, respectively).

One aspect of Saranda's communist history can be seen opposite the post office on Rruga e Flamurit: **Memorje 78**, a concrete pillbox, half-excavated so that you can look through a grille into its interior. Inside, there is an information panel with photographs of different types of bunker and diagrams of their design; see box, page 197, for more information.

Boats can be hired for day trips at the little harbour (eg: the *Ajla*; m 069 64 46 410). They set off between 09.00 and 10.00 each day; the tourist information office at the harbour can advise. These excursions typically include one or more of the nearby beaches to which there is no road access, such as Kakomeja; the boatmen leave when they have enough passengers to make it worth their while. The going rate is 5,000 lek per passenger.

BUTRINT

The ancient city of Butrint, one of UNESCO's World Heritage Sites, is far and away the most-visited archaeological site in Albania, with visible remains spanning two-and-a-half millennia – from the first settlers in the late 6th or early 5th century BC to Ali Pasha Tepelena (see box, page 218) at the beginning of the 19th century AD. Then the site became overgrown and half-forgotten, visited only by the occasional artist (including the British poet Edward Lear), until 1928, when the Italian Archaeological Mission, led until his death by Luigi Maria Ugolini, began to uncover the city's hidden treasures. After World War II, Butrint was once again abandoned and forgotten until the Albanian Centre for Archaeology began excavating there in 1956. Archaeological research has continued at the site ever since.

Informative and well-presented panels guide the visitor through the city; the small museum, on what was once the acropolis, illustrates Butrint's history through beautiful artefacts; further interesting sites lie across the Vivari Channel, which connects Lake Butrint with the sea, and can be visited on foot or by boat. There is so much to see in and around Butrint that anyone with more than a fleeting interest in history or archaeology could easily spend a whole day (or more) there. Anything less than 3 hours is likely to feel rather rushed and unsatisfactory.

An information leaflet, with a map of the site, is available at the ticket office at the entrance to the site. Tickets may be purchased in advance at w cultureticketsalbania.al. The website of Butrint National Park (w butrint.al) has extensive information about the archaeological site and the habitats in the park but, weirdly given how many foreigners visit Butrint in non-pandemic years, the information is only in Albanian. To find out about the site before your visit, the on-site information panels are reproduced in the 'Archive' section of the website of the Butrint Foundation (w butrintfoundation.co.uk), a charitable trust set up in 1993 to save Butrint from the neglect and looting that threatened its survival at the time. The Butrint Foundation's excellent publications can be ordered via this website and are also often on sale in the courtyard outside the Butrint Museum.

GETTING THERE AND AWAY The ancient city of Butrint is about half an hour's drive from Saranda, 24km on a good, asphalted road that runs alongside Lake Butrint and through the village of Ksamili. Cyclists might prefer to use the back road, along the eastern shore of the Butrint Lagoon, which has much less traffic and lets you approach the site on the cable ferry (page 225).

Buses between Saranda and Butrint leave hourly in each direction until 18.30; the one-way fare is 100 lek. In Saranda, there are bus stops at the junction of Rruga Mit'hat Hoxha and Rruga Jonianët; opposite the synagogue and basilica site; and opposite the Butrinti Hotel. The last bus back to Saranda from Butrint leaves at 19.30. Any Saranda **taxi** will do the run; you should agree the fare before setting off. Either you could negotiate a charge for extra waiting time with the driver or, if you have a mobile phone, you could arrange to call him when you are ready to be collected. The town's main taxi rank is on the corner of the central park in Saranda, opposite the Myrtaj supermarket.

For those coming from northwestern Greece with their own transport, the route via the small border crossing at **Qafëbota**, a short drive from Igoumenitsa on the Greek mainland, is a very attractive way to approach Butrint. It would be worth making a short detour to see the old stone-built houses (*kulla*) in the Shehat neighbourhood of **Konispoli**, just over the Albanian side of the border. The route passes the villages on the Vrina Plain before you transfer on to the cable ferry to

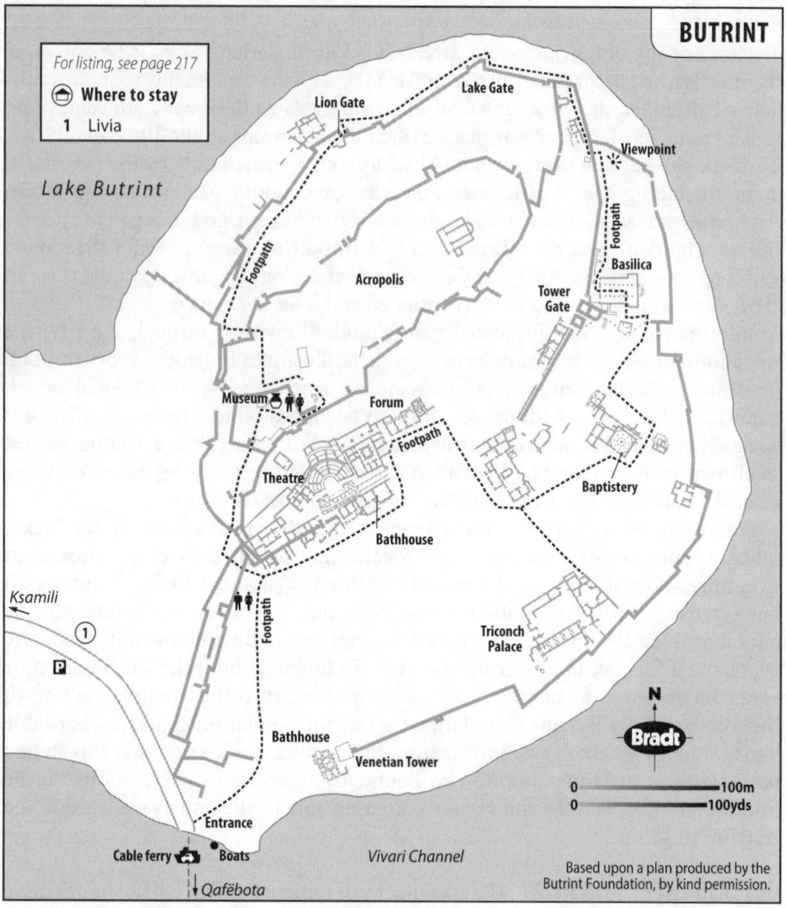

reach the entrance of the Butrint site. By public transport, the daily buses between Igoumenitsa and Saranda use the Qafëbota crossing.

In the tourist season, Butrint becomes very busy; thousands of visitors pass through the site on the peak days. If you can be flexible with your time, it is better to visit either first thing in the morning, before the tour groups arrive from Corfu, or later in the afternoon, when they have left.

GETTING AROUND AND OTHER PRACTICALITIES A reasonably surfaced path leads around the site. Most of it is fairly flat, apart from a slight climb up to the viewpoint for the aqueduct and back down to the Lake and Lion Gates. However, the museum is on the city's acropolis, on the summit of the hill above the monumental centre. The usual access to it is through the Lion Gate and up several flights of steps, with intermittent handrails. Visitors with limited mobility may find it easier to use the steps to the west of the theatre.

A toilet block has been installed near the entrance to the ancient agora, but it is not always open. The only reliable toilets within Butrint are on the acropolis. The Livia Hotel, a few minutes' walk from the site entrance, serves meals (**$$$$**) and drinks, and obviously has toilets for customer use.

You should be sure to have enough drinking water with you, especially in high summer when it can become extremely hot. There is nowhere to buy water within the site. You may also wish to stock up on insect repellent; Butrint is low-lying and surrounded by water, ideal territory for mosquitoes and other biting insects.

For boat trips to Diaporit and Ali Pasha's Castle, see page 225. Plays are staged in the Butrint theatre; until 2020, there was an international drama festival every summer, Butrinti 2000. Details of future events may be promoted on the festival's Facebook page (f Butrinti Summer Festival); the tourist offices in Saranda (page 216) should also have information about this.

THE CITY (⌚ 08.00–sunset daily; museum ⌚ 08.00–16.00; 700 lek for non-Albanians, inc museum admission) Butrint is first mentioned in the 6th century BC as a harbour; its location at almost the narrowest point of the Straits of Corfu made it a strategic crossroads between the Ionian islands, particularly Corfu itself, and the wealthy trading cities of Epirus. Pottery from the 7th and 6th centuries BC has been found on the acropolis hill, but any traces of such an early settlement were built over in antiquity.

In the 5th century and into the 4th century BC, Butrint was effectively part of Corcyra (Corfu), the Corinthian colony across the Straits. Later, the city became integrated into the Epirote Alliance, as part of the Chaonian territory whose capital was Phoinike. In 167BC, Rome's wars with Macedonia came to an end with the final victory for Rome, and Butrint, like the rest of Epirus, became part of a Roman-administered province.

The earliest building below the acropolis was a **sanctuary** to the god of medicine, Asclepius, in what developed into the city's monumental centre. In the 4th century BC, or slightly later, a **defensive wall**, with imposing gates at regular intervals, was built around the expanding lower city – a stretch of this, with large irregularly shaped blocks, can still be seen as you enter this area. Worshippers came to the sanctuary to be healed and, to meet their other needs, various other buildings were erected: a temple, in front of the shrine; a hostel for pilgrims or priests to stay – the so-called Peristyle Building; and, between them, a **theatre**, built with donations made to the god. An inscription on the theatre seats dates its construction to the early 2nd century BC, although this was almost certainly an extension of an earlier, simpler theatre. To the side of the walkway leading into the theatre, inscribed blocks form part of the wall; these record the freeing of slaves, more than 500 of them, between 163BC and 44BC. Behind the Peristyle Building, a long portico (a stoa) once ran, with a well set into the hillside within it; the ropes that hauled water from this well over the centuries have worn deep grooves into its marble door.

Wealthy Romans – including Cicero's friend Atticus – had been buying up land at Butrint throughout the 1st century BC, and in 44BC the city became a Roman colony. The official language became Latin and Butrint began to mint coins. In the city centre, the Hellenistic agora (market) was remodelled and turned into a Roman forum. During Ugolini's excavation of the theatre, several statues were found within it, including three portrait heads of the Emperor Augustus, his wife Livia and his general Agrippa, which have been dated to 27–12BC. Agrippa is in the National Archaeological Museum in Tirana; Augustus and his wife are displayed in the Butrint Museum (the head of Livia, looted in the 1990s, was recovered in 2000). Shops sprang up around the forum and a bathhouse was built next to it, paved with a black-and-white mosaic. The mosaic, like all the mosaics at Butrint, is kept covered to protect it; the hypocaust with which the baths were heated has been partly reconstructed. To feed the baths and fountains with water, Roman engineers constructed an **aqueduct** to bring water from springs 4km away across the Vrina Plain, near the modern village of Xarra. Some of the piers that carried the aqueduct can still be seen, looking across the water towards Xarra from a viewpoint on the path around the site. The aqueduct was extended into the city in the 1st century AD and piers from that extension survive near the Great Basilica.

In the 1st century AD, the city spread across the Vivari Channel and a whole new suburb began to develop on the Vrina Plain. In the old lower city, the theatre was expanded, with a new stage and seating for 2,000 or so spectators, and more bathhouses were built. The city continued to grow and its wealthiest citizens commissioned prestigious villas on both sides of the Channel. One of these, at Diaporit on the eastern shore of Lake Butrint, can be visited by boat. Another lies southwest of the monumental centre; when it was first constructed, it was a traditional Roman villa, with elegant, mosaic-floored rooms arranged around a central courtyard. It is known as the **Triconch Palace** because, around AD420, it was expanded into a much more substantial building that included a dining room (*triclinium*) with three scalloped niches. The palace even had its own water gate, by which visitors arriving by boat could enter the building straight from the water's edge. Strangely, in view of all the work that had been done to create this beautiful residence, it was abandoned shortly before it was completed; carved window frames had been installed but the floors were never paved and the walls were left unpainted. The most likely reason is that the rising water table brought construction to a halt.

Perhaps as a way of coping with seasonal changes in the water table, the people of Butrint now began to build their houses of perishable timber. The city was not plunged into poverty – far from it, as attested by archaeological finds, including many (datable) coins – but from the 6th century onward, the only stone buildings were Christian structures. The most important of these are the **Great Basilica** and the associated, though not adjacent, **Baptistery**. The latter was the largest baptistery east of Rome, apart from Hagia Sofia in Constantinople (now Istanbul). Unfortunately for the visitor, its magnificent mosaic floor is kept covered with sand and plastic sheeting, the only cost-effective way to protect it from the elements. Happily, however, a photographic reproduction of the mosaic is displayed in the Butrint Museum. The baptistery's design is as symbolic as the mosaic's, with two concentric rings of eight granite columns – eight being the symbol of salvation and eternal life – and seven concentric bands in the mosaic that culminate in the eighth circle of the font. The fountain set into the wall, directly opposite the entrance and thus forming the other end of the building's principal axis, is almost unique in a baptistery and must represent the Fountain of Life referred to in Genesis. The mosaic, too, is full of Christian symbolism: cockerels, which represent rebirth and resurrection; birds and fish representing the faithful; and two large compositions on the principal axis, showing drinking peacocks (symbols of Paradise) and stags (symbolising the faithful who thirst after God).

Some of the motifs in the baptistery mosaic were also used in the Great Basilica; these similarities allow both buildings to be dated to the second quarter of the 6th century. The basilica is huge, 31.7m long and 23.7m across, and is dominated by a pentagonal apse with arched windows; two of the original large windows were blocked in, and the middle one replaced, when the basilica was refurbished in the 13th century.

Not long after these magnificent Christian monuments were erected, Butrint's fortunes took a turn for the worse. In the 6th century, a new city wall was quickly built around the lowest-lying parts of the peninsula, obviously to defend the city from attackers. A further refortification took place in the 13th century and a new castle was built on the acropolis; reconstructed in the 1930s, this castle now houses the Butrint Museum. These walls were conserved just a few years ago and a path has been cleared around much of their length, so that visitors with a little more time at their disposal can explore this aspect of the site. The Venetian Republic purchased Butrint, along with Corfu, in 1386 and built the tower at the entrance to the site, the triangular fortress on the other side of the Vivari Channel and, probably, the fortress at the mouth of the channel that is known as **Ali Pasha's Castle**. All these fortifications hark back to the first defensive wall, built in the 4th century BC. The path around the site and up to the museum passes three of the gates in this ancient wall: the main entrance to the city, Tower Gate, near the baptistery; the Lake Gate, which Ugolini called the Scaean Gate, after the *Aeneid*; and the Lion Gate, so-called from the carved lintel of a lion sinking its teeth into a bull's neck, which was placed there long after the gate was first constructed. The carving is typical of Greek archaic art of the 6th century; it is thought that this relief may have come from a building associated with the sanctuary on the acropolis.

BEYOND THE CITY The triangular fortress and the remains of the aqueduct, across the Vivari Channel, are easy to visit on foot. A delightfully low-tech cable ferry plies to and fro across the channel; the charges range from €0.50 for foot passengers, through €1 for cycles and €3 for saloon cars, to €10 for mobile homes. The gate into the triangular fortress is in the wall furthest from the ferry jetty – the southern side. Within the walls is a courtyard, in the centre of which is a circular building (perhaps a *hamam*, or steam bath, added later by the Ottomans). The western wall contains several small vaulted chambers, probably originally used as gunpowder magazines, workshops or stores. In the southwestern corner is an unusually shaped tower; there are good views of the city of Butrint from its upper floor and from the fortress battlements.

To reach the piers of the Roman aqueduct, continue along the edge of the Vivari Channel until you reach the fish traps and the building beside them, where there are beehives. Cross the little bridge there, and head slightly inland along a track that leads to an excavated area of the Roman suburb on the Vrina Plain. By the 2nd century AD, this included villas and a public bathhouse, with a large cistern that was supplied with water from the aqueduct. If you look along the wall of the cistern, you will see the bases of the aqueduct piers in a line running towards Xarra, the village on the hill. It is about 15 minutes' walk from here back to the cable ferry.

The expansion of Butrint in the 1st century AD meant new building not only on the Vrina Plain, but also at Diaporit, on the eastern shore of Lake Butrint. A large villa has been excavated here, with a bath complex, a peristyle and a mosaic-floored *triclinium*. The boatmen who hang around the entrance to the city can take you out to Diaporit.

They also offer trips to **Ali Pasha's Castle**, which is on a little island at the edge of the marshes and can only be reached by boat. The trip out to the fortress meanders through the wetlands, with good opportunities to see waterbirds, and offers an entirely different perspective of the Butrint area. The fortress itself is beautifully constructed and is well worth exploring. The entrance to the Vivari Channel – with Ali Pasha's Castle, the triangular fortress and the reconstructed Butrint Castle – can be seen from the deck of the Saranda-Corfu ferry (the view from the hydrofoil is not so good) and gives a good idea of the geography of the channel and the city.

In 2000, as part of the Albanian government's efforts to protect Butrint, the archaeological site and the surrounding area were given national park status. The park now extends for 86km² and, in addition to its archaeological significance, has a wide variety of animal habitats and great biodiversity. It is listed as a Wetlands Site of International Importance, under the Ramsar Convention. Proposals emerge from time to time to develop trails around the park, of varying distances and levels of difficulty. The staff at the site ticket office may be able to advise on this.

AROUND SARANDA

Ksamili Until a decade or so ago, Ksamili, 17km south of Saranda on the road to Butrint and only six nautical miles (*hexamilion*) from Corfu, was a charming hamlet, with a few dozen houses, a lovely little sandy beach and one restaurant. Then, like many other formerly idyllic spots on the Albanian coast, a frenzy of building overwhelmed it. It is now full of hotels and holiday apartments that sit empty for nine or ten months of the year. If you can find your way through them, Ksamili is a nice place to stop for a swim or a meal on the way to or from Butrint, especially outside the peak tourist season.

The **Rilinda Restaurant** ($$$) has the best location, opposite one of the islands that close off and protect Ksamili Bay; the restaurant runs a bar on the island during the summer, to which you can swim or take a pedalo or rowing boat. Fresh fish and seafood feature prominently on the menu. To find the Rilinda using public transport from Saranda, get off the bus at the first of the two stops in Ksamili and head right until you reach the sea.

Mursi The largest villages on the Vrina Plain are Xarra and Mursi. The latter is particularly attractive, with its two old churches and lake. For those driving to or from Greece via Qafëbota (page 221), Mursi is almost exactly halfway between the border and the main Butrint site. It is a Greek-speaking village; a memorial in the square commemorates villagers who were captured trying to escape to Greece during the communist period and died in prison or internal exile – as the memorial puts it, 'those who sought Europe and didn't even see daylight'.

Just at the turn-off into Mursi on the main road, the family-run, friendly **Nefeli Restaurant** ($$$) offers a menu of local produce including vegetables from the restaurant's own garden, fish, eels and mussels from Lake Butrint, local olives and cheese, homemade focaccia, and good house wine. A post-lunch coffee will probably rack up more food-miles than the entire meal.

Phoinike (🕘 summer 09.00–18.00 daily, winter 08.00–16.00 daily; 300 lek) The ancient city of Phoinike was the capital of Chaonia, one of the three largest states (*koina*) in the Epirote Alliance. It was built on a hill that controlled the valley between Butrint to its south and the mountains that run into the Ionian Sea, to its north. Its fortifying walls were built at the end of the 4th century BC and the beginning of the 3rd, with the huge polygonal stones common to Epirote cities (there are stretches of similar walls at Butrint). The middle of the 3rd century BC was the high point of Phoinike's power. The city became the capital (or one of the capitals) of Epirus in 232BC and minted its own coins. In 205BC, it was here that the peace treaty was signed that ended the First Macedonian War: the Peace of Phoinike. The building where it was signed is known as the *thesauros*, although it was a small temple rather than a vault.

The Chaonians constructed not only fortification walls and the *thesauros*, but also a huge theatre, built into the natural curve of the hillside. The stone seats were later plundered for re-use, which meant it was not obvious there was a theatre there at all until it was excavated in the 1980s. The first couple of rows of seats have survived. Also visible is the line that marks the highest row of seats, 192m above the stage, which is itself 30m wide. The theatre held 17,000 spectators, testament to the size and importance of the city around it.

The Romans extended the city and restored the theatre. Later still, in the 5th or 6th century, a basilica was built next to the ancient *thesauros*, which by then was being used as a baptistery. It is difficult to make sense of the remains of the basilica because this area was used during the communist period as a military base. Tunnels were dug under the ancient site and bunkers were installed all around the hilltop. Luckily, there is a helpful information panel showing the outline of the basilica and the older temple.

Similar information panels are installed above the theatre and at other points of interest around the large site (3km long). In particular, excavations since 2002 have shed new light on Phoinike's residential buildings. Small signs on the paths, in English and Albanian, show directions to the remains of all the buildings. A stepped path with handrail leads up to the site from the car park and ticket office; a wooden walkway, again with handrail, gives access to the theatre.

The views from the acropolis and the theatre are superb; the Butrint Lagoon can be seen quite clearly, as can the southernmost villages of the Albanian Riviera. Of course, this is why both the Chaonians and the communists chose the site for their fortifications.

The modern village of Finiqi is on a minor road that links the Saranda–Delvina road and the main Saranda–Gjirokastra road. From the village, an asphalted road, suitable for any normal vehicle and offering wonderful views, leads up to the entrance to the site. There is also a footpath up from the village, a 30–45-minute walk. Buses to Finiqi leave Saranda roughly every 2 hours from 07.00 to 13.30. The last bus back to Saranda leaves Finiqi at 14.00.

St Nicholas Church, Mesopotami (100 lek) The Church of St Nicholas (Kisha e Shënkollit) stands, surrounded by cypresses, on a hillock just outside the village of Mesopotami. It was first documented in 1281, but was built on the site of an earlier church – indeed, some of the limestone blocks used in its construction came from an even older building, perhaps in the nearby city of Phoinike. Some of these blocks bear curious carvings that are thought to pre-date the arrival of Christianity here. On the eastern wall (outside the altar), you can see an eagle, a lion, a dragon and an even weirder mythical creature, apparently strangling itself with its own tail. Inside the church, a central pillar is constructed around a stone column; the plasterwork of the pillar has been removed in places to reveal some of the original decoration and a Greek inscription. Some frescoes survive behind the altar.

Coming from Saranda, the turn-off for the church is a few hundred metres beyond the village, where a sign reading '300m, Manastir' (Albanian for 'monastery') indicates a track up to the right. It is gated but, when the caretaker is there, this should be unlocked and you can open it yourself. To be sure of there being someone there to issue your ticket and let you into the church, it is better to go in the morning. Mesopotami is easy to get to by public transport; take one of the many buses that run between Saranda and Gjirokastra and ask to be dropped off at 'Manastir', ie: the start of the track.

The Blue Eye (100 lek/car, 50 lek/person) The Blue Eye (Syri i Kaltër) is an unusual underwater spring, set in shady woods just off the main road between Gjirokastra and Saranda. The water bubbles up through a deep pool, making a curious circular shape, deep blue at its centre and almost electric blue around the edges, like the pupil and iris of an eye. The rocks from which the spring rises are more than 45m below the surface and the pool has never been fully explored.

The Blue Eye is a pretty spot, with oak trees fringing the pool and flowers growing on the banks. It is surrounded by woodland and by the streams that flow from the spring and onwards into the River Bistrica. In the old days the area was reserved for the party elite to hunt and fish in, and ordinary Albanians were banned, which is usually a good indicator of how nice a place is.

The turn-off for the Blue Eye is indicated by a large brown 'tourist attraction' sign, just before the road begins to climb up to the Muzina Pass (22km from Saranda). It is 2km from the turn-off to the car park; the road is reasonable. A path leads through the trees to wooden platforms that give a good view of the Blue Eye from above. There is a restaurant with toilets.

Islamic historical buildings, Delvina Two very significant Islamic sites can be visited either with one's own transport or by taxi from Delvina, a small town about 20km from Saranda, high in the hills above the Bistrica Valley. The **Rusan Mosque** was built in the 16th century and is mentioned by the 17th-century Ottoman traveller Evliya Çelebi. Also known as the Gjin Aleksi Mosque, it was restored in 2020. Its dome has a beautiful ceiling, inscribed with the 99 names of Allah; it can be admired more closely from the *makfil*, the women's gallery. Slim, agile visitors can climb the tightly winding stairs to the top of the minaret. From here, there is a good view of the different levels of the mosque's roof and of the hexagonal buildings in the grounds. These are Bektashi *tyrbe*s, of later date than the mosque; one of them contains the graves of several Bektashi *babas*.

On the other side of Delvina is the **Xhermëhalla Islamic Complex**. The buildings within it include a mosque, a ruined *madrasa*, or Islamic school, a bathhouse and several Bektashi *tyrbe*s, as at Rusan. During restoration work in 2010, a hitherto unknown fountain was revealed, below the entrance to the mosque and *madrasa*; this was where the faithful washed before entering the mosque to pray. There are good views from Xhermëhalla of the ruins of the Byzantine **Delvina Castle**, perched imposingly on a crag. It is possible to hike up to the castle, but there is not much to see once you get there apart, of course, from the views.

Both the Rusan Mosque and the Xhermëhalla Islamic Complex are very close to Delvina: only 5 or 10 minutes' drive. Simple accommodation is available in Delvina at the Shameti Hotel (📞 0815 22380; **$**), centrally located with good views from the terraces on the upper floors.

THE RIVIERA

To the north of Saranda is the Albanian Riviera, one of the most beautiful coastlines of the whole Ionian Sea. There are not many good consequences of Albania's isolation and poverty under communism, but this unspoilt coast was one. A handful of small resorts, including the Workers' Camp (page 47) at Dhërmiu, offered suitably unblemished families the chance of a fortnight or so at the beach. The section of the coastal road between Himara and Borshi was a closed military zone, because of the submarine base at Porto Palermo. Himara was a sleepy village and even Saranda was a quiet, low-rise town.

In the last 20 years, however, one after one, the lovely beaches of the Riviera have been developed for tourism. Even the smallest bays have cafés and restaurants on the beach. From the southern outskirts of Saranda to the seafront promenade of Vlora, the coastline is an almost unbroken ribbon of hotels, restaurants and exclusive villa developments. Accommodation ranges in price from simple rooms in private houses to luxury hotels. Many beaches have temporary, summer-only campsites. Prices increase dramatically in summer and it is advisable to book in advance. Although most hotels say they will accept credit cards, the systems do not always work reliably so it is essential to carry sufficient cash. There are ATMs in Himara.

GETTING THERE AND AWAY The journey from Saranda to Vlora takes about 4 hours by car; the road is well surfaced, but narrow and steep over the Llogoraja Pass. Those who do not want to stop in Himara should take the bypass that curves above the town. The Albanian government has announced tenders several times for a 'Llogara Tunnel' through the mountains, most recently in June 2021. If it is ever completed, it will cut about an hour from the journey.

Using **public transport** on this route means that you can enjoy the wonderful views without having to concentrate on the road. The buses that use the coast road usually display a sign on the dashboard reading 'Bregdet' ('coast') to differentiate them from the buses that go via Fieri and Gjirokastra. The first Bregdet bus of the day leaves Saranda at 06.00 and continues to Tirana; in the other direction, the Bregdet bus leaves Tirana's North/South bus station at 06.15. The next Bregdet bus leaves Saranda at 07.00; there is then a gap until a bus for Himara at 10.30. The last Bregdet bus of the day leaves Saranda at 14.30. From Vlora, the first Bregdet departure of the day is at 06.45.

Any bus will let you off in any of the small towns on its route, or at the road-ends for the beaches or the castles. Similarly, you can get *on* a bus anywhere along its route; ask locally for the time it is expected where you are. It is unwise to rely 100% on the last bus of the day, especially in summer when they are often full and you may be left stranded at the roadside, without alternative transport. Foreign travellers, even those who speak some Albanian, should prepare themselves to have to pay well over the odds for part-journeys on the Bregdet buses.

The coast road is a lovely route for **cyclists**. There are some very steep stretches, but the magnificent scenery is a good excuse to stop for lots of rests. Drivers are usually courteous to cyclists, but caution is required; cycling after dark is certainly not advisable. It is about 140km from Saranda to Vlora.

Leaving Saranda, the road at first curves inland, through the village of Shën Vasili – the site of a prison camp in the communist period, then called Përparimi ('Progress'). After Shën Vasili, it climbs gradually above the deeply indented bays and the view from above is unforgettable. Rivulets run from the mountains and lose themselves in the fine sand of the beaches. The hillsides between Lukova and Piqeras are covered in olive groves, planted on terraces that were cut by detachments of students from Tirana at around the same time as the villages of the Greek coasts were being covered in concrete.

BORSHI Just before the village of Borshi, just over an hour from Saranda, a minor road up to the right leads up to **Borshi Castle**, sometimes also referred to as Sopoti Castle. The first written reference to it is in 1258 and the hill on which it stands was already fortified by the 4th century BC. However, what can be seen today dates from the 18th century. The mosque just within the entrance was built at that time; the painted ceiling and walls must have been beautiful when the fresco was in better condition. The whole castle is rather neglected and overgrown, but the views from it are spectacular, out across the Ionian Sea to Corfu in one direction and, in the other, towards the mountains that run the length of the Riviera. There is a paved footpath up from the car park to just short of the castle entrance, with stone benches on which to rest and enjoy the views. If you are on foot, the best place to start is the Ujvara Restaurant; ask the waiters to show you the short cut up to the road. It takes about half an hour to walk up to the castle entrance from the restaurant. The Ujvara is a lovely place to stop for a meal ($$$) or a drink, with its tables arranged on terraces surrounded by waterfalls (the eponymous *ujvara*); the service is friendly and some English is spoken.

BAY OF PALERMO After Borshi, the road drops down to the coast and rounds the Bay of Palermo, where Ali Pasha Tepelena (see box, pages 218) built one of his imposing fortresses on a promontory connected to the mainland by a narrow – and easily defensible – causeway. The promontory closes off part of the bay to create a sheltered harbour, still used today by local fishermen, and a pleasant pebbly beach. Cars can be parked either at the restaurant on the main road – a good place, with its shady terrace and impeccable toilets, for a drink or meal after your visit – or just beyond the causeway, beside a restored church (said to have been built by Ali Pasha for one of his wives, a Christian) and ruined 20th-century buildings, with communist-era slogans still visible under the more recent graffiti. It is a few minutes' walk up a rough track to the **castle** (100 lek). An information board has been installed at the start of the track, with helpful plans of the fortress and a brief history of it in English and Albanian. There is another board with plans as you enter the fortress.

The interior of the castle consists of a huge vaulted chamber with archways leading off it into smaller rooms and dark tunnels (a torch is essential), well worth exploring thoroughly. A stone staircase leads up to the battlements, from where part of the outer walls can be reached. The views are stunning. The islands that can be seen in the distance are Greek territory, lying off the northwest of Corfu. Not surprisingly, there are dense arrays of bunkers on the hillside overlooking the bay. The fortress itself was used as a military depot during the Italian occupation, and probably afterwards, too.

From the castle (and at certain points along the road) you can see a huge tunnel blasted into the cliffs on the northern side of the bay. It was built as a shelter for the submarines that the Soviet Union based in the Adriatic from the late 1950s. When the Soviet Union broke off relations with China and Albania sided with China, the USSR naturally took the view that it should get its submarines back. After a stand-off lasting several weeks, four of the eight submarines were left behind. These events were dramatised in the 1979 film *Face to Face* (*Ballë për Ballë*), scripted by Ismail Kadare.

HIMARA *Telephone code: 039*

Himara is the largest town between Saranda and Vlora, with a high school, district hospital, ATMs and so forth. If you find Saranda overdeveloped, this is the place to come. It has good hotels and restaurants, the standard of service is better than at some other resorts on the Riviera, and the local people are friendly and helpful.

The swimming in Himara is excellent, with clear blue water that stays warm until late in the year. Non-swimmers, however, should note that the beach slopes very sharply into the sea, unlike the gentle Adriatic coast further north. There is no longer much of a beach left in the town centre, where most of it has been replaced with a vast expanse of promenade, but the terraces of the bars and restaurants behind it are pleasant spots to sit and admire the sea. The beach just to the south of the town, called Potami, is pebble, but the hotels there provide sun-loungers

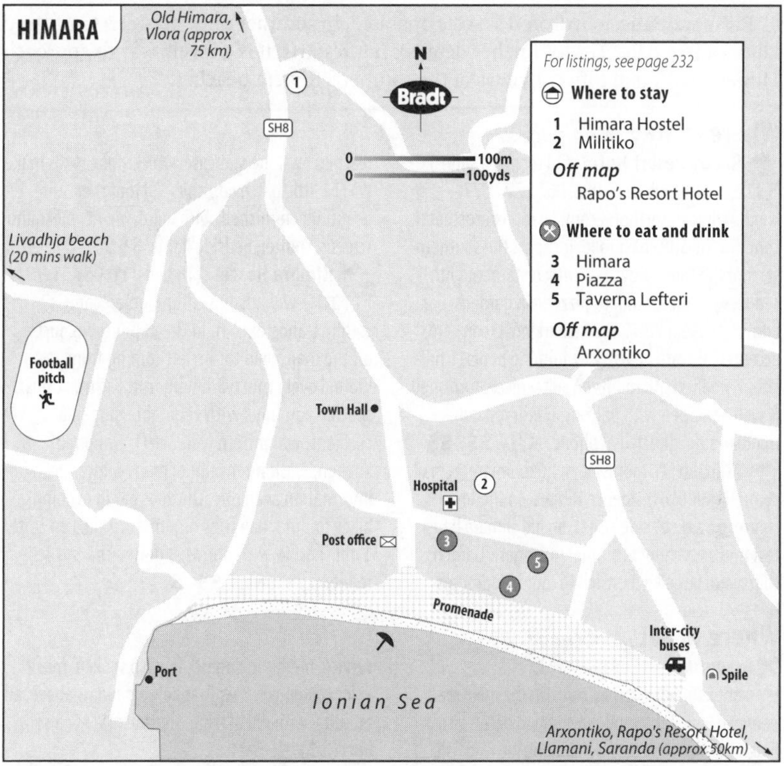

and the sea is crystalline. Quieter beaches nearby include Livadhja to the north, 25 minutes' walk beyond the football pitch, and Llamani, a beautiful cove 10 minutes' drive south.

Excavation in the cave of **Spile** (which means 'cave' in Greek, the mother tongue of most of the local people) revealed evidence of habitation in the Neolithic period. The cave is right next to the main road as it meets the promenade. The gate is locked; when there is someone there to open it, admission is 100 lek. **Old Himara**, above the modern town, is often referred to as 'Himara Castle' and, in the 5th–4th centuries BC, when Himara was part of Chaonia, it really was fortified. Procopius of Caesarea, in the 6th century AD, mentions it as one of the fortresses rebuilt by Justinian. It now has an astonishing number of churches in varying stages of dilapidation, some with beautiful frescoes. It is a pleasant and scenic walk of 30–45 minutes from Spile to Old Himara.

Getting there and away The road between Saranda and Vlora is asphalted and in good condition all the way. Himara is about 1½ hours from Saranda and about 2 hours from Vlora. See page 229 for details of public transport from Vlora and Saranda along the coast road. There is a daily bus to Himara from Tirana at 13.00. The journey time to or from Tirana has been cut by at least an hour, thanks to the new bypasses around the cities of Fieri and Vlora. There is also a daily departure from Tirana to Qeparoi, via Himara, at about midday and, in summer only, another at 17.00. Direct buses link Himara with Athens and other Greek cities.

Pre-pandemic, a hydrofoil service operated, in summer only, between Corfu and Himara (see page 214 for further details). If it restarts, it is a lovely way to approach Himara, with magnificent views of the southern Riviera beaches.

Where to stay *Map, page 231*

Rapo's Resort Hotel (48 rooms, 3 suites) 322857; m 069 89 73 986, 067 27 77 077; e info@raposresorthotel.com; w raposresorthotel.com. On the SH8 coast road, just past the southern start of the Himara bypass. Lifts; restaurant with sea-view terrace; outdoor pizzeria in gardens; bar. English spoken; Wi-Fi; secure parking; credit cards accepted. Private beach, 2 swimming pools (1 full-size, 1 smaller). All rooms en suite, nicely furnished & well equipped with balcony, hairdryer, iron, minibar, safe, direct-dial phone, AC, TV. **$$$$$**

Militiko (7 rooms) e militikohimare@gmail.com; f Militiko residence Himare. In the town centre, on a quiet side street; an old Himara house, restored by architect (& hotel manager). Garden, courtyard, large kitchen/living room; bedrooms reached by stone staircases; thick stone walls make Wi-Fi a little patchy upstairs. All rooms en suite, beautifully furnished, with hairdryer, AC, mosquito screens, shutter, bedside lights. **$$$**

Himara Hostel (18 beds) m 069 51 71 901; e wehadsomuchfun@gmail.com; w himarahostel.com. In the upper town, just off the main road to the left coming from Vlora. Lovely courtyard with fruit & citrus trees; spacious grounds with vegetable garden & chickens; water from well. Wi-Fi; equipped kitchen, washing machine; maps & local information available. Outdoor bar in evenings; bikes for hire; day trips organised. 2 dbls en suite; 1 dbl sharing with dorms; 3 dorms sharing 3 toilets & 2 showers. **$$–$**

Where to eat *Map, page 231*

Arxontiko m 069 83 97 183; e arxontikohimare@gmail.com. On the main road between Spile & Potami; sea-themed décor; also hotel. Excellent fish & seafood menu inc wild fish; good house wine; friendly, enthusiastic staff. **$$$$**

Piazza m 069 25 47 365, 067 39 18 997; e piazza_restaurant@hotmail.gr; f Restaurant Piazza. On the seafront promenade; tables outside on shaded terrace with sea view; nicely decorated indoors. Wide range of seafood dishes, pasta & pizza; huge portions; home-produced wine; good service, menus in English, English spoken, free Wi-Fi for customers. 3 well-appointed rooms above, all en suite, with dbl glazing, shutters, TV, AC; also 2 apts (**$$**). **$$$**

Taverna Lefteri On pedestrian street parallel to the promenade. Fish & seafood as well as grilled meat, pasta & traditional dishes such as *mish turli* (page 49). Informal atmosphere, good house wine. **$$$**

Himara On pedestrian street parallel to promenade. A good bakery, with the usual range of bread & buns, plus excellent *byrek*. **$**

THE NORTHERN RIVIERA North of Himara, the marvellous scenery continues, with dramatic mountains rising up from the coast and the deep blue sea shimmering in the sunlight. The road goes through the pretty villages of Vunoi and Dhërmiu; below them, and below the road, are lovely beaches, with fine, clean sand, transparent blue sea, plenty of accommodation and lively nightlife in the summer. Jala beach is 5km from the main road, just before the first houses in Vunoi; Dhërmiu beach, sometimes known by its Greek name, Dhrimadhes, is 1.5km from the road. Both beaches are clearly signposted and both roads are well surfaced. There is no public transport to the beaches; those travelling by bus should ask to be let off at 'Plazh' ('beach') and then walk, or try to hitchhike, down the hill.

A few kilometres beyond Dhërmiu, the road begins to climb towards the Llogoraja Pass. On the right, perched on the hillside, is the village of Palasa. To the left is Palasa beach, about 3.5km from the highway, which is now effectively privatised. The luxury villas with their sea views are a far cry from the wild shore where, in 48BC, Julius Caesar landed from Brundisium (now Brindisi), in pursuit of his rival Pompey (page 9). Caesar led his legions from here over the Llogoraja Pass to Oricum; you can follow in their footsteps, more or less, although the paths are not at all clear. It would be easier in reverse, from Llogoraja; see below.

Where to stay and eat There are many hotels and private rooms at both Jala and Dhërmiu beaches. Temporary **campsites** open during the summer at these and most other beaches on the Riviera; some are quite luxurious and offer the option of renting a furnished tent, rather than pitching your own. Many hotels and guesthouses on the Riviera beaches can be reserved through the usual international booking websites or the Tirana-based Albania Holidays (page 30). Out of season, many guesthouses and hotels close. In July and August, it is highly advisable to reserve accommodation in advance.

Shkolla Vuno (3 dorms) Vunoi; m 068 40 63 835; e tiranabackpacker@hotmail.com; w tiranahostel.com; ⌚ Jun–Sep. This backpackers' hostel is a repurposing of the old village school, which closed in 2011 due to the declining school-age population. Well-equipped kitchen; b/fast inc; tables, benches & hammocks in courtyard; outdoor showers with solar-heated water; toilet block; camping in olive grove. English spoken. Visitors can participate in activities to benefit the local community: clearing up litter, clearing paths, or repairing buildings. Hiking to Jala & Gjipe beaches or into mountains; kayaks available to rent. **$**

LLOGORAJA The hairpin bends ahead of Palasa lead to the Llogoraja Pass, over 1,000m above sea level. A tourist information kiosk and viewpoint are in a lay-by on the left as the road climbs above the beaches. To your right are the bare peaks of the Çika Mountains, 2,045m at their highest point, with pines and firs shrouding the hillside below them. To your left the cliffs drop almost sheer into the Ionian Sea, as wine-dark as it was when Odysseus sailed it. The whole area around the top of the pass – over 1,000ha – is designated as a national park. It is rich in wildlife (roe deer, foxes, squirrels, wild boar and wolves are common) and would make an excellent base for a few days' hiking. Hang-gliding from the clifftops out over the sea can be arranged (enquire at your hotel).

A short hike that requires no more than reasonable fitness and sensible shoes is to Caesar's Pass (Qafa e Çezarit), where Julius Caesar is thought to have led his legions over the mountains from their landing at Palasa. The (unmarked) path leads up from the right-hand side of the road, roughly opposite the Sofo hotel and restaurant. The walk through the pinewoods takes 20–30 minutes, before you emerge on to more open ground and a viewpoint, with stunning views of the tip of the Karaburuni Peninsula and the start of the Adriatic.

A good circular hike goes up to Qafa e Thellë ('the Deep Pass'), along the ridge to the phone masts, then down to the top of the pass. The path starts from an obvious point between the Iliria Restaurant and the Hotel Alpin; it has been paved and is generally in reasonable condition, although sensible footwear should obviously be worn. It is possible to hike over Qafa e Thellë to the start of the Karaburuni Peninsula and Caesar's landfall at Palasa, but the paths on the other side of the mountain are difficult and unclear; a local guide should be hired.

There is no public transport specifically to Llogoraja, but several buses a day run between Vlora and Himara, Qeparoi or Saranda; see page 229 for details. If you do not plan to stay overnight, you should ascertain on arrival the expected time of the last bus on which you can return or continue onward.

Where to stay and eat *Map, page 212*

There are several hotels within the national park, interspersed with restaurants all offering, in season, specialities of spit-roasted lamb and kid. Both hotels listed here have good restaurants.

Llogora Tourist Village (22 rooms, 3 suites, 16 chalets) 033 225 790; m 069 33 44 400; e info@llogora.com; w llogora.com. Set in over 1ha of beautiful grounds on the edge of the forest, with deer wandering freely. Restaurant with international menu & traditional dishes; bar, tennis court, indoor pool, gym, children's play area; babysitting service. Some English spoken; Wi-Fi in public areas. Guided treks, hang-gliding & jeep excursions can be arranged. Each chalet has 1 dbl & 1 twin bedroom, living room with TV, CH, fridge, bathroom with shower, furnished veranda angled away from the chalet next door. Hotel rooms all en suite with TV, CH, good-sized balcony, bedside lights. **$$$**

Hotel Alpin (20 rooms) m 069 20 55 936, 069 23 90 561; e info@hotelalpin-al.net. Helpful English-speaking management; hiking guides can be arranged; good restaurant, tables outside on large veranda in summer. All rooms en suite with satellite TV, CH, fridge; some have balcony with views over national park. **$$**

ORIKUMI *Telephone code: 0391*

The road emerges from the forests of Llogoraja into the different environment of the Adriatic coast. The Karaburuni Peninsula is where the Ionian and Adriatic seas divide. It forms a sheltering curve around the Bay of Vlora, creating a safe harbour that was first used in the 6th century BC: Oricum. The modern town of Orikumi, with its long pebble beach, is a popular holiday resort, especially with Albanian families. It has a health centre, ATMs, mobile phone agencies and a post office.

Getting there and away Orikumi is about 1km beyond the southern end of the Vlora bypass. The town's main street is the first left after the roundabout where the bypass diverges from the coast road; to get to the archaeological site or the beach, it is better to take the next left, then right at a roundabout with an anchor on it, continuing until you get to the sea.

By **public transport**, any Bregdet bus for Vlora will drop passengers off at the start of Orikumi's main street. Buses that use the bypass will drop passengers off at the roundabout where it begins, a few minutes' walk from the junction into the town. Buses run all year round between Vlora and Orikumi. In Orikumi they wait on the main road at the junction with the main street; the bus stop in Vlora is behind the university. The last bus for Vlora leaves Orikumi at 15.30 and leaves Vlora for Orikumi at 17.15. The journey takes about half an hour and the fare is 100 lek.

Where to stay and eat

California (15 rooms) Rr Pashaliman; m 068 54 27 504, 069 46 57 141 (WhatsApp), 068 54 27 504 (WhatsApp); e leftersadikaj@hotmail.com; f Hotel California orikum albania. Comfortable, nicely decorated hotel, set in extensive, tree-shaded grounds; run by an Albanian-Canadian family. Riverside arbour; swimming spot with small beach; terrace restaurant surrounded with olive trees. Ample free, secure parking; reliable Wi-Fi throughout. Closed in winter. Rooms of varying sizes, all en suite with AC, TV; most have balcony with mountain/river views. **$$**

Argeli (31 rooms) Rr Pashaliman; 22205; m 069 72 66 630; e hotelargeli2020@gmail.com; f hotel Argeli Orikum Vlore Albania. At the bridge into Orikumi on the coast road from Vlora; usually open all year round, but in winter best to phone ahead to confirm. Bar; secure parking; children's play area; restaurant/pizzeria in summer. Wi-Fi rather unreliable in rooms. All rooms en suite; all have balcony with drying rack; AC, TV, fridge. **$**

Te Poli Just beyond the bridge as you enter Orikumi from Vlora, it offers a wide range of fish & seafood, including some wild varieties. Closed in winter. Some English spoken. **$$$**

Veip Isaraj year-round. Just off the main street in Orikumi, it serves fresh grilled fish, generous salads & traditional dishes such as pilaf. Some English spoken. $$$

What to see and do At the far end of Orikumi's beach, where the Karaburuni Peninsula begins to curl up to the north, is an active naval base and, within it, the archaeological site of **Oricum**. This ancient city was founded in the 6th century BC by colonists from the Greek island of Euboea. It developed into an important trading post thanks to its geographical position and excellent harbour, protected by the peninsula that the Greeks called Acroceraunia ('the thunder-riven heights') and the Ottomans named Karaburun ('the black cape'). By the 3rd century BC, Oricum was minting its own coins. Philip V of Macedon occupied it for a while during the First Macedonian War (214–205BC); later, during the Roman Civil War, it quickly surrendered to Julius Caesar after he landed with his troops at Palasa, on the other side of the Llogoraja Pass (page 232).

Oricum was first excavated in the 1950s, but systematic research has been conducted there over the last decade or so, led by the Albanian Institute of Archaeology and the University of Geneva. The city's best-known monument is an ornamental fountain, or **nymphaeum**, built into the hillside and facing the sea. Until it was re-excavated in 2014, this had been identified as a small ceremonial theatre. The modern excavations have revealed part of the avenue that led from the city's northern gate to the nymphaeum and beyond. The Albanian and Swiss archaeologists have identified three distinct phases of construction of this gate – Hellenistic, late antique and medieval – and part of the city walls, which extend a further 30m underwater. Above the nymphaeum, a beautiful flight of rock-cut steps, complete with a water-channel carved into the rock to supply the fountain, leads up to the acropolis. Two medieval houses have been excavated there. Three deep wells have also been discovered, although there is no longer any water in them.

Although it is in a military area, the archaeological site is open to the public (200 lek). You should carry your passport or ID card to show the guards at the gate. There are helpful information panels at various points around the site. In summer, a guide is usually on duty within the site from about 09.00 until about lunchtime on weekdays.

The last stretch of beach is on a spit of land separating the sea from a marshy, reeded area called the **Pashaliman Lagoon**. Pashaliman was the name the Ottomans gave to the ancient harbour – 'a harbour so good it is worthy of a Pasha' – and the naval base also retains this name. The lagoon is an important site for waterfowl and other birds, especially the cattle egret (*Bubulcus ibis*). These attractive herons can even be spotted from the coast road to Vlora, helpfully grooming the cows in fields by the roadside. The reed beds are also home to warblers, pygmy cormorants and marsh harriers. An information panel at the beach, at the junction with the road from the centre of Orikumi, gives more information about the species that can be observed there.

On the edge of the marshland, the 12th-century **church of Marmiroi** perches on a hillock. Three lovely frescoes survive within: a Virgin with Child, John the Evangelist and (somewhat restored) St Michael. Its high cupola can be seen from far off, but it is a little tricky to get to because of the reed beds that surround it. There is a footpath from the western edge of the town – cross the irrigation canal and follow the path around the reed beds until you come to a solid path through the reeds. Alternatively, a rough vehicle track leads off from the beachfront just before the entrance to the naval base; it does not go all the way to the church, so you will need to find your own way around the reed beds to the solid path.

With the completion of the Vlora bypass, expected by summer 2022, the coast road along the Bay of Vlora will be used mainly for tourism purposes. A string of hotels lines it, starting in **Rradhima**, with its long pebble beach thronged with sun-loungers in peak season. Rradhima's roadside restaurants – Labëria and Portokalli – offer traditional southern Albanian dishes, including spit-roasted lamb or kid in season. The fish market at the little harbour will grill fish on the spot for customers to enjoy at one of the tables set out nearby or to take away to eat at their holiday apartment. Boats leave from this harbour on day trips to Karaburuni (page 246). The tourist information kiosk near the harbour (🕘 summer only) can provide details about these and other sightseeing options in the vicinity. The old village of Rradhima, high above the beach resort and also accessible from the bypass, offers magnificent views of the bay, Karaburuni and Sazani.

TRAGJASI In the low hills above Orikumi is the village of Tragjasi. Cooler than the seaside, it is popular in summer with Albanian holidaymakers and becomes very lively, with performances by well-known Albanian singers and bands.

Getting there and away There are two routes to Tragjasi from Orikumi. One is to return to the Vlora bypass and follow it for about 1km to another roundabout. The other is to leave Orikumi by the bridge over the River Izvori, then take the first right which leads to the same roundabout. Tragjasi is signposted and the start of the village can be seen from this roundabout.

By public transport, there are rural **buses** to Tragjasi from Vlora, via Orikumi, at noon and 16.30; they leave Tragjasi for Vlora at 07.00, 07.30 and 14.30. The fare from Vlora to Tragjasi is 150 lek. Alternatively, a taxi from Orikumi should cost no more than 300 lek.

Where to stay and eat

Grand Hotel Tragjasi (21 rooms) m 069 72 12 905, 069 64 34 802; e hoteltragjasi@hotmail.com; f Hotel Hotel Tragjasi; 🕘 Jun–Sep. In the main village square (free parking), with the river running through landscaped grounds. English spoken, good Wi-Fi throughout. Good restaurant ($$$) with traditional & Italian menu; outside tables arranged on riverside are shaded by trees; live music in summer. Spacious rooms, all with generously sized, well-equipped en suite, good-sized balcony, TV, AC; generous b/fast inc. **$$**

Beni Tragjasi. Grilled meat & salads all year round, spit-roasted lamb & traditional dishes in summer. Covered terrace, also tables in the park across road. $$

Te Rrapi i Izvorit Tragjasi. Tables outside, in summer, in idyllic setting under the eponymous plane tree (*rrapi*), beside one of the springs that feeds the River Izvori; also sizeable indoor restaurant, open at weekends off-season. Home-cooked traditional specialities including free-range chicken, fresh dairy produce, homemade bread & *byrek*, huge salads. $$

What to see and do The atmospheric ruins of **Tragjasi i Vjetër** ('Old Tragjasi') are higher up than the modern village, about 300m above sea level. It is thought to date from the 14th or 15th century and to have been burned and rebuilt three times during the Ottoman period. It was then burned down twice more during World War II: in 1939 by the Italians, and in 1942 by the Germans. War-weary and impoverished, rather than rebuilding again, the villagers moved downhill, closer to their fields, and built new homes to create the modern village. Old Tragjasi was abandoned. The road to it is not asphalted, but it can be tackled in any reasonably sturdy car as far as the cemetery, still in use by the modern villagers. The old village can be seen from here, on its hilltop, but is separated from the cemetery by a riverbed (dry in summer) which is crossable only by 4x4. From the river it is a fairly steep climb up to the ruined houses. It takes about three hours to walk there from the modern village.

The **Castle of Gjon Boçari**, although signposted from the junction with the main road, cannot be visited at the time of writing. The site is fenced off and a locked gate blocks the path that leads to it.

VLORA *Telephone code: 033*

Vlora has a long history, but its main claim to fame is as the place where Albanian independence was proclaimed in 1912. The city has three very different museums and is a good base for several interesting excursions. It sits towards the north of the Bay of Vlora, with beautiful views of the Karaburuni Peninsula and the island of Sazani, which together close the bay off to the west. Vlora's geographical position – roughly midway between Tirana and Saranda, and only 75km from Italy – makes it a convenient entry point into Albania.

Then known as Aulon, the town existed in antiquity – the Roman poet Martial, who wrote in the late 1st and early 2nd centuries AD, refers to it (in Epigram XIII. CXXV) as producing fine wool and wine; true to form, he says he'd rather have the wine. By the 4th century AD it is mentioned frequently as a landing port from the Italian ports of Otranto and Brindisi and, especially, as a stopping-off point on the road between Apollonia and Butrint. During the reign of the Emperor Justinian (AD527–65), it was one of the eight largest cities in the province of New Epirus and was the seat of a bishopric. It was taken by the Normans in 1081 and went on to suffer the same fate as Albania's other coastal cities, changing hands several times over the centuries. Vlora has always been a particularly attractive prize, because Sazani Island, in the Bay of Vlora, controls maritime access to the Adriatic.

It was the first Adriatic port to fall to the Ottomans, in 1417. Ali Pasha Tepelena (see box, page 218) took it in 1810 and held it until he was captured and killed in 1822. On 28 November 1912, delegates from all over Albania met in Vlora and declared their country's independence from the Ottoman Empire. Unfortunately for the provisional government and its prime minister, Ismail Qemali, achieving independence was not quite as simple a matter as announcing it. Vlora and – of course – Sazani were occupied by Italy in 1914, and it was 1920 before the Italians could be dislodged. Indeed, Albania's sovereignty over Sazani was not wholly secure until after World War II.

Vlora's recent past has been equally turbulent. In March 1991, while most of the world was concentrating on the Gulf War, 20,000 or so young Albanians commandeered ships in the harbours of Vlora and Durrësi and took them to Brindisi. In February 1997, riots in Vlora against failed pyramid-saving schemes developed into a civil uprising that engulfed the whole country and destabilised it for many months. At the same time, Vlora's proximity to southern Italy made it a natural base for Mafia-type operations, and it became the centre of an international network of clandestine emigration and the trafficking of women. For a few years, until a clampdown in 2002, it was effectively under the control of armed gangs. Vlora and the surrounding beaches are now safe and visitors need have no special concerns.

GETTING THERE AND AWAY

By sea Car ferries run daily between Vlora and the Italian port of Brindisi throughout the year, excluding Sundays in low season. They leave Brindisi at around 23.30 every night and dock in Vlora at about 07.00 the following morning. The return journey to

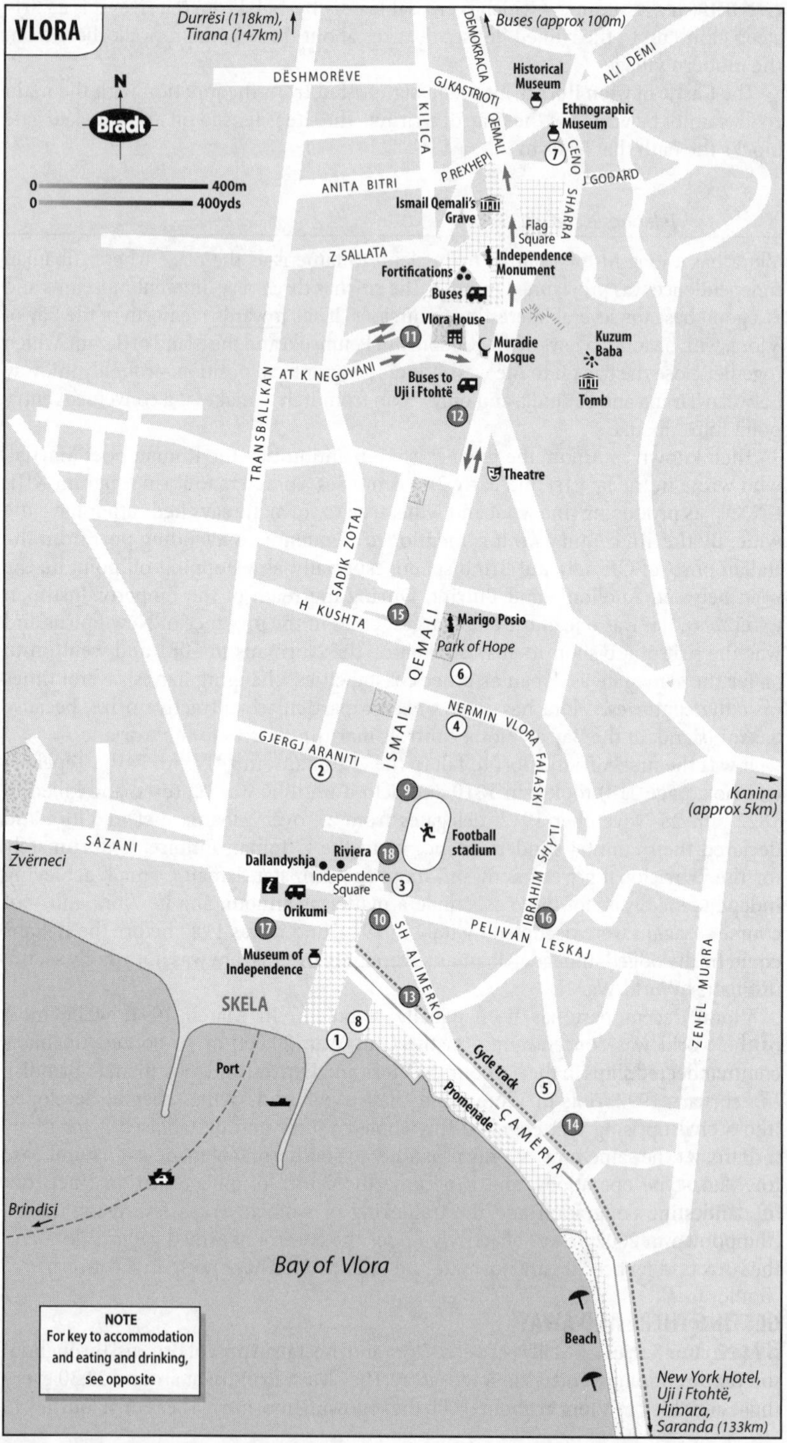

VLORA
Durrësi (118km), Tirana (147km)
Buses (approx 100m)
N
Bradt
0 400m
0 400yds
DËSHMORËVE
GJ KASTRIOTI
DEMOKRACIA
J KILICA
QEMALI
Historical Museum
ALI DEMI
Ethnographic Museum
CENO
7
P REXHEPI
J GODARD
ANITA BITRI
Ismail Qemali's Grave
SHARRA
Flag Square
Z SALLATA
Independence Monument
Fortifications
Buses
Vlora House
11
Muradie Mosque
Kuzum Baba
Tomb
AT K NEGOVANI
Buses to Uji i Ftohtë
12
Theatre
TRANSBALLKAN
SADIK ZOTAJ
H KUSHTA
15
Marigo Posio
Park of Hope
6
ISMAIL QEMALI
NERMIN VLORA
4
FALASKI
GJERGJ ARANITI
2
9
Kanina (approx 5km)
Football stadium
SAZANI
Zvërneci
Riviera
18
Dallandyshja
Independence Square
3
IBRAHIM SHYTI
16
Orikumi
10
17
PELIVAN LESKAJ
Museum of Independence
SH ALIMERKO
ZENEL MURRA
SKELA
13
8
1
Port
Cycle track
5
Promenade
14
ÇAMËRIA
Brindisi
Bay of Vlora
NOTE
For key to accommodation and eating and drinking, see opposite
Beach
New York Hotel, Uji i Ftohtë, Himara, Saranda (133km)

VLORA
For listings, see from page 240

Where to stay

1 Bologna
2 Martini
3 Partner
4 Riviera
5 Studio Vlora Apartments
6 Tozo
7 Vlora
8 Vlora International

Off map

New York

Where to eat and drink

9 Bold Bistro
10 Çamëria
11 Holiday
12 Kristal
13 Novus
14 Pastificio Elidoni
15 Rimini
16 Salvadore
17 San Giorgio al Porto
18 Tre Forchette

Brindisi is faster; the ferries leave Vlora at around 13.00 and arrive at about 18.30. A range of cabin accommodation is available. The one-way passenger fare in deck class ranges from €50 in low season to €70 in high season, plus embarkation taxes; return fares booked at the same time are reduced. Fares, schedules and online bookings are available on the Italian ferry website w traghetti.it.

By land There are frequent buses to and from **Tirana**, from early in the morning until the afternoon. The last Tirana bus leaves Vlora at 16.00. In Tirana, they leave from the North/South bus station; in Vlora, small inter-city buses to Tirana leave from the side of Flag Square. The fare is 500 lek and the journey takes about 2½ hours. There are also buses to and from all other major towns in southern and central Albania, until at least early afternoon. Hermes Travel operates a minibus service between Vlora and Tirana Airport. The fare is 1,000 lek each way; the last departure from Vlora (Flag Square) is at 14.30. Contact details are at w hermesaeroport.com. Full-size inter-city buses arrive at and leave from a rather disorganised terminus on Rruga Demokracia, a long way from the city centre.

The road between Vlora and **Saranda** is one of Albania's scenic highlights, over the Llogoraja Pass and along the Riviera. Buses to Saranda leave Vlora at 06.45 and 08.30 every day – see page 229 for details of buses in the other direction. There are also buses from Vlora to Himara and other towns on the Riviera. With the completion of the Vlora bypass in 2022, buses beween the Riviera will no longer reliably pass through Vlora city centre.

Buses and minibuses ply frequently along the coast of the Bay of Vlora to Orikumi. The bus stop is behind the university building, across the road from the Riviera shopping centre.

GETTING AROUND Vlora is a large city, and the distances between the sights in the centre, the port and the beaches are too great for all but the most enthusiastic walker. There are several taxi ranks around the city; one is at Independence Square, where the promenade meets the Boulevard. Bikes can be hired near here (150 lek/hr).

Urban buses are frequent, with a flat fare of 30 lek. The most useful route for the visitor is the 'Uji i Ftohtë' bus; Uji i Ftohtë is how Albanians refer to a spring of drinking water and, in Vlora's case, this is a fountain with carved stone lions, at the point where the coast road divides into two one-way routes. The Uji i Ftohtë bus starts and terminates here, runs along the city beach (Plazhi i Ri), then the Boulevard all the way to the Muradi Mosque, and onwards to a stop near the main inter-city bus terminus. The bus stops along the coast road are very obvious, with illuminated screens and space for the buses to pull in, but quite a long distance apart; on Boulevard Ismail Qemali, the stops are more frequent but less well indicated. The buses on this route can get very crowded in high summer.

TOURIST INFORMATION A tourist information kiosk (🕘 summer only) is located near Independence Square (Sheshi Pavarësia), behind the university. The staff do not seem to be particularly knowledgeable or to speak especially good English, but they may be more helpful on matters such as car hire or hotel reservations. Any travel agency in Vlora (eg: Dallandyshja Travel, in the Riviera shopping centre; ☎ 222 222; m 068 20 05 319) can provide timetable information about, and tickets for, all ferry departures, from Saranda and Durrësi as well as from Vlora. See page 247 for information about boat trips to the Karaburuni Peninsula.

The website of the Municipality of Vlora (w vlora.gov.al or bashkiavlore.org) has extensive information, although only in Albanian, about things to do and places to visit in the area.

WHERE TO STAY *Map, page 238*

Choosing where to stay in Vlora really comes down to what you want to do while you are there. The hotels in the city centre are handy for museums and public transport; those at the seaside often have lovely views over the Bay of Vlora and the Karaburuni Peninsula. The city beach is fringed with a wide, tree-lined promenade, with many hotels all along it. Those with their own transport might prefer to head further down the coast to one of the many hotels that line the Bay of Vlora. Reductions in room rates can often be negotiated outside the peak tourist season of July and August.

City

Partner (57 rooms) Rr Pelivan Leskaj; ☎ 408 282; m 069 40 78 108; e reservation@hotelpartner.al; w hotelpartner.al. English spoken; lift; restaurant; bar; spa; Wi-Fi. Business facilities; laundry service; car hire; parking; safe at reception. Good-sized rooms, all with large en-suite bathroom, some with bathtub; good lighting, hairdryer, AC, flatscreen TV, bedside lights, thick curtains, fridge. Some rooms have sea view. B/fast inc. **$$$**

Martini (20 rooms) Rr Gjergj Araniti; ☎ 224 017; m 069 20 83 049, 069 20 38 877; e hotel_martini@hotmail.com; f hotelmartinivlore. English spoken; good Wi-Fi throughout; nicely decorated with original art. Free parking; friendly, helpful management. All rooms en suite with AC, TV with good range of channels inc BBC World), fridge, bedside lights; most have balcony. Generous b/fast inc. **$$**

Riviera (14 rooms) Rr Nermin Vlora, pranë Shkollës Industriale; ☎ 408 212; m 069 38 96 622, 069 62 25 202; e hotel.riviera@yahoo.com. Restaurant; some English spoken at reception. All rooms en suite with twin beds, AC, TV. **$$**

Tozo (15 rooms) Bd Ismail Qemali; ☎ 223 819; m 069 85 67 520; f Hotel Tozo Vlore. Set back from boulevard behind the little Park of Hope. Restaurant, terrace bar; parking; Wi-Fi; professional management. All rooms en suite with AC, TV, good curtains; some have balcony. **$$**

Vlora (15 rooms) Rr Justin Godard; m 069 33 43 947. Restaurant, comfortable 1st-floor bar with large terrace overlooking Independence Monument; lift; some English spoken. Convenient for museums & bus terminus. Good-sized rooms, all en suite with LCD TV, AC, Wi-Fi, balcony, fridge. **$$**

Seaside

Bologna (40 rooms) Pranë Portit Detar (next to seaport); ☎ 409 600; m 069 73 02 897; e hbvlora@gmail.com; f BolognaHotel. Contemporary boutique hotel in fabulous setting right next to the port, at the end of the promenade; large terrace bar & good restaurant overlooking sea; stylish reception area (good English spoken); parking; conference room; lift; Wi-Fi. Generously proportioned, beautifully designed rooms, all with nice en-suite bathroom, AC, flatscreen TV, minibar & balcony; most have great views across the Bay of Vlora. Cooked b/fast inc. **$$$**

New York (85 rooms) Rr Aleksandër Moisiu; ☎ 406 648/9; m 068 40 13 306, 069 21 71 363; e info@hotelnewyork.al; f Hotel New York-Vlore. Just before the tunnel on coast road. Professional, helpful staff; good English spoken at reception. Restaurant with sea view; outdoor pool, poolside pizzeria & BBQ (summer only); popular bar with terrace; business centre, conference facilities. Wi-Fi throughout; lift; laundry service; free secure parking. Garden, children's play area, terrace. Most rooms have balcony, many have magnificent sea views. All rooms en suite with AC, safe, flatscreen TV, minibar, desk, drying rack for beachwear. **$$$**

Vlora International (60 rooms, 6 suites, 6 apts) Sh Isa Boletini; 424 408; m 069 20 90 838; e hotel@vlora-international.com; w vlora-international.com. English spoken. Wi-Fi, parking, restaurant, bars, terrace; lift, conference rooms, business facilities. Indoor pool, hot tub, spa. Good-sized rooms, some with balcony, all have good-sized en-suite bathroom, AC, LCD TV, safe, phone, fridge, bedside lights. **$$$**

Studio Vlora Apartments (3 rooms) Rr Shaban Demiraj; m069 77 09 255; summer only. Each studio has a fully equipped kitchen with table & chairs, washing machine, cleaning materials; en-suite shower room, TV, AC; small shared balcony with washing lines.**$**

WHERE TO EAT *Map, page 238*

In addition to the listings here, the restaurants in the upmarket hotels are open to non-residents. Along the seafront promenade, apart from the hotel restaurants, there are many pizzerias and grills.

Salvadore Rr Pelivan Leskaj; 408 808; m 069 87 51 441; noon–16.00 & 19.00–late. Restaurant attached to fish wholesalers; you choose your fish or seafood from the ice boxes on display, priced by the kg, then enjoy a starter or aperitif at your table while your fish is cooked to order (small preparation charge added to displayed price). Seafood pasta or risotto can also be prepared. Some English spoken. Smoking ban not enforced. Also has 10 hotel rooms. $$$$

San Giorgio al Porto Lagja Pavarësia; 403 422. In a basement, across street from university. Formal dining; service can be slow. Good range of seafood & fish (some wild), fresh pasta, proper Italian risotto, interesting salads & vegetables; Italian wine list. $$$$

Tre Forchette Bd Ismail Qemali; m 067 50 03 333. Just off the Boulevard (look for the logo of the eponymous 3 forks). Formal dining, professional service; tables also on covered terrace. Very interesting Italian-inspired menu: homemade pasta, arancini, carpaccio, fresh fish & shellfish, steaks & other meat dishes. $$$$

Holiday On the corner opposite mosque & Eqërem Bey Vlora house. Tables outside in nice sheltered gardens; grilled meat, pizzas & salads. A lovely spot for coffee or beer; very convenient for inter-city bus terminus. $$$

Novus Off Rr Çamëria (behind the little square at the city end of promenade). Traditional Albanian & Italian-inspired dishes; traditional desserts; good house wine. Casual, friendly ambience, illustrated menu, good value. $$$

Pastificio Elidoni Rr Shaban Demiraj, just off Rr Çamëria; m 069 25 18 887. Excellent homemade pasta, ravioli, gnocchi, imaginative salads. Friendly service, good value. $$$

Rimini Rr Hasan Kushta. Good pizzas, huge salads, also some pasta options; friendly staff. $$$

Bold Bistro Bd Ismail Qemali; w boldbistro.al. Good choice of b/fast deals; range of BioTea herbal teas. Covered terrace, heated in winter; impeccable toilets. $$

Çamëria Off Rr Pelivan Leskaj. Simple & friendly; traditional dishes (pilaf, *paçe koke*, liver), grilled meat; some English spoken. Very good value. $$

Kristal Bd Ismail Qemali. Self-service buffet; traditional meals such as *pastiço* & pilaf, also pizzas & sandwiches. Tables inside & out; friendly staff. $$

WHAT TO SEE AND DO

Museum of Independence (Muzeu Pavarësia; Rr Ismail Qemali, Skela; 08.00–11.00, 17.00–22.00 Mon–Sat; 18.00–22.00 Sun; 200 lek) When the First Balkan War started in October 1912, the Albanians realised that, if they did not obtain independence from the Ottoman Empire, their territory would be swallowed up by their Balkan neighbours. Ismail Qemali (1844–1919), one of 26 Albanians elected to the Ottoman parliament after the Young Turk revolution of 1908, travelled to Vienna and Budapest to obtain diplomatic support for Albanian independence.

On his return to Durrësi, he found that Serbian troops were approaching the Adriatic, and he made his way across the treacherous marshes (long since drained) of the Myzeqeja Plain to the relative safety of Vlora. It was thus that on 28 November 1912, Albanian independence was proclaimed in Vlora and Skanderbeg's ancient emblem, the double-headed black eagle, was raised at the spot that is now called Flag Square (Sheshi i Flamurit). Albania's first government, led by Ismail Qemali, set up its headquarters in the only building available, the quarantine hospital in the port. This modestly sized villa is now the Museum of Independence.

The most interesting thing about the museum, for the majority of non-Albanians, is that several of the rooms have been kept as they were when they were used by those first ministers. Ismail Qemali's chair is still there behind his desk, and his bookcase still has books in it. On the long table in the Cabinet Room is the pen with which official documents were signed, and next to it, the government seal with its double-headed eagle symbol. Photographs of each of the first ministers hang on the wall; there are many other interesting photographs and paintings on display throughout the museum.

Ethnographic Museum (Rr Ceno Sharra; m 069 54 36 974; ⌚ 09.00–16.00 Tue–Sat, 09.00–14.00 Sun; 100 lek) The Ethnographic Museum in Vlora is located in the house where, in 1908, the Labëria Patriotic Club was set up. Towards the end of the 19th century, after the crushing of the Prizren League, the Albanian nationalist movement switched its focus from political demands to cultural campaigning. 'Patriotic clubs' were set up in towns around Albania and in other Ottoman cities with a significant Albanian population, including Istanbul itself, where it was called the 'Albanian Committee'. The Labëria Patriotic Club was named after the region of which Vlora is the main town. It provided evening classes to people who wanted to learn how to read and write in Albanian, their mother tongue – no fewer than 50 Vloran women registered for these classes, and the head-teacher was Marigo Posio (page 246).

The signs to the museum refer to it in English as 'House of Labëria Club'. However, the collection on display mainly consists of ethnographic objects and traditional costumes. The first room on the ground floor contains household items such as wooden milk-churns and copper trays. The room on its left is devoted to agriculture; in addition to examples of agricultural implements, including a tobacco-cutting machine, it has a meticulous scale model of a farmstead, showing the separate buildings for family and guests, little models of livestock, and even tiny hanks of tobacco drying under the eaves.

The room on the right acknowledges Vlora's role as a fishing town. The centrepiece is a boat carved about 30 years ago from a single tree trunk, an ancient technique that was still in use until very recently. Larger versions of the nets on display are still used – the circular net is cast from the boat over a shoal, and the fishermen move the mast up and down to lure the fish into the centre of the net, so that as many as possible are trapped before they pull it in. The long trap and the multi-pronged fork hung on the walls are used to catch eels in the lagoons of Narta and Pashaliman; the eel trap has two layers of mesh and, as the eel swims in, the pressure of its head tightens the inner layer so that it cannot escape. Of course these ingenious techniques are rather bad news for eels and fish, but they are a lot better than dynamite, which in the 1990s replaced traditional fishing methods along much of the Albanian coast.

Upstairs, the 'men's room' of the house was where (male) guests were entertained, and some of the original furniture can be seen there, including a tray for serving raki and a *sofër* – a low, circular dining table – inscribed with the owner's name in the Greek alphabet and the date 1896. Guests sat in order of age on the cushioned seats around the walls; the host sat on the left of the fireplace and his most distant relative sat on its right.

The 'women's room', across the hallway, has some interesting examples of traditional Vloran costumes – as women grew older, they wore darker and darker shades of cloth – and dowry chests. The old tradition was that every bride had an Albanian flag and an embroidery of Skanderbeg (page 136) in her dowry chest, and some of these are exhibited, too. Finally, the 'workroom' has as its centrepiece a genuine loom, with examples of traditional carpets and *qilime* (rugs).

Historical Museum (Rr Perlat Rexhepi; ⌚ 09.00–16.00 Tue–Sat, 09.00–14.00 Sun; 100 lek) Located in what was once Vlora's town hall, the Historical Museum is a good place to find out about the archaeology and history of the whole area.

On the left of the entrance is the museum's collection of Neolithic and Bronze Age artefacts. Maps and photographs on the walls explain the most significant sites for each period. There are finds from the Bronze Age tumulus at Vajza and from the ancient city of Amantia (see box, page 244). Amphorae and other items retrieved from recent underwater excavations are also displayed in this room. The city of Vlora has seen little excavation, because it has been continuously inhabited throughout its history, but fragments of Roman artefacts are constantly unearthed whenever a building contractor or utility company digs more than a couple of metres down. Some of these casual finds are displayed in a case near the door.

Across the hallway, the second room has scale models of traditional houses and of the 12th-century church of Marmiroi (page 235), bells from Venetian clock towers, and inscriptions from mosques, churches and – rare in Albania – a Jewish gravestone inscribed in Hebrew. Vlora's status as a major trading centre meant that it had a large Jewish population during the Ottoman period, but few traces of this thriving community have survived. A lovely, though headless, statue of Artemis/Diana, goddess of the hunt, with her dog by her side, was excavated by Luigi Ugolini, the Italian who led the first excavations of Butrint. Recent acquisitions have come to the museum from the Vlora family, descendants of wealthy 19th-century landowners whose best-known scion was the politician and writer Eqërem Bey Vlora (1885–1964). When the family was renovating its ancestral property in the city – the beautiful house which can be seen, through its gates, between the Muradie Mosque and the Independence Monument – they donated a number of pieces to the Historical Museum. These include a Roman head of Dionysus and a 19th-century marble carving of a child's head.

Exploring Vlora Like most of Albania, Vlora has experienced a lot of new building in the past 25 years, and viewing the city from above is a good way to make sense of its geography. **Kuzum Baba** was a Bektashi cleric, whose *tyrbe* (tomb) is on the summit of the hill above the Muradie Mosque. Steps from Boulevard Ismail Qemali, across the road from the mosque, lead to a statue of Dede Ahmed Myftar, who was the leader of the world Bektashi community from 1947–80. You can continue from here on foot to the top of the hill, where the Bektashis' regional headquarters is housed, in an attractive yellow and green building set in peaceful gardens. Outside, a paved ramp leads to Kuzum Baba's tyrbe, with a shrine beside it full of lit candles. The large terrace of the restaurant here (or, if you are feeling brave,

AMANTIA *Carolyn Perry*

Visiting the remote and evocative site of Amantia is much easier now that the road from Vlora has been resurfaced. The ancient city has been identified with a site near the modern village of Ploça, on the top of a long limestone ridge. The settlement of Amantia is a huge site, and though there are not many standing remains, it is fascinating to visit all that is left of an important walled hilltop settlement with a sanctuary area, a stadium and a number of monumental tombs.

The city, seat of the Amantes tribe, was located in a strategic position overlooking two important routes along river valleys – the Vjosa (ancient Aoos) and the Shushica (ancient Polyanthos) – connecting the interior with the coast in the borderlands of Illyrian and Epirote territory. Ancient sources refer to Amantia variously as an Illyrian city and a Greek colony. Archaeologists have found some evidence for settlement in the Archaic period, but the majority of the remains that can be seen today are from the 4th to 3rd centuries BC, when the settlement became urbanised.

The archaeological site is in two parts: the road leads to the ticket office and car park, situated below the summit of the ridge and next to the stadium. Though the **stadium** has been robbed of many of its stone seats, one end is very well preserved, with 17 banks of seating on the west side and eight on the east. Steps allowing access to the upper rows of seats can be made out at intervals. Originally about 60m long, the stadium has been dated by inscriptions to around 300BC. The remains of monumental stone tombs near the east end of the stadium indicate the importance of this public area.

Returning to the ticket office, the road continues up the hill to the **settlement**, which is 621m above sea level. Some sections of the ancient wall are visible on the way. The wall, of conglomerate ashlar blocks, enclosed the top of the ridge in a circuit of some 2,200m punctuated with gates, towers and indented traces. Some parts of the hilltop may have been fortified in the 5th century BC, but the main period of construction seems to be the 4th century BC, with some repairs carried out under Justinian in the 6th century AD. There is a working farm within the walls,

its roof) offers the best viewpoint, over the whole city and beyond, to Karaburuni, Sazani, Zvërneci and Narta. It is also possible to drive up to the restaurant from the other side of the hill.

The building where the flag was first raised was badly damaged while the city was being bombarded by Greece in December 1912, and it was knocked down in 1932. The area cleared by this demolition has been kept as a large open space and is called Flag Square. Dominating the square is the **Independence Monument**, an imposing bronze cast in the Socialist Realist style. Around its base stand various key figures in the independence movement, including Ismail Qemali and the Kosovar hero Isa Boletini; above them, on a rock, a flag-bearer makes ready to hoist the double-headed eagle of Albania. Vlora's football team is called Flamurtari ('the Flag-bearer') in honour of the anonymous patriot who first raised the flag of independence. Beside the monument, near where the demolished house once stood, the Albanian flag flies from a small column. Ismail Qemali himself is buried, beneath a Socialist Realist statue of a warrior, in the park behind this column.

The beautiful 19th-century house across the street from the Independence Monument is the property of the Vlora family. On the other side of Flag Square, a couple of streets – Rruga Justin Godard and Rruga Ceno Sharra, where the but someone will lead you through the animal pens to the famous arched gate in the southeast section of the wall. As you walk, look out for flattened areas hewn in the rock as platforms for rooms, also rock-cut steps and a couple of cisterns.

Retrace your steps and walk to the northwest part of the site to see the remains of the foundation platform of the **Temple of Aphrodite**. They are best viewed from above as it is quite a steep climb down the hill. Outside and below the city walls, the temple would have been beautifully situated with views over the valley. The temple, of the Doric order, was identified as dedicated to Aphrodite by an inscription recording repairs. Adjacent are the remains of an early Christian **basilica** of the 5th/6th century AD, seemingly built on top of another temple. Amantia was the seat of a bishop from at least the mid 4th century, but by the end of the 6th century, the city was in decline and the bishopric was transferred.

On the way to the site, you will pass the monument of **Drashovica** on your left. This impressive Socialist Realist monument, by Mumtaz Dhrami, commemorates two Albanian victories: the liberation of Vlora from the Italians in 1920, and over the Germans in October 1943 following a prolonged engagement. Around 7,000 Italian prisoners of war, who had been imprisoned in barracks in Mavrova and Drashovica, were freed following the Albanian action, during which the Germans suffered heavy losses.

PRACTICAL INFORMATION To reach Amantia, take the SH76 from Vlora along the course of the River Shushica, following signs towards Mavrova, and continue until just beyond the village of Vajza. Amantia is signposted off the main road and is visible to the left, on the long limestone ridge. Admission costs 300 lek. The road is asphalted all the way to the site. There is no public transport.

As you come out of Vajza, you will see **Taverna Shpella** on your right. This is the last chance for refreshments and a bathroom stop, as there are no facilities on site at the time of writing.

Ethnographic Museum is – have been repaved with stone setts and the houses repaired and restored. This is pretty much the only part of Vlora where its 19th-century architecture can be appreciated.

At the southern end of the park is a short stretch of **wall**, whose foundations may date back to the 4th century AD, with 6th-century additions in brickwork. These ancient fortifications were rebuilt and extended in the 16th century, with eight towers forming an octagon. This refortification was one element of major building work in Vlora ordered by Suleiman I, the Magnificent (ruled 1520–66), to secure Ottoman trade to and from the port. Exiting the park by the side street which runs between the Holiday restaurant and the Vlora family's house will bring you to another building project of the same time: the beautifully proportioned Muradie Mosque, with its elegant minaret of carved stone. It is said to have been designed by the great architect Sinan (1489–1588). He built mosques, bathhouses, bridges and *hans* (inns) throughout the empire, and is considered to be one of the founders of Ottoman architecture. The minimalist decoration within consists of elegant plasterwork fluting and Koranic calligraphy on the ceiling dome.

If you continue down the main road, towards the port, you will pass the theatre. A hundred metres or so further, in a small park (the Park of Hope) on the same side of the street, is an attractive bust of **Marigo Posio**. She was born in 1878 and brought up in Korça, where she married and became involved in the nationalist movement. She and her husband attracted the attention of the Ottoman authorities, and moved to Vlora to shake them off. When the local Patriotic Club was founded in 1908 (page 242), Marigo Posio taught Albanian literacy at the night school there, under the outward guise of giving embroidery classes. Her real contribution to the art of embroidery, however, was the double-headed eagle on the flag that was raised in Vlora on 28 November 1912 – a painting of her embroidering the Albanian flag hangs at the top of the stairs in the Museum of Independence. The original flag was handed down by Ismail Qemali to one of his many sons, and is now lost. Marigo Posio died in 1932 and was buried between two olive trees on the island of Zvërneci.

Around Vlora Those with their own transport (including bicycles) will find it easy to explore a little further afield.

Kanina Castle is about 5km from the city centre; neatly paved steps lead up to the castle from the car park. Kanina was the seat of a bishopric in the 12th century and changed hands several times during the slow collapse of the Byzantine Empire, until it fell to the Ottomans in 1417. It was used as an Italian garrison during World War II and then, in the communist period, it was a surveillance centre for the Albanian air force. On a clear day, its strategic location provides wonderful views over the city and out to Karaburuni and Sazani in the west; northwards to the Narta Lagoon and Zvërneci; and across the River Vjosa towards the mountains of Mallakastra in the east.

The **Narta Lagoon** is one of a string of important wetland sites along the Albanian coast. It has become especially well known in recent years for its huge colony of flamingos. Plans to build a new airport just to the north of the lagoon were fiercely opposed by Albanian and international conservation organisations. Narta has been exploited for its salt since Roman times – the salt-works on its eastern side, now operated by an Italian company, are clearly visible from the highway between Vlora and Fieri. Most of the salt is exported to neighbouring countries, for use on their roads in winter.

At the southern tip of the lagoon is the island of **Zvërneci**, with its church and monastic buildings, which, by tradition, was the last resting place of Vlora's most illustrious sons and daughters – Marigo Posio is one of those buried here. Flamingos can often be seen in this part of the lagoon. The monastery was once home to a community of Orthodox monks; after 1967, it was used as an internment camp for political prisoners. The buildings have now been restored and a footbridge has been built to link the island with the mainland. Behind the church, steps lead up to the peaceful woods which cover the rest of the island.

To get to Zvërneci from Vlora, follow the main road west from the roundabout with the Riviera shopping mall; it leads through unprepossessing industrial outskirts to a forest of pines and firs which shelters a long sandy beach. Beyond the forest lies the village of Zvërneci and, about half a mile beyond that, a small car park and the footbridge to the island. There is no public transport to the island; it takes about 2 hours to walk from the Riviera mall.

KARABURUNI The northern tip of the Karaburuni Peninsula (Kepi i Gjuhëzës) is where the Adriatic and Ionian seas meet. The peninsula, which shelters the southern end of the Bay of Vlora, was a closed military zone during the whole of the communist period. In recent years, it has become a popular destination for holidaymakers staying in Vlora and the resorts around the bay; between June and

September or October, several companies run scheduled day trips from Vlora and Radhima to the beaches on the eastern shore of the peninsula. 'Pop-up' restaurants operate at these beaches in summer. The beaches and caves on the western shore can be accessed by boat from Dhërmiu beach (page 232). For those wishing to hike in the wilderness of Karaburuni, see the box on page 248.

The boat trips typically spend most of the day at a beach on Karaburuni; most of them use Shën Vasili beach. Before going to Karaburuni itself, the boats stop at **Sazani Island**, 13 nautical miles from Vlora. There is a beach near the mooring point. Alternatively, for a fascinating glimpse into military life in communist Albania, you can visit the **former naval base**. It was a functioning town, home to 2,500 inhabitants – naval men and officers with their families – and had its own school, with its own air-raid shelter, its own power plant, a shop and cinema, which had been built by the Italians before they were ejected, a fully equipped hospital, a refectory, houses for the officers and apartments for the men. The officers' families even had their own beach. Water was brought by boat from Vlora and stored in the cisterns, the tops of which can be seen as you walk up the hill to the town. The base was abandoned in 1997, after the civil uprising that year, and today there is only a small naval force on the island.

Some boats then visit the **Cave of Haxhi Aliu,** near the tip of the peninsula. Haxhi Aliu was an 18th-century pirate from Ulqini (now in Montenegro) and this sea cave, 100m long, was one of his hideouts. You can swim in the cave; the walls have small stalactites.

Another cave, at **Grama**, on the western (Ionian) shore of the peninsula, was used during World War II as a base by British and US special forces (see boxes, pages 13 and 14). Code-named 'Sea Elephant', the Grama cave was chosen not only for its extreme remoteness, but also because it was larger (and, one hopes, had fewer lice and scorpions) than SOE's first base on the peninsula, code-named 'Seaview'. The walls of the Grama cave have thousands of inscriptions, carved into them over the centuries by passing sailors, soldiers and merchants – the earliest are said to date from the 3rd century BC. Some of the smaller boats can get to Grama from Vlora; they require a minimum of eight passengers to make it worth their while. There are also day trips to Grama from Dhërmiu.

Practicalities From **Vlora**, the excursions leave from the port (next to the Bologna Hotel) at 10.00 and return around 18.00, typically charging 2,000 lek per person. There are boats to suit every taste, from large party boats with music, foam parties, etc, including a three-masted 'pirate boat', to small craft that travel faster and can access the Cave of Haxhi Aliu. The travel agencies in Vlora can book them for you, or you can pay on the day; each company has its own ticket-stance at the approach to the port. From **Radhima**, the Regina Hotel (m 069 26 56 757) operates daily departures, subject to a minimum number of 20 passengers, from its own jetty. They leave around 09.30 and land back in Radhima around 18.00. Small boats also do trips to Karaburuni from Radhima; ask around at the harbour at around 08.00.

Aquamarine Adventure m 069 71 14 050; w aquamarine-adventure.al. DJ & bar on board; access to cave by rubber dinghy; private beach on Karaburuni.

Avventura m 068 62 57 889; f Avventura II. Small & fast, this family-run boat gets to Sazani before all the other vessels & goes right into the sea cave.

Julka Unique m 068 55 55 559; f Julka Unique. This trimaran – claimed to be the only one in Albania – has live music & folk dancing during the trip; toilets; bar.

HIKING ON KARABURUNI

With thanks to Eva de Hullu and Joost Smets

The Karaburuni Peninsula offers a fantastic opportunity to hike in one of the wildest parts of Albania. A rough vehicle track links the Pashaliman naval base with what remains of **Shëngjini**. Still marked as a village on some maps of Albania, Shëngjini was a military base during the communist period. All the buildings were deliberately demolished when the base was abandoned, leaving only remnants of walls and a strikingly dense concentration of bunkers of various shapes and sizes. The 'bunker strategy' described in the box on page 197 can be seen clearly here, with large bunkers watching out over the shores dotted with smaller ones. Bunkers that contained heavier weaponry look out over the bay and Sazani. Their inner walls once carried instructions – now roughly painted over – on how to operate the weapons.

Before reaching Shëngjini, you walk through a smaller deserted military post. Around the military buildings are fig trees, perhaps planted by soldiers decades ago – a welcome treat, with their sweet fragrance, in this harsh environment. If you are planning to stay overnight, the ruins of Shëngjini would be a suitable spot to pitch your tent; just 100m beyond them, alternatively, is a rare field of something vaguely resembling grass – most of Karaburuni is covered with trees or thorn-bushes. There are many butterflies and other insects.

About 30km from Orikumi (it looks shorter on maps, but the road keeps turning in discouraging bends) and 5–6km beyond Shëngjini, the Karaburuni Peninsula reaches its most remote point. The track passes high above Haxhi Aliu's Cave, at sea level; the steep cliffs mean the cave cannot be reached from above. At the cape, tunnels overlook the narrow strait between Karaburuni and Sazani. Inside, posters explain how to set landmines, how to tell various chemical weapons apart and how to make a built-up area safe following a gas attack. Red-painted quotations by Enver Hoxha still grace the walls. Strange white flowers grow all around, 1.5m high, with huge red bulbs.

It is trickier than it seems to leave Karaburuni without walking into the naval base by mistake. After some fishermen's huts, you come to some military buildings. Beyond these, it looks at first as if you're walking straight into the base; however, this is the correct track for avoiding it. You descend nearly to sea level, past more buildings, and then turn right, slightly uphill, keeping the barbed wire to your left. A bend in the road will lead you slightly above the military base and around Pashaliman Lagoon. The detour around the lagoon adds at least 5km to the walk, but it is far quicker in the long run than being arrested and interrogated for trespassing on the base.

FIERI *Telephone code: 034*

The centre of the Albanian oil industry, Fieri lies at the western edge of Europe's largest onshore oil field. Although it is not the most attractive city in the country, it is a good base from which to visit Apollonia and Ardenica. Byllis and Divjaka-Karavasta are also close by. Birdwatchers will want to visit the Narta Lagoon, famous for its huge colony of flamingos.

Apollonia was founded in the 6th century BC and became one of Roman Albania's most important cities; a medieval monastery next to the ancient site houses an excellent museum. The 18th-century monastery at Ardenica, the only one in Albania where monks still reside, has frescoes painted by the Zografi brothers.

GETTING THERE AND AWAY There are buses to Fieri from almost every other city in Albania. From Tirana, they leave at least hourly from the North/South bus station. From Berati, similarly, buses depart at least every hour between 07.00 and 15.00; they use the minor road via Roskoveci and take about 90 minutes. After years of delays, Fieri at last has its bypass, which means that buses to or from further south (eg: Vlora or Gjirokastra) no longer go through the city.

The Likometaj company operates a minibus service every 2 hours between Fieri (the first departure at 03.30) and Tirana Airport. The fare is 1,000 lek each way. To reserve a seat, call in at Likometaj's office on Rruga Jakov Xoxa in Fieri or phone 222 408 or m 069 67 40 073.

Apollonia is about 12km west of Fieri, on a reasonably good, asphalted road. It is signposted at the turn-off to the site, in the village of Dërmenas. The new Fieri bypass was originally intended to cut right through the archaeological site. Thankfully, this appalling plan was averted and the new road loops to the west of the site. Those driving to Apollonia from north or south, rather than coming from Fieri, can turn on to the Apollonia road directly from the bypass (well signposted).

Ardenica is about half an hour's drive north of Fieri and about an hour from Tirana. The turn-off for the monastery is signposted from the SH4 highway, in Albanian and English. There is no public transport to Apollonia or Ardenica. The main taxi rank in Fieri is just south of the main square, Sheshi Pavarësia, where the university building is.

WHERE TO STAY AND EAT

Hotel Fieri (58 rooms) Rr Jakov Xoxa; 222 394; m 068 20 85 860; e reservation@hotelfieri.com; w hotelfieri.com. On Sheshi Europa, very central location, overlooking the river. 24-hour reception; English-speaking, helpful staff; restaurant, terrace & indoor bars, conference rooms. Generous buffet b/fast inc. All rooms en suite (some with bathtub as well as shower), with TV, fridge, safe, good curtains, bedside lights. 12 'economy' rooms in annexe (**$$**), 46 larger 'standard' rooms in main hotel (**$$$**).

Toska Fish Restaurant Rr Llambi Bego, Lagja Kastriot; m 069 63 63 615; e restorantoska@gmail.com. Excellent food on a slightly out-of-the-way backstreet, a few blocks west of the university. Wide choice of fish (wild as well as farmed), seafood, homemade pasta, risottos & salads; generous portions; attentive staff. $$$

WHAT TO SEE AND DO

Ardenica Ardenica is the only monastery in Albania where there are still monks in residence. It is surrounded with high walls, but it is usually possible to gain access by knocking on the wooden gate. Within the monastery complex is its church, built in 1744 and dedicated to the Birth of Mary Theotokos (Mother of God).

According to traditions, the monastery was founded in the 13th or 14th century, possibly on the site of a pagan temple. Stones from still more ancient sites were used to build it; fragments of column capitals and Byzantine Greek inscriptions can be seen in the southern wall (nearest the entrance). During the atheism campaign of 1967, the bishop saved the monastery by convincing the people who came to destroy it that Skanderbeg had been married there in 1451. Instead, it was turned into a military barracks and returned to the Albanian Orthodox Church only in 1996.

The church is a long building of creamy-coloured stone, with a colonnaded narthex. The walls within are covered with paintings by Kostandin and Athanas Zografi, brothers from Korça who were famous in their lifetimes throughout the Balkans. The paintings depict various saints and Biblical scenes including a series showing the sufferings of Christ. The beautiful gilded iconostasis was also carved around 1744, as were the throne and the icon-stand; many of the icons in it

ALBANIAN OIL

Albania's hydrocarbon resources have been exploited since before the arrival of the Romans, who traded for bitumen with the Illyrians in inland settlements such as Byllis. Bitumen (also known as asphalt) was used in the ancient world for construction and to waterproof ships. Naturally occurring bitumen can still sometimes be seen seeping from the earth in the oilfields between Fieri and Kuçova.

After the Roman period, there is no record of petrochemical exploitation in Albania until the early 20th century. After World War I, foreign oil companies, including what later became BP, were awarded drilling concessions; by 1939 Albania's annual oil production was over a million barrels. Under communism, the oil industry was of course nationalised and made a significant contribution to the country's GDP. By the 1990s, however, in common with other Albanian industries, outdated equipment and practically non-existent environmental standards meant the oil industry was not internationally competitive. It took a decade or more for oil production to start to pick up again.

Around 200,000 people are employed in Albania's oil industry. Petroleum assets and wells are owned by the state company Albpetrol, part of the Ministry of Infrastructure and Energy. Almost all of Albania's crude oil is produced by the Chinese-owned Bankers Petroleum (sold by its former Canadian owners in 2016). The country's two main refineries, an oil refinery at Ballshi and a bitumen refinery in Fieri, have also changed hands since the 1990s. The entire industry is blighted by accusations of sharp practice and a total absence of transparency.

However, for visitors to the country, it is interesting to see the many small oil rigs scattered above Albania's oilfields. The road up to Byllis, where the country's hydrocarbon industry first began, 2,000 years ago, offers particularly good viewpoints for these installations.

were made by another famous Albanian artist, Kostandin Shpataraku. A wooden staircase in the narthex leads to more frescoes, a *Last Judgement* and the icon of the church above the entrance.

Beyond the church and its bell tower, added in 1924, is an elegant cloister of stone arches, supporting a wooden terrace that gives shade to the monks' cells on the first floor.

Apollonia (🕘 Oct–Mar 09.00–17.00 daily, Apr–Sep 08.00–20.00 daily; 300 lek) The city of Apollonia was the second Greek settlement on the Illyrian mainland, after Epidamnos (now Durrësi). Founded, according to tradition, in 588BC and named for the god Apollo, it was settled first by Corinthians, who were followed by others, especially from nearby Corcyra (Corfu). At the time, Apollonia lay only a kilometre from the River Aoos (the Vjosa, in Albanian) and it became a major port. The city grew in importance and, by the time of the Roman conquest in the middle of the 2nd century BC, its coins were in wide circulation, especially in the Danube provinces where Roman coinage was not accepted. With its rival Dyrrachium (the Romans' name for Durrësi), it was one of the starting points of the Via Egnatia, the great arterial road that linked the Adriatic coast with Byzantium.

In addition to its importance as a trading and military port, the Roman elite considered Apollonia a centre of higher learning. The young Octavian studied there before he was given the title of Augustus – indeed, he had to rush back to Rome to claim power after the Ides of March, 44BC, when his adoptive father, Julius Caesar, was assassinated. Most of the remains that can be seen at Apollonia date from the Roman period. Augustus later awarded Apollonia the status of a 'free and immune city' – immune, that is, from the obligation to pay taxes. Apollonia's status meant that – unlike Dyrrachium and other colonies – it continued to elect its local authorities, its everyday language was Greek, not Latin, and its coins had Apollonia's own symbols on them.

In late antiquity, a series of earthquakes shifted the course of the River Aoos – the River Vjosa – far to the south and left Apollonia without the port which had brought its prosperity. The ancient city now stands forlorn on its hill overlooking the fertile Myzeqeja Plain and, a few miles to the west, the Adriatic.

The ancient city Apollonia is a complex, multi-layered site and it is estimated that only about 10% of the city has been excavated to date. Good information panels, in Albanian and English, have been installed around the site, with computer-generated images of how archaeologists believe the buildings would have looked at the time they were being used. These make it very much easier to get a sense of the layout of the city. A large map at the entrance to the site shows the various buildings, with a key in Albanian and French.

The city was first excavated by the French archaeologist Léon Rey, between 1924 and 1938. It was Rey and his team who uncovered the building that immediately draws the visitor's eye: the **Bouleuterion**, where the city council met. It was built in the late 2nd century AD by the brother of a military commander who had died on Rome's eastern front. Both brothers held the position of *agonothetes*, the official who presided over and judged the games, and so this building is also sometimes known as the Monument of the Agonothetes. We know all of this from the Greek inscription on the pediment above the columns. These were restored in the 1970s by Albanian archaeologists, who fortunately made it very obvious which bits are restored and which are original.

Behind the Bouleuterion, and built around the same time, is a little theatre known as the **Odeon**. This was not the city's public theatre, but a venue for cultural and musical events for the elite, seating only about 300 people. The line of four marble-clad column bases, between these two buildings, is all that remains of a triumphal arch, through which all traffic into the square would have had to pass.

Leading off this civic area to the northwest is the portico known as **Stoa B**. At 75m long and 12m wide, the stoa predates the Bouleuterion and Odeon by some five centuries. Built to a Corinthian pattern, its ground floor was separated with Doric columns into two parallel walkways. Above these walkways, an upper promenade, probably with Ionic columns, allowed Apollonia's rich citizens to enjoy the marvellous views over their thriving port and the Adriatic Sea. The whole structure backed on to the slope of the hill leading up to the city's acropolis; to reinforce it, 17 niches were built into the hillside on the ground floor. The stone for these was brought, by sea, from the Karaburuni Peninsula, 70km away. During Léon Rey's excavations, several busts of famous philosophers were found around these now-empty niches, placed there to inspire intellectual conversations.

A restored arch at the northwestern end of the stoa marks the site of one of the shops that once stood there. In the area around it are the remains of a cistern, in which rainwater was collected (Apollonia has no aqueduct), and a rectangular building that had a mosaic floor and which archaeologists believe may have been a shrine. The city's public **theatre** can be reached by following the track between the end of the stoa and the arch. It was built in the 3rd century BC, on a magnificent site on the western edge of the city, and held about 10,000 spectators. The curve of the seats can still be seen, cut into the hillside facing the Adriatic, but most of the stonework of the theatre's structure has gone, re-used over the centuries for other buildings. The 18th-century governor of Berati, Kurt Pasha (page 265), notoriously removed huge quantities of stonework from Apollonia for his own building projects.

Like all Greek cities, Apollonia had a reserved area called the *temenos*. This was dedicated to a god, or to several gods, and was not in everyday use. In Apollonia, the *temenos* was on the hill to the east of the Bouleuterion, which Rey called Hill 104. It was surrounded by a wall, part of which can be seen by following the path uphill from the Bouleuterion, on either side of the beautiful archway which was the entrance to the *temenos*. Neatly cut from limestone and sandstone, some of the rectangular blocks are marked with a monogram consisting of the Greek letters D and A: 'belonging to the state of Apollonia' – in other words, the *temenos* wall was a public work.

This path follows the *temenos* wall to the eastern edge of the city. In the valley below was the necropolis, or cemetery, used from the Iron Age onwards. There is an array of communist-era bunkers on the opposite side of the valley. A little further on are the remains of the city's southeastern **gate**, with its watchtowers. In ancient times, the Vjosa River curved round the head of this valley and the gate provided access to and from the port. Looking south across the valley from this gate, you will see a single column on a little hill. This is the only surviving column of a Greek temple, built (probably in the 5th or 4th century BC) to mark the entrance to the harbour. Known today as the Temple of Shtyllas (*shtylla* means 'column' in Albanian), it may have been dedicated to the city's patron god, Apollo, or to the god of the sea, Poseidon.

The later buildings The site **museum**, located on the first floor of the monastery building, is full of well-presented information about the history of Apollonia and its excavations. There are three rooms of lovely, interesting artefacts: imported and locally made Greek vases, bronzes and busts; armour, including a 4th-century shield, which was excavated in hundreds of pieces and took 27 years to restore; a case of coins minted in Apollonia and elsewhere; and, in the gallery outside, burial markers (*stelae*) with fascinating inscriptions. You should try to allow at least 45 minutes to look around the museum. Outside, the 13th-century **church** and the 14th-century refectory are also well worth a look. The wellhead in the exonarthex of the church is a repurposed Doric column from the ancient city; you can lift the lid to see the rope-marks worn into the marble by years of lowering and raising buckets. On the church wall behind it is a patch of 13th-century fresco, depicting three Byzantine emperors. There are beautiful frescoes in the refectory, including scenes from the life of Christ and various saints; the eyes of some of the saints were scratched out by believers, who would mix the paint and plaster from them with water and drink this potion as a miracle cure.

There are two cafés at Apollonia: one, named after Léon Rey, is at the summit of 'Hill 104' (the *temenos* hill) and has good views; the other is straight ahead as you enter the fenced-off area of the archaeological site. There are reasonable toilets behind this bar, which visitors to the site may use; the monastery building also has public toilets.

BYLLIS

(🕘 Mar–Oct 08.00–18.00 daily, Nov–Feb 08.00–16.00 daily; 300 lek) Byllis is a vast archaeological site spread over 30ha of hilltop overlooking the River Vjosa.

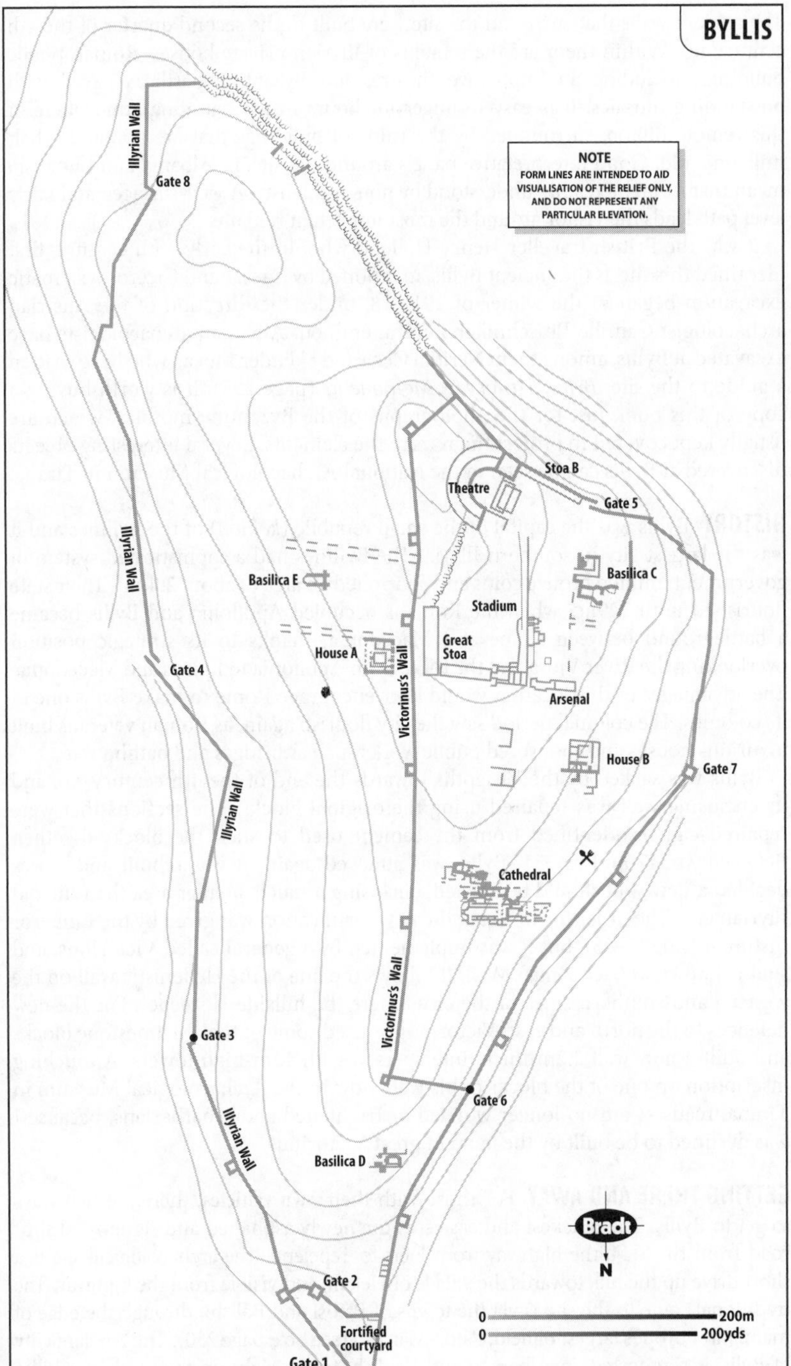

BYLLIS
NOTE
FORM LINES ARE INTENDED TO AID VISUALISATION OF THE RELIEF ONLY, AND DO NOT REPRESENT ANY PARTICULAR ELEVATION.
Illyrian Wall
Gate 8
Stoa B
Theatre
Gate 5
Illyrian Wall
Basilica C
Basilica E
Stadium
Great Stoa
House A
Gate 4
Victorinus's Wall
Arsenal
Illyrian Wall
House B
Gate 7
Cathedral
Victorinus's Wall
Gate 3
Gate 6
Illyrian Wall
Basilica D
Bradt
N
Gate 2
0
200m
0
200yds
Fortified courtyard
Gate 1
P

The ancient walls that surround the site were built in the second quarter of the 4th century BC. Within them are the remains of Illyrian private houses, Roman public buildings, including an impressive theatre, and Byzantine basilicas paved with outstanding mosaics. It is easy to linger for hours in the haunting atmosphere of this remote hilltop, surrounded by the ruins of buildings that are two-and-a-half millennia old. Good interpretative panels around the site, in Albanian and English, mean that it can be readily understood by non-specialists. A well-surfaced and fairly level path leads the visitor around the most important remains.

It was the British traveller Henry Holland who, in the early 19th century, first identified this site as the ancient Byllis, mentioned by Caesar and Cicero. Systematic excavation began in the winter of 1917/18, under the direction of the Austrian archaeologist Camillo Praschniker. Several eminent Albanian archaeologists have excavated at Byllis, among them Neritan Ceka and Skënder Muçaj, who have written a guide to the site, *Byllis: History & Monuments* (page 295). It is worth buying a copy of this book just for the photographs of the Byzantine mosaics, which are usually kept covered to protect them from the elements. Several interesting objects discovered at Byllis can be seen in the National Archaeological Museum in Tirana.

HISTORY Byllis was the capital of the small republic (*koinon*) of the Byllines and it was the largest city in southern Illyria. The Byllines had a sophisticated system of government, minted bronze coins and controlled an area of about $20km^2$. Their state flourished until 229BC, when the Romans occupied Apollonia and Byllis became a battleground between Rome and Macedonia, thanks to its strategic position overlooking the River Vjosa and the route from Apollonia to Epirus and Macedonia. The advantages of this location would later encourage Rome to make Byllis one of its colonies. The colonial period saw the city flourish again, as Roman veterans built luxurious houses and sponsored public works such as bridges and bathhouses.

Byllis was sacked by the Visigoths towards the end of the 4th century AD, and its enclosing wall was repaired using the original blocks. The sections that were repaired can be identified from the cement used to stick the blocks together. Between AD547 and AD551, Byllis was attacked again. It was rebuilt and it was decided a new wall should be erected, enclosing a much smaller area than the old Illyrian city. The order to construct the new fortification was given by the Emperor Justinian (AD527–65), but it was implemented by a general called Victorinus, and so it is known as Victorinus's Wall. It follows the line of the Hellenistic wall on the western and southern sides of the city, where the hillside is steeper. For the new defences to the north and east, Victorinus re-used some of the old limestone blocks and built a new wall 2.2m thick, interspersed with 12m-high towers. A touching inscription on one of the blocks of his wall, now in the Archaeological Museum in Tirana, reads: 'I am no longer worried or frightened about barbarians, because I was destined to be built by the hand of great Victorinus.'

GETTING THERE AND AWAY For those with their **own vehicles**, there are two ways to get to Byllis. The quickest and easiest is the newly asphalted and signposted slip-road from the SH4, the highway from Fieri to Tepelena. The archaeological site is a short drive up the hill, towards the village of Hekali, and visible from the highway. The traditional route to the site is via the towns of Patosi and Ballshi, through the edge of mainland Europe's largest oilfield, Patos-Marinza (see box, page 250). The 'Ancient City of Bylis' is signposted, in Albanian and English, to the right on the brow of a hill a couple of kilometres south of Ballshi. It is about 5km from the junction to the site; the road is well surfaced and a 4x4 is not required. 'Nodding-donkey' oil rigs can be seen in the fields below. Beyond the Byllis junction, the old road to Tepelena has not been maintained since the highway was opened and it is now in very poor condition.

By **public transport**, there are buses to Ballshi from Fieri – the journey takes about an hour. Local taxis can be hired in the centre of Ballshi, beside the war memorial. Those on a tight budget could walk to the junction and then try to hitchhike to Hekali, about 1km short of the entrance to the site, or simply walk the 5km up the hill. Hekali has a rural bus service, which probably leaves Ballshi around lunchtime; the owner of the café at the junction is very helpful and may be able to advise on bus timings.

Admission tickets are sold at the restaurant just beyond the entrance gate to the cathedral. Admission is free on the last Sunday of the month, except in the summer, and on certain dates such as International Museums Day. The restaurant has reasonable toilets, a fridgeful of cold drinks and a small stock of publications about archaeology in Albania, including, usually, *Byllis: History & Monuments,* mentioned opposite. The food on offer (**$$$**) is simple but of excellent quality, and service is quick and efficient.

WHAT TO SEE AND DO The walls that enclosed the Illyrian city form a rough triangle more than 2km around. On the southern edge there is a gap in the wall where the hillside drops away in a steep cliff for about 200m. The Hellenistic (Illyrian) walls were 8–9m high, built with large rectangular blocks of limestone. These were laid in two lines 3.5m apart, and the gap between the rows was then filled with small stones laid at right angles to the blocks. There were six entrance gates, each guarded by a tower, and additional towers were built at the corners of the walls, to protect and strengthen them.

Between 230BC and 167BC, Byllis's protection was enhanced with the addition of a fortified courtyard at the northern apex of the triangle of its walls. The courtyard was guarded in its turn from a round tower, nearly 9m in diameter and 9m high. The remains of this fortified courtyard are on the right of the modern road as you approach the site.

From the site entrance next to the café, follow the path to the *agora*, the area of the city which the Byllines reserved for public spaces and civic buildings. A wall divided this public area from the residential quarter, which was laid out in a grid, with the houses in blocks known as *insulae*. Covering 4ha, the agora was completed during the 3rd century BC, with buildings including the **Great Stoa** (to the east), the Stadium and the vaulted Cistern. On the southern edge of the agora, the Theatre is perhaps the most imposing of Byllis's ancient monuments.

The limestone vaults of the **Cistern** were originally covered with stone tiles to form an underground reservoir, with a capacity of about 1,200m^3, which supplied the city with water. Even more remarkably, the roof of the reservoir formed the northern part of the Stadium. Limited suitable space meant that Byllis's **Stadium** had only one track, rather than the more usual oval form. The spectators stood on the steps rising up to the east of the track, which continued as far as the Theatre. The steps were made of rectangular limestone blocks; some can still be seen. Associated with the Cistern is a much later **Bathhouse**, which dates from the reconstruction of the city during Justinian's reign; the baths used water from the Cistern, which was thus still in working order seven centuries after it had been built.

To the west of the Stadium steps is another underground building, known as the **Arsenal**. Although it was originally built in the middle of the 3rd century BC, it was rebuilt at the beginning of the 1st century AD, when the beautiful wall at the far end was constructed in *opus reticulatum*, the 'netting' pattern that gives it its Latin name.

The **Theatre**, also dating from the middle of the 3rd century BC, would have held about 7,500 spectators. The semicircle of its seating used the slope of the hill as a natural rake; the seats themselves were almost all broken up and re-used over the years for other buildings (including Victorinus's Wall). One section of VIP seating, with carvings on the back, can be seen at the foot of the slope. The best view of the layout of the theatre is obtained by climbing up to the top of the seating rows. The semicircular *orchestra* – the space where the chorus stood during the performance – was drained by a stone-lined channel. In the Hellenistic period, the stage was a 3m-high platform supported on columns. When the theatre was rebuilt during the Roman colony, this stage was replaced with a stone base and a brick backdrop.

The capacity of the theatre shows that it was intended not only for the citizens of Byllis, but also for people from other Bylline towns, who would normally have entered the city by the nearest gate to the theatre, now known as **Gate 5**. This is the best preserved of the Illyrian gates and clearly shows the double entrance created by running a corridor between the two parallel lines of the wall. This structure protected the gate from attacks with catapults or fire and meant that invaders could be picked off from above if they tried to storm the gate. In addition, a tower stood on the arch of the gate. A stoa led from the gate to the entrance to the theatre seats. Gate 5 was rebuilt when the Roman colony was established and the Latin inscription on its southern flank reads: 'Augustus, son of the divine emperor Caesar, gave it' ('it' being the reconstruction).

Several basilicae were built at Byllis during the Byzantine period; five have been excavated to date. They are all paved with beautiful mosaics, but (sadly for visitors) these are normally kept covered with protective layers of sand and plastic sheeting. The largest and most impressive Byzantine structure at Byllis is the religious complex known as the **Cathedral**. It is fenced off from the main part of the site, just before the café, and it consists of a church (Basilica B), a baptistery and an episcopal palace. It is of great archaeological importance, because of the complexity of its architecture, the richness of its decorative elements and the large number of objects excavated, which included many coins.

The Cathedral was built in three distinct phases: the original construction, in the late 4th century, was a three-naved church with a narthex (entrance) and portico, and a simple baptistery; in the AD470s, this was expanded with an atrium and galleries; and finally, when the Cathedral was rebuilt during Justinian's reign, the episcopal complex was added. In its completed state, the basilica was a long, narrow building – an astonishing 67m in length – with side-naves, narthex, exonarthex (the room leading into the church, separating it from the outdoors) and porticos, and with galleries on the upper floor. The body of the church (*naos*) is 24.7m long and consists of three differently sized naves, the central one measuring 7.75m across. The naves were separated from each other by columns set on a high base; these columns were not only carved, but also painted, following the Illyrian tradition. At the southern end of the central nave is a platform on which the lectern stood. The atrium is a rectangular hallway surrounded by four porticos, one of which is the exonarthex. A staircase led from the northeastern corner of the exonarthex to the first floor and galleries of the church.

The floors of several sections of the church are paved with magnificent mosaics, which are usually covered to protect them from the elements. One shows a rustic scene; others depict the fishermen of Nazareth and the brothers Simon and Andrew (and an especially cute jellyfish); smaller panels bear different kinds of animals and birds. The basilica's walls were decorated with frescoes, but only a few of these remain, geometric patterns from the first phase of construction.

In AD586, Byllis was sacked and burned once again, this time by invading Slavs. After this destruction, the city was abandoned and the bishopric moved to the nearby town whose name, Ballshi, is derived from the ancient city's name.

BERATI *Telephone code: 032*

Berati is one of the oldest cities in Albania and one of the most attractive; the view of its white houses climbing up the hillside to the citadel is one of the best-known images of Albania. The citadel walls themselves encircle the whole of the top of the hill. Within them are eight medieval churches, one of which houses an outstanding collection of icons painted by the 16th-century master Onufri. Berati also has an excellent Ethnographic Museum and several other interesting buildings, including two of the oldest mosques in Albania. Thanks to their historical value, the religious buildings in the citadel were protected from the worst ravages of the atheism campaign, and in 1976 the government designated Berati a 'museum city', which saved the town centre from communist urban planning.

Berati has been inhabited since the Bronze Age, over 4,000 years ago. The great Tomorri massif, which rises behind it, was a sacred mountain from very early times and it still hosts a huge Bektashi festival every August. The first traces of building on the citadel date from the second half of the 4th century BC, when the Illyrian Parthini controlled the area.

Berati thrived in the Middle Ages, thanks to its strategic location at the point where the trading routes from the south met the lowland plain. This made it an appetising conquest for successive invaders. The Bulgarian Empire took the city in AD860 and held it – barring a 40-year period during which it was reconquered by Byzantium – until 1018. Berati's second return to the Byzantine fold lasted longer, despite a determined attack by the Angevins, who besieged the citadel for seven months in 1280–81. By the mid 14th century, however, as Byzantium's power waned, Berati and much of the rest of Albania became part of Stefan Dušan's 'Empire of the Serbs and the Greeks'. (For more background to this confusing period in Albania's history, see page 9.)

After Stefan Dušan's death in 1355, the whole of what is now southeast Albania, reaching as far as Kastoria (now in northern Greece) came under the control of the Muzakaj family of Berati, one of the powerful Albanian clans that emerged as the only functioning authorities in the period before the Ottoman conquest. The citadel of Berati fell to the Ottomans in 1417 and, despite an attempt to retake it, led by Skanderbeg in 1455, it remained in their hands for nearly 500 years. The mountains of the Berati region were a hotbed of partisan activity during World War II, and the city was the first seat of the Interim Government that came to power in October 1944, under the leadership of Enver Hoxha.

The name of the city may come from the Turkish word *berat*, meaning an order conferring a decoration, a sort of royal warrant; or it might derive from 'Beligrad', the name the Slavs gave the town, although there is debate about whether this is philologically possible. Berati was recognised as a UNESCO World Heritage Site in July 2008.

GETTING THERE AND AROUND Berati is easy to get to from almost everywhere in central and southern Albania, with good **bus** connections with Vlora, Durrësi and Elbasani as well as Tirana. The buses from Tirana leave every 45 minutes, from 04.30 until about 14.30, from the North/South bus terminal. The journey takes about 2 hours and the fare is 400 lek.

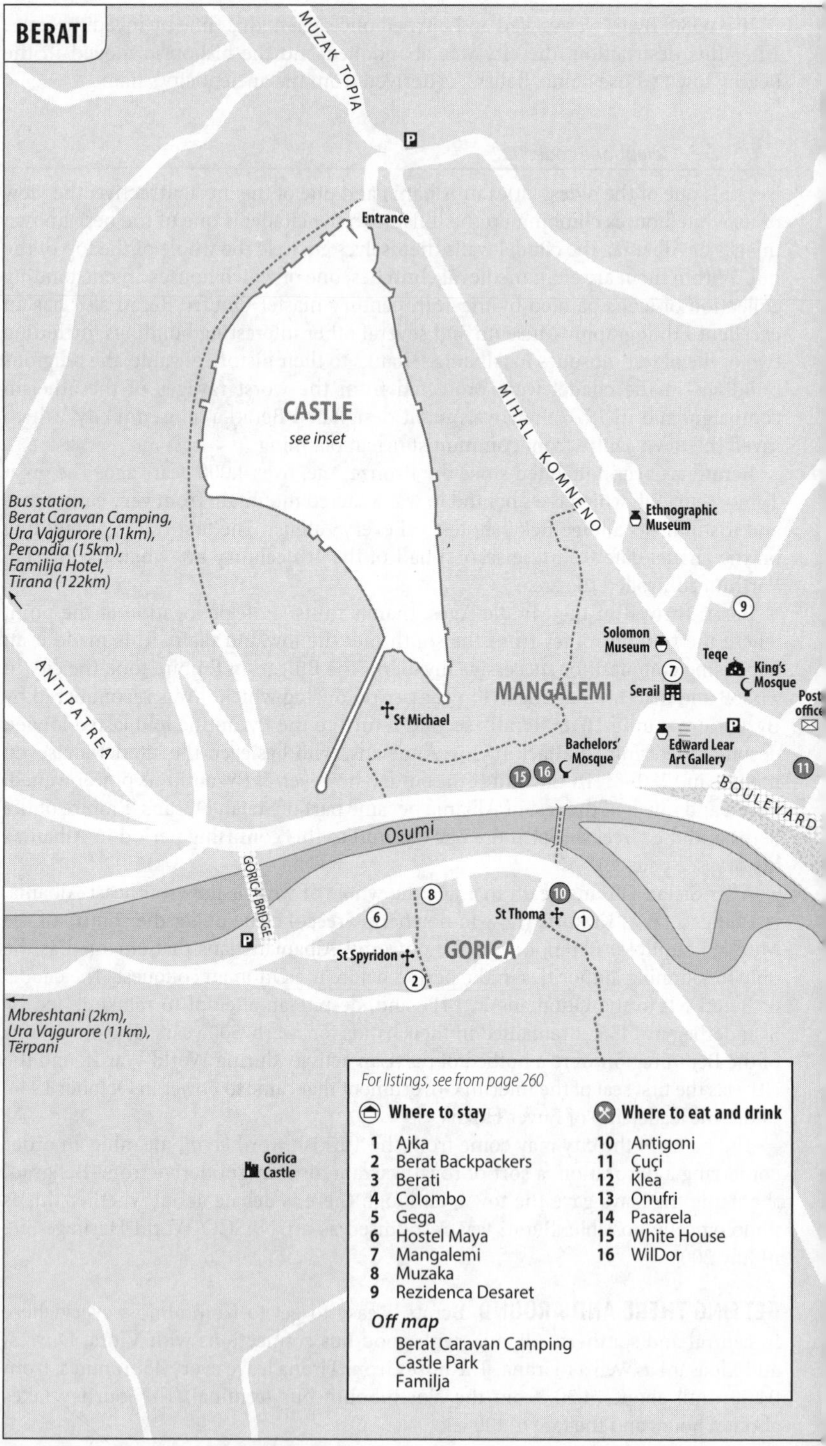
BERATI
MUZAK TOPIA
Entrance
CASTLE
see inset
MIHAL KOMNENO
Bus station,
Berat Caravan Camping,
Ura Vajgurore (11km),
Perondia (15km),
Familija Hotel,
Tirana (122km)
Ethnographic Museum
Solomon Museum
Teqe
King's Mosque
Serail
MANGALEMI
Post office
St Michael
Bachelors' Mosque
Edward Lear Art Gallery
ANTIPATREA
BOULEVARD
Osumi
GORICA BRIDGE
St Thoma
St Spyridon
GORICA
Mbreshtani (2km),
Ura Vajgurore (11km),
Tërpani
Gorica Castle
For listings, see from page 260
Where to stay
1 Ajka
2 Berat Backpackers
3 Berati
4 Colombo
5 Gega
6 Hostel Maya
7 Mangalemi
8 Muzaka
9 Rezidenca Desaret
Off map
Berat Caravan Camping
Castle Park
Familija
Where to eat and drink
10 Antigoni
11 Çuçi
12 Klea
13 Onufri
14 Pasarela
15 White House
16 WilDor

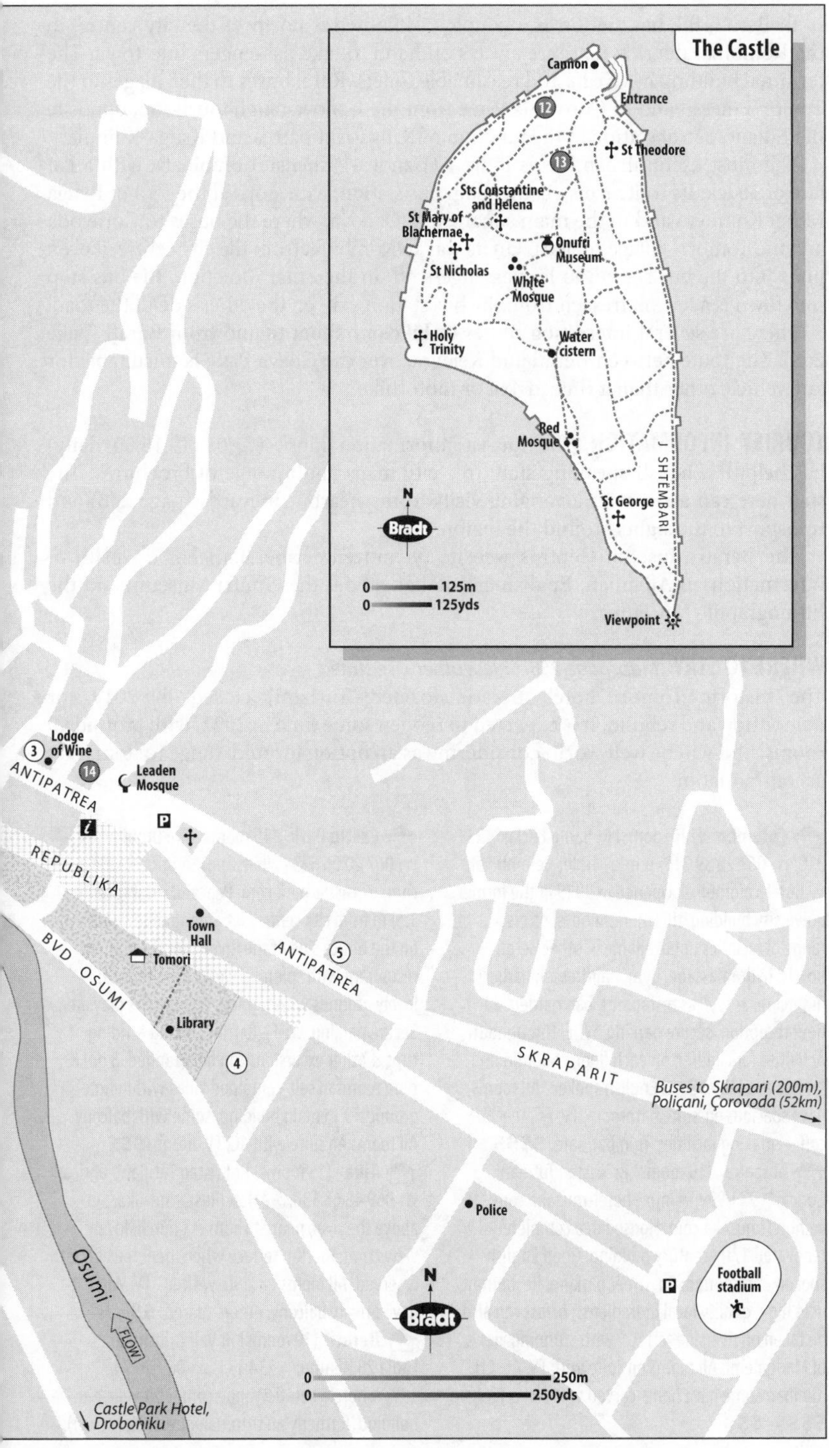

The Castle
Cannon
Entrance
12
13
St Theodore
Sts Constantine and Helena
St Mary of Blachernae
Onufri Museum
St Nicholas
White Mosque
Holy Trinity
Water cistern
Red Mosque
J SHTEMBARI
St George
Viewpoint
N
Bradt
0 125m
0 125yds
Lodge of Wine
3
14
Leaden Mosque
ANTIPATREA
REPUBLIKA
Town Hall
Tomori
BVD OSUMI
ANTIPATREA
5
Library
4
SKRAPARIT
Buses to Skrapari (200m), Poliçani, Çorovoda (52km)
Police
Osumi
FLOW
N
Bradt
Football stadium
0 250m
0 250yds
Castle Park Hotel, Droboniku

In Berati, the bus station is a couple of kilometres north of the city centre, in the Kombinat district; taxis are always on hand to take passengers into town. The terminal building has a café and reasonable toilets. Rural buses to the villages in the Tomorri massif and to Çorovoda leave from the Uznova neighbourhood, opposite the Edjano petrol station at the junction of Rruga Antipatrea and Rruga Rilindja.

The most useful urban bus is Linja 1 (Uznova–Axhensi–Kombinat), with a flat fare of 30 lek. Its route runs via the main bus station, with stops at the foot of Rruga Mihal Komneni and in the main square, and Uznova, where the buses to Çorovoda and the Tomorri villages depart. On its way to Kombinat from the city centre, it even pulls into the bus station to let passengers off; in the other direction, the bus stop into town is a few metres left from the bus station exit, on the other side of the road.

There are several interesting routes **by bike** or **on foot** to and from Berati (page 268). The route between Berati and Këlcyra, over the Gllava Pass, is unsuitable for any vehicle other than a rugged 4x4 or motorbike.

TOURIST INFORMATION The tourist information kiosk (🕘 08.00–16.00 daily) has helpful, English-speaking staff, free city maps and a range of brochures. The staff here can assist with arranging visits to the nearby vineyards (page 266) and transport to the sights around the region.

The Berati Museum Centre's website (w muzeumet-berat.al) has a wealth of information, in Albanian, English and Italian, about the Onufri Museum and the Ethnographic Museum.

WHERE TO STAY *Map, page 258, unless otherwise stated*

The historic Tomori hotel, Berati's former 'Turizmi', closed in 2019 for demolition and rebuild. It is expected to reopen some time in 2022, with around 90 rooms, and will be well worth considering as an option for mid-range to upmarket accommodation.

Colombo (120 rooms) Rr Santa Lucia; ☎ 231 010; m 067 20 39 215; e info@hotel-colombo.al; w hotel-colombo.al. Opened in 2019 in the former university building, this modern hotel offers a range of facilities not available in other Berati hotels: hydromassage, gym, hairdresser, barber, nightclub, as well as restaurant, bar, garden. 24-hour reception, secure parking, Wi-Fi throughout. Activities for children on each floor, childminding service available. Good English spoken. All rooms have spacious en-suite bathroom, TV, AC, tea- & coffee-making facilities, minibar, safe. **$$$$**

Muzaka (10 rooms) Rr Kristaq Tutulani, Gorica; ☎ 231 999; e info@hotel-muzaka.com; w hotel-muzaka.com. Housed in a completely renovated 17th-century building. Good English spoken at reception; on-street parking. Restaurant uses high-quality local ingredients; b/fast can also be taken on riverside terrace, with stunning views of Mangalemi. All rooms en suite with TV, AC, CH, minibar; some have hand-carved wooden ceilings. **$$$$–$$$**

Castle Park (15 rooms) Rr e Drobonikut; m 067 20 06 623 (WhatsApp); e info@castle-park.com; w castle-park.com. Peaceful rural setting 1.5km from city centre, set among pinewoods on the Gorica side of the River Osumi. Excellent restaurant with splendid views from terrace; lovely grounds with terraces & children's play area. Secure parking; Wi-Fi. Rafting, hiking & riding trips & other excursions can be arranged. 8 dbl & twin rooms in self-contained villas within hotel grounds; 7 in main building, some with balcony. All rooms en suite with AC, TV, fridge. **$$$**

Ajka (15 rooms) Rr Kristaq Tutulani, Gorica; m 069 48 65 130; f HotelRestorantAjka. Set above the river, near St Thoma's Church; lovely views from rooftop terrace where generous b/fast is served. All rooms en suite with AC, TV, Wi-Fi; 2 have private balcony, others shared. **$$**

Berati (10 rooms) Rr Veli Zaloshnja, Lagja 28 Nëntori; ☎ 234 131; m 069 20 74 199; e hotel_berati@yahoo.com. 300-year-old building, formerly an Ottoman guesthouse (*han*), now carefully restored. The bar & flagstones in the restaurant are of stone from Mt Tomorri. Secure on-street parking, safe storage for bicycles & motorcycles. Reception open 24h; b/fast of local/homemade produce inc. Same management as Lodge of Wine shop. All rooms en suite with AC, TV, some have traditional fireplace, some have balcony. **$$**

Gega (26 rooms) Rr Antipatrea; 231 902; m 069 53 84 435; e hotel.gega@yahoo.com. Bar, restaurant with Italian menu, Wi-Fi, free parking. All rooms have nice en-suite bathrooms, AC, flatscreen TV, fridge. **$$**

✱ **Mangalemi** (20 rooms, plus 6 in annex) Rr Mihal Komneno, Mangalemi; 232 093; m 068 23 23 238; e hotel_mangalemi@yahoo.com; w mangalemihotel.com. Berati's first private hotel, still family-run, in sensitively restored historic buildings; English spoken. Good restaurant with traditional specialities; bar with excellent selection of rakis. *Çardak* (covered balcony), courtyard, roof terrace with views of castle & city; laundry service; generous b/fast inc. All rooms en suite (some also with bathtub), with AC, TV, Wi-Fi, desk, safe, minibar, good curtains. **$$**

Rezidenca Desaret (15 rooms) RR. 22 Marsi 4, Lagja 13 Shtatori; 237 593; m 069 77 72 732; e rezidencadesaret@ymail.com; f RezidencaDesaret. Spectacular setting high up in Mangalemi. English spoken, good restaurant & bar, peaceful garden; secure parking inc; Wi-Fi throughout. Large, well-appointed rooms, all en suite with AC, TV; most have balcony with lovely views over city. **$$**

Berat Backpackers (7 rooms) Gorica 295; w beratbackpackers.com; closed in winter. In a Grade II-listed building with vine-covered terraces; directions on website. Day tours to surrounding area. 3 dorms, 4 private rooms, all sharing bathroom facilities; bed linen inc; camping spaces. B/fast inc. **$**

Familja [map, page 212] (30 rooms) Rr Kombëtare Ura Vajgurore-Kuçova; m 069 20 11 933; e hotelfamilja@hotmail.com. Walking distance (1km) from junction of the highway with the road to Kuçova. Friendly, English-speaking management; good restaurant, secure parking. All rooms en suite with AC, TV, Wi-Fi. **$**

Hostel Maya (6 rooms) Rr Kristaq Tutulani, Gorica; f MayaHostelBerat. One of few hostels in Berati open all year round. Traditional Gorica house, shady courtyard, well-equipped kitchen. 2 dorms, 4 dbl/twin rooms, each with small private bathroom. **$**

Berat Caravan Camping [map, page 212] Ura Vajgurore; m 069 87 56 409; e info@sarandaholidays.com; w beratcaravancamping.com; all year. Set in a beautiful garden; 12km from Berati, close to good bus route. Bar & restaurant; Wi-Fi, fridge use, electricity inc; self-catering & BBQ facilities; laundry; 2 showers, 2 toilets, hot water. 3 simple guest rooms also available. **$**

WHERE TO EAT *Map, page 258*

Antigoni Gorica; m 069 24 44 522, 069 36 25 189; e antigoni.restaurant@outlook.com. Fairly formal dining in restaurant, more relaxed on outdoor terraces; splendid views of Mangalemi from upper-terrace bar. Grilled meat, roast lamb & kid, vegetarian menu incl stuffed aubergine, pepper or vine leaves. Very popular with local families & foreign groups; advance booking advisable. **$$$$**

WilDor Rr Antipatrea. Interesting menu with some less commonly found traditional dishes such as *mish çomlek* (page 49) & rabbit; also pizza, salads, stuffed vine leaves. Good Albanian wine list; quirky décor. **$$$$**

Çuçi Rr Antipatrea; m 069 24 33 341. Opposite the post office; the best place in Berati for very traditional dishes such as *paçe* (sheep's head soup), veal brains & lamb's liver. The nicely printed menu (in English & Albanian) also has less adventurous but no less tasty options: grilled & baked meat, *qofta*, pilaf & huge salads. Excellent value given its city-centre location. **$$$**

Klea In the castle, roughly straight ahead from entrance (signposted); 234 970; m 069 76 84 861. Friendly, English-speaking management, superbly prepared traditional dishes, good house raki; nice modern toilets. In summer, tables outside in lovely courtyard with views over Osumi Valley. Also has hotel rooms (**$$**). **$$$**

Onufri In the castle, on the right as you head towards the Onufri Museum; also known as Koço Plaku, after the owner. Huge spreads of traditional dishes in cosy, welcoming atmosphere. **$$$**

Pasarela Rr Gaqi Gjika. Opposite the Leaden Mosque, on the 3rd floor; lift. Some tables outside on the terrace, with good views of city & castle.

Tasty, good-value Albanian specialities such as stuffed peppers & aubergines, *tavë kosi* & *fergesë* (page 49), as well as the usual grilled meats. $$$

White House Rr Antipatrea; 234 570. Just beyond pedestrian bridge. Italian-based menu, wood-fired pizzas, good risotto & pasta. $$$

WHAT TO SEE AND DO

The castle (admission 200 lek) The citadel of Berati was first fortified in the 4th century BC by the Illyrian Parthini. At the same time, they also fortified the hill opposite, on the left bank of the River Osumi; the remains of the massive walls there, known as Gorica Castle, can still be seen among the trees. The pair of fortresses ensured that the whole river valley could be controlled and defended.

To get to Berati Castle on foot, the easiest way is to walk up Rruga Mihal Komneno (also known as Rruga e Kalasë, 'Castle Street') – the steep cobbled road through Mangalemi, one of the city's protected 'museum zones'. It is possible to drive this way, although by car it is better to use the longer road that curls around the back of the hill on which the castle stands. If you are entering Berati from the north, the turn-off is just after the bus station; it is signposted off the main road (in Albanian and English) for 'Kala, Castle'. This road meets Rruga Mihal Komneno at the car park for the castle. From there, it is a short though rather steep walk to the entrance gate and ticket office. On foot, there are short cuts up the winding stone staircases through Mangalemi, and then through the trees below the citadel, but it is difficult to find the way without a guide.

On the wall by the archway that is the outer entrance to the castle, a cross can be seen with the initials MK. This probably dates from a refortification of the citadel undertaken in the 13th century, during the reign of Michael II Comnenus Ducas, Despot of Epirus (page 9). The walls follow the contour of the hilltop in a rough triangle and a network of narrow cobbled streets connects the stone-built houses within them. The citadel is still home to many families, the more enterprising of whom sell souvenirs or run guesthouses or cafés.

Of the 42 churches that the castle walls once contained, only eight remain and, with one exception, they were locked up after the atheism campaign of the late 1960s. The exception was the Church of the Dormition of St Mary (Kisha e Fjetjes së Shënmërisë), a three-naved basilica that was built in 1797 on the foundations of a 10th-century church and which now houses the **Onufri Museum** (w muzeumet-berat.al; summer 09.00–13.00 & 16.00–19.00 Tue–Sun, winter 09.00–16.00 Tue–Sat, 09.00–14.00 Sun; 200 lek), signposted from the inner entrance to the castle.

Onufri was the greatest of a group of Albanian icon-painters – many of them anonymous – of the 16th century. He worked throughout the Balkans, but many of his finest icons were painted for the churches of the Berati citadel. Onufri followed and developed the Byzantine traditions of icon-painting, but his work is special because of his mastery of colour; the red paint he used has the technical name of 'Onufri red'.

The museum was redesigned in 2016 and the exhibition now covers two floors. Over a hundred beautiful icons, from churches in Berati and the surrounding area, are displayed. The earliest are from the 14th century, before icon-painters began to put their names to their work (this is because their purpose was to glorify God, not themselves). Later painters whose names we know, apart from Onufri, include his son Nikolla, David Selenica, Kostandin Shpataraku and the Katro (or Çetiri) family from Korça. Some of the icons combine traditional Byzantine iconography with Ottoman images – a round table, like the *sofër* that can be seen in the Ethnographic Museum, in an icon of the Last Supper (anonymous, 18th century), and the minarets of mosques peeking above the city walls in the icon called 'The Life-Giving Source'.

The collection also includes liturgical items, such as crucifixes and Bible covers, examples of the beautiful work of Berati's silver- and goldsmiths.

A preview of some of these lovely icons and objects can be enjoyed on the Berati museums' website (w muzeumet-berat.al); the museum shop has a good selection of cards and books about Albanian art. There are toilets behind the shop.

The entrance to the museum is through the church, which is also worth looking around. The ornate iconostasis (altar screen) at the far end was carved in walnut wood and decorated with gold leaf by master craftsmen from the Berati School of the 19th century. The three main icons were the work of Onufri and placed in the church at the time it was built; others were done in the mid 19th century by Johan Katro. The two manuscripts known as the *Codices of Berat* were discovered in 1968, buried behind the altar – the 6th-century *Purple Codex* is one of the oldest such manuscripts ever found, anywhere – and are now conserved in the State Archive in Tirana.

A walk around the perimeter walls to the **viewpoint** will give you a feel for the size and layout of the castle, as well as offering great views of the city below and the mountains across the river. The 13th-century **Church of St Michael** nestles into the hill below and can be seen to good effect from the Gorica quarter across the river. A path leads up to this church from the main road, but it is treacherous and the church is usually locked. Above the viewpoint, just within the walls, is the **Church of St George** (Shën Gjergji; 14th century), which was converted into a restaurant during the communist period but has now been restored by the parishioners. The Church of St Theodore (Shën Todri) has some surviving frescoes by Onufri. **St Mary of Blachernae** (Shën Mëri Vllaherna) is the oldest church in the castle; local tradition holds that this church was built to celebrate the defeat of the Angevin besiegers in 1281. It was rebuilt in 1578, as the inscription about the narthex door reveals, and its frescoes were painted by Nikolla, Onufri's son.

Returning now to the perimeter path, the huge bust of Constantine the Great (AD306–37) below the walls was installed in 2003, on the curious grounds that he was one of the Illyrian emperors (even though he was from Niš, hundreds of miles from Berati in what is now Serbia). The beautiful **Holy Trinity church** (Shën Triadha) now comes into view, on the slope of the hill just below the inner fortification of the castle (the English text on the information board refers to this area as the 'citadel'). This part of the castle was built at roughly the same time as the church, in the 13th century. Berati fell to the Ottomans in 1417 and the conquerors wasted no time in refortifying the citadel. They also built two mosques there, the Red and White mosques. Now ruined, both date from the 15th century and are among the oldest in Albania. The **White Mosque**, so-called because of the beautiful white stone of which it was built, stands at the corner of the inner fortification opposite the water cistern. The remains of the **Red Mosque** lie just outside this area; it was badly damaged by German bombs during World War II.

Near the Red Mosque is an underground water cistern, dug deep into the rock on which the castle stands, and supported with brick columns and elegant arches. In the 1930s, the Italians adopted a different approach to ensuring the citadel's water supply; they piped spring water across-country from Mount Shpiragu (the 'striped' mountain that faces Mount Tomorri to the west). Sections of the piping can still be seen in the area around the cistern. Information panels have been installed outside each of the churches and at some other points around the castle.

Set into an archway in the outer walls, above the first entrance gate, is a **cannon** that bears the date 1684 and which local tradition claims is English. In fact it may well have been made by the British gun founder Thomas Western (1624–1707).

Western carried out contract work for export to the Republic of Venice in 1684; some of his Venetian mortars can be seen in Corfu (two are in the Old Fortress and another in Sanrocco Square) and one is displayed in the Tower of London. The cannon in Berati is probably a large saker, a widely used gun that fired a cast-iron solid shot of 6–9lb. The emblem engraved on it seems to be the Lion of St Mark, the symbol of the Venetian Republic. The saker may have been captured in battle from Venice (which briefly occupied nearby Vlora in 1690–91), or simply acquired through trade. (I am grateful for the advice of Nicholas Hall of the Royal Armouries.)

Ethnographic Museum (w muzeumet-berat.al; ⌚ May–Oct 09.00–18.00 daily, Oct–Apr 09.00–16.00 Tue–Sat, 09.00–14.00 Sun; 200 lek) Just off Rruga Mihal Komneno is a beautiful traditional house, built in the 17th or 18th century and converted in 1978 into Berati's Ethnographic Museum. A visit to the museum is an excellent opportunity to learn about Berati architecture and find out more about people's way of life until only a few decades ago. It was a family home until 1978; as in many other cases, the family was moved into an apartment to make way for the museum. They were eventually compensated for the loss of their property, but not until 2001.

Like traditional houses elsewhere in Albania, the ground floor was not used for living in, but for storage and household activities such as pressing olive oil or distilling raki. Part of the ground floor of this house has been converted to represent an Ottoman bazaar, with examples of traditional costumes and displays about the crafts traditionally practised in Berati, such as metalwork, felt-making and embroidery.

The first floor, where the family lived, is accessed by an external stone staircase that leads to the *çardak* – a vast balcony on which they spent most of their time in the warmer months of the year. Raised covered sections, called *qoshke*, functioned like outdoor rooms, with carpets, divans and windows. In the centre of the first floor is the kitchen, lit by a skylight; on either side of the kitchen is a toilet – one for guests, the other for members of the family. All the rooms are furnished with items that the inhabitants used in their day-to-day lives, such as looms for wool and silk, cooking utensils and dinner services. Two rooms were used for entertaining guests and have screened galleries (*mafil*) in which the women of the household sat while their menfolk ate and drank in the room below. In one of these visitors' rooms is a beautiful dinner service of engraved copper, set out on a *sofër* – a low, circular table around which the diners sat on the carpeted floor. The door of this room is ingeniously designed so that, when the head of the family opened it to his guests, it closed the access to the steep wooden steps to the women's gallery. Laminated information sheets and panels, in English and Albanian, explain the items on display.

Solomon Museum (Rr Mihal Komneno; m 069 30 79 580; €2, lek also accepted) At the time of writing, this is the only museum in Albania that presents the lives and work of the country's Jews. The museum was founded by the late Simon Vrusho, a prominent member of the Jewish community in Berati, and is run by his widow. It moved to its current premises in 2019; it takes about half an hour to look around and provides a good introduction to this little-known aspect of Albania's history.

The exhibition consists mostly of nicely presented photos of Berati Jewish families and of local people who helped Jewish refugees during World War II. It also features the Kabbalist Sabbatai Zevi (1626–76), who came to Berati from

Vlora, following his expulsion from Constantinople. Sabbatai was born in Smyrna (now in Turkey) and claimed to be the Jewish Messiah; his followers were known as Dönme ('converts'). In Berati, he is believed to have been buried in Bilça, just outside the city, although some scholars maintain that he died and was buried in Ulqinj, now in Montenegro.

Edward Lear Art Gallery (🕘 08.00–14.00 Tue–Sun; free) The British poet Edward Lear (1812–88) was a professional artist, especially sought after for his natural history studies (compared by contemporaries to the best work of Audubon). Lear visited Albania twice and made many pencil sketches and watercolours of the places he visited and the people he saw. Two of his watercolours, and a self-portrait drawing, are displayed at the entrance to the gallery named after him. Most of the exhibition, however, is of work by 20th-century artists from Berati and elsewhere in Albania. There are some fine works on display and those interested in modern art will enjoy an hour or so looking round the gallery's collection.

Historic mosques Berati's historic mosques are located fairly close together near the modern town centre. The **Bachelors' Mosque** (Xhamia e Beqarëve), on the main boulevard, was built in 1827 for the use of the city's (unmarried) shop assistants, and its external walls are beautifully decorated with wall paintings. The **Leaden Mosque** (Xhamia e Plumbit), so-called from the covering of its dome, dates from the first half of the 16th century. It is mentioned by the great Ottoman explorer Evliya Çelebi (1611–82). The oldest of the three – and one of the oldest mosques in Albania – is the **King's Mosque** (Xhamia e Mbretit), at the foot of Rruga Mihal Komneno, the street up to the castle. It has a beautifully carved and painted wooden ceiling, and a large women's gallery. It is possible to see inside the mosque immediately after prayer times; at other times it is usually locked, although it can be opened for group visits.

The two-storey building with the arched porch across the courtyard from the King's Mosque was a *teqe* of the Sufi order of the Khalwati (or Halveti). It has a beautifully painted ceiling surrounded by frescoes, stained-glass windows and painted wall-cupboards. The inscription above the door reveals that the *teqe*'s construction was funded by Ahmed Kurt Pasha, who governed Berati and much of the rest of central Albania in the second half of the 18th century (see box, page 218, for more about the Albanian *pashaliks*). It is thought that he was buried in a now-empty grave behind the *mihrab*. Ahmed Kurt Pasha was also responsible for building the Gorica Bridge and the governor's palace (Seraglio, *Sarayet*) on the other side of Rruga Mihal Komneno, using stonework he plundered from Apollonia. The buildings of the Mangalemi Hotel once formed part of the pasha's palace. There are informative and helpful panels, in English and Albanian, next to the various historic buildings around the town.

Gorica Three neighbourhoods of Berati are designated as 'museum zones', with restrictions on the alterations which may be made to the properties within them. Mangalemi and Kalaja (the castle) are two; the third, Gorica, lies on the other side of the River Osumi. The two sides of the town are connected by the **Gorica Bridge**, a narrow stone bridge built in the 18th century to replace the wooden bridge that had been used until then. A new road bridge in the western outskirts of the city has replaced the Gorica Bridge for most vehicles.

After the Ottoman conquest, Gorica became the Christian quarter; two churches survive there. There are information panels outside each of them, with a floorplan of the church and a map showing its position within Gorica. The opening hours below, also posted on the church gates, are more of an indication of intent than a reliable guide. It may be possible to contact a key-holder by calling the mobile number on these signs. The little **Church of St Thoma** (⌚ 08.00–10.00 & 17.00–19.00) is tucked into a corner of the cliff at the eastern end of Gorica, at the steps down from the footbridge. A shrine behind the church marks where a local saint is said to have left his footprint in the rock. The gate of St Thoma's is a good viewpoint for the Castle and the houses of Mangalemi below it. The **Church of St Spyridon** (⌚ 08.00–10.00 & 16.00–18.00) has an inscription in the narthex which dates its construction to 1864. To find it from the riverbank, look for the steep, narrow Rruga e Kishës (Church Street), roughly halfway between the modern footbridge and the historic Gorica Bridge.

AROUND BERATI

Perondia Those who are interested in Byzantine religious architecture might like to visit the 12th-century church in the nearby village of Perondia, about 15km from Berati, on the right off the road to Kuçova from Ura Vajgurore. The church is usually kept locked, but it is sometimes possible to gain entry by asking around in the village for the key-holder. The interior is in poor repair. A carved wooden iconostasis dates from 1786; a small amount of badly damaged fresco survives on the walls. The icon of The Birth of St Mary in the Onufri Museum came from this church.

Vineyards Berati is well-known for the quality of its wine. Vineyards (*kantina*) which offer visits and wine-tastings include **Çobo** (w cobowineryonline.com), in Ura Vajgurore; **Nurellari** (w nurellariwinery.com), in the village of Fushë-Peshtani, roughly halfway between Berati and Poliçani; and **Alpeta** (f Kantina e Veres Alpeta; also a restaurant and guesthouse), in the pretty hillside village of Roshniku, about 30 minutes' drive from Berati. The Lodge of Wine shop, on Rruga Antipatrea, has a good selection of wines from these and other Albanian vineyards.

Rafting Several agencies offer rafting excursions through the spectacular canyons on the River Osumi. The best time of year for these is in spring (March to May), when the river is high with meltwater. The water is lower, and safer, in May and June. The doyen of these companies is the Tirana-based Outdoor Albania (page 30), which offers qualified and experienced guides for rafting and, in summer, river-hiking trips. The Castle Park hotel just outside Berati also offers rafting trips.

The mountains Mount Tomorri is a long, complex massif, most of it over 2,000m high. It runs roughly north–south to Çorovoda from Lake Banja south of Elbasani, with its highest peak, Çuka e Partizanit (2,414m), pretty much halfway along it. An easy way to see some of the spectacular mountain scenery of the Berati area is by taking the good, asphalted road towards Çorovoda (about 45km). This takes you through the district of Skrapari, a centre of partisan activity during World War II; there are many communist-era war memorials in the villages and by the roadsides.

About halfway between Berati and Çorovoda is the little town of **Poliçani**, one of communist Albania's main arms production centres. The huge factory complex on the valley floor once employed 4,500 people; now the factory lies almost idle. A far more profitable business nowadays is the quarrying and preparation for export of decorative stone tiles, which you will see stacked by the roadsides as you drive through the area. There are buses from Berati to Poliçani, roughly every hour from 07.00 to 14.30. The fare is 150 lek.

After Poliçani, the river valley narrows and the mountains become even more dramatic. **Bogova** is a pleasant stopping-off point; you can hike to the pretty waterfall and then have a drink or something to eat in one of the roadside cafés. There are also a couple of small hotels in Bogova (for example, Qato, by the river in Novaj; m 069 20 84 547, 069 23 88 457; **$$$**).

The largest town in Skrapari, **Çorovoda** is an excellent base for outdoor activities such as rafting and hiking, or for visits to nearby attractions. It has simple but comfortable hotels, nice cafés and restaurants, friendly, helpful inhabitants, and at least one ATM, on the street leading to the main square from the bus terminus. Buses leave Berati for Çorovoda at 08.00, 09.00 and 11.00 and take about 2½ hours each way. They then return to Berati; the last bus leaves Çorovoda at 14.30. The fare is 300 lek. These buses depart from the eastern outskirts of Berati, in the neighbourhood called Uznova, near the regional hospital (Spitali Rajonal). The useful Linja 1 urban bus (page 260) stops in Uznova. Rural buses operate from Çorovoda to the main villages in Skrapari.

Beyond Çorovoda, the roads are unasphalted and some are very rough, suitable only for 4x4. There are many lovely spots for picnics, but not many places where food or water can be bought. At the **Osumi Canyon**, several kilometres of stunning multi-coloured cliffs drop down to the fast-flowing River Osumi below. Rafting excursions to the canyons can be arranged at the right times of year. Viewpoints over the canyon start about 20 minutes' drive from Çorovoda, along the fair road to Çepani.

A couple of kilometres out of Çorovoda, again on a reasonable road, is a fine Ottoman bridge, **Ura e Kasabashit**: 26m long, across three elegant arches. When it was built in 1640, this bridge linked Berati with trans-continental trade routes, through Voskopoja and the Via Egnatia. Now it's in the middle of nowhere.

A longer, more challenging route is the road that curls around the eastern flank of the Tomorri massif and ends just beyond the tiny village of Gjerbësi. It's a rough road, reaching 1,200m above sea level at one point, but the scenery is spectacular, with beautiful cliffs that give way to strangely coloured mountains of an almost lunar barrenness. Little villages and farms cling to the mountains on either side of the River Tomorrica. The surfaced road continues up Mount Tomorri as far as the Kulmaka *teqe*, where the Bektashi saint **Abaz Aliu** is buried. This is one of the holiest sites of Bektashism, the focal point of a great pilgrimage every August. A 4x4 vehicle is needed to reach the *teqe*; from Çorovoda, you should allow at least 4 hours there and back. The bar in Gjerbësi can arrange meals, given a couple of hours' notice.

Where to stay, eat and drink

Flora (7 rooms) Beside Çorovoda bus terminus; m 068 33 99 752. Restaurant; b/fast can be prepared on request. All rooms en suite with TV, fan, Wi-Fi. **$**

Osumi (12 rooms) Sh Riza Cerova (main square), Çorovoda; 031 222 220; m 068 20 77 403, 069 76 76 231. Çorovoda's first private hotel, established in 2000. Restaurant, free parking, Wi-Fi throughout; helpful management; mountain water from spring, generator. All rooms en suite with AC, TV. **$**

Riza Malo Beside Çorovoda bus terminus. Fresh meat, carefully prepared; generous salads with delicious local tomatoes; friendly management. **$$$**

Drita e Tomorrit Just off Çorovoda's main square, by the river. A lovely place for a coffee or drink, with riverside tables shaded by grand old trees, & tufted ducks wandering among the chairs. **$**

Walking, hiking and cycling Various options are open to those who would like to walk in the countryside around Berati without embarking on a serious hiking expedition. One suggestion is to start at the Gorica end of the new road bridge, then take the minor road to the left, heading roughly west (not the road along the river, which leads to Ura Vajgurore). After some destroyed barracks and other military buildings, with tunnels into the hillside visible on the other side of a small river, the road starts to climb. After an hour or so you reach a pretty reservoir, just before the village of Mbreshtani, which is a good spot for a picnic. An alternative walk is to the village of Droboniku, a few kilometres up past the Castle Park hotel (page 260); this is especially nice in springtime when the cherry trees are in blossom.

For experienced, well-equipped hikers, Mount Tomorri offers magnificent opportunities, but the seriousness of this mountain should not be underestimated. There are no neatly marked footpaths, no hiking maps and no mountain rescue service. Your hotel in Berati or Çorovoda may be able to arrange a guide for you. Outdoor Albania (page 30) offers hiking, ski-touring and climbing expeditions in the Tomorri massif. Appropriate footwear and clothing are essential, and you should be in reasonable physical shape. Do not assume that you will have mobile-phone signal; leave a note of your planned route with someone – perhaps the management of your hotel.

To start you on your hike, there are daily buses around lunchtime (generally between noon and 13.00) to many of the villages around Mount Tomorri: for example, to Roshniku, Tomorri, Karkanjozi or Kapinova. These buses leave from the main bus station in Berati. Another option is to begin to hike from Bogova or Çorovoda; see page 260 for information about buses on that route.

Until the 20th century, Berati was connected with the trade routes to its north and south by ancient tracks across the mountains. Many of these are still used by local people and some are passable on motorbikes or 4x4 vehicles as well as on foot. Adventurous, fit and well-equipped cyclists might also like to consider these options. See the regional map for Southeast Albania (page 178) for a rough indication of these routes.

One of these ancient trading routes runs along the River Tomorrica, between the modern towns of Çorovoda and Gramshi, at the southern end of Lake Banja. See page 267 for details of the start of this route, between Çorovoda and Gjerbësi. Thereafter, it is only passable in dry summer weather, since it follows the river, crossing and recrossing it, and there are no bridges between Gjerbësi and Gramshi. It takes the villagers about 6 hours on foot from the Gjerbësi Bridge to Gramshi (note that Albanian villagers are very fast walkers). It is essential to be prepared for delays or breakdowns on this route, since there is almost no habitation and there is unlikely to be any other traffic. From Gramshi you could continue north to Elbasani, or you could head for North Macedonia or northern Greece along the River Devolli. See page 190 for information about the latter route.

Another possibility, on foot only, is to cross the Ostrovica mountain range from Çorovoda to Vithkuqi or Voskopoja, in the district of Korça. The road is reasonable as far as the village of Potomi, in Skrapari district. A minibus operates between Çorovoda and Backa (check times in Çorovoda). From Backa a path leads east-northeast to Çemerica; the track to Vithkuqi goes off to the east there. For Voskopoja, continue through Marjani, a beautiful stone village, to Gjergjavica. From there it is an easy walk to Voskopoja (thanks to John Shipton for sharing his notes on this route). Two days should be allowed for this hike.

Another route connects Çorovoda with the district of Përmeti, continuing south on the Çepani road and then on to Frashëri or to Këlcyra via Prishta; it is about

40km from Çorovoda to Përmeti as the crow flies. The Italian-built road over the 900m-high Gllava Pass to Këlcyra is, at the time of writing, passable only with a rugged 4x4 vehicle or motorbike – or, of course, on foot.

GJIROKASTRA *Telephone code: 084*

The austere and beautiful town of Gjirokastra began to spread downhill from its castle in the 13th century. The castle still broods on its hill, overlooking the whole city and the river valley below. From that vantage point, the grey stone of the houses below and the grey slates of their roofs blend into the hillside, distinguished from it only by their whitewashed walls. Gjirokastra's architecture and haunting atmosphere are described by one of the city's most famous sons:

> This was a surprising city, which seemed to have come out of the valley unexpectedly, one winter's night, like a prehistoric being, and clambered up with difficulty, stitching itself on to the side of the mountain. Everything in this city was old and made of stone, from the streets and fountains right up to the roofs of its big houses, a century old, which were covered with stone tiles the colour of ash, like so many huge carapaces. It was difficult to believe that under these hard shells the soft flesh of life thrived and was renewed.
>
> Ismail Kadare, *Kronikë në gur* (*Chronicle in Stone*)

Gjirokastra first enters history in 1336, in the memoirs of John Cantacuzenus. He was the son of the governor of the Morea, the Byzantine province in the Greek Peloponnese, and would later become Emperor John VI Cantacuzenus. In the 15th century, the city was besieged and then captured by the Ottomans, but unlike many other hitherto important Albanian towns, Gjirokastra flourished under its new rulers. It was the administrative centre of a province (*sanjak*) covering what is now central and southern Albania, and it became a major trading centre.

By the 17th century, the city had 2,000 houses, and the bazaar was constructed at this time. It was subsequently destroyed by fire, and the shops and other buildings that remain in the old bazaar area, Qafa e Pazarit, date from the early 20th century. Most of the large traditional houses were built in the first half of the 19th century.

In the 20th century, Gjirokastra produced two particularly well-known sons. **Enver Hoxha** (see box, page 84) was one of the leaders of the partisan resistance in World War II and went on to run Albania for 41 years, until his death in April 1985. The site of the house where he was born in 1908 is now the Ethnographic Museum, and a good example of Gjirokastra traditional architecture. **Ismail Kadare** (see box, page 276) is the only Albanian writer who is at all well known in the English-speaking world; he stayed in Albania until late 1990, at which point he left the country for France where he still spends most of his time. Other local heroes are Çerçiz Topulli, who led an uprising against the Ottomans in 1908 and whose statue stands in the square named after him, and the two young women who are commemorated with a monument in the same square, Bule Naipi and Persefoni Kokëdhima, hanged by the Germans on suspicion of being partisans.

Gjirokastra became a UNESCO World Heritage Site in July 2005. It had been awarded the status of a 'museum city' by the Albanian government in 1961, which gave legal protection to its architectural heritage and kept new building out of the historic centre. Thanks to this, and no doubt also to its steep cobbled streets, the old town has retained its charming atmosphere.

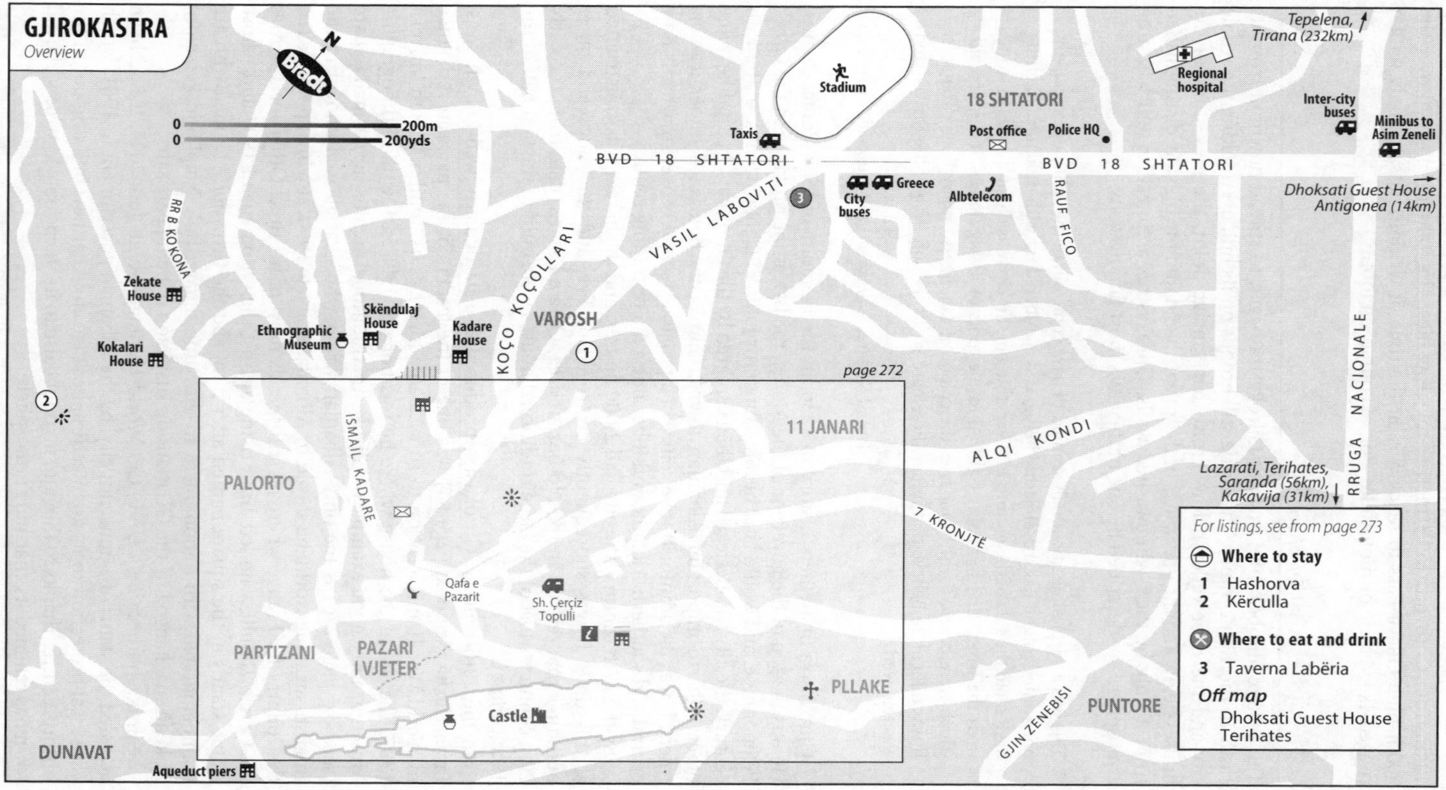
GJIROKASTRA
Overview
Bradt
N
0 200m
0 200yds
Stadium
18 SHTATORI
Regional hospital
Tepelena, Tirana (232km)
Inter-city buses
Minibus to Asim Zeneli
Taxis
Post office
Police HQ
BVD 18 SHTATORI
BVD 18 SHTATORI
Greece
City buses
Albtelecom
RAUF FICO
Dhoksati Guest House
Antigonea (14km)
VASIL LABOVITI
RR B KOKONA
Zekate House
Kokalari House
Ethnographic Museum
Skëndulaj House
Kadare House
KOÇO KOÇOLLARI
VAROSH
page 272
11 JANARI
ISMAIL KADARE
PALORTO
ALQI KONDI
RRUGA NACIONALE
Lazarati, Terihates, Saranda (56km), Kakavija (31km)
7 KRONJTË
Qafa e Pazarit
Sh. Çerçiz Topulli
PARTIZANI
PAZARI I VJETER
PLLAKE
Castle
PUNTORE
GJIN ZENEBISI
DUNAVAT
Aqueduct piers
For listings, see from page 273
Where to stay
1 Hashorva
2 Kërculla
Where to eat and drink
3 Taverna Labëria
Off map
Dhoksati Guest House
Terihates

> It was a steep city, perhaps the steepest in the world, which had broken all the laws of town planning. Because of its steepness, it would come about that at the roof-level of one house you would find the foundations of another; and certainly this was the only place in the world where if a passer-by fell, instead of sliding into a roadside ditch, he might end up on the roof of a tall house. This is something which drunkards knew better than anyone.
>
> It really was a very surprising city. You could be going along the street and, if you wanted, you could stretch out your arm a bit and put your hat on top of a minaret. Many things here were unbelievable, and a lot was dream-like.
>
> Ismail Kadare, *Kronikë në gur* (*Chronicle in Stone*)

GETTING THERE AND AWAY There are various ways to get to Gjirokastra from **Greece**. The daily **bus** service from Ioannina, 90km away, leaves at 06.00 from just outside the main bus station. Alternatively, Greek KTEL buses run several times a day up to the border at Kakavija; taxis and buses wait on the Albanian side of the border to run people the 30km up to Gjirokastra. The buses are scheduled to leave Kakavija at 07.30, 10.30, 14.00 and 16.30. To get to them, you have to walk across the border and uphill, past all the taxi drivers, to the petrol station; youthful porters hang around on the Albanian side to transport heavy luggage. There are also buses to Gjirokastra from Thessaloniki and Athens.

Buses ply the route between **Saranda** and Gjirokastra every hour or so, from 05.00 until 14.00; the fare is 300 lek. The journey takes about 1½ hours, on a good asphalt road along the River Bistrica and then over the Muzina Pass into the Drinos Valley. If you have your own transport, the alternative route through the town of Delvina offers good views across the Bistrica Valley. Work to upgrade the road via Delvina began in 2021; when it is complete, this is likely become the principal route from Saranda to the SH4 highway. Mountain bikers or hikers might consider the track across the Mali i Gjerë range from Delvina to the village of Lazarati, a few kilometres south of Gjirokastra.

From **Tirana**, the buses to Gjirokastra leave from the North/South bus terminal from early morning until early afternoon. They take between 4 and 5 hours. A bus runs every day except Sundays between Gjirokastra and Korça; it leaves Gjirokastra at 07.00. See page 199 for more information about this long but beautiful journey through the magnificent scenery of the Gramoz Mountains.

Gjirokastra's main bus terminus is beside the highway, in the northern outskirts of town. The buses to Greece leave from a stop on Boulevard 18 Shtatori, opposite the stadium.

GETTING AROUND Inter-city buses cannot drive up into the old town, but there are always taxis waiting to ferry people up from the bus terminus. Any bus coming from Saranda or Kakavija will drop passengers off at the foot of the hill going up to the old town. It is a very long, steep climb on foot. City buses ply between Boulevard 18 Shtatori and Sheshi Çerçiz Topulli, via the highway and this junction, with a flat fare of 30 lek. In the old town, there is a taxi rank in Sheshi Çerçiz Topulli.

People in Gjirokastra, like everywhere else in Albania, navigate by neighbourhoods (*lagja*) or landmarks. Those who are driving themselves should note that, in the old town, most streets are very narrow and steep; indeed, some are flights of steps. For pedestrians, these are useful short cuts between the old and new towns; driving a vehicle requires deep local knowledge and impeccable hill starts.

TOURIST INFORMATION The tourist information kiosk is on Sheshi Çerçiz Topulli (🕘 08.00–16.00 Mon–Fri, 10.00–14.00 Sat). A map of the old town is posted at the

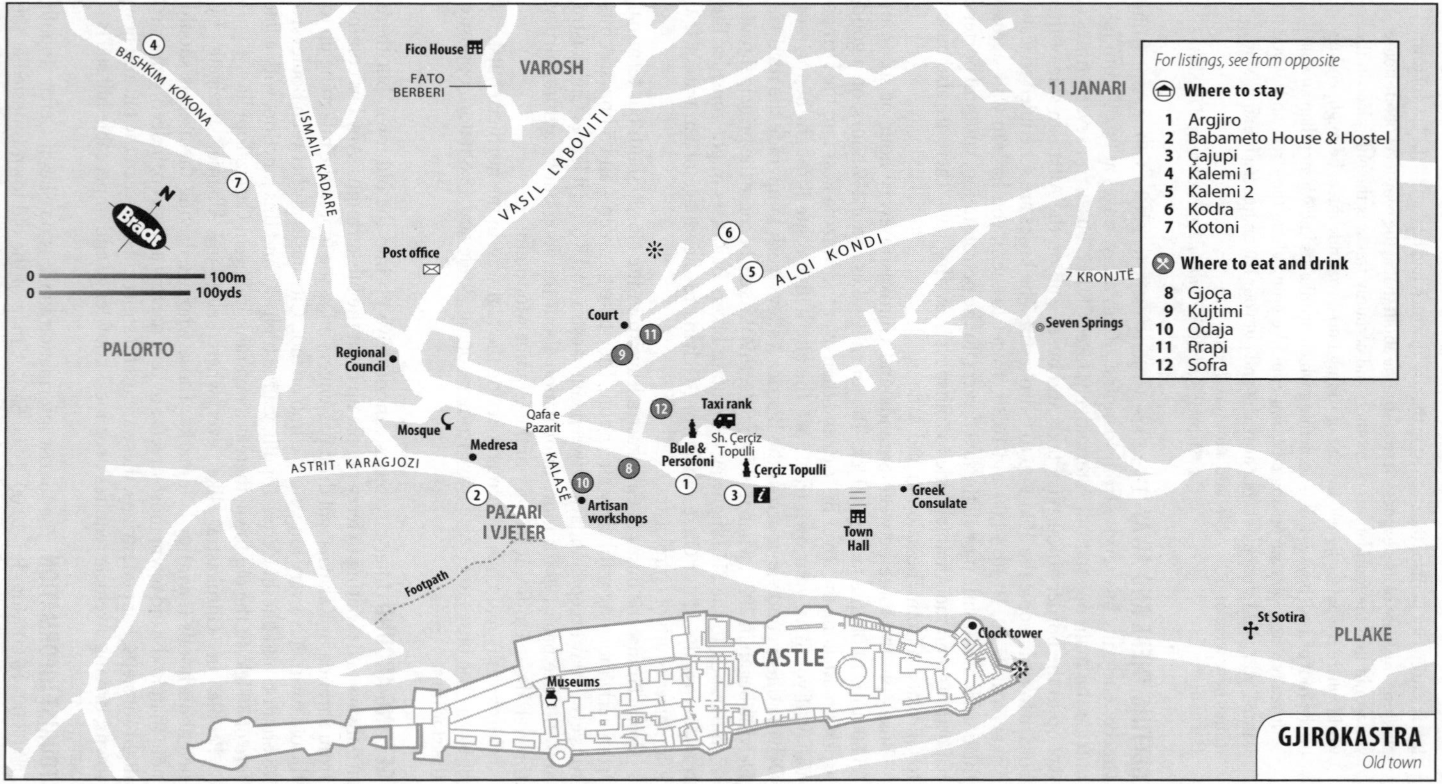
GJIROKASTRA
Old town
For listings, see from opposite
Where to stay
1 Argjiro
2 Babameto House & Hostel
3 Çajupi
4 Kalemi 1
5 Kalemi 2
6 Kodra
7 Kotoni
Where to eat and drink
8 Gjoça
9 Kujtimi
10 Odaja
11 Rrapi
12 Sofra
BASHKIM KOKONA
ISMAIL KADARE
VASIL LABOVITI
ALQI KONDI
ASTRIT KARAGJOZI
KALASË
11 JANARI
7 KRONJTË
Fico House
FATO BERBERI
VAROSH
PALORTO
PAZARI I VJETER
PLLAKE
Post office
Court
Regional Council
Mosque
Medresa
Qafa e Pazarit
Taxi rank
Bule & Persofoni
Sh. Çerçiz Topulli
Çerçiz Topulli
Artisan workshops
Town Hall
Greek Consulate
Seven Springs
Footpath
CASTLE
Museums
Clock tower
St Sotira
0 100m
0 100yds
N
Bradt

western end of Sheshi Çerçiz Topulli, next to the statue of Bule and Persefoni. The **Gjirokastra Foundation** (w gjirokastra.org) offers cultural tours of varying lengths, including culinary tours. Its website has a wealth of information about the city, in English and Albanian. The Foundation supports the artisans whose workshops are around Qafa e Pazarit and on Rruga e Kalasë (Castle Street). They include lacemakers, a woodcarver and a stonemason, who make exquisite pieces of art as well as small souvenirs. A couple of the shops on Qafa e Pazarit (eg: AlbTour) provide tour-guiding services, in English and other languages, and sell guidebooks (including this one).

Caravan Travel (page 30) organises excursions on horseback, with English-speaking guides, to places of interest in the Gjirokastra area. For experienced riders, the highlight is a week-long tour along the old trading routes in the Zagoria and Pogoni mountains, with visits to Labova e Kryqit and other beautiful churches, and finishing at Antigonea. Bespoke tours can also be arranged.

WHERE TO STAY *Map, opposite, unless otherwise stated*

Argjiro (49 rooms) Rr Gjin Zenebisi; 267 022; m 069 57 06 315; e hotelargjiro@gmail.com; w hotelargjiro.al. Central location; 1885 building used as hotel in communist era, completely rebuilt in 2016. Lift; bar; restaurant; roof garden with views of old town; conference room; laundry service. Wi-Fi throughout, free parking, good English spoken. All rooms en suite, some with bathtub; AC, flatscreen TV, phone, bedside light; some have balcony. **$$$**

Kalemi 2 (14 rooms, 2 suites) Rr Alqi Kondi, Qafa e Pazarit; 266 010; m 068 22 34 373, 068 40 11 413; e info@kalemihotels.com; w kalemihotels.com. Sympathetic restoration of a beautiful Category 2 house (page 277), reroofed in slate; each room has a hand-carved wooden ceiling in a different design. B/fast room, laundry service, good English spoken; Wi-Fi, parking; magnificent views of castle from upper floors & terrace. Lavish b/fast inc. All rooms en suite with LCD TV, AC, desk, fridge; suites have bathtub as well as shower. 2 rooms on ground floor (**$$**); all others on upper floors with views. **$$$**

Kërculla [map, page 270] (10 rooms, 2 suites) Rr Bashkim Kokona; m 069 44 10 222; f kercullaresort. A new building in a traditional style, in an amazing mountaintop setting above the city. Big restaurant on ground floor; more intimate dining room upstairs, with open fire; bar. 2 large terraces; large outdoor pool with views of city & mountains; BBQ; children's play area. Business facilities; laundry service. Wi-Fi, ample parking. Suites in separate building nearby. Rooms beautifully finished, each with a different pattern of stone; all en suite & with balcony (more views), plus flatscreen TV, AC, heating, phone, minibar, safe. **$$$**

Çajupi (34 rooms) Sh Çerçiz Topulli; 269 010; m 067 26 43 431, 068 20 54 962; e info@cajupi.com; w cajupi.com. Unbeatable location on main square; English spoken at reception. Restaurant on top floor with good menu & views; bar with traditional décor; lift to all floors; Wi-Fi throughout. All rooms en suite (some also have bathtub), with AC, flatscreen TV; some have small balcony & city view, others overlook forest on castle hill. **$$**

Kalemi 1 (15 rooms) Lagja Palorto; 266 010; m 068 22 34 373, 068 40 11 413; e info@kalemihotels.com; w kalemihotels.com. A traditional Gjirokastra house, lovingly restored by the owner; 1 dbl room has a beautiful carved ceiling. Magnificent views of the city & the castle from the balconies on the upper floors. Bar; Wi-Fi, parking; good English spoken. Lavish b/fast with fresh bread inc. All rooms en suite (some have bathtub, as well as shower), with TV, CH; some also AC. **$$**

Kodra (12 rooms, 1 suite) Rr Alqi Kondi; 262 115; m 069 40 62 661, 069 69 48 718; e info@hotelkodra.com; w hotelkodra.com. Built into the base of the platform which, until 1991, supported a huge statue of Enver Hoxha. Good restaurant (**$$$**) with traditional décor; Wi-Fi throughout; parking; laundry service; direct access to terrace bar above hotel with great views; English spoken. All rooms en suite with TV, AC. **$$**

Kotoni (7 rooms) Lagja Palorto; m 069 27 69 814; e info@hotelkotoni.al; w hotelkotoni.al. Traditional house with views of castle & old town. Rooms have original features such as carved ceilings. B/fast room & terrace restaurant; English spoken. All rooms en suite with flatscreen TV, AC, Wi-Fi. **$$**

Babameto House & Hostel (6 rooms) Lagja Pazari i Vjetër; 262 090; m 069 36 55 915, 069 23 73 093; e info@gjirokastra.org; w gjirokastra.org. A historic 19th-century Gjirokastra house, fully restored in 2013; also Cultural & Heritage Centre. Kitchen, bar, Wi-Fi, lockers, ironing board; towels & sheets provided. Traditionally furnished sitting room, courtyard. Bike hire available. 2 rooms en suite, with balcony; 2 dorms sharing showers & toilets. **$**

Hashorva [map, page 270] (3 rooms) Lagja Varosh; 262 314; m 069 35 62 098; e hotelhashorva@yahoo.com. A traditional Gjirokastra house, partially modernised; bedrooms have carved wooden doors & other traditional architectural features; pleasant garden. Parking, Wi-Fi, laundry service. 2 twin rooms share a large, simple bathroom, 1 dbl room is en suite. **$**

WHERE TO EAT *Map, page 272, unless otherwise stated*

Gjirokastra is proud of its traditional dishes and several restaurants offer them. *Pashaqoftë* is soup with small meatballs; *qifqi* are little rice patties, fried in olive oil; *sarma* are stuffed vine leaves, like the Greek *dolmades*; *shapkat* is a kind of pie with spinach; and *tigani* is pan-fried pork with onions. *Oshaf* is a dessert made with sheep's milk and dried figs.

Kujtimi Qafa e Pazarit. Good salads, traditional Gjirokastra dishes such as *qifqi*, plus whatever is available & fresh – fish, mussels, frogs' legs. Most tables outside on the lovely vine-shaded terrace. **$$$**

Odaja Rr e Kalasë. Above stonemason's & woodcarver's workshops on street of artisans. Traditional Gjirokastra dishes such as *qifqi* & *tigani*; friendly family owners; wood-burning stove in winter. **$$$**

Rrapi Qafa e Pazarit, under the plane tree (*rrapi*). Pasta, salads & Gjirokastra specialities such as *shapkat* & *sarma*. **$$$**

Gjoça Qafa e Pazarit. Small restaurant with extensive menu – traditional Gjirokastra dishes, plus pasta, grilled lamb, fish. Friendly, helpful owners. **$$**

Sofra Sh Çerçiz Topulli. Traditional Gjirokastra dishes; small private dining room, hand-carved ceiling, traditionally furnished with low seats & *sofra* (low wooden table), annex to larger, modern bar/restaurant. Family-run, good value. **$$**

Taverna Labëria [map, page 270] Rr Vasil Laboviti, in the new town, opposite the stadium. Specialises in chargrilled meat, innards, etc. **$$**

Out of town *Map, page 270*

Dhoksati Guest House m 069 20 93 976, 069 73 66 270; e landikoci10@yahoo.com; f dhoksatiguesthouse. Family home in village visited by Lord Byron; friendly & welcoming; homemade southern Albanian food from local ingredients; handmade souvenirs, honey etc for sale. **$$**

Terihates Terihat; 0884 231 390; m 069 20 79 874/5. In a Greek-minority village south of town. Excellent traditional dishes such as *kukurec* (Albanian equivalent of haggis) made from lamb or kid; also pasta, pizza, etc. **$$**

WHAT TO SEE AND DO

The castle (May–Sep 09.00–19.00 daily, Oct–Apr closes earlier; 200 lek)

Gjirokastra's castle perches above the city, controlling the Drinos Valley below and the passes through the Lunxhëria Mountains opposite. It is no longer inhabited, unlike the citadels of Kruja and Berati, but it was used as a garrison and a prison until very recently. Excavations have indicated that the citadel may have been inhabited as early as the Iron Age, in the 8th–7th centuries BC; it was probably fortified in the 5th century BC and extended during the Despotate of Epirus (page 9). Further enlargements and improvements were made in the early Ottoman period and in 1811 Ali Pasha Tepelena (see box, page 218) undertook extensive building work. Much of what can be seen today is the work of Ali Pasha's architects and engineers.

The entrance to the castle can be reached via the steep, cobbled road that winds up the hillside from the top of Rruga e Kalasë (Castle Street), where the artisans' shops are. For those on foot, it is faster to use the steps that start almost exactly opposite the end of this street. The ticket office is just inside the castle entrance.

Turning right after the ticket office leads you into dark vaults built by Ali Pasha. The high tunnel to the left at the start of the vaults was originally the castle's main southern gate. A little further on, a Bektashi *tyrbe* stands in a small garden, up some steps on the left. The rest of the vaults are fun to explore, but they are unlit and rather treacherous underfoot.

A left turn after the ticket office brings you into a dimly lit gallery lined with World War II artillery pieces. Right at the end of the gallery is a rare example of a Fiat L6/40 tank, used by the Italian army from 1941 to 1943. A collection of older weapons forms part of the exhibition in the **Museum of Armaments**, housed in the former prison above this gallery. Tickets (200 lek) are sold separately from admission to the castle; the museum ticket office is at the exit of the vaulted gallery, just after the Italian tank.

The ground floor of this building is now the **Museum of Gjirokastra**, an extensive overview of the city from its prehistory to the very recent past. The curators have made up for the slight sparseness of actual artefacts by creating a series of really informative panels. Almost every aspect of Gjirokastra's development is covered, from the geological composition of the stones that pave its streets, through the life and times of Ali Pasha Tepelena, the stories of the families who built the city's beautiful houses and, finally, the events of the communist and post-communist periods. There are even some women featured, notably the writer Musine Kokalari (1917–83), imprisoned and persecuted by the communist authorities, and 'Gjirokastra's first feminist', Urani Rumbo (1895–1936). The exhibition is so extensive that most visitors will want to spend at least an hour looking around – ideally longer.

The **prison** was built in 1929 to accommodate King Zog's enemies, and then used enthusiastically by the Wehrmacht during World War II; in the summer of 1944, the Germans were holding 500 prisoners in the 50 cells here. The prison remained in use until 1968, when the first National Folk Festival took place in Gjirokastra Castle and it was felt that political prisoners were not entirely compatible with this happy event. It was transformed into the Museum of Armaments, which opened in 1971. The exhibition begins with the post-1912 struggles by people in different parts of Albania to consolidate their independence, notably the 'Vlora War' of 1920 against Italian occupation. However, the museum focuses mainly on World War II, with armaments taken from Italian or German troops and some British weapons that were supplied to the partisans by the Special Operations Executive (SOE). After touring the exhibition, the guide will take you to see some of the prison cells: a chilling experience. A gruesome display case at the end of this section contains the clothes worn by Bule and Persefoni, the young women hanged by the Germans in 1944.

It will be with some relief that you emerge from the gallery on to a small terrace. In the corner sits a two-seater jet that the communist regime claimed was an American spy plane, forced down in 1957. The US air force's version of events is that the pilot, Major Howard Curran, 'strayed' into Albanian airspace during a routine flight to Naples from a US base in southern France and was forced to land by Albanian MIGs. Major Curran was released after being held for a couple of weeks; his plane, however, stayed where it was, at Tirana Airport, before the Albanian government decided that it should be displayed in Gjirokastra. Beyond the plane, a path leads into an open area, largely taken up with the staging for the folk music festival which takes place here every four years (the 2020 festival was held in May 2021). Another Bektashi *tyrbe* nestles against the castle wall, behind the staging.

ISMAIL KADARE

The Albanian writer who is best known outside the Albanian-speaking world is Ismail Kadare (the stress is on the last vowel of both his names), who was born in Gjirokastra in 1936. He studied literature at the University of Tirana and went on to study at the Gorky Institute in Moscow. He returned to Albania after the break with the Soviet Union in 1961 and worked as a journalist, as well as publishing a volume of poetry. His first novel, *The General of the Dead Army*, was written between 1962 and 1966, and brought him immediate renown. It was later made into a film, in which Marcello Mastroianni played the eponymous general, seeking the remains of Italian soldiers fallen during the Fascist occupation of Albania.

Following the success of his first novel, Kadare became the editor of the Albanian literary review *Les Lettres Albanaises*, and went on to write over a dozen novels, as well as short stories and essays. Many of his works are heavily allegorical and it is difficult for non-Albanians to grasp the layers of meaning in them; his novels *The Monster* (banned in Albania for 25 years) and *The Palace of Dreams*, and the work of literary criticism *Aeschylus*, are examples of these rather obscure, but ultimately rewarding, works. Some of his other novels, on the other hand, are much more accessible to the foreign reader and give very interesting insights into aspects of Albanian daily life in the latter half of the 20th century. *Chronicle in Stone*, about growing up in Gjirokastra, and *Broken April*, about the revenge culture of the northern highlands, are good to start with. *The Concert* sheds some light on Albania's break with China (page 17) and how it affected Albanian professionals. *The Castle* is about Albania's resistance to the Ottoman invasion – the eponymous castle is Skanderbeg's seat at Kruja. The more recent (2003) works *Agamemnon's Daughter* and *The Successor* are fictionalised accounts of the fall from grace of Mehmet Shehu, Albania's prime minister from 1954 to 1981.

Ismail Kadare was allowed to travel widely by the communist government, and he could have defected from Albania on several occasions, but he chose not to. He was one of a group of writers and other influential people who lobbied for cultural liberalisation in the late 1980s. Towards the end of 1990, when communist regimes had collapsed all over central and eastern Europe, and it was obvious that even in Albania the end could not be far off, he left the country and obtained political asylum in France, where he still spends much of his time. Many young Albanians who took part in the struggle for democracy were hurt and baffled by what they saw as Kadare's abandonment of them. His 1991 book *Albanian Spring* (out of print in its English translation) outlined his reasons for leaving the country but, like much of Albania's recent history, it remains a very controversial matter.

Kadare is frequently mentioned as a contender for the Nobel Prize for Literature. In 2005, he was awarded the inaugural Man Booker International Prize and, in 2016, the French Legion of Honour.

Beyond the stage is the **clock tower**, another of Ali Pasha's improvements to the castle, although it was heavily restored in the 1980s. Below it, the structure of a very old church – possibly dating back to the Byzantine phase of fortification – has recently been identified. A viewpoint at the eastern extreme of the castle offers panoramic views of the Drinos Valley and the Lunxhëria Mountains beyond.

A well-used panel indicates the position of various places that can be seen, including Antigonea.

In addition to the vaults, the clock tower and other improvements, Ali Pasha also built an **aqueduct**, which brought water from springs on Mount Sopoti, 10km away, to huge cisterns under the central area of the castle. The aqueduct was demolished in 1932, unfortunately; the bases of three of its piers still stand at the southwestern tip of the castle, a few minutes' walk from the entrance towards the neighbourhood of Dunavat. You can return to the city through a tunnel *under* the castle, reasonably well lit and beautifully restored.

Gjirokastra dwelling houses Although based on standard Ottoman architectural principles, the beautiful 19th-century houses of Gjirokastra are unique. Berati's houses are lovely too, but their structure is different and the topography of the town makes them seem more uniform. In Gjirokastra, no traditional house is quite like another, although they have been classified according to certain design characteristics such as the number of wings that they have.

Many of the best examples of Gjirokastra domestic architecture were built in the first three decades of the 19th century. The Pazari i Vjetër (Old Bazaar) quarter, for example, dates mostly from around 1830. The houses are characterised by their defensively designed lower floors, with narrow entranceways and small windows set high in the wall. The entrance arches (*qemeret*) are made of dressed stone, often worked with great skill and refinement, and engraved with images of animals or birds; their wooden doors are also decorated with carvings. The ground floor of the house was traditionally used for storage and had a cistern (*stera*) into which rainwater was piped from the roof. The size of the cistern was an indicator of the status of the family that owned the house. The roofs themselves are of grey stone slates, supported on a wooden frame.

The living quarters, as is usual in Albanian vernacular architecture, are on the upper floors. In Gjirokastra there are usually two or three floors in total, with a few four-storey houses. Some of the houses are simple vertical structures; a widespread variant has a single wing added to this central structure, while the wealthiest families built houses with two wings. The Zekate house, right up at the top of the Palorto quarter and visible from many vantage points in the old town, is an outstanding example of the latter style.

Internally, each house is laid out in a way that reflects the family structure of the time. The main room was the 'winter room' (*dimërorja*), also called the 'fire room' (*dhoma e zjarrit*), with an ornate fireplace (*oxhaku*) that decorated the room as well as warming it. The number of chimneys and windows was another status symbol for Gjirokastra's wealthy families. One or more living rooms were used by family members for day-to-day activities. Guests were received in a separate room (*oda e miqve*), which was always the most beautifully decorated in the house. The walls were sometimes adorned with frescoes, and the ceiling was often of carved and sculpted wood. Reception rooms often had a wooden gallery – sometimes closed, sometimes open – where the women of the household could keep an eye on proceedings; this was especially useful when the men below were discussing the possible betrothal of their children. The rooms were linked by wide corridors and covered balconies (*nëndivani* and *divani i sipërm*), which were also used as living areas in hot weather. Three-storey houses with double wings also had open balconies set between the two wings.

On paper the traditional houses of Gjirokastra enjoy quite strict legal protection. Fifty-one of them have Category 1 listing, meaning that no external modifications are permitted; over 350 others are listed in Category 2, where some modification is allowed as long as the façade is not altered. In practice, however, these beautiful buildings are at great risk from neglect, abandonment and fire. Illegal building work also takes place within the supposedly protected Museum Zone of the town.

Traditional houses can be found throughout the old town, especially in the Partizani, Dunavat and Palorto neighbourhoods. Some have been converted into hotels – see page 273 for details. Many others are unoccupied and can only be seen from the outside. Two original houses which have been restored and can be visited are described below; others may well open to the public in due course.

The **Kadare house** (Rr Fato Berberi 16; 🕘 09.00–19.00 daily; 200 lek) has now been rebuilt and opened to the public. This is where Ismail Kadare (see box, page 276) was born, to a professional family (his grandfather was a judge) and where, in his early teens, he wrote his first story. The house was badly damaged in a fire in 1999; the ground floor and basement have been painstakingly reconstructed, funded by UNESCO and the Albanian state, and you can see the rainwater cistern, the pantry and the beautiful external staircase. Photographs illustrate the reconstruction process. The first floor has been completely rebuilt, but it gives an impression of how the living space was distributed. Some original items which belonged to the family are on display, including an intricately decorated wooden chest.

The Kadare house is not easy to find. The easiest route is to head downhill from the square where the Regional Council is, past the post office; Rruga Fato Berberi is a small, winding street to the left. The first imposing traditional house on this street is the colourful **Fico house**; the Kadare house is a little further, on the other side of the same street.

Another reconstructed traditional house is now the **Ethnographic Museum** (🕘 09.00–19.00 daily; 200 lek), on the site of the house where Enver Hoxha was born. The original building was destroyed by fire in the 1960s and it was rebuilt as a showcase for the classic features of a traditional Gjirokastra house. The museum contains many interesting items from daily household life and has (old) maquettes of three types of traditional architecture, including the Zekate house (see opposite).

The nearby **Skëndulaj house** (🕘 09.00–19.00 daily; 200 lek), built originally around 1700 and partly rebuilt in 1827, was formerly the Ethnographic Museum. It was confiscated in 1984 from the family who had lived in it for generations; they recovered it in 1992 and have restored it beautifully. The external architecture of this house has a couple of unusual features: lines of chestnut wood set into the wall every metre, to strengthen it, and a window and slit in the corner of the building through which the cistern could be cleaned and its water level checked. The cistern has a capacity of 130,000 litres and is piped into the house through a tap. One wall of the cistern is also the wall of the pantry; an ingenious method of keeping food cool. Another interesting architectural feature is the underground shelter, a vaulted cellar; on the floors above it are kitchens whose ceilings are also vaulted, making the whole structure incredibly strong. Many of the household implements displayed in the kitchens – the coffee-roaster, for example – were used by the family until just a decade or so ago.

The Skëndulaj house has 64 windows, nine chimneys and six toilets (long-drop toilets, admittedly, but nonetheless quite impressive for the early 19th century). Some of the reception rooms also have an en-suite steam room (*hamam*), as well as galleries (*mafil*) and cupboards for storing bedding (*musandra*). The *divan*, or covered balcony, overlooks the city and connects with every room on that floor. It has a raised platform on which the mother of the household would sit in the mornings with her daughters-in-law to share out the day's tasks. The most elaborately decorated room, the *oda e miqve*, has no fewer than 15 windows, some with stained-glass lozenges. The frescoes on the fireplace, which are original, are full of symbolism: pomegranates and pomegranate flowers are believed to bring luck to your children, while candles symbolise the development of the family. The *mafil* was enclosed in glass in 1985, after the house had been requisitioned by the government; originally it had a wooden grille like the galleries in the other rooms. The *oda e miqve* was used for betrothal ceremonies, which would take place in the raised part of the room. The ceiling above this part of the room has two ceiling roses, rather than the usual single rose, to symbolise that two people will now live under the same roof.

The **Zekate house** (200 lek), an imposing double-winged house at the top of Palorto, was built in 1810 by one of Ali Pasha Tepelena's administrators, Beqir Zeko. The tall arches of the entranceway support the weight of the upper rooms. On the ground floor, to the right of the entrance, is the large rainwater cistern; the family's status is further displayed by the stained-glass windows, elaborate fireplaces and carved wooden ceilings. The reception rooms have wooden galleries and *musandra*. The winter rooms have adjacent toilets and steam rooms (*hamam*). The top, third, floor is astonishing: the summer *divan* has spectacular views, particularly from the dais in the corner where the head of the household would sit with his most important guests. Finally, the remarkable reception room on this floor has beautiful frescoes on the walls and fireplace; an elaborate gallery and *musandra* over the entrance to the *oda* and its en-suite toilet; a magnificent carved and gilded ceiling; painted doors and coloured-glass windows. The Zekate house was restored in 2005. It does not have set opening hours, but the elderly couple who own it live next door and are usually somewhere around.

Town hall air-raid shelter (🕘 summer 08.00–20.00 daily, winter 09.00–14.00 Mon–Fri, 09.00–17.00 Sat, 09.00–15.00 Sun) During the communist years, when town halls across Albania were known as 'Executive Committees', air-raid shelters were built under them so that the Committee Members and staff could continue to administer their town in the event of enemy bombardment. It is said that the shelters under the Executive Committee of Tirana, which nowadays houses the administration of the Albanian Parliament and other national institutions, were connected to Enver Hoxha's villa in 'The Block' (page 83).

The city of Gjirokastra was no exception. Its air-raid shelter, now open to the public, is in fact a huge labyrinth of underground corridors with small offices opening off them. Many of the offices still have the signs on their doors indicating which department or functionary would have worked within; even the telephone switchboard operators would have relocated down to the bunker. The functionaries would have slept, as well as worked, in their little windowless offices. In the centre of the labyrinth is a large meeting hall, beyond which are the offices of the party officials who made up the Executive Committee itself. Private stairways (now blocked-up) led down to this VIPs' corridor from their offices above ground. The whole structure was designed to resist the impact of missiles of up to six tonnes; exploring the complex gives a unique insight into the Hoxha regime's permanent state of alert for enemy attack. Maps at the entrance show the entire network of tunnels under the city.

The Seven Springs (7 Krojët) Part of a Muslim's preparation for prayer involves purification by washing, which means that running water can be found in or near every mosque. Gjirokastra's 'Seven Springs' were built into the foundations of a

17th-century mosque. The mosque was destroyed in 1967, but the springs have survived and some are still in use. An inscription in Ottoman Turkish above the main fountain includes the line 'The one who built the pool shall be happy.' Across the stream is a bathhouse, or *hamam*, unfortunately not open to visitors.

AROUND GJIROKASTRA

Antigonea (w antigonea.com; ⌚ 08.00–16.00 Mon–Fri, 09.00–15.00 Sat–Sun; 200 lek) In 295BC, the king of the Molossians, one of the three main peoples of Epirus, founded a city and named it after his wife, a princess of both the Macedonian and Egyptian royal families. The Molossian king was Pyrrhus, whose later battles against expansionist Rome would come to be known as 'Pyrrhic victories'; his wife's name was Antigone and the new city was called Antigonea.

For more than a hundred years, Antigonea was a major economic and cultural centre. Then, after Rome's victory in the Third Macedonian War (171–168BC), Epirus was unfortunate enough to be on the route of the victorious army's return home. Even though the Epirote Alliance had not been involved in that phase of the war, 70 of its cities were sacked and 150,000 of its citizens were taken to Rome as slaves. Antigonea's neatly planned streets and luxurious houses were reduced to rubble and its fortifications levelled.

In a beautiful and highly strategic setting, on a mountainside overlooking the Drinos Valley opposite Gjirokastra, Antigonea is one of a handful of archaeological sites in Albania which has been extensively excavated and also has good interpretative materials for the non-specialist visitor. Well-designed information panels, placed at various significant points throughout the site, explain the history and function of the buildings.

The main things to see are the remaining sections of the city's fortifications and the remains of several impressive buildings. The best stretches of the city walls are those around the acropolis, near the site entrance, and right at the other, southern end, where you can see how the Romans destroyed the main gate to the city and pushed over the top of the wall. Near this gatehouse are the remains of a stoa (a covered walkway), which is a very clear example of the Epirote dry-stone building technique, using large polygonal stones.

The path through the city takes the visitor past a group of houses. It was while one of these houses was being excavated, in 1968, that the site was identified as Antigonea, thanks to the discovery of 14 bronze *tesserae* imprinted with the name of the city; these are thought to have been voting tokens, used in the city's decision-making processes. The path continues down some steps to the so-called House of the Peristyle, with its colonnade that would have surrounded a garden or courtyard in the interior of the house. Note the large stone nearby with differently sized holes in it; this was for measuring out accurate quantities of various types of foodstuff such as oil, flour and so forth – the Molossians' Trading Standards Authority.

The city's main street ran north–south from the acropolis to the main gate; part of it can be seen below the House of the Peristyle, while excavations in 2013 revealed another section further to the south. In what was the centre of the city – the agora – another stoa, nearly 60m long and double-storeyed, was built up on an artificial terrace, above the line of the hill, so that it had spectacular views and could be seen from far around. Houses and workshops were built on a grid pattern around the agora, some of them with imposing columns that can still be seen. Almost at the end of the site is a palaeochristian basilica, triconch in shape and with mosaic floors (normally kept covered, unfortunately), from around AD500.

A useful leaflet with a map of the site and information about the main buildings and fortifications is included in the admission fee. The website gives brief information about the site, in English, and about other things to see in the area. It takes about half an hour to get to Antigonea by car from Gjirokastra; the road is signposted, for 'Parku Arkeologjik Antigone', from the main highway, near the bus terminus. The road is asphalted all the way to the site entrance and there is ample parking there. It is a lovely drive, through beautiful scenery and past several traditional villages with attractive Byzantine churches. It is also possible to hike up to Antigonea; it takes about 1½ hours. The footpath starts at the Archaeological Park's office, in the village of Asim Zeneli, and leads over the hills to the archaeological site, emerging behind the site office and the old fountain.

Tepelena Tepelena was the home town and secondary residence of Ali Pasha Tepelena (see box, page 218), who was Governor of Ioannina from 1788 to 1822. Ioannina, now in northern Greece, was at the time the capital of the administrative district (*sanjak*) that covered much of southern Albania. Ali Pasha took a special interest in architecture and was responsible for building, or rebuilding, many castles and fortresses, including the one in Tepelena.

A large bronze statue of a reclining Ali Pasha dominates the usual entry point to the town. The statue is based on a famous painting of Ali Pasha by the French artist Louis Dupré, but his position is reversed so that he appears to be gazing towards his native village on the hillside on the other side of the Vjosa valley. From the statue, it is a short walk along the main street – inevitably called Rruga Ali Pasha Tepelena – to the castle. Its massive walls encircle an area of 4–5ha. It is still inhabited and there is no charge to visit it. The stone-setted streets within it were relaid in 2020–21; the area around the castle has been landscaped and public toilets installed. There is a viewpoint from which can be seen the river valley and the bridge over the Vjosa, also originally built by Ali Pasha Tepelena. Steps lead from here, rather precariously, to the highway below.

Getting there and away Tepelena is 30 minutes away from Gjirokastra and about an hour from Përmeti. Buses from Tirana for Tepelena leave from the North/South bus station. Any bus heading to or from Gjirokastra or Përmeti will drop off or pick up passengers on the main road at the entrance to Tepelena.

Libohova The small town of Libohova, in the Bureto mountains on the other side of the Drinos Valley from Gjirokastra, would make an excellent base for those who prefer the countryside to cities. You would need your own transport; bikes would be ideal, as long as your thigh muscles are in good shape. There are **buses** to Libohova from Gjirokastra every morning, but getting *around* the area is another matter. The journey by car takes less than an hour; the bus takes a bit longer.

The main square in Libohova is dominated by the huge plane tree in its corner. This tree is said to be the largest of its kind (*Platanus orientalis*) in the Balkans, and to be 500 years old. It is 25–30m high and its branches extend for several metres in all directions. The terrace restaurant below it is made even cooler by the water that is channelled straight from the spring and past the tables. The views from the square across the Drinos Valley are spectacular on a clear day.

In the 19th century, Libohova was a much larger town than it is today, and the feudal landowners – the Libohova family – enhanced its importance through some clever diplomacy, marrying into the family of Ali Pasha Tepelena. This was a smart move that gave the town the protection of the most powerful man in southern

Albania at the time and allowed it to prosper. Ali Pasha's sister, Shanica, was buried in the Libohova family graveyard, which is 5 minutes' walk from the town square, up past a Bektashi *tyrbe* and then down towards the stream. Unfortunately the graveyard has been neglected for many years and is very overgrown – you should ask someone to show you where it is, since if you try to follow directions you will probably walk right past it. It is no longer possible to tell which of the graves is Shanica's.

Ali Pasha's other legacy to Libohova was its **fortress**, the west wall of which can be seen from the road as you drive into the town. The entrance to the fortress is through someone's backyard (the owners seem to have no objection to tourists blundering through their property), downhill from the main square. There is nothing left of the interior of the fort itself, apart from some bricked-up archways, but the walls are very imposing – smooth blocks of grey stone about 2m thick in places.

The Hotel Libohova on the town square (4 rooms; m 069 54 64 605; f Bar Restorant Hotel "Libohova"; all rooms en suite with TV & AC; **$$**) is comfortable and has lovely views out over the Drinos Valley. The owner also runs the terrace restaurant (**$$$**) under the plane tree in the square. The salad ingredients are locally produced and delicious, as is the cheese which is processed at a factory at the foot of the hill.

Labova e Kryqit (200 lek) The parishioners of Labova e Kryqit ('Labova of the Cross') say that the construction of their church was ordered by the Emperor Justinian (AD527–65), who donated a fragment of the Holy Cross to the church and was married in it. The building that stands here today, however, is much later, perhaps 13th century. Dedicated to the Birth of Mary, it is built with the red bricks, laid in patterns, which are so characteristic of early churches in Albania, and it is roofed with the grey slates that give Gjirokastra its beautiful austerity. An even later exonarthex (portico) runs the length of the front wall.

Inside the church is a magnificent iconostasis of ornately carved and gilded wood, dating from 1805 and decorated with dragons and eagles. On each side of the iconostasis, and behind it, are beautiful frescoes, and on the arch behind the throne are images that blend the pagan beliefs of the people with Christian symbolism. More frescoes decorate the walls of the nave. The works of art in the church have been conserved and restored and, when the restorers removed one of the icons for treatment, they found a much older icon (possibly 16th century) hidden underneath it and now displayed beside it – a crowned figure representing, so the story goes, the Emperor Justinian himself. Another icon shows St Paraskevi, martyred in the 2nd century, with her head in a bowl (and a second head, still attached to her neck).

Subsidence over the centuries has made the cupola lean very noticeably, and the building has had to be reinforced on several occasions; an inscription indicates that such reinforcement was carried out in 1783, but it has continued into modern times. Some of the reinforcement work can be examined in the gallery of the church and the bell tower.

The church is set in a walled garden, and both the garden gate and the church itself are kept locked. The family that holds the key lives nearby; the telephone number may be posted on the gate, or you can ask anyone in the village to find them to let you in.

Labova e Kryqit is about an hour's drive from the main north–south highway. The last half hour is mostly unpaved. There is a public fountain and a café in the square.

The *teqe* at Melani As you come down the hill from Labova or Libohova towards the highway, a minor road off to your left leads to one of the holiest sites of

Bektashism, the *teqe* at Melani. Built in the early 19th century, it occupies a splendid site, high on an isolated hill commanding glorious views of the Drinos Valley. Traces of fortification can be seen lower down around the hill, parts of which date back to the 4th century BC.

The *teqe* is a large building in which the faith's followers study, pray, meditate and listen to the teaching of the *baba* (father). The building is not always open, and the best time to visit is on one of the Bektashi holy days, when hundreds of believers make their way to Melani. These are social as well as religious occasions; people come with their family and friends, and bring picnics that they enjoy under the poplar trees which surround the *teqe*. There is a *tyrbe* (shrine) in front of the *teqe*, the burial place of one of the early *babas* there. You should remove your shoes before entering either the *tyrbe* or the *teqe* itself, and avoid stepping on the threshold.

The Melani *teqe* was damaged and looted during the atheism campaign of the late 1960s. When freedom of worship was restored, local believers collected money and materials and rebuilt the *teqe* with their own hands, sleeping in turns there every night to make sure their work was not vandalised. Many of those who helped with the restoration were from Lazarati, a Bektashi village a couple of miles south of Gjirokastra.

Hadrianopolis In 1970, a landslide revealed the remains of a classical theatre in the Drinos Valley, south of Gjirokastra, and academics were baffled as to what it was doing there. Ancient sources mentioned a city, built during the Emperor Hadrian's reign (AD117–38) and called Hadrianopolis after him, and located it somewhere between Apollonia and Butrint; but surely this theatre in the middle of nowhere could not possibly have anything to do with a city? It was not until 2002, when the site of the theatre was drained and some of the area around it was excavated, that the first archaeologists began to realise that they really were looking at a city. They had, after all, discovered Hadrianopolis.

The lovely little theatre retains many of its original features – the entrances to the first and second rows of seating, the stage with its entrances for the actors and, below it, for the prompters, and the paved *orchestra*. Performances are occasionally staged in the theatre nowadays. Beyond the theatre, a beautiful stretch of wall, in a herringbone pattern, is part of the forum; there are hypocausts here, too, showing where the bathhouse was. Other buildings that have been excavated include part of the wall that surrounded the city, an ancient cemetery outside that wall and two temples. Hadrianopolis seems to have gone into some decline in the 3rd century, but the settlement survived into the 6th century. Its name lives on in the modern Albanian 'Dropulli', the collective name for the villages that flank the river between Gjirokastra and the Greek border.

The site, unattended, is about a kilometre up a rough track from the village of Sofratika, just off the highway to Greece. Rural buses serve Sofratika from Gjirokastra; it would be an easy walk to the site from the village, or from the junction on the highway.

Appendix 1

LANGUAGE

THE ALPHABET Although the Albanian alphabet has a large number of letters (36), each consonant is always pronounced in exactly the same way, whatever its position within a word. A few of them do not have exact equivalents in English and, for these cases, approximations are given in the list below. Vowels can be long or short but, with one exception, they are very easy to pronounce.

The only vowel which might cause difficulty is ë, which represents the sound which philologists call '*schwa*'. It is the vowel sound a native English-speaker makes in the second syllable of the word 'understand'; a native French-speaker makes the same sound in the first word of '*je comprends*'. For speakers of Slavic languages, it is like a vocalic 'r' without the 'r' sound (like the semivowel in the Serbo-Croat word '*trg*'). There are two problems with ë. One is that at the end of a word it is scarcely pronounced at all, but it can affect the length of the vowel in the previous syllable. The other is that, unlike most Indo-European languages, the *schwa* in Albanian can be stressed; this is hard for non-native-speakers to get right, because we are used to *schwas* snuggling in between consonants without anybody noticing they are there.

Fortunately, it is so unusual for any foreigner to be able to string together more than a few Albanian words that any slight mispronunciation of ë or anything else is invariably overlooked in the torrent of congratulations.

PRONUNCIATION

A as in c**u**t or c**a**rt
B as in **b**ig
C as the 'zz' in pizza
Ç as in **ch**urch
D as in **d**og
Dh the 'th' in **th**at
E as in g**e**t or as in s**ay**
Ë as in 'the' in 'th**e** cat sat on th**e** mat'
G as in **g**old (always hard)
Gj – the 'du' in 'en**du**re' is an approximation
I as in h**i**t or m**ee**t
J the 'y' in **y**ear (not **j**am)
K as in **k**ite
L as in **l**og
Ll – a double 'l' sound, a bit like a Russian or Serbo-Croat 'dark' L
M as in **m**at
N as in **n**ot
Nj the 'ni' in u**ni**on
O as in h**o**t or th**ough**t
P as in **p**at
Q – the 'tu' in 'ma**tu**re' is an approximation
R as in **r**oad
Rr – a trilled double 'r'
S as in **s**un
Sh as in **sh**ine
T as in **t**in
Th as in **th**ick
U as in b**u**sh or m**oo**n
V as in **v**ote
X the 'ds' in ki**ds**
Xh as in **j**u**dg**e
Y – the French sound in '**tu**' or the German 'ü' as in 'd**ü**nn'
Z as in **z**oo
Zh – the 's' in plea**s**ure

DEFINITE AND INDEFINITE ARTICLES In Albanian, the definite article ('the' in English) does not (normally) go before the word it defines but is suffixed to it. Thus, 'the Boulevard' is '*Bulevardi*', while any old 'boulevard' is '*bulevard*'. This feature is not unique to Albanian – it is found, for example, in Swedish and Romanian. Different prepositions, as well as taking different cases of the noun, also require either the definite or the indefinite form. This is not something which the visitor need worry about unduly, except to be aware that the rules apply to place names as well as to every other noun.

When they are speaking English or another foreign language, Albanians tend to use the definite form of place names – that is, they will refer to 'Gjirokastra' rather than 'Gjirokastër', and 'Kukësi' rather than 'Kukës'. When they speak Albanian, of course, they use whichever form of the word is grammatically appropriate, but most other languages do not have the grammatical framework which allows them to do that. This book therefore uses the definite form of all place names except for Butrint, which is so consistently called this in every English-language publication that it would be confusing to refer to it here as 'Butrinti'.

However, on road signs, bus signs and railway timetables and the like, the destination will always appear in the indefinite form. This is because it is invisibly governed by the preposition *në*, meaning 'to' or 'in', which must be followed by the indefinite. So, for example, the buses run *nga Tirana në Durrës* ('from Tirana to Durrësi') and then return *nga Durrësi në Tiranë* ('from Durrësi to Tirana'). All Albanian-produced maps, and most foreign-produced ones, too, consistently use the indefinite form. In many cases the difference is quite small and it is easy to tell which place is meant. Some which are not so obvious are listed at the end of this Appendix.

PHRASEBOOKS AND LANGUAGE COURSES The best phrasebook available commercially outside Albania is the *Albanian–English, English–Albanian Dictionary & Phrasebook*, by Ramazan Hysa, published in 2000 by Hippocrene Books.

Albanian grammar is difficult, and moving beyond simple phrases requires serious study. *Colloquial Albanian*, by Isa Zymberi, is the best book that is readily available in the UK and North America, although its idiom tends towards the Kosovar. It can be purchased with or without the accompanying CD (which is even more Kosovar). Other language course books can be purchased in Tirana.

WORDS AND PHRASES

Essentials

Good morning	*Mirëmengjesi* (until about 11.00)
Good afternoon	*Mirëdita* (until about 16.00 or 17.00)
Good evening	*Mirëmbrëma*
Good night	*Natën e mire* (when leaving people at the end of the evening)
Hello	*Përshëndetje*
Goodbye	*Mirupafshim*
What is your name?	*Si e keni emrin?*
My name is …	*Emri im është …*
Where are you from?	*Nga jeni?*
I am from …	*Jam nga …* [see town and country names in the next section, and use the definite form]
How are you?	*Si jeni?*
Pleased to meet you	*Gëzohem*
Thank you	*Faleminderit*
Please	*Ju lutem*
Don't mention it	*S'ka gjë*

Excuse me	*Më falni*
Cheers!	*Gëzuar!*
Yes	*Po*
No	*Jo*
I am looking for …	*Po kërkoj …*
I don't understand	*S'kuptoj*
Slowly, please!	*Avash, ju lutem!*
Do you understand me?	*A më kuptoni?*

Questions

how?	*si?*	when?	*kur?*
what [is …]?	*çfarë* [është …]?	why?	*pse?*
where?	*ku?*	who?	*kush?*
which?	*i cili/e cila?*	how much?	*sa?*

Numbers

1	*një*	11	*njëmbëdhjetë*
2	*dy*	12	*dymbëdhjetë*
3	*tre*	13	*trembëdhjetë [etc]*
4	*katër*	20	*njëzet*
5	*pesë*	21	*njëzetenjë*
6	*gjashtë*	30	*tridhjetë*
7	*shtatë*	40	*dyzet*
8	*tetë*	50	*pesëdhjetë*
9	*nëntë*	100	*(një) qind*
10	*dhjetë*	1,000	*(një) mijë*

Time

What time is it?	*Sa është ora?*
It's …	*Ora është …*
am/pm	*paraditës/mbasditës*
today	*sot*
tomorrow	*nesër*
yesterday	*dje*
(the) morning	*mëngjesi*
(the) evening	*darka*

Days of the week

Monday	*e hënë*	Friday	*e premtë*
Tuesday	*e martë*	Saturday	*e shtunë*
Wednesday	*e merkurë*	Sunday	*e dielë*
Thursday	*e enjtë*		

Months of the year

January	*Janar*	July	*Korrik*
February	*Shkurt*	August	*Gusht*
March	*Mars*	September	*Shtator*
April	*Prill*	October	*Tetor*
May	*Maj*	November	*Nëntor*
June	*Qershor*	December	*Dhjetor*

Getting around

Public transport

Ticket (single/return)	*biletë (vajtja/vajtja e ardhja)*
I want to go to …	*Dua të shkoj në …* [and use indefinite form]
How much is the ticket?	*Sa kushton bileta?*
What time does it leave?	*Në çfarë orë niset?*
What time is it (now)?	*Sa është ora?*

from	*nga*	plane	*avion*
to	*në*	ferry	*traget*
bus station	*agjencia (e udhëtarëve)*	car	*makinë*
railway station	*stacioni i trenit*	taxi	*taksi*
airport	*aeroporti*	arrival	*mbërritja*
port	*porti, skela*	departure	*nisja*
bus	*autobus*	here	*këtu*
minibus	*furgon* or *kombi*	there	*atje*
train	*tren*	Bon voyage!	*Rrugë të mbarë!*

Self-drive

Is this the way to … ?	*Kjo është rruga për në …* [and then use indefinite form]?
Where is there a petrol station?	*Ku ka pikë karburanti?*
Please fill up the tank	*Të lutem mbushe plot serbatorin*
I'd like … litres	*Do desha … litra*
diesel	*naftë*
leaded petrol	*benzinë me plumb*
unleaded petrol	*benzinë pa plumb*
I have broken down	*kam pësuar defekt*

Road signs

Give way	*Jep përparësinë*	Exit	*Dalje*
Danger	*Rrezik*	Detour	*Rrugë e tërthortë*
Entry	*Hyrje*	One way	*Rrugë një kalimshe*
No entry	*Nuk lejohet hyrja*	Keep clear	*Mos zij rrugën*

Directions

Where is … ?	*Ku është … ?* [then use definite form]?	north/south	*veri/jug*
		east/west	*lindje/perëndim*
straight on	*drejt*	opposite	*përballë*
left	*majtas*	behind	*prapa*
right	*djathtas*	in front of	*para*
… at the traffic lights	*… në semaforë*	near	*afër*
… at the roundabout	*… në rrumbullakë*		

Signs

Entrance	*Hyrja*
Exit	*Dalja*
Open	*Hapur*
Closed	*Mbyllur*
Ladies (toilet)	*Gra(të)*
Gents (toilet)	*Burra(t)*
Information	*Informacion*

Accommodation

Where is the X hotel?	*Ku gjendet hoteli X?*
Please show it to me on the map	*Ju lutem ma tregoni në hartë*
Do you have a … room?	*A keni një dhomë …?*
… single … (room)	*… teke*
… twin …	*… dyshe*
… triple …	*… treshe*
… double …	*… dopio/matrimonial*
… with an en-suite bathroom?	*… me banjë brenda?*
How much per night?/per person?	*Sa kushton nata?/veta?*
Where is the bathroom?	*Ku është banjo?*
Is there water?	*A ka uji?*
Is there electricity?	*A ka drita?*
Is breakfast included?	*E përfshihet mëngjesi?*
I'm leaving today	*Sot largohem*

Food

Do you have a table for X people?	*A keni tavolinë për X veta?*
I don't eat meat	*Nuk ha mish*
I don't eat fish	*Nuk ha peshk*
I don't eat dairy products	*Nuk ha bulmet*
[Please] bring me a …	*ma sillni një …*
fork	*pirun*
knife	*thikë*
spoon	*lugë*
May I have the bill?	*Më bëni llogarinë?*

bread	*bukë*	meat	*mish*
butter	*gjalpë*	lamb	*… qengji*
cheese	*djathë*	veal	*… viçi*
olive oil	*vaj ulliri*	pork	*… derri*
pepper (ground)	*piper*	suckling pig	*… gici*
salt	*kripë*	kid	*… keci*
sugar	*sheqer*	chicken	*… pulë*
ice cream	*akullorë*		

Drinks

water	*uji*	tea	*çaj*
still mineral water	*uji mineral pa gaz*	coffee	*kafe*
sparkling water	*uji me gaz*	espresso	*kafe ekspres*
ice	*akull*	Turkish coffee	*kafe turke*
milk	*qumësht*	beer	*birrë*
fruit juice	*lëng frutash*	wine	*verë*

Shopping

I'd like to buy it	*Dua ta blejë*
How much is it?	*Sa kushton?*
I don't like it	*Nuk më pëlqen*
I'm only looking	*Po shikoj*
It's too/very expensive	*është shumë e shtrenjtë/ është shumë i shtrenjtë*
It's cheap	*është i lirë/është e lirë*

I'll take it	*Do ta merr*
I'd like more	*Dua më shumë*
I'd like less	*Dua më pak*
I'd like a smaller one	*Dua një më të vogël*
I'd like a bigger one	*Dua një më të madh*

Where is … ? / *Ku është … ?*

… the bank	*… banka*
… the post office	*… posta*
… the church	*… kisha*
… the mosque	*… xhamia*
… the embassy	*… ambasada*
… the exchange office	*… zyra këmbimi*
… the telephone centre	*… Telekomi*
… the museum	*… muzeu*
… the archaeological museum	*… muzeu arkeologjik*
… the ethnographic museum	*… muzeu etnografik*
… the historical museum	*… muzeu historik*
… the art gallery	*… galeria e arteve*
… the castle/fortress	*… kalaja*

Emergencies

A&E clinic	*Urgjenca*
Please help me	*Ju lutem më ndihmoni*
Call a doctor	*Thërrohuni mjekun*
There's been an accident	*Ka pasur një fatkeqësi*
I'm lost	*Jam e/i humbur*
Go away!	*Iku!* (although the author's experience is that the annoying person is more likely to go away if s/he is addressed in a language which is not Albanian)
police	*polici(a)*
policeman	*polic(i)*
fire brigade	*zjarrfikësit*
ambulance	*autoambulancë*
thief	*hajdut*
hospital	*spital*
I am ill	*Jam i sëmurë* (if the speaker is male); *Jam e sëmurë* (if the speaker is female)

Health

diarrhoea	*diarrea*	asthma	*astmë*
nausea	*krupa*	epilepsy	*sëmundja e tokës/ sëmundja e hënës*
(a) doctor	*mjek*		
(a) prescription	*recetë*	diabetes	*sëmundja e sheqerit*
(a) pharmacy	*farmaci*	I'm allergic	*Jam alergjik*
painkiller	*analgjesik*	… to penicillin	*… penicilinës*
antibiotic	*antibiotik*	… to peanuts	*… kikirikesh*
antiseptic	*antiseptik*	… to bee-stings	*… thumbëve bletësh*
condom	*prezervativ*		
contraceptive	*mjet kontraceptiv*		
suntan lotion	*krem dielli*		

Other

I want to make a phone call	*Dua të bëj një telefonatë*
I do not understand	*Nuk kuptoj*
I do not speak Albanian	*Nuk flas shqip*
Do you speak English?	*A flisni anglisht?*
… French?	*… frengjisht?*
… Italian?	*… italisht?*
… Russian?	*… rusisht?*
OK	*Në rregull*
Of course	*Patjetër*

Adjectives (all in singular indefinite form)

beautiful	*i/e bukur*	hot	*i/e ngrohtë*
old	*i/e vjetër*	cold	*i/e ftohtë*
new	*e re/i ri*	difficult	*i/e vështirë*
good	*i/e mirë*	easy	*i/e lehtë*
bad	*i/e keq*	far	*larg*
early (in the day)	*herët*	near	*afër*
late (in the day)	*vonë*		

SOME PLACE NAMES IN ALBANIA

Definite	Indefinite	Italian	Greek (transliterated)
Shqipëria	**Në Shqipëri**	**Albania**	**Alvania**
Dhërmiu	Dhërmi		Dhrimadhes
Dibra	Dibër		
Durrësi	Durrës	Durazzo	Dhirrachion
Gjirokastra	Gjirokastër		Argirokastron
Himara	Himarë		Cheimarra or Chimara
Korça	Korçë		Koritsa
Ksamili	Ksamil		Eksamilion
Lezha	Lezhë	Alessio	
Llixhat	Llixhe		
Llogoraja	Llogara		
Saranda	Sarandë	Santi Quaranta	Agii Saranda
Shëngjini	Shëngjin	San Giovanni	
Shkodra	Shkodër	Scutari	
Tirana	Tiranë	Tirana	Tirana
Vlora	Vlorë	Valona	Avlona

SOME PLACE NAMES IN GREECE

Definite	Indefinite	English	Greek (transliterated)
Greqia	**(Në) Greqi**	**Greece**	**Ellas**
Athina	Athinë	Athens	Athina
Janina	Janinë	Ioannina	Ioannina
Korfuzi	Korfuz	Corfu	Kerkira
Kosturi	Kostur	Kastoria	Kastoria
Selaniku	Selanik	Thessalonica or Salonica	Thessaloniki

SOME OTHER USEFUL PLACE NAMES

English	Albanian
Europe	***Evropa***
England	Anglia
Great Britain	Britania e Madhe
Edinburgh	Edimburgu
Ireland	Irlanda
Northern Ireland	Irlanda e Veriut
London	Londra
United Kingdom	Mbretëria e Bashkuar
Republic of Ireland	Republika e Irlandës
Scotland	Skocia
Wales	Uellsi
The world	***Bota***
Australia	Australia
Canada	Kanadaja
New York	Njujorku
Istanbul	Stambolli
Skopje	Shkupi
USA	Shtetet e Bashkuara të Amerikës
New Zealand	Zelanda e Re

Appendix 2

FURTHER INFORMATION

BOOKS London-based I B Tauris has traditionally been the most significant publisher of works about Albania in English. It is worth checking their website (**w** ibtauris.com) from time to time to see if they have published anything new which interests you.

General history

Ceka, Neritan *The Illyrians to the Albanians* Migjeni, 2005. An authoritative and fascinating account of the ancient history of this ancient land.

Crampton, R J *The Balkans Since the Second World War* Longman, 2002. A readable introduction to a complicated area and a complicated history, covering Albania, Bulgaria, Romania and Yugoslavia, as well as Greece.

Durham, Edith *Burden of the Balkans*, 1905; available from various print-on-demand publishers. The history of the Balkans through Edith Durham's rather partisan eyes; at least you know which side she's on!

Durham, Edith *Twenty Years of Balkan Tangle* George Allen & Unwin, 1920; available from various print-on-demand publishers. Edith Durham's account of the historical developments in the Balkans during the disintegration of the Ottoman Empire, many of which she witnessed or even participated in.

Imber, Colin *The Ottoman Empire 1300–1650* Palgrave Macmillan, 2002. An excellent general history of the rise of the Ottoman Empire, with interesting chapters on its administration and military structure.

Malcolm, Noel *Kosovo: A Short History* Macmillan, 1998. Explains the later Ottoman period better than anyone else; also good on the political aspects of the Albanian nationalist movement.

Norwich, John Julius *Byzantium: The Decline & Fall* Penguin, 1996. The third and final instalment of Lord Norwich's accessible and reliable history of the Byzantine Empire, covering the confusing period when most of Albania changed hands several times. The family trees are invaluable; the bibliography is good, too.

Pettifer, James *The Kosova Liberation Army* Hurst & Co., 2012. A history of the KLA from 1948 to 2001, written by a defence specialist and Balkans expert. Mostly about Kosovo, obviously, but also gives fascinating insights into Albanian military theory and the fevered atmosphere of Tirana in 1998–2000.

Vickers, Miranda *The Albanians: A Modern History* I B Tauris, reprinted 2001. Detailed, reliably researched and well written. An excellent guide to Albania's complicated history in the 20th century, and an indispensable companion for anyone trying to understand why Albania is the way it is now.

Vickers, Miranda and Pettifer, James *Albania: From Anarchy to a Modern Identity* Hurst & Co, 2nd edition, 1999. Good account of the transitional period from the late 1980s to 1996.

Vickers, Miranda and Pettifer, James *The Albanian Question: Reshaping the Balkans* I B Tauris, 2007. A carefully researched and riveting account of the last decades' events in the Albanian-speaking lands, including the pyramid-scheme riots in 1997 and the attempted coup in 1998, as well as the Kosovan War and refugee crisis.

Winnifrith, T J *Nobody's Kingdom: a History of Northern Albania* Signal Books, 2020. A comprehensive history of northern Albania, examining the cultural differences between the country's south and north.

World War II

Bailey, Roderick *Smoke without Fire? Albania, SOE & the Communist Conspiracy Theory* in S Schwandner-Sievers and B Fischer (eds) *Albanian Identities: Myth, Narrative and Politics* Hurst & Co (New York), 2002

Bailey, Roderick *The Wildest Province: SOE in the Land of the Eagle* Jonathan Cape, 2008. The definitive account of what SOE did in Albania, based on recently declassified records and interviews with survivors.

Bethell, Nicholas *Betrayed* Random House, 1985. An account of the British and US attempts to infiltrate saboteurs into Albania between 1949 and 1953.

Fischer, Bernd J *Albania at War 1939–1945* Hurst & Co, 1999. The only modern academic history of Albania from the Italian invasion of 1939 to the end of World War II.

Foot, M R D *SOE: The Special Operations Executive 1940–46* Greenwood Press, 1984. Includes SOE's work in Albania.

Mangerich, Agnes Jensen, with Rosemary L Neidel and Evelyn M Monahan *Albanian Escape: The True Story of US Army Nurses Behind Enemy Lines* University Press of Kentucky, 2006. A stranded American nurse's account of occupied Albania.

Shehu, Mehmet *La Bataille pour la Libération de Tirana* Editions Naim Frashëri (Tirana). Detailed account of the Battle for the Liberation of Tirana in 1944, written by one of the participants. Hard to obtain, may be available in the UK through inter-library loan.

Memoirs by SOE agents See boxes, pages 13 and 14.

Amery, Julian *Approach March: A Venture in Autobiography* Hutchinson, 1973

Amery, Julian *Sons of the Eagle: A Study in Guerilla War* Macmillan, 1948

Davies, Edmund F *Illyrian Adventure: The Story of the British Military Mission in Enemy-Occupied Albania* Bodley Head, 1952

Glen, Alexander *Footholds Against a Whirlwind* Hutchinson, 1975

Hibbert, Reginald *Albania's National Liberation Struggle: The Bitter Victory* Pinter, 1991

Kemp, Peter *No Colours, No Crest* Cassell, 1958

Kemp, Peter *The Thorns of Memory* Sinclair-Stevenson, 1990

Oakley-Hill, D R *An Englishman in Albania* I B Tauris, 2004

Smiley, David *Albanian Assignment* Chatto & Windus, 1984

Historical background

Achtermeier, William O *The Turkish Connection: The Saga of the Peabody-Martini Rifle* in *Man at Arms Magazine* Vol 1, No 2, 1979

Dumas, Alexandre (père) *Ali-Pacha* in *Causes Célèbres* Veuve Dondey-Dupré, 1840. Romanticised but fun version of Ali Pasha Tepelena's career. Available as an ebook in English translation for Kindle (w amazon.co.uk). The French original has been digitised by Google.

Durham, Edith *Albania & the Albanians* I B Tauris, 2004. An edition, by Bejtullah Destani, of Edith Durham's articles and letters, most of them unavailable for over 60 years. A fascinating historical document.

Fleming, K E *The Muslim Bonaparte: Diplomacy & Orientalism in Ali Pasha's Greece* Princeton University Press, 1999. Critical biography of Ali Pasha Tepelena. Can be ordered through the publisher's website (w pup.princeton.edu).

Lubonja, Fatos *Second Sentence: Inside the Albanian Gulag* I B Tauris, 2009. A memoir of life as a prisoner in the forced-labour camp of Spaçi (page 147). Harrowing but essential reading.

Pettifer, James (ed) *Albania and the Balkans* Elbow Publishing, 2013. Essays in honour of Sir Reginald Hibbert, the SOE agent and (later) diplomat. Ambitious in scope, will have something to interest almost everyone.

Rees, Neil *A Royal Exile* Studge Publications, 2010. Published to mark the 70th anniversary of the exiled King Zog's arrival in England. Oral and archive history of the 'royal' family's six-year stay in the Thames Valley and Chilterns.

Tomes, Jason *King Zog* Sutton Publishing, 2003. Biography of Ahmet Zogu, who crowned himself King of the Albanians in 1928. Power struggles, intrigues, pistol fights and assassinations.

Cultural background

Allcock, John and Young, Antonia *Black Lambs & Grey Falcons* Berghahn Books, 2000. A collection of essays about women travellers in the Balkans, including Edith Durham, Margaret Hasluck and Rose Wilder Lane.

De Waal, Clarissa *Albania: Portrait of a Country in Transition* I B Tauris, 2013. A wealth of information and unique observation drawn from the author's anthropological fieldwork in rural Albania since the 1990s.

Hasluck, Margaret, edited by Robert Elsie *The Hasluck Collection of Albanian Folktales* CreateSpace Independent Publishing Platform, 2015. Some 115 folk tales collected and translated into English by Hasluck and her friend Lef Nosi (see box, page 104).

Hasluck, Margaret *The Unwritten Law in Albania* Cambridge University Press, 2015. Hasluck's posthumous masterwork, a comprehensive study of the legal system among the mountain clans, including blood feud (see box, page 104). Engagingly written, with many insights into daily life in the Albanian mountains.

Kadare, Ismail. Almost anything by this great Albanian writer gives an insight into the culture and history of the country. *Broken April* and *Chronicle in Stone* are especially illuminating on the north and on Gjirokastra, respectively. His novel *The Successor* is a fictionalised account of the mysterious death of Mehmet Shehu, and is worth reading for that reason although it is not one of his best works. It and some of his other novels, translated into English from the French versions, are published by Canongate. Affordable paperbacks of the Albanian–French translations are published in the *Livre de Poche* series.

Kanun of Lekë Dukagjin. It is difficult to find good translations of the *Kanun*. The best is a parallel edition, with Albanian on one page and the English version opposite, published in the US by Gjonlekaj Publishing Co (1989). The International Bookshop in Tirana's Skanderbeg Square stocks it, but outside Albania it is hard to obtain.

Various authors *Albania: A Patrimony of European Values* Tirana, 2001. A useful overview of aspects of Albanian culture such as literature, fine art and music. On sale in Tirana bookshops.

Young, Antonia *Albania: World Bibliographical Series* ABC-Clio, 1997. A bibliographic guide to cultural and historical aspects of Albania. Out of print, but may be available in reference libraries.

Young, Antonia *Women Who Become Men* Berghahn Books, 2000. Interviews with some of northern Albania's 'sworn virgins', a fascinating insight into this dying tradition.

Zymberi, Isa *Colloquial Albanian* Routledge, 1991. Language course which gives a thorough grounding in Albanian grammar.

Travel writing

Carver, Robert *The Accursed Mountains* Flamingo, 1999. Sensationalist and negative account of travelling in Albania and meeting Albanians, none of whom the author appears to like. Albania was not like this in 1996, when he was there, and it is not like this now.

Cusack, Dymphna *Illyria Reborn* William Heinemann Ltd, 1966. An uncritical but fascinating glimpse of communist Albania before the atheism campaign – she hears church bells ringing and *muezzins* calling the faithful to prayer, and describes Tirana as being full of minarets. Her encounters with ordinary Albanians are described in a delightfully positive light.

Durham, Edith *High Albania* Edward Arnold, 1909; available from various print-on-demand publishers. Classic and enthralling account of travels in northern Albania in the early 20th century.

Hanbury-Tenison, Robin *Land of Eagles: Riding Through Europe's Forgotten Country* I B Tauris, 2014. An account of the journey on horseback by the author and his wife, from the far north to the far south of Albania, peppered with adventure and mishap, discovery and unexpected encounters.

Hussain, Tharik *Minarets in the Mountains: A Journey through Muslim Europe* Bradt Guides, 2021. Longlisted for the 2021 Baillie Gifford Prize, this is a magical and eye-opening account of a journey exploring the region's cultural heritage, unveiling forgotten Muslim communities, empires and their rulers.

Lane, Rose Wilder and Dore Boylston, Helen *Travels with Zenobia: Paris to Albania by Model T Ford* University of Missouri Press, 1983 (out of print). The authors – one the daughter of Laura Ingalls Wilder, the other the creator of the Sue Barton novels – drove across Europe to Albania in 1926.

Lear, Edward *Edward Lear in Albania – Journals of a Landscape Painter in the Balkans* I B Tauris, 2008. Lear, famous for his nonsense poetry, was a professional artist, who visited Albania in 1848 and 1857, and made a large number of drawings and watercolours of Butrint, Berati and elsewhere. This welcome reissue of his detailed and humorous journal of his 1848 trip is illustrated with some of his own sketches and paintings.

Ward, Philip *Albania* Oleander Press, 1983 (out of print). A rare record of a visit to communist Albania.

Guidebooks

Ceka, Neritan *Apollonia: History & Monuments* Migjeni, 2001. Scholarly guide to the archaeology and history of Apollonia, an invaluable companion to the site. On sale in Tirana and in Albanian museum bookshops.

Ceka, Neritan *Buthrotum: History & Monuments* Migjeni, 2006. Scholarly guide to the archaeology of Butrint. On sale in Tirana and in Albanian museum bookshops.

Ceka, Neritan and Muçaj, Skënder *Byllis: History & Monuments* Migjeni, 2004. Scholarly guide to the history and buildings of Byllis; has photographs of the Byllis mosaics, usually kept covered. On sale in Tirana and in Albanian museum bookshops.

Gilkes, Oliver *Albania: An Archaeological Guide* I B Tauris, 2012. Detailed notes on archaeological sites, large and small, throughout Albania, especially strong on the southwest of the country. Includes many site plans and very useful advice on access.

Gilkes, Oliver et al *Gjirokastra: the essential guide* Gjirokastra Conservation and Development Organization, 2009. A pocket guide to the city of Gjirokastra and the surrounding region. Small but full of information about the places to visit, some with site plans, and illustrated with modern and historic photographs.

Hansen, Inge Lyse (series editor) *Hellenistic Butrint, The Butrint Baptistery and its Mosaics, The Rise and Fall of Byzantine Butrint* and *Venetian Butrint* Butrint Foundation, 2007–2009. An indispensable series of archaeological guides to the whole of the Butrint site, in English and Albanian. Scholarly and beautifully illustrated.

Via Egnatia Foundation *Via Egnatia on Foot: A Journey into History* Via Egnatia Foundation (w viaegnatiafoundation.eu), 2nd edition 2017. Part 1 covers the 475km from Durrësi to Thessaloniki. Detailed route notes with topographic maps and GPS co-ordinates, historical and cultural context and practical information.

Other Balkan country guidebooks For a full list of Bradt's Balkan and other European guides, visit **w** bradtguides.com/shop.

Abraham, Rudolf and Evans, Thammy *Croatia: Istria, with Rijeka and the Slovenian Adriatic* (2nd edition) Bradt Guides, 2017

Bostock, Andrew *Greece: The Peloponnese, with Athens, Delphi and Kythira* (4th edition) Bradt Guides, 2019

Clancy, Tim *Bosnia & Herzegovina* (6th edition) Bradt Guides, 2022

Clancy, Tim *Via Dinarica: Hiking the White Trail in Bosnia & Herzegovina* Bradt Guides, 2018

Evans, Thammy *North Macedonia* (6th edition) Bradt Guides, 2019

Knaus, Verena and Warrander, Gail *Kosovo* (3rd edition) Bradt Guides, 2017

Letcher, Piers with Abraham, Rudolf *Croatia* (6th edition) Bradt Guides, 2016

Mitchell, Laurence *Serbia* (6th edition) Bradt Guides, 2022

Rellie, Annalisa *Montenegro* (6th edition) Bradt Guides, 2022

WEBSITES

Travel information

w punetejashtme.gov.al The website of the Albanian Ministry of Foreign Affairs has information (in English) about entering Albania, the contact details for Albanian embassies throughout the world, and information about the Ministry's activities.

w tirana-airport.com The official website of Tirana International Airport, hosting a wealth of useful information, including a full list, with contact details, of airlines that operate scheduled flights into Tirana, information about onward travel, and real-time arrivals and departures.

Tourist information

w albania-holidays.com Offers tours throughout the country, city tours of Tirana and bespoke arrangements. Hotel reservations can be made through its sister website **w albania-hotel.com**.

w albaniantourism.com The Albanian Ministry of Tourism's website has information about archaeological and historical sites, cultural events and museums. Also contact information for selected hotels across the country, though these cannot be booked through the site.

w hostelworld.com Reservation site for several Albanian hotels as well as hostels.

General background

w albania.usembassy.gov/index.html Information about the United States's activities in and policy towards Albania.

w balkanspeacepark.org A network of academics, artists, environmental activists and local people living and working in the valleys and villages of northern Albania, Montenegro and Kosovo. See box on page 173 for more about B3P.

w https://cia.gov/library/publications/the-world-factbook/geos/al.html The CIA factbook on Albania, with a reasonably up-to-date summary of recent history and the Agency's assessment of the current state of affairs.

w frosina.org Designed for the Albanian diaspora in the US; has articles about Albania, folk tales and recipes.

w gov.uk/government/world/albania News from the British embassy in Tirana.

w instat.gov.al Albania's National Statistical Institute has a wealth of data on its website, much of it in English as well as Albanian.

w iucn.org The International Union for Conservation of Nature & Natural Resources; gives information about endangered species all over the world, including Albania.

W lcweb2.loc.gov/frd/cs/altoc.html US Library of Congress Country Study of Albania; from 1992, but useful historical background.
W osce.org/albania Information about the mandate and the activities of the OSCE Presence in Albania.
W reenic.utexas.edu/countries/albania.html The REENIC (Russia and East European Network Information Centre) site has links to a huge range of other websites.
W tiranatimes.com The best of Tirana's English-language online newspapers. Some of the content is accessible only to subscribers, but they provide news summaries.

Index

Page numbers in **bold** indicate major entries; those in *italic* indicate maps.

INDEX OF ADVERTISERS

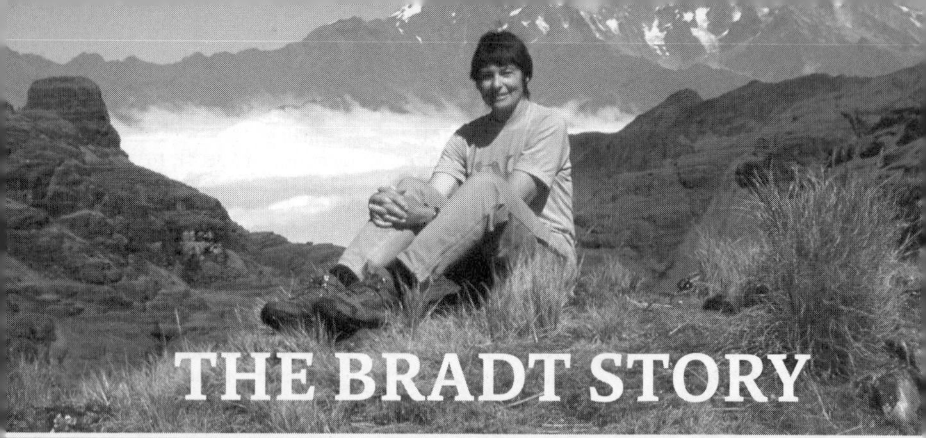

THE BRADT STORY

In the beginning

It all began in 1974 on an Amazon river barge. During an 18-month trip through South America, two adventurous young backpackers – Hilary Bradt and her then husband, George – decided to write about the hiking trails they had discovered through the Andes. *Backpacking Along Ancient Ways in Peru and Bolivia* included the very first descriptions of the Inca Trail. It was the start of a colourful journey to becoming one of the best-loved travel publishers in the world; you can read the full story on our website (bradtguides.com/ourstory).

Getting there first

Hilary quickly gained a reputation for being a true travel pioneer, and in the 1980s she started to focus on guides to places overlooked by other publishers. The Bradt Guides list became a roll call of guidebook 'firsts'. We published the first guide to Madagascar, followed by Mauritius, Czechoslovakia and Vietnam. The 1990s saw the beginning of our extensive coverage of Africa: Tanzania, Uganda, South Africa, and Eritrea. Later, post-conflict guides became a feature: Rwanda, Mozambique, Angola, and Sierra Leone, as well as the first standalone guides to the Baltic States following the fall of the Iron Curtain, and the first post-war guides to Bosnia, Kosovo and Albania.

Comprehensive – and with a conscience

Today, we are the world's largest independently owned travel publisher, with more than 200 titles. However, our ethos remains unchanged. Hilary is still keenly involved, and **we still get there first**: two-thirds of Bradt guides have no direct competition.

But we don't just get there first. Our guides are also known for being **more comprehensive** than any other series. We avoid templates and tick-lists. Each guide is a one-of-a-kind expression of an expert author's interests, knowledge and enthusiasm for telling it how it really is.

And a commitment to wildlife, conservation and respect for local communities has always been at the heart of our books. Bradt Guides was **championing sustainable travel** before any other guidebook publisher. We even have a series dedicated to Slow Travel in the UK, award-winning books that explore the country with a passion and depth you'll find nowhere else.

Thank you!

We can only do what we do because of the support of readers like you – people who value less-obvious experiences, less-visited places and a more thoughtful approach to travel. Those who, like us, take travel seriously.

Bradt GUIDES

TRAVEL TAKEN SERIOUSLY